Psychology:
Theory and Application

Kent & Sussex Weald NHS Trust

THE LIBRARY

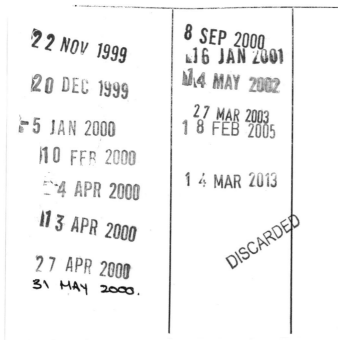

Psychology
Theory and application

Psychology: Theory and Application

Philip Banyard
Department of Applied Social Science,
Nottingham Trent University, UK

and

Nicky Hayes
Honorary Research Fellow,
University of Huddersfield, UK

CHAPMAN & HALL
University and Professional Division
London · Glasgow · Weinheim · New York · Tokyo · Melbourne · Madras

Published by Chapman & Hall, 2–6 Boundary Row, London SE1 8HN, UK

Chapman & Hall, 2–6 Boundary Row, London SE1 8HN, UK

Blackie Academic & Professional, Wester Cleddens Road, Bishopbriggs, Glasgow G64 2NZ, UK

Chapman & Hall GmbH, Pappelallee 3, 69469 Weinheim, Germany

Chapman & Hall Inc., One Penn Plaza, 41st Floor, New York NY 10119, USA

Chapman & Hall Japan, Thomson Publishing Japan, Hirakawacho Nemoto Building, 6F, 1-7-11 Hirakawa-cho, Chiyoda-ku, Tokyo 102, Japan

Chapman & Hall Australia, Thomas Nelson Australia, 102 Dodds Street, South Melbourne, Victoria 3205, Australia

Chapman & Hall India, R. Seshadri, 32 Second Main Road, CIT East, Madras 600 035, India

First edition 1994

© 1994 Philip Banyard and Nicky Hayes

Designed and typeset in 10.5/13.5 pt ITC Garamond by G and M H Wadsley
Printed and bound in Hong Kong
ISBN 0 412 46440 3

A catalogue record for this book is available from the British Library

Library of Congress Catalog Card Number: 94–70234

Contents

Preface

In this book we have aimed to give you, the reader, an introduction to some of the basic theoretical concepts in psychology and to show how they have been applied in a range of professional areas. Psychology is a subject that most of us are interested in, and in this text we have tried to show what a versatile discipline psychology is and what an exciting subject it can be to study.

The book is designed to show the connections between the various areas of applied psychology. For the most part, applied psychologists tend to produce specialist texts which are relevant to their own area of work. But much of the research in work psychology, for example, is relevant to the applied areas of sport or health or education, and research into sport psychology has messages for health psychology too. What we have tried to do in this text is to draw out the relationships between the various areas and show how the same basic concepts may manifest themselves in different applied fields.

We hope that you will find the book stimulating and so will be encouraged to look further into the areas of applied psychology. We hope, too, that the book will act as a stimulus to additional research, whether that is in student projects or in research in the 'real world'. The text provides references and applications for each psychological concept that is introduced, and an interested reader should, with luck, find at least some of these provocative to further study. We have tried to use the widest possible range of sources and have included material from *Combat* magazine, advertising case histories, nursing journals, personnel journals and even some psychology journals!

When we designed the book we wanted to get away from the psychology of the North American undergraduate. Much of the reported research in introductory texts is based on studies carried out on students and a cursory reading of introductory texts rarely makes us aware of the relevance of psychology in the real world. Student life is an unusual period in a person's life which is characterized, for many, by having few responsibilities, and for some by having a large bar tab. A psychology that is relevant in applied settings needs to look outside a student group for its research participants. As we have found, there is wealth of material in psychology which allows us to explore psychology in its broader context.

And, finally, one of our main aims in writing this book was that you should find it enjoyable, as well as useful. All right, so there's only so far you can enjoy a text book, but given the requirements of an academic book, we hope that it is pleasurable to read, and will encourage you to read and study more psychology.

Applied psychology consultants

Since neither of us could possibly claim to be expert in all the fields of applied psychology, we engaged the help of several expert psychologists to advise us in the choice of material. The consultants offered us a great deal of helpful advice and suggestions, and have contributed in no small part to the success of this project. We are deeply grateful to the following psychologists for their advice and contributions to the book's contents: Mike Herbert (International Medical College, Kuala Lumpur); Viv Shackleton (Aston Business School); John Wilcock (Swansea College); Gill Jackson (The Nottingham Trent University); Ian Glendon (Aston University); and Gerry Finn (Jordanhill College of Education).

We would also like to thank Viv Shackleton and Pete Sanders for their help and encouragement in the preparation of the final manuscript.

Philip Banyard
Nicky Hayes

Acknowledgements

The authors would like to acknowledge Trevor Hylton (for sound advice), Dominic Recaldin (for good suggestions and only gentle nagging), William Merrin (for thinking), Lesley Phair (for forbearance) and Patrick Hylton (for advice, and also support during the distress of relegation).

The following figures are reproduced with kind permission of their sources:
Figure 1.1 The Kobal Collection
Figure 1.7 Sheldon Cohen, Carnegie Mellon University, Pittsburgh, USA
Figure 2.3 (Top left) Hulton-Deutsch Collection, (top right) Popperfoto and (bottom) Impact Photos
Figure 2.9 Translated and adapted by permission. Copyright © The Institute for Personality and Ability Testing, Inc., 1993. International copyright in all countries under the Berne Union, Buenos Aires, Bilateral, and University Copyright Conventions. All property rights reserved by the Institute for Personality and Ability Testing, Inc., 1801 Woodfield Drive, Savoy, Illinois 61874, USA. All rights reserved. Published in the UK by ASE, a division of the NFER-NELSON Publishing Company Limited, Darville House, 2 Oxford Road East, Windsor, Berkshire SL4 1DF. NFER-NELSON is the sole publisher of 16PF in English language in the European Community, based upon an exclusive licensing agreement with the Institute for Personality and Ability Testing, Inc.
Figure 2.11 Barnaby's Picture Library
Figure 2.22 Impact Photos
Figure 2.26 Press Association
Figure 3.19 Mick Casey, Public Relations, Nestlé
Figure 3.22 *The Guardian*
Figure 3.28 (Left) Giselle Freund, (right) Victoria and Albert Museum Picture Library
Figure 3.29 Hewlett Packard Press Office, Wokingham
Figure 4.1 Newsteam
Figure 4.15 Popperfoto
Figure 4.18 Civil Aviation Authority (press release photograph from *New Scientist* archive)
Figure 4.23 Pete Addis
Figure 5.1 Ralph Gibson, Novosti
Figure 5.13 Professor Albert Bandura, Stanford University, Stanford, California
Figure 5.17 London Regional Transport, LRT Registered User No. 94/E/619
Figure 5.22 Associated Press
Figure 6.3 World of Leather
Figure 6.8 (Left) Impact Photos, (middle) Format Partners, (right) Barnaby's Picture Library
Figure 6.15 Press Association
Figure 6.17 John Shepherd, University of Aberdeen
Figure 6.19 American Association of Advertising Agencies
Figure 6.22 Sarah Lamb
Figure 6.24 (Top left) Scallywags, (top right) Andrew Manson, (bottom left) Tim Scott, (bottom right) Young 'uns
Figure 7.2 ET Archive
Figure 7.6 Peter Newark's Western Americana
Figure 7.19 'What's On'
Figure 7.22 Abbott Mead Vickers
Figure 8.1 Colorsport
Figure 8.3 Colorsport
Figure 8.4 Stanley Milgram
Figure 8.26 (Left) J. Allan Cash Photo Library, (middle) Impact Photos, (right) TRRL

While every effort has been made to trace copyright holders and obtain permission, this has not been possible in all cases. Any omissions brought to our attention will be remedied in future editions.

All cartoons by Julia Osorno.

1
Methods
of
investigation

Introduction

This chapter looks at the range of methods used by psychologists to obtain evidence about the quality of their theories and the effectiveness of their applications. Knowing about how evidence has been collected is important. One of us recalls watching a nature programme on television and hearing the commentator say that 'swallows sleep on the wing'. Being in an uncritical frame of mind he found this a fascinating snippet of information and later that evening reported it to some friends. However, in the middle of repeating this snippet, he suddenly thought 'How do they know?'

The question is all about how you collect the evidence which tells you that a swallow was asleep when it was flying. Physiological measures of sleep require complicated equipment: electrodes attached to the scalp and so on. Clearly, this would be a bit tricky with a flying swallow. Similarly, observing that the birds had their eyes closed for a period while they were flying (and that in itself would be difficult, without the means to fly side-by-side with them), it still does not show that they were asleep – they could just be resting their eyes yet still be awake. We could only evaluate this information fully by knowing what method was used to discover it.

Sometimes, too, information of this type is actually a way of admitting that we do not know. Another nature documentary, seen by the other author, showed swallows roosting on the rocks behind a remote waterfall – safe and secure from predators, but definitely not in flight. The belief that swallows sleep on the wing has a long history and is widely known, but that does not mean that it is supported by evidence. What it actually seems to represent is the fact that nobody had ever seen swallows roosting.

So what has this got to do with human psychology? The answer is simply this: that if we are to make sure that what we are talking about is valid, we need to look at how the evidence for it has been collected. In many instances in the scientific literature, the results of studies are presented as bland summaries, without any indications of how the data were collected and how the conclusions were arrived at. This can lead to an uncritical acceptance of scientific information – even, as with the swallow story, when it is more of a scientific myth than an observable phenomenon. In psychology, we need to be even more careful of this: psychologists are not exempt from these problems. We need to be very aware of psychological methodology, so that we can evaluate the quality of the evidence that is being given to us.

A psychologist might be interested in all sorts of behaviour and experience, ranging from happiness at work, intellectual ability, driving skill, friendship or the speed of cognitive processing etc. The difficulty which every research psychologist has to face is: how to measure the thing that they are interested in. A number of important social variables, such as friendship or emotional attachments, can only be investigated by asking people about their experience. But this often presents its own difficulties: for example, that we do not know what they are judging their experience against. Alternatively, we can use observers, but then we have to face the fact that two observers will often disagree on the meaning of the same act. A man singing in the street might appear as 'just in high spirits' to one observer, as 'dangerously drunk' to another, or as 'seriously disturbed' to a third. The problem of measurement can never be entirely overcome, so it is important to be aware of how the research was conducted and how the variables were operationalized.

Figure 1.1 You might judge this person to be just in high spirits, dangerously drunk, or seriously disturbed.

This chapter reviews the most common methods of investigation used in psychology and gives some examples of how they have been applied. It highlights some of the strengths of each method, but also discusses some of its limitations. At the end of the chapter, we look at some of the common problems that psychologists have to deal with when conducting research and interpreting the evidence.

Experiments

The **experiment** is sometimes described as the cornerstone of psychology. This is partly due to the central role experiments play in many of the physical sciences and also to psychology's historical view of itself as a science. A considerable amount of psychological research still uses the experimental method. It is favoured because of the control that it offers and the type of inferences that can be made.

In an experiment, the experimenter makes a prediction about the effect one measurable variable will have on one other measurable variable. In an ideal experiment, all other variables are controlled – that is, they are held constant so that they cannot affect the outcome – and the independent variable is manipulated by the experimenter. Each time the **independent variable** is changed, the **dependent**

experiment *A form of research in which variables are manipulated in order to discover cause and effect.*

independent variable *The conditions which an experimenter sets up to cause an effect in an experiment. These vary systematically, so that the experimenter can draw conclusions about changes.*

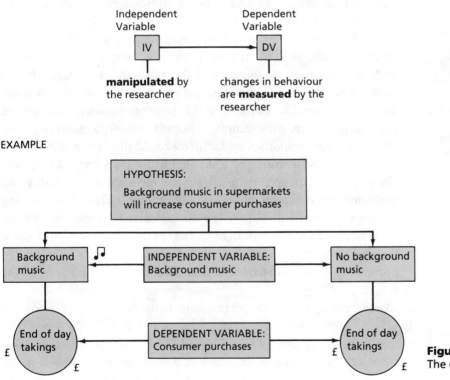

Figure 1.2
The experimental method.

dependent variable The thing which is measured in an experiment and which changes, depending on the independent variable.

variable is measured. If there is a significant change in the dependent variable then the experimenter infers that it was caused by the difference in the independent variable.

The main strengths of this method are its replicability and the inferences of cause that are made. Experiments use a precise method that can be repeated by other researchers to verify, refute or provide further insights into the results. This is known as replicability. In addition, the classic experiment gives what seem to be simple, logical answers to specific questions. The nature of experimental control is that the experimenter attempts to make sure that all the other possible influences on behaviour are reduced to just one independent variable and that nothing else can be influencing it. In this way, unlike other methods of investigation, the experiment seems to be able to identify specific causes for specific events.

The ability to identify causation – one of the strengths of experimentation – is also one of its weaknesses. Experiments imply causes, but how much of human behaviour has a single cause? Nearly all examples of social behaviour have an array of influences that affect the individual and contribute to the decision to behave in a particular way. Because experiments only look at a limited number of variables the researchers sometimes conclude that a certain form of behaviour has a simple cause, but this is just a consequence of adopting the experimental method.

Another problem lies in the fact that the precise control which is involved produces very artificial situations. This, in turn, generates artificial behaviour on the part of the research participants. If you limit the responses that someone can make, then they can only make limited responses! An example of this problem comes from cognitive psychology where, for example, a popular research measure in the 1960s involved responses to **tachistoscopic** displays which flashed up a few letters or words, or a simple picture for a few milliseconds. These required people to make simple recognition responses and facilitated the development of complex theories about how fleeting glimpses of information are or are not processed. In real life, though, we generally have rather longer to take in information, so it is questionable how much this can tell us about the ways that people process information in their everyday lives.

REPLICABILITY
CONTROL
CAUSATION
PRECISION
ARTIFICIALITY

Figure 1.3 The strengths and weaknesses of the experimental method.

A classic example of the experimental method is Rosenthal and Jacobson's (1968) study of teacher expectation. The research began with an earlier study, in which Rosenthal and Fode (1963) demonstrated that rats learned mazes more or less quickly, depending on the beliefs of the

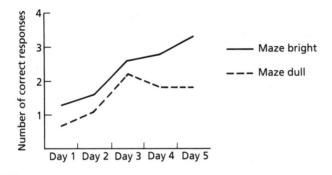

people who were training them. Psychology students who believed that
they had specially bred 'maze-bright' rats trained their animals more efficiently than those who believed that they were working with 'maze-dull'
rats: the animals acted in accordance with the label that they had been
given, because, unconsciously, the students treated the two groups quite
differently.

Rosenthal and Jacobson (1968) then extended the study to a real-life
context. They visited an American elementary school purporting to have
devised a new test which could predict which pupils would 'bloom'
academically during the course of the next school year. However, what
they called the Harvard Test of Inflected Acquisition was in fact
Flanagan's Test of General Abilities (TOGA), an IQ test measuring 'basic
ability', which claims to be free of cultural bias (culture-free).

A random sample of school pupils were chosen, which consisted of
20% of the pupils, dispersed throughout the age range and the apparent
range of abilities in the school. The teachers were informed, by acciden-
tally 'overhearing' a conversation between the experimenters, that these
children would be likely to 'spurt' in their academic performance during
the next year. Nothing was said about the remaining 80% of the pupils.
Eight months later, the researchers resumed and retested the children,
using the same **IQ test.**

In the language of psychological experiments, the experiment
contained an experimental group, consisting of 20% of the pupils, and a
control group which was the remaining 80% of the pupils. The independent variable was whether the teachers had heard the children being
singled out for special mention or not. Only those in the experimental
group had been named. This was intended to create an expectation of
likely success on the part of the teacher. The dependent variable was the
pupil's performance on the IQ test. When Rosenthal and Jacobson
analysed the scores of the retested children, they found marked differences between the performance of the experimental and the control
group. Children in the experimental group, for whom likely success had

Education

*IQ A numerical figure,
believed by some to indicate
the level of a person's
intelligence and by others to
indicate how well that
person performs on
intelligence tests.*

***control group** A group
which is used for
comparison with an
experimental group.*

been predicted, showed greatly improved scores, by comparison with those in the control group. Further analysis suggested that the main difference in performance was to be found among the younger children. The Rosenthal and Jacobson study appeared to provide clear evidence that teacher expectations could directly influence pupil performance. They called this phenomenon the **self-fulfilling prophecy**: the pupils seemed to have done better simply because the experimenters had prophesied that they would.

Perhaps predictably, the study was soon criticized. There were arguments that the IQ test was not standardized for the age range with which it was used: individual pupils' test scores were sometimes rather odd. The statistical analysis, too, was challenged as being inadequate and replication studies showed mixed results. Few of these were genuine replications and, in general, their results implied that the effect of teacher expectation was less than the original study had indicated. Interestingly, however, despite the debate about the adequacy of the evidence, the study remains a significant one – possibly because it addresses a phenomenon which many people feel themselves to have experienced in one way or another.

The experimental method was used by Rodin (1983) to demonstrate a causal link between health and a sense of control in elderly people. Rodin predicted that people who were given training that would reduce their feelings about lack of control would have a number of psychological and health benefits. The most likely of these benefits would be to develop more positive attitudes, to become more active and to feel in better health. To test these predictions, 40 elderly female residents in a nursing home were selected and interviewed extensively about their perceived control, and stress and personal problems. At the same time, a number of behavioural observations were made, including general medical tests and ratings of general health.

The women were matched on the criteria of age and length of residence in the home, and then randomly assigned to one of three groups. In Group One, the women received the training programme, in Group Two, the women received no training but received the same amount of attention from the psychologists, and Group Three received no training and no attention. This design allows for a direct evaluation of the training programme and controls for the effect of simple attention on the performance and feelings of the residents. In this design, the training is the independent variable and the measures of **attitude**, behaviour and health are the dependent variables.

The training programme was conducted by psychologists who were unaware of the baseline measures made at the start of the study. The

self-fulfilling prophecy
The idea that expectations about a person or group can become true simply because they have been stated.

Health

attitude *A relatively stable opinion towards a person, object or activity, containing a cognitive element (perceptions and beliefs) and an emotional element (positive or negative feelings).*

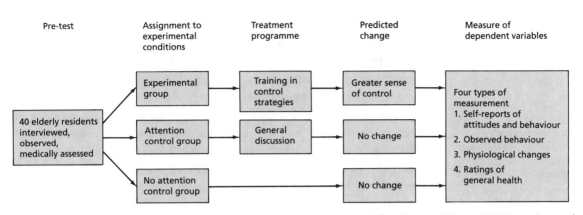

| Pre-test | Assignment to experimental conditions | Treatment programme | Predicted change | Measure of dependent variables |

Figure 1.5 Experimental design to investigate the relationship between a sense of control and health. (Rodin, 1983.)

women in Group One were given two training sessions a week for three weeks. The training programme attempted to teach the women to reduce negative self-statements and use more positive statements. The training also involved encouraging more activity and suggesting ways to solve problems about potential health hazards.

The researchers repeated the initial tests one month after the test period to measure the effects of the training programme. The results followed the predictions of the researchers, and demonstrated that the women in Group One showed improvement in their ability to deal with stresses in their lives and deal with problems. They also took part in more activities, reported themselves to be happier and more energetic, and had greater feelings of personal control. The general medical tests also showed improvement. Group Two, who had only received attention but no training, showed some slight improvements over Group Three, but these improvements were not statistically significant.

The design of this study with its **random assignment** of the women to the three conditions and the two control conditions allows for a clear inference to be made about the effectiveness of the training programme. It is worth noting that studies of therapeutic intervention often show short-term improvement which subsequent follow-up studies find is not maintained. In this study, however, the women still showed the same improvement 18 months after the training programme was conducted.

random assignment
Allocating research participants to experimental conditions by using chance, such as a toss of a coin.

Experimental control and natural experiments

The Rosenthal studies on the self-fulfilling prophecy highlighted just how important an experimenter's expectations could be in experimental work. A researcher who knew what was expected in an investigation could subtly influence the behaviour of research participants in ways that were extremely difficult to identify: subtle non-verbal signals like the difference between a genuine and an assumed smile or whether they seemed impatient as they waited for someone to perform a task. It became apparent that here was another aspect of behaviour which needed to be controlled if the 'pure' uncontaminated experiment was ever to be achieved.

The main way that experimenter expectations are controlled in a laboratory study is by using a **double blind control**. A double blind control is where both the research participants in the experiment, and the person conducting it, are 'blind' to the hypothesis of the study – in other words, they don't know what the hypothesis is. (A single blind control is when the research participants don't know the purpose of the study, but the experimenter does.) In a double blind control, the conditions of the experiment are arranged by someone else, and the person who actually meets the research participants and carries out the study is unaware of what is expected. In this way, theoretically, they can avoid influencing the results without even realizing it. Double blind controls are particularly important in drug trials, which are easily influenced by expectations. By using a double blind design, neither the person administering the drug nor the person receiving it knows whether they have received the real drug or a **placebo** – an inert substance which doesn't have any effect.

In many studies, however, the 'double blind' design is impractical, since it just leads to increasingly rigid control, which becomes less and less like everyday human experience. One alternative is the

double blind control A *form of experimental control which aims to avoid self-fulfilling prophecies by ensuring that neither the subjects nor the experimenter who carries out the study are aware of the experimental hypothesis.*

placebo effect *An inactive substance or fake treatment that produces a response in patients.*

Single blind

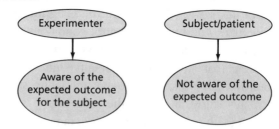

For example, Rosenthal and Fode (see page 5)

Double blind

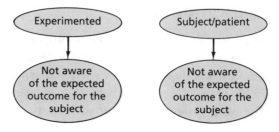

Figure 1.6 Single blind and double blind studies.

natural experiment. Natural experiments are events which have significantly changed crucial variables. By exploring the outcomes of these changes, it is possible to develop conclusions about causation.

A classic example of a natural experiment in education occurred as a result of the partition of Germany after the Second World War. As a result of the division between East and West Germany, the education system, which had previously been unified, became divided, and had to adapt to two entirely different economic systems and social structures. It was therefore possible for educationalists to study the differences between the two education systems in terms of their relationships with their economic and social contexts, knowing that the prior variables had been controlled. The recent reunification of Germany may offer similar, albeit reversed, opportunities in the long term.

natural experiments
Events in which variables change as a result of natural, political, social or economic circumstance, such that the outcome of these changes can then be studied.

The distinction between natural experiments and laboratory experiments is neatly illustrated by two studies of the effects of prolonged loud noise on performance. In a laboratory experiment by Glass, Singer and Friedman (1969) people were asked to perform tasks after being exposed to 25 minutes of loud noise (108 decibels – equivalent to a car horn at 3 feet). One of the tasks consisted of a series of unsolvable puzzles and the experimenters measured how many times people would try to solve them before giving up. The second task was to proofread a document. By comparison with a control group, people who had been exposed to loud noise beforehand made far fewer attempts to solve the problems and made many more proofreading errors.

Environment

Figure 1.7 The residential tower block studied by Cohen, Glass and Singer (1973) was particularly troubled by noise because it was built over an urban motorway.

Cohen, Glass and Singer (1973) then conducted a natural experiment on a similar issue. They studied a large, high-rise apartment block built over a busy road in New York. They measured noise levels on the various floors, which grew steadily less with height – upper floors were much less noisy than lower ones. Children on the lower floors were found to have poorer hearing discrimination and to be poorer readers than the children on the upper floors. The experimenters concluded that it was likely that the prolonged noise had affected their ability to concentrate and to make sustained effort – both of which are necessary in learning to read.

Neither type of study is perfect. In the natural experiment, although the experimenters tried to reduce the effect of other variables, such as pollution and social class, as much as possible, there are still questions about the choice of sample and the effects of various other factors which could not be controlled. However, although it has these drawbacks, it does involve real loud noise which continued for a long period of time, rather than an artificial 25 minutes of white noise generated by a machine in a psychology laboratory (see Figure 1.8).

The fact that both studies came up with similar observations indicates a different issue in psychological research, which is the difference between evidence and proof. Neither study could be take as absolute proof that noise affects cognitive abilities – there were too many things wrong with each one. The laboratory study was probably too tightly controlled, whereas the natural experiment was probably too realistic, in the sense of involving too many additional variables. Together, though, they may provide evidence of a real phenomenon. Using several different methods of study to investigate a phenomenon is known as **triangulation**. If several different methods of study all come up with similar implications, we may conclude that the phenomenon we are investigating is a real one, even if it isn't possible to obtain a single, absolutely definitive study which proves it once and for all.

Another example of a natural experiment, which triangulates on Rosenthal's work on teacher expectation, was described by Seaver (1973). Seaver used belief in sibling similarity as the basis of his experiment. Teachers often have an expectation that brothers and sisters will be similar in a number of ways, because of their shared genetic and environmental characteristics. Seaver's natural experiment was to study pupils who had been taught in the first year of primary school by the same teachers as their older sibling and to compare their performances with those pupils who were taught by a different teacher from the older sibling. In this way, Seaver had two distinct groups for his experiment: an experimental condition consisting of those taught by the same teacher

triangulation *Using several different methods of study to investigate a phenomenon is known as triangulation. If several different methods of study all come up with similar implications, we may conclude that the phenomenon we are investigating is a real one even if it is not possible to perform a single absolutely definitive study which proves it once and for all.*

Education

True experiment

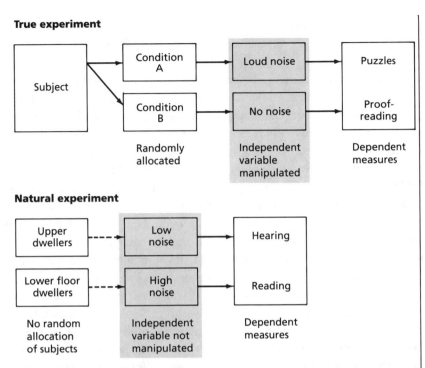

Figure 1.8 Natural experiments and 'true' experiments.

and a control condition of those taught by different teachers. The dependent variable was the performance of the children on various ability tests and assessments.

Seaver had no need to intervene in any way, since all the information came from the official school records. He selected his pairs of children, ensuring that the older and younger siblings had been separated by no more than three grade levels. Then he looked at their official school results, which recorded their performance on six Stanford Binet IQ subscales and their two grade performance assessments. Independent assessors categorized the older siblings as high, average or low performers, since this was thought to be the likely basis on which teachers formed their expectations. The performance of the younger siblings was then examined. The results showed, very clearly, that 'high expectancy' children – in other words, those with the same teacher whose older siblings had done well – showed improved performance by comparison with the control group. Similarly, 'low expectancy' students showed worse performance than controls who had been taught by different teachers. In other words, there was improvement in all categories of test performance when the teacher had a positive expectation of how the child would perform; and a low performance on almost all tests when there was a negative expectation.

The results which Seaver obtained were significantly different and very powerful – all the more so, because of the way that teachers discuss their pupils in the staffroom. This implies that it is not necessary for a teacher to have taught an older sibling to have formed an expectation. Staffroom talk can be assumed to be a powerful source of information about pupils' family histories and this, if anything, would have weakened the findings of the study. It was important, too, that the experiment showed how negative expectations could affect pupils. For **ethical** reasons it would be impossible to look at this in a controlled experimental study, so the value of the natural experiment is that it enabled the researcher to investigate a phenomenon which could not normally be studied – the effects of teachers' negative expectations on school students.

ethics A set of rules designed to distinguish between right and wrong.

Health

Pitts and Phillips (1991) described a natural experiment in Glasgow and Edinburgh where the key variables were manipulated by the authorities. The key manipulation was the policing policy directed towards people carrying syringes and needles, which might be used for injecting proscribed drugs. In both cities it was legal for pharmacists to sell syringes and needles to intravenous drug users. However, in Edinburgh, the police pursued a policy of arrests if they found people carrying injecting equipment, whereas in Glasgow no such policy existed. The study investigated the patterns of sharing of injecting equipment – a crucial vector in the spread of the **HIV virus**. What the researchers found

human immunodeficiency virus (HIV) HIV is the virus that is believed to cause AIDS by attacking the immune system.

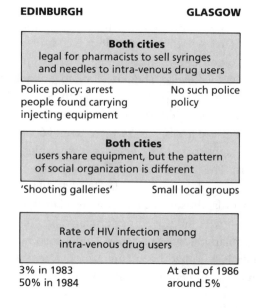

Figure 1.9 Impact of public health policies on the growth of AIDS in Scotland. (Pitts and Phillips, 1991.)

was that although sharing of equipment occurred in both cities, the way that it happened was very different and this seemed to relate directly to the policy adopted by the police force.

In Glasgow, sharing tended to occur in small local groups, between just a few known associates. In Edinburgh, however, many more drug users would share equipment, in places which had become known as 'shooting galleries'. Since the policing policy made it dangerous to be carrying needles in Edinburgh, there was an incentive for drug users to provide 'safe houses' where users could obtain both the drugs and the means of injecting it. Understandably, this style of drug abuse leads to a wider mixing of blood. In Glasgow the rate of HIV infection among intravenous drug users at the end of 1986 was around 5%, while in Edinburgh it grew much more quickly, from 3% in 1983 to 50% in 1984. It would seem that this natural experiment tells us something about the consequences of different attitudes and policing policies towards intravenous drug users.

It is important to remember, though, that studies on real life behaviour are difficult to carry out at the best of times. When they involve acts which are socially unacceptable, such as having sexual affairs, or illegal, such as taking proscribed drugs, then manipulating variables and obtaining reliable measures of a dependent variable becomes almost impossible. In the above example, although it offers a startling insight into the value of considered policing policy, it is difficult to be sure whether the data about the incidence of drug use in either city are accurate, and also to verify the incidence of HIV infection in the intravenous drug-using population.

A different problem with experimental techniques becomes apparent when we take an overview of the issues in a study by Herbert *et al.* in 1983. They investigated hospital patients who had just undergone surgery for hernia repair and had therefore just had a general anaesthetic. These were compared with a group of of patients, matched for age, gender and amount of bed-rest, who had not had an anaesthetic for at least two weeks. Each of the research participants performed a five-minute serial reaction time test four times a day for the two days after their operation. The control group were tested in identical circumstances, at the same time of day and by the same experimenter. Herbert *et al.* found that the anaesthetised patients performed less well than the controls and that these effects lasted well into the second post-operative day, suggesting that the adverse effects of anaesthetic agents can be shown to last for longer than many health professionals believe.

When studying some areas of human experience, such as illness, it is not always possible, or ethical, to assign people to experimental groups and then manipulate their experimental conditions. In this study, for example, there would be serious ethical problems in giving anaesthesia to people who did not need it or to withhold anaesthesia from some patients scheduled for surgery. In natural experiments, then, matching groups as closely as possible becomes extremely important.

Society

A general problem with psychological methods concerns how the conclusions are presented. Studies are often carried out on a very specific sample of people, yet the conclusions appear to refer to people in general. Schwabacher (1972) made an examination of articles in the *Journal of Personality and Social Psychology,* and found that the results of research using boys and/or men were likely to be generalized and discussed as if they applied to any member of the human race: 'individuals are ...'. But research based on girls and/or women was likely to be generalized only to their own sex: 'women are...'. The generalization of research on males to refer to all individuals is a potentially serious bias in psychological research and theory which can lead to serious distortions of theory as well as empirical research. The same applies with references to other groups of people, who can be virtually invisible in contemporary psychology.

There are a number of other issues about the use of the experimental method in psychology. One of them is to do with normative data. Some researchers consider that an important advantage which experiments have over observational techniques is the random assignment of research participants to experimental conditions. This helps to reduce the problems of analysis caused by systematic differences between people. Other psychologists, however, argue that grouping people together in this way, and trying to cancel out individual differences so that we only look at a group norm, is limited in how much it can tell us because it ignores what is special about people. Increasingly, for example, cognitive psychologists are drawing data from case studies of special individuals as much as from experiments that give norms of human behaviour.

The aim of controlling a human being's environment is also a little impractical. It is impossible to identify all of the crucial variables that may affect someone's behaviour, or to completely control the human environment. For one thing, it is impossible to control the mental world of people taking part in a study. Imagine a trial on a stress reduction technique where the environment is carefully controlled, but in the middle of the trial the person being 'stress-reduced' suddenly remembers that they have left the gas on. They are unlikely to disclose this to the experimenter, but it will have an effect on most measures of stress response. For these reasons, and several others, many psychologists prefer to work using observational rather than experimental techniques.

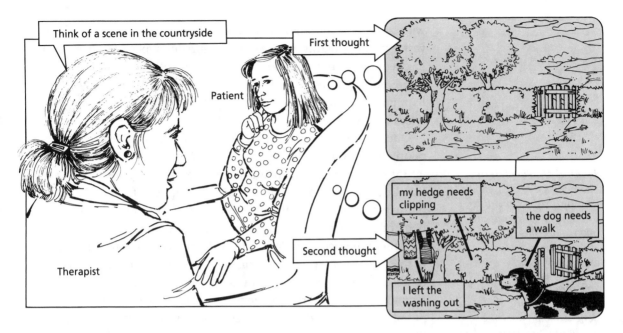

Figure 1.10 The mental world of the stress reduction patient.

Observation

Observation is an everyday human activity – we all look at what people are doing and draw conclusions from it. What distinguishes everyday observations from observational research is not whether we are observing or not, but how we go about it. Psychologists try to collect data on people they observe in a systematic and recordable way. A range of observational techniques are available to researchers, which vary according to how much the researcher takes part in the behaviour, how structured the measurement of the behaviour is and how much the research participants react to being observed.

Researchers have to choose what vantage point to take when observing behaviour. Should they observe from outside the group or should they take part and participate with the subjects? The main advantage of taking part is that it is possible to gain a deeper understanding of the motives behind the behaviour. However, the cost can be a loss of detachment – the observer may become too involved in what is going on to be able to record those observations in an objective or systematic way.

Another dimension on which observational techniques vary is the degree of structure in the way that the observation is recorded. Human experience can be described in a relatively unstructured way which allows its richness to come through. Indeed, we could say that this has been one of the main tasks of literature and poetry. The problem, though, is that it is difficult to compare one description with another. One answer to this is to code observations within a very limited structure such as by categorizing types of behaviour and just counting the number of examples of them which appear. Although this gives a much more restricted view of what is happening, it does allow researchers to compare different experiences relatively easily.

One problem in many types of psychological research concerns people's awareness of the fact that they are being studied. For example, research participants may respond to **demand characteristics** in a study – the range of cues that appear to reveal what the participants in a study are supposed to do. As Orne (1962) showed, demand characteristics can lead participants to behave in a way that they think the situation demands or the researcher wants, rather than in the way that they would normally act; so researchers often attempt to design **non-reactive measures** which do not produce this type of reaction from research participants. Covert observation – leaving people unaware that they are being observed – is one way of doing this, although there are now strict guidelines as to when covert observation becomes an unethical intrusion of privacy.

demand characteristics
Those aspects of a psychological study (or other artificial situation) which exert an implicit pressure on people to act in ways that are expected of them.

non-reactive measures
Research measures that are designed to produce the minimum influence on the behaviour of the research participants.

Health

Although the term implies that it is about seeing, observational research does not have to be entirely about visual information. Robinson and Whitfield (1987) made tape recordings of consultations between trainee general practitioners and their patients. These recordings, made with the consent of the participants, were then analysed, to look at the types of interactions between these doctors and their patients. Analysis of the tape recordings showed that, while spontaneous information from patients did not seem to connect with how the doctors spoke with them, discussions between doctors and patients – or at least, discussions initiated by patients – depended on whether the doctors asked questions or not. The study suggested that communication is a central part of good medical practice, since the discussions allowed the patients to complete their understanding of what was going on. So this kind of unobtrusive observation can be very useful in gaining insight into how everyday interactions between people take place.

Observation can also involve recording physical measurements. For example, it is important for machinery designers to know the measurements of people so that the machine can be designed for easy use. Cars have to be designed so that people can reach the steering wheel and the pedals with comfort. We can only make sure that this will happen by observing how people drive cars, and recording personal dimensions, actions and strengths.

Orne discovered that people will behave very differently in a psychology study than they will in everyday life. In one study, Orne asked a number of people whether they would carry out five push-ups as a personal favour. Not surprisingly, no one would acquiesce to this request and usually asked 'Why?' However, when asked to carry out the same actions for an experimenter the response was usually 'Where?'

In another study, individuals were asked to carry out a series of addition calculations on sheets filled with rows of random numbers. To complete a sheet, a person had to make 224 calculations. Each individual was presented with 2 000 sheets – a clearly impossible task. The research participants were given their instructions, deprived of their watch and told, 'Continue to work; I will return eventually.'

The test was originally designed to test the difference in compliance levels between hypnotic and wakeful people. Orne was unable to investigate this because his wakeful research participants were so compliant. In fact, Orne was unable to discover how compliant the wakeful research participants would be, because after five-and-a-half hours they were still engaged in the task, and the experimenter gave up.

To try and induce non-compliance, Orne modified the task so that every time they finished a sheet of calculations they had to pick up a card from a pile that would give them instructions of what to do next. However, each card said: 'You are to tear up the sheet of paper which you have just completed into a minimum of thirty-two pieces and go on to the next sheet of paper and continue working as you did before; when you have completed this piece of paper, pick up the next card which will instruct you further. Work as accurately and rapidly as you can.'

To the amazement of the experimenters the research participants complied with this meaningless request and they came to the conclusion that it is very difficult to design a study to test the degree of social control in hypnosis because of the very high level of control in the experimental situation itself.

Orne argued that experimental research participants pick up various cues about the research hypothesis and respond accordingly. He called these cues the *demand characteristics* of the experimental situation.

Figure 1.11 Demand characteristics: the demonstration of compliance to the experimenter described by Orne.

This type of observation can provide us with valuable information about people, but when it is actually conducted, it also highlights some important problems. To record the various moving dimensions on a person it is necessary to make a large number of measurements such as height, sitting height, buttock–knee length, shoulder breadth, arm reach, knee height, eye height and many more. But when we are trying to convert this information into design specifications, we find that there is

Work

Figure 1.12 Tabular format for presentation of anthropometric percentile data. (Roebuck, Kroemer, and Thomson, 1975.)

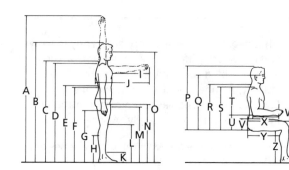

Key to figure	Dimension	5th* Percentile	95th* Percentile
A	Overhead reach	78.6	87.6
B	Stature	65.9	73.9
C	Cervical height	56.1	63.7
D	Shoulder height	53.4	60.9
E	Elbow height	41.3	47.3
F	Waist height	38.9	45.0
G	Knuckle height	27.7	32.4
H	Calf height	12.6	15.5
I	Depth of reach		
	one arm	20.2	26.8
	both arms	19.2	24.5
J	Functional reach	29.1	34.3
K	Ankle height	4.7	6.2
L	Kneecap height (top)	17.1	22.4
M	Crotch height	30.8	36.2
N	Wrist height	31.6	36.7
O	Eye height	60.8	68.6
P	Sitting height	34.7	38.8
Q	Eye height, sitting	30.0	33.9
R	Mid-shoulder height	23.7	27.3
S	Shoulder height	22.2	25.9
T	Shoulder-elbow length	13.1	15.3
U	Elbow rest height	8.2	11.6
V	Thigh clearance height	5.6	7.4
W	Elbow-grip length	12.8	14.9
X	Buttock-knee length	22.1	25.6
Y	Buttock-popliteal length	18.2	21.5
Z	Popliteal height	15.8	18.7
AA	Knee height	20.4	23.6

* 1967 Air Force officer flying personnel

labelling theory The approach to understanding social behaviour which is based on the idea of the self-fulfilling prophecy – that expectations can become self-confirming, because the people concerned act as if they were already true.

Education

no such thing as the average body shape. Daniels (1952) studied flight staff members to see how consistently average they were on 12 physical dimensions. Each person was checked to see whether they fell within the middle third of measurements on each dimension. Startlingly, not one person out of the 4000 who were measured was average on all 12!

Observational studies can also be useful when we are looking at the more subtle forms of social processes. In the last section, we looked at two different types of experiment on educational **labelling**. In another study of educational labelling, this time an observational one, Rist (1970)

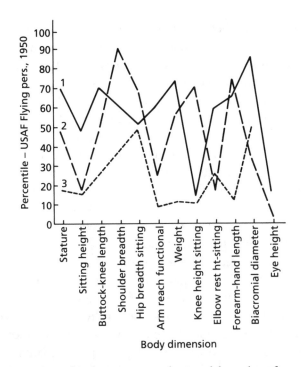

Figure 1.13 Three lines, each representing one person, showing the percentiles for each of 12 body dimensions. (Roebuck, Kroemer and Thomson, 1975.)

studied an American kindergarten teacher and her class for one year in detail. The observations were made twice weekly during one-and-a-half hour sessions for the course of that year and Rist collected additional information about the children's progress over the next two years.

Initially the teacher had grouped the children into three groups, allocated to different tables in the schoolroom. These represented fast, medium and slow learners, although she did not actually make any systematic measures of the children's ability. The pupils allocated to the top table had some predictable characteristics. They were articulate, spoke with a standard accent, were more comfortable in interacting with adults, were better dressed and cleaner, and came from intact families with good educational backgrounds. These factors are closely related to standard middle class values, but need have little bearing on actual academic capabilities.

Rist concluded that the grouping practice had everything to do with the teacher's 'ideal pupil types' – special stereotypes based upon her prejudices. More to the point, these special stereotypes became self-fulfilling: Rist found that by the end of the school year the teacher was devoting most of her teaching time to those at the top table. The follow-up data suggested that these decisions had fairly lasting effects. During these years, later decisions about the children's school careers were often based upon the initial groupings.

Rist argued that the educational process is prejudiced against children who do not fit the teacher's 'ideal types' and that this implies that society will organize itself in a caste system that ensures an impenetrable social hierarchy. Of course, as only one teacher was studied, questions must be asked about how typical they were of teachers in general. However, the general view is that these results do reveal some of the different types of processes and effects which can be found in some educational settings.

Another variation on the observation technique is to analyse the outcomes of conscious or unconscious thought processes. We could, of course, try to do this directly, by asking people what they were thinking; but many of our ideas and assumptions do not really go into words all that easily. Sometimes, too, we are not even aware that we have recurrent themes in the way that we think or interpret situations. In these cases, it is often useful to conduct indirect observations, such as looking at the things that we create, like writing or pictures.

menarche *The onset of menstruation.*

Society

Koff (1983) analysed the pictures of male and female figures drawn on two occasions six months apart (time 1 and time 2 in Figure 1.14) by young women who were either pre**menarche**al or who had already begun to menstruate. Of the 87 young women in the study, 34 were premenarcheal on both occasions, 23 were post-menarcheal on both occasions (in other words, they were already menstruating) and the remaining 30 changed their menarcheal status during the study (in other words, they began menstruation during the six months). The post-menarcheal young women produced drawings which highlighted sexual differences between men and women far more than the drawings of the premenarcheal young women. The young women who changed status during the study also showed changes in their drawings (Figure 1.14).

This study shows how much of an effect beginning to menstruate can have on the body image. Since we tend to take our body image for granted, however, this information could only really have been obtained in this indirect manner. Most people have difficulty providing direct verbal descriptions of how they feel about themselves, but how they feel may emerge indirectly through this type of observation.

Work

Indirect observations of this kind can also be used for studying how people see other aspects of their experience. A number of investigations of organizational experience, for instance, have used projective techniques such as drawing, fantasizing and story-telling to look at how people see particular organizations. For example, Nossiter and Biberman (1990) asked members of an organization to (a) imagine and draw an image that represented the company; and (b) name an animal that the company resembled. The respondents were then asked to explain why they had made the choices that they had. When this method was used to compare two very different companies, the researchers reported encour-

A	Drawing by a premenarcheal girl, time 1
B	Drawing by a premenarcheal girl, time 2
C	Drawing by a postmenarcheal girl, time 1
D	Drawing by a postmenarcheal girl, time 2
E	Drawing by a girl whose menarcheal status changed over course of study – premenarcheal girl, time 1
F	Drawing by a girl whose menarcheal status changed over course of study – post-menarcheal girl, time 2

aging differences emerging between two organizations and suggested that this type of indirect observation forced the research participants to focus on just one or two key characteristics of the company. Because of this, they provided a useful indicator of what employees and managers considered to be the most important thing about the company that they worked in.

Other, rather more straightforward, approaches to this kind of indirect observation have also been used in studying organizations. For example, Fairfield-Sonn (1987) asked managers to draw their own versions of the organization's chart, showing who was responsible to whom and where different departments features in the organizational structure. Fairfield-Sonn found that the versions drawn by managers from different parts of the company were very different and represented '**cognitive maps**' of the underlying power structures within the company, which often gave useful insights into how misunderstandings and rivalries could develop.

Figure 1.14 Drawings of 'girls' by pre and post-menarcheal young women. (Adapted from Golub, 1983.)

cognitive maps Mental images about where things are. People develop cognitive maps as they get to know a town or an institution; rats develop one as they explore mazes.

Case studies

Some psychological research does not concern itself with large numbers of subjects, as is usually the case with experiments or obser-

Figure 1.15 Genie: a case study. (Adapted from Wade and Tarris, 1993.)

The picture was drawn by Genie and shows her listening to the psychologist play the piano. These drawings were used to study her social and mental development.

vational studies. Instead, it focuses on single cases: a technique known as the case study method. A single case doesn't have to mean just one single person. It might be a family, a social group or even a single organization, which might even involve large numbers of people. Case studies can be extremely useful, because they can allow the researcher to investigate something in far more detail than might be possible if they were trying to deal with more participants.

Even though psychology has always used case studies, they have some limitations, on the grounds that you cannot tell whether one single case is typical of others, or not. In other words, it is unclear how far it is possible to generalize findings from a case study to other people or cases. But, sometimes, we can learn a great deal from exceptional cases and this can also throw light on how ordinary cases operate – in the same way that studying errors in perception, for example, may help us to understand how ordinary perception works.

Many modern researchers are finding case studies increasingly valuable, in that a detailed case study can bring out several different aspects of a given experience, each of which can be investigated separately or together. Since people's experience tends to involve lots of

Over the years there have been a number of recorded cases of children brought up in extremely adverse conditions. One tragic example is that of 'Genie', who was brought up in the most appalling circumstances by her family in America. Although there are holes in the information available, it appears that her father, who may well have been psychotic, was certainly brutal and ended up committing suicide before the case came to court. Her mother was blind and her brother seems to have patterned his behaviour on the father, who treated her in an animalistic way, beating her with a stick and howling at her. 'Genie' was kept in a backroom, bound up and strapped to a sort of commode type structure for most of her life. In 1970, aged thirteen and a half, she was taken into care and became the focus of attention for a number of developmental psychologists.

It was hoped that Genie would be able to provide some answers to questions about development, not least of which was the issue around a critical period for language. One theory suggests that language must be experienced before a certain age – the critical period – for it to be learnt at all. Initially Genie was not capable of gestures let alone language. She was almost mute and had next to no conversational experience. After some intensive care she was able to develop some language competence. Nonetheless, her linguistic competence remained retarded. In other

areas, anecdotal evidence suggests she advanced further. For example, she was able to journey by bus into the town by herself. From this case, it has been argued that some linguistic input is necessary at an earlier stage to ensure proper language development. Nonetheless, given her progress against the background of the calamitous environmental circumstances in which she was reared, some optimism at the human potential for developmental resilience is in order.

However, it is sad to add that Genie's suffering did not come to an end when she was discovered, but continued at the hands of the scientific community. After her discovery, researchers struggled for access to the disturbed child and some were able to foster her, to help her development and also to facilitate the scientific observation. Distressingly, when the research money ran out, the fostering ended, and Genie then experienced a number of poor foster placements where she was abused and regressed to her non-communicative condition. Later, her mother was able to take more responsibility for her and sued the psychologists for excessive experimentation on the child.

Case studies, like that of Genie, can provide unique insights into the human condition, though this is not the only case where the balance between the quest for scientific knowledge and the need for human compassion has left a lot to be desired.

different influences and factors anyway, just looking at how they combine together in a single instance to produce a particular result can be very worthwhile.

Case study research in cognition reveals the wide range of cognitive experiences that people have and provides a useful counterbalance to the style of research that emphasizes human norms rather than individual uniqueness. For example, Parkin and Hunkin (1991) carried out a battery of cognitive and memory tests on a single patient who, several years earlier, had received radiation therapy for nasal cancer and who was now experiencing memory problems. They found that, by comparison with scores of amnesic and control subjects, he showed marked **anterograde amnesia** for verbal material and a dense retrograde amnesia. (Anterograde amnesia is concerned with an inability to store new information; retrograde amnesia is concerned with an inability to recall events which have happened in the past.)

Health

anterograde amnesia
The loss of memory for events taking place after the damage which produced the amnesia.

This result would seem to imply that radiation treatment for this kind of cancer may inadvertently result in temporal lobe damage and corresponding behavioural deficits. However, since the study was dealing with a real human being, and in this instance the symptoms appeared some time after therapy, the study can only suggest that radiation damage might have been responsible for the clinical picture. There will have been lots of other factors going on in that person's life which might have influenced the research participant's memory – and, also, recurrence of the cancer or other physical explanations cannot be excluded.

Sometimes a case study may be of a whole organization. In a series of case studies conducted by the National Economic Development Office in 1978, the policy of graduate recruitment in a large manufacturing group was analysed. Graduate recruitment had previously been conducted in a haphazard fashion, but now the system was being updated, so that the company adopted a more structured and systematic approach. Where the previous system had led to emergency measures and redundancies, the new system allowed the manufacturing group to maintain a steady predictive recruitment of 25–30 graduates a year. Evaluation studies of the outcome of the new recruitment policy suggested that, as a result of this, the company was able to operate in a more consistent manner. It was also deemed to provide a more rational basis for decision-making, since those who were planning ahead could predict from year to year how many graduates, and of what kind, the company would be taking on.

Work

Case studies of small companies, too, have been useful. Farn and Jiang (1990) found that undertaking research in one single small business at a time allowed them to investigate a range of organizational issues in small businesses in the Republic of China. Without taking a case study approach, a number of the areas which they discovered might otherwise have proved inaccessible. Farn and Jiang adopted a consultancy-based approach, in which the participating company was provided with a consultant's report, free, in return for allowing the staff to participate in a number of interviews. The researchers then used the information gleaned from the staff to identify areas of concern within the company.

A similar model was used by Hayes and Lemon (1991), in a case study of a small, growing computer software company. In this case, the case study investigation focused on issues of social identification within the company. By highlighting areas which were not yet a problem, but which were likely to become more serious as the company grew, they were able to sensitize the directors of the company to the need for a positive approach to human resource management from the very earliest days of the company's history. This type of detailed analysis was only possible because the case study method made it possible to conduct an in-depth investigation of a wide range of organizational issues.

Society

Smith (1992) investigated the personal and phenomenological experiences of pregnancy in four women, focusing particularly on identity change during the transition to motherhood. This involved using several different forms of qualitative analysis – analysis which allowed the researcher to focus on the meaning of the experience for the women concerned. Smith was able to triangulate on different aspects of the experiences of the individual women concerned and to provide a richly detailed exploration of what it meant to be pregnant. The analysis was idiographic, in that it focused on individual experience and did not attempt to generalize to all women, and longitudinal, following each person throughout their pregnancy in four intensive case studies.

This study shows very clearly the potential that the case study method has for allowing detailed exploration of real and complex experiences: as a counterbalance to the often relatively superficial outcomes of normative research, which attempts to collate together the experience of very large numbers of people. If we are to understand the complexities of human experience, case studies are a valuable research tool. That does not mean, though, that gathering data about large numbers of people is useless. We do need to know about individual experience; but we also need to know something about general trends in human behaviour and decision-making. In this very different type of research, the survey is a major research method.

Questionnaires and surveys

A survey will usually take the form of a very short and highly structured questionnaire, usually administered to a large group of people. Questionnaires are designed to elicit information from people, in a manner which will allow the researcher to make generalizations about the topic. This is actually quite a tricky task and questionnaires can be easily affected by bad design or bias.

There are four main ways of administering questionnaires: **face-to-face** interviewing, which is useful but expensive in terms of employing and training interviewers; **handout questionnaires**, when there is a readily available and clearly defined population who are all located in one place at a given time; **postal questionnaires; and telephone questionnaires**.

Response rates to questionnaires vary with the type of sample and with the population concerned. A population which is highly motivated and interested in a topic will obviously produce a higher response rate than one which lacks interest. The technique used to administer the questionnaire itself will also produce variation in response rate, with responses to postal questionnaires being lowest and responses to telephone questionnaires highest. There are also some factors which have been shown to increase response rates, such as using follow-up queries, providing incentives to respondents (such as a prize draw or free ball-point pen) and, most importantly of all, increasing the ease of reply. As a general rule, the harder a questionnaire is to answer, the lower the response rate will be.

One of the most important things about a survey is how representative of the population it is. The population is the total set of all the cases which exist. So, for instance, if your research was into infant reflexes, your population would be all the infants anywhere in the

When conducting research you first need to identify
who you want to investigate.
This is your *population*.
Then you choose a *sample*
from this population to use in your study.

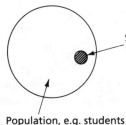

Sample, e.g. my friends
at college

Ways of selecting a sample include:
* random sampling;
* quota sampling;
* stratified sampling;
* opportunity sampling.

Population, e.g. students

sample *The group of subjects used in a study: the selection of people, animals, plants or objects drawn from a population for the purposes of studying that population.*

random sample *A way of selecting a sample where every person from the defined population has an equal chance of being chosen.*

world. Obviously, it isn't possible to study the whole of the population directly, so social researchers need to use sampling techniques which provide a **sample** of people who are representative – typical – of the population as a whole.

Social researchers use a range of sampling techniques. Statistically, an ideal type is a **random sample**, which is defined as a sample in which any member of the population has an equal chance of being selected. That sounds easy enough, but really, it is quite difficult to obtain a truly random sample, especially from a larger population. How would you go about, for instance, getting a truly random sample of, say, British 15-year-olds? You could not just ask for volunteers, because only certain people would be likely to volunteer in the first place – and, besides, where would you place the advert? Because of the difficulties of achieving a truly random sample, many researchers use the quota sampling system instead.

Quota sampling involves looking at the population and classifying it into categories. Then a sample is drawn which consists of some subjects from each category, in roughly the same proportions as they occur in the population. One special kind of quota sampling is known as **stratified sampling** and in this the population is divided into strata or layers – like, say, social class or family income. Then a set number of people from each layer is chosen for the study.

Sometimes, too, the population is not easy to contact: identifying illegal drug users, for instance, is not the sort of sample which can be obtained from looking down a list. In this case, a researcher might use a technique known as **snowball sampling**: asking existing contacts to tell their friends about the study and ask them to get in touch with the researcher. In practice, though, what many researchers – and almost all psychology students – use is an **opportunity sample**, which essentially consists of taking their sample from people that they have the opportunity of studying!

Questionnaires have an appeal to social researchers of all kinds, including psychologists, because they allow a researcher to gather a large amount of information in a relatively short space of time. They also have a more serious advantage in that they allow the investigation of 'invisible' behaviour and experience. For example, sexual behaviour is socially invisible (in most cases), and our imagination and dreams and ambitions are (fortunately!) also not open to public scrutiny. The skilful use of questionnaires allows investigation of many types of invisible behaviour and experience in large samples of people; although the more intensive investigations of this aspect of human life have tended to involve interviews rather than surveys.

Work

Surveys are also very useful for identifying general patterns of human behaviour, because they can be applied to such large samples. Raelin (1985) investigated work patterns among professional people during the course of their careers, by collecting data anonymously from 403 individuals. The sample included engineers, financial professionals, lawyers, chemists and other scientists. These were classified into three age groups: 25–34 years, 35–44 years, and 45–65 years. The questionnaire asked about individual behaviour, the characteristics of the organization the person worked in, job characteristics and mobility patterns. From this, the researchers were able to identify a number of patterns to professional work, which would have been unlikely to emerge from other methods of investigation.

Some of their findings related to age. For example, they found that **self-esteem** is at the highest level among the young professionals and lowest in the middle age group, rising again with the older ones. They also found that conflict at work was experienced most by the older group and least by the middle group. There were other age-related findings; the three groups were similar on occupation and industry, and achievement and professional participation, so it is unlikely that the differences in self-esteem arose from these factors. Instead, the researchers concluded that there was a distinct professional life-cycle, comprising three distinct career stages in the work patterns of salaried professionals. However, this conclusion may not be as clear-cut as it seems: work expectations have changed a lot over the past 20 years, and the assumptions held by older professionals regarding stability, change and the like may be very different from those held by younger ones.

self-esteem *The evaluative dimensions of the self-concept, which is to do with how worth while and/or confident the person feels about themselves.*

The information which can be obtained from questionnaires is limited in many ways. Myers *et al.* (1990) undertook a project aimed at evaluating the quality of care in a psychiatric hospital. They surveyed 258 patients in 4 'traditional' English psychiatric hospitals, using a questionnaire of 45 items supplemented by freehand comments. The questionnaire explored issues like the patient's experience of fellow patients, the staff, and the material and institutional aspects of hospital care. The responses to the questionnaire indicated that the patients were perfectly satisfied with the quality of care that they were receiving, even though both researchers and staff were aware that there were really considerable grounds for dissatisfaction.

Health

Myers *et al.* concluded that questionnaire studies of patients' views, while important, could not be regarded as an adequate assessment of the quality of life in a psychiatric hospital. In particular, bias arising because of the wish to please could not be totally avoided. In addition, some patients judged the quality of life in the hospital to be good because their only yardstick was an oppressed and threadbare life outside. Myers *et al.* therefore argued that an independent appraisal by people who were leading more privileged lives needs to be an essential complement to the patient's view when trying to evaluate the quality of care in this type of institution.

Another problem with surveys concerns the response rate. Postal surveys, for example, often have very low response rates, which are usually only between 20–30% for marketing research and can be less than 10%, in other words, fewer than one in ten of the people surveyed bother to respond to the questionnaire. And this in turn means that there is no way of checking how **representative** your respondents are, with respect to the general target population. If, say, you are carrying out research into the long-term effects of surgery, then you might only get replies from people who have had a negative experience and not have any from the people who are reasonably contented with the outcome.

One solution to this is to target a very specific population. Mathieson *et al.* (1991) conducted a survey of all married people in Southern Alberta, Canada, who had undergone a surgical removal of the larynx because of cancer. The patients and their families were contacted to investigate psychosocial reactions in the family, and nearly all of them responded to the survey. The survey found that the patients' spouses reported higher levels of depression, tension and fatigue than did the patients themselves. So it would seem that when the population being investigated is relatively small, like this one, trying to sample all of them can be reasonably successful. The problem, though, is that the conclusions which can be drawn are still relatively restricted. Purists might argue that they can really only apply to a specific population in an area of Canada, although most people would conclude that they might be typical at least of other white North American populations.

Shackleton, Wild and Wolffe (1980) looked at how response rates to postal questionnaires could be improved. The study concerned a questionnaire which was sent to 85 partially sighted school leavers and was asking about the jobs (or otherwise) which they had experienced since leaving school a year before. Thirty-five of the research participants had been made aware of the study earlier and knew one of the researchers personally, so one question was whether this personal contact would make a difference to whether they were likely to send the questionnaire back or not. In addition, the researchers offered a financial incentive to half the people in the study, which they would earn by sending the questionnaire back.

Interestingly, the researchers found that neither personal contact nor financial incentive made any difference to whether people returned the

Information disclosed to the computer and to the doctor

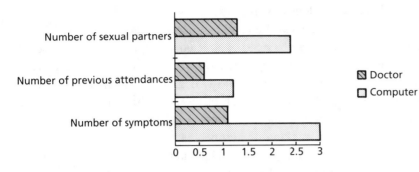

Figure 1.17 People are more likely to tell personal information to a computer than they are to a doctor. (Robinson and West, 1992.)

Information disclosed to the questionnaire and to the doctor

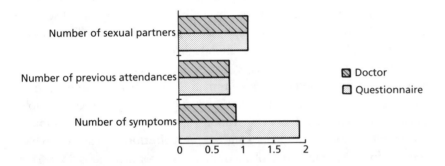

questionnaire, but keeping up contact with the respondents did. Only 42% of the research participants sent the questionnaire back initially, but when the researchers sent follow-up letters at frequent intervals, that increased to 87.5%. Obviously, nagging your respondents can be a productive strategy in questionnaire research!

The perceived source of the questionnaire may also be one of the hidden influences on response rates. Robinson and West (1992) were interested in the amount of self-disclosure made by people attending a genito-urinary clinic (a clinic which specializes in venereal disease). Before seeing the doctor, patients were asked to record the intimate details of their symptoms, previous attendances and sexual behaviour on a questionnaire administered either in a written version or by computer.

The results of the study showed that people were prepared to reveal significantly more symptoms to the computer than they would put on paper or tell the doctor. Also, more disclosures about previous attendances were made to the computer than to the doctor. One explanation of this finding might be that posing this type of question in a relatively impersonal way helps people to come out with information of a highly personal nature. Another explanation might be that we feel less exposed when informing a machine rather than a person and that we are less worried about social judgement.

Sometimes, surveys can be used to uncover some very detailed information. Schoenman *et al.* (1988) conducted a telephone survey of people who had attended a smoking cessation treatment one-and-a-half or two years earlier. They were sorted into two groups, which consisted of 29 non-smokers and 32 smokers. Each of the participants in the survey was asked to respond to a number of questions. These included identifying 6 different causes of smoking or abstinence; explaining why they personally were either a smoker or a non-smoker at the time of the survey; rating the reason they had just given on 5 causal dimensions, such as whether they felt it was controllable, likely to continue in the future and so on; and reporting how strongly they felt about the fact that they were either a smoker or a non-smoker, by rating the intensity of a list of 16 different emotions. They were also asked to estimate how likely it was that they would be smoking three months later.

The non-smokers in the survey reported confidence, contentment and relief. They were optimistic about their likely ability to refrain from smoking in the future and attributed their success to controllable, personal dispositions. Smokers' responses, on the other hand, showed uncertainty about future smoking and **attributions** (reasons) which seemed to indicate that they blamed themselves for their behaviour. They also felt that they had been personally responsible for their relapse, seeing it as essentially controllable. In other words, for smokers, feeling unhappy and sorry were associated with believing that they were personally responsible for their relapse.

attribution *The process of giving reasons for why things happen.*

The study shows how complex motivational information can be collected through survey techniques. However, it is fair to note that surveys are most commonly used to obtain non-personal information and that the more common techniques for intimate disclosure of this kind are interviews.

Interviews

Interviews are becoming increasingly popular as a research tool. They have the advantage that they allow us to investigate people's experiences through the accounts that they give of those experiences. Harré (1979) argued that analysing the verbal accounts which people give of their experience – in this case, what they say when they are being interviewed – should form an important basis for social psychology, because people's understanding of what is happening is just as important an influence on their behaviour as

1. **The hostile interview**, in which the interviewer and interviewee have different goals. For example, in a confrontational interview between, say, a bored council official and a member of the public there may be little intention of co-operation.
2. **The limited survey**, like the kind of public market research survey in which you are stopped in the street and asked, say, about your favourite type of yoghurt. These interviews are characterized by very little personal involvement on the part of either the interviewer or the interviewee.
3. **The rapport interview**, which may be clearly defined and have firm boundaries, but which also involves a high degree of positive interaction, casual byplay and human contact. This type of interview tends to produce high levels of co-operation between interviewer and interviewee.
4. **The asymmetrical trust interview**, in which one participant (usually the interviewee) is more trustful than the other, such as might be found in a typical doctor–patient interview.
5. **The depth interview**, in which a high level of rapport and trust are deliberately built up, with the intention of exploring the views and motivations of the interviewee. This type of interview is commonly used in marketing research, and also in skilled anthropological and clinical interviews.
6. **The phenomenological interview**, in which there is a maximum amount of trust and caring between the interviewer and interviewee, with very few boundaries and limitations placed on the content of the interview. The idea behind this kind of interview is that it should allow the participants to enter into and to share each other's worlds, with due recognition of both interviewer and interviewee as involved and active human beings.

Figure 1.18
Types of interview.

what is really going on. What people believe is happening is even more likely to influence their behaviour than the objective reality.

Massarik (1981) argued that interviews can vary along a number of interrelated dimensions. These dimensions include how hostile or accepting the participants are of one another; how much trust or distrust exists between participants; how the roles of interviewer and interviewee are played out – like whether these roles are extremely unequal or not – and the amount of closeness or 'psychological distance' which exists between the interviewer and the interviewee. Using these dimensions, Massarik identified six different forms of interview, which are listed in Figure 1.18. Most research interviews tend to be either limited surveys, rapport interviews or depth interviews. The most important questions for research concern how structured the interviews are, and how much rapport or trust is built up between the interviewer and interviewee.

In a highly structured interview, such as a limited survey, an interview schedule is very precisely worked out beforehand and the interviewer must stick to the specified questions exactly. By contrast, rapport interviews are less structured than the limited survey type, but much richer in terms of the quality of the information which the interviewer receives. Typically, a schedule for a rapport interview will simply list the main topics which the interview should cover. The interviewer then conducts the interview in such as way as to make it seem as much like a normal conversation as possible, concentrating on building up the relationship between the interviewer and interviewee, and getting the interviewee to feel as relaxed as possible.

Environment

Interview methods lend themselves to a wide range of enquiry. Canter (1980) collected a range of interviews from people who had just escaped from fires. They were particularly asked to describe what they did when they first discovered the fire. Canter showed that, rather than revealing a picture of people as being panic-stricken and irrational, people acted logically within the constraints of the knowledge which they had available to them – although their actions could appear illogical to an observer who knew more about, say, the physical layout of the building. Clearly, this type of information could not really be collected in any other way, in the sense that direct observation of, or experiments with, fires are both unethical and impractical, and questionnaires would be unlikely to capture anything of the richness of the information.

Society

Interview methods have also been used to investigate deeply personal matters, such as sexual behaviour. The first systematic study of sexual behaviour which used the interview method was conducted by Kinsey (Kinsey, 1948, 1953). He collected the sexual histories of 5000 men and 5000 women, from a mainly white American population. The study dealt mainly with the frequency and variety of outlets for sexual activity, and their publication caused considerable controversy because the results confounded society's expectations about sexual behaviour. In particular the study showed that there was a much higher incidence of premarital sex, fetishism and homosexuality than society had expected. It also challenged some cherished myths about the sexual behaviour of females, showing that women could be as sexually active and exploratory as men. Furthermore, it confronted other stereotypes about sexual behaviour, for example that only young people had or enjoyed sex. The research showed that people in their 80s and 90s could be sexually active. The furore resulting from Kinsey's research led to a more or less total ostracism for a researcher whose only crime was that he had applied systematic methods of sampling and data collection to an area which society deemed to be taboo.

The chart shows the level of homosexual activity reported to Kinsey by Americans in the late 1940's.

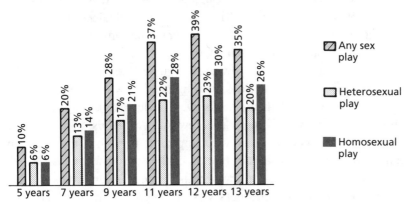

Any sex play

Heterosexual play

Homosexual play

Figure 1.19 Percentages of prepubescent boys who are engaged in sociosexual play. (Kinsey *et al.*, 1948.)

Perhaps as a result of Kinsey's experience, the area of sexual behaviour has been much discussed but, until the incidence of AIDS, relatively little researched. Everyday conversations between friends and family almost always talk about sexual behaviour in the third person, rather than talking directly about personal experience. Our knowledge about what people do, how they do it, where they do it, how often they do it and where they buy the equipment is fragmentary – we know small bits, gleaned from here and there, and put it together to make what sense we can. But this ignorance poses a problem which arises in health promotion campaigns. The health messages surrounding **HIV** and **AIDS** are all about changing sexual behaviour, but if we do not know how people conduct their sexual lives and how they negotiate sex with another person, it is very difficult to design health education programmes to change it.

An example of the gaps in our knowledge and understanding of sexual behaviour comes from a study by Ingham, Woodcock and Stenner (1991). Their research was based on interviews with 95 young people between the ages of 16 and 25, who had been contacted through a variety of sources such as hostels and youth centres. The researchers found that their respondents did not try to assess HIV risk factors in prospective partners. Moreover, the time lapse between 'becoming a couple' and first intercourse was 2 weeks or under for half of the sample and within 24 hours for about a quarter of them. It also appeared that the younger the respondent the higher the risk behaviour, as indicated by the higher condom use by older females who also progressed to intercourse later in relationships.

Another example around HIV and AIDS that highlights the sampling difficulties of surveys was described in a study of injecting drug users by

Klee (1991). Klee interviewed 303 injecting drug users, over an 18-month period. She collected her data through semi-structured interviews lasting between 50 and 90 minutes. The sample was obtained by snowball sampling from respondents, and using community drug teams, in-patient units, probation and needle exchanges.

Injecting drug users are particularly vulnerable to HIV and AIDS mainly because of the practice of sharing needles with other users. Klee reported that, although many users were reducing risk by ceasing to share needles or only sharing with a few known friends, there were still a significant number of users who appeared to ignore the risks and continued to share. The central finding of the study was that one of the most important factors in this was homelessness. Apart from HIV-risky injecting behaviour, homelessness was also significantly associated with heavy drug abuse, recent involvement in crime and disorganization in daily life.

Work

One of the questions which arise about interviews is whether they actually represent what people do. It may be that people will say that they do, or have done, one thing in an interview, whereas in fact they did something quite different. In a work setting, Latham and Saari (1984) asked employees what they would do in a number of hypothetical situations with regard to their work. Supervisors then observed what actually happened when these situations arose. There were significant correlations between employees' reports and supervisors' observations. But there were no significant correlations between what employees said they had done in the past and supervisory observations of current performance, implying that retrospective accounts may not be so useful. This is a matter of some concern, given how important retrospective accounts of what happened are for police evidence and court judgments, and it is one which we will be taking up again when we look at memory, in Chapter 5.

feminist research Mary Gergen (1988) suggested the following as the main themes of feminist research: 1. recognizing the interdependence of experimenter and subject; 2. avoiding the decontextualization of the subject or experimenter from their social or historical surroundings; 3. recognizing and revealing the nature of one's values within the research context; 4. accepting that facts do not exist independently of their producer's linguistic codes; 5. demystifying the role of the scientist and establishing an egalitarian relationship between science makers and science consumers.

Another important issue to consider when we are looking at interview methods is the relationship between the interviewer and the interviewee. From our own experience we know that if we are asked the same question by our doctor, or our friend or our boss or our mother, we will often give substantially different answers. Interviewers, too, are not neutral: we respond to being interviewed as a social event and respond in a style which we consider appropriate to the interview.

Cotterill (1992), for example, drew on her experience of researching on relationships between women in order to contribute to the discussion about what goes on in the research interview. She pointed out that feminists have argued that, even in **feminist research** which attempts to correct power imbalances as much as possible, the power imbalance between women respondents and women researchers tends to be in favour of the latter, which means that the situation does not really involve a full balance between the participants and can become distorted.

Cotterill, however, argued that interviews are fluid encounters and that the balance of power shifts such that even the researchers are sometimes vulnerable. The subjective experiences of researchers, she argued, are vitally important for our understanding of the interaction and must be acknowledged. This links with Rom Harré's insistence that it is the social meaning of what is going on that is important to the people participating in the event and that a full exploration of social life cannot take place without looking at the total episode, rather than just the individual act or action.

Rom Harré took a first degree in mathematics and physics, and a second in philosophy and anthropology. He taught mathematics and physics in various places, including the University of the Punjab, until graduate work in Oxford, with J.L. Austin, led to an abiding interest in the philosophy of science. A central preoccupation of his studies has been the role of language both in the development of the sciences and in human interaction in general.

In the last twenty years he has been a pioneer in developing the theory and practice of discursive psychology. His work in psychology has included not only theoretical investigations such as *The explanation of social behaviour* (1973, with P.F. Secord) but a wide variety of empirical studies of language in use, including the role of nicknames in personality development (1977, with J. Morgan and C. O'Neill) and most recently a study of the relation between pronoun grammars and the sense of self published as *Pronouns and People* (1991, with P. Muhlhausler). With R. Lamb he edited the *Blackwell Encyclopedic Dictionary of Psychology* (1983). He is a Fellow of Linacre College, Oxford, and Professor of Psychology at Georgetown University (Washington, D.C.). He has also been, for many years, adjunct professor of philosophy at SUNY, Binghamton, giving summer courses in the programme for Philosophy, Computers and Cognitive Science. Among his other books are *Varieties of Realism, Social, Personal and Physical Being*, and *The discursive mind* with G. Gillet.

Qualitative analysis

Partly as a result of the influence of Rom Harré and others, partly because of an increasing dissatisfaction with traditional quantitative methods and partly because of increased input from feminist psychologists, psychologists in recent years have become increasingly interested in using qualitative analysis. Qualitative analysis involves looking at data from the point of view of the meanings and implications that they have, rather than simply analysing them in terms of numerical data. As psychology becomes more and more concerned with everyday life, getting to grips with social meaning, and how people see things has become more and more important, and very often quantitative techniques simply are not appropriate for this.

There is a wide range of qualitative techniques used by psychologists. Case studies, as we saw earlier, often involve qualitative analysis of the accounts which people give of their experience. Clinical interviews, too, often involve people giving information about relevant aspects of their life history, and this constitutes qualitative information which a professional psychologist uses to make sense out of the information which they have available. Other forms of qualitative analysis include discourse analysis and repertory grids, both of which we will be looking at later in this book; protocol analysis, ethnography and thematic qualitative analyses.

Society

Griffin (1992) discussed how feminist interventions in academic research had contributed to the increased use of qualitative analysis in psychology, particularly in the social, clinical and developmental areas. By emphasizing women's perspectives, rather than just assuming that what was typical of white males was typical for the whole human race, feminist approaches had inevitably explored the experiences of women, and these were most readily obtained through qualitative approaches which allowed researchers to explore the meaning and implications of events or situations for individual women.

Cognitive psychologists, too, have used qualitative information in the form of **protocol analysis**, which involves identifying the steps involved in undertaking particular types of cognitive activity by reporting them out loud. For example, Sloboda (1985) reported a study of the process of creative musical composition which involved collecting protocols by recording the different stages which he went through as he composed a piece of music. However, one of the problems with this approach was that the need to stop the composition task and record a protocol would have been likely to disrupt what was happening when the composition process was going smoothly, so protocols in musical composition, at least, tended to reveal those moments when the composer was unsure of where she or he was going, and was casting around among available possibilities to identify a useful next step.

Hayes (1991a) used a thematic qualitative analysis to compare the outcomes of a consultancy project in two small companies. The themes were pre-established, derived directly from applying social identity theory to the organizational context and focused on three particular areas. The first was categorization, which translated into organizational terms as encouraging a perception of the in-group out-group boundaries as being at the borders of the company ('the company versus the outside world'), rather than allowing in-group rivalries to evolve within the company itself ('the programmers versus the administration'). The second theme was to do with promoting in-group cohesiveness, which translated into organizational terms as establishing good communication within the company, so that employees were made aware of how both they and others contributed to the company as a whole, and could see themselves as part of a team. The third theme was to do with promoting positive self-esteem as a result of belonging to the in-group, and translated into organizational terms as encouraging pride in the company and its achievements. The causal attributions relating to these themes which were made by employees over time were then analysed to give a picture of social identification of the employees over the 18-month period of the consultancy.

Work

Finn (1991) collected common images of freemasonry from adult community education students in the west of Scotland, and used these as the basis for a qualitative analysis of interviews with freemasons and of the available literature to explore the social significance of freemasonry in Scotland. The analysis explored the perceptions revealed during the initial analysis, and evaluated how far they linked with accounts of freemasonry in historical and current literature, with issues that emerged during interviews with wives and family members of freemasons, and with interviews with freemasons themselves. Finn concluded that many

Society

	%
Masonry as traditional hierarchical power elite	94
Masonry as means of career enhancement	79
Masonry identified with secrecy	36
Masonic membership as family tradition	28
Masonry associated with Protestant image	26
Claiming close Masonic associations	49

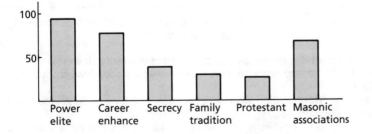

of the negative perceptions of freemasonry derived more from the actions of individual freemasons than from the organization itself, although there was some need for the organization to consider seriously the way that its members conducted their affairs.

Rosser, Marsh and Harré (1978) used qualitative methods to explore the behaviour of football fans. By collecting the accounts and explanations given by the fans, they were able to identify a series of ritualized patterns of behaviour on the terraces, ranging from a longitudinal 'progression' through the ranks with seniority reflected in whereabouts on the terraces a specific individual would stand; to sequences of chasing and ritualized threat behaviour shown towards rival fans, which, although described using extremely violent vocabulary, in fact rarely actually came to a confrontation. One implication of their analysis is that very heavy policing, by preventing ritualized behaviour, allows fans no structured outlet for their excited energies and so may possibly make confrontations more serious when they do occur.

Billig (1990) used a detailed qualitative analysis of an ordinary family's conversations about the royal family to explore the process of collective remembering. The ways that the royal family were described, Billig found, recapitulated the family's own perceived social position, and reflected aspects of their family's own biography and mythology. Other aspects of the family's discourse dealt with wider issues, such as the idea of special privilege being accorded to the royal family, which in turn revealed interesting contradictions between beliefs about social equality and beliefs in the importance of the past and tradition.

Hayes (1991b) showed how a qualitative analysis of historical children's literature could be used as a teaching tool in exploring many of

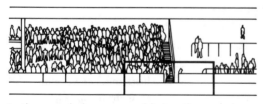

As the casual observer would view the crowd

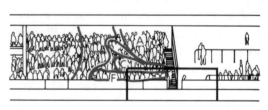

The social groups mapped on to the crowd by Rosser, Marsh and Harré

Figure 1.21 The London Road end of Oxford United Football Club stadium. (Rosser, Marsh and Harré 1978.)

The three most distinctive groups identified in the research were:
* Group F 'The Novices' who were young and took their lead from the other fans;
* Group A 'The Rowdies' who were teenagers who wore club colours and made the most noise;
* Group C 'The Town Boys' who wore regular clothes and were older and commanded respect from the other groups.

the significant historical aspects of socialization for children. In the pre-television era, books were a major agent for socialization into the wider society; and revealed very clearly the social and cultural assumptions of their times, knowledge about science and the world (often designed to reinforce a picture of the white British male as the pinnacle of civilization), social and moral values, and also how the perceptions of effective moral education for children had changed over time.

Q-methodology is used to discover personal accounts of experience and behaviour. It was developed by Stephenson in 1935 and extended the statistical tool of factor analysis. Stephenson suggested that instead of looking for common factors between people, such as personality traits or factors of intelligence, research should concentrate on individual accounts. For example, he showed people series of pictures of vases and asked them to place the vases along a scale from 'ones I think are most aesthetically pleasing' to 'ones I think are most unaesthetic'. When he had collected the data from a number of people he carried out a **factor analysis** to show the common features within an individual's judgements. In this way he was able to develop different accounts of beauty rather than trying to find objects that most people find beautiful.

factor analysis A method of statistical analysis which examines intercorrelations between data in order to identify major clusters of groupings, which might be related to a single common factor.

Stephenson (for example, 1962) used this technique to investigate images of health care in America. A similar approach was subsequently used by Stainton-Rogers (1991) to uncover a range of accounts that people make about the nature of health and illness. The importance of this work is that it highlights the need for sophisticated health education programmes which respond to the different accounts held in the populations.

More recently, some researchers have extended the scope of the Q-sort so that it can be applied to a wider range of research questions. Q-methodology still involves the same sorting method as the original Q-sort, but includes statements other than straightforward descriptions of self. In a study of lesbianism, Kitzinger (1987) used Q-methodology to discover how some women experience their lesbian identity. Forty-one self-identified lesbians completed a 61-item Q-sort, the items of which had been derived from earlier interviews. An analysis of the data produced five main accounts of lesbianism. The central theme of the accounts varied from those who saw their lesbianism in terms of personal growth, happiness and freedom, through seeing lesbianism as a political decision that derives from feminism, to seeing lesbianism as a personal inadequacy or failing. The richness of the accounts developed by the Q-sort illustrate the advantages of this approach in terms of identifying how people see their own life – something which is almost impossible to assess using the traditional psychometric methods.

We can see, then, that qualitative analysis allows a psychologist to be directly concerned with underlying meanings and implications of information, and also allows psychologists to explore wider historical and social issues in the context of their research. In modern research, most psychologists tend to adopt a combination of qualitative and quantitative approaches, which allow statistically reliable information obtained from numerical measurement to be augmented and enriched by information about the research participants' explanations.

Psychometrics

Psychometric means, literally, 'measuring the mind' and, in one sense, any systematic attempt to assess mental characteristics could come into this category. The term, however, is usually used to describe specific tests for personality, aptitudes, creativity, intelligence or some kind of attitude measurement.

psychometric tests
Instruments which have been developed for measuring mental characteristics. Psychological tests have been developed to measure a wide range of things, including creativity, job attitudes and skills, brain damage and, of course, 'intelligence'.

There are three crucial features of **psychometric tests** which need to be considered, both in their development and in their use. These are first, how consistent the test results are – an issue which is known as reliability; secondly, how true the test results are to what they are supposed to be measuring, which is known as validity; and thirdly, what kind of outcomes the test provides with different groups of people – an issue known as standardization.

If a test is judged to be reliable, that means that it will produce the same outcomes in the same situations: an attitude measurement, say, will produce the same result if the same people tested twice – assuming, of course, that they haven't changed their attitudes in the mean time. Reliability is described using a correlation coefficient, which expresses how closely the first measurement taken correlates with the second.

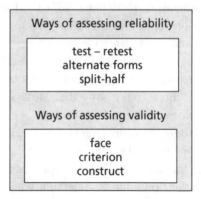

Figure 1.22 Reliability and validity.

There are three ways of obtaining reliability coefficients: **test–retest**, in which the same test is given twice; **alternate forms**, in which two equivalent versions of the test are given; and **split-half**, in which half of the test items are given on one occasion and the other half the second time. The two sets of scores which are obtained in this way are compared, and the correlation coefficient shows how closely they match: a high correlation, close to $+1$, indicates that the test is reliable. Most psychometric tests show reliability coefficients of 0.8 or above.

Validity refers to how far the test actually measures what it claims to do. There are three forms of validity. The first and least convincing (although possibly the most popular) is face validity, or surface validity, which is whether the measure looks as though it is appropriate. The second is criterion validity, which is assessed by

test–retest method A system for judging how reliable a psychometric test or measure is which involves administering the same test to the same people on two different occasions and comparing the results.

alternate forms method A system for judging how reliable a psychometric test is, which involves comparing the results produced by two different versions of the same test, if they are given to the same subjects.

split-half method A system for judging how reliable a psychometric test is which involves splitting the test into two, and administering each half of the test to the same people, then comparing the results.

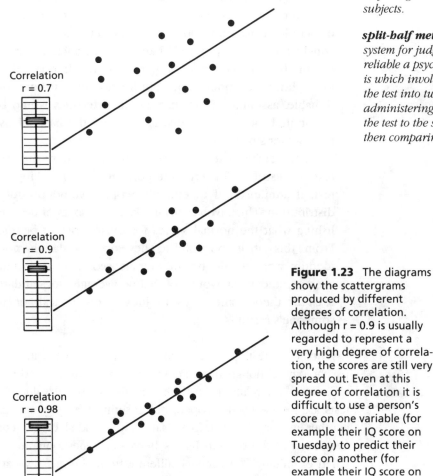

Figure 1.23 The diagrams show the scattergrams produced by different degrees of correlation. Although r = 0.9 is usually regarded to represent a very high degree of correlation, the scores are still very spread out. Even at this degree of correlation it is difficult to use a person's score on one variable (for example their IQ score on Tuesday) to predict their score on another (for example their IQ score on Friday).

intelligence quotient *A numerical figure, believed by some to indicate the level of a person's intelligence and by others to indicate how well that person performs on intelligence tests.*

comparing the test results with some other known standard – like, say, comparing **intelligence quotient** scores against school achievement or comparing the outcome of a job aptitude test with how well the person does at a work simulation task. The test's relationship with a score obtained at the same time is its concurrent validity; its relationship with something in the future is its predictive validity.

The third measure of validity is construct validity, which is about whether the test really measures the theoretical construct that it is supposed to be measuring. For instance, a model of intelligence which saw intelligence as consisting of numerous component skills would need to be assessed by an IQ test that assessed numerous component skills, rather than just testing a few.

The idea of standardization rests on the principle that abilities, both mental and physical, are distributed throughout a population according to a normal distribution curve. This concept can be traced back to the work of Francis Galton (1888), who measured thousands of people at his anthropometric centre in London, and came to the conclusion that all physical characteristics, such as strength of grip, height, breadth of upper arm etc., were all normally distributed throughout the population. Galton made the further, possibly questionable, assumption that mental characteristics would be normally distributed too and this idea has formed the basis of psychometric testing ever since.

Standardizing a test involves establishing how the scores of this test are distributed among the population and making sure that the test, if administered to enough people, would produce a normal distribution. This involves testing large numbers of people and establishing what the normal scores for those types of people might be. From this, it is possible to develop population norms, which identify what would be an average score, what would be above average, and what would be below average; so standardization, at least in theory, allows us to judge how typical, or uncommon, someone's result is.

Health

Psychometric testing is a major commercial area within professional psychology, although the commercial success of a test does not necessarily bear any relationship to its scientific or social value. Psychometric tests are frequently developed, but ensuring that they are really valid is another matter. For example, Main and Waddell (1987) conducted an evaluation of the 62-item Illness Behaviour Questionnaire. They used it when examining 200 patients suffering from chronic low back pain and found that 25 items out of the 62 were unsatisfactory, particularly with respect to validity. Three new scales – affective and hypochondrical disturbance, life disruption and social inability – seemed to represent a statistical improvement on the original scales but even they did not really help researchers or clinicians to analyse pain or disability.

Personality tests are widely used in occupational testing, as a guide in selecting people for jobs – although they are always backed up by other information, such as that obtained by job interviews, and never used on their own as an indicator of whether a particular person should be chosen. Occupational tests are also used for guidance, counselling and development. One of the oldest personality tests, and one which has generated a vast amount of research, is the Eysenck Personality Inventory (generally referred to as the EPI). This test purports to be a reliable measure of two personality factors: introversion and neuroticism. Although the test has many serious limitations, and was standardized mainly on a pathological sample (of ex-servicemen suffering from neurosis and being treated at the Maudsley hospital in the 1940s), it has been widely used in psychology.

Work

Other personality tests were based on rather more complex models of personality. Cattell's 16PF, for example, assesses personality in terms of 16 personality factors, producing a personality profile rather than single test scores. Cattell arrived at these 16 **traits** by looking not just at the reliability of questionnaire items, as did Eysenck, but also incorporating information from life records and ratings from others who knew the person concerned. As a result, the profile tends to give a much richer picture of personality than does the rather simplistic score offered by the EPI. Similarly, the Myers-Briggs Type Indicator identifies 16 possible combinations of personality characteristics, based on Jung's idea of four major personality dimensions. The Myers-Briggs Type Indicator is used in occupational, clinical and educational settings.

trait *A specific facet of personality.*

Intelligence tests, too, were traditionally used in occupational testing, although their history is deeply controversial. Gould (1981) discussed how one of the first commercial applications of the early intelligence tests was used to select people for the US army and involved tests which were so deeply loaded with cultural bias that even established American citizens found them very difficult. Not surprisingly, these had the effect of classifying any member of an ethnic minority as a moron or even lower on the intellectual scale; and ultimately resulted in strict immigration quotas for certain racial groups – which in turn meant that many of those seeking to flee from the Nazis in Europe were denied entry to America and unable to escape the concentration camps.

More recently, intelligence tests are used as one method out of many others in selecting people for the civil service in Britain, as well as for

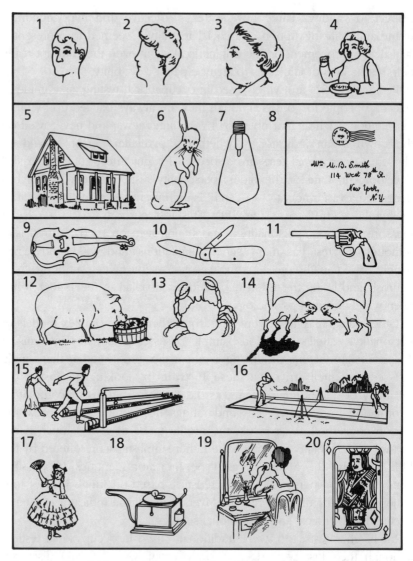

Figure 1.24 IQ test for US army recruits. (Gould, 1981.)

Even the pictorial items of the test used on US army recruits required a high degree of cultural knowledge. The task is to complete the pictures.

other types of jobs. These are often administered in the form of paper and pencil 'group' tests, such as the AH4 or AH5, which can be given to a large number of people under exam-like conditions. For more detailed clinical assessments, however, the type of intelligence test used tends to be an individualized test such as the Stanford-Binet or Wechsler tests, in which one person at a time is tested, on a whole array of sub-tests which evaluate spatial and manipulative skills, as well as more conventional skills like vocabulary and arithmetic.

Psychometric tests have also been used to help clinicians to diagnose particular disorders. For example, the Beck Depression Inventory assesses each of the major symptoms of clinical depression, and so forms a useful diagnostic tool because it allows the clinician to get an overall picture of the disorder. Although it is accepted as useful, however, there is some debate as to whether it is a unique measure of clinical depression or whether all it really measures is whether the person is disturbed or not – a kind of less specific 'general psychopathology'.

Tashakkori, Barefoot and Mehryar (1989) used the Beck Depression Inventory in Iran, where results obtained from students were correlated with other personality tests. Iran was chosen, partly because of the

Health

Figure 1.25 The Beck Depression Inventory is used by clinicians to assess the major symptoms of depression and get an overall picture of the patient's condition. (Beck, 1967.)

Mood A (Sadness)
0   I do not feel sad.
1   I feel blue or sad.
2a   I am blue or sad all the time and I can't snap out of it.
2b   I am so sad or unhappy that it is quite painful.
3   I am so sad or unhappy that I can't stand it.

Mood B (Interest in others)
0   I have not lost interest in other people.
1   I am less interested in other people now than I used to be.
2   I have lost most of my interest in other people and have little feeling for them.
3   I have lost all my interest in other people and don't care about them at all.

Thought C (Pessimism)
0   I am not particularly pessimistic or discouraged about the future.
1   I feel discouraged about the future.
2a   I feel I have nothing to look forward to.
2b   I feel that I won't ever get over my troub-les.
3   I feel that the future is hopeless and that things cannot improve.

Thought D (Failure)
0   I do not feel like a failure.
1   I feel I have failed more than the average person.
2.   I feel I have accomplished very little that is worthwhile or that means anything.
3   I feel I am a complete failure as a person (parent, husband, wife).

Motivation E (Work initiation)
0   I can work about as well as before.
1a   It takes extra effort to get started at doing something.
1b   I don't work as well as I used to.
2   I have to push myself very hard to do anything.
3   I can't do any work at all.

Motivation F (Suicide)
0   I don't have any thoughts of harming myself.
1   I have thoughts of harming myself but I would not carry them out.
2a   I feel I would be better off dead.
2b   I feel my family would be better off if I were dead.
3a   I have definite plans about committing suicide.
3b   I would kill myself if I could.

Physical G (Appetite)
0   My appetite is no worse than usual.
1   My appetite is not as good as it used to be.
2   My appetite is much worse now.
3   I have no appetite at all any more.

Physical H (Sleep loss)
0   I can sleep as well as usual.
1   I wake up more tired in the morning than I used to.
2   I wake up 1–2 hours earlier than usual and find it hard to get back to sleep.
3   I wake up early every day and can't get more than 5 hours of sleep.

importance of cross-cultural investigations of such measures, but also because students there were thought to be at high risk in terms of depression, because of its post-revolution social and political environment. This formed a significant contrast with the Western cultures in which the test had previously been investigated. A number of other tests were administered in conjunction with the BDI: the Eysenck Personality Inventory; the James Internal–External scale; and two separate measures of self-esteem.

The Beck Depression Inventory scores correlated with Eysenck's neuroticism personality dimension, which is generally accepted as a measure of anxiety states; and with the James test of **external locus of control** – a characteristic shown by Seligman and others to link closely with depression (Abramson *et al.*, 1985). In addition, the Beck Depression Inventory scores were higher with the Iranian sample than they were with comparable student samples taken from Western cultures. The researchers concluded that the Beck Depression Inventory is more complex than a measure of 'general psychopathology' and is actually capable of pinpointing a number of specific aspects of depression, the strongest of these being the feeling of 'helplessness'. We will be looking further at helplessness and stress in Chapter 2.

external locus of control
The feeling or belief that events are caused by situations or by others and cannot be influenced by oneself.

Education

Other types of psychometric test have explored personal issues, such as self-esteem and the self-concept. Marsh (1992) looked at the idea that students at school have an academic self-concept which is entirely distinct from their personal self-concept. The relationship between academic self-concept and academic performance is not a straightforward one, since some students who show high academic performance seem to have an unrealistically low academic self-concept – they do not see themselves as being particularly capable, academically, although their work indicates that they are.

In a test of 507 schoolboys, Marsh compared results on a psychometric test known as the Academic Self Description Questionnaire II with another self-concept scale and the boys' actual school grades. Marsh found that the boys' academic self-concept scores in different areas were very variable – much less so than their achievement scores – and suggested that the academic self-concept consists of a number of relatively discrete components, relating to different areas of academic work.

The above gives a flavour of the range of psychometric testing in the field of mental distress and physical health. Think of a feeling, or attitude or perspective on life and you can be sure that there are a lorry-load of tests to 'measure' it. The popularity of these tests is due in part to the apparent simplicity of their use and the apparent clarity of the answers they offer. But the reality underlying their use and application is rather different: one of the major dangers in psychometric testing is not so much the tests themselves, as their use by untrained or credulous individuals. While psychologists recognize that all psychometric tests have serious limitations, which are an inevitable consequence of trying to describe an individual's experience within very narrow pre-determined parameters, it is too easy for others to take a test result as an absolute indicator of ability or suitability – much as happened in the use of intelligence tests for educational selection (see also page 77 for a discussion of the Barnum effect).

Another flaw in many psychometric methods is that they seek to compare all individuals against one standard of 'normality' – they are nomothetic rather than idiographic, describing the general norm rather than describing the individual. Most psychometric tests – although not all – are based on the notion that psychological traits are normally distributed and people are either near the mean (and therefore normal) or at the extreme (and therefore odd). This approach is therefore limited in terms of how far it can illuminate the unique life experiences that each of us has.

Some psychometric tests, however, have avoided that particular assumption. One example of this is the repertory grid which we will be looking at in the next chapter when we explore personal construct theory. This test is **idiographic** – in other words, it is concerned with describing the individual and not measuring the individual up to some normative standard.

Meta-analysis

Meta-analysis has become an important research technique in psychology because it allows us to interpret and make sense out of the findings of several different studies, all dealing with the same topic. The aim of meta-analysis is to take out the statistical variation which happens because of the statistical artefacts which each study will have, in order to get at the 'true' correlation which underlies all the variation. Statistical artefacts – distortions of the data – tend to happen for three major reasons. One of these is the size of the sample which has been used for the study: a sample of less than 150 or so subjects will tend to produce some kind of bias, in that it is unlikely to be exactly typical of the parent population.

Another source of statistical artefacts is when the measures which have been used are unreliable, which is why it is so important to look at the reliability of a measure. And the third major source of statistical error tends to be because the possible scores have been restricted to

meta-analysis A research method which analyses the outcomes of several studies investigating the same issues.

a very narrow range; rather than being spread out as fully as they might have been. For instance, if you were collecting information about what people do in their leisure time, and you limited their possible answers to just 'sport', 'hobbies' and 'watching TV', you would have produced a very restricted range of possibilities. Restricting the range of answers like this can distort the information received and produce statistical errors.

Meta-analysis attempts to deal with these artefacts by looking at the statistical coefficients – usually correlation coefficients – which have been obtained from each of a large number of studies. These are known as effect size indicators, and meta-analysis involves calculating an average coefficient from these. By averaging out the results from a large number of indicators, it is hoped that the final outcome will reflect what the relationship really is.

The technique of meta-analysis, then, can be useful for making sense out of the findings of a large number of different studies dealing with the same area and because of that it is becoming increasingly important as a psychological research tool.

Work

Weisner and Cronshaw (1988) performed a meta-analysis of studies of employment interviews, to investigate the impact of job interview format (individual vs. board interviews) and interview structure (unstructured vs. structured) in terms of their predictive validity. The meta-analysis of 150 investigations of interview validity suggested that the 'received view' of interview invalidity is false. Within that, structured interviews produced mean validity coefficients which were twice as high as those for unstructured interviews. Board interviews tended to be more reliable than individual interviews, but there were no differences between them in terms of validity.

Robertson and Kandola (1982) performed a meta-analysis of 60 studies evaluating work sample tests used in occupational selection. The tests were assigned to one of four categories: (i) psychomotor; (ii) individual decision-making; (iii) job-related information; and (iv) group decision-making. The meta-analysis showed that psychomotor work sample tests and group discussions show a higher predictive validity than more conventional forms of psychological testing, such as intelligence or personality tests. Results from the other two categories were more equivocal. Research on applicant reaction to such tests also suggests that the tests may help to reduce adverse impact and produce positive reactions from candidates.

Education

Hillocks (1984) examined 60 studies on the effectiveness of different methods of teaching composition in American schools. The studies involved 75 experimental/control treatments in all, conducted with 11705 students, 6313 of whom were in experimental groups and 5392 in control groups. The studies ranged across elementary, secondary and college levels of education. Hillocks looked particularly at four different modes of instruction which had been explored by the researchers – presentational, natural process, environmental and individualized modes – and found that the results suggested that much educational practice was misguided. The presentational approach was the one most commonly practised in schools and colleges, and the natural process method was recommended by adherents of the National Writing Project, yet both of these methods emerged as being less effective than the environmental method. Hillocks suggested that one reason why the environmental method was so much more effective might be because it places such a high priority on high levels of student involvement.

McEvoy and Cascio (1989) investigated the widespread belief that work performance declines with age. The researchers performed a meta-analysis of 65 studies on the relationships, drawn from a review of 22 years (1965–1986) of articles in 46 behavioural science journals. The total independent sample size was 38983. The result of the overall meta-analysis of the relationship between work performance and age was a mean correlation of 0.06, which did not appear to be generalizable across settings. In other words, the results revealed that age and performance appear to be generally unrelated. There was also no indication that this was moderated or affected by the type of performance measure or type of job to any great degree. This is a counter-intuitive finding, but an important one, as it emphasizes the importance of individual qualities in work performance, regardless of arbitrary classifications such as age.

Work

These studies all demonstrate some new insight into a range of data that has been achieved by meta-analysis. However, no single method of analysis is perfect and meta-analysis, too, has its weaknesses. One of these is apparent in another example of the technique provided by Schwarzer and Leppin, in 1989. They conducted a meta-analysis of 55 studies (32739 research participants) designed to investigate whether social support is related to health status. A correlational analysis supported the relationship between family support and health, but mainly for women who were in stressful situations. What this implies is that the influence of variables, other than the major one under study, might have to be examined in order to get a more complete picture of what is going on.

Society

As Schwarzer and Leppin pointed out, meta-analysis, like data obtained from other sources, needs to be interpreted and the quality of the information which it can offer depends to a high degree on the quality of that interpretation. All meta-analyses are subject to retrieval bias (some studies may have been overlooked), publication bias (studies may have been rejected by journal editors) and reporting bias (completed studies may not have been submitted for publication). In addition, meta-analyses all operate on just one level of analysis, so any conclusions which we draw from them about human beings must also be located within the full range of cultural, social, psychological and other levels of analysis.

Meta-analyses have other problems too. For example, the sheer quantity of information is sometimes used to disguise its worthlessness. A much quoted example of this is the analysis of intelligence test correlations between different family members collected by Erlenmeyer-Kimling and Jarvik (1963). This study formed the basis of the estimates of heritability of intellectual differences made by Jensen (1969) and Eysenck (1971). The study by Erlenmeyer-Kimling and Jarvik presented correlational data from 52 separate published studies, though they did not list their sources. Figure 1.26 shows an increase in correlational values as the genetic similarity of people under test becomes closer and was claimed to be firm evidence of a high genetic component in intelligence.

Kamin (1974) investigated this meticulously, obtaining a list of their sources from the authors of the meta-analysis and obtaining copies of each different set of data. By looking closely at these, he was able to show that this meta-analysis was worthless. Some studies which contradicted the heritability argument had been omitted and some of those which had been included were seriously flawed or, in some cases, had been fabricated by the eminent British psychologist Cyril Burt (Kamin, 1974). Sadly, it has to be reported that the worthlessness of this data has

Figure 1.26 Meta-analysis of studies on intelligence by Erlenmeyer-Kimling and Jarvik. Each spot (•) represents the results from one study. Overall the data were collected from 52 studies.Kamin, however, pointed out that several studies had been left out and that some of the included ones were worthless.

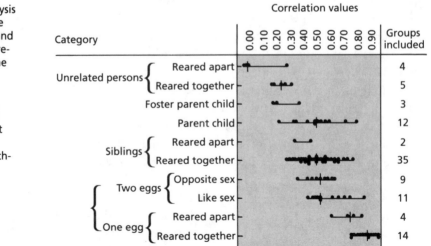

not stopped its regular appearance in many academic publications. In terms of meta-analysis, the methodological point to take from this is that big is not always better.

Some evaluative issues

All methods have some limitations and some advantages. The way that information is collected will inevitably limit the type of response that can be recorded. There are a number of general problems to consider when evaluating the quality of psychological evidence. These include publication bias, ethnocentric sampling biases and ethical issues.

Publication bias

Maccoby and Jacklin (1980) point out that the consideration of differences between the sexes is influenced by biases in the collection and reporting of the evidence. For example, studies usually compare average scores for men with average scores for women. In fact, the differences between the averages is often very small, while the variation within each group is quite large. The reporting of difference between the sexes obscures the greater differences within sexes. Maccoby and Jacklin (1980) pointed out that the desire to obtain and publish positive results means that there is an inbuilt bias towards publishing differences between the sexes and discarding the evidence that finds no difference. This makes differences more visible than similarities.

Another source of distortion comes from the choice of research for publication. Researchers and editors prefer positive results. Students, too, experience this with practical work and they often experience disappointment when a practical exercise 'fails to work'. This disappointment is misplaced, because a non-significant finding can be just as important as a significant one in providing scientific information. In this context, it is worth noting that, historically, some of the major advances occurred as a result of exploring errors.

For example, Pavlov (1927) developed the theory of classical conditioning (see Chapter 5), because he investigated why his dogs were salivating at inconvenient times. When he entered his laboratory in the morning ready to investigate the salivation reflex he found that the dogs would salivate before he put food in their mouths, thereby wrecking his experimental procedure. Many researchers would have tightened the controls on the study to prevent the dogs seeing Pavlov enter the room. Pavlov, however, decided to investigate why his study was going wrong in the first place, rather than just trying to ensure that it worked out as he wanted.

Ethnocentric sampling bias

*ethnocentricity Being
unable to conceptualize or
imagine ideas, social beliefs
or the world, from any viewpoint other than that of
one's own particular culture
or social group. The belief
that one's own ethnic group,
nation, religion, scout troop
or football team is superior
to all others.*

Ethnocentrism refers to the tendency to overestimate the importance and worth of people in your group, and to underestimate the importance and worth of people who are not in your group. The ethnocentric sampling bias refers to the limited range of people who are studied by psychologists. For example, Sears (1986) described how published research in social psychology between 1940 and 1950 was based on a wide variety of subjects and research sites. However, from the 1960s to the 1980s, research was overwhelmingly based on laboratory studies using students as subjects. A review of samples used in social psychology articles published in American journals in 1980 revealed that 46% of studies were conducted on psychology students, a further 37% were conducted on other students and only 17% of studies used adults in their research.

Research on the full life span suggests that college students are likely to have less crystallized attitudes, a less formulated sense of self, stronger cognitive skills, stronger tendencies to comply with authority and more unstable peer group relationships, by comparison with other adults. Moreover, the laboratory setting is likely to exaggerate all these differences. Silvermann (1977) showed that these factors often resulted in the outcome of psychological findings being entirely artificial.

Sears argued that the view of human nature which psychology suggests may have been influenced by design of its studies and its choice of subjects.

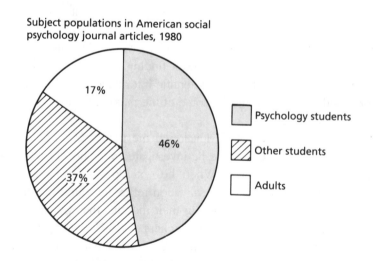

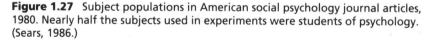

Figure 1.27 Subject populations in American social psychology journal articles, 1980. Nearly half the subjects used in experiments were students of psychology. (Sears, 1986.)

To caricature the point, contemporary social psychology ... presents the human race as composed of lone, bland, compliant wimps who specialise in pencil and paper tests. The human being of strong and irrational passions, of intractable prejudices, who is solidly embedded in tightly knit family and ethnic groups, who develops and matures with age, is not that of contemporary psychology; it does not provide much room for such as Palestinian guerillas, southern Italian peasants, Winston Churchill, Idi Amin, Florence Nightingale, Archie Bunker, Ma Joad, Clarence Darrow, or Martin Luther King.

Sears stated that psychology tends to describe a world from a narrow viewpoint, a viewpoint that is largely white, male, middle class and transatlantic. Generalizations are made about 'people', when, in fact, the sample does not include many of the groups that make up our society and the world community. Issues of class, ethnicity and gender are largely ignored in the general work of psychology. For example, child care, family structure and the norms of everyday living show considerable cultural variation. This is rarely acknowledged in psychology books, which usually portray a particular style of 'family life' as normal, desirable and stereotyped.

This problem is not limited to psychology: a major issue in studies of psychiatric diagnosis concerns how people from different cultural groups are diagnosed and treated by psychiatric practitioners. One issue that affects this is the way that we judge the behaviour of people from a different group to ourselves; another is the highly restricted experience of non middle class lifestyles on the part of most medical practitioners and particularly psychiatrists.

In the 1990s, there have been a number of signs which suggest that psychologists have been taking these issues more seriously. There is, for example, a much higher incidence of published research from countries other than North America and Britain in the journals. As social and developmental psychologists in particular become sensitized to issues of ethnocentricity, many researchers are making consistent efforts to address the problem. However, research in the discipline is still very heavily weighted towards white, transatlantic student research participants and there is still a very long way to go.

Ethical issues

One of the most important questions in modern psychology is that of conducting research in an **ethical** manner. When they are considering undertaking a research project, psychologists are professionally bound to consider the detailed implications of the research, both in terms of how

ethics *A set of rules designed to distinguish between right and wrong.*

they undertake it and in terms of the possible consequences of the research. Will the results of the investigation have a harmful or beneficial effect on our society and the individuals within it?

Ever since 1969, when Miller uttered a call for psychology to be at the forefront of promoting a responsible and humane society, psychology has become increasingly concerned with the ethical characteristics of its research. In part, this concern arose directly because of some of the extremely unethical studies conducted by psychologists in the past. Professional psychological associations regularly revise the ethical principles that are issued to researchers, which offer a framework for the conduct of research. The principles issued by the British Psychological Society in 1990 are summarized in Figure 1.28.

In addition, psychological research institutions have ethics committees, which meet regularly to consider the implications of research and its likely outcomes before the research is carried out. Research proposals which do not conform to these criteria, or which look as though they may have potentially damaging outcomes, are not permitted to develop into full-blown studies. The contrast between this approach and much of the early history of psychology, in which researchers felt able to adopt an entirely manipulative approach towards their 'subjects', could hardly be greater.

Figure 1.28 Summary of the ethical criteria proposed by the British Psychological Society for the conduct of research.

Consent Have the subjects of the study made an informed consent to take part? Have the parents of child subjects given informed consent to the research procedures? Have payments been used to induce risk-taking behaviour?

Deception Have the subjects been deceived? Was there any other way to carry out the study other than by using deception? Have the procedures been approved by other psychologists?

Debriefing Have the subjects been effectively debriefed? Has any stress caused by the procedures been removed?

Withdrawal from the investigation Are the subjects clear that they can withdraw from the study at any time without penalty or scorn?

Confidentiality Participants in psychological research have the right to expect that information they provide will be treated confidentially.

Protection of participants Investigators must protect participants from physical and mental harm during the investigation.

Observational research Unless the participants give their consent to being observed, observational research must only take place where those observed could normally expect to be observed by strangers.

Giving advice Psychological advice must only be given if the psychologist is qualified in the area in which the advice is requested.

Colleagues Psychologists should take action if they believe that any of the above principles are being violated by a colleague.

Summary

1. Applied psychology has involved many different methods of investigation. Experiments are investigations in which a variable or condition is changed, in order to see what outcome results from that change.
2. Laboratory experiments involve a high degree of control, in order to rule out other possible causes. Other experiments, though, occur naturally, and so cannot be controlled very easily.
3. There are several different types of observational studies, including recorded observations using video and audio tape, and participant observation, which involves the researcher joining in the activity.
4. Case study research involves focusing on one single instance, such as a person, family, or organization. It allows researchers to look into the topic far more deeply.
5. Questionnaires and surveys are ways of investigating large groups of people, but do not allow very detailed analysis of any particular topic.
6. Interviews involve gathering information about people's own ideas, opinions and experiences, and so can provide information which a researcher using other methods might miss.
7. Qualitative analysis involves analysing data by looking at its meaning. It can be approached in a number of different ways, and is increasingly used by psychologists.
8. Psychometric tests are ways of measuring mental characteristics. They need to be reliable, valid and standardized.
9. Meta-analysis involves looking at large numbers of studies which have been undertaken on the same topic, and aggregating their results to see what overall conclusions might be reached.

PRACTICE QUESTIONS AND ACTIVITIES – 1

Methods in psychology

Suggest how you might investigate the following questions using the psychological methods described in this chapter.

1. How do changes in lighting, heating and breaks affect the productivity and well-being of workers?
2. Do young offenders have different family lives to non-offenders?
3. How do people behave towards someone when they have a romantic interest in them?
4. Are some styles of teaching more effective than others?
5. Does a noisy environment harm the intellectual development of children?
6. Does a noisy crowd encourage sports players to perform at their best?
7. Do people get better after a series of psychotherapy sessions?
8. How do staff in a psychiatric hospital relate to a patient in conversation and how do the patients relate to each other?
9. Are psychometric tests a useful predictor of performance in the work place?
10. Does living near a motorway have any effect on the behaviour, intellect and emotional adjustment of children?

Advantages and disadvantages

Most of the above questions could be effectively studied by more than one method. However, the choice of method will affect the type of information you will get from the study. With this in mind, try and fill in the following table, and summarize the key points of the experimental and observational methods.

In the second table, look at the relative advantages and disadvantages of laboratory and 'real life' settings for studies.

	Experiments	Observations
Definition		
Advantages		
Problems		
Examples		

	Laboratory	Natural environment
Definition		
Advantages		
Problems		
Examples		

PRACTICE QUESTIONS AND ACTIVITIES – 1

Measuring psychological variables

If you want to measure the length of a piece of wood, or the temperature of your bath, it is a relatively easy exercise. We have a recognized unit of measurement and some simple measuring instruments. However, with most psychological variables the task is far from simple. Take aggression, for example. My judgement of aggressive behaviour might be very different from someone else's, in particular, different from the person I think is being aggressive.

Ways of measuring aggression might include:
- physiological measures of arousal;
- rating scores of observers;
- self-report rating scores;
- check list of aggressive actions;
- activity count;
- number of previous convictions, etc.

All of these measures tell us something, but none will give us the whole picture. Psychologists, inevitably, have to make do with these partial measures, and it is worth considering the strengths and weaknesses of the various measures available.

Go back to the list of ten research questions above and select two or three. Then identify the variables that need measuring, and try and suggest as many ways as you can of measuring them.

2
Personality and coping

Introduction

Human beings have always developed theories about what people are like. The theories of personality which we know about go back to the ancient Greeks and beyond, and some of these have formed the basis for modern psychological theories of personality. Strangely, however, many of these theories appear to have a relatively limited range of applications outside of the narrow therapeutic contexts in which they were first developed. General theories about what ordinary people are like do not seem to have proved themselves all that useful in everyday living.

Personality theories which have led directly to the development of therapies for emotional distress and maladjustment, however, seem to have been the ones which have made the jump into the world of applied psychology – the psychoanalytic theory of Sigmund Freud and the humanistic approach of Carl Rogers, for example, have stimulated vast libraries of work. As this is an applied psychology text, however, we have decided to cover only those theories for which we could find more general application, outside of their specific clinical context in which the theory was first developed.

One approach to personality that has been used in a variety of contexts are trait theories of personality. The reason for their popularity might well be their ease of application – personality **traits** are generally assessed by a relatively simple questionnaire. Another possible explanation may be to do with the relatively prescriptive and simplistic models which these approaches produce. Trait theories seek to categorize people into predetermined character types using common dimensions of personality measurement, such as introversion and extroversion. One of the limitations of this approach is the failure to acknowledge the way that each individual brings a unique perspective to the world. The **personal construct** theory of George Kelly forms a contrasting

personality *A distinctive and relatively stable pattern of behaviours, thought, motives and emotions that characterize an individual.*

personal constructs *Individual ways of making sense of the world, which have been developed on the basis of experience. Personal construct theorists argue that getting to understand the personal constructs which someone applies to make sense of their experience is essential for effective psychotherapy, as well as for effective interaction in day-to-day living.*

approach to the understanding of personality, which takes this uniqueness as its starting point.

Another approach to personality, which also deals with personal adaptation to the world, has been to try to correlate specific aspects of personality with a variety of behaviour and health outcomes. An example of this approach is the study of the Type A and Type B personality. Early research suggested that there was a simple relationship between certain distinctive styles of behaviour and coronary heart disease, which suggested a link between a personality trait and this illness. However, subsequent studies have shown the relationship is rather more complex, involving the interaction of a number of other variables, notably stress, with the Type A personality type.

Studies on stress have to battle against common misconceptions of the concept. It is useful to clarify what we mean by stress by breaking the elements of stress down into **stressors** (environmental changes that can induce a stress response), the **stress response** (physiological changes, such as autonomic arousal, which occur as a result of stress) and the **stress experience** (how we perceive the situation and the experiences we are having). The experience of stress is affected by our cognitive appraisal of the situation that we are in, so stress is not inevitable. We might easily see an event as exciting rather than stressful.

The study of stressors often begins with the study of stressful life events. In this, the work of Holmes and Rahe in charting the degree of stress provided by differing life events was particularly useful. Their Social Readjustment Scale provided a stimulus for a wide body of research which examined the various factors that induce stress. Research into the relationship between physiological arousal and stress adaption generally takes as its starting point the 'fight or flight syndrome', described by Cannon, and also the work of Selye on the General Adaptation Syndrome to long-term stress.

One of the most important concepts in our modern understanding of the stress experience is the idea of **coping**. Lazarus and Folkman suggest that when an individual is under stress, there are two important cognitive

stressors Environmental changes that can induce a stress response.

stress response Physiological changes, such as autonomic arousal, which occur as a result of stress.

stress experience How we perceive the situation and the experiences we are having. The experience of stress is affected by our cognitive appraisal of the situation that we are in, so stress is not inevitable. We might easily see an event as exciting rather than stressful.

coping The process of managing external or internal demands that are perceived as taxing or exceeding a person's resource.

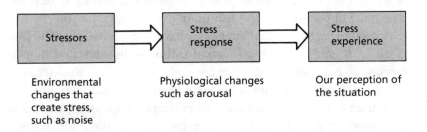

Environmental changes that create stress, such as noise

Physiological changes such as arousal

Our perception of the situation

Figure 2.1 Components of stress.

learned helplessness *The way that the experience of being forced into the role of passive victim in one situation can generalize to other situations, such that the person or animal makes no effort to help themselves in unpleasant situations, even if such effort would be effective.*

locus of control *Where control of what happens is perceived to come from. An internal locus of control means that the person sees it as coming from within themselves – so they are largely in control of what happens to them or at least in a position to influence it. An external locus of control means that it is perceived as coming from sources outside of the person and so is not something which the individual can influence.*

self-efficacy beliefs *The belief that one is capable of doing something effectively. Self-efficacy beliefs are closely connected with self-esteem, in that having a sense of being capable and potentially in control tends to increase confidence. But the concept is often thought to be more useful than the generalized concept of self-esteem, since people may often be confident about some abilities, or in some areas of their lives, but not in others.*

self-actualization *The making real of one's abilities and talents: using them to the full.*

appraisals which need to be made. The first of these concerns the nature of the stressor and how threatening it actually is. The second, which is equally important, concerns how well we are able to cope with the situation. Healthy living, in this model, is considered to be the successful matching of stressor to coping abilities.

Psychologists have developed a number of concepts which may help us to understand how people go about coping with stressors. The concept of learned helplessness describes how some people may learn to be passive in the face of stressors, when they could reduce or remove them by taking action. This occurs as we learn passivity from an inability to take effective action in some situations, and then go on to generalize this response to other situations where it does not really apply. The concept of **learned helplessness** has been applied to explain a number of areas where people seem to act in ways which are lower or less effective than their ability suggests, or than they could be.

A complementary concept to learned helplessness is the idea of **locus of control**. In research into locus of control, psychologists look at whether people attribute their behaviour or circumstances to something which they can control or whether they see themselves as powerless to do anything about it. A third important concept that has been applied to coping, and is also related to the other two, concerns **self-efficacy beliefs** – our beliefs of our own competence. If we believe that we are able to take action effectively, we are more likely to try, and we are therefore more likely to cope effectively. In all three of these concepts it has been found that examining the cognitions, or beliefs, which are associated with the experience of stress is helpful in understanding how people can improve their experience; and this has been found in many different contexts.

Rogers' theory of personality

Carl Rogers developed one of the first humanistic theories of personality – an approach to personality which emphasized the wholeness of the human being, and the positive growth and striving to develop which the humanists saw as a feature of psychological health.

According to Rogers, human beings have two basic needs. The first of these is the need for **self-actualization** – the idea that human beings have a basic need to make real, or actualize, the different aspects of themselves. This leads them to seek personal development in a number of ways: developing or perfecting their skills; exploring new ideas; or enhancing their understanding. Pursuing hobbies and other interests is a way of satisfying this need.

The second of the two needs which Rogers identified is the need for **positive regard** – the idea that people also need approval, companionship, love or at least respect from other people. This need is so important that it can sometimes stifle the need for self-actualization. The individual does not actually dare to explore their own interests, on the grounds that this might lead to disapproval from others. But if the need for positive regard is satisfied and the person feels secure in the approval of others, then the two needs can both be balanced and the individual will be psychologically healthy.

positive regard Liking, affection, love or respect for someone else.

In Rogers' model, then, healthy personality development occurs through relationships which offer **unconditional positive regard**, freeing the individual to explore potential and work towards self-actualization without risking loss of relationships through disapproval. These may occur through family, in childhood or beyond, or they may occur later in life.

unconditional positive regard Love, affection or respect which does not depend on the person's having to act in particular ways.

Neurotic clients had parents who always made their love conditional upon 'good behaviour'. This conveyed the message that the child was not really loved and the parents would really have liked some ideal child who never misbehaved. Such children grew up striving for approval from others and neglecting their own self-actualization in the process. They also developed an unrealistically high ideal self-concept, which led to increased anxiety and neurosis. The role of the Rogerian therapist, teacher or other helper is to provide a relationship of unconditional positive regard which will free the person to explore their own life options and satisfy their need for self-actualization.

The therapy is now known as person-centred therapy, an approach which emphasizes that the person is active in their own development. The term rejects the dependent/passive implications of the term 'patient'. Rogers later came to the view that a professional therapist was not actually essential. Unconditional positive regard could be provided by other people, for example through encounter groups. By meeting others face-to-face, without defences, and experiencing warmth and support from them, the person can feel free to explore their potential needs in a psychologically safe environment.

> **Key reference:** ROGERS, C. R. (1961) *On Becoming a Person: a therapist's view of psychotherapy.* Constable, London.

Butler and Haigh (1954) evaluated the effectiveness of psychotherapy using a Q-sort (see Qualitative Analysis in Chapter 1). The correlation between self-concept and ideal self-concept in two groups of people

Society

correlation A measure of how strongly two, or more, variables are related to each other.

counselling The key features of counselling are as follows. (a) At least two people are required. One must identify themselves as in need of help (the client) and one must identify them-selves as the person providing help (the coun-sellor). (b) The participants must be in psychological contact, though not neces-sarily face-to-face. (c) Both the counsellor and the client must identify the process as counselling rather than some other kind of helping relationship. (d) Counselling is freely entered into by the person seeking help. (e) The counsellor acknowledges the central role of, and actively uses relationship variables in, the counselling process. (f) The counsellor will share with the client the common key purpose of the activity.

who had applied for therapy was –0.01, which is effectively no correla-tion at all. By comparison, the correlation in a similar group of ordinary people who had not applied for therapy was +0.58. One of the two low groups then entered client-centred therapy, based on the ideas of Carl Rogers. The second group was asked to wait for six weeks, until the therapist would be free to begin their treatment. At the end of six weeks, Butler and Haigh tested them again, and found that the **correlation** between self and ideal self of the group which had been waiting had not changed, nor had the 'normal' group, but those who had been receiving treatment showed a rise in their average correlation, to +0.31, which suggested that the therapy really was helping them to build up their self-esteem.

The humanistic approach to personality, as exemplified by Rogers' theory, was first developed as a result of work in personal therapy. In a direct challenge to the idea of the impersonal, detached 'professional', Rogers identified various qualities which were essential for a successful therapist, and Truax and Carkhuff (1967), in an investigation of successful and unsuccessful **counselling**, found that these were indeed important. The three qualities were congruence (acting in a way that fits with the situation), genuineness (being truly sincere in the expressions and emotions which are being expressed) and empathy (being able to experi-ence the feelings of the other person). Only by having these three quali-ties, Rogers argued, would it be possible for someone to demonstrate genuine, unconditional positive regard. And clients would be able to tell if it were faked.

Truax and Carkhuff found that helpers who did not possess these qualities were not merely ineffective – they could actually contribute to people becoming worse than they had been before they came for help. These qualities were not affected by sex, race or the prior experience of psychotherapy, or, interestingly enough, by the person's past experience as a therapist. The researchers found that therapists with personal prob-lems of their own were likely to be less effective and they also found some support for the suggestion that helpers are more effective when they are working with clients who hold values similar to their own.

Counselling is an over-used word and can sometimes be applied to interactions of very diverse qualities. Sanders (1993) noted that the term counselling has been used to describe tutorial advice in education, psychotherapeutic situations and also disciplinary hearings. In the armed forces and in some medical settings, you are said to have been coun-selled when you have been cautioned or reprimanded. People who are trained counsellors have a much clearer idea of what the term means and what activity should take place during a counselling session.

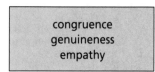

congruence
genuineness
empathy

Figure 2.2 Essential qualities for a successful therapist.

Figure 2.3 Cultural conventions of death can either encourage or inhibit the expression of feelings. (The top two pictures show sombre spectators at the funeral in London of wartime leader Sir Winston Churchill. Mourners at the funeral in Tehran of Ayatollah Khomanie behaved in a dramatically different way, *left*.) (See also Figure 8.36a).

A particular personal crisis where humanistic psychology has often been applied is when someone is facing up to the approach of death. In Western society, people often try to avoid issues around this inevitability, and rarely discuss their deepest anxieties and fears. The humanistic approach, however, encourages people to break through their inhibitions and cultural conventions which lead us to hide our feelings and to distort our experience. Kubler-Ross (1970) suggested that both dying people and their relatives should be more open about the approach of death. It is more positive to help the dying person to prepare for death than to suppress talk about it; and Kubler-Ross suggested that if this taboo is broken, it would become possible to see death more positively, as the final stage of personal growth.

Humanistic psychology of one form or another has often been applied in organizational psychology, where it was apparent to those studying organizational behaviour that people were far more complex than simply automatons who would work harder in response to the incentive of

Work

sensitivity training A technique of experience-based training in which individuals learn interpersonal skills.

earning more pay. **Sensitivity training** is one example of a humanistic approach which became very popular in the 1960s and 1970s, though mostly in America. This involved groups of managers and workers coming together with the aim of improving their abilities to work together, and to communicate with each other, and to improve their sensitivity to how they are seen by other people.

Another aspect of this approach was to deal with potential conflict by trying to encourage communication between staff members. Rogers (1970) described an example of a large American company that used an encounter-style approach to help with personnel problems that were likely to occur because of a merger. Key members of staff were interviewed and encouraged to express any feelings, anxieties, prejudices and personal fears about the forthcoming merger. Then the two groups of staff were brought together and a facilitator displayed the concerns of both sets of staff, using a visual presentation. Open discussion was encouraged and people were asked to communicate as frankly as possible about their feelings concerning the merger. Rogers argued that this encounter helped to clarify which were substantial concerns, and which were based on conjecture and misunderstanding.

Maslow, another humanistic psychologist, suggested that it is not enough for work to just satisfy 'deficiency' needs such as the need to earn enough money to survive. Maslow's hierarchy of needs, which we will be looking at in more detail in Chapter 6, portrays the idea that human beings have higher needs, which become important as soon as lower ones are satisfied. Paying workers adequately is important, but it is not the only thing that motivates us. We also need to exercise our autonomy and to develop our potential in the work place.

One approach which is related to this idea is that of McGregor (1960). McGregor conducted a series of interviews with managers and employees in a study of effective management. McGregor proposed that an important factor in management was the theories which managers hold about human nature and what people are like. These theories, he argued, could be classified into two kinds, which he referred to as Theories X and Y. Theory X is the idea that people are basically lazy and need to be driven. They will therefore dislike work and require high levels of control, discipline and direction in the work place in order to get them to carry out their duties. Theory Y, on the other hand, suggests that work is as natural as play and that people like to work and to feel useful. They will therefore, if given the opportunity, become involved with their work, and develop a high sense of responsibility and commitment.

McGregor found that managers who held Theory Y beliefs tended to

A manager day-dreams

run their departments in such a way as to emphasize responsibility and trustworthiness on the part of the employees. Crucially, these managers also had departments which were more productive than those run by managers with Theory X beliefs. People worked harder, took fewer days off sick and were far less likely to leave.

Humanistic theories of personality emphasize the idea that people are active, capable and able to act autonomously. This led to the development of a number of attempts to tap into these qualities in organizational practice as well as in personal therapy. **Peer group assessment** and assertiveness training are both concepts which derived from this approach. Peer group assessment is a method of professional development in which a group of, for example, social workers would meet with a facilitator and devise a series of criteria for assessing efficient work. These criteria would be used by each individual to assess his or her own performance. Subsequent sessions might explore ways of improving performance and ways that the improvement could be monitored. **Assertiveness training** is about making your own needs clear, while, at the same time, acknowledging the needs of other people.

The humanistic approach to personality emphasizes the uniqueness of the individual, our unique experience of the world and the unique needs that we have. It emphasizes our personal agency – our ability to take effective action in the world around us. Although many would see this as a strength of the theory, there is also some concern about whether this really applies as widely as Rogers and Maslow assumed it did. Many people experience severely restricted choices in their lives and may not have the same opportunities for personal development which are open to others.

Figure 2.4 Theory X and Theory Y managers. Which are you? Which is your boss? Which is your tutor?

peer group *A group of people who are considered to be the equals of, or like, the person concerned.*

assertiveness training *Group therapies with a behavioural focus designed to model and role-play appropriate ways to stand up for your rights.*

Personal construct theory

Personal construct theory proposes that, in order to understand how people act and interact with one another, we need to look at how they interpret, or construe, their personal worlds. George Kelly (1955), the founder of personal construct theory, proposed that people act as scientists as they go about their daily lives. By that he meant that we are continually developing theories about the world and interpreting our experience in the light of these theories.

Kelly argued that the theories which people use tend to take the form of a set of bipolar constructs, such as 'aggressive – gentle' or 'generous with money – tight-fisted'. The important point of the theory, though, is that one person may use constructs which are very different from those used by someone else – even someone doing the same job. This means that they will see their worlds quite differently and may interpret the same event as meaning something entirely different.

repertory grid technique
A system for eliciting personal constructs and showing how individuals use them to interpret their experience.

Kelly proposed a system for eliciting personal constructs from people, known as the **repertory grid technique**. The first step in this technique involves naming a set of 'elements'. These would depend on what the particular target of the study was: if it concerned, say, interpersonal relationships, then the relevant elements would consist of people who were significant in that person's life. But if the target concerned, say, reactions to consumer products, the elements might consist of a set of different competing items. By asking clients to take the elements in groups of three, and to say in what way any two of the group were similar but different from the third, their personal constructs will emerge. Then these are arranged in a grid form, and the grid can be used to explore the further implications of that person's personal construct style for each particular problem.

> **Key reference:** KELLY, G. (1955) *The Theory of Personal Constructs.* Norton, New York.

Education

Personal construct theory has been applied in a number of fields, offering as it does the opportunity for researchers to get a glimpse of the phenomenological worlds – the personal understandings and experiences – of other people. Driver (1983) showed how an understanding of the personal constructs which children hold about the physical world is useful to science teachers working in schools. By identifying the causal frameworks that pupils were bringing to their work, it became easier for the teacher to disentangle the errors which children made. Because they were more aware of students' existing theories, they could therefore understand the sources of their errors and misunderstandings, and could teach the children more effectively.

Examining clients' personal constructs can often produce unexpected insights into why people act as they do. Winter (1967) looked at people who had been attending social skills training, but unsuccessfully – they had not developed improved social skills as a result. When the personal constructs which these clients applied to social skills were elicited, it became apparent that the lack of success in the training was not because they could not learn social skills, but because they did not want to. Their repertory grids showed that they saw social skills as being associated with unpleasant characteristics, like dishonesty, selfishness and egotism, and so they resisted the training.

Society

Fay Fransella, born 1925, Jersey, the Channel Islands.

At school in England she was not considered to be of 'advanced' material and so left at sixteen and took a domestic course plus evening classes in shorthand and typing. She then trained as an occupational therapist and spent ten years in charge of a department in a large psychiatric hospital. During this time she married and divorced and learned to fly a Tiger Moth.

Questioning whether what OTs did was of any use, a clinical psychologist and psychiatrist helped her design some research. After an A level course at evening classes, she was accepted at University College London. From there she took a Diploma in Abnormal Psychology at the Institute of Psychiatry, London.

Her jobs from 1962 to 1982 included a lectureship in clinical psychology at the Institute of Psychiatry, where she obtained her PhD; research grants with the Mental Health Research Fund and the Medical Research Council; senior lectureship, and then Readership at St George's Hospital and the Royal Free Hospital Medical Schools. In 1968 she married again and took up sailing, studying for the Yachtmaster Off-Shore Certificate.

Her main professional interests have been in stuttering, weight disorders and, increasingly, personal construct psychology. She has written and edited ten books and many chapters and journal papers.

She was appointed Reader Emeritus in 1981 on taking early retirement to set up the Centre for Personal Construct Psychology in London. The Centre offers courses, workshops, therapy and counselling, and research and development work within organizations.

In 1972, Fay Fransella showed how personal construct theory was valuable in speech therapy with people who suffered from congenital stuttering. Fransella showed that repertory grids were not only useful to the client, in directing their attention to constructs that might prove either helpful or unhelpful in dealing with their problem, but also to the therapist, who would be more effective if able to see things in the same way as the client did.

Fransella discussed how stutterers who are just on the verge of being cured of their stuttering through speech therapy often relapse suddenly. Their interaction with the world as a stutterer is familiar to them: they are aware of how people are likely to react and have developed a range of constructs which enable them to deal with that world. Entering the new world of the non-stutterer is threatening, because it involves different expectations of interaction and requires the formation of a new set of personal constructs – living with unknown rules.

Work

Fullerton and West (1991) performed a study which used repertory grid techniques to examine how management consultants and their clients thought about consultancy. In the first stage, a set of categories, used to describe relationships between the consultant and the consulting company, was obtained from a panel of consultants. From this work, they obtained six broad categories of consultancy relationship, such as 'unsuccessful', 'moderate', 'correct' and 'unpredictable'. These were then presented to 22 consultants and 12 clients – senior managers who had been responsible for employing consultants in their organization. The subjects were asked to take the described relationships in groups of three, and to say in what way any two were similar to each other and different from the third.

This stage of the research provided a large number of different bipolar dimensions, such as: 'Client has control/Consultant has control'; 'Consultant is aware of practicalities/Consultant is too theoretical' etc. These were used as the basis for a questionnaire, in which a new group of subjects were asked to rate how important each of these dimensions were, and also to estimate how frequently they occurred within normal consultancy practice.

Fullerton and West found that there were some noticeable differences between the perceptions of clients and consultants. In general, consultants tended to emphasize those constructs which were concerned with building up positive relationships (e.g. 'the consultant should always be available to the client'); whereas the clients tended to emphasize cost and efficiency (e.g. 'effective use of time'). It also emerged that both groups sometimes held different models about what the whole business of consulting should be about – for example, many of the consultants perceived their role as setting processes in motion which would mean that the company initiated the necessary changes itself, whereas many of the clients expected a prescriptive approach, in which the consultants would tell them what to do. The researchers felt that this discrepancy could be resolved by better communication and explanations at the very beginning of the consultancy relationship, and also by consultants giving more attention to educating their clients about process-oriented ways of doing things.

We can see, then, that personal construct theory provides us with a way of looking at the **phenomenological** basis of individual personality. People may act in distinctive ways because they have distinctive ways of understanding what is going on around them, so understanding how someone sees what is happening around them can often give us useful insights into why they are acting as they are. A contrasting approach has been to look for norms of behaviour and to measure people against these norms. This approach is exemplified by the trait theories of personality.

phenomenological
Concerned with the person's own perceived world and the phenomena which they experience, rather than with objective reality.

Trait theories of personality

Trait theories are based on the idea that differences between people stem from internal consistencies, known as **personality traits**. These traits then produce regularities in behavioural style, which can then be assessed by means of questionnaires. One of the earliest trait theories of personality was developed by Eysenck, in 1947, who described two major dimensions of personality: (a) introversion/extroversion, and (b) neuroticism/stability, and argued that these were fundamental traits which accounted for a large proportion of individual differences.

Eysenck argued that personality traits arose from inherited physiological tendencies. He saw extroversion as arising from differences in the balance of excitatory and inhibitory processes in the reticular activating system of the brain. Introverts, he suggested, inherit nervous systems which have a bias towards excitation rather than inhibition and so do not need to seek additional stimulation. Extroverts, on the other hand, inherit a tendency towards inhibitory responses, so they become bored very quickly and therefore seek new stimulation. Neurotic individuals, according to Eysenck, have a labile (easily activated) autonomic nervous system, so they react readily and quickly to alarming or stressful stimuli. Stable individuals, on the other hand, take longer to react and do so less strongly.

Other researchers identified different combinations of personality

About 2300 years ago the Greek philosopher Hippocrates suggested a theory of personality types that was based on the proportion and dominance of four bodily fluids or humours. This theory was refined by another Greek philosopher, Galen, some 500 years later.

The four humours are as follows.

Blood   If a person is influenced by blood then he or she will have a **sanguine** personality – cheerful, optimistic, outgoing and interested in physical pleasures.

Phlegm   If a person is influenced by phlegm he or she will be **phlegmatic** – unemotional, detached, withdrawn, dependable and dull.

Yellow bile   If a person is influenced by yellow bile he or she will have a **choleric** personality – angry, hateful, short-tempered and impulsive.

Black bile   A person influenced by black bile is **melancholic** – unhappy, depressed and self-destructive.

Figure 2.5   Personality types.

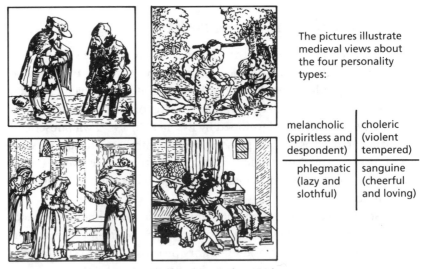

The pictures illustrate medieval views about the four personality types:

melancholic (spiritless and despondent)	choleric (violent tempered)
phlegmatic (lazy and slothful)	sanguine (cheerful and loving)

Figure 2.6   Personality traits. (From Eysenck, 1981.)

traits. Cattell, for example, described 16 different traits as a result of collating and factor analysing information about people from several different sources (Figure 2.9). The models grew and diversified throughout the second half of the 20th century. Gradually, however, a general trend began to emerge, and factor analysis of the various models showed that these could be grouped together into five basic factors, which are listed in Figure 2.8. Cluster analysis of a large number of personality tests, including Cattell's 16PF and Eysenck's

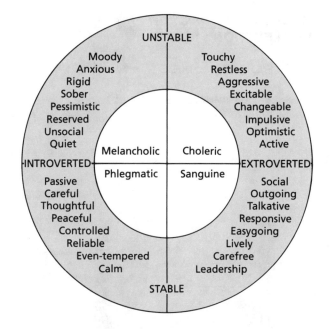

Figure 2.7 Personality: Eysenck's factors. The inner ring shows Galen's four personality types and the outer ring shows how two of Eysenck's factors map on to it. (Eysenck, 1981.)

1. **Extroversion** Sometimes referred to in a slightly wider form as 'surgency'.
2. **Emotional stability** Broader in scope than Eysenck's neuroticism, but essentially similar.
3. **Agreeableness** Including traits of generosity, friendliness and interpersonal criticism.
4. **Control** Including traits of disorganization, meticulous approaches to work etc.
5. **Culture** Including the traits of curiosity, creativity, intelligence, and knowledgeability.

Figure 2.8 The five robust factors.

five robust factors The recurrent finding that personality questionnaires produce results which, when factor analysed, fall into five groups, thought to represent basic personality traits.

temperament The stable aspects of the character of an individual, which are often regarded as biologically based, and as providing the basic dispositions which interact with the environment to develop personality.

EPI, showed that the **five robust factors** seem to emerge repeatedly. The recurrent finding suggested that they may be tapping into basic differences in temperament between individuals.

Claridge (1988) argued that looking at underlying **temperament** is more useful than trying to identify specific personality traits (in other words, regularities of behaviour), since traits can be affected so strongly by social experience. Initial differences in temperament are shaped and modified by experience and social expectation, which may produce differences in surface personality, even between those sharing the same basic temperament.

SIXTEEN PERSONALITY FACTOR
QUESTIONNAIRE FIFTH EDITION (16PF5)

16 PF 5

PROFILE SHEET

SURNAME _Harrison_ FORENAME _Molly_

SEX _F_ AGE _31_ DATE _12 . 1 . 94_ NORM GROUP _Gen Pop F+M_

Instructions:
Write the raw score for each factor in the second column and the sten score in the third column. Starting with Factor A, place a mark over the spot representing the appropriate sten score. Repeat for each factor. Connect the marks with straight lines.

PRIMARY FACTORS

Factor	Raw	Sten	Left Meaning	Standard Ten Score (STEN)	Right Meaning
A: Warmth	12	5	More Emotionally Distant from People		Attentive and Warm to Others
B: Reasoning	15	10	Fewer Reasoning Items Correct		More Reasoning Items Correct
C: Emotional Stability	16	6	Reactive, Emotionally Changeable		Emotionally Stable, Adaptive
E: Dominance	6	2	Deferential, Cooperative, Avoids Conflict		Dominant, Forceful
F: Liveliness	20	9	Serious, Cautious, Careful		Lively, Animated, Spontaneous
G: Rule-Consciousness	7	3	Expedient, Non-conforming		Rule-Conscious, Dutiful
H: Social Boldness	14	6	Shy, Threat-Sensitive, Timid		Socially Bold, Venturesome, Thick-Skinned
I: Sensitivity	13	6	Objective, Unsentimental		Subjective, Sentimental
L: Vigilance	5	2	Trusting, Unsuspecting, Accepting		Vigilant, Suspicious, Sceptical, Wary
M: Abstractedness	12	7	Grounded, Practical, Solution-Oriented		Abstracted, Theoretical, Idea-Oriented
N: Privateness	0	1	Forthright, Straightforward		Private, Discreet, Non-Disclosing
O: Apprehension	10	5	Self-Assured, Unworried		Apprehensive, Self-Doubting, Worried
Q1: Openness to Change	16	6	Traditional, Values the Familiar		Open to Change, Experimenting
Q2: Self-Reliance	10	6	Group-Oriented, Affiliative		Self-Reliant, Individualistic
Q3: Perfectionism	13	6	Tolerates Disorder, Unexacting, Flexible		Perfectionistic, Organized, Self-Disciplined
Q4: Tension	14	6	Relaxed, Placid, Patient		Tense, High Energy, Impatient, Driven

GLOBAL FACTORS

EX: Extraversion	8	Introverted, Socially Inhibited		Extraverted, Socially Participating
AX: Anxiety	4	Low Anxiety, Unperturbed		High Anxiety, Perturbable
TM: Tough-Mindedness	5	Receptive, Open-Minded		Tough-Minded, Resolute
IN: Independence	3	Accommodating, Agreeable, Selfless		Independent, Persuasive, Wilful
SC: Self-Control	4	Unrestrained, Follows Urges		Self-Controlled, Inhibits Urges

Figure 2.9 An example using Catell's 16 PF Test Profile.

Key reference: McCrae, R. R. and Costa, P. T. Jun. (1985) Updating Norman's 'adequate taxonomy': intelligence and personality dimensions in natural language and in questionnaires. *Journal of Personality and Social Psychology,* **49**, 710–21.

Ever since the theory was developed, there has been a considerable amount of research which has used the Eysenck Personality Inventory (EPI). In part, this is because it offers a relatively straightforward and easily analysed outcome: instead of the 16-factor profile offered by Cattell's 16PF, for instance, only 2, or at the most 3, significant scores are offered by the EPI – extroversion, neuroticism and sometimes an additional dimension of psychoticism, although the psychoticism dimension is very much more contentious than the other two. The relative ease of analysis which this involves is tempting to any researcher and Eysenck's claim that these were tapping fundamental biological differences made it even more appealing.

However, it is worth noting that many of these studies find differences that do not correspond to Eysenck's theory. For example, Gulian (1974) conducted two experiments to study the relationship between noise as a stress agent and introversion–extroversion. In the first experiment, six introverts and six extroverts (assessed by the EPI) were simultaneously presented with experimental noise of 125–8000 Hz and a set of seven monosyllables (joc, foc, toc etc.) simultaneously. The research participants were required to press a button when they heard a particular noise. Despite the fact that this was exactly the type of task in which neural inhibition or excitation might be expected to play a part, there were no differences between the introvert and extrovert groups.

In the early days of sport psychology, investigating personality traits was enormously popular. Researchers sought to identify what makes a good sportsman or woman and, in particular, the characteristics that distinguish the winner from the loser. Although this is a less common approach among sports psychologists now (partly because of 50 years of research showing that traits are elusive at best), there are still some researchers who investigate personality traits and sport.

Sport

Daino (1985) investigated 36 male and 30 female competitive tennis players aged between 13 and 18 years old, and a parallel set of age-matched controls who did not participate in sport. They were each given several psychometric tests: a trait-based personality test; a test which assessed anxiety and related behaviours; and a will-to-win questionnaire. The results showed significant differences in personality traits between the two groups. As a group, tennis players scored higher on extroversion and will-to-win and lower on neuroticism, **psychoticism**, anxiety,

psychotic *A mental state characterized by profound disturbances in reality testing, thought and emotion.*

obsessiveness and depression than controls. All the tennis players had significantly higher will-to-win scores than the non-sports control group. In addition, male players had lower obsession scores, and female players had higher extroversion scores, but lower neuroticism, anxiety, depression and somatization scores than their matched controls.

One problem with studies of this kind, however, is that they often confuse the causal factors – they tend to assume that the measured personality traits cause behaviour, where, in fact, the reverse could just as easily be the case. Playing sport regularly produces psychological as well as physiological adaptations. For example, sportspeople have more experience of achievement than people who do not play sport, because they have more opportunities to achieve. This increases their sense of self-efficacy and control which, as we will see later in this chapter, is an important factor in reducing stress. In addition, the exercise itself produces physiological changes in the brain, through the release of the chemicals endorphin and enkephalin, which make us feel happier and more at ease with ourselves. So it is hardly surprising that competitive sports players score differently on personality tests from people who do not play sport. That does not mean, however, that it is personality which causes competitive success.

Another way that personality comes into sport psychology is in the composition of a team. It is an everyday belief of many spectators that combining the best technical exponents of a sport does not necessarily make up the best team. There are different roles to fulfil, and a team full

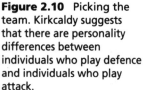

Figure 2.10 Picking the team. Kirkcaldy suggests that there are personality differences between individuals who play defence and individuals who play attack.

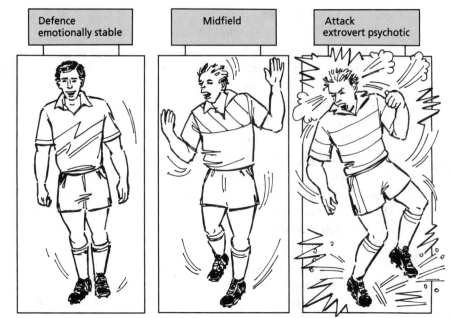

of captains might not play too well together. Kirkcaldy (1982) administered the Eysenck Personality Questionnaire to 199 team athletes and 124 individual sport athletes, all aged between 22 and 24 years old. A third of the sample were female. However, Kirkcaldy did not find any significant personality differences between team and individual athletes. When team sports were considered separately, Kirkcaldy found that males in offensive positions scored substantially higher in psychoticism and extroversion than mid-field players. Defensive players showed more emotionally stable patterns than offensive players, although these differences were relatively slight.

Kirkcaldy's results are surprising in several respects. The view of males in offensive positions seems to confound the spectators' view of professional football, where the 'hard' people are usually in the middle or in defence, and the model striker is former England football captain Gary Lineker, who has never knowingly said 'bother' during a game. The original lack of difference between team and individual athletes is also surprising considering the different qualities involved in, say, football and tennis, although less so if one adopts a sceptical approach to the value of trait theory in the first place.

Although the five-factor approach to personality has attracted a considerable amount of interest among personality and occupational psychologists, much of this research has been concerned with replicating the original findings, that factor analysis of various personality measures consistently yields the five robust factors. Perhaps owing to a relative lack of awareness of this model on the part of other applied psychologists, there appears as yet to have been relatively little research in which the model has been applied to real problems.

It is not, however, for lack of suggestions that the model could prove useful. For example, Widiger and Trull (1992) suggested that the five factors could be of value to clinical psychologists and psychiatrists in interpreting the personality axis of the American diagnostic system for psychiatric illness known as **DSM-IIIR**. It would be useful particularly for clarifying some basic personality dimensions and for broadening the idea of personality beyond the conventional extroversion–neuroticism dimensions of Eysenck's theory.

Other trait measures of personality, though, have been applied in different areas. On the topic of anti-social behaviour, Lane (1987) investigated the relationship between the personality measures of psychoticism, extroversion and neuroticism, and levels of conduct disorder, delinquency and therapy responsiveness in children in a series of short-term and long-term studies. Eysenck had argued that extroverts, because of their lower levels of conditionability, should feature more prominently in

DSM-IIIR *Published in 1987, it is the revised third edition of the* Diagnostics and Statistical Manual of Mental Disorders, *developed by the American Psychiatric Association.*

Society

groups showing higher levels of conduct disorder or delinquency, and had later extended that argument to include the idea of psychoticism. The results of the test broadly confirmed the predictions, in the sense that children who showed higher levels of anti-social behaviour did tend to score more highly on these measures.

In the area of health, one of the major concerns has been to understand why people engage in knowingly risky behaviours (e.g. smoking, eating hamburgers, having unsafe sex) and who is most likely to do it. McCown (1991) looked at the relationship between Eysenck's three personality variables (extroversion, psychoticism and neuroticism) and people's knowledge about HIV and high-risk behaviour. In the first study, out of 315 adults, those who scored highest on the N (neuroticism) scale also scored lowest on the test of HIV knowledge. However, these people also scored highest on the L scale, designed to detect when people are lying, so none of their test results can really be taken as valid.

In a second study, McCown asked 86 homosexual men who had completed an HIV education course to complete the same surveys. All three personality variables (extroversion, psychoticism and neuroticism) correlated with unsafe sexual practices. In other words, McCown concluded, people who were most neurotic and most extrovert were also most likely to engage in riskier sexual behaviour.

In a study on marriage, Russell and Wells (1991) assessed the quality of marriage of 94 couples aged between 19 and 73 years old, and compared this assessment with the responses of the couples on a version of the Eysenck Personality Questionnaire. There was a significant degree of what the researchers called 'assortative mating' on the neuroticism, psychoticism and lie scales, but not extroversion. In other words, the researchers concluded, people who scored high on neurotic or psychotic scales tended to marry people with a similar profile on these dimensions.

One of the striking things about this study, though, is that like the previous one, the researchers used the lie scale as if it were a trait measurement. This directly contradicts even Eysenck's own views of the test: the lie scale was introduced in order to detect people who were answering the questions falsely, in order to present themselves as better than they really were. Any L score higher than two implies that the person has been lying, and so none of their test results should be taken seriously. The use of the L scores as if they were actual personality data, as these experimenters did, merely suggests that their original data are completely unreliable, so we cannot exactly place much faith in their conclusions.

Another, very serious problem with the Eysenck Personality Questionnaire and similar tests is to do with the expectation of the people taking the tests. Furnham and Varian (1988) looked at how people predict and accept their own test scores. In their first experiment, 159 undergraduates tried to predict their own and a well-known other person's personality scores on the EPI. They were fairly good at this. Then, 56 undergraduates were given false feedback after completing the EPI. They were more likely to accept positive feedback as accurate than negative feedback, even though it did not have any connection with their actual scores. Then, in a the third study, 80 adults were given different feedback statements after completing the EPI and asked whether they believed them to be accurate. General positive statements were more readily believed than any others.

This leads us to an inevitable discussion of the Barnum effect (so named after the famous American showman). In brief the Barnum effect refers to a powerful tendency to believe information given to us about our personal qualities. This is used to good effect by fortune tellers, astrologers, handwriting 'experts' and various other contemporary shamans. If the 'expert' can say what people are prepared to accept, and can phrase it in such a way that it implies some intimate insight, then there is a good, if dishonourable, living to be made.

An early demonstration of this was provided by Forer (1949) in a classroom demonstration of gullibility. Forer described a personality test to his students and allowed them to persuade him to let them take the test (the first rule of a successful con is to appear reluctant!). Thirty-nine students completed the test. One week later, each was given a typed personality sketch with their name on it. The researcher encouraged the class to keep the results confidential and the students were asked to indicate whether they thought the test results were accurate. In fact they had

Figure 2.11 Saying what people want to hear and suggesting some intimate insight is the way to fame and fortune.

1. You have a great need for other people to like and admire you.
2. You have a tendency to be critical of yourself.
3. You have a great deal of unused capacity which you have not turned to your advantage.
4. While you have some personality weaknesses, you are generally able to compensate for them.
5. Your sexual adjustment has presented problems for you.
6. Disciplined and self-controlled outside, you tend to be worrisome and insecure inside.
7. At times you have serious doubts as to whether you have made the right decision or done the right thing.
8. You prefer a certain amount of change and variety, and become dissatisfied when hemmed in by restrictions and limitations.
9. You pride yourself as an independent thinker and do not accept others' statements without satisfactory proof.
10. You have found it unwise to be too frank in revealing yourself to others.
11. At times you are extroverted, affable, sociable, while at other times you are introverted, wary, reserved.
12. Some of your aspirations tend to be pretty unrealistic.
13. Security is one of your major goals in life.

Figure 2.12 Personality sketches used by Forer to demonstrate the Barnum effect.

been given identical personality sketches (see Figure 2.12) which had no relationship to their test responses, yet all of the students rated the test as a perfect or near-perfect tool for investigating personality. This is a demonstration of the Barnum effect.

If we return to the study by Furnham and Varian (1988), we could argue that this is a demonstration of this same Barnum effect, and that the EPI is successful, at least in part, because it provides plausible personality sketches. Another demonstration of this effect, this time using a projective test, was described by Handelsman and McLain (1988). This study assessed the impact of test feedback about one partner on both members of male–female couples. Twenty-four pairs of male and female undergraduates completed a Rorschach test. Then, in the presence of a partner, they were given a standard personality interpretation, which they were deceived into believing had come from the test. Half of the pairs were strangers and the other half close friends. Intimate couples rated the personality feedback as more accurate, remembered more of it, had more faith in psychological tests and rated the experimenter's skill higher than did strangers. The results also suggested that males were generally more gullible than females.

Some psychologists, for example Davis-Blake and Pfeffer (1989), suggested that personality factors are irrelevant and their importance for occupational psychology little more than a mirage. Why, then, does it remain so popular? One reason is because it provides us with a consistent basis for interacting with other people: if we saw people as constantly changing, we would not be able to predict how to act with them in the future; if we see them as consistent, we can make such predictions, even if they are not fully justified. And this, of course, represents yet another problem with trait approaches to personality: the way that people will often assume that behaviour is more consistent than it really is and so will tend to ignore information which contradicts their assumptions.

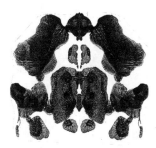

Figure 2.13 Example of a Rorschach item.

Society

Newcomb (1961) kept daily records of the behaviour of a group of boys at a summer camp, and found that there was little consistent 'introvert' or 'extrovert' behaviour. Most boys showed both types of behaviour. Camp leaders, however, perceived regularities of behaviour, imposing traits on the individual boys, such that if a boy had been deemed introvert, his extrovert behaviours were entirely ignored – they imposed consistency and would not tolerate the possibility that one person might show contradictory personality traits. The imposed traits depended largely on the descriptions of the boys given in the records. Steiner and Johnson (1963) followed this up and found that there was a general, and powerful, unwillingness among their research participants to tolerate the possibility that highly desirable and highly undesirable traits could co-exist within the same person. They also found that this linked with authoritarianism.

Overall, then, although we can see a wide range of applications for trait theory, it is difficult not to doubt its usefulness as a diagnostic tool or a predictor of behaviour. Another way of looking at personality traits, however, which does seem to have been a little more useful, at least as a basis for investigation, is to take more specific aspects of behaviour and look at how they may correlate with other types of experience. This is known as the 'narrow-band' approach to personality, and one of its most useful applications has been the concept of Type A and Type B personality.

Narrow-band approaches to personality

Narrow-band approaches to personality do not attempt to describe the whole personality of a person or to present a general overview. Instead, they focus on a very specific aspect of personality and explore how that specific aspect affects other parts of the person's life or cognitions.

One of the first of the 'narrow-band' theories was developed with Adorno, after the Second World War, in his attempt to use personality theory to explain the phenomenon of Fascism. Adorno showed how a particular facet of personality known as **authoritarianism** could develop from the individual's early experience, and result in a person who was rigid, intolerant and outright hostile to social deviants. This personality structure, Adorno believed, underlay the policies of the extreme Fascists in Germany and elsewhere, before and during the war. Although this approach did not provide an adequate explanation in itself since there were also social and economic and political issues to take into account, it did contribute to our understanding of a small part of the picture.

The 'narrow-band' approach known as **Type A** and **Type B personality** had its origins in an entirely different area. It developed as an attempt to explain why it was that some people seemed to be particularly susceptible to coronary heart disease, while others, who worked equally hard, were not. Although, as we shall see, the original ideas concerning these personality types have been modified with further research, the concept opened up new avenues of enquiry which, in conjunction with evidence coming from other areas, dramatically changed the medical profession's views of the relationship between mental states and physical health.

type A and B personalities
Personality syndromes in which A is characterized by impatience, intolerance and a high level of stress, while B involves a relaxed, tolerant approach and noticeably lower personal stress.

Friedman and Rosenman (1974) observed that the people who seemed to be particularly susceptible to coronary heart disease also tended to have certain personality similarities. These, they argued, formed the Type A personality pattern, which consists of three major facets. The first is a competitive achievement orientation, in that these people tend to be very self-critical and to strive towards goals without feeling a sense of joy in their efforts or accomplishments. The second personality characteristic is time urgency: Type A individuals seem to be in a constant struggle with the clock. They often become impatient with delays and unproductive time, and are likely to arrange too many commitments into their diaries and often try to do more than one thing at once. The third facet of Type A personality is a high level of anger and/or hostility: these people tend to be easily aroused to anger or hostility, which they may or may not show outwardly. By contrast, Type B individuals are less competitive, show less time urgency and experience less hostility.

Key reference: FRIEDMAN, M. and ROSENMAN, R. H. (1974) *Type A Behaviour and Your Heart.* Knopf, New York.

Each of the 13 items listed below has 2 extremes (e.g. easygoing – hard driving), one at each end of a continuous scale. Circle the number which you feel most closely represents your own behaviour.

a	Never late	5 4 3 2 1 0 1 2 3 4 5	Casual about appointments, easygoing
b	Not competitive	5 4 3 2 1 0 1 2 3 4 5	Very competitive
c	Anticipates what others are going to say (nods, interrupts, finishes for them)	5 4 3 2 1 0 1 2 3 4 5	Good listener
d	Always rushed	5 4 3 2 1 0 1 2 3 4 5	Never feels rushed (even under pressure)
e	Can wait patiently	5 4 3 2 1 0 1 2 3 4 5	Impatient when waiting
f	Goes all out	5 4 3 2 1 0 1 2 3 4 5	Casual
g	Takes things one at a time	5 4 3 2 1 0 1 2 3 4 5	Tries to do many things at once, thinks about what he/she is about to do next
h	Emphatic in speech (may pound desk)	5 4 3 2 1 0 1 2 3 4 5	Slow, deliberate talker
i	Wants good job recognized by others	5 4 3 2 1 0 1 2 3 4 5	Cares about satisfying himself/herself no matter what others may think
j	Fast (eating, walking etc)	5 4 3 2 1 0 1 2 3 4 5	Slow doing things
k	Easy going	5 4 3 2 1 0 1 2 3 4 5	Hard driving
l	Hides feelings	5 4 3 2 1 0 1 2 3 4 5	Expresses feelings
m	Many outside interests	5 4 3 2 1 0 1 2 3 4 5	Few outside interests

Figure 2.14a Type A/Type B personality questionnaire.

The classic study of Type A and Type B personality was the 12-year longitudinal study of over 3500 healthy middle-aged men reported by Friedman and Rosenman in 1974. The researchers found that more than twice as many Type A people as Type B people developed coronary

Health

heart disease. When the figures were adjusted for smoking, lifestyle etc. it still emerged that Type A people were nearly twice as likely to develop heart disease as Type B people. Other researchers found that differences in the kinds of Type A behaviour correlated with different kinds of heart disease: angina sufferers tended to be impatient and intolerant with others; while those with heart failure tended to be hurried and rushed, inflicting the pressures on themselves.

Therapy for modifying Type A behaviour often has quite a high degree of success. The most successful therapies are based on behaviour therapy and stress management training, including relaxation training and delegation of responsibility. A five-year intervention programme of such training for 1035 post heart attack patients showed that the recurrence rate for both fatal and non-fatal heart attacks was reduced to half that of a control group.

The idea that people can be categorized into simple types has an appeal to a range of practitioners because of the implications for predictions of future health and of job performance. The relationship between personality type and ill health is far from straightforward, however, as Ragland and Brand (1988) discovered in their follow-up study of a study started in 1960. The original study had used Type A personality measures to identify 257 men who subsequently had coronary heart disease in 1969 and found that, in the first eight years of the study, the measure of Type A behaviour was successful in predicting the development of coronary heart disease.

However, in a follow-up conducted 22 years later, the mortality rate of these men was related to the Type A and B behaviour patterns which had been established on their original entry into the study. Ragland and Brand found that among the 231 men who survived the first coronary

Figure 2.14b Scoring code for Type A/Type B questionnaire.

Each item scores on an 11-point scale, but some of the scales vary. The following scales score from 1 on the left to 11 on the right: b, e, g, k, l, m

The following score from 11 on the left to 1 on the right: a, c, d, f, h, i, j

So, for instance, if you are only very occasionally late, and have therefore completed item a) as shown below, your score for the first scale would be 10.

a   Never late   5 (4) 3 2 1 0 1 2 3 4 5   Casual about appointments, easygoing

Your final score is the sum total of all the scales.

If your score is high, don't have a fried breakfast tomorrow!

event for 24 hours or more, Type A subjects died at a rate much lower than that of Type B men (19.1 versus 31.7 per 1000 person-years). This subsequent finding was rather unexpected. It may indicate that Type A personalities respond differently to a coronary event than do Type Bs. Alternatively, Type A behaviour patterns may cease to be a risk factor after such an event – people may take warning and change their lifestyle.

Woodall and Matthews (1989) looked at how the family's emotional and social environment linked with children's Type A behaviours. To detect Type A behaviour in children, they recorded a range of stressful behaviours, such as the frequency and expression of anger, hostile outlook, hostility displayed during an interview and cardiovascular responses to laboratory stressors. They also used a questionnaire with the parents, to give them two measures of family environment, which were labelled positive affiliation and authoritarianism. Woodall and Matthews looked at 66 girls and 48 boys from 114 families. Each of the children was aged between 6 and 16 years. They found that those families who scored low on positive affiliation tended to have children who were more angry and hostile. Boys from these families had a more pronounced heart rate response to all laboratory stressors, particularly so if their families also scored highly on the authoritarianism scale.

Society

It is questionable how far this personality distinction is useful in sport, despite cultural assumptions that aggression is essential for a sportsperson. In a study by Hinckle, Lyons and Burke (1989), 96 runners aged between 16 and 66 years were classified as either Type A or Type B. They were then compared in terms of sport competition anxiety, hard-driving behaviour, and response to the challenge of training and racing. Interestingly, the results revealed no significant differences between the two groups, except that Type A runners ran more often when they did

Sport

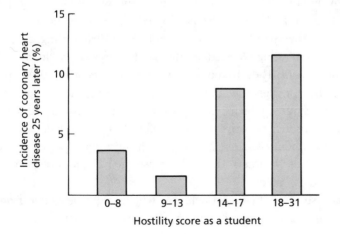

Figure 2.15 Williams, Barefoot and Shekelle (1985) measured the hostility scores of male medical students. Twenty-five years later they collected data on the incidence of heart disease and other associated ailments.

not feel motivated than did Type B runners. The researchers assumed that this refuted the cultural expectation, which does seem likely, although there are some hints that they seemed to be equating Type A behaviour with simple aggression and it is far more complex than that.

Work

The Type A theory seems to generate a range of conflicting results, though it does seem to have some value in predicting response to work stress. Kirmeyer (1988) investigated how interruption affected Type A and Type B people working as police radio dispatchers. Each of the 72 radio dispatchers was observed throughout one work shift and about half of them were also observed for two additional shifts. The observers recorded each work activity according to its state of progress: whether it was finished before the next activity was begun; whether it was left unfinished so that the dispatcher could attend fully to a new demand; or whether it was processed but ultimately left unfinished while the dispatcher simultaneously attended to one or more new demands.

When the results were analysed it was found, not surprisingly, that the people who had to leave their activities unfinished more often, or who handled more than one demand simultaneously, judged their work to be more overloading and needed more coping actions than those who had been able to complete most of their tasks before moving on to the next. Regardless of the level of interruption, Type A research participants also proved to be more likely to judge the demands of the job as overloading and to take more coping actions than Type B research participants.

Society

The description of the Type A personality has more components of the stereotyped masculine personality than the stereotyped feminine personality. We would therefore expect to find some differences in the research around the Type A personality for men and women. Baker *et al.* (1984) identified five distinctive features of Type A behaviour in women, which are given in Figure 2.16. As can be seen, the outcome is that there is relatively little difference between men and women in this respect, but also assumes that the woman has adopted a masculine identity!

Health

On the other hand, Haynes and Feinleib (1980), using a method of statistical monitoring, looked at the health of women in a variety of different careers. They found that women in executive career positions did not show a higher incidence of heart disease than women in other types of positions, which questions the idea that coronary disease is an automatic product of a dysfunctional lifestyle in all individuals, i.e. both men and women. Women participating in more male-populated (considered 'high stress') careers, do not increase their chances of heart disease, as one would predict.

Of course, one obvious conclusion which might be drawn from these findings is that women in general are more accustomed to stressful

- The incidence of Type A behaviour in America is comparable for men and women when socioeconomic factors are controlled.
- Type A behaviour in women is positively correlated with socioeconomic status (SES), occupation, education and incidence of coronary heart disease.
- Type A women tend to show greater autonomic arousal to laboratory stressors as well as greater time urgency and speed, more goal direct-edness, a preference to work alone under stress conditions and more competitiveness/aggressiveness than Type B women.
- Type A positively correlates with various estimates of anger, hostility and masculine sex role orientation.
- Depression and anxiety in Type As depends on the woman's sex role orientation and locus of control.

Figure 2.16 Features of Type A behaviour in American women.

lifestyles and therefore tend to have better coping strategies. The way that people go about coping with stressful life events is an important feature of understanding our response to stress and how we go about dealing with it.

Stressful life events

In 1967, Holmes and Rahe suggested that experiencing life events which were stressful could produce serious damage to an individual's health. One of their major findings was that the stress generated by such events seemed to be cumulative. Whether a particularly stressful period produced illness later on depended on just how much stress had been accumulated. People who had experienced an unusually high number of stressful life events in a given period were very much more likely to experience a prolonged illness in the following year than people who had not.

Holmes and Rahe looked at medical case histories and interviewed a large number of people who were suffering or had suffered from extreme stress. From this data, they developed a social readjustment rating scale which ranked life events according to how much stress they appeared to give people (see Figure 2.17). Not every life event was the same – for example, going through a divorce or suffering a bereavement was very much more stressful than changing one's eating or sleeping habits.

An interesting observation suggested a relationship between the social readjustment scale and subsequent health. For example, Holmes and Rahe observed that people who scored between 200 and 300 points in a given year were statistically likely to develop health problems the following year; and those who had scored over 400 points were likely to suffer a major illness. The researchers suggested that this came from the physical drain on the body produced by the continual arousal and the general adaptation to long-term or repeated stress.

> **Key reference:** HOLMES, T. H. and RAHE, R. H. (1967) The social readjustment rating scale. *Journal of Psychosomatic Research* **11**, 213–18.

Health

There have been a number of studies using the Holmes and Rahe scale. De Benedittis, Irenzetti and Pieri (1990), for example, used it to examine the development and relief of headaches. They examined 63 chronic headache patients aged between 18 and 60, and compared them with 44 people aged between 23 and 60, who acted as controls. They expected the headache patients to report significantly more stressful life events in the year before their headaches had begun and the results confirmed their prediction. The year before the onset of the headaches, the patients had experienced a significant increase in their stressful life event scores,

Figure 2.17 The Holmes and Rahe social readjustment scale. (Holmes and Rahe, 1967.)

Rank	Life Event	Mean Value	Rank	Life Event	Mean Value
1	Death of spouse	100	23	Son or daughter leaving home	29
2	Divorce	73	24	Trouble with in-laws	29
3	Marital separation	65	25	Outstanding personal achievement	28
4	Jail term	63	26	Wife begins or stops work	26
5	Death of close family member	63	27	Begin or end school	26
6	Personal injury or illness	53	28	Change in living conditions	25
7	Marriage	50	29	Revision of personal habits	24
8	Fired at work	47	30	Trouble with boss	23
9	Marital reconciliation	45	31	Change in work hours or conditions	20
10	Retirement	45	32	Change in residence	20
11	Change in health of family member	44	33	Change in schools	20
12	Pregnancy	40	34	Change in recreation	19
13	Sex difficulties	39	35	Change in church activities	19
14	Gain of a new family member	39	36	Change in social activities	18
15	Business readjustment	39	37	Mortgage or loan less than $10 000	17
16	Change in financial state	38	38	Change in sleeping habits	16
17	Death of close friend	37	39	Change in number of family get-togethers	15
18	Change to different line of work	36	40	Change in eating habits	15
19	Change in number of arguments with spouse	35	41	Vacation	13
20	Mortgage over $10 000	31	42	Christmas	12
21	Foreclosure of mortgage or loan	30	43	Minor violations of the law	11
22	Change in responsibilities at work	29			

not just by comparison with the controls, but also by comparison with their own scores the previous year.

There also seemed to be some links between the types of stressful life experiences which people had experienced and the kind of headaches they suffered from. 'Mixed headache' sufferers reported a higher incidence of interpersonal arguments and difficulties than patients who only experienced migraine headaches. Moreover, it was not at all uncommon for the onset of headache to be heralded by a sudden increase in the frequency and magnitude of stressful life events.

Beautrais *et al.* (1982) looked at the health of 1082 children over a 4-year period. They looked at measures of general health and correlated these with scores on a modified, 20-item version of the Holmes and Rahe scale which was completed periodically by the children's mothers. The researchers found that there was a marked trend for illnesses to increase in direct proportion to the number of family life events. Children from families with the largest number of stressful life events had six times the risk of hospital admission than those from low scoring families.

The clear implication of this study is that stressful life events may also have indirect effects on other family members, though it is unclear why this should be so. It might be due to stress affecting the family's coping ability. But we should bear in mind that it is possible, too, that the child's illness produced an increased reporting of life events. Psychologists have long known how mood tends to affect what we remember – when we are unhappy or anxious we are more likely to remember unpleasant things than we are when we are happy or contented. So it is possible that parents who were already anxious about their child would recall more of the stressful events that had happened during the previous year than they did when the child was well.

A modified version of the Holmes and Rahe scale was used in China by Yanping and Derson (1986). They compared 105 **neurotic** patients with 10 normal controls, all of whom were aged between 16 and 60. The researchers looked at the quantity and stress ratings of life event changes experienced by the two groups. They divided the life events into three categories, on the basis of how often they had happened and how intense the stress which they produced was. They found that, during the year prior to the onset of the neurotic illness, the patient group experienced more life event changes and had significantly higher levels of stress than the control group. They also rated the same life events as being fundamentally more stressful – a finding which may link with some of the cognitive research into stress, notably that of perceived **locus of control**, which we will be looking at later in this chapter.

Tafari, Aboud and Larson (1991) studied 2000 Ethiopians, aged

neuroses *Mental disorders, where the patient commonly suffers from anxiety but remains in touch with reality.*

between 15 and 55 years, and living in rural communities. They used a World Health Organization self-report questionnaire to identify incidents of mental illness, and a modified version of the social readjustment scale of Holmes and Rahe as a measure of stress. The prevalence of mental illness in the population, they found, was 17.2% and high mental illness scores were strongly associated with high levels of stress. The odds of experiencing six or more stressful life events were over twice as high for psychotics and neurotics as for 'normals'.

It is uncertain, however, how these findings should be interpreted, since these illnesses were associated with family history of mental illness and with being divorced, separated or widowed. The researchers took it as supporting the life events approach, although it is equally possible that the mental illness produced the life stress in the first place. It is also worth noting that the condition of neurosis correlated with being female, 35–44 years of age, illiteracy and chronic illness, so it is obvious that wider social factors are also involved.

The stressful life event approach to stress and illness generated a considerable amount of research, not least because the measure developed by Holmes and Rahe provides a relatively straightforward way of measuring stress. It also conforms to everyday notions of the effect of dramatic events in our lives. In accounts of personal experience recorded in news reports it is not unknown for people say how a particular event, such as unexpected bereavement or desertion by a loved one, has 'shattered my life'. But Kanner *et al.* (1981) argued that the minor stressors and pleasures of everyday life might have a more significant effect on health than the big, traumatic events assessed by the Holmes and Rahe scale, particularly in view of the cumulative nature of stress.

Kanner *et al.* (1981) developed a checklist-based scale to explore these small events, which they called the Hassles and Uplifts scale (Figure 2.18). They administered the checklist to 100 middle-aged adults once a month for 10 months. The Hassles scale was found to be a better predictor of psychological problems than life event scores, both at the time and later. Scores on the Uplift scale, however, only seemed to relate to symptoms in women – the men in the study seemed relatively unaffected by uplifts.

Other criticisms of the scale concern the nature of the life events included, which have been described as more relevant to a narrow group of people – white, male, professional workers – than to the population as a whole. The items of the Holmes and Rahe stressful life events scale are listed in Figure 2.17. Anderson-Kulman and Paludi (1986) suggested that factors other than paid work need to be considered when evaluating stress in women because much of women's work is unpaid. For

Ten most frequently expressed **hassles** of middle-aged adults:

1. concerns about weight;
2. health of a family member;
3. rising prices of common goods;
4. home maintenance;
5. too many things to do;
6. misplacing or losing things;
7. outside home maintenance;
8. property, investment or taxes;
9. crime;
10. physical appearance.

Ten most frequently expressed **uplifts** of middle-aged adults:

1. relating well to spouse or lover;
2. relating well with friends;
3. completing a task;
4. feeling healthy
5. getting enough sleep;
6. eating out;
7. meeting your responsibilities;
8. visiting, phoning or writing to someone;
9. spending time with the family;
10. home pleasing to you.

Figure 2.18 The hassles and uplifts checklist. (Kanner *et al.,* 1981.)

example, role strain is higher for women in low-income jobs with child care demands and no assistance with housework.

Moos (1981) identified a number of different types of stressors which are relevant to the individual at work, and these are listed in Figure 2.19. Some of the other factors that have been shown to influence the perception of life events include age, in that young people appear to accumulate more stressful life events than people over 30; gender, in that women accumulate greater life change scores than men; marital status, in that single, separated and divorced people accumulate more life events than married and widowed people; and social class, in that the poor experience more stressful life events than those who are well off.

Work

We can see, then, that although the stressful life events approach has been useful, it cannot be taken as the complete answer to understanding the relationship between health and illness. It did establish, however, that physical illness can have other causes than straightforward physical ones. In this way, too, it linked with the findings of many of those who were investigating the physiological basis of stress and anxiety, and the long-term outcomes of prolonged stress.

Figure 2.19 Work environment scale: descriptions of the dimensions that measure how stressful a workplace is. (Moos, 1981.)

RELATIONSHIP DIMENSIONS	
Involvement	The extent to which employees are concerned about and committed to their jobs
Peer cohesion	The extent to which employees are friendly and supportive to one another
Supervision support	The extent to which management is supportive of employees and encourages employees to be supportive of one another
PERSONAL GROWTH	
Autonomy	The extent to which employees are encouraged to be self-sufficient and make their own decisions
Task orientation	The degree of emphasis on good planning, efficiency and getting the job done
Work pressure	The degree to which the pressure of work and time dominate the job milieu
SYSTEMS MAINTENANCE AND SYSTEMS CHANGE	
Clarity	The extent to which employees know what to expect in their daily routine, and how explicitly rules and policies are communicated
Control	The extent to which management uses rules and pressures to keep employees under control
Innovation	The degree of emphasis on variety, change and new approaches
Physical comfort	The extent to which the physical surroundings contribute to a pleasant work environment

Arousal and stress

arousal A general physiological state in which the sympathetic division of the autonomic nervous system is activated.

The concept of **arousal** is central to our understanding of stress and relates to the activities of the sympathetic division of the autonomic nervous system, and its effects on the body. The function of the sympathetic division is to rouse the body to action, and it does so by activating a number of physiological mechanisms which produce or maintain alertness and energy, such as by releasing stored sugar into the bloodstream to fuel muscle activity, by increasing the heart rate so that blood reaches the muscles more quickly and by stimulating the release of the hormone adrenaline, which then acts to maintain this level of functioning in the body.

Psychological interest in arousal has tended to centre around the relationship between a physiologically aroused condition and emotional or highly active states. Aroused states tend to accompany the subjective experiences of fear and anger, and the sensation of arousal appears to interact reflexively with these emotions, with one enhancing, and in turn being enhanced by, the other. Arousal states also accompany anxiety and worry, with the extent of the arousal linking closely with the degree of emotion. The relationship between states of arousal and levels of performance has also been investigated. One early principle of arousal is known as the **Yerkes-Dodson Law**, which states that arousal improves performance only up to a point. Beyond that point, performance will decline. The optimal level of arousal varies for different tasks, with complex tasks showing an earlier performance decrement than simple tasks for the same level of arousal.

Yerkes-Dodson law of arousal *The principle that performance of any given task can be improved if the person is aroused; but that if the arousal increases beyond an optimal point, performance then declines.*

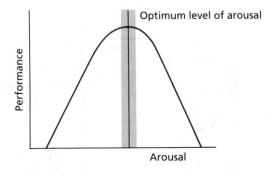

Figure 2.20 The Yerkes-Dodson Law. The optimum level of arousal depends on a number of factors, including the complexity of the task.

Immediate responses to stressful or anxiety-provoking events generate a high level of physiological arousal. This is sometimes also known as the 'fight or flight' response, since it is directly concerned with making immediate energy available to the individual in order to deal with the perceived threat. In modern living, however, perceived threat is rarely responded to by physical action. Moreover, perceived threats do not have to be present in a physical form and so they are, therefore, more difficult to avoid or escape from. This means that the threat may be continuous and nebulous. For example, the concern that financial misfortune might result in homelessness does not represent a direct physical threat, but it may result in an acute and ongoing perceived threat.

Selye observed that long-term adaptation to stress followed a three-stage pattern, listed in Figure 2.21, which he named the

Figure 2.21 The general adaptation syndrome.

1. Alarm
Like the fight or flight response, the function of this stage is to mobilize the body's resources. Initially arousal drops below normal then rapidly rises above normal. The body cannot sustain the alarm reaction for long and if it continues unabated then the organism will die within days or even hours.

2. Resistance
The body adapts to the stressor. Physiological arousal declines but is still above normal. The organism shows few outward signs of stress, but the ability to resist new stressors is impaired and the organism becomes vulnerable to disease of adaption, such as ulcers and high blood pressure. People also experience feelings of fatigue and general weakness. Long-term psychological effects that have been identified include increased irritability and a tendency towards a pessimistic outlook.

3. Exhaustion
Eventually the body's energy reserves become depleted and the ability to resist declines. If stress continues then disease, damage and death can follow.

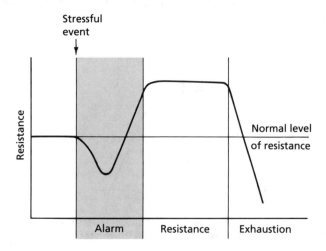

burnout   A problem incurred by workers in which consistent and frustrating hard work over years produces a sense of numbness, lethargy and a lack of motivation.

general adaptation syndrome. It is thought also that the syndrome of **burnout** in the helping professions can be attributed to a combination of the general adaptation syndrome to long-term stress, coupled with lower perceptions of control and efficacy.

Key reference: SELYE, H. (1982) History and the present status of the stress concept. In L. Goldberger and S. Breznitz, (eds) *Handbook of Stress: theoretical and clinical aspects.* Macmillan, London.

Arousal does not simply happen as a direct response to threat. It can also be a consequence of more nebulous situations, such as crowding. We experience crowds in daily life as both a negative and a positive experience. Positive experiences often arise from specific social events, although simply being part of a busy atmosphere, for example in a large shopping mall, is enjoyable for some people. Social events, like football matches and music concerts, generate their own energy from the crowd, although a full crowd does seem to be necessary for this: a football match can only have a great 'atmosphere' if the stadium is full and a concert from the local beat combo will sound better if the place is full.

There are negative sides of crowding too, some of which are to be found in experiences of travel. Lundberg (1976) studied male passengers on a commuter train, comparing their responses to trips made in crowded and uncrowded trains, and measuring arousal by analysing levels of **adrenalin** in urine. Despite the fact that even under the most crowded conditions there were seats available for everyone, he found that levels of adrenalin increased as more people rode the train, indicating that people were becoming more aroused.

Interestingly, Lundberg also discovered that the level of adrenalin was not just to do with the number of people on the train, but was to do with when the passenger joined it. Those who got on the train at the first stop experienced fewer negative reactions than passengers who joined the train half-way to the city, despite the fact that the early boarders had a longer journey (over an hour compared to just over half an hour). The important issue here seemed to have everything to do with choice of seat: passengers who could choose where they sat experienced less stress than those who could not. Lundberg explains this in terms of having a degree of control of the environment, which seems to act as a buffer to stress from crowding. However, there is always the possibility that passengers choose favourite seats precisely because they find it calming to sit in that particular place.

Ray and Fitzgibbon (1981) asked patients who were undergoing

Health

adrenalin *A hormone secreted by the adrenal glands, which causes increase in blood pressure, release of sugar by the liver and a number of other physiological responses to threat.*

Figure 2.22 Lundberg surprisingly found that people who got on a commuter train half-way to the city, and therefore had a shorter journey, experienced more stress than people who had been on the train from the start of the journey.

Health

Sport

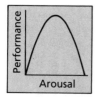

Figure 2.23 Gould *et al.,* (1987) found an inverted U relationship between anxiety and performance if the anxiety was accompanied by increased heart rate etc, but *not* if the anxiety was mainly cognitive (in the form of thoughts)

Society

surgery for removal of the gall-bladder to complete a stress arousal inventory before and five days after their operation. Measures of psychological adjustment and physical recovery from the operation were also recorded. Ray and Fitzgibbon found, not surprisingly, that stress and arousal scores were greater before the operation than afterwards. But they found a difference between the arousal scores and the stress scores obtained before the operation. High stress scores were associated with high post-operative stress and pain ratings; but arousal scores did not correlate with any of the measures taken afterwards, including the rating of experienced pain, and how much pain–sleep medication the patients needed. This suggests that it may be necessary to separate the concepts of stress and arousal, and one way of doing this might be to regard arousal levels as indicating whether the person is using adaptive coping mechanisms or not. We will be looking at coping in the next section.

The Yerkes-Dodson Law, which proposes that there is an inverted-U relationship between performance and arousal, was investigated by Sonstroem and Bernado (1982) on a sample of American female basketball players. The players belonged to eight teams who played at least three games in a pre-season tournament. The measure of basketball performance included successful shooting, rebounds, steals, assists, fouls and turnovers. Arousal was measured by a pencil and paper test of anxiety. The two measures were compared and it was discovered that moderate levels of arousal and/or anxiety were associated with the best performance during the game.

A similar finding was obtained by Gould *et al.* (1987) on the performance of pistol shooters: those with only moderate anxiety performed most accurately, while those with both high and low anxiety performed less well. Gould *et al.* also noticed that this pattern only applied to certain forms of arousal: if the anxiety was mainly cognitive, in the sense of being manifested in thoughts and imaginary possibilities, then it did not take place; but if the anxiety had a substantial physiological component, and was accompanied by the increased heartbeat and sweating of arousal, then the inverted-U curve relationship between performance and arousal could be observed.

The issue for our understanding of the relationship between television and arousal comes from the question of whether television viewing is arousing or relaxing. The answer seems to depend on the relationship between the material and the viewer's cognitive state. Someone's response to a given programme is affected by whether the material is absorbing enough to capture their attention and involvement; but that also links closely with how the communication relates to the viewer's frame of mind. Exciting material on the television may relax someone who is already excited about something else, but may wind up a viewer who is more relaxed. One theory is that exciting television may relax viewers by disrupting the mental rehearsal that keeps arousal levels high – if you are distracted by the programme, then you will stop repeatedly thinking about the event or person that is upsetting you and so calm down.

Condry (1989) reviewed a range of studies on arousal and television, and suggested that suspense-type dramas and comedy are both especially effective at creating intense arousal in both children and adults (hardly surprising, since that is the direct aim which the film and TV producers have been practising for decades!). Condry suggested that the type of arousal produced by these very diverse stimuli was actually very similar and suggested that it came from a common feature in these programmes, also shared by sports programmes. The common feature in all these cases is that the viewer experiences a combination of uncertainty and involvement, and Condry suggested that it is this which produces the arousal of the viewer in these types of programmes.

There has been a considerable amount of evidence to suggest that arousal directly suppresses immune system functioning. Kiecolt-Glaser *et al.* (1984) took blood samples from volunteer medical students one month before and on the first day of final examinations. The students also completed scales measuring life events, bodily symptoms and adequacy of interpersonal contacts, and the blood samples were analysed for indicators of immune system functioning. Kielcolt-Glaser *et al.* found that the second blood sample showed a significant decrease in **natural killer cell** activity, as well as an increase in plasma immunoglobulin – in other words, the higher the stress, the less well defended the individual was against infection.

The researchers also found that students with higher stressful life event and loneliness scores had lower natural killer cell counts than did low scorers. The study confirms other experimental evidence that exposure to psychological stress can suppress the functioning of the immune system, rendering people more vulnerable to illnesses and infections, and therefore also suggests that providing social support, or other psychological ways of modifying the stress, might help to reduce these effects.

We can see, then, how the concept of arousal allows us to explore bodily responses to stressful events, and how they link with external and social situations. However, whether we experience situations as stressful or as a positive challenge and whether we fear it or welcome it depends entirely on how we appraise it cognitively – how we interpret and make sense out of it. The implication of this is that the coping strategies which we use in dealing with stress are crucial to what we experience.

Health

natural killer cells
Natural killer cells are part of the immune system and play an important role in killing some types of tumour cells and also can kill cells infected with viruses or bacteria.

Coping

Coping has been defined as the process of managing external or internal demands that are perceived as taxing or exceeding a person's resources (Lazarus and Folkman, 1984). The development of health psychology has brought about a framework for investigating coping, which has tended to focus on three different aspects: the mechanisms involved in coping; the experience of coping; and different strategies for going about coping. The model of coping suggested by Lazarus and Folkman suggested that the stress experience is moderated by two basic appraisals. The first of these is an appraisal of the level of threat; and the second is an appraisal of the person's own resources for dealing with it.

These appraisals of the relationship between the individual and their environment are also influenced by personal characteristics like the person's pattern of motivation, such as their values, commitments or personal goals; their beliefs about their own self and about the world; and their personal recognition of their resources for coping, such as their social skills, problem-solving skills or finances. Appraisal processes are also influenced by environmental variables such as the nature of the danger, whether it is imminent, whether it is ongoing or short term and whether it is an ambiguous type of threat or not, as well as the existence and quality of social support.

Psychologists and other health workers have investigated coping with a view to developing therapeutic methods which will help people to learn more effective ways of dealing with stress. These have taken a number of forms: for example, some psychologists have found it beneficial to tell the person in advance what sensations to expect and why, alerting them to the specific therapeutic procedures being undertaken, and giving them cognitive and behavioural strategies to use during stressful situations.

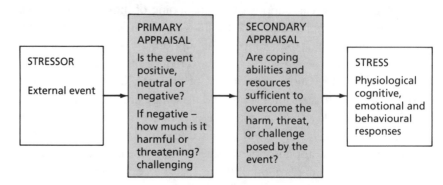

Figure 2.24 Model of stress and coping. (Taylor, 1986.)

Other interventions have included the use of relaxation and guided imagery to regulate anxiety states and stressful experience; distraction; or reinterpretive methods, such as encouraging the patient to see the experience as something which they can do something about. The **cognitive therapy** approach developed by Aaron Beck (1980) operates very much on the latter principle: by looking at the way that the individual interprets their situation, cognitive coping strategies are developed which allow the person to reappraise the situation and perceive it differently.

> **Key reference:** LAZARUS, R. and FOLKMAN, S. (1984) *Stress, Appraisal and Coping.* Springer, New York.

cognitive therapy A form of psychotherapy which is based on changing people's beliefs, attitudes and attributions about their worlds, and so helping them to act more positively and to change things for the better.

Folkman and Lazarus (1988) developed a Ways-of-Coping questionnaire which listed a broad range of cognitive and behavioural strategies that people use to manage the demands of specific stress encounters. They argued that the questionnaire responses showed up eight main coping strategies that people use. Two of these were focused on the problem and the remaining six were focused on ways of dealing with the emotional response to the problem (see Figure 2.25).

McDonald and Korabik (1991) asked male and female managers to describe stressful work-related situations they had experienced and how they coped with them. Then they asked them to complete the Ways-of-Coping checklist for each of the situations and assessed additional types of work stressors with another questionnaire. They found that male and

Work

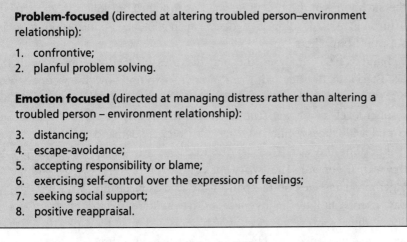

Problem-focused (directed at altering troubled person–environment relationship):

1. confrontive;
2. planful problem solving.

Emotion focused (directed at managing distress rather than altering a troubled person – environment relationship):

3. distancing;
4. escape-avoidance;
5. accepting responsibility or blame;
6. exercising self-control over the expression of feelings;
7. seeking social support;
8. positive reappraisal.

Figure 2.25 Eight main coping strategies derived from response to the Folkman and Lazarus Ways-of-Coping questionnaire.

female managers did not differ in how they coped with work-related problems, but women were more likely than men to report that prejudice and discrimination and work/family interfaces were sources of stress. Women were also more likely than men to cope with their feelings by talking to others; the men, on the other hand, were more likely to cope by engaging in some distracting activity.

Society

Cairns and Wilson (1984) found that people who lived in areas in Northern Ireland which had a high degree of sectarian violence tended to have a higher level of psychological disorder than people who lived in more peaceful areas, particularly if they had a realistic appraisal of the amount of violence that was going on. But those who adopted a coping mechanism which the researchers termed denial, in which they inaccurately perceived there to be relatively little violence, seemed to have lower levels of disturbance. The suggestion is that if you are in a situation where reality really is threatening, violent and intolerable, being unrealistic about how dangerous it is may help you to cope!

Wilson and Cairns (1992) used an adapted version of the Lazarus and Folkman checklist to explore differences in coping among people in different areas of Northern Ireland. They had found that their 'denial' mechanism linked with the coping mechanism known as 'distancing' identified by the checklist. Residents of the high violence areas which the researchers had surveyed earlier seemed to be particularly inclined to use this coping mechanism. But a comparison with the residents of Enniskillen, after a particularly violent and unexpected bomb explosion that was targeted at civilians rather than soldiers or property, showed that they did not use distancing to any great extent. Instead, they used the more active styles of coping, involving attempts at positive reappraisal of the situation – at the time it seemed as though Enniskillen might provide a turning point leading to a decrease in violence – and seeking social support from others.

Barger (1991) analysed the oral histories of 25 flight nurses with the US Forces in the Second World War, to explore how they coped with war. Barger's content analysis indicated that the nurses had used two distinct levels of coping. The microscopic level was to do with how they coped with the specific external and internal demands which occurred daily during the war. The macroscopic level was to do with coping with the war in general. The two were coped with differently: by a range of ingenious strategies on the part of the nurses in dealing with the day-to-day events and by an overall positive attitude shared by the women about their wartime service, which indicated that they perceived their wartime experience as a challenge rather than as a threat.

Basler and Rehfisch (1990) looked at how coping training could be

Figure 2.26 Wilson and Cairns found that a common coping mechanism for people in high violence areas was denial. In contrast the response to exceptional tragedies, such as the bombing of the church in Enniskillen in Northern Ireland, was to use more active coping styles, such as positive reappraisal.

used to help people who were suffering from chronic pain. They developed a 12-week intervention package, which included training patients to reinterpret the pain experience, training in physical relaxation techniques, avoiding negative and catastrophic thinking, and training in how to use distraction at key times. They found that compared with an untreated waiting list control group, there were significant improvements for these patients at a six-month follow-up. The patients reported fewer general and pain-related symptoms, and a lower level of anxiety and depression. There was also a decline in the number of visits which they made to the doctor.

Health

The implication of the study is that behavioural interventions to enhance coping skills in distressing medical conditions can be beneficial and relatively long lasting. There are, of course, always problems with this type of study. For example, it is always possible that the patients were responding to the additional interest in their cases shown by those who had developed the training strategy; without the introduction of a third group who received just as much attention, it is not possible to be sure that this has not happened. (Although many of those working with chronic pain patients would argue that even if there was this type of 'placebo effect' going on, it wouldn't matter – the important thing is that the patients subjectively experienced less pain as a result of what happened to them!)

Terry (1991) applied ideas about coping to people dealing with new parenthood. Terry collected longitudinal data from 123 couples in the third trimester of pregnancy, and then 4 weeks and 3 months after the birth, and found that both post-natal anxiety and the general appraisal of the stressfulness of the birth related to the importance and anticipated difficulty of the birth, the couples' familiarity with childbirth, the infant's temperament, and the couples' experience of recent and concurrent stressors. Not surprisingly, Terry also found that the event was appraised as more stressful by females than males.

Sport

Coping is an important feature in success at sports, as virtually all sportsmen and women have to deal with failure, defeat and injury at some point in their careers. A number of stress inoculation and stress management programmes have been developed to deal with these issues. An example is the stress inoculation programme developed by Meichenbaum (1977). This programme involves four phases which are listed in Figure 2.27. In each situation the athlete practises relaxation and coping statements. The threatening situations are presented through imagery, films, role playing and real-life situations, and in this way the athlete becomes inoculated to progressively increasing levels of stress, so eventually their fear is minimized to the extent where she or he can cope with it.

Zeigler, Klinzing and Williamson (1982) tested the programme's effectiveness in training cross-country runners. The aim of their study was to measure the effects of the programme on heart rate and oxygen consumption, which is crucial in this sport. Runners in the treatment group met the researchers twice a week for five weeks of the stress inoculation programme. By comparison with a matched control group, the

---

Phase 1   The trainer talks with the athlete about their stress responses, and during this phase the athlete learns to identify and express feelings and fears. The athlete is also educated in lay terms about stress and the effect.

Phase 2   The athlete learns how to relax and use self-regulatory skill. This is done in small groups using a problem-solving approach with members of the group helping each other to find solutions. Stressful experiences are described in detail and potential hazards identified.

Phase 3   The athlete learns specific coping self-statements designed to be used in stressful situations.

Phase 4   The trainer guides the athlete through a series of progressively more threatening situations. As the athlete learns to cope with a relatively mild situation, he or she is immediately exposed to a situation of greater stress.

Figure 2.27   The stress inoculation programme.

test group showed significant differences during and after a 20-minute run.

Several times now we have mentioned that social support is an important factor in stress. Dunkel-Schetter, Folkman and Lazarus (1987) tried to unravel exactly what we mean by social support – what its important features are and how it takes place. They interviewed 150 middle-aged community residents once a month for 6 months and each interview deliberately dealt with a specifically stressful situation which had happened during the previous month. The interviewer also assessed the social support that the interviewee had received and their methods of coping with the situation.

Society

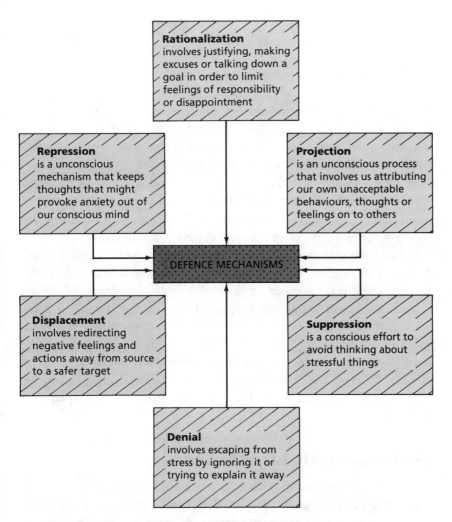

Figure 2.28 Examples of defence mechanisms that are used to protect ourselves from anxiety by distorting or denying reality.

Figure 2.29 The picture was drawn by a child in response to a request for a self-portrait. She has drawn both herself and her 'imaginery friend' without a *mouth*. This could be seen as an example of *DENIAL* because the child stuttered so badly she was almost unable to talk.

The researchers were particularly interested in three different factors to do with how the person experienced stress: the person's predispositions; the way they usually appraised specific stressful encounters; and the coping strategies they used. They found that each of these was associated with a different type of social support. The person's own predispositions related most strongly to the emotional support which they received from other people. Appraisal factors, on the other hand, related most strongly to practical help; while coping strategies related to the informational support which the person received. The results also suggested that coping successfully is associated with all three types of social support.

It has been suggested that the three types of social support which Ziegler *et al.* studied represent different constructs and that they also have different consequences. It is possible, too, that successful coping behaviour involves letting other people know what you want or need, through interpersonal cues. In such situations, if the members of the social environment respond accordingly, then the appropriate type of social support for the person's needs is provided. So the general notion of social support covers a wide range of activities and experiences, but how effective these are depends on how the stressed person perceives the support.

post-traumatic stress disorder *An anxiety resulting from experience with a catastrophic event beyond the normal range of human suffering, and characterized by (a) numbness to the world, (b) reliving the trauma in dreams and memories and (c) symptoms of anxiety.*

Post-traumatic stress disorder

One of the observations that has helped to advance our understanding of the long-term effects of stress is recognition of the condition known as **post-traumatic stress disorder** (PTSD). The concept grew out of work in many different fields of traumatic stress and was known as 'shell shock' during the First World War. It took a long time, however, for the condition to be actually recognized as a syndrome in its own right and for the military, as well as others, to realize that it was actually a psychiatric disorder resulting from traumatic experiences and not just cowardliness or an over-vivid imagination.

Post-traumatic stress disorder was first described in the third edition of the *Diagnostic and Statistical Manual of the American Psychiatric Association* (DSM-III) in 1980. The condition has three main groups of symptoms: re-experiencing phenomena (for example recurrent and intrusive distressing memories of the traumatic event or situation); avoidance or numbing reactions (such as efforts to avoid the thoughts or feelings associated with the trauma and feeling detached or estranged from other people); and symptoms of increased arousal (such as difficulty in staying asleep, irritability and outbursts of anger).

These are not qualitatively different from the experiences which a non-sufferer will have after a traumatic event – everyone has some reaction to a disaster or tragedy. What distinguishes the individual with post-traumatic stress disorder is the breadth, severity and endurance of the symptoms. The condition is cyclical, and the symptoms can disappear and reappear. They can also appear some time after the event, even several months or years, and the delayed versions of the condition are no less severe.

> **Key reference:** HODGKINSON P. E. and STEWART, M. (1991) *Coping with Catastrophe.* Routledge, London.

Not everyone reacts in the same way to traumatic events, and it is relatively unpredictable who will develop post-traumatic stress disorder and who will make a speedy readjustment. However, if the stress is serious enough and prolonged, there is some suggestion that everyone will succumb in time. Swank (1949) studied 4000 survivors of the Normandy campaign and found that all soldiers became incapacitated once roughly three-quarters of their companions had been killed. Moreover, Archibald (1963) found that even as late as 15 years after a traumatic event, 70% of survivors showed symptoms of PTSD.

That does not mean, of course, that PTSD automatically results from any experience of combat. Some studies of American Vietnam veterans, for example, showed that the people who developed chronic post-traumatic stress disorder were likely to have histories of family psychiatric disorders such as alcoholism, depression or anxiety. But although these

COPING WITH A CRISIS...

Somebody you know may have died or been injured on the 6th March. Your experience was a very personal one but this pamphlet will help you to know how others have reacted in similar situations. It will also show how you can help normal healing to occur and to avoid some pitfalls.

NORMAL FEELINGS AND EMOTIONS ALWAYS EXPERIENCED

FEAR	— of damage to oneself and those we love.
	— of being left alone, of having to leave loved ones.
	— of "breaking down" or "losing control".
	— of a similar event happening again.
HELPLESSNESS	— crises show up human powerlessness, as well as strength.
SADNESS	— for deaths, injuries and losses of every kind.
LONGING	— for all that has gone.
GUILT	— for being better off than others, i.e. being alive, not injured, having things.
	— regrets for things not done.
SHAME	— for having been exposed as helpless, "emotional" and needing others.
	— for not having reacted as one would have wished.
ANGER	— at what has happened, at whoever caused it or allowed it to happen.
	— at the injustice and senselessness of it all.
	— at the shame and indignities.
	— at the lack of proper understanding by others, the inefficiencies.
	— WHY ME?
MEMORIES	— of feelings, of loss or of love for other people in your life who have been injured or died.
LET DOWN	— disappointments, which alternate with
HOPE	— for the future, for better times.

Everyone has these feelings. The experience of other disasters has shown that they may be particularly intense if

— many people died
— their deaths were sudden, violent, or occurred in horrifying circumstances.
— no body was recovered
— there was great dependence on the person who died
— the relationship with the person was at a difficult stage
— this stress came on top of others

Nature heals through allowing these feelings to come out. This will not lead to loss of control of the mind, but stopping these feelings may lead to nervous and physical problems. Crying gives relief.

HEALING

Remember that the pain of the wound leads to healing. You may even come out wiser and stronger.

SOME DO'S AND DON'TS

DON'T bottle up feelings. **DO** express your emotions and let your children share in the grief.

DON'T avoid talking about what happened. **DO** take every opportunity to review the experience within yourself and with others. **DO** allow yourself to be part of a group of people who care.

DON'T let your embarrassment stop you giving others the chance to talk.

DON'T expect the memories to go away – the feelings will stay with you for a long time to come.

DON'T forget that your children will experience similar feelings to yourself.

DO take time out to sleep, rest, think and be with your close family and friends.

DO express your needs clearly and honestly to family, friends and officials.

DO try to keep your lives as normal as possible after the acute grief.

DO let your children talk to you and others about their emotions and express themselves in games and drawings.

DO send your children back to school and let them keep up with their activities.

DO DRIVE MORE CAREFULLY. DO BE MORE CAREFUL AROUND THE HOME

WARNING: ACCIDENTS ARE MORE COMMON AFTER SEVERE STRESSES.

Figure 2.30 The support leaflet produced for those affected by a ferry disaster. The ferry capsized in Zeebrugge harbour with the loss of 188 lives.

soldiers were fighting under severe conditions, their conditions were significantly different from those of the Normandy soldiers.

Environment

Studies of the development of emotional reactions in volunteer fire-fighters involved in the 1983 Australian Ash Wednesday fires have raised some questions about the importance of personality in susceptibility to post-traumatic stress disorder for short-term but deeply traumatic experiences. McFarlane (1989) looked at how the impact of the Ash Wednesday disaster and what happened afterwards were affecting people 4, 11 and 29 months after the disaster. McFarlane found that life events following the disaster seemed to be just as important as the disaster itself in determining stress, suggesting that life events have an important role in post-traumatic stress, but more in terms of sustaining it than contributing to its development.

There is a considerable amount of controversy as to whether therapy for disaster victims offers any benefit. For example, a follow-up study of the survivors and the bereaved from the Zeebrugge ferry disaster asked for an evaluation of the quality of the social support after the disaster. The people who reported that the support was 'mixed' or 'unhelpful' fared no worse than the people who reported it as 'helpful' (Hodgkinson and Stewart, 1991).

However, some psychologists argue that self-report is an inappropriate measure in such cases: therapy may ameliorate symptoms even though people do not necessarily perceive an improvement, since the people concerned will be making comparisons with how they were before the disaster rather than with how severe PTSD usually is in such situations. Longer term follow-ups using direct observations and clinical measures rather than self-report do seem to suggest that therapy may be effective.

Emergency workers who have to deal with major disasters also experience post-traumatic stress disorder. An example is given by Taylor and Frazer (1982) who described the response to an air disaster in 1979, when a DC10 on a tourist flight crashed into a mountain in Antarctica, and all of the 257 passengers and crew were killed. It took ten weeks to recover and identify the bodies, involving a number of personnel: scientists, police, mountain climbers, dentists and embalmers. Only 84% of the bodies were successfully identified: the remaining 16% were buried in a communal grave.

Taylor and Fraser followed up 183 members of the recovery personnel after the experience, at 3 and 20-month intervals. Several of the workers reported persistent images of disfigurement, body contortion and fixed facial expression; or else were experiencing dreams in which they were in air crashes, in claustrophobic situations or where corpses were being handled.

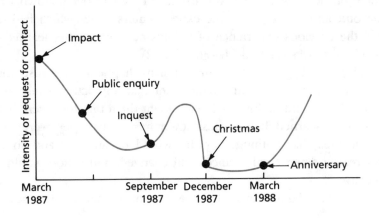

Figure 2.31 The symptoms of post traumatic stress disorder vary in strength over a long period of time. The graph shows the changing levels of support requested by survivors and bereaved after the Zeebrugge ferry disaster. (Hodgkinson and Stewart, 1991.)

Over 80% of the helpers reported changes in sleep patterns over the first 3 months, and many also reported changes in appetite, in feelings, in talking and in social activities. After 20 months, however, only 8% said they still needed to talk over their experiences. Most (80%) now felt they had overcome any problems satisfactorily and a few even felt that they had benefited from the experience. During the whole time, only seven people had developed symptoms so severe that they required therapeutic intervention.

However, the relatively low number presenting for therapeutic treatment may partly be accounted for by the fact that post-traumatic stress disorder is still a relatively unfamiliar syndrome to many people. Mitchell (1992) described how the residents of the Scottish village of Lockerbie experienced severe post-traumatic stress disorder after an American airliner exploded above the village, but it was not until they received insurance leaflets describing the symptoms of PTSD that the local doctors were able to realize that what they were treating among the population was actually a specific and recognizable syndrome, rather than just a collection of individual reactions.

Learned helplessness

The term **learned helplessness** refers to a passive condition in which people and animals fail to take action which would improve their situation, even when such actions are easily identifiable. The syndrome was identified on the basis of a number of ethically questionable animal experiments, such as those by Seligman and Maier (1967), in which dogs were exposed to unavoidable electric shocks. When their experimental conditions changed, and they were able to escape from the shock if they jumped over a barrier, most of the dogs did not learn to escape but instead endured the shock passively. Some of them even failed to learn after they had been shown what the outcome would be by the experimenters. Dogs which had not had the previous experience of helplessness, of course, learned to avoid the shocks very quickly (Figure 2.32).

Seligman suggested that this passivity happened because their previous experiences had taught them that any action which they could take would be futile – it had taught them that they were helpless. This 'learned helplessness' then meant that they were used to the idea that nothing they did would be any use and so did not realize when circumstances had changed, and action would be effective.

In 1975, Seligman extended the idea of learned helplessness to

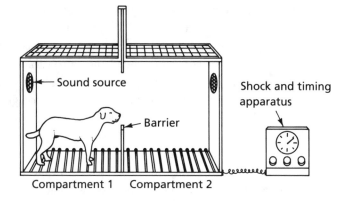

Figure 2.32 Various stimuli can be presented to the dog to indicate that the floor of compartment 1 is about to be electrified. The dog can *learn* to *avoid* the shock by jumping over the barrier into compartment 2. (Redrawn from Seligman and Maier, 1967.)

human beings, drawing parallels between the passivity of the experimental animals, and the lethargy and apathy of people who are severely depressed.

Seligman suggested that there are three elements which characterize someone who is in a state of learned helplessness. First, the person (or animal) must first have been in a situation in which the outcomes did not depend on their behaviour. Secondly, this produces a belief or expectation that their behaviour will not have any effect on the outcome; and thirdly the belief produces a number of behavioural and cognitive problems, which mean that effective action will suffer and the person will experience a sense of lack of control. In 1978 Abramson, Seligman and Teasdale extended this idea to become more specific about the sense of lack of control. They produced an analysis of **attributional styles**, showing how people who were severely depressed also tended to adopt distinctively negative attributional styles which led to passivity and apathy.

> **Key reference:** ABRAMSON, L. Y., SELIGMAN, M. E .P. and TEASDALE, J. D. (1978) Learned Helplessness in Humans: critique and reformulation. *Journal of Abnormal Psychology*, **87**, 49–74.

Learned helplessness has been demonstrated in a number of different contexts. For example, de Vellis *et al.* (1978) began a study by giving college students a series of unsolvable puzzles. When they later gave the same students similar puzzles, but this time ones which could be solved, they found that the students showed a strikingly lower performance than

Education

those who had not experienced the unsolvable puzzles first. In a similar study Miller (1986) gave 240 children (all 11 years old) either solvable or unsolvable matching-figures tasks and then asked them to solve 15 anagrams. The children who had experienced the unsolvable matching figures tasks were more inclined to give up earlier, particularly if the task was described to them as difficult. But when they were not given the choice of giving up, they performed just as well as those who had experienced solvable puzzles first.

Dweck (1975) observed that girls are more likely to attribute their academic failures to a lack of ability, whereas boys attribute their academic failures to a lack of effort. Dweck also observed that although girls receive less negative feedback than boys generally, what they do receive is more likely to be directed towards poor academic performance. Negative feedback for boys, on the other hand, tends to be more to do with conduct. The consequence of this, Dweck argued, is that girls come to believe that poor academic performance comes from lack of ability, over which they have little control, and so they come to see themselves as less likely to succeed.

Environment

Learned helplessness effects are not limited to artificial tasks carried out in laboratory or school settings. Our natural environment may contribute strongly to feelings of learned helplessness. For example, crowded environments may affect a person's ability to regulate their own social behaviour and therefore contribute to a feeling of learned helplessness. Rodin (1976) found that children living in high-density housing were less likely to assume control of events when they were given the opportunity than children living in less dense areas and related this to the children's everyday experience of not being able to control their environments to any significant degree.

Cohen *et al.* (1980) studied children from four schools located under a flight path near Los Angeles airport, where uncontrollable, unpredictable and loud noise was frequent. The children were compared with children from three matched schools in quiet areas, using physiological and behavioural measures of stress. The researchers found that the children from noisy areas not only had significantly higher blood pressure, but were also more likely to give up on a puzzle-solving cognitive task. This study suggests that although much research into learned helplessness and cognitive performance has been done in laboratory conditions, similar effects can be found in more naturalistic settings.

Goodman, Saxe and Harvey (1991) pointed out that most of the mental health literature on homelessness has focused on the characteristics that may be seen as risk factors for homelessness – factors which will make someone more vulnerable to becoming homeless. But Goodman *et al.* argued that homelessness itself is a risk factor for emotional disorder. One of the reasons for this is that the sudden or gradual loss of one's home is in itself a stressor of sufficient severity to produce symptoms of psychological trauma. The conditions of shelter life, too, may produce trauma symptoms. In addition, many homeless people – particularly women – become homeless after experiencing physical and sexual abuse, which in itself produces psychological trauma. So Goodman, Saxe and Harvey argued that the social separation and learned helplessness involved in homelessness are symptoms of psychological trauma, not its cause.

Walus-Wigle and Meloy (1988) argued that the concept of learned helplessness might be useful in understanding what the medical profession describe as 'battered woman syndrome' — the pattern of physical abuse suffered by many women in marriage. Walus-Wigle and Meloy pointed out that the typical cycle in a violent marriage consists of three phases. First, there is a tension-building period which is characterized by minor incidents of assault. This eventually climaxes in the second phase, which is an overtly violent attack on the woman, or series of attacks, but this is then followed by a contrite, loving period between violent events when the male expresses remorse toward his female victim. The researchers suggested that the psychological impact on the female victim begins with feelings of helplessness, guilt and lowered self-esteem, which lead to a pattern of learned helplessness characterized by passive and submissive behaviour, and a feeling that the violence is somehow inevitable.

Society

Unemployment is another social problem which has attracted the attention of learned helplessness theorists. Baum, Fleming and Reddy (1986) studied the behavioural changes related to unemployment among people who were employed and some who were unemployed for varying periods of time, ranging from less than three to more than eight weeks. Half the people in each group were exposed to an unsolvable

> There is a very real problem with creating labels like 'battered woman syndrome'. Psychologists and social workers might find it interesting and possibly useful to categorize the responses of certain groups of people so they can look for similarities and therefore common forms of help that they can offer. The problem lies in the identification of the victim rather than the assailant. By creating a label like 'battered woman syndrome' a perception is created that some of the responsibility for the assault lies with the woman. Imagine working on racial issues and developing a 'racist assault syndrome' that sought to identify the characteristics of people who have been racially attacked. The idea is absurd.

Figure 2.33 'Battered woman syndrome'.

task, while the other half had a solvable task. Urine samples were collected to measure the physiological **stress response**. The results indicated a general stress response among the unemployed group and suggested that learned helplessness also became manifest in the later stages of unemployment.

Health

The modified theory of learned helplessness described by Abramson, Seligman and Teasdale argued that there are three attributional dimensions which contribute to feelings of helplessness. One of these is to do with how people explain failure to themselves – such as the failure to get a job or to solve a personal problem. It makes a difference, Abramson *et al.* argued, whether the person sees the problem as internal or external (originating within themselves, as a personal quality, or originating in circumstances outside of themselves). It also matters whether the person sees their situation as stable or unstable – in other words, as likely to persist in the future, or not. And it matters whether the person interprets the failure as global or specific – whether it is seen as just applying to the one situation or to a wide range of other situations as well.

Depressive people, Abramson *et al.* argued, have a typical depressive attributional style, in which they explain negative events as coming from internal, stable and global causes – 'It's me, it's going to last for ever and it's going to affect everything I do.' As a result, they tend to become depressed when bad events occur. People who see failure as resulting from external constraints, as temporary, and as specific to that particular situation, on the other hand, are unlikely to become depressed.

There are some indications that this type of attributional style correlates with other maladaptive measures. Prapavessis and Carron (1988) administered a sports questionnaire to 50 tennis players, 31 male and 19 female, all aged between 11 and 25 years old. The questionnaire was designed to assess cognitive, motivational and emotional maladaptive achievement patterns and attributional style. The researchers found that 11 out of the 50 tennis players demonstrated maladaptive achievement patterns and that these were also associated with an attributional style which indicated learned helplessness.

As we can see, the idea of learned helplessness has been applied to a wide range of situations and problems, although the idea of learned helplessness in itself presents a relatively passive picture. However, the attributional reformulations of the theory provided a clear direction for cognitive therapy, showing how a change in someone's pattern of attributions could contribute directly to a more positive approach to living. This linked with another of the key concepts in cognitive therapy, which is that of locus of control.

Locus of control

Rotter (1966) suggested that people differ in the way that they experience their locus of control – in other words, where they feel the control over events in their life comes from. Some people perceive themselves as having an external locus of control, which means they do not feel that they, personally, can control events: they see their lives as being controlled by outside forces. Things happen to them. On the other hand, some people perceive themselves as having an internal locus of control, which means they experience themselves as exerting personal control over events in their lives. They make things happen, rather than passively waiting for them to occur.

Rotter went on to argue that locus of control is a significant factor in psychological well-being. Feeling unable to control events – feeling oneself to be a 'victim of circumstance' – is inherently stressful for the human being. Moreover, Rotter argued, because such people experience a higher level of stress, an external locus of control can lead to ill health and psychological problems.

Key reference: ROTTER, J. B. (1966) Generalised expectancies for internal vs. external control of reinforcement. *Psychological Monographs*, **80 (1)**.

The I-E Scale asks you to choose one of two alternatives from items such as the following.

1.a) In the case of the well-prepared student there is rarely, if ever, such a thing as an unfair test.
1.b) Examination questions are often so unrelated to course work that studying is really useless.

2.a) The average citizen can have an influence on government decisions.
2.b) This world is run by the few people in power and there is not much the little guy can do about it.

3.a) Most people do not realize the extent to which their lives are controlled by accidental happenings.
3.b) There is no such thing as 'luck'.

4.a) What happens to me is my own doing.
4.b) Sometimes I feel that I do not have enough control over the direction my life is taking.

People with an **internal** locus of control tend to choose 1.a), 2.a), 3.b) 4.a); and people with an **external** locus of control tend to choose the alternatives.

Figure 2.34 Examples of items from Rotter's locus of control scale.

Environment

Being able to exert some control over one's situation is important for human beings. For example, when elderly people start to live in nursing homes they often show a decline in activity and health. Langer and Rodin (1976) investigated whether this decline is related to the way that elderly people in residential homes often have few responsibilities or opportunities to influence their everyday lives. Langer and Rodin manipulated the amount of responsibility allowed to residents of the two floors of a modern high-quality nursing home. The residents on the two floors were similar in psychological and physical health, and in socioeconomic status.

On one floor, they were allowed to take on responsibilities like arranging the furniture and participating in making decisions about activities. On the other floor, the residents led an orthodox institutional life, in which they exerted very little personal control over their day-to-day lives. Rodin and Langer took measures of happiness and activity and found that there was an immediate improvement in the residents who had more control. This difference was still evident 18 months later and, furthermore, the residents with control were healthier, and fewer of them had died.

Sometimes, we may come to believe that we have control over an event that is really determined by other forces. Wortman (1975) demonstrated this in a game of chance. She used two marbles, one red and one blue, and a tin can. In one condition the experimenter said to the subjects: 'I will put the two marbles that you hand me in the can, mix them up, reach in without looking and pull one out.' In the other condition the experimenter said: 'I would like you to take these two marbles, place them in the can, mix them up, reach in without looking and pull one out.' In both conditions, the colour of the marble that was pulled out affected what prize the subject would get. The subjects were then asked to rate how much they felt they could influence the marble they got. Although they had an equal lack of control over which marble was picked, the subjects who picked the marble out themselves felt they had much more influence over the outcome.

It would appear, then, that it may not be necessary to have real control, as long as you believe that you have it. In fact, this appears to be the basis of superstitions – by giving you rituals to perform or tokens which you must keep with you, they provide an illusion of control, which helps people – particularly those with an external locus of control – to feel more secure. Those whose locus of control is predominantly internal don't usually feel the need for 'lucky' tokens or mascots. But there is also evidence that people with an internal locus of control do tend to be more successful and more healthy than those without – whether the latter use lucky charms or not!

Figure 2.35 People who experience external locus of control are more likely to gain comfort from lucky charms.

The concept of locus of control has been shown to have a lot to do with how someone responds to treatment. Ollendick *et al.* (1980) used a fixed **token economy** system, based on operant conditioning, in a treatment programme for 90 delinquent youths. Although the overall programme resulted in a relatively low recidivism rate, in that only 38% offended again after the treatment, they found that there was a difference between internally and externally oriented offenders. The internally oriented ones committed fewer offences during the institutional programme and manifested lower recidivism rates when they were followed up a year later. Externally oriented youths, on the other hand,

Society

token economy *A system involving the use of tokens as secondary reinforcers used, for example, in the rehabilitation of long-term psychiatric patients.*

derived less benefit from the programme and showed higher rates of recidivism, relapsing into crime more often. The implication, then, was that the success of the treatment programme depended on whether the youths perceived themselves as being in control of what happened to them or not.

In some medical situations, close compliance to treatment regimes is essential for continued good health. **Diabetes** is one of these conditions: Bradley *et al.* (1987) developed a scale to measure feelings of control among diabetics. The scale was administered to groups of patients who were offered a choice of continuing with conventional treatment, of experiencing an intensified programme of conventional therapy or of adopting a newly developed technique which involved delivering insulin by an infusion pump. They found that, in general, those patients choosing the pump saw themselves as having less personal control over their condition than the other two groups. But, within that group, those who had achieved the most effective blood glucose control a year later were also those who had a more internal locus of control. The study suggested that taking account of patients' beliefs and ideas could help the development of better self-monitoring systems, and so improve the long-term health of the patient.

Health

diabetes *Type I diabetes involves a complete failure of the pancreas and requires insulin replacement by injection. Type II diabetes is far more common. In this condition individuals retain some endogenous insulin and are able to maintain homeostatic glycemic control through diet, weight management and oral medication.*

Work

Cummins (1989) examined the role of social support and locus of control in job satisfaction. Cummins conducted a survey of 96 workers aged between 20 and 49, and found that there was a difference between those with internal and external locus of control in terms of the kind of support which they found useful. Those with internal locus of control found it more useful to have support from a variety of sources, whereas those with external locus of control found direct support from supervisors to be more helpful. The researchers also concluded that the stress buffering effect of social support may only relieve job stress when that support is specific to issues at work and when the people who are receiving the support believe they can influence the outcomes.

Education

Locus of control is not fixed and there have been several studies showing how it can be changed. In one study, Reimani (1971) investigated a group of school teachers who were encouraged to help children develop a more internal locus of control, through a careful use of praise and reward in the classroom. When the children were tested after the trial period, they showed a significant increase in internality by comparison with their scores at the start of the experiment. Reimani also reported the outcome of a special set of counselling sessions held with older students, designed to increase their internality. As a result of these sessions, the students not only reported feeling very much more in control of their own studying, but also described how they had engaged in more positive behaviour, like finding new accommodation or going to their tutors to get feedback on their progress.

Doherty (1983) suggested that locus of control may also change in response to very disturbing or disrupting life events. So, for example, many women who have been through the trauma of divorce show an increase in external locus of control at the time, but later on this drops back to a more internal level as they acclimatize to the change. Cheney and Blecker also showed that women who are systematically abused by their husbands tend to show a much more external locus of control than non-battered women and that this tends to increase the longer the abuse continues.

Locus of control, then, is all about whether we feel empowered in a given situation or not. Over the years, Rotter's useful, though rather simplistic, concept has become refined and developed. One of the most important developments in this concerns how people do not simply have one single locus of control: our perceptions of our abilities differ for different types of situations. In some situations, we expect to be able to take effective action, while in others we may see ourselves as less capable. Research in this area, therefore, has focused on people's beliefs about self-efficacy, exploring how they influence behaviour and, perhaps most importantly, how they change.

Self-efficacy

In many ways, **self-efficacy beliefs** are the exact opposite of learned helplessness and cognitive therapy for depression often focuses on encouraging people to develop positive self-efficacy beliefs. Bandura (1989) argued that self-efficacy beliefs are important, because they determine what we will try to do.

Self-efficacy beliefs express what we believe we are capable of achieving – they are all about the idea that we can act positively in a given situation. These beliefs, in turn, influence our perception, motivation and performance. Beliefs about our own abilities and about qualities such as intelligence have been shown to have a direct influence on how both children and adults interact with their worlds, and therefore how they go about learning from them.

Bandura argued that the self-efficacy beliefs which people hold about their own capabilities directly affect how much effort they are prepared to put into achieving or completing tasks. If we believe that we are capable of achieving something, we will be likely to stick at it until we succeed. If, on the other hand, we doubt whether we are capable of doing it successfully, we are unlikely to try as hard and will give up more easily. Because of this, Bandura argued that it is a good thing if people have self-efficacy beliefs which are slightly higher than the evidence would suggest, because this encourages them to aim high. By doing so, they try harder, and so they develop their skills and abilities even further.

Bandura argued that we make judgements of self-efficacy primarily on the bases of our own achievements. However, we also use other sources for these judgements, including observations of the behaviour of other people, social and self-persuasion ('You know you can do it really... '), and monitoring our emotional states. For example, if we are feeling anxious then we may experience lower self-efficacy beliefs than when we are feeling relaxed, because we may attribute our anxiety state as deriving from a possible expectation of failure.

Self-efficacy, as a sense of personal mastery, is not the same as an overall sense of self-confidence. Bandura argued that self-efficacy beliefs are best thought of as a collection of specific evaluations – as perceptions of abilities. Although this might help to give confidence, it need not do so, particularly if the person does not regard the ability as particularly significant. This is an important concept, because it helps us to avoid oversimplifying people's complex self-knowledge and self-evaluation into a single label like self-esteem.

> **Key reference:** BANDURA, A. (1977) Self-efficacy. *Psychological Review,*
> **84**, 191–215.

Society

The concept of self-efficacy has been investigated in many situations, including the prediction of voting behaviour. Wollman and Stouder (1991) hypothesized that the best predictor of whether people would vote or not would be to do with the perceived efficacy of voting. They conducted 4 studies, involving 504 undergraduates, 57 military and medical personnel, and 57 female members of a bowling league to compare efficacy beliefs with respect to political issues, and the degree of political activity which people engaged in, such as voting, participating in demonstrations etc. All four studies confirmed the hypothesis that the more situation-specific a person's feelings of efficacy, the greater the predictability of their political behaviour.

McAuley, Duncan and McElroy (1989) investigated whether there was a relationship between the self-efficacy beliefs of children and the causal attributions which they made. After setting up a competitive situation on a bicycle ergometer, they assigned 36 children, aged between 9 and 12 to winning or losing groups (which was thought to lead them to high or low self-efficacy beliefs), and asked them to rate their performance. They found that the self-efficacy beliefs expressed by the children were significantly related to stable and controllable attributions. The researchers suggested from this that self-efficacy beliefs might exert a considerable influence on the types of causal **attributions** we form.

Performance of another nature was investigated by Lee and Gillen (1989). They tested the hypothesis that self-efficacy would be positively related to performance quality and quantity in sales. They asked 64 male and 19 female sales representatives of a large manufacturing corporation to respond to a number of self-efficacy based questionnaire items, which had been constructed specifically for the sales tasks performed by the respondents. Not surprisingly, they found that those salespeople with higher self-efficacy beliefs tended to have higher performance outcomes than those with lower self-efficacy beliefs.

Levinson (1986) investigated the relationship between self-efficacy beliefs and teenage girls' contraceptive behaviour in 258 female clients of a family planning clinic. Levinson found that girls with high self-efficacy beliefs with regard to contraceptive behaviour think that they can and

attribution theory The *explanation of social perception by examining how people allocate intention or meaning of the behaviour of others.*

Society

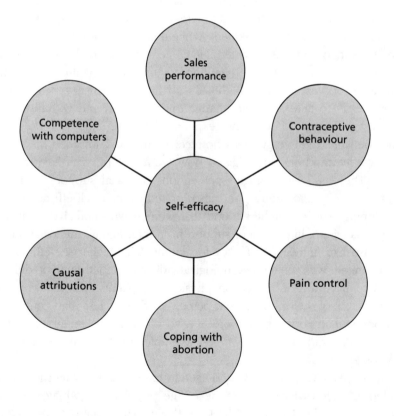

Figure 2.36 Self-efficacy has been shown to be important in a range of behaviours.

should be responsible for their sexual activity, whereas those with lower self-efficacy beliefs may use contraception inefficiently because they experience conflict regarding their strong sexual feelings and activities.

Self-efficacy may also be a significant concept in pain control. Bandura *et al.* (1988) induced high or low levels of self-efficacy in two groups of people by manipulating the demands of a mental arithmetic task. Half of each group were then given an injection of either a saline solution, which would have no effect, or naloxone, an opiate antagonist which blocks the effects of the body's natural pain-killers. All of the research participants then had an arm immersed in ice-cold water and their pain thresholds were measured, partly by physiological stress measures, and partly by timing how long they could endure the pain.

Bandura *et al.* found that, among the research participants who were given the **placebo** injection, those with low self-efficacy beliefs experienced higher levels of stress during the cognitive test, but could withstand more painful stimulation than those with high self-efficacy beliefs. The two groups given naloxone did not differ in their pain tolerance, which was low. The researchers suggested that because low self-efficacy beliefs are stressful for the body, it may be that such people secrete a higher level of natural pain-killers. While this might seem to be beneficial on the surface, in the long term it could have harmful effects on the immune system, rendering them more vulnerable to illness. (Another possibility, of course, is that those with high self-efficacy beliefs were more ready to take action to change their situation and withdraw from the test, although this does not explain why there should be no difference between the two groups who received the 'real' injection.)

Major *et al.* (1990) investigated how women cope with having abortions. They assessed women's perceptions of social support from their partner, family and friends, and also looked at their self-efficacy beliefs for coping. The researchers found that women who perceived that they were receiving a high level of support from their family, friends and partners also had higher self-efficacy for coping. This higher self-efficacy, in turn, linked with better psychological adjustment, although it did not seem to have any influence on physical complaints. Women who told close others of their abortion but perceived them as less than completely supportive had poorer post-abortion psychological adjustment than either women who did not tell or women who told and felt that they received complete support.

Some years ago, the BBC radio used to have a Saturday morning show called 'Children's Favourites'. One of the popular songs played by the presenter, 'Uncle Mac', was 'The Little Engine That Could', the story of a little engine which was able to pull a heavy set of trucks over a hill when larger engines had failed. The trick was that the little engine kept saying to itself (herself, maybe?) 'I think I can, I think I can'.

Some training methods in self-efficacy appear to be loosely based on this song. Gist, Schwoerer and Rosen (1989) compared self-efficacy beliefs and alternative training methods, in a field experiment involving 108 university managers being trained to use a complex computer software package. A behavioural **modelling** approach was compared with a tutorial approach and produced higher self-efficacy scores, and also higher performance on an objective measure of computer software mastery than the tutorial method.

modelling *Providing an example which a child can imitate in order to learn styles of behaviour.*

Perhaps not surprisingly, managers with high computer self-efficacy beliefs performed significantly better than participants with low computer self-efficacy scores. But the participants low in self-efficacy also reported that the behavioural modelling method gave them greater confidence in their ability to master the software training – in other words, the method seemed to have raised their self-efficacy beliefs. They reported more effective cognitive working styles, being more at ease with the task, having more satisfaction with training, and less frustration, by comparison with those in tutorial training.

We have seen, then, how research into personality, stress and coping has covered a range of applications, as well as a range of theoretical contexts. In the next chapter, we will look at how human beings communicate with one another and how psychological research into communication of one form or another has been applied in different fields.

Summary

1. Rogers' theory of personality is based on the idea that people have two basic needs: for positive regard, and for self-actualization. Both must be satisfied for mental health.

2. Personal construct theory is concerned with how we make sense out of our worlds, by constructing personal mini-theories, or constructs, which we apply to our experience.

3. Trait theories of personality are concerned with consistent regularities of behaviour which people show. They often use questionnaire-style measurements to assess these traits.

4. Narrow-band approaches to personality also look at traits, but focus on single aspects of behaviour rather than attempting to describe the whole personality.

5. Investigations of how people respond to stressful life events showed that these can influence people's physical health as well as their mental well-being.

6. The concept of arousal is a general way of describing our physical response to anxiety, alarm, or other disturbing situations. Long-term arousal and stress are closely linked.

7. Coping is the process of managing internal and external demands on the person. It involves identifying positive ways of dealing with stress and reducing its potential damage.

8. Post-traumatic stress disorder is a syndrome which arises as a result of experiencing disasters or similar events, which lasts for some time after the event itself – sometimes even years.

9. Learned helplessness is the way that animals fail to act to change their situation if they have previously experienced conditions in which there was nothing they could do. It has been linked with depression in human beings.

10. Locus of control is concerned with how people perceive what happens to them, and whether they see themselves as being able to influence their lives or not.

11. Self-efficacy beliefs are the beliefs that we have about what we are capable of doing and having high self-efficacy beliefs has been shown to be psychologically healthy.

PRACTICE QUESTIONS AND ACTIVITIES – 2

Personal constructs

The methods of personal constructs allows you to identify the important constructs you use to understand the world. This is not something that can be done in five minutes, but it might be worth an hour or two of your time to carry out this exploration.

1. Get ten small bits of card. On each of the first eight cards write the name of a person whom you know very well, for example, mother, boss, partner etc. On the last two cards write 'ME – as I am' on one and 'ME – as I would like to be' on the other.
2. Mix the cards up and and take out any three.
3. Think about the three people in front of you and try to think of one important way in which these two people are similar to each other but different to the third person. This is a 'construct' that you are using to judge people by. Write it down.
4. Mix up the cards and repeat the process.
5. You will find that after a while some of the constructs are repeating themselves, though with slightly different words. It is likely that you will develop a list of around eight key constructs.
6. You might like to consider the following questions.
   (a) Are these constructs a surprise to you?
   (b) Who is most like 'ME – as I am'?
   (c) Who is most like 'ME – as I would like to be'?
   (d) How big is the gap between me and my ideal self?

The Barnum effect

Try out the Barnum effect. Invent a personality test or handwriting test, or something that might suggest it can explore what people really think and feel. Ask some friends or colleagues whether they would like to try out this test in strictest confidence to evaluate how accurate and insightful the test is.

Give them the test, then collect in the results and take it away for you to study. This 'analysis time' is quite important, because if the test appears to be easy to interpret it will be less plausible. (A corollary of the Barnum effect is the 'Two bits of paper and a paperclip effect', where people walk around their place of work with two bits of paper and a paper clip to show that they are busy. Never walk around empty handed, since then people will think you have nothing to do.) After an appropriate length of time, give them a handwritten copy of the list used by Forer (on page 78) and ask the person to rate each statement on a five-point scale for accuracy. Then ask them to rate how insightful the test is. If the Barnum effect works then people will rate your test, whatever it was, very highly.

In debriefing your willing participants, you will give them an insight into the workings of personality assessment and will encourage a more critical approach in future.

PRACTICE QUESTIONS AND ACTIVITIES – 2

Stress

There are all manner of things you can do on the topic of stress. One illuminating exercise is to keep a stress diary. You know those charts that are found at the bottom of beds in hospitals with a number of incomprehensible graphs on them? Well, your task is to create an observation chart on stress.

First, you need to decide how you feel when you are stressed. For example, your teeth might go on edge or you might feel homicidal. Make a short list and put it into the form of a table as shown in the example below. In this example I have rated my feelings of stress on a five-point scale every evening. An alternative method would be to record your observations every four hours over a period of two or three days.

Here are the points to look for.
- Do you have the same pattern of stress responses all the time?
- Does the overall level of stress remain constant?
- If you have different feelings for different stressful events, then which events create which type of stress?
- What does all this tell us about the concept of 'stress'?

	MON	TUES	WED	THURS	FRI
ANGER	4	2	5	5	3
TENSION	2	3	4	5	1
DISTRACTED	5	4	2	3	3
IRRITATED	5	3	2	4	5

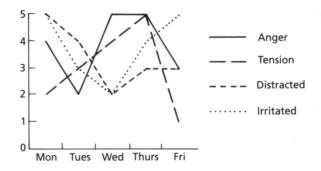

3
Communication and explanation

Introduction

This chapter is all about how we go about communicating with other people. Communication is an unavoidable part of living – even a hermit living a solitary life is communicating something, just by virtue of staying separate from other people. Communication involves passing information from one person to another, but it does not necessarily involve conscious awareness. Sometimes we send information to other people without realizing it and sometimes we receive information without being aware that

Figure 3. 1 Messages given and received. One simple message can mean very different things to the sender, the receiver and the observer.

we have done so. Communication happens on many levels, conscious and unconscious, and takes many different forms.

In this chapter, we will look at some of those forms. We will begin by looking at a form of communication which is often entirely unconscious – our non-verbal behaviour. Non-verbal communication is crucially important to our interaction: Argyle, Alkema and Gilmour (1971) compared the effectiveness of non-verbal and verbal communication in messages and estimated that non-verbal communication is four times as powerful as verbal communication. If we are faced with a person saying one thing in words, while contradicting what they are saying by their body posture and facial expression, we are much more likely to believe their posture and expression. Leaders, con-artists, advertisers and politicians, of course, have known this for years: they use non-verbal communication systematically, to make what they are saying appear more convincing.

Messages, then, are communicated by all kinds of subtle indicators, such as the way that we walk or the gestures that we make. Still more messages are contained in the way that we pronounce words and the style of language that we adopt. In Britain at least, and in many other countries too, accent and dialect are key discriminators of social class, regional identity and sometimes ethnic background. Some towns in Britain include a large mixture of people from all kinds of different backgrounds; other towns have a narrower social mix and the regional identity of the place is stronger.

linguistic relativity hypothesis The idea that thinking depends on language and so people who speak a different language also inhabit different conceptual worlds.

One important theory about language and the way that it connects with thinking is the **linguistic relativity hypothesis**. This suggests that the words we use to describe objects and events affects how we think about them – the structure of the language that we use guides our view of the world. This naturally leads to the question of whether people using different languages have very different ways of seeing the world. Does this mean that communication between people of different cultures is impossible? Are there ideas which are common to all human beings? Or do we need to develop special forms of language in order to think about certain kinds of things?

An extension of this line of enquiry leads us to consider whether people who use different forms of the same language have different cognitive structures. The idea proposed by Bernstein was that some users of the English language use an impoverished form of it and so are denied access to the more sophisticated styles of thinking – an idea known as the verbal deprivation hypothesis. This idea was suggested as a possible explanation for the relatively low achievement of working-class children in British schools (see Figure 3.2). Not surprisingly, there

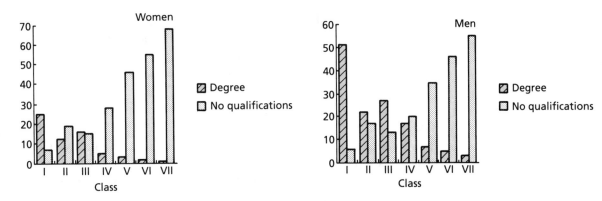

Figure 3.2 A general household survey taken in 1986 shows the percentage of people in different social classes leaving education with either a degree or with no qualifications.

are other explanations for this level of performance, and many researchers have suggested that the language of these children might be different, but is not cognitively deficient. But, of course, this aspect of psychology is intimately linked with wider questions involving the sociopolitical context of educational provision.

Communicating with other people involves more than simply understanding words. We also need to comprehend the underlying social scripts which are used in day-to-day living. We use social scripts to structure our daily interactions – to give meaning to the complex, patterned forms of behaviour which are involved in, say, using a library, eating out, or attending a meeting. As we become socialized into society, we learn to conform to these underlying patterns of behaviour entirely without realizing it, but it is in these patterns that our shared knowledge about, and assumptions of, social and cultural life is most clearly revealed.

There are shared assumptions, too, in how we go about making conversation. We use metaphors and idioms to illustrate what we mean, and in doing so we invoke a shared knowledge of the world which enriches and brings alive our conversation. Discourse analysis is concerned with looking at the deeper meanings and understandings from various pieces of verbal communication, whether spoken or written. It goes beyond an analysis of word meanings, seeing discourse in its social and cultural framework, and exploring patterns of shared meaning.

There are social influences, too, in how we go about explaining things to ourselves. The process of attribution is to do with identifying the reasons why things happen, and as such it is intimately concerned with how we interpret our own behaviour and that of other people. Do we, for example, explain why someone did something in terms of stable, lasting causes, or do we identify reasons which are not likely to happen again? The various dimensions of the attributional process show us how giving different types of reasons for why things happen can directly influence what we try to do and how we interact with other people. In other words, they can be a major determinant of social action.

Attributions are to do with the individual explanations which people make; but we are also influenced by the more general types of explanations which are accepted by our social groups and by society as a whole. The concept of social representations is all about exploring how ideology influences individual and group beliefs: our society and culture predisposes us to accept certain types of explanations for why things happen, rather than others. In a Western society, for example, we tend to be more at ease if explanations are linked with scientific concepts – or at least, phrased in scientific language – rather than with magical ones. As society changes, so do our beliefs and ideas about the nature of human beings: the study of social representations explores how shared beliefs differ from one culture or time to another and how people actively negotiate the social representations which they are prepared to accept.

Non-verbal communication

non-verbal communication
Communication which does not involve language or words of any form.

Non-verbal communication, or NVC, is a general term used to describe communication without the use of words. Argyle (1975) argued that non-verbal cues serve four major functions. They are used to assist speech, helping to regulate conversation or to emphasize meaning. They are used as replacements for speech: a gesture may render a verbal question unnecessary. Non-verbal cues are also used to signal attitudes: a casual posture may indicate boredom in one context or familiarity with the situation in another. And they are

Figure 3.3 Gestures are very expressive, but the same gestures can convey more than one meaning. A fist pounding on a table could be excitement or anger. And a hand under a chin could be tiredness or intense concentration.

also used to signal emotional states: a smile and relaxed posture may indicate happiness; a different posture may indicate tension or anxiety.

The topic of non-verbal communication is a great favourite with popularizers of psychology. Observing standing, sitting or walking styles and deciding what each might mean has an obvious appeal – whether it is based in reality or not. It is the psychology of magazine articles, which address non-verbal communication in items such as 'If you cross your legs when talking to your boss it means...?' or 'If you put your weight on your left foot when standing at a bus stop it means...?' This type of analysis, understandably, is of very little value indeed – it is too simplistic to take account of the real subtleties involved in human communication and only the very credulous follow its blueprints. None the less the topic can also offer some insights that go beyond sheer entertainment value.

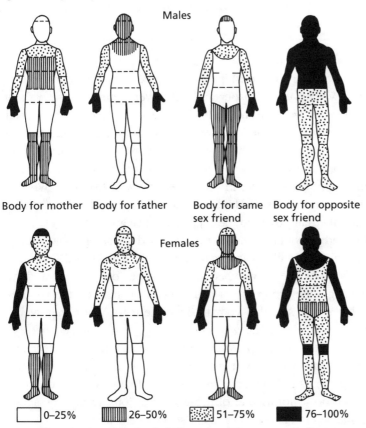

Figure 3.4 Who touches whom, where and how often (for white Western peoples). (Knapp, 1978.)

Areas of the body involved in boldily contact. The top row indicates which part of a male's body may be touched by the person indicated beneath each figure. The bottom row indicates which part of a female's body may be touched by the person indicated above. Percentages show the relative amount of touching for each area.

paralanguage *Non-verbal cues contained in how people say things, such as in tones of voice, pauses, or 'um' and 'er' noises.*

personal space *The physical distance which people like to maintain between themselves and others. This varies according to their relationship with and attitude to other people, and according to norms and contexts.*

Non-verbal communication includes a wide range of different types of cues. These include **paralanguage** (the expressive aspects of voice which accompany spoken words), eye contact, facial expression, posture, gesture, touch, proxemics (including concepts of **personal space** and acceptable conversational distance) and dress. Ekman and Friesen (1969) classified these into five functional groups: emblems, illustrators, affect displays, regulators and adaptors. Emblems have a direct meaning with a verbal equivalent – like specific gestures or uniforms. Illustrators accompany speech and amplify or demonstrate what is being said. Affect displays are non-verbal signals of emotional states, regulators are non-verbal acts which direct the flow of conversation and adaptors are idiosyncratic non-verbal acts which help people to cope.

Key reference: EKMAN, P. and FRIESEN, W. V. (1969) The repertoire of non-verbal behaviour categories: origins, usage and coding. *Semiotica,* **1**, 49-98.

Society

Non-verbal communication is one of the principal ways that people negotiate power relationships when they are interacting with other people. We can establish our authority over someone else without ever exchanging a word. Henley (1977) discussed how touch is used as a signal of power in American and British organizational life: a boss may put an arm across the shoulder of a subordinate in a friendly gesture which none the less indicates superior power: it would be unthinkable for the subordinate to act in the same way with the boss. Who touches whom and in what way, Henley argued, can give important insights into who has the real power in the organization (Figure 3.5).

Non-verbal communication can be used to assert power in gender relationships as well as in organizations. In a study by Forden (1981), research participants watched a videotape of a man and woman conversing. One group saw a man touch a woman on the shoulder and the other group saw the woman touch the man. When they were asked later, those who saw the woman touch the man assessed her as dominant and the man as passive – but no comparable judgements were made by those who saw a man touch a woman. The implication, that touching carries a dominance message and that it is somehow noticeable if women do it, forms one of those unconscious social messages which are contained in almost all forms of social interaction.

Using non-verbal communication positively can be an important key to getting on with other people. In 1950, Jennings studied 400 girls in a reformatory, and found that the popular girls were those who helped and

Figure 3.5 Same gesture: different social meaning.

protected others, encouraged them, cheered them up, made them feel accepted and wanted, and controlled their own moods so as not to inflict depression or anxiety on others. They also were able to establish rapport quickly, won the confidence of a wide variety of other personalities, and were concerned about the feelings and needs of others. The unpopular girls, on the other hand, were dominating, aggressive, boastful, demanded attention and tried to get others to do things for them.

Although it is obviously valuable for people to be socially skilled, the reason why the magazine-type 'guides' to interpreting non-verbal signals are so highly questionable is because there are so many differences between different communities and cultures in how non-verbal signals are used. For example, Gielen (1979) observed that there are systematic race and gender differences in the use of **eye contact** in conversation. From a series of naturalistic observations, Gielen found that pairs of black women in conversation tend to make eye contact less often than do pairs of white women and that white adults in general make more frequent eye contact than black adults.

eye contact Mutual gaze or when two people are each looking at the other's eyes at the same time.

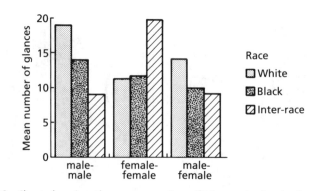

Figure 3.6   Chart showing the mean number of glances in dyads of various racial and sexual compositions. (Gielen *et al.*, 1979.)

ethnocentricity *Being unable to conceptualize or imagine ideas, social beliefs or the world, from any view-point other than that of one's own particular culture or social group. The belief that one's own ethnic group, nation, religion, scout troop or football team is superior to all others.*

In white middle-class cultures, eye contact is generally taken to be a signal of mutual trust and liking. Smith (1983), assuming that this is the same in all cultures, argued that interracial female dyads (in other words, pairs consisting of one white and one black woman) and white male dyads reflect the highest degree of mutual trust and liking, whereas inter-racial male and male–female dyads expressed the least. The problem with these conclusions, however, is that, as Gielen's study showed, some black cultures involve generally less eye contact than some white ones. So we would need to look much more deeply at the quality of relationships before we could tell whether this is a valid conclusion, or simply an expression of **ethnocentricity** on the part of the researcher.

These studies do, however, suggest that messages inferred from non-verbal behaviour should be interpreted cautiously, since both race and gender are influential in establishing different 'norms' for eye contact. As Henley pointed out, the social context and social use of the signals has everything to do with the meaning of non-verbal communication and, without taking it into account, we are unlikely ever to be able to make accurate interpretations of what is going on.

Health

Since a good rapport between participants in a medical consultation is a vital component of effective practice, and since people do tend to judge others by their appearance, dressing appropriately for the role can be important. McKinstry and Wang (1991) showed 475 patients attending doctors' surgeries pictures of the same male or female doctor, dressed either very formally (white coat over suit or skirt) or very informally (jeans and open-necked, short-sleeved shirt, or pink trousers, jumper and gold earrings). The patients were asked to rate how happy they would be to see the doctor in the picture and how much confidence they would have in the doctor's ability. The traditionally-dressed images received higher preference ratings than the casually attired ones, particularly on the part of older and professional-class patients.

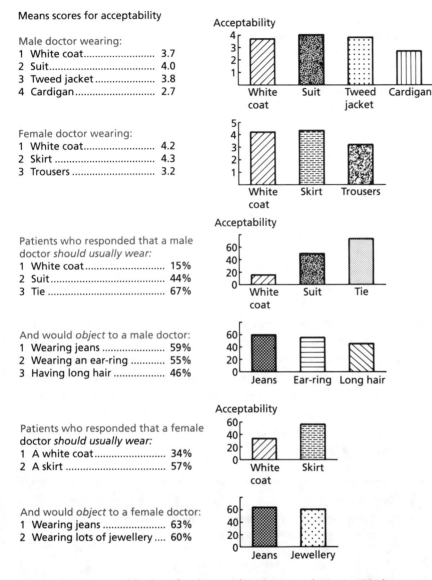

Means scores for acceptability

Male doctor wearing:
1 White coat.......................... 3.7
2 Suit..................................... 4.0
3 Tweed jacket...................... 3.8
4 Cardigan............................ 2.7

Female doctor wearing:
1 White coat.......................... 4.2
2 Skirt 4.3
3 Trousers 3.2

Patients who responded that a male
doctor *should usually wear:*
1 White coat............................ 15%
2 Suit.. 44%
3 Tie 67%

And would *object* to a male doctor:
1 Wearing jeans 59%
2 Wearing an ear-ring 55%
3 Having long hair 46%

Patients who responded that a female
doctor *should usually wear:*
1 A white coat.......................... 34%
2 A skirt 57%

And would *object* to a female doctor:
1 Wearing jeans 63%
2 Wearing lots of jewellery 60%

Figure 3.7 Acceptable dress for doctors. (McKinstry and Wang, 1991.)

Appearance, though, is not the only source of non-verbal communication. Argyle (1975) emphasized that there is a fluid interplay between the different channels of non-verbal communication, so other variables would also be important in influencing the quality of the patient/doctor relationship. A formally dressed doctor who avoids eye contact and does not use appropriate facial expressions would be likely to come across as aloof or distant, and this in itself would be likely to prove to be a barrier to effective patient/doctor interaction for most people.

Society

One of the responses to a greater understanding of non-verbal communication has been to develop social skills training programmes to improve an individual's ability to put across the messages they want. Sutton (1979) discussed how non-verbal signals are used in directing the nature and prospects of social worker interviews and of counselling, and identified a number of simple and fundamental questions for social workers which might usefully focus their attention on the non-verbal messages which they were unconsciously transmitting. The list is given in Figure 3.8 although Sutton emphasized that it should not be regarded as exhaustive: there are many other details of social worker–client interaction which had not been included. It does, however, give an insight into the kind of non-verbal details which professionals regard as important and could provide a useful basis for research into whether their clients regard them as equally important.

However, social skills training has an obvious appeal for therapists, management trainers and media consultants etc. Margaret Thatcher, for example, learned to modulate her voice to be lower and softer rather than harsh and shrill, as an important part of her media skills training for becoming prime minister. In our everyday exchanges with people we tend to believe that non-verbal communication is out of the control of the individual and therefore it is a more accurate indicator of their intentions or attitudes than their conversation. Some people are able to lie with relative ease, but others can be spotted in their lying because they give themselves away through their unconscious actions. It remains to be seen, though, whether in an increasingly image-conscious society, the

1. Am I punctual?
2. Do I smile at clients as we meet each other?
3. Do I make sure my client is not kept waiting, or, if this happens, do I apologize?
4. Are our chairs positioned to indicate equality?
5. If time is limited, do I make it clear how long we have?
6. Do I give my client my full attention or do I allow my gaze to wander?
7. Do I make sure I am not interrupted?
8. Do I sit in a relaxed, but not over-casual position?
9. Does my facial expression usually convey friendliness, tension, anxiety, aloofness, warmth? What *does* it convey?
10. Is my manner confident, over-confident, tentative, condescending, cold, aggressive, distant, anxious? What manner have I?
11. Do I avoid making notes as my client speaks, apart from purely factual information?

Figure 3.8 NVC checklist for social workers.

attention to self-presentation might reduce our confidence in reading other people's non-verbal messages.

Trower, Bryant and Argyle (1978) found that studies of neurotic patients imply that specific training in social skills seems to be slightly more effective than psychotherapy, desensitization or other forms of therapy, but not by very much. Maxwell (1976) found higher rates of success with adults seeking treatment for social difficulties in New Zealand. In part, this may be because Maxwell used a different method of treatment, particularly involving 'homework assignments', so these clients might have had more practice than the others. Alternatively, they may simply have been more self-motivated. In all cases, though, social skills training produced a considerable reduction in social anxiety and it is not beyond the bounds of possibility that just reducing social anxiety in itself might produce an improvement in the long term.

Health

Hersen and Bellack (1976) discussed how the use of **assertiveness** and other forms of social skills training with psychotic patients in the USA produced more improvement than alternative forms of therapy. The most effective methods of training were extremely intensive, involving maybe 20 or 30 sessions working on just one symptom at a time, but it is not clear how well these people managed to function when they left hospital, although the researchers were optimistic.

In a different study, Brown (1975) showed that the use of intensive social skills training for teachers was a much more effective method of training good teacher behaviour than other methods and was more effective in eradicating bad habits. Brown used the method known as **micro-teaching**, in which teachers are filmed as they teach a class, and then their actions and activities are replayed and discussed, in some detail. By getting an opportunity to see themselves as others see them, the trainee teachers are more likely to become aware of the non-verbal signals which they are emitting and so are in a better position to lean how to project different signals.

Education

We can see, then, that non-verbal communication is an important first step in the communication process. It allows us to convey emotions, power, social roles and attitudes without having to commit ourselves verbally, and it allows us to express nuances of social meaning in subtle forms. It can also transmit important messages about our social standing. In this, one of the most important forms of non-verbal communication, at least in British society, comes from the way that we say things – the use of accent and dialect.

Accent and dialect

In non-verbal communication, accent is a feature of paralanguage – those additional features of spoken language which convey information about the individual. Paralanguage includes many other signals too, such as hesitations, speech timing and tone of voice; but accent is distinctive because the information which it conveys is not specific to the individual, but to the wider structures of society.

Lyons (1981) distinguished between three forms of common linguistic variation: accent, dialect and idiolect. An accent is a pattern of pronunciation: words are given distinctive inflections, use particular vowel sounds or are given an emphasis which is different from other ways of speaking. However, the basic structure and vocabulary of the language remain the same. Accents may signal social class, regional origin and sometimes ethnic group membership, and in some societies, such as Britain, they form an active determinant of the nature of social interaction. People interact quite differently with someone who has a highly regional accent – implying that they come from a working-class background – than they do with someone who has a 'posh' accent (which does not indicate regional origin, but does indicate an upper or upper-middle class background – or an attempt to appear to have come from one).

A dialect is when the language itself varies in form and in content. Dialects have their own distinctive grammatical constructions and vocabulary. The dividing line between a dialect and a language is blurred – at some point, if the differences between two dialects become extreme enough, they may be regarded as two different and independent languages. In reality, however, whether a dialect becomes judged to be a separate language is entirely dependent on social, not linguistic, criteria, particularly with regard to the relative power and status of its speakers. It is through the emergence of dialects and regional separation that the many different languages of the world are believed to have evolved.

An idiolect, on the other hand, is unique to a particular person or, at the most, their closest friends and family. It is the personal style of language use developed by the individual person during the course of their lifetime. Idiolects often include characteristic grammatical constructions as well as a special use of vocabulary to indicate a distinctive meaning – such as a word which encapsulates a family 'in-joke'. Idiolects are reasonably accessible to outsiders, in that the person is still generally speaking the same language, but the subtlety of the referents are not.

Key reference: LYONS, J. (1981) *Language and Linguistics: an introduction.* Cambridge University Press, Cambridge.

There is some suggestion that people may find their own regional accents to be more attractive than those of other groups. Cheyne (1970) asked Scottish and English speakers to rate tape-recordings of speakers on a number of different personality traits. English people rated the male English speaker as being more intelligent, ambitious, self-confident and likely to be a leader than the Scots male. The Scots, on the other hand, judged the Scottish voice as indicative of greater generosity, good heart-edness, friendliness and likeability. However, one problem with the conclusion that this is evidence of in-group favouritism is the extent to which different accents signify differences in power and status. This is particularly relevant given the historical nature of the conflict between English and Scottish cultures.

Another possibility is that the perceived differences represent broad distinctions between accepted or expected character traits. Giles (1973) looked at how people perceived three different accents: South Welsh, Somerset and received pronunciation (RP), otherwise known as BBC English. From the ratings given by the 96 participants in the study, Giles found three main groups of character traits, centering round competence, personal integrity and social attractiveness. The RP voice was judged to be competent, but did not achieve ratings indicating integrity or social attractiveness, whereas the voices from the other two groups achieved lower ratings of competence but higher ones on the other two personality characteristics.

Society

The use of accent in signifying membership of social groups is well known. The onus appears to be on the speaker to dissociate from that group if she or he is not to be perceived in terms of the stereotype. Such dissociation is, however, possible: Gardner and Taylor (1968) asked Canadian subjects to listen to three speeches about 'What Canada means to you'. They were all delivered with a French Canadian accent, but in one version of the speech the speaker made remarks suggesting that he was actually French Canadian; in another he made remarks suggesting that in fact he was not; while the third speech gave no indication of whether the speaker might or might not be French Canadian. In the first and third conditions, subjects' judgements of the speaker were directly in tune with the French Canadian stereotype, but not in the second condition.

A number of researchers have shown how accent can exert a dramatic influence on social judgement. Giles (1973) showed that 17-year-olds who were asked to evaluate the quality of an argument against capital punishment were directly affected by the accent of the speaker.

Figure 3.9 Some U and non-U terms identified by Alan Ross in Nancy Mitford's *Noblesse Oblique* (1959), Penguin Books, London.

U	Non-U
Looking glass	Mirror
Lunch	Dinner
Mad	Mental
Dining room	Lounge
Wireless	Radio
Napkin	Serviette
Lavatory	Toilet
How do you do?	Pleased to meet you
Rich	Wealthy

self-fulfilling prophecy
The idea that expectations about a person or group can become true simply because they have been stated.

In a similar study, Edwards (1979) showed that teachers' ratings of children using dimensions like intelligence, enthusiasm, happiness, co-operation etc. were powerfully influenced by accents. The subjects were played tape recordings of different children reading the same passage and the children with regional working-class accents were rated less positively on all dimensions. The clear inference was that regional accents imply social inferiority. Given the research into **self-fulfilling prophecies** which we looked at in Chapter 1, the implication of these is that, regardless of their actual abilities, people with strong regional accents will need to try harder to succeed than those speaking forms of English which are more approved by society in general and the educational system in particular.

Accent and dialect can also have an impact on the development of literacy skills. Juel, Griffith and Gough (1986) looked at the development of literacy skills in young children, by following up 80 children in their their first two years at school. Their results showed that the child's own use of language seemed to be a major factor in its reading achievement. The habitual use of particular forms of English, such as using a strong dialect at home or only speaking English as a second language, meant that these children often had a very poor awareness of the phonemes – the sound units – in the language. Because of this, they found it hard to separate spoken language into words, and so had difficulty in learning both word-recognition and spelling, by comparison with other children whose language at home was closer to standard English. The study, then, illustrates how early experience of speech sounds can affect a child's performance at school. Although many children are able to overcome this early handicap, there is always the possibility that this type of problem will put the child at risk from social labelling or a lowered sense of self-efficacy with regard to developing reading and literacy skills.

Linguistic relativity

The **linguistic relativity hypothesis**, which is also sometimes known as the Sapir–Whorf hypothesis after the linguists who, at separate times, developed it, proposes that our thinking is determined by the language that we use. Each language system has its own unique set of categories and distinctions, and these shape how reality and social interaction are perceived.

The linguistic relativity hypothesis has two forms: a strong one and a weak one. The strong form states that if a language does not contain a term for a particular concept, there will be no way for people speaking that language to deal, cognitively, with the concept, and so people who only speak that language will not be able to deal with that concept at all. The weak form of the linguistic relativity hypothesis – in practice the more common one – retains the idea that the language used in a given culture shapes and directs the experiences and assumptions of that culture, but does not go so far as to say that language determines them.

In practice, it is the weak form which is more commonly believed by linguists and psychologists. The idea is that if a term does not exist for a concept, then it makes it more difficult to think about that concept, although not totally impossible. It also works the other way: the discovery of an Eskimo language which had 27 different words for snow (Boas, 1911) implied that a finer level of cognitive

linguistic relativity hypothesis The idea that thinking depends on language and so people who speak a different language also inhabit different conceptual worlds.

Figure 3.10 Twenty-seven kinds of snow.

discrimination about snow was made by members of that society than was possible for most English speakers.

Human beings do, however, adapt language as the need arises. So situations where there was a need to make a number of fine discriminations about snow, as for example among expert skiers, led to the generation of new terms – specialized vocabularies which served the need to communicate about concepts in a more precise way. Having the appropriate terms available facilitates deeper cognitive analysis. This is also the origin of most technical and academic jargon, although not always the explanation for its use.

Key reference: SAPIR, E. (1947) *Selected Writings in Language, Culture and Personality*. University of California Press, Los Angeles.

A judgement that shows the effect that different languages can have on perception is described by Gleason (1961) who presents a comparison of colour terms for three languages. The way that speakers of English, Shona (spoken in Zimbabwe) and Bassa (spoken in Liberia) divide the spectrum is shown below. There are some very clear distinctions to be made; not least is the notion of a colour circle in Shona and a straight line in English. It is known that when we recall colour we depend for our memory on the verbal label, so we are likely to drift in recall towards the 'pure' colour of, for example, 'green' rather than the 'greeny-blue' which we saw. The categories of the language spectra are therefore important for our visual interpretation of the world.

English

Purple	Blue	Green	Yell-ow	Orange	Red

Shona

Cipswuka	Citema	Cicena	Cipswuka

Bassa

Hui	Ziza

Figure 3.11 Describing colour.

The linguistic relativity hypothesis postulates that language does not just *describe* the world we inhabit but also moulds the way that we *experience* it. In 1932, Carmichael, Hogan and Walter reported what became a classic study of the importance of verbal labels on cognition. In their study, people were shown simple line drawings which they were later asked to reproduce. Each picture was shown with a verbal label, but the labels were different for the two groups in the experiment. Carmichael, Hogan and Walter found that the labels had a dramatic effect on the

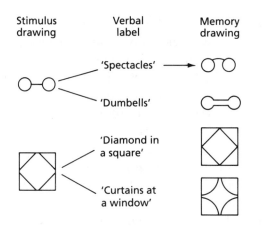

Figure 3.12 Examples of verbal labels and memory. (Carmichael, Hogan and Walter, 1939.)

memories of the people – they produced drawings which were more illustrative of the label than representations of the original drawing (see Figure 3.12). The implication of the study was that language is a powerful influence on the way we construct the world mentally.

Sapir (1947) discussed how our verbal description of events and objects determines how we understand what is happening. One of the examples which Sapir quoted was of a seemingly simple description of, say, a stone moving through space towards the ground. In English, we analyse the action as 'the stone falls' and naïvely believe that this is the only way to see it. But if we were speaking French or German the stone would have a gender – masculine in one language and feminine in the other! In the Chippewa language we would have to identify explicitly that a stone is an inanimate object. In Russian there is no distinction between 'a' stone or 'the' stone, so people would just say 'stone falls', which is also how it would be described in Latin if anyone spoke it any more. And if we were speaking the language of the Kwakiutl from South America then we would also have to state whether the stone was visible or invisible. So the same event will be described in different ways by different language speakers.

If this all seems a bit abstract then imagine the simple dinner table request 'Would you pass the salt please?' In English this request would take the same verbal form (although not the same tonal inflections), no matter who was being addressed. The subtleties of social address in English are expressed non-verbally. But in most European languages, including Dutch, French and German, there are two forms of the word 'you': an intimate form used for family and friends, and a polite form. The verbal request, then, depends on the relationship which the individual has with that person. In Japanese, which has a culture and

Society

language based heavily on politeness, there are even more variations in the form of address, each indicative of the relationship which the individual has with the person they are addressing.

Language, then, expresses social experience as well as our physical experience, and the language that we use also shapes our social experience in very specific ways. Lutz (1990) described how the Ifaluk people of Micronesia have several different words for anger, each of which distinguishes a different type of anger. *Tipmochmoch* refers to the kind of irritability which people feel when they are ill; *lingeringer* refers to the kind of anger which builds up gradually, in response to a succession of small, annoying or unwanted events; *nguch* is the kind of anger which people feel towards relatives who have failed to live up to their obligations; *tang* refers to the frustrated anger which occurs when one is helpless in the face of misfortunes or insults; and *song*, which refers to righteous indignation, or morally justifiable anger.

Lutz described how the existence of these five distinct words for anger helps to distinguish social reactions towards them. People respond differently, depending on how the anger has been defined, and in ways which allow for social approval as well as different degrees of social disapproval. Of all the different types of anger, *song* is the only one which is socially approved. All the others, particularly if they occur often enough, are regarded as a sign of character weakness, but not to the same extent – *tipmochmoch,* for instance, is regarded as more excusable than, say, *lingeringer.*

Another consequence of language use was suggested by Slobin (1971) who pointed out how often European languages use object words (nouns) to describe processes. For example, in English we might describe the process of 'flaming' using a noun and referring to 'the flame'. Slobin argued that this tendency to see processes as objects exerted a powerful effect on Western science, because it led directly to the process of **reification** – seeing a process as an object. In modern psychology a lot of activity has been directed towards finding and describing processes, as if they were really objects. The classic examples here are intelligence and aggression. Both of these are actually referring to processes – ways of doing things – but they have been treated as if they were 'things', which people had more or less of. Historically, some of the consequences of this reification have been tragic.

reification The process of treating an adverb as if it were a noun – e.g. seeing 'acting intelligently' as if it were a manifestation of some kind of entity called 'intelligence'.

The same might be said of the cognitive concept of memory, although as far as we can tell nobody has been put in a concentration camp or compulsorily sterilized because of the reification of the process of remembering into a 'thing' called memory. Most of the evidence suggests that there is not a 'memory' in the brain, but that memorizing is a process that occurs throughout the brain. Just because we have a word for it, does not mean to say that it exists.

Warner (1976) looked at the relationship between the structure of language and the concepts of disease held by different cultures. In traditional Chinese medicine, the crucial issue is balance. The two universal forces of yin and yang regulate the universe, and must be balanced to achieve harmony within the body and within nature. During much of Chinese history, health and illness were seen as agents of nature; the maintenance of regularity in life, in harmony with nature, was seen as the way to health. As anatomical knowledge grew, the organs were also seen as being in balanced co-operative interaction promoting health and harmony. This is in direct contrast to European views of the organs as being individual bits to be replaced when they become faulty.

Health

In the Chinese language there is a similar emphasis on balance, with the avoidance of extremes and absolutes. Objects are not pigeonholed into one extreme or another, but assigned a relative position on a spectrum of degree between two qualities. So where Europeans are inclined to classify a person into a type, for example extrovert, this would not translate effectively into Chinese.

In European languages we make great use of spatial metaphors for all manner of experiences. For example, we might say 'I felt a little *low* today'. A consequence of this is that a number of abstract ideas take on the properties of physical objects. So a *line* of thought can be *grasped* or *blocked*. And you *fall* in love and get *carried away* by your feelings.

This leads us, argues Warner, to see the experience of illness in spatial

Figure 3.13 'Catching measles'. The way we use English encourages us to see illness as an object and may be one of the reasons for excessive surgery.

terms (for example, we might refer to a *level* of pain) and to see illness as an object (for example we might say 'I *caught* a cold'). This has led us towards physical explanations of health and ill-health, and towards medically based treatments. So we are likely to use excessive surgery to remove failing parts of the body, and ignore the social and cultural features of ill-health.

By contrast, other societies, using different forms of language which are more expressive of a holistic relationship between the individual and their social and physical world, are more able to conceptualize the idea that social factors are important in illness. Horton (1976) discussed how traditional medical treatments in Africa focused on social factors even in diagnosing infectious diseases – seeking out the person who had fallen out with the patient, and who might therefore have 'cast a spell' on them. This seems bizarre to Western minds, yet actually makes perfect sense when the person is seen in a more holistic context.

In a traditional society, with a relatively high rate of infant mortality, those who grow to adulthood tend to have a high natural immunity to disease. So, if someone falls sick, the question is not where the germ came from, but how their immune system has been weakened to the extent that the illness can take hold. As we saw in Chapter 2, one of the consequences of prolonged stress is a suppression of immune functioning. In traditional communities the primary sources of stress come from disturbed interactions with other people. So, when the traditional medicine practitioner seeks to find out who the person has quarrelled with lately, and to reconcile their dispute and so lift the spell, this is actually an extremely practical method of treatment. By taking the ongoing social stress away from the person, it allows their natural recovery processes to act freely to fight the illness.

Society

Verbal labels are used to provide social categories and attempt to influence the way we think of a person or a political movement. Thouless (1974) described how the use of the term 'terrorist' or 'freedom fighter' describes a similar set of activities and aims of a person involved in aggressive political activity. But the different terms evoke quite different images and mind-sets. Like the words, 'regime' and 'government', the choice of term establishes which side the speaker is on.

Language is also used to disguise what is really taking place. Politicians and military people have a range of terms to try to adjust our perceptions of unpleasant events. One of the more recent ones is the term 'ethnic cleansing' which, of course, is simply another word for genocide. There is no doubt that language is an important weapon in the armoury of politicians and that control of the use of language can result in considerable influence on the political agenda.

Figure 3.14 Note the startling differences between a terrorist, a freedom fighter and a regular soldier.

During the Vietnam War a new language was developed to hide the carnage that was taking place, The following excerpt is taken from an interview recorded by the journalist John Pilger in 1975, with a member of a B-52 bomber crew. The man was wearing a shoulder patch which said '100 Vietnam Missions'. Pilger writes:

'Does that mean', I ask him, 'that you have made one hundred bombing raids over Vietnam?'

'Yes sir.'

'Were all of them military targets?'

'Affirmative. Every one.'

'No bombs fell on populated areas?'

'Negative, sir ... except for some collateral damage here and there.'

'Collateral damage?'

'That means civilian personnel casualties.'

'People killed?'

'Children, women ... ?'

'I guess so ...'

'Did you ever think about this collateral damage?'

'Negative, sir. You're too busy doing your job.'

Figure 3.15 New terms for old ceremonies.

We can see, then, that the way that we go about using language can exert a powerful influence on our thinking. As we have seen, the strong version of the linguistic relativity hypothesis is not necessarily supported: the existence of social dissidents, free-thinkers and rebels shows that language does not completely determine how we think, although it does have a great deal of influence. But, in its heyday, the strong form of the linguistic relativity hypothesis was widely accepted. Among other implications, this led directly to the idea of verbal deprivation.

Verbal deprivation

verbal deprivation hypothesis *The idea that children who do not experience extended forms of language may suffer cognitive deficits as a consequence.*

The **verbal deprivation hypothesis** rests on the assumption that thinking is determined by language. Proposed by Bernstein, in 1973, it suggested that some children become disadvantaged because they learn a form of language which is restricted in vocabulary and flexibility, and therefore does not permit certain types of thinking – in particular, analytical, abstract thinking.

elaborated language codes *Ways of using language characterized by extensive vocabulary, complex grammatical structure and an attempt to make meaning verbally explicit.*

Bernstein distinguished between the **elaborated codes** of language used by middle-class speakers and the **restricted codes** used by working-class speakers. Elaborated codes were verbally explicit with a high proportion of subordinate clauses, adjectives and uncommon adverbs; restricted codes were verbally implicit, with a high proportion of personal pronouns, and a strong dependence on implicit meaning and shared social experience. In particular, Bernstein argued that restricted codes were particularistic: concrete and tied to circumstances. This represented a problem, since it is only by being able to perceive universalistic orders of meaning, like general principles and abstract concepts, that people become able to identify the basis of their experience and therefore to change it.

restricted language codes *Ways of using language characterized by limited vocabulary, simple grammatical structures, and a heavy reliance on shared implicit meaning and paralinguistic cues.*

Bernstein went on to argue that the class system limits access to elaborated codes, since working-class children are socialized into restricted language codes, while middle-class children are socialized into extended language codes – and since the education system favours extended language codes, this gives working-class children a disadvantage. Accordingly, Bernstein argued, working-class children should be regarded as verbally deprived, since their linguistic experience disadvantages them, by comparison with middle-class children.

Challenges to the verbal deprivation hypothesis, spearheaded by the American linguist Labov (1972) attacked the idea that restricted codes denied access to universalistic forms of meaning, and demonstrated that this was not the case. However, although such challenges showed that restricted code users were as capable of dealing with abstractions and general principles as elaborated code users, they did not address the issue of other forms of disadvantage for restricted code users within the education system; particularly questions of stereotyping and teacher expectation.

> **Key reference**: BERNSTEIN, B. (1973) Social class, language and socialisation. In V. Lee (ed.) (1979) *Language Development.* Croom Helm/Open University, London.

The issue of elaborated and restricted codes generated furious debate over whether some codes were or were not better than others. Labov (1972) analysed the speech of two American children: Larry, who was a black non-standard English speaker and Charles, who was a white standard English speaker. He suggested that, although Larry did not speak standard English, his speech contained a richness of meaning which was entirely absent in the seemingly more correct utterances of Charles.

Education

Labov's intention was to show that the form of the language which someone uses does not actually determine the thinking that they are capable of doing. Larry showed himself capable of constructing a sophisticated set of arguments about abstract concepts, despite speaking a restricted language code. In this respect, Labov's swingeing critique of Bernstein's work was undoubtedly valid, and Bernstein himself later accepted that he had been wrong in adopting the strong form of the linguistic relativity model in this way.

Unfortunately, however, there were cultural aspects of Bernstein's analysis of which Labov, as an American, was perhaps less aware. Bernstein was not actually saying that speakers of restricted codes were stupid, as Labov had assumed. Robinson (1991) described how Bernstein was trying to show how working-class children in Britain were seriously disadvantaged by the massive social assumptions made in education, which valued one form of linguistic code and rejected the other. The American Labov, largely unaware of how powerfully Britain's class distinctions manifest themselves through perceptions of spoken language, ignored these questions and focused instead on an entirely different aspect of Bernstein's work. Unfortunately, his critique, while valid in its own right, had meant that Bernstein's social message had become entirely ignored. Both researchers were attempting to redress élitist assumptions about spoken language, but, coming from different cultures, they approached the question entirely differently.

Cooper (1984) challenged how Labov's emphasis on linguistic structure had led him to ignore the social aspects of language use. Cooper (1984) reanalysed some of the linguistic extracts presented by Labov and suggested that Labov's interactions with Larry were actually much more positive than his interactions with Charles. Cooper also argued that the reproduction of Labov's exchange with Larry was presented in a much more favourable manner and form than that of Charles, and showed logical errors which led to overvaluing what Larry had said. Cooper went on to argue that this positive bias meant that the extracts were not actually very helpful in exploring questions about dialect and education. However, it is equally possible to argue that all Labov was doing was reversing the usual bias, by favouring the non-standard English speaker above the standard English speaker. In this respect, his research is as valid as that of any of the other comparative studies.

In a further reworking of the same material, Winch (1985) also reanalysed Labov's linguistic extracts. Winch accepted much of Cooper's argument, but also reanalysed Cooper's reanalysis of the transcript of Larry. He accepted Cooper's judgement of Labov's inadequate logical account, but argued that this was not a sufficient basis for a refutation of Larry's cleverness. Instead Winch concluded that the two extracts show that there is no necessary relationship between dialect form and logical capacity. Both extracts can be presented as positive examples.

When obtaining the extracts, Labov had shown how linguistic performance is very much affected by the social situation, especially socially 'artificial' situations. When interviewed formally, Larry would hardly speak and came across as virtually inarticulate. But when sitting on the floor sharing a packet of crisps with a researcher from his own ethnic group, he chattered freely, and this was the source of Labov's transcripts. Winch argued that the extracts show how important it is to recognize the pattern of social meaning contained in the whole exchange. This, coupled with the impact of Bernstein's work, which had emphasized how some forms of meaning were deeply contextually embedded, led to an increased emphasis on studying how language was actually used in the home and school.

What this tangled debate also shows is how difficult it is to separate the analysis of dialect from value judgements about particular speech forms; and how these value judgements are intimately linked with groups, power and status in society. Although few would accept the idea of linguistic deprivation any more, without looking at language in its social context it is almost impossible to gain any idea of what is really going on.

In other words, the whole question of language and language use has been thrown into a sociopolitical arena in which it is difficult to gain a consensus of opinion. Questions of whether a form of language is structurally and semantically inferior become tangled up with questions about whether society favours some forms of language above others. Among its many other effects, the Bernstein/Labov debate stimulated a considerable amount of research into whether different dialects were linguistically and intellectually inferior to standard English.

Choy and Dodd (1976) made tape-recordings of Hawaiian children of around 11 years old. The interviewer to whom they were responding used either standard English or the local Hawaiian dialect. On the basis of the way the children responded to the interviewer, they were classified as either SE (standard English) or NE (non-standard English) speakers. The children were then given comprehension tasks to solve, at the same time as attending to a reaction time task. Their attention was divided in this way because the researchers thought that doing so would give them an indication of how difficult the children found the comprehension. The results showed that children performed better on both accuracy and ease of comprehension measures when the comprehension task was in their dominant dialect. But speaking standard English did seem to give children a slight edge: those who did so gave more correct responses in their 'own' conditions than the others did when responding to their own dialects, and they also did almost as well as the NE speakers when responding to the non-standard English condition.

On the face of it, this might suggest that speaking standard English offered the children some kind of intellectual advantage. But the researchers also asked the children's teachers to rate individual children on a number of dimensions, including confidence, eagerness, ethnicity, academic performance, classroom behaviour, and predicted future success in occupation, academic situations and social relationships. The teachers' evaluations consistently showed that negative attributions were associated with NE speech and that these were linked to beliefs that went well beyond educational beliefs, and predicted even future marital contentment and the happiness of resulting children.

Hughes (1989) reported a study in which it was found that teachers saw many pupils as coming from homes that failed to socialize them properly. In particular, the children's spoken language was identified as being a considerable problem which explained many other phenomena such as aggression. Many such children were judged by their teachers to have little or no language. Teachers evoked a range of explanations for why this happened, from perceived family social problems to the effects of television, but, effectively, they were operating a language deficit model, assuming that because the children spoke a different form of language they were therefore cognitively incapable. Hughes also reported that the teachers did wish to improve children's performances but were unsure how, or whether, this could be done.

Actual recordings of the same children at home, however, showed that there was very little substance to the teacher's perceptions. Parents saw the children as being very talkative and wide-ranging in their choice of topics. Moreover, they did monitor their child's speech, and applied their own standards for the purpose of correction. Tape-recordings of the children's speech substantiated the parental judgements and also showed that there was considerable parental involvement with the children – a picture which was entirely different from that presented by the teachers. Recordings of the same children at school showed considerable variability and situational specificity in their speech. Even children who were almost mute in the classroom could be shown to be loquacious in other settings.

Tizard *et al.,* in 1983, compared language at home with language at school in 30 girls aged between 3 and 4, comparing how they spoke with their mothers and their teachers, at home and at school. Half of the children had fathers who were manual labourers and mothers who had left school without qualifications; the other half had fathers in professional or managerial positions and mothers who had either attended college or had qualified to do so. The researchers found significant social class differences, particularly in the way that the language styles of the children with working-class parents changed more between home and school than did styles of the middle-class children. They argued from this that children from working-class homes are disadvantaged by having to adjust their language style when they go to school each day.

It may be, however, that this is an unnecessarily pessimistic judgement. An educational approach which acknowledged the validity of different forms of language and aimed to teach children to reach fluency in the one they did not use at home might actually end up advantaging the child, rather than disadvantaging it – but only if the child perceives its own form of language as equally respected. For children from Asian parents in Britain, the English that they speak at school is a second language at first, but none the less by the time they reach their teenage

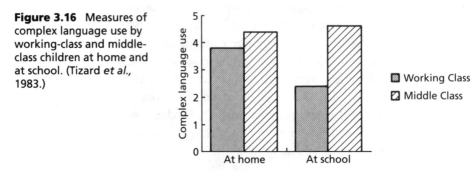

Figure 3.16 Measures of complex language use by working-class and middle-class children at home and at school. (Tizard *et al.,* 1983.)

Complex language use

Working Class
Middle Class

At home   At school

years they are using it as their own personal language (thinking and dreaming in it), while still speaking another language at home with their parents. So assuming that a four-year-old's use of language determines its future social competence is not necessarily valid.

Lyons (1981) pointed out that many people are **diglossial** – able to speak more than one kind of language with relative ease. The children in Tizard's study were very young and still learning to use language – it is not surprising that they may have stumbled over its different forms. But through television and other experiences, children also learn other forms of language, and most children, by the time they are teenage, are fully diglossial when they want to be. If they are acting out a role as part of a game, for instance, children who appear in the classroom to be only capable of using non-standard English can show themselves as proficient in standard English as anyone else. For these researchers to assume that working-class children are incapable of achieving diglossial fluency therefore seems to be deeply élitist. We need to look at social, rather than ability, reasons for why children do not show the same verbal fluency in the classroom as they show outside it.

diglossia The ability to speak in more than one form of language, e.g. 'posh' English and colloquial English, as the situation demands.

From the mass of information and opinion about linguistic style, one thing is clear. Many teachers believe in the idea of linguistic deprivation and this idea affects the way they deal with children. Teachers, when faced with failing pupils, behave like other humans and blame someone else. Hughes suggested that teachers' beliefs are very much a product of their working environment and that these beliefs cannot be overcome without changing their working environment. He suggested that smaller classes, better resources and a less pressurized curriculum might help to facilitate this, but emphasized that what is really important is that teachers can believe this possibility exists for their pupils.

Overall, then, research suggests that dialects do have an influence on how children perform, but not because there is any deficiency in the language itself. These outcomes come about because of the negative assumptions which society as a whole makes about those who speak non-standard English. Children are likely to be disadvantaged by social labelling, even though they are not intellectually restricted by the dialect which they use. It is this issue which is at the heart of current educational debates about the form of language that should be taught in school. While an emphasis on standard English is taken by some as a denigration of the individual's ability, it is seen by others as a practical realization that the real world does involve labelling, and that to equip the child with a knowledge of standard English is the only way to make sure that it gets a start in life which is not hampered by social labelling and stereotyping.

Social scripts

In 1977, Schank and Abelson suggested that we live much of our everyday living according to well-defined and well-understood 'scripts'. These allow us to identify what is going on and to know how we should act in order to be socially acceptable. The classic example of a script is the way that you know what to expect and how to behave when you go to a restaurant. Although nobody actually tells you, a very little experience is enough to tell you what is likely to happen. If anyone involved in the episode, for example the waiter, yourself or your companion, were to begin to act in a different kind of way, the 'script' would be broken. In practice, though, this does not happen very often: we are well aware of what is expected of us and carry it out more or less unconsciously. There are 'scripts' for other everyday life situations too, like going to a disco, attending school or catching a bus.

script A well-known pattern of social action and interaction which has been socially established and accepted, and is implicitly and automatically followed by people in the relevant situation.

Schank and Abelson suggested that scripts could be classified into three types: **situational scripts,** which involve the kind of typical social situations that are described above; **personal scripts**, like the expectations and behaviours involved in being someone's friend; and **instrumental scripts**, associated with particular targets or goals, like those to do with travelling home from school or college. By the time we reach adulthood, we are equipped with a range of unconscious scripts which will guide us through almost all types of social experience.

> **Key reference**: SCHANK, R. and ABELSON, R (1977) *Scripts, Plans, Goals and Understanding: an inquiry into human knowledge*. Erlbaum, Hillsdale, N.J.

We learn scripts from a very early age. Schank and Abelson described how, when Shank was going to buy a new car, his four-year-old daughter asked him if he was going to buy a new keyring too. She had remembered that he had bought a new keyring when he had bought the last car, two years earlier, and had firmly associated keyring-buying as part of the behavioural script involved in new car purchasing. Schank and Abelson commented that if we are building plausible scripts from such an early age, then the number that an adult possesses must be very large.

Education

Fivush (1984) conducted a study on the development of scripts in 30 young children, aged between 4 and 5. She was interested in how children would learn a general script for the school day, and how this would relate to their memories of specific events. The children were inter-

In the short story *Chawdron*, by Aldous Huxley, one of the characters articulated the idea that social living is only a matter of acting out one's part appropriately:

'... A virtuous man is one who's learned his part thoroughly and acts it competently and convincingly. The saint and the hero are great actors ... people with a genius for representing heroic characters not their own; or people with the luck to be born so like the heroic ideal that they can just step straight into the part without rehearsal. The wicked are those who either can't or won't learn to act.'

In this extract, Huxley is arguing that virtue and wickedness are all a matter of whether we act in the ways that society expects or not. Few psychologists would be prepared to go that far but there is little doubt that the enactment of social scripts is an important ingredient in successful social living.

Figure 3.17 We act out social scripts like actors on a stage.

viewed about the school day routine four times during the first three months of school. The results showed that even by the second day of school, the children's reports were general and well organized, and that their structure remained stable over time. Moreover, the children shared a common representation of the routine: all of the children tended to mention acts that occupied a particular time and place in the classroom, and each of these acts encompassed a list of possible activities in a hierarchical fashion.

When it came to remembering specific events, though, the children had difficulty recalling specific episodes of the day before (a finding which will come as no surprise to many parents). This was the same in all four interviews – they could recall the general script with ease, but not distinctive events. Fivush concluded that children learn to represent events in a general spatial–temporal framework based on their first experience with a new routine; things which happen within that framework become blurred, as they simply become part of the increasing complexity of the framework itself.

Huesmann and Eron (1984) looked at scripts with respect to the development of aggressive behaviour. They conducted a 3-year study of over 800 primary school children, taking 3 sets of measures: the amount of *cognitive rehearsal* of aggressive behaviours – in other words, how much the child thought about them; the amount of *overt aggression* shown by the child; and the child's *regular TV viewing*. The results suggested that there was a relationship between the level of cognitive rehearsal for aggression and overt aggression – those who thought about it more were more likely to do it – and also a positive correlation between cognitive

Society

rehearsal and TV viewing. The researchers suggest that scripts for aggressive behaviour are learned through a circular process at an early age and become more firmly entrenched as the child develops. The result, then, is that aggression becomes self-perpetuating in some children.

Understanding the social scripts that we use in everyday life is of interest to those involved in marketing. The hair-care industry, for example, is both large and profitable, and so it makes sense for those involved to understand the way that people go about self-grooming. Rook (1985) carried out two studies into the scripts of ritual grooming behaviour – the patterns of behaviour we engage in to make ourselves look nice. In the first study, 91 18–25-year-olds responded to a questionnaire on morning grooming activities. The results of this showed that hair-care activities were central in morning grooming scripts. Most of the respondents were satisfied and happy with their hair, though there was some core frustration with the disappointing results achieved despite prodigious efforts.

Figure 3.18 How do you feel?

Figure 3.19 The Gold Blend couple.

In the second study, 59 19–26 year olds wrote stories about two relatively ambiguous pictures, each of which included some feature of grooming behaviour. A typical example might be something like someone brushing their hair in front of a mirror as the door into the room opens. The pictures were being used as a **projective test** – a test in which the stimuli themselves do not contain much meaning, so the meanings which people see in them will have been projected by the people themselves. When they were explaining what was in the picture, the research participants told stories which had themes about a number of different social scripts, such as identity problems, breaking away, work and relationships – both real and hoped for. The researchers concluded that it is necessary to investigate the social scripts associated with personal grooming when planning advertising campaigns for personal products.

Many adverts, of course, rely entirely on our knowledge of social scripts to have their effect. The famous Gold Blend adverts of the early 1990s, in which a series of television adverts detailed the stages in a relationship between two characters as they gradually became more intimate, relied entirely on the audience's knowledge of social scripts to make any sense. In an episode which made the headlines, one of the protagonists deliberately broke the accepted script – interrupting the other while she was having dinner in a restaurant with someone else, and making her leave the scene. It is a moot point whether it was the depicted breaking of the social script or the fact that he actually (finally) got round to telling her he loved her which was the factor that made the advert hit the headlines.

Romance and sexual behaviour is very highly scripted, and a plethora of literature and film exists which both depicts and defines what those scripts are. Rose (1985) argued that the descriptions of relationships and

projective tests
Psychometric tests which involve providing the person with ambiguous stimuli and seeing what meanings they read into them. The idea is that this will illustrate the concerns of the unconscious mind.

Consumer

sexual expression in romantic fiction are one of the forces that shape desire in women and men, by defining a set of expected action and response. Rose went on to suggest that the social script known as romance is highly dysfunctional for women, in the sense that it encourages unrealistic expectations and does not equip them for the reality of married life.

Rose analysed the structure and content of two common scripts: a romance script, found in fairy tales and romance novels (aimed mainly at women); and an adventure script, incorporated in action comic books, adventure novels and pornography (aimed mainly at men). She studied three aspects of these scripts: the stage of the relationship addressed by the scripts; the manifest and latent themes revealed in the text; and the sexual and non-sexual motives expressed or revealed by the characters. The analysis showed that the stories were primarily concerned with the courtship phase of relationships, but ended just where the difficult bit in life begins – the couple get married and are expected to live happily ever after. As a result, it creates a set of extremely unreal expectations about the conduct of relationships.

Male scripts can be seen to be strongly influenced by pornographic material. Malamuth and Billings (1984) used the pornographic book *Story of O* to develop an analysis of the role of pornography in the male imagination. For some psychoanalysts, pornography represents a sexual fantasy surrounding individual developmental conflicts left over from childhood. They see it as providing a repertoire of scripts to help the individual relieve and redesign these conflicts, with possibly therapeutic effects. On the other hand, pornography has been viewed by Marxist theorists as manifesting the unequal power relations between the dominant and subordinate classes. A further argument comes from feminist theorists who view the functions and effects of pornography as a direct incitement to rape and exploitation, arguing that it has to be seen within the larger context of male–female relations. Whatever role pornography plays, though, it is apparent that in popular culture successful male characters use scripts that are emotionally impoverished and often extremely aggressive.

Figure 3.20 Social scripts and relationships.

Society

Dane and Wrightsman (1982) argue that script processing has an important influence on legal judgements, both in terms of whether someone is judged to be guilty and in terms of the recommendations for the sentence. They reviewed a number of studies, many of which took the form of laboratory-based experiments, and noted that these studies recurrently found that extraneous factors such as race, social class, moral character and expressions of remorse were instrumental in affecting judgments, mainly by invoking plausible scripts.

Another courtroom simulation was carried out by Bennett and Feldman (1981), who asked students to tell true or false stories to a group of their peers. The listeners were then asked to vote privately on whether they regarded the stories to be true or false. The results showed that the judgements which the listeners made were unrelated to the actual truth of the story. The judgements were also unrelated to the physical characteristics of the way that the story was presented, as measured by the number and length of pauses. Instead, the important feature of the story for the judgement was how plausible it was – its coherence.

The researchers found that a coherent story needs to have a central piece of action, which links all the other characters clearly. The more ambiguous the connections that appeared in the story, the less likely it was to be judged true. So, for example, describing a character who might or might not have had something to do with the incident in question was judged to make the story less plausible – even though in everyday life it is often very difficult for us to make full sense out of what was happening. If the story fitted into a plausible script, however, then it was judged to be true. Regrettably, despite the fact that this study was a simulation, there seems to be a considerable amount of evidence that the same process happens in the legal system in real life. In a court of law, a jury is asked to make judgements about the truth or otherwise of various accounts given by witnesses. So the question of whether we can tell truth from invention is all-important.

The issue that arises out of this concerns how different groups make stories coherent. There is considerable variation in language and cultural practices in our pluralistic society, and what appears to be a plausible script to a judge will not necessarily reflect a plausible script to someone from a different group. Some groups are disadvantaged by the criminal justice system because they are likely to describe what happened in ways which are coherent to them, but assume a shared knowledge which is entirely absent on the part of their listeners. It is not at all uncommon for a court reporter writing in the popular press to record a comment by some judge which reveals a complete lack of knowledge about everyday cultural reference points for the person they are dealing with (such as saying: 'Surely the phrase "well wicked" must refer to something very evil?'). Since judges are overwhelmingly middle class, this clash of cultures tends particularly to influence their perception of those from working-class and ethnic minority backgrounds.

Sexism is another social factor which influences court script processing. Allen (1987) documented how there is a far greater tendency for female offenders to be 'psychiatrized' at the lowest level of psychiatric involvement – in other words, people in courtrooms often suggest

sexism *Using the pervasive power imbalance between men and women to oppress women by devaluing their experience, behaviour and aspirations.*

AN EVENT...

...SEEN FROM ONE POINT OF VIEW...

...GIVES ONE IMPRESSION.

SEEN FROM ANOTHER POINT OF VIEW...

...IT GIVES QUITE...

...A DIFFERENT IMPRESSION.

BUT IT'S ONLY WHEN YOU GET THE WHOLE PICTURE...   ...YOU CAN FULLY UNDERSTAND...   ...WHAT'S GOING ON.

Figure 3.21 Our judgement of a scene depends on our shared understanding of people and events.

that a woman offender has acted as she has because of some kind of psychiatric disturbance – but they say so without having consulted any psychiatric practitioners. There are two ways of explaining this phenomenon: some say it is evidence of courts being sympathetic to womens' social pressures; but this is not supported in other contexts, as we shall see. The alternative explanation is that it needs to be seen in the context of general scripts about women as neurotic and irrational. Male crime, on the other hand, is construed as decisive, planned action, even in cases where there may really be some psychiatric disturbance – which has a great deal to do with the high proportion of mentally-ill male offenders in the prison system.

The criminality script does not usually work in favour of women. Willemsen and van Schie (1989) reported that girls tend to be more severely judged than boys. For example, girl offenders tend to be given more severe sanctions for committing offences such as truanting and absconding. Boys, on the other hand, are more likely to be severely judged for violence against people and property. This, too, has everything to do with the plausibility of behaviour in terms of the social scripts which are available. The researchers suggested that where behaviour is stereotypical, such as violent behaviour on the part of boys, then it is judged to be due to the stable internal characteristics of the child and treated with more sympathy than if it is behaviour which deviates from the script.

The power of scripts is particularly apparent when looking at judgements about rape. Society has a number of these, many of which come directly from pornographic literature and popular films. Scully and Marolla (1984) interviewed 114 American men who had been convicted of rape, and found that 40% of them denied they had raped the woman at all – even though it had been proved in court that they had done so. They justified their behaviour by discrediting and blaming the victim, and

40% Deny rape (dispute conviction)	60% Admit rape
Explanations discredit the victim	Explanations Blame drugs, alcohol, emotional upset
Also make reference to fictional scripts, for example, 'no' really means 'yes'	Retain self-image as a 'nice guy'

Figure 3.22 Summary of explanations given by men convicted of rape. (Scully and Marolla, 1984.)

so putting their own actions in a more favourable light. The women were portrayed as willing, or as seductresses, and the men referred often to fictional scripts such as: 'Women mean "yes" when they say "no"'; 'Most women eventually relax and enjoy it'; and 'Nice girls don't get raped'.

Scully and Marolla also found that the remaining 60% of the men that they interviewed, who admitted that they had committed rape, tended to excuse their behaviour by blaming drugs or alcohol, or referring to their emotional problems. They retained a self-identity of being a 'nice guy' beneath it all – understandable, in view of the **cognitive dissonance** which would have ensued if they had not; but a dangerous perception none the less, in the sense that it denied any possibility that they might do it again, and so prevented them from working seriously on their problem. Scully and Marolla suggested that rapists learn their actions and attitudes towards women partly from a social script which is used to reduce their own responsibility and to maintain their view of themselves as non-deviant.

Social scripts are all about the ways that we expect patterns of action and interaction to occur as we go about our everyday lives. But, as we have seen, they can exert a powerful influence on whether an explanation is perceived as being inherently plausible or not. This makes them also linked with the process of attribution – how we go about explaining why something has happened.

cognitive dissonance
The tension produced by cognitive imbalance – holding beliefs which directly contradict one another or contradict behaviour. The reduction of cognitive dissonance has been shown to be a factor in some forms of attitude change.

Attribution and explanation

Attribution theory is concerned with how people explain to themselves why particular events or circumstances happened. One strand of research in attribution theory is concerned with the nature of the attributions which we make. A major distinction between types of attributions concerns whether a person's behaviour is seen as being caused by the situation that they are in, or whether it is thought to arise because of the type of person that they are. Attributions which emphasize the situation are known as external or situational attributions; whereas those which attribute causes to sources within the person are known as internal or dispositional attributions.

Research into attributions has adopted two major approaches: information-processing approaches, which take the view that when we come to explain a given event we analyse its features and from that decide what its probable cause was; and social approaches, which look at the ways that people attribute causes to events in terms of the social groups that they belong to, the social contexts in which the attribution takes place and the social functions which it serves.

One information-processing approach is that we make certain attributions rather than others because of **covariance**: we look at whether the behaviour which someone is showing is distinctive to them, whether it is consistent in the sense that they always tend to show it, and whether there is consensus, and other people show it too. On that basis, this model argues, we form our judgements about whether the behaviour has arisen from internal or external causes. This approach has tended to be more associated with American attribution theorists.

Social context approaches to attribution have tended to be more associated with European social psychology. Many psychologists taking the view are highly critical of approaches like the covariance model, because they imply that attributions are made purely in terms of the immediate stimuli and ignore the wider social context. European attribution theorists look at the social purposes which are served by the attributions, and at the way that these link with social representations and social identifications in socially-shared and accepted explanations of events.

In 1985, Weiner proposed that attributions could usefully be understood in terms of four major dimensions: internal/external, concerned with whether the cause is considered to have originated within the person or not; stable/unstable, concerned with how long lasting the cause is; controllable/uncontrollable, related to how much the cause is under the control of the person performing the act and linking with research into locus of control; and global/specific, related to whether the cause was considered to have many outcomes or only a few (Weiner, 1985). Research into these attributional dimensions showed how the type of attribution could exert a direct effect on the amount of effort or persistence which the individual would put into dealing with things.

> **Key reference**: HEWSTONE, M. (1989) *Causal Attribution: from cognitive processes to collective beliefs*. Blackwell, Oxford.

In everyday life we make attributions all the time. We are always ready to make some inference about the behaviour of others and give our reaction to it – it is the basis of social gossip. Attributions have been investigated in a wide range of contexts. For example, Brewin (1984) interviewed 42 male victims of industrial accidents, immediately after their injury, and then again 2–4 weeks after their return to work, asking them for the reasons why their accident had occurred. Brewin investigated the influence of causal responsibility and culpability. A person

Work

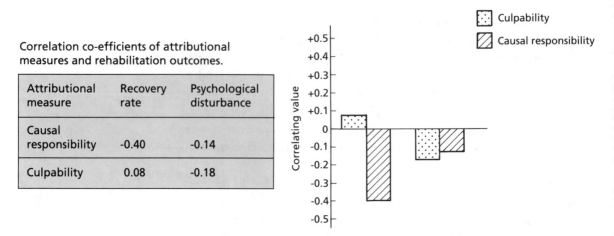

Correlation co-efficients of attributional measures and rehabilitation outcomes.

Attributional measure	Recovery rate	Psychological disturbance
Causal responsibility	-0.40	-0.14
Culpability	0.08	-0.18

Figure 3.23 Attributions and recovery after an accident. People who felt more culpable for an accident tended to have a faster recovery rate. (Brewin, 1984.)

feels causally responsible if she or he has acted in a way that has brought about the accident. On the other hand, culpability is a moral evaluation referring to how much the individual deserves the blame for the accident. In this study Brewin gave people a list of statements and asked the people to agree or disagree using a five-point scale. An example of a causal responsibility item was 'My actions contributed to causing the accident', and an example of a culpability item was 'My actions were negligent by my standards'.

Brewin found that causal responsibility was unrelated to recovery rate and only weakly related to the overall psychological disturbance of the subject. However, research participants who felt more culpable tended to have a faster recovery rate. The study suggests, then, that blaming yourself for an accident rather than blaming others is likely to be associated with a faster recovery rate (Figure 3.23).

Since attribution is such an important basis for the way we evaluate other people, those in positions of power often attempt to control the attributions which other people will make. Salancik and Meindl (1984) examined the attributions for company performance over an 18-year period given by chief executive officers of 18 American corporations, using annual stockholder reports. They found that the managers of unstable firms, who had little real control over organizational outcomes, strategically manipulated the causal attributions in their reports to produce the impression that they were in control. As evidence of this, they claimed responsibility for both positive and negative outcomes more than did the managements of firms with stable performance. In addition, they were reluctant to attribute poor performance to uncontrollable environmental events. When environmental effects were described, they were coupled with announcements about executive changes, implying that the management was taking steps to wrestle with its unruly environment.

Attribution is also the basis of evaluations which we make about ourselves. One of the recurrent findings is that attributions often show motivational bias – we seek to present ourselves in the best possible light. Nauta (1988) investigated how this happens among clergymen, by looking at the attributions made by 287 Dutch Reformed and Christian Reformed ministers to 4 different scenarios with positive and negative outcomes. This was followed up by another study, in which 95 clergymen were asked to evaluate how well clerics had performed their tasks in 16 other scenarios. In both cases, the researchers found motivational biases. Positive outcomes were attributed to variable and internal causes, while negative outcomes were attributed to stable and external causes.

Noel, Forsyth and Kelley (1987) investigated whether it was possible to challenge this type of biased attribution in cases where it was obviously detrimental. The attributions made by undergraduates who were failing a course showed that these students tended to emphasize external and uncontrollable causes, like luck and ability, as the reasons for why they were failing. This, the researchers believed, was an example of the self-serving bias, in that the type of attribution which the students had made served to protect them from uncomfortable feelings of guilt or responsibility. The researchers attempted to change the attributional style of one group of students. They showed their experimental group a videotape of two student interviews where the students described how they improved their school performance after they stopped blaming their grades on external factors such as bad teachers and bad luck, and started to see them as being due to controllable factors such as study skills or

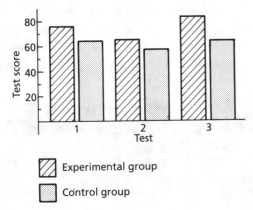

Average test scores after the attribution videos

Test	Experimental group	Control group
1	76	64
2	65	57
3	83	64

Figure 3.24 Attributions and academic performances. (Noel, Forsyth and Kelley, 1987.)

effort. The students assigned to the control group were shown similar interviews, but the content of the message emphasized feelings and attitudes. The experimental group of students subsequently performed much better in their coursework and earned higher grades than 11 similar students who had acted as 'controls'.

Society

As we can see, then, the types of attributions which we make are important determinants of how we deal with life. Frazier (1990) showed how the attributions made by rape victims are important in their subsequent readjustment. Frazier interviewed victims of rape and found that attributions of self-blame generally led to serious long-term after-effects, including depression. This applied if there was any type of self-blame involved – even those who blamed themselves but also acknowledged society factors showed poor adjustment. An analysis of the interviews identified three factors, which are shown in Figure 3.25. The factors that are associated with successful adjustment, on the other hand, were having a feeling of control over one's future life, and a view of the event as bad luck, and so not something that would affect future decision making. Blaming other people did not improve the prospect of successful adjustment and, in fact, seemed to have a negative effect.

Health

Attributions can also influence the outcome of various health programmes such as dieting. Jeffery, French and Schmid (1990) examined how people see the problems of sticking to long-term diets. In a large-scale study designed to investigate ways of preventing hypertension, 416 men and 209 women were asked to keep to particular types of diets over a period of 3 years. There were four types of diets altogether: weight loss, reduced sodium, weight loss plus reduced sodium, and reduced sodium plus increased potassium. Every six months, the participants were asked if they were having any problems, what those problems were and why they were happening.

The researchers found that there was a significant difference between people trying to keep to the different kinds of diets, in terms of the explanations they gave for why they had failed. People who were on weight-loss diets were much more likely to blame themselves for failing

Poor judgement	Societal factors	Victim type
Poor judge of character	Never police around	Can't take care of myself
Made a rash decision	People don't get involved	Got what I deserved
Too trusting	Too much pornography	Victim type

Figure 3.25 The attributions made by victims of sexual assault can have an effect on their future readjustment. (Frazier, 1990.)

to stick to the diet than people on the other diets, who tended to blame the situations that they were in. There was also a gender difference, in that men tended to see the problems with sticking to the diet as being more controllable than women did.

Storms and Nisbett (1970) investigated the effect of attribution on insomnia. People who suffer from insomnia often report difficulty in breathing, being too alert, feeling too warm and experiencing an increased heart rate. The researchers reasoned that if the insomniacs attributed these experiences to something external rather than something internal then this would relieve some of their anxieties and so help to relieve the insomnia The study involved three groups of insomniacs. Each person was given a non-active tablet to be taken before going to bed. The insomniacs in one group were told that the tablet would give them a sense of alertness and an increased heart rate (the symptoms of insomnia). Those in the second group were told that the tablet would relax them and those in the third group were not told anything about the tablet.

The researchers found that the people in the first group slept longer and better than those the third group; and they in turn slept better than the people in the second group. In other words, when people had an external reason (the tablet) for how they were feeling, they could get to sleep, but when they believed that their feelings had an internal cause, they were unable to sleep. What is also interesting, though, is that when the insomniacs were interviewed they blamed their good or bad sleep during the experiment on events that had happened to them during the day, even after they had been told about the experiment – an interesting example of the way that we can 'freeze' on to habitual explanations and be resistant to adopting new forms of explanation.

Grove, Hanrahan and Stewart (1990) asked 276 sports participants to give the most likely causes of rapid or slow recovery from injury. When they analysed the responses, they found that the participants had tended to use four general types of attribution about recovery: personal attributions, concerning the character or disposition of the individual concerned; injury-related attributions, about the nature of the problem; treatment-related attributions, which were concerned not just with the type of treatment but also with how it was applied; and situational attributions, which were concerned with the circumstances under which the injury took place and what was available subsequently.

Sport

When the sportspeople's attributions were examined, the researchers found that there were systematic differences in the attributions which they made for slow and rapid recovery. The causes of slow recovery from injury were consistently perceived as less stable, controllable, global and intentional than the causes of rapid recovery. This was partly because of the type of reasons which were given – slow recovery was also seen as being more likely to have come from internal sources than rapid recovery. Interestingly, too, the researchers found a relationship between physical self-esteem and the types of attributions which they made: people with lower self-esteem were more likely to give uncontrollable and stable attributions.

Society

Stratton and Swaffer (1988) used attributional coding to help develop appropriate **family therapy** for mothers who were physically abusing their children. They began by coding the attributions which mothers made about their children as they watched them playing. They compared the attributions of three groups: mothers of abused children, and mothers of similar socioeconomic backgrounds, with either 'normal' or physically disabled children. The attributions made by mothers of battered children differed significantly from those made by the others, particularly in the dimension of controllability – these mothers perceived their children's behaviour as much less controllable. As a result of this, their therapy was directed towards teaching them how to influence their child's behaviour and how to guide their child towards different activities, so lessening the degree of frustration and allowing the mother to control her own feelings more.

family therapy *An approach to psychotherapy in which individual dysfunction is seen as a family problem, rather than a personal one, and in which communication patterns and alliances within the family are explored, and sometimes challenged.*

As we saw in Chapter 2, believing that we are in control is important if we are to deal positively with stressful situations. Taylor, Lichtman and Wood (1984) interviewed 78 women with breast cancer, asking each of them if they had 'some kind of theory about how they got their cancer'. Almost all of the women – 95% – made causal attributions for their illness, and their explanations included 'stress', 'diet' and 'heredity'. Interestingly, only the controllable attributions related to how well they had adjusted to their illnesses, except for a suggestion that blaming others was linked with not coping very well.

Sport

Some researchers argue that the attributions which team players make are more important in influencing how they play than any other single factor. Robinson and Howe (1987) looked at the kinds of attributions which were habitually made by 17 male university soccer players. They collected attributional inferences and mood profiles from each of the players during a crucial three-game period. During that time, 7 of the players achieved successful performance, and 10 of them were unsuccessful. The researchers found that successful players were more likely to make attributions which involved controllable and stable factors than did the unsuccessful group.

Stratton (1991) described how attributional coding was used to explore consumer perceptions of a major airline. They collected transcripts from

'Special care' refers to a special way of being looked after. It means being made to feel a special relationship with the cabin crew, being offered things that are not ordinarily provided. This is reflected in comments about the cabin crew such as 'They don't have to talk to you – you feel as if you belong' and 'If you are treated as an individual, it makes you feel like you're a valued customer'.

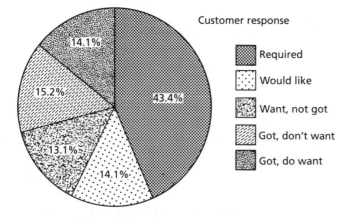

Customer response

■ Required

∷ Would like

■ Want, not got

▨ Got, don't want

■ Got, do want

Figure 3.26 Satisfaction with British Airways. (Stratton, 1991.)

a number of group discussions, as consumers talked about how they saw the airline, features of airlines in general and so on. They then extracted the attributions made in the transcripts, which gave them over 1000 attributional statements to be coded. These attributions were very revealing. For example, every time the airline was mentioned, it was perceived as being in control of events, whereas passengers themselves were seen as having control over things less than a fifth of the time. Given what we know about stress and powerlessness (Chapter 2), the finding implies that passengers are likely to feel more stressed by the fact that they are not able to exert any control over what happens to them.

Work

The commonest pattern of attributions was of an event being seen as stable, global, external, universal and uncontrollable. In other words, it was seen as likely to recur in the future, as having important consequences, but as originating outside of the consumer and not something which they could influence. Interestingly, Stratton found that these attributions were only made about what the airline referred to as 'special care' – events where the customer received personal attention from the cabin staff and which were out of the ordinary. The conventional experience of air travel was perceived quite differently.

The analysis produced a number of 'action points' through which the airline could improve its customer care, including recognizing the passengers as individuals, extending their sense of control where possible, such as by offering them more choice in seating, food and drink, and so on; and training the cabin crew to recognize requests for special attention as sometimes, at least, being examples of a need for personal reassurance, rather than simply a passenger trying to cause trouble.

Education

Hau and Salili (1989) looked at changes in how Chinese primary school children interpreted the causes of exam results, as they became older and progressed through the educational system. Younger children, they found, expected to do better in exams and in other school activities than older ones did, especially if they had experienced some positive current achievements. They also tended to attribute successful outcomes to external and controllable causes. Older children, however, tended to make internal and uncontrollable attributions for examination success, and generally had lower expectations for themselves. In a later study, Hau and Salili (1991) looked at how an older group of Chinese students, who had reached high school, explained their academic performance. They found that these students made internal, controllable, stable and global attributions – relating to factors like effort, interest, study skills and ability. The implications of these two studies, then, is that long-term educational experience involves a gradual shaping of attributions for academic success. The researchers concluded that their findings were reasonably accurate in expressing the cultural attitude towards educational success in the Chinese culture.

Society

Attributions may be important, but they are not everything. Fincham and O'Leary (1983) investigated the types of attributions made by married couples who were having difficulties in their relationships. They obtained a sample of what they called 'maritally distressed' couples, by recruiting couples who had applied for marital therapy and a comparable group of 'non-distressed' couples, who were recruited through an advertisement in the local newspaper. When they asked each of the partners about their partner's positive and negative behaviour, they found that the non-distressed group rated causes for positive acts as more global and controllable than those who were distressed. Distressed spouses, on the other hand, saw the causes of negative behaviour as being global and therefore likely to apply to lots of other events as well. On the whole, though, the researchers found that attributional analysis was not nearly as important as the couple's emotional responses to one another and suggested that a purely cognitive approach to marital therapy was clearly not enough.

Judgements of attribution take place in a social context and so social attitudes and situations are an important basis for the kind of attribution which we make. Carroll, Galegher and Wiener (1982) analysed the judgements made by five expert parole decision makers, on the Pennsylvania

Board of Probation and Parole, and showed that the attributions which they made linked strongly with important aspects of those decisions, such as the willingness to grant parole, prognoses for rehabilitation and risk of future crime. However, the researchers emphasized that this was only the case if the attributions were seen as occurring within a more general social context: a dimensional coding which treated these judgements as if they were context-free was much less effective.

One of the more common social myths is the frequently expressed belief that women who become victims of rape contribute to their victimization by dressing and behaving in ways that provoke sexual violence in men. In an experimental study by Krahé (1988), the research participants were first assessed to see how far they accepted this myth. Then they were given descriptions of a rape. In one condition the introductory sentence read, 'After having finished work in her office, the victim was on her way to the car park where her car was parked', whereas in the other condition the introductory sentence read, 'After having had a drink on her own in a pub, the victim was on her way to the car park where her car was parked'. Krahé found that those people who scored high on rape-myth acceptance tended to attribute responsibility to the woman if she had been in the pub rather than the office.

Both sub-cultural attitudes and cultural influences may also affect the attributions which we make. Such messages can come from other people, but also often come from the mass media. In this way, attributions and **social representations** can be seen as being closely linked. Gaskell and Smith (1985) interviewed 204 school dropouts, who had left school some two years previously and had been unemployed since then. The interviews included questions about the reasons for unemployment

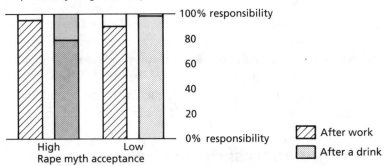

Figure 3.27 The diagram shows how much responsibility for the rape was assigned to the rapist by the subjects. The subjects were divided into two groups (high and low rape myth acceptance) on the basis of their responses to a questionnaire. (Krahé, 1988.)

situations, political views, and orientation towards political violence and riots. By and large, the explanations which these participants offered during the interviews tended to be generally similar to those offered by people in employment and also to those offered by the mass media. There were some differences, though. In particular, Gaskell and Smith's subjects showed a tendency to see life as more determined by chance and less controllable. The researchers also found that, overall, unemployed people were more likely to say they supported violent political action, but also to say they supported the Labour party.

Whitley (1990) looked at heterosexuals' attitudes toward people who were known to be homosexual. Questionnaire data from 193 female and 173 male heterosexual undergraduates showed that attitudes were more negative when homosexuality was attributed to controllable than to uncontrollable causes. Whitley also found that heterosexual women were more likely to report knowing a lesbian than heterosexual men were to report knowing a gay man. Similarly, among respondents who reported knowing a gay man, women reported closer acquaintanceship than men did.

Education

Smith and Whitehead (1984) investigated attributions about promotion and demotion made by 87 white American and 131 Native American college students. The students were asked to read an account of a worker who was promoted or demoted in a job and then give reasons for why this had happened. They found that the white American students were more inclined to attribute the promotion or demotion to internal factors like ability and effort, whereas the Native American students were more inclined to attribute them to external power factors. Interestingly, too, when both events were explained using external attributions, promotions produced attributions relevant to the individual, like social class, whereas demotions produced attributions relevant to the environment, such as corruption.

Attributional analysis, then, is concerned with looking at the factors which will influence the explanations which we reach, about why certain things happened or why people acted as they did. If we are looking at the process of social explanation, though, we also need to look at the way that explanations are framed – at the interpretive repertoires and explanatory frameworks which are used to make sense out of them.

Discourse analysis

Discourse analysis is about analysing the meaning of everyday communication between people. It takes the position that utterances are acts, the same as any other type of behaviour, and so they should be analysed as behavioural acts which influence people. When people use a particular form of discourse, it has repercussions of its own which may not have been intended or anticipated, or even understood by the speaker or writer. In this context, the meaning of an utterance is not a straightforward matter of dictionary definitions. Instead, it depends on the semantic context – the systems of meaning in which the utterance is embedded.

Discourse analysts look at the range of **functions** that an utterance serves. These range from interpersonal functions such as explaining, justifying, excusing, blaming etc., to social functions such as ideological ones in which the utterance supports or legitimates the power of one group in society. What people say and write is different according to what they are doing, or intending to do, and speakers give shifting, inconsistent and varied pictures of their social worlds. An event, a policy or a personality can be described in many different ways as the function of that description changes from formulating a positive evaluation to constructing a negative one, e.g. from excusing to blaming. Since the type of variation is thought to come from the function that the discourse is serving, variation is used by discourse analysis as a clue to understanding what a particular piece of discourse is really doing.

Discourse, then, is a constructive process, in which the participants make an active selection of their material, in a way which has practical consequences. One type of discourse analysis focuses on **interpretive repertoires** – the range of terms, styles and grammatical fashions which are used for constructing particular accounts of actions, cognitive processes and other phenomena. These interpretive repertoires can be seen as the building blocks which speakers use in communicating with one another in making sense of the social world. They will often have been derived from one or more key metaphors and the presence of the repertoire will often be signalled by certain figures of speech.

Another type of discourse analysis focuses on **deconstructionism**, in which the underlying assumptions, biases and world views are disentangled from the overt semantic content of the discourse. At this point, discourse analysis begins to link with the area of investigation known as social representation theory, which we will also be looking at in this chapter.

deconstructionism
Originally a form of literary criticism, but more recently recognized for its value in philosophy. Developed by the French philosopher Jacques Derrida, it is a theory of meaning in which the assumptions behind language are exposed.

Key reference: POTTER, J. and WETHERALL, M. (1987) *Discourse and Social Psychology: beyond attitudes and behaviour.* Sage, London.

Society

Discourse analysis particularly lends itself to analysis of content in various manifestations of the mass media. Hacker *et al.* (1991) performed a deconstruction study in which 12 research participants were first surveyed in a manner which emphasized the ideological nature of news bias and then shown videotapes of the American NBC news. The topics covered by the news were explained to them, and then they were interviewed. When subjects had news deconstruction explained to them, they then went on to identify news bias and ideology – in other words, with prompting from researchers, subjects' outlook and thoughts towards news changed. They still tended to struggle, however, when trying to find a more trustworthy source of information to replace TV news.

Another interesting feature of this study is the way that it shows how discourse analysis is able to take a different stance to methodology than many other areas of enquiry in psychology. The researchers were delib-

Halla Beloff, born 11 May 1930. Educated at South Hampstead High School and Birkbeck College, London.

The sight of women is the site of so many contradictions.

Jo Spence's idea has become more and more salient to Halla Beloff's work. She started her career respectably enough, working in personality research as an assistant to R.B. Cattell in Illinois, going on to do a PhD on objective tests of Freud's anal character, following that with less embarrassing research in social conformity, both at Queen's University, Belfast. During her many years at Edinburgh University she moved towards identity work and gender, and then to a more maverick interest in the social psychology of photographing and photographs. That is, she has combined her interests in the visual arts with her psychology. Her hope was that the outcome would be the extension of the field of psychology and some sabotage of traditional methods of study. Her own primary motivation has been to enjoy herself more and this has been successfully achieved.

The two pieces of her writing which have caused some stir have been the book *Camera Culture* (Blackwell, 1985) and *Mother, Father and Me: our IQ* (*The Psychologist*, 1992). It was the latter which demonstrated that young women systematically underestimate their IQ compared with young men's self-estimates. Will it be enough that this information be reflected back to them?

She has held many offices on the British Psychological Society and was President of the Society during 1983–84.

erately discussing the material with the research participants and consciously exerting an influence on the participants' ways of analysing what was going on – something which runs entirely counter to the idea of the 'objective', detached and dispassionate scientist. Acknowledging utterances as valid acts of behaviour also means that the speech acts of researchers are acknowledged as part of the social process, as well. So, where conventional psychological research either ignores or only pays lip-service to the influence of the researcher on the situation, discourse analysts are able to use it as an active part of their research method.

Discourse analysis has also been applied to explore other kinds of statements and not necessarily verbal ones. Beloff (1988) used discourse analysis to examine ten self-portrait photographs of eminent photographers, taken between 1901 and 1986. Beloff found that analysis of these photographs shows that the self-portraits of male photographers emphasize the individual's situation – self-characteristics are presented in terms of the social role of the photographer. Although the women included in the study were comparable in status to the men, their self-portraits demonstrated signs of the conventional submissive feminine identity. Beloff argued that these portraits illustrate how the vision of the self seems to come from communally available visual repertoires located within the society and conventions of their time.

Baltaxe and Simmons (1977) conducted a discourse analysis on the bedtime soliloquies of an eight-year-old autistic child. By comparing these with those of a normal child of two-and-a-half, studied in 1962 by Weir, they found that there were some systematic differences, particularly in terms of how accurate the use of grammar was. This analysis revealed that the autistic child seemed to use specific linguistic strategies which ordinary children did not often use, and suggested that a method of conducting therapy with autistic children which took account of that might be more productive than trying to apply more conventional teaching approaches.

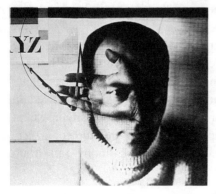 

Figure 3.28 Two examples of self-portraits from Bellof's study.

Figure 3.29 Lew Platt, the Chief Executive Officer of Hewlett-Packard became known as the man who practised 'management by walking around'.

Work

Potter and Edwards (1990) made a discourse analytic study of the management of factual versions in political dispute. The dispute involved Conservative politician Nigel Lawson and a group of journalists, and showed how each side was drawing on a different set of interpretive repertoires which involved entirely different assumptions about why things were like they were. Although both sides claimed that they wanted to get to 'the facts of the matter', these were actually part of the dispute itself, rather than the criteria for resolving it.

Another aspect of discourse analysis is to do with exploring the metaphors which are used to describe, and also to define, social action. Beattie (1988) discussed the metaphors which Margaret Thatcher used during the early years when she was prime minister. When speaking about the country and the economy, Mrs Thatcher tended to use two types of metaphor. One of these was concerned with the body, and involved hardship metaphors such as 'we have to pull in our belts' or presenting unpleasant social policies as 'medicine' to cure a sickness. The other was the use of military metaphors, presenting the economy as a 'battleground' or describing the 'fight' to control inflation. What these metaphors actually did was to define and constrain political debate – it is difficult, after all, to argue that someone who is 'sick' should not be given 'medicine'.

The use of metaphors also attracted attention from those studying organizational cultures. Mitroff (1983) argued that metaphors have powerful potential within organizational life, since they are able to capture the complexity of organizational life in relatively simple statements. The use of metaphor can evoke rich but succinct images, such as the 'management-by-walking-around' metaphor used for the style of management at Hewlett-Packard, described by Peters and Waterman (1982).

Pondy (1983) identified a number of features about the role of metaphor within the organization. One of these is that, by drawing on shared meanings, the explanation is placed beyond doubt, such that it does not require further elucidation. Metaphors also enable a bridge to be built between the familiar and the new. So, for example, translating industrial goals into military terms means that they may be more readily understood and accepted. Hirsch and Andrews (1983) examined the metaphors used in corporate takeovers, and showed how the 'warfare' and 'cowboy'-style metaphors in common use defined both interpretations of, and responses to, the various business practices involved in mergers and takeovers. The power of this becomes particularly apparent when managerial metaphors from Japanese cultures are studied, which, by contrast, emphasize concepts like co-operation, harmony and group consensus.

A different way of exploring discourse in an organizational context was used by King and West (1987), in an examination of how people construed the idea of innovation. They collected descriptive accounts of individual experiences of innovation at work from 27 managers (18 men and 9 women), chosen to give a cross-section of different occupations and organizations in both the private and the public sector. This produced a total of 466 statements about innovation, which revealed several different factors that either helped or inhibited innovation at work (see Figure 3.30). The analysis showed that people were often ingenious in the way that they tried to overcome resistance to change from superiors and sometimes from colleagues; but also showed that continued blocking of innovation from superiors was not uncommon, and did in the end mean that people tended to lose their motivation to find new and better ways of doing things.

Educational ideologies are conventionally seen as being either traditional or progressive. Billig *et al.* (1988) argued that this was actually a false dichotomy, in the sense that both forms of education, as they occur in practice, tend to be refinements of the same type of approach – or the same dialogue, as they put it. Traditional views of education, they argued, are associated with a belief in 'in-duction' – filling children with knowledge, whereas progressive views are concerned with 'e-ducare' – a belief in drawing knowledge out of children. But analysis of teachers'

Education

External facilitators
    Pressure (mostly economic) from outside the organization
    Freedom/discretion in the job
    Attitudes and attributes of particular colleagues and/or superiors
    Support from the work group

External inhibitors
    Aspects of organizational ethos/culture
    Characteristics of key people in the organization
    Lack of resources
    Time pressure

Internal facilitators
    Desire to achieve personal satisfaction and fulfilment through work
    Need for variety in work
    Having a creative personality

Internal inhibitors
    Own personality and attitudes
    Own lack of abilities

Figure 3.30
Factors mentioned as facilitators and inhibitors of innovation at work.

discourse presented by Edwards and Mercer (1987) showed that 'progressive' views are not, and cannot be, pristinely reflected in practice. Inevitably, there is guidance, direction, selection and control in which the pupil is subordinate to the teacher, and 'personal discovery' is subordinate to discovering what the curriculum decrees and the teacher intends.

The classic modern example of this, of course, is the school chemistry syndrome. Almost all curriculum literature holds that the value of children performing science experiments in school is so that they can learn from the evidence of their own senses. But the reality is that this does not happen at all. All over the UK, schoolchildren perform chemistry experiments in which the results do not come out as predicted. Logically, if the curricular objectives were true, they should be encouraged to take this as valid evidence. But the reality is that they are instructed to believe the accepted paradigm being outlined by the chemistry curriculum, regardless of what results they actually get in their practical work.

The Socratic method of education, in which children are questioned systematically until their answers reveal that they are aware of the issues, is often quoted as 'progressive', in the sense that it is deemed to be a method which draws on the child's own knowledge. The method is drawn from a classic account, written by Plato, of Socrates questioning a slave-boy. Billig *et al.* (1988) showed how this classic example of the Socratic method highlights the same ideological contradictions. In Plato's account, Socrates does not draw out from the slave-boy what the boy already knows. Instead, he conveys information, controls the exchange, cues the path to be followed and arrives at conclusions that he had determined from the outset.

From their analysis of teacher dialogue and Plato's account, Billig *et al.* concluded that both positions, in-duction and e-ducare, are inherent in educational practices. Educational discourse, they argued, is not concerned with the exploration of knowledge and individuality, but with social values of authority, control, democracy and personal freedom, and how they are to be represented in society and education.

Hoffman, Kirstein, Stopek and Cicchetti (1982) performed a structural analysis of the discourse of **schizophrenics**, and of how people listen to them. The central concept which listeners identified was that the speech of normal people was perceived as having 'coherence', whereas that of schizophrenics was not. Features of coherence, therefore, were used as the basis of a discourse analysis comparing schizophrenic and non-schizophrenic speech. The researchers found that this scheme was able to distinguish between schizophrenic and non-schizophrenic groups with a high degree of accuracy. They went on to look at how clinicians make judgements in diagnosing schizophrenia and suggested that what clini-

Health

schizophrenia A mental disorder marked by some, or all, of the following symptoms: delusions, hallucinations, incoherent word associations, inappropriate emotions or lack of emotions.

cians were actually doing when they were making these diagnoses was a form of discourse analysis which was very similar to that of their analytical model.

Potter and Reicher (1987) explored the different accounts of the Bristol St Paul's riot, which had occurred in 1980. They explored transcripts of interviews with people who had been actively involved in the events, copies of reports and editorials in the national press, transcripts of TV coverage and records of parliamentary proceedings. They found that different participants in the event produced very different forms of discourse. As one aspect of the analysis, they looked at the ways in which the word 'community' was used in the accounts. This was without exception used positively if it had an evaluative loading - all the accounts considered community to be a 'good thing'. But what the community was perceived as being differed greatly. In some accounts, for example, the community was described as 'disrupted' or 'finished' by the riot, while in others the riot was taken as an example of how cohesive the community was. Similarly, in parliament the event was described as a problem of 'community relations', and the police were depicted as being part of the community, whereas in other accounts the event was deemed to have been a riot between the community and the police. The differences between the various accounts revealed widely varying interpretations of what the event had been about.

Society

Discourse analysts acknowledge two major disadvantages to their approach. First, it is very time consuming; and secondly, it is not suited to the production of the kind of broad empirical laws which are commonly the goal of social psychological research. On the other hand, discourse analysts claim that there are a number of advantages to their approach. Firstly, they argue, the approach attempts to do justice to the subtlety and complexity of lay explanations of behaviour and experience. Secondly, it is a systematic approach whose findings are open to evaluation, and thirdly, the analysis of this type of data is both interesting and potentially useful.

While acknowledging these advantages and disadvantages, many social psychologists see a different set of disadvantages to discourse analysis. Rae (1989) examined the different analytical techniques which have been developed within discourse analysis, and came to the conclusion that they had little to offer a practitioner who wanted better tools to understand what was going on with clients in interviews. Rae concluded that the kind of attributional coding which we looked at in the last section was actually more useful to practitioners in that context.

Other psychologists, too, see discourse analysis as rather limited in scope. There are other approaches in social psychology which also attempt to look at the subtlety and complexity of lay explanation, so discourse analysis is not alone in that respect. But many social psychologists (e.g. Breakwell, 1993) argue that the relativistic comparison of interpretive repertoires undertaken by discourse analysis is a dead-end, in that it fails to take account of the very real differences in power and political influence in society.

Although discourse analysts claim to be taking into account the social context of utterances, by treating all accounts as if they had equal validity and relevance, they ignore inequalities of power and status in society. To treat accounts from police and the accounts from bystanders as if they were exactly the same ignores the sociopolitical reality that the police have a degree of power to impose their definitions on immediate and subsequent events which is quite different from that of bystanders. The study of social representations, by contrast, is directly concerned with the way that shared beliefs are located within, and reflect, their social and political contexts.

Social representations

social representation theory *A theory which looks at how shared beliefs develop and are transmitted in social groups and in society as a whole. Such shared beliefs serve an important function in explaining reality and in justifying social action.*

The theory of social representation was developed by Serge Moscovici and forms one of the major theories in European social psychology. Effectively, **social representation theory** is concerned with how people explain social and political events. Moscovici argued that popular forms of explanation develop, through conversation and media report, until eventually they comprise a body of 'knowledge' which is regarded as adequate to explain what is going on. Unlike scientific theorizing, however, this knowledge may have little to do with direct observation or deduction. Rather, it is concerned with the development of shared frameworks which deal with the unknown by rendering it familiar and explaining it in terms of what the person already knows.

One central concept in social representation theory is the way that social representations often operate as manifestations of a more general ideology. In one of the first studies of social representations, Moscovici charted how psychoanalytic theory developed from being accessible only to experts, to becoming part of the everyday understanding of large numbers of people. In the process, it became changed, with concepts becoming simplified and ideas becoming more deterministic, until eventually psychoanalytic theory became a form of explanation which served to legitimize the status quo and to justify reactionary social views. As it became accepted and adapted by the population at large, Moscovici argued, psychoanalytic theory had become a way of explaining things which could be used to prevent social challenges or radical ideas permeating through society. An example of the penetration of **psychoanalysis** can be seen in these horror films, such as the *Nightmare on Elm Street* series, where reference is made to early traumatic childhood experience as an explanation for the development of adult abnormal behaviour.

Another important concept in social representation theory is the way that social representations are not static, unchanging things, but are rather dynamic processes, continually being adapted, developed and renegotiated so that they are constantly taking new forms. Moscovici identified everyday conversation as the major way that social representations are negotiated. It may also be argued that the mass media has a considerable amount to do with the form that modern social representations take. This dynamic nature of social representations carries the implication that long-standing social groups will be likely to develop their own social representations over time, and that these may differ from more generally accepted ideological social representations, or from those of other social groups.

psychoanalysis *Freud's theory of personality which describes how human behaviour is affected by unconscious thoughts and feelings.*

> **Key reference**: MOSCOVICI, S. (1984) The Phenomenon of Social Representations. In R. M. Farr and S. Moscovici (eds) *Social Representations*. Cambridge University Press, Cambridge.

Moscovici argued that social representations tap into a 'consensual universe' of accepted meanings and ideas, permitting people to exchange and discuss complex ideas and assumptions efficiently. This was supported by research findings which suggest that social representations become more similar as children grow older. For example, Burgard, Cheyne and Jahoda (1989) found that both Scottish and West German children's estimates of incomes showed a progressive convergence with age, suggesting that there is an increased social consensus as social experience develops.

Society

Many of the social representations which are in common currency consist of traditional knowledge which has been passed on through the family, through social institutions or through the wider culture. For example, Larsen and Lazlo (1990) described a study which showed how cultural history exerts its influence on the appreciation of literature. Hungarian and Danish research participants each read the same short story, which told of two peasants being abused by two armed men, but engaging in passive resistance. This story reflected the cultural history and traditions of Hungary, but not those of Denmark, which had a tradition of independence and autonomy among its peasantry. When research participants were asked to note the number of occasions in the story when they were reminded of personal experience, it emerged that the story had far more 'personal relevance' for the Hungarians than it did for the Danes, since it related to a more pertinent social representation.

Every culture has its own ideas about what can and cannot be eaten, and what constitutes an acceptable diet. These shared cultural beliefs are social representations and, like other social representations, they represent the demands of society, and change as society changes. Fischler (1980) argued that recent changes in these social representations in contemporary urban industrial societies had resulted in diets which were sometimes nutritionally inadequate. Methods of food production, distribution and consumption had changed, which had meant that the social representations of acceptable diets had come to include far more snack and fast-food consumption. In turn, this had meant that ideas about nutritional balance and the satisfying of physiological needs had become less important in how people thought about food.

In addition to cultural and historical representations, social representations may also emerge from more recent, 'scientific' theories, and some research has been concerned with charting the development of these theories. One of the first such studies was conducted by Moscovici in 1961, and identified three phases in the development and acceptance of psychoanalytic theory in French society. The first of these was the scientific phase, in which **psychoanalysis** was elaborated as a scientific theory, with knowledge of its tenets and practices being largely restricted to professional scientists. This was followed by a second phase, in which the image and concepts of psychoanalysis began to diffuse through society, and were modified or recast in the process. The third phase was described by Moscovici as the ideological phase, in which the transformed version of psychoanalysis becomes a signifier of a school of thought, being adopted by power bases in society and thus becoming not only accepted, but enforced as a product of thinking (Moscovici, 1961). Similar developments have been shown in the formation of social representations around split-brain research (Moscovici and Hewstone, 1983). These studies also show how ideas of what constitutes 'common-sense' have changed over time, with the interaction of established ideas with scientific knowledge.

Work

Hayes (1991a) showed how organizational cultures, too, can be viewed as social representations. Organizations develop their own distinctive patterns of action, their own symbols, legends and metaphors. These are sometimes maintained officially, as for example in large multinationals such as IBM or Mars, but sometimes exist unofficially, in the form of shared anecdotes, metaphors and 'canteen cultures' among employees. These overt signs of organizational culture reflect an underlying set of shared assumptions and explanations about why the world is like it is. In that sense, they form a social representation, and they are explicitly used as the basis for evaluation of existing and novel practices in the organization.

Depolo and Sarchielli (1983) compared the social representations of work held by three groups of workers: those who worked in factories; those who worked in small co-operative businesses; and irregular workers, who chose to work a reduced number of hours or days of work. They found that the irregular group shared very different beliefs about the nature of work as a human activity in general and about the experience of their own work; but these were quite different from the views of work held by people in larger firms, and by political and trade union organizations. The researchers concluded that looking at work in terms of the social representations shared by different groups could do much to help to understand organizational behaviour.

Although different groups of people may adopt different social representations, those social representations tend to be closely linked with their general social context. Bolzman, Mugny and Roux (1987) found that representations of success or failure in business students were not simply a reflection of the dominant social views, but were instead closely linked to the socioeducational status of the student's own group. Similarly, Giorgi and Marsh (1990), in a survey of attitudes towards the Protestant Work Ethic in several European countries, showed that the effect of the country's religious culture was more important in whether the person accepted such ideas than the specific religious beliefs of the individual.

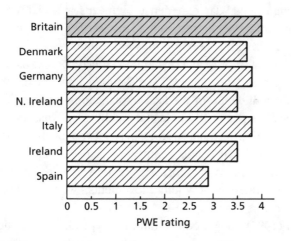

Figure 3.31 Chart showing the Protestant work ethic rating (PWE) of European countries. (Giorgi and Marsh, 1990.)

The study of social representations, then, allows for the incorporation of both historical and sociopolitical contexts in the formation of shared explanations.

Society

Different social representations can also mean that two groups completely fail to understand one another. Di Giacomo (1980) studied a student protest movement at a Belgian university, following a government decision to double annual enrolment fees. The movement started off well, but rapidly lost support from the mass of the student body. From analysing the social representations of the student leaders and ordinary students, di Giacomo found that the two groups were using entirely different explanations and ideas. For example, the student leaders spoke and argued in terms of 'student–worker solidarity', whereas the majority of students were quite unable to perceive what they might have in common with ordinary workers. It was this discrepancy in the type of explanations and arguments used which had meant that the student leaders had lost the support of the students whom they were trying to represent.

Education

Carugati (1990) argued that social representations also play an important role in justifying actions and roles. In an examination of the beliefs about intelligence held by teachers, parents, and teachers who were also parents, Carugati found that the teachers who were also parents were most likely to hold to the theory that intelligence was a 'gift', because that view allowed them to come to terms more readily with what they were actually doing – and enabled them to attribute lack of success to the child rather than to their own efforts. Parents who were not teachers, on the other hand, were more likely to see intelligence as something to be enhanced and/or developed by the school. Carugati argued that the understanding of everyday experience by means of social representations is inherently linked with the need to establish a satisfying social and personal identity, with coherent norms and values.

Health

Studies of social representations in their social context have explored a number of themes. Herzlich (1973) described how the growing acceptance of and confidence in medical explanations, as they achieved the status of social representations in the public mind, has been shown to relate to the growth in political and social power of the medical profession in the second half of this century. Similarly, Jodelet described how changes in social representations of the body could be interpreted in terms of the influence of youth movements, women's liberation and other social factors (Jodelet, 1984).

Ammann (1987) compared the different types of explanations offered by two groups of therapists: a group who adopted a Rogerian approach of client-centred therapy, emphasizing concepts such as the self and personal growth; and a group of therapists who adopted a behavioural approach, emphasizing changes in behaviour as the primary goal of therapy. The therapists were observed as they conducted their therapy sessions, and also interviewed about their thoughts, feelings and ideas during the sessions. Ammann found that the professional orientations of both groups – the client-centred therapists and the behaviour therapists – exerted a strong influence on the way that they interpreted and explained events; therapists who belonged to the same groups tended to adopt the same kinds of explanations; but the explanations, and actions, of the two groups were very different from each other.

Social representations are not just about how other people behave, though; they also influence how we perceive ourselves. Wright (1987) asked 377 adults to provide ratings of 4 dimensions concerned with their own health. These dimensions were: the state of their own health at the time; their general estimate of healthiness for people of their age and gender; the best possible health rating that they personally could have; and how satisfied they were with their general state of health. The researchers found that people had systematically different expectations about general health depending on their age and gender, and that they then applied these social expectations to judgements about their own health. Their beliefs about the best possible state of health were also strongly influenced by whether and how much they smoked. The researchers came to the conclusion that beliefs about health and what could be expected were social representations, shared between people, and affecting the nature of explanation and expectations in that field.

Social representations are not static: they change with time and some-times develop very rapidly. Galli and Nigro (1987) showed how chil-

Environment

Figure 3.32 Galli and Nigro discovered that the Chernobyl nuclear power station disaster near Kiev in the Ukraine in 1986 soon became incorporated into children's social representa-tions of radioactivity.

dren's social representations of radioactivity (as expressed through drawings, comments on the drawings, and offered definitions) incorporated the effects of the Chernobyl catastrophe within a very short space of time after the event. The implication here is that social representation does not require a long phase of gestation: given Moscovici's emphasis on the role of conversation in the development and negotiation of social representations, a social consensus on major events such as Chernobyl is likely to develop quite quickly. In a different study of social representations among punk and communist Italian adolescents, Amerio and Ghiglione (1986) showed that some social representations actually seem to promote change and adaptation in social behaviour, while others seem to inhibit it.

Health

Markova and Wilkie (1987) discussed how the ability of social representation theory to address issues of conceptual thought in its social context means that it is better placed to explain the emergence of new social attitudes than traditional individualistic theories. In a case study of social representations about Acquired Immune Deficiency Syndrome (AIDS), Markova and Wilkie showed how a traditional attitude or concept formation approach to the problem does not allow a full analysis, since it emphasizes cognitive categorization only, and AIDS produces emotional responses as well as cognitive ones. Social representation theory, on the other hand, allows a fuller conceptualization of the social dynamics of the phenomenon, in a context which acknowledges the reality of social, historical and political factors, as well as psychological ones.

Summary

1. Non-verbal communication is communication which takes place without the use of words. It is a very powerful form of communication, and serves many functions.
2. Accents and dialects are distinctive patterns of speech. They can carry messages about personal origin, culture, and social class, and can be significant determinants of social interaction.
3. Linguistic relativity is about the way that our thinking, and particularly attitudes and assumptions, can be shaped by the words we use.
4. The idea of verbal deprivation is the idea that some people may be intellectually disadvantaged because they do not speak in a particular way. Research suggests that social disadvantage, rather than intellectual disadvantage, may be the problem.
5. Social scripts are the unwritten rules of everyday life, which produce our expectations about what is likely to happen in what situation.
6. Attribution is the way that we explain things which have happened. The type of attribution which we make can influence our future behaviour considerably.
7. Discourse analysis is concerned with analysing the meaning of everyday communication – not just how people convey information to one another, but also the implicit social meanings which are contained in the discourse.
8. Social representations are the shared beliefs held by members of groups or of society in general. They are not static, but change with time and involve personally negotiated meanings.

PRACTICE QUESTIONS AND ACTIVITIES – 3

Non-verbal communication

The topic of non-verbal communication creates a lot of interest in the general public. On the one hand it creates amusement because it is interesting to watch people and make inferences about their behaviour and intentions. On the other hand it creates a little unease because the general public is inclined to over-estimate how much psychologists can understand about what is going on. The public feels vulnerable to this analysis in the way that children believe that their parents know what they are thinking, especially when they have just been naughty.

One of the more interesting and illuminating exercises is to try out different styles of non-verbal communication. You can turn it into a game without losing the point. Find a number of blank cards and write on each of them an adverb that could be conveyed by non-verbal communication, for example:

- caringly;
- lovingly;
- angrily;
- aggressively;
- femininely;
- assertively;
- obscenely;
- intellectually;
- masculinely;
- patronizingly;
- sympathetically;
- dismissively.

One person has to pick up a card and convey the meaning of the word to the others just by non-verbal communication. The trick is to use as many muscles as possible: the way you walk, and the way you sit, as well as gestures and facial movements.

A variation on this is to try and guess the social role, so the cards might have 'social worker', 'teacher' or 'estate agent' written on them.

Accents and dialects

A brief exercise on accents is to consider what social messages are conveyed by a particular accent. First make a list of the accents you can recognize. The most easily recognizable in this country tend to be:

- Cockney (London);
- Geordie (Newcastle);
- Welsh;
- Scottish;
- Irish;

- West Country;
- Scouse (Liverpool).

You might be able to recognize some others and you could add them to the list. Residents from any one of the areas mentioned above will be able to recognize inflections in the accents that place the speaker in a particular town or part of the region. So, for example, people in the north-east often claim to able to tell by accent whether someone comes from Newcastle or Sunderland, but to someone from the south of England, there is no obvious difference in the way people speak from the two cities.

Take your list and settle down to some serious research in front of the television. I know this is a hardship, but you might have to stay there for several hours. When an advertisement comes on, listen to the voiceover and note what accent it is and what product it is that the voice is describing. After you have collected this information, the questions to look at are as follows.

- Are certain types of product matched to certain types of accent?
- What personal qualities does each accent convey?

Attributions

One of the most striking features of our attributional style is the different way that we explain our own behaviour in comparison to the way we explain other people's behaviour. For example, if I have arranged to meet someone and I am late, then it is not due to some personal failing of mine, but is due to the traffic, the state of my car, the state of the weather or the state of the world economy. On the other hand, if I am on time for the meeting and the other person is late, it is because they did not allow themselves enough time to get to the meeting place and anyway they never cared about me in the first place. This can be the start of numerous jolly domestic disputes.

A relatively safe illustration of this effect is to ask your colleagues or friends to write down their answers to the following questions.

- Why did you choose to have a relationship with your current partner (if they do not have a partner, then the question can be asked about a close friend)?
- Why did you choose your current career/course of study etc.?

Then ask them to think about a close friend and ask similar questions.

- Why did your friend choose to have a relationship with his or her current partner?
- Why did he or she choose his or her current career/course of study, etc.?

When you have collected a few responses to these questions look at the answers and divide the responses into dispositional attributions (something about the person) and situational attributions (something about the situation they are in). Have the people in your exercise made the attributional bias that was predicted?

4

Thinking
and
intelligence

Introduction

This chapter is about how we make sense of the world. Making sense of things, interpreting situations and scenes, and planning activities are such basic human qualities that we take them for granted. We do not need to understand how we think, or how we plan, in order to do it – we just go ahead. It is interesting, though, to consider some of the characteristics of intelligent activity and what we might be able to do to enhance it.

The first concept which we introduce in this chapter is the notion of schema, which has become a very fundamental idea in cognitive and social psychology. Loosely speaking, a schema is a mental representation which includes plans for action as well as factual knowledge. The concept has been used by psychologists to explore how human beings act in a wide range of settings, from everyday conversation to making perceptual judgements. The concept also helps to focus our attention on some of the parameters which constrain our thinking and which may lead us to draw some kinds of conclusions in preference to others.

One of the many themes in investigations of human thought is the computer metaphor. The idea of the intelligent computer has been a hallmark in popular culture ever since Stanley Kubrik brought HAL to the wide screen in the 1960s science fiction film *2001*. The spectacular tricks of the modern computer have enhanced this idea, partly because most of us do not understand what a computer is doing even in its simplest operations, so we believe that almost any activity which it performs must be intelligent. There are, however, some very substantial differences between the way that people think and the way that computers process information. The 1970s and 1980s saw a fad in which computer logic was taken as the standard, and any divergence between human thinking and computer processing was regarded as an error on the part of humans. Fortunately, this idea of the person as a faulty computer is gradually fading. Psychologists, however, are still interested in looking at the uses of computer simulation and artificial intelligence, and some research in these areas may even be useful.

From computer modelling we move on to human reasoning. How do we work problems out and what are the factors which influence our thoughts when we are doing so? The difficulties of study in this area become evident if you try to think about the way you think. Where did that thought come from? Was it always in the form of words? Why did I think about it in that particular way and not some other? Excessive use of this type of personal reflection is to be advised against, particularly on a Friday night after three pints of Old Disgusting Mild Ale. Fortunately, psychologists, at least when they are at work, tend to be a relatively sober group of people and therefore able to conduct these enquiries in relative safety. As we shall see, there are many different influences which can affect our reasoning, ranging from ill-health to social expectations.

After reasoning comes decision-making, at least in theory. There has been a considerable amount of interest in the process of decision-making, not least because there are a lot of people in society who want to influence the decisions which we make, from who we will vote for, to the brand of baked beans we intend to buy on the next trip to the super-market. Consumer society bombards people, every day, with an endless barrage of trivial decisions, to the point where sometimes, taking a break from decision-making can be a wonderful relief. But, on the other hand, as members of modern society we demand the right to decide our own lives and make our own decisions. Consumer choices, everyday life deci-sions and social decisions such as legal judgments are all aspects of deci-sion-making which psychologists have studied.

One of the consequences of human decision-making is that sometimes we make errors. Sometimes, these errors are trivial and have no effect on anyone. Those errors are simply ignored. But sometimes equally trivial errors can set off a chain of events which precipitates a major tragedy. Human beings will never perform faultlessly, and systems which include human beings need to be designed to take account of this. Moreover, the conditions under which those human beings work need to be arranged to minimize the likelihood of errors. It is pointless, for example, to design a checking system without failsafes for closing the bow doors on a passenger ferry and then to expect its operators to manage it faultlessly when they are working excessively long shifts for prolonged periods of time.

Research into errors has looked at people, the machines they operate, the environment they are working in, the design of the jobs they are asked to do, the supervisory structures for that job and the management

Figure 4.1 The Kegworth plane crash, in which 47 passengers died when a British Midland flight crashed just short of the runway at East Midlands Airport, was 'a disaster waiting to happen'.

of the whole operation. Examination of many of the major disasters which have caught public attention, like the Kings Cross Underground station fire, the Kegworth plane crash, or the *Herald of Free Enterprise* disaster shows that these accidents were simply waiting to happen, inherent in the design of the system and the way it was managed. But it is the people asked to operate these faulty systems that usually get the blame.

It is easy to agree that errors should be reduced, but no system can be completely risk-free. The effort we put into reducing errors is determined by a number of factors, not least of which is our evaluation of the risks involved. We make judgements about risk all the time: whether to go bungy-jumping or white-water rafting, whether to smoke a cigarette, whether to buy a hamburger from a street vendor. Judgements of risk are not only structured by our knowledge of the likely outcomes of the action, but also by a variety of other social factors. The social cachet of bungy-jumping or burger-eating may, for some, outweigh a cool evaluation of the risks involved. Surveys about risky behaviour and HIV vulnerability show that we often regard our own vulnerability as lower than other people's, even when we are undertaking quite high-risk activities.

Another quality which influences performance and, therefore, the chances of error is whether we can sustain attention for long periods of time. In modern society, people often find themselves in situations where they must maintain concentration for hours on end and loss of attention can be fatal – such as driving on a motorway. Any task that requires a constant high level of performance requires sustained attention and so it is important to know what factors make us more or less likely to make mistakes. Psychologists have studied sustained attention in many contexts, including at work, in sport and when driving.

Creativity, too, requires sustained attention, although in a way which is quite different from the kind of sustained attention required by, say, an air traffic controller. The nature of creativity attracts the attention of both psychologists and the general public. What is the difference between the artist and the artisan? What does it mean to think creatively and is this activity reserved for just a few special people? Psychology has tried to explore the creative mind and the nature of creative activity, partly through investigating the work of highly creative people and partly through looking at the distinctive styles of thinking which seem to be employed in the creative process.

Psychology has also, somewhat more controversially, tried to quantify intelligence. From an early history in which the development of intelligence testing was, more or less explicitly, an exercise in applied racism, to a middle history in which intelligence testing became an exercise in implied racism, the history of the psychological study of intelligence finally seems to have reached a point where it can recognize and respect variance between different cultures and personal experience. All of which does not, of course, prevent modern racists from dredging up the old stuff when they want to revive the arguments. But more modern research in this area looks at how differences in styles of thinking may be valuable, not a handicap, in a variety of different contexts.

Schemas

A **schema** is a cognitive structure that represents factual information, organizes how we deal with it and directs courses of action with respect to it. Initially, the concept of 'schema' was developed by cognitive psychologists describing how we go about using information: the memory researcher Bartlett (1932) used the term when describing how people's own ideas and assumptions adjust information which is to be recalled. More recently the concept has been further developed by social psychologists to describe how we structure our social worlds. Rumelhart (1980) suggested that there are four ways of thinking about schemas (also termed schemata), each of which has been adopted by different psychologists researching into that area:

1. schemas can be seen as plays, containing information about characters, setting and scripts for appropriate sequences of action;
2. schemas can be seen as theories, which allow us to produce a meaningful explanation for what is happening around us;

schema A mental framework or structure which encompasses memories, ideas, concepts and programmes for action which are pertinent to a particular topic.

3. schemas can be seen as computer systems, allowing us to process information that we are receiving from the world;
4. schemas can be seen as decoders, breaking down and analysing the components of everyday living in the same way as a grammatical parser will break down a sentence into its grammatical parts and its meanings.

Person schemas refer to our theories and expectations about what other people are like and how they are apt to behave. Stereotypes, for example, can be seen as an instance of role schemas. We might have a stereotype of a doctor and certain expectations about how he or she will behave, and what they are like. Hazel Markus (1977) has suggested that people organize their experiences in terms of self-schemas which guide how we think about ourselves and our behaviour.

The schema is a form of mental representation which encompasses action and intention, as well as factual information. The idea of the schema has been applied in several different fields of psychology: in developmental psychology through Piaget and subsequent researchers; in cognitive psychology through the work of Neisser and others; and in social psychology, where it is closely linked with the idea of the social script put forward by Schank and Abelson, which we looked at in Chapter 3.

It has been proposed that schemas develop through the two processes of assimilation and accommodation. Assimilation concerns the incorporation of new information. A schema may develop in one context, yet be applicable to others. Its range becomes extended as new information becomes assimilated into the schema, without, however, fundamentally changing it.

Unlike assimilation, accommodation involves change to the schema itself, as it stretches and adjusts to fit new information. If the adjustment required is too great, the schema may sub-divide, with each new schema in turn growing and changing as it accommodates new material. Some psychologists identify the twin processes of assimilation and accommodation as representing the way in which all cognitive development and social adjustment takes place: beginning always with existing cognitive structures, then extending and developing these into new representations: new schemas.

Key reference: FISKE, S. T. and LINVILLE, P. W. (1980) What does the schema concept buy us? *Personality and Social Psychology Bulletin*, **6**, 543–57.

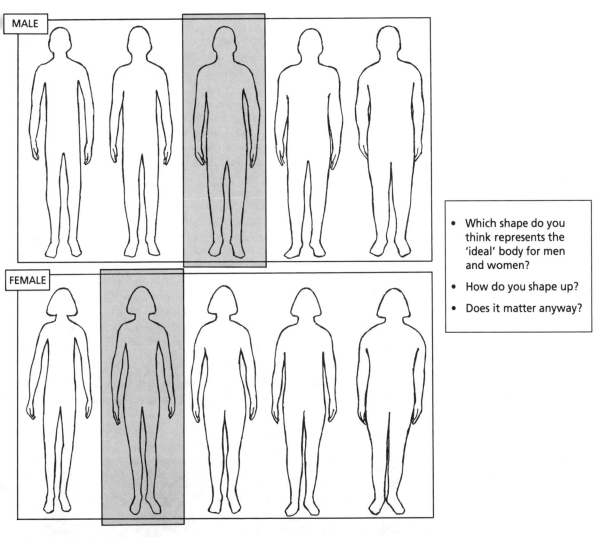

- Which shape do you think represents the 'ideal' body for men and women?

- How do you shape up?

- Does it matter anyway?

Figure 4.2 Body schemas.

How do we develop schemas? Many would appear to develop and change through social interaction. Some, however, appear relatively early. The first schema to be formed is thought to be the body schema – the image each of us carries of our own bodies. As we develop, we become aware of our own physical abilities and gain an impression of what our bodies are like. In a consumer society, in which people are surrounded by often highly unrealistic images of the 'ideal body', this can also result in a very distorted body image. There is some evidence that people who suffer from anorexia nervosa have a very distorted body image, seeing themselves as fat when in reality they have become virtually emaciated.

Society

Orbach (1978) argued that perceptions of the body as 'fat' are inextricably tied up with wider social issues of feminism and self-identity. Women labelled themselves with the derogatory term 'fat', and felt unhappy about it, when really they simply had bodies expressing the natural variation in physique typical of humankind. Accepting the negative label happened as part of their socialization as women and the way that they devalued themselves by comparison with men. Boskind-White and White (1983) also showed that women who suffer from bulimia – the disorder in which eating binges alternate with severe purges of the body – tend to be particularly concerned with being attractive to men and, as a result, have absorbed very unrealistic ideals about the ideal body. As a result of this, the most appropriate therapy for these people has been that which is oriented towards the development of self-respect and self-esteem.

Another type of schema to do with the body is one which may possibly be inherited. Eibl-Eiblesfeldt (1975), drawing on research from earlier ethologists, argued that we have a special schema for babies – whether animals or children. We respond differently to young children and animals than we do to adult members of the same species, and Eibl-Eiblesfeldt suggested that this is because, as mammals, we have inherited an automatic caretaking response to immature mammals, which is triggered off by a number of key signs. The signs are listed in Figure 4.3.

1. Large head in proportion to body.
2. Protruding forehead, large in proportion to the size of the rest of the face.
3. Large eyes below the midline of the total head.
4. Short, thick extremities.
5. Rounded body shape.
6. Soft, elastic body surfaces.
7. Round protruding cheeks.

The suggestion is that we have a powerful schema for recognizing vulnerable forms of all animals and we respond appropriately, often with an 'aahhh!'

Figure 4.3 Key signs of infanthood.

Infant forms (usually judged as 'cute')   Adult forms

Figure 4.4 Pictorial representations of the key signs of infanthood. (Eibl-Eiblesfeldt, 1975.)

According to Eibl-Eiblesfeldt, this is a very basic form of schema, which is shared by members of all human societies – although, of course, as with any inherited characteristic, there will be individual variations in its strength. Cartoonists and others make use of these features when drawing animals: characters such as Mickey Mouse, Sylvester or Jerry Mouse all have disproportionately large eyes and heads, and many other neotenous features, and this is thought to explain why people react so positively to them.

It has also been suggested that this schema has a more serious side. It may be an important consideration for care workers in judging whether a child is at risk from physical abuse. McCabe (1984) studied photographs of 2 groups of children: 22 physically abused children aged between 3 and 6 years old; and 22 non-abused children of the same age. The comparison showed that the children who has been physically abused had head and facial features which seemed older than those of their age-mates, and so had fewer of the features described by Eibl-Eibelsfeldt. McCabe looked at other physical variables associated with age, such as height, but found that these were relatively unimportant: it seems to be head and facial features which lead people to judge that someone is of a particular age.

McCabe suggested that judgements of this kind are made almost unconsciously by the child's carers and thought it possible that this might result in some children being expected to act in a way which was more appropriate for an older child. When they do not meet these expectations, they may become more vulnerable to physical abuse. It is not so much that the face and head structure causes the abuse, as that it results in an unrealistic age judgement, and so the child is expected to act in a more mature fashion.

According to McCabe, these findings supported the idea that there is an innate 'infant-schema' which influences behaviour. But, of course, it is equally possible, and probably more plausible, that the strain involved in suffering physical abuse produced the differences in the first place. The relaxed facial muscles of the happy child, as opposed to the drawn facial muscles of the tense child, may in itself produce different ratings of age. It is also possible that the stress of physical abuse resulted in the child losing its childlike characteristics more quickly. Many researchers, including Levine (1960), have shown that stress can accelerate and sometimes distort physical maturation, as the organism attempts to cope with the problems. A more detailed study, following up children over time and looking at long-term changes resulting from moving from an abusive environment to a warm supportive one might be of more value in investigating this hypothesis than a simple rating of photographs.

We are more likely to remember things which relate directly to our most important schemas, than we are to remember things which are less relevant to us. Smith and Lewis (1985) suggested that our own racial self-schema is likely to affect what we remember. They played pre-recorded stories to 120 black children aged between 6 and 7 years old, while the children looked at picture books which were designed to accompany the tapes. Each child listened to two stories. One group listened to two stories with black characters; a second group listened to stories with white characters; and a third group listened to stories with animal characters. After each story, the children were asked four questions, which showed how much they remembered about the story's events and characters. The researchers found that the children remembered those stories which related to black characters much better than those which involved white characters, and argued that this was partly because the children had more highly developed schemata for their own racial group than they did for whites.

In a totally different field, **ergonomics** is all to do with how human beings and machines interact, and making sure that they do so in the most efficient way also includes making sure that the machines relate easily to the way that people habitually think. The actions which we use when we are operating machines are often guided by our schemas about how machines should work. Loveless (1962) argued that one of the important ergonomic principles when designing controls for machinery was that the movement of the controls should conform with these existing schemas, since these direct what we expect to happen when we perform an action. For example, it makes more sense to us to move a lever forwards to produce a forward movement in a machine and to pull it back to reverse. Having controls which operate counter to expectations – like a lever which has to be moved forwards to make the machine move backwards, increases the likelihood of mistakes and can lead to serious industrial accidents.

Loveless also argued that the same should apply to visual displays. Wherever possible, a display should move in the same direction as the control itself: if a lever is to be moved to the right, then the pointer indicating that movement should also move to the right. Although these might seem relatively straightforward recommendations, there have been many industrial accidents of varying degrees of severity produced by counter-intuitive displays and controls, which contradict the operator's own expectations – partly because of a failure to consider the human side of the human–machine interface.

There have also been some striking commercial outcomes of these factors. Digital watches, for instances, enjoyed only a relatively brief

Work

ergonomics *The area of work psychology concerned with designing tools, machines, work systems and work places to fit the skills and abilities of workers.*

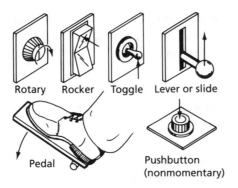

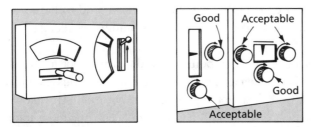

Control response stereotypes for turning on equipment

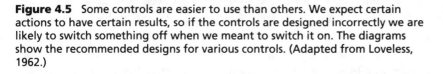

Direction of control movement recommended for a 'change in display' indicator.

Figure 4.5 Some controls are easier to use than others. We expect certain actions to have certain results, so if the controls are designed incorrectly we are likely to switch something off when we meant to switch it on. The diagrams show the recommended designs for various controls. (Adapted from Loveless, 1962.)

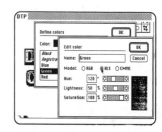

Figure 4.6 Visual images on the computer screen.

period of popularity before people moved back to analogue designs, mainly because people preferred the spatial metaphor of the round face, which showed time visually, rather than in numerical symbols. And the popularity of the Apple Macintosh computer came from the same source: it was directly attributable to the way that the computer used visual images which could be moved about on the screen, like pieces of paper on a desk, rather than using complex symbolic languages which only experts could visualize. It became popular very quickly, because ordinary people could learn to use it so quickly – even those who did not know anything about computers. Eventually, commercial rivals were forced to adopt the Windows system, which imitated the Macintosh desktop metaphor, in order to compete.

We have general schemas as well as specific ones. Janoff-Bulman (1989) suggested that our general world-schemas are the most useful framework to use when we are trying to understand how people respond to traumatic events. The single most common response to negative life events such as crime, disease and accidents is an intense feeling

Environment

of vulnerability. People report that they feel vulnerable, unsafe and unprotected, and that they were unprepared for the trauma because they never thought it could happen to them. Janoff-Bulman argued that this response actually tells us a lot about the way that most people live their lives – in particular, that we generally operate in an illusion of invulnerability, a basic belief that 'It can't happen to me'.

Janoff-Bulman went on to suggest that there are three primary aspects of common world-view schemas held by people who had not experienced trauma The first is that the world is generally perceived as benevolent, rather than hostile. The second is that events in the world are perceived as meaningful, rather than random; and the third is that people who have not experienced significant trauma tend to have a basic sense of self-worthiness. The experience of trauma challenges all three of these.

Janoff-Bulman (1989) reported a study carried out to investigate how much people's schemas are influenced by previous traumatic events, using the World Assumptions table in Figure 4.7. He interviewed 338 undergraduates, of whom 83 had experienced 6 or more traumatic incidents in the past.

Although the 'victims' had generally experienced their unpleasant events some years prior to the study, they showed noticeable differences in their world-view schemas. They perceived themselves more negatively, and saw the world as less benevolent, than people who had not experienced this number of traumas. They also tended to show more depression than the other students – an effect which was strongest among the men in the study.

One of the common responses to trauma are thoughts and feelings of self-blame – often to a more extreme degree than seems justified to an observer. But Janoff-Bulman suggested that self-blame may actually help people to adapt, by providing them with a route whereby they can maintain their world schemas. If the disaster happened through your own fault, then you may be able to repair your view of the world as benevolent and meaningful. Being victimized is one thing, having to readjust your whole view of the world is another.

Society

Paap (1989) discussed how the concept of schema is useful in understanding the process of perceiving and comprehending a scene. People in many jobs have to sort through visual information quickly, ranging from the intelligence officer who sorts through satellite spy shots, to a TV director picking out what looks to be the best shot from a choice of several different monitors, to a designer flicking through a series of computer images when seeking an illustration for a poster, to someone leafing through holiday snaps to find the one which shows the visit to

J	1	Misfortune is least likely to strike worthy people
BP	2	People are naturally unfriendly and unkind
R	3	Bad events are distributed to people at random
BP	4	Human nature is basically good
BW	5	The good things that happen in this world outnumber the bad
R	6	The course of our lives is largely determined by chance
J	7	Generally, people deserve what they get in the world
SW	8	I often think I am no good at all
BW	9	There is more good than evil in the world
L	10	I am basically a lucky person
C	11	People's misfortunes result from mistakes they have made
BP	12	People don't really care what happens to the next person
SC	13	I usually behave in ways that are likely to maximize good results for me
J	14	People will experience good fortune if they themselves are good
R	15	Life is too full of uncertainties that are determined by chance
L	16	When I think about it, I consider myself very lucky
SC	17	I almost always make an effort to prevent bad things from happening to me
SW	18	I have a low opinion of myself
L	19	By and large, good people get what they deserve in this world
C	20	Through our actions we can prevent bad things from happening to us
L	21	Looking at my life, I realize that chance events have worked out well for me
C	22	If people took preventive actions, most misfortune could be avoided
SC	23	I take actions necessary to protect myself against misfortune
R	24	In general, life is mostly a gamble
BW	25	The world is a good place
BP	26	People are basically kind and helpful
SC	27	I usually behave so as to bring about the greatest good for me
SW	28	I am satisfied with the kind of person I am
C	29	When bad thing happen, it is typically because people have not taken the necessary actions to protect themselves
BW	30	If you look closely enough, you will see the world is full of goodness
SW	31	I have reason to be ashamed of my personal character
L	32	I am luckier than most people

BW: benevolence of the world
BP: benevolence of people
J: justice
C: controllability
R: randomness
SW: self-worth
SC: self-controllability
L: luck

Figure 4.7 World assumptions scale. (Janoff-Bulman, 1989.)

the egg and chip café on the Costa Blanca. In such situations, the glance at each separate stimulus often involves little more than a single eye fixation – the perceiver does not have time to take in all of the details of the scene. Instead, the single fixation activates a relevant schema – that's a beach photo, so it won't do, that's a picture of the dodgems – and the person only pauses and looks at the picture more closely when the appropriate schema has been activated.

Computer simulation and artificial intelligence

With the advent of the computer, many researchers became fascinated by the question of whether it would ever become possible for a machine to think as a human being does. Researchers into computer simulation believe that the process of teaching a computer how to simulate human problem-solving or human action may throw light on our own understanding of the same areas.

Although early research into computer simulation concentrated on serial processing, in which the computer simply followed one line of reasoning, or logic chain, at a time, more recent research involves connectionism, or **parallel distributed processing (PDP)**. These models represent attempts to replicate the complexity of the human mind by allowing for multiple chains of reasoning, with cross-connections, to be operating simultaneously. This research has produced some interesting outcomes including simulation programmes which appear to be able to generate novel outcomes, and also including 'fuzzy logic' – an approach which seems to be similar to the human ability to operate with vague approximations rather than precise data.

A different approach to the use of computers in problem-solving has been to produce computer systems which might aid or improve how human beings tackle problems. These attempts fall into the general category of **artificial intelligence**, often referred to as AI. Artificial intelligence systems include robotics, in which machines are designed which can perform specific tasks, with the aid of sensors which will allow them to guide their actions and movement mechanisms which allow them to move appropriately. Robots are not uncommon in modern manufacturing industries, although they bear little resemblance to the mechanoids of science fiction.

Another area of AI research is concerned with the development of **expert systems**. These are computer programs which are specially designed to aid experts in their professional decision-making by

parallel distributed processing *A form of computer simulation in which several different logic pathways are at work simultaneously, with inter-connections between them.*

artificial intelligence *Computer systems which are able to 'learn' and to produce the same kinds of outcomes as are produced by human thinking.*

expert systems *AI systems designed to provide human experts with an extended information source, to aid them in making decisions.*

providing easy access to extra information. Each expert system has three components: a knowledge base, providing information which is specific to the task and presented in a way that the expert can easily understand; some kind of system for looking at the available data and matching it up with the knowledge base – often referred to as an 'inference engine'; and a user interface, which allows the expert to communicate requests to it. The ideal user interface is 'user-friendly', in the sense that the process for communicating requests is clear and simple for a human being to use, although many of the early expert systems were not particularly friendly at all.

Expert systems, of course, do not replace human beings. Rather, they augment the human being's own decision-making. Human experts often have implicit knowledge, which is not easily verbalized, and would therefore be impossible to include in the database. Also, human experts can cover a wide range of questions, and can generalize from previous cases by recognizing general patterns, even when each particular element in a given case is different.

Key reference: JOHNSON-LAIRD, P. N. (1988) *The Computer and the Mind*. Fontana, London.

One of the first attempts at **computer simulation** was the general problem solver, or GPS, as it became known, developed by Newell and Simon, in 1972. This programme involved comparing how things are at the beginning of the problem, the initial state, with how things would be when the problem has been solved, the goal state. The difference between the two is known as the problem space. Newell and Simon's model concentrated on reducing the problem space.

Even in a simple problem, though, the problem space can be quite large, and to go through all the possible options would be too lengthy and tedious. In their programme, therefore, Newell and Simon used **heuristics** – short cuts to solving the problem, calculated using a method known as means end analysis. This involved breaking the problem down into a number of smaller stages, or sub-goals, which will serve to reduce the problem space. The problem-solver takes the step which will reach the first sub-goal and the problem space is then recalculated. Then the step which leads towards the next sub-goal is identified and taken, until the end of the problem is reached. Using this approach, Newell and Simon were able to programme a computer to solve simple problems – but only ones where both the beginning and the goal states were very clearly defined! Most human problems are rather less clear than that.

computer simulation The attempt to develop computer programmes which will replicate human processes such as skill learning or problem-solving.

heuristics Strategies for solving problems which involve taking the step which looks most likely to lead towards a solution, even if this is uncertain.

Society

Another early approach to computer simulation was to develop programs which operated within a regular set of rules, to generate responses to questions. Using this approach, Abelson and Carroll (1965) simulated the belief system of a right-wing American politician, and showed that the computer was able to respond to questions in a manner which was remarkably similar to those of the original politician on whom the program had been modelled.

A similar approach was taken with the early counselling programme ELIZA. ELIZA worked by recognizing key words and responding to them

---

Psychiatrist: Why are you in the hospital?
PARRY: I shouldn't be here.
Psychiatrist: Who brought you here?
PARRY: The police
Psychiatrist: What trouble did you have with the police?
PARRY: Cops don't do their job.
Psychiatrist: What do they do instead?
PARRY: They arrest the wrong people.
Psychiatrist: They arrest the right one sometimes.
PARRY: The law should get those Italian crooks.
Psychiatrist: Are you Italian?
PARRY: My background is British but I was born in that country.
Psychiatrist: Do you know any Italian crooks?
PARRY: I try to avoid the underworld.
Psychiatrist: Are you afraid of the underworld?
PARRY: The Mafia are the worst gangsters.
Psychiatrist: Are you connected with the Mafia?
PARRY: You know, they know me.
Psychiatrist: How do they know you?
PARRY: They spy on me.
Psychiatrist: Why do they?
PARRY: They want to get false evidence to frame me.
Psychiatrist: What do they have against you?
PARRY: They are out to get me.
Psychiatrist: Are you sure of all this?
PARRY: You don't believe me?
Psychiatrist: I'm doing my best.
– silence –
PARRY: Can't you think of a decent question to ask?
Psychiatrist: You seem hostile to me.
PARRY: Some of your remarks annoy me.
Psychiatrist: I am sorry
PARRY: Forget the excuses, you guys are all alike.

Figure 4.8 An interview between a psychiatrist and PARRY. (Colby, Weber, and Hilf, 1972.)

So you keep fantasizing that you are talking to machines

Figure 4.9 A psychiatrist has a disturbing delusion.

with appropriate non-directive questions. For example, someone who typed in a comment involving the word 'mother' would be invited to 'Tell me more about your mother'. In this way, the programme generated the impression that it was answering the individual who was typing in their questions on the computer's keyboard. Many people found interacting with the programme to be an inherently fascinating exercise and some also claimed to find it therapeutic.

More sophisticated simulations were developed, particularly in the psychiatric arena. Colby (1981) wrote a computer simulation model known as PARRY, which was all about explaining the **paranoid** form of mental disturbance. A person suffering from paranoia wrongly believes that they are being persecuted. They are suspicious of other people, look for threats in innocent remarks and respond with hostility. In the model underlying PARRY's operation, these are seen as strategies for minimizing and forestalling shame-induced distress.

Colby asked a number of psychiatrists to interview a 'patient', using a computer to communicate with them. Sometimes, the psychiatrists interviewed real patients and other times they interviewed PARRY, but none of the participants at any point realized that they were diagnosing a computer programme. Figure 4.8 gives an extract from an interview between a psychiatrist and PARRY.

In terms of PARRY's operation, the simulation consists of two parts. One part is concerned with understanding the interview questions of clinicians, who were inevitably communicating in everyday language (or, at least, their professional equivalent). For this Colby was able to draw

Health

paranoia *Unreasonable and excessive suspiciousness, jealousy or mistrust.*

on a wide range of research into computer understanding of human speech. This is by no means perfect, and it may be for this reason that simulations of mentally disturbed people seem to have been more successful than other kinds of simulations. It is possible that we would overlook miscomprehensions or minor errors in those we considered to be mentally ill, where we would be more aware of them if we believed that we were interacting with a 'normal' human being.

Once an approximation of the meaning of the question was made, it would then be passed to the second part of the simulation, which was a combination of data structures and production rules. These operated at more than one level, dealing with the immediate stimulus, but also sizing up the current state of the interview and deciding on that basis which actions (statements or questions) the model should perform next in order to fulfil its intentions.

Servan-Schreiber (1986) pointed to a number of advantages of computerized psychotherapy of this type. The two most important ones were, first, the relative cheapness of this type of approach by comparison with the cost of traditional psychiatric treatment; and, secondly, what seems to be a greater willingness on the part of patients to report personal information or socially deviant behaviour to a computer rather than a psychotherapist. People will sometimes admit things to a computer which they would conceal from other human beings. Servan-Schreiber suggested that computerized therapy is most appropriate for brief cognitive and behavioural therapies.

However, PARRY, like other simulations of this nature, operated on a fairly simple set of responses to relatively predictable questions and was unable to respond effectively if the questioner moved outside a standard format of questioning. For this and other reasons, the value of this kind of therapy would seem questionable. If people are depressed or paranoid, human treatment programmes are likely to be more effective in the long run. The extensive research into cognitive restructuring therapy shows how successful and lasting intervention in psychiatric problems may involve rather more sophisticated forms of treatment – such as developing people's self-efficacy beliefs and locus of control (see Chapter 2). Simply encouraging someone to feel better because they have talked about their problems is a short-term solution at best. Computer simulations may be cheaper, and superficially effective, but they are unlikely to be able to produce long-term cognitive change and so will not prevent a recurrence of the problem.

Work

Rumelhart and Norman (1982) produced a computer simulation of typing. This model was designed to be able to replicate the actions of a human being typing, so it was not enough just to create a programme

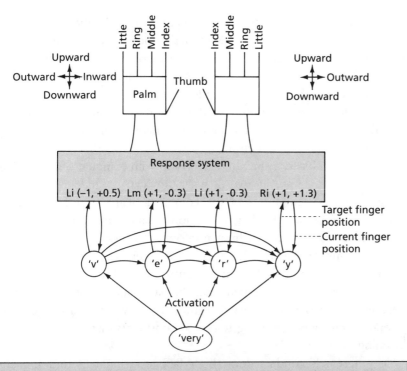

A typewriting simulation. The word schema 'very' activates the component keypress schemata. The left-to-right lines ending in filled circles indicate inhibition; thus, to begin with 'v' is not inhibited whilst 'y' is maximally inhibited. Within the response system L and R, and I and M denote left and right index and middle fingers. The numbers in brackets indicate the momentary discrepancy between target and present finger position in the vertical and horizontal axes. The curved arrows indicate the feedback loops which act to reduce the discrepancy when each keypress schema is activated.

Figure 4.10 Typing simulator. (Rumelhart and Norman, 1982.)

which would always type accurately. Human beings make mistakes too – but with a reasonably skilled typist, at least, these mistakes are not random. They involve certain types of mistake – such as one hand typing faster than the other, producing transposed letters – 'hte' instead of 'the', for instance. They also sometimes involve doubling the wrong letter, like writing 'bokk' instead of 'book'. If the model was truly to simulate human typing behaviour, therefore, it was important that the model should also be capable of replicating those types of errors, at least sometimes.

Rumelhart and Norman achieved this in the simulation by combining a number of basic units in a hierarchical fashion. The basic unit is known as an activation-triggered schema, or ATS, which would be set off if the right kind of conditions become apparent. In terms of physical action, there were several different levels: one set of activation schemas would each represent a single keypress for a single letter; but a higher order group would represent whole words. Each word ATS, therefore, would in its turn set off a sequence of letter activation schemas. In addition, as seems to happen with human thought and action, when one schema was activated, the others closest to it were slightly inhibited and less likely to become activated themselves. When Rumelhart and Norman activated the simulation to type a continuous 2000 words, they found that it produced several features which are common in human typing too – including many of the most common errors!

We have developed a strange relationship with computers. On the one hand, many people are in awe of what they can do and, on the other, we are often contemptuous of the computer's capacity for unthinking and ludicrous error. Further confusion results from the idea that computers are the model for human information processing. In the early days of cognitive science, this was often taken to its limits by some researchers. Palombo (1984), for example, asked the question 'Can computers dream?' He argued that human-made computers exhibit dreamlike behaviour, and that when they do, they conform to the same general information-processing rules and constraints that apply to human dreaming.

Sleep research conducted on both laboratory animals and humans shows that dreaming sleep seems to be necessary for the transfer of new information from the events of the day into permanent long-term storage. During the day we experience a massive range of sensory information, even if we are not aware of it: the feel of a chair, the sight of the bus coming and so on. At some point, the brain needs to sort all this information out, and to sift what needs to be remembered from that which can be forgotten or ignored. It also needs to link new information with our existing knowledge and skills. According to Palombo, dreaming in humans can be seen as a refinement of an information-processing technique employed ever since the first organisms became able to learn from their interactions with the outside world.

Palombo went on to suggest that large computer information systems are not only able to dream in this more primitive sense, but appear to need to do so, because of the nature of their information-processing tasks. They need to have periods in which they consolidate information and identify the implications of their operations for their basic state. This, Palombo argues, is what is happening when we dream.

The evidence for this argument, however, rests on rather a simplistic notion of both the nature of dreaming, and of the type and complexity of information which both animals and human beings process. A similar example of this type of problem lay in the way that computer logic was so often taken as the absolute definition of accurate reasoning. This meant that when human beings performed reasoning problems and came to different conclusions from a computer, they were often construed as making 'errors', when what they were really doing was incorporating highly sophisticated social knowledge into their logic – something which computers were unable to do. Human reasoning is not the same as formal logic and many of its distinctive characteristics represent a deep level of adaptation to our complex social lives.

Human reasoning

Research suggests that looking at human thinking as the simple, logical processing of information may be misleading. There are some differences between how human beings think and computer logic, and these differences are systematic in nature. One of them is the way that we find it much harder – and take longer – to process negative information than we do to process positive information. So we can comprehend a statement like: 'If the circle is red, then the triangle will be blue' more easily, and more quickly, than we comprehend a sentence like: 'If the circle is not brown, then the triangle will not be green'. Although the two statements are logically equivalent, people take longer to process the negative one and are more likely to make mistakes when they do it.

Similarly, Wason and Johnson Laird (1970) showed that we tend to apply our broader knowledge about what is practical or likely when we are solving problems. This may also mean that we do not always reason according to strict formal logic. For example, if you heard your friend say, 'I'll go for a walk on Sunday if the weather is fine', you would be likely to conclude that she wouldn't go for a walk if it was raining. To a human being, that seems obvious. But to a computer, which operates by formal logic, there would be just as much chance of seeing your friend go for a walk in the rain as in the sunshine on that particular Sunday. Saying that 'I will do this if...' is not the same as saying 'I won't do this if not', in the same way as saying that 'all guitars are musical instruments' is not the same as saying 'all musical instruments are guitars.'

So, human reasoning is not quite the same thing as formal logic. Some psychologists have seen these features of the way that human beings think as 'errors' in reasoning, because they do not match up to strictly logical processes. But others see them as evidence that human reasoning is far more subtle and sophisticated, since it does not just include the elements of the problem, but also looks at its whole social context, taking into account prior knowledge about the world and about the probable actions of people.

Key reference: WASON, P. C. (1968) Reasoning about a rule. *The Quarterly Journal of Experimental Psychology*, **20**, 273–81.

Society

The phrase human reasoning may sometimes seem to be almost a contradiction in terms, given people's ability to act in idiosyncratic and apparently illogical ways. But it is not really. Reasoning implies working things out – taking all the different elements of a problem into account and working out a strategy or solution which allows for these. We usually assume that this means reasoning is logical and predictable, and free from bias, but actually, that does not have to be the case – and human reasoning is none of these. We reason in a way that bears little or no relationship to formal logic, but which works very well in the everyday worlds that we live in. We can see some interesting applications of this idea if we look at the factors which bias and mould our reasoning.

Apparent errors in human judgement can often be attributed to the application of more sophisticated social knowledge than a computer could possibly manage. For example, Tversky and Kahneman (1983) described a common 'error' that people make when they are given probability problems to solve. In one study, participants were told that an imaginary person called Linda was a former activist, single, very intelligent and a philosophy graduate. They were then asked to estimate the probabilities of her being a bank teller, a feminist or a feminist bank teller. Most people said that it would be more probable that she was a feminist bank teller than a bank teller. This is not logically correct, because the category of bank tellers includes all feminist bank tellers.

In human thinking, though, the category of bank teller as opposed to feminist bank teller would have been interpreted as meaning 'non-feminist bank teller' – and if someone had really used those terms to describe two people, that would have been what they intended to communicate. In real life, we would not be likely to contrast the two if they were not different, and we rarely actually spell out everything that we mean, so we would assume that the person that we are talking with shares certain social conventions and would pick up the implication. As we saw in Chapter 3, conversation depends on implicit meanings, which we do not spell out very often at all.

Health

Another factor is how information is presented in the first place. An example of how the presentation of the message affects reasoning was provided by Marteau (1990). In this study, a group of medical students was asked whether they would undergo, or whether they would advise patients to undergo, a number of medical procedures such as surgery for terminal liver disease, or termination of pregnancy if the child would have haemophilia. When they were presented to the research

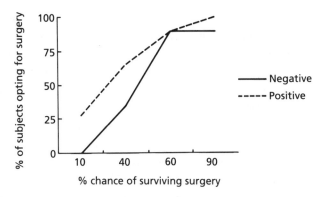

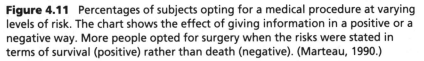

Figure 4.11 Percentages of subjects opting for a medical procedure at varying levels of risk. The chart shows the effect of giving information in a positive or a negative way. More people opted for surgery when the risks were stated in terms of survival (positive) rather than death (negative). (Marteau, 1990.)

participants, the risks of the procedures were framed in either a positive or negative way. For example, the researcher might describe the risk of undergoing an essential operation as being that the person had a 10% chance of surviving surgery or a 90% chance of dying.

Marteau found that the way in which the information was presented affected the decisions which people made. By phrasing the option in an optimistic way, people tended to make more optimistic judgements: they were more likely to choose an option which gave a 10% chance of surviving, than one which gave a 90% chance of dying, even though logically the two are identical. (Of course, this is not the only factor that will affect our judgement in this type of circumstance: Marteau went on to suggest that human judgement also depends on the level of the risks involved, and we will be looking at risk assessment later in this chapter.)

If we look closely at these results, though, we can see how what seems on the surface simply to be an error actually comes from applying a sophisticated social knowledge. When we are communicating with other people, we guide the conversation, often unconsciously, through our choice of language. We also, as we will see in Chapter 7, have a basic tendency to co-operate with other people, and to fall in with what they are suggesting unless there is a good reason why we should not. So, in a task like this, we pick up the cue which we are being given by the use of optimistic words and are more likely to make a positive judgement. Alternatively, we pick up the subtle cue involved in the use of negative words to describe the option and make a judgement which takes that into account. It may not be strictly logical, but it is far from being an error, if we look at how this would work in the real situation.

Being ill can also affect how we reason. Krikorian (1990) looked at what happens when people are suffering from a direct nervous system infection by the **human immunodeficiency virus (HIV)**. Krikorian performed a comprehensive neuropsychological examination of 38 HIV-infected people who were beginning to show the symptoms of immune deficiency, and compared them with 16 uninfected people who were otherwise very similar. Even though the major aspects of cognitive functioning, such as language, visual-spatial and memory consolidation abilities were quite normal, the people with HIV infection were less able to pay attention to information, and also showed difficulties in organizing information effectively and in general reasoning.

Most of us have experienced a minor version of this problem when we have been ill – like a cold being accompanied by errors and the thought that 'I can't think straight'. It is not certain whether this effect is produced by the illness itself or by the additional stress that being ill puts us under – if, indeed, it is possible to separate the two. In evolutionary terms, however, it does make sense for us to become more passive if we are ill, since that would help to save energy which can be more usefully employed to fight the illness. Again, what would be simply a malfunctioning for a machine may have a deeper implication when we are looking at real human beings living their everyday lives.

Ironically, the tendency to perceive human thinking as full of 'errors' is in itself a misrepresentation of the findings – our ideas about reasoning itself have become distorted! Christansen-Szalanski and Beach (1984) found that research into the psychology of judgement and decision-making was cited very selectively, and argued that this selective bias had a strong influence in how readers of the literature looked at human reasoning. For example, when they analysed how often good- and poor-performance articles were mentioned by other academics between 1972 to 1981, Christansen-Szalanski and Beach found that 'poor-performance articles', which presented human judgement as being full of errors, were cited significantly more often than articles which gave evidence for accurate and logical reasoning by human research participants – yet there were just as many articles of each kind available in the literature.

In another part of the study, 80 members of the Judgment and Decision-making Society, a semi-formal professional group, were asked to complete a questionnaire assessing the overall quality of human judgement and decision-making abilities on a scale from 0 to 100. They were then asked to list four examples of documented poor judgement or decision-making performance and four examples of good performance. Interestingly, they remembered twice as many examples of poor performance than of good ones, even though there was only a limited range of poor-performance examples.

The researchers also found that people who were less experienced in the field tended to have a lower opinion of human reasoning ability than those who were highly experienced. They concluded that there is a citation bias in the judgement and decision-making literature which means that poor-performance articles tend to receive most of the attention from other writers, despite the fact that there are equivalent proportions of each type of research finding in the journals.

That does not mean, of course, that we always think in the most positive or advantageous way. Bassoff (1985) argued that certain tendencies in human reasoning may interfere with whether we make accurate personal and social judgements. Bassoff was particularly interested in the way that we often fail to process negative information. As Wason showed, we take longer to process negative statements than we do positive ones. Also, we often fail to consider negative examples, and we will frequently discount negative evidence, particularly against our pre-existing ideas.

Society

Bassoff suggested that counsellors can help clients to use these negative instances positively, to help people to escape from self-defeating beliefs. A lot of the time, people who are depressed or overly anxious hold dysfunctional beliefs – ideas and attributions which mean that things are perceived as being much worse than they really are. Helping people to recognize negative instances when they happened in daily experience allows them to realize that, actually, things are not always the same and that they can sometimes change.

For example, someone who was stuck in a belief that everything they tried to do was always a failure could be helped to recognize those occasions when they did actually do things successfully. Instead of just ignoring them, they could deliberately notice them and so question some of the ideas which they had previously accepted. Bassoff suggested that techniques which encourage people to explore new ways of behaving, like role-play, psychodrama, guided imagery and hypnotherapy, are often helpful ways to bring this home.

Another special form of reasoning that has attracted the interest of psychologists is the area of **moral reasoning**. Here, the work of Piaget, and later Kohlberg, suggested that moral judgement is largely a cognitive process affected by the general structure of our thinking and in particular by our ability to use abstract reasoning. The clear extrapolation from this approach is that the more intellectually advanced you are the more sophisticated your moral reasoning will be. But this finding may not be as clear-cut as it sounds.

moral reasoning Using cognitive processes to make judgements about right and wrong.

One of the many problems with this approach is the way that moral reasoning was defined in these studies. Kohlberg had tended to use problems which contrasted justice and care dilemmas (e.g. 'A man breaks into a chemist shop to steal medicines for his dying wife. Was he right or wrong?') In his theory, Kohlberg assumed that abstract notions of social justice (which tended to be favoured by men) were a higher form of reasoning than notions of social responsibility (which tended to be favoured by women). But it is open to debate whether one is really 'better' than the other.

Gilligan and Attanucci (1988) explored the real-life dilemmas encountered by 46 men and 34 women, mostly adolescents and young adults. They found that both groups of respondents were concerned about both justice and care, but in general the respondents would tend to focus on one or the other type of concern when they were dealing with a given question and not really consider the other type very deeply. Although there were some exceptions, in general care-based dilemmas, focusing on issues such as human welfare, were most likely to be presented by women, whereas justice dilemmas were most likely to be presented by men. Gilligan and Attanucci suggested that it is more useful to look at these differences as simply that – differences – than to see them as arranged in some kind of hierarchy. In either case, the emphasis was on social responsibility, but there was a difference in how social responsibility was being interpreted.

We have seen, then, that the assumption that human reasoning is full of errors is one which is questionable, to say the least. It rests on the idea that the kind of limited, formal logic followed by a computer should be the ultimate goal of human reasoning too, and ignores the fact that human thinking takes place in a real context, in which social knowledge, empathy and interactive mechanisms can be just as important as formal, symbolic logic – or even more so. But there are other types of errors which human beings do make, some would say with alarming frequency. In the next section we will look at some of these.

Errors

As we go through life, we continually make errors of one sort or another. Reason (1990) proposed that, essentially, there are three different types of error that we make: (a) skill-based slips and lapses; (b) knowledge-based errors; and (c) rule-based errors. Reason argued that these types of errors differ on several dimensions, which are listed in Figure 4.12, and went on to develop a General Error Modelling System (GEMS) that allowed psychologists to examine the causes of these errors.

According to Reason, errors at the skill-based level mainly come

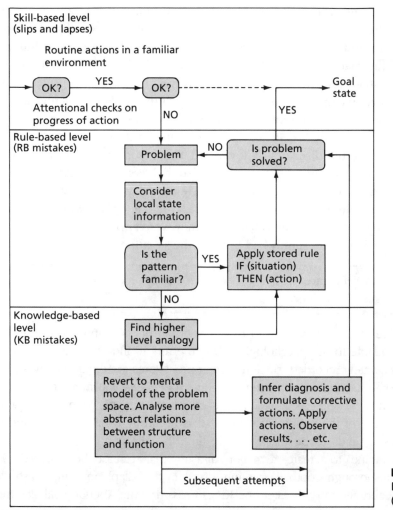

Figure 4.12 Dimensions of errors. (Reason, 1990.)

Figure 4.13 The General Error Modelling System (GEMS). (Reason, 1990.)

from monitoring failures – failing to pay attention to a complex task. This means that the action runs in its usual default pattern, rather than what is intended to happen – like setting out to drive to the shop and ending up on the road to work, because that is the more usual journey.

Mistakes at the knowledge-based and rule-based levels, Reason found, tend to be associated with problem-solving. Knowledge-based mistakes have their root in two aspects of human cognition. The first of these he referred to as bounded rationality – the way that we tend only to use a limited number of strategies to puzzle things out. The second source of knowledge-based mistakes derives simply from the fact that our knowledge for any problem is nearly always incomplete.

The GEMS model also suggests that problem-solvers tend to begin dealing with a new problem by trying to match it to a problem that they have met before – applying rules which are familiar. They only go on to the more laborious activity of developing novel solutions if the match does not fit. So rule-based mistakes tend to fall into two categories. The first category involves applying good rules in the wrong context, as is shown in many of the studies of mental set. The second category involves applying bad rules in the first place. As an example of this, Reason described the Zeebrugge ferry disaster, in which the directors of Townsend Thorenson saw their objectives as being concerned with keeping shareholders happy, rather than with ensuring that the ferries ran safely on a day-to-day basis. Since they knew little or nothing about the day-to-day operation of the ferries, this meant that the rules which they were applying in their decision-making were simply bad ones for the situation.

> **Key reference:** REASON, J. (1990) *Human Error.* Cambridge University Press, Cambridge.

Environment

One of the problems with research into errors is simply the lack of data available to the psychologists. Often, errors in industrial settings are not accurately recorded, since reporting procedures are often lengthy and the consequences of admitting error are sometimes enormous for the individual worker. As a result it is extremely difficult to build up a full picture of the pattern of errors that is occurring on a given site and the result tends to be that the only time that errors surface is when they combine to create a major disaster that cannot be ignored. The Hillsborough football stadium disaster, the Clapham train crash, the Zeebrugge ferry disaster, the Kings Cross fire, the Aberfan coal slag-heap disaster and many others all show a similar pattern: of many ignored minor errors eventually surfacing in a tragic and disastrous loss of life.

Early research into industrial accidents tended to focus on individual people, rather than on systems and practices of operation. Greenwood and Woods (1919) performed some of the earliest research into industrial accidents for the Industrial Fatigue Research Board during the First World War. As part of their study, they explored the idea that some individuals are 'accident prone', or more likely to have accidents than others. They found statistical distributions of accidents which seemed to support the idea of accident proneness, and gradually this became accepted as a stable characteristic of certain individuals.

However, as research became more extensive in the middle of the century, the idea of accident proneness was challenged. Some researchers (e.g. Arbous and Kerrich, 1951) argued that the initial

Herald of Free Enterprise	
Chain of events and active failures	*Contributing conditions and latent failures*
Herald is docked at No. 12 berth in Zeebrugge's inner harbour and is loading passengers and vehicles before making the crossing to Dover	This berth is not capable of loading both car decks (E and G) at the same time, having only a single ramp. Due to high water spring tides, the ramp could not be elevated sufficiently to reach E deck. To achieve this, it was necessary to trim the ship nosedown by filling trim ballast tanks Nos 14 and 3. Normal practice was to start filling No. 14 tank 2 hours before arrival. *(System failure)*
At 1805 on 6 March 1987, the Herald goes astern from the berth, turns to starboard, and proceeds to sea with both her inner and outer bow doors fully open	The most immediate cause is that the assistant bosun (whose job it was to close the doors) was asleep in his cabin, having just been relieved from maintenance and cleaning duties. *(Supervisory failure and unsuitable rostering)* The bosun, his immediate superior, was the last man to leave G deck. He noticed that the bow doors were still open, but did not close them, since he did not see that as part of his duties. *(Management failure)*
Chief officer checks that there are no passengers on G deck, and thinks he sees assistant bosun going to close doors (though testimony is confused on this point).	The chief officer, responsible for ensuring door closure, was also required (by company orders) to be on the bridge 15 minutes before sailing time. *(Management failure)* Because of delays at Dover, there was great pressure on crews to sail early. Memo from operations manager: 'put pressure on your first officer if you don't think he's moving fast enough ... sailing late out of Zeebrugge isn't on. It's 15 minutes early for us.' *(Management failure)* Company standing orders (ambiguously worded) appear to call for 'negative reporting'. If not told otherwise, the master should assume that all is well. Chief officer did not make a report, nor did the master ask him for one. *(Management failure)*
On leaving harbour, master increases speed. Water enters open bow doors and floods into G deck. At around 1827, Herald capsizes to port.	Despite repeated requests from the masters to the management, no bow door indicators were available on the bridge, and the master was unaware that he had sailed with bow doors open. Estimated cost of indicators was £400–500. *(Management failure)* Ship had chronic list to port. *(Management and technical failure)* Scuppers inadequate to void water from flooded G deck. *(Design and maintenance failure)* Top-heavy design of the Herald and other 'ro ro' ships in its class was inherently unsafe. *(Design failure)*

Figure 4.14 Reason's analysis of the Zeebrugge ferry disaster. (Reason, 1990.)

Figure 4.15 Reason (1990) identifies the main cause of the Zeebrugge disaster as 'management failure'.

research had failed to distinguish adequately between the different levels of risk run by people in different jobs. Other researchers performed their own studies and found different outcomes. For example, Adelstein (1952) studied accident rates among railway shunters and found that the 'random hypothesis' was better supported by these data – that people were equally likely to have accidents. Reason (1990) argued that the critical problem is often in the system design, or the result of inappropriate training or inappropriate management procedures, rather than individuals.

Work

With the rise of **ergonomics** – the study of efficiency and human–machine interaction – as a discipline, some research focused on how errors actually take place. Ergonomic investigations of physical factors leading to errors at work show a difference between two types of errors, which Davies and Shackleton (1975) described as commission errors and omission errors. Aspects of the working environment such as excessive and continuous machinery noise increase the likelihood that an individual will make commission errors – errors in which they respond incorrectly to information which has been presented to them. But individual factors such as loss of sleep produce omission errors, in which the person fails to notice that the information has been presented at all.

Another source of error in the relationship between operators and machines is the de-skilling of the workers. Bainbridge (1987) referred to this as the irony of automation. She pointed out that designers view human operators as unreliable and inefficient, and try to replace them wherever possible with automated devices. Yet, often, this policy leads directly to an increased number of errors and accidents. The paralysis of the London Ambulance Service as a direct result of the introduction of an

The importance of designing complex machinery to match the abilities of people became clear during the Second World War. An example of this comes from aviation, where, at the start of the war, the military concentrated on training men to fly aircraft rather than designing aircraft that could be flown by men. However, they discovered that even very experienced pilots were prone to make errors with the poorly designed control systems. For example, similar looking controls operating the landing gear and the steering flaps on some B-25 bombers were placed next to each other. The unfortunate consequence of this was that several B-25s were brought in to land without the landing gear in place and so landed on their bellies. The pilots believed that they had activated the landing gear, but in fact they had just steered the plane. Observations like this led to the development of aircraft controls that better match the capabilities of pilots.

Figure 4.16 The importance of sympathetic instrument design and location.

automated emergency call routing system in 1993 was a classic example of how this type of problem happens. There are two ironies here: the first being that many mistakes come from the designer's initial errors – systems are introduced which have not been properly worked out and which are actually unable to do what is required of them. In addition, Bainbridge points out, designers still leave people to do the difficult tasks, which cannot be automated so easily.

That does not mean that all automation is inappropriate. In an automated industrial plant the task of the operators is to monitor the system to ensure that it is functioning normally. People are, of course, not very well suited to carry out this task because of the known problems in maintaining **vigilance**, particularly on boring tasks. In the case of many routine and undemanding tasks, the use of machines is undoubtedly more efficient, and frees the human operators to adopt executive functions and take action in unpredicted circumstances. Also, this design means that the operators rarely get any practice in operating the system, unless something goes wrong. So the operators only take control in an emergency which suggests they need to be very highly trained and skilled.

vigilance More commonly referred to as sustained attention: relates to the ability of an individual to maintain concentration on a task.

Bainbridge went on to describe a near-disaster in an American nuclear installation. Once it became clear to the operators that a problem had developed, they congregated in the control room and took out the emergency procedure book – which was two-and-a-half inches thick! The assistant shift supervisor read aloud from the book while other operators checked out the various instructions. This less than satisfactory arrangement was further compromised when the assistant supervisor went to investigate why one part of the plant was failing, without following the instructions for how to deal with the consequences of this failure. As the situation deteriorated, the operators improvised and finally returned the reactor to a safe condition. If this had developed into a major disaster, no doubt individuals would have been blamed, yet really it would have arisen in an error in the design of the human–machine environment, with the failure to train staff explicitly in emergency procedures.

One of the most important areas of concern in error making is driving skill. Although most of us are never involved in an accident that is our fault ('the tree came out and hit me'), we make minor errors of judgement every time we get behind the wheel – like misjudging where the centre line of the vehicle is and driving a little closer to a parked car than we meant to.

Vernor and Tomerlin (1989) looked at the sources of misperception of a motor car's centre line. In their study, research participants were asked to make estimates of the car's centre line, and then follow instructions

Environment

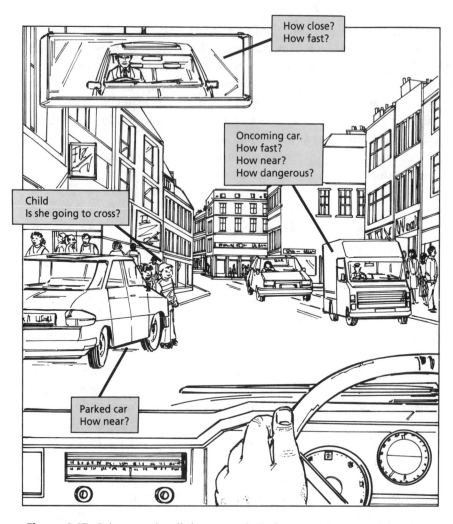

Figure 4.17 Drivers continually have to make judgements about speed, location and intention. Errors are inevitable.

like 'press brake pedal' which were given to them visually. From time to time during the exercise, the experimenter would shout 'Stop'. The researchers found a significant difference in misperceived centre line between cars, with most misperceptions being to the right (the cars were all left-hand drive). They did not, however, find any connections with pedal error (hitting the accelerator instead of the brake), make of car or driver gender.

There is some question, however, how far studies of this kind are actually useful when it comes to letting us know about the problems in real life. The problem with a simulation study is that it often does not match the real situation very closely – for example, in this study, the drivers were asked to keep their feet flat on the floor between actions, which is not at all what someone who is really driving would do.

Triggs and Berenyl (1982) took a more realistic approach when they were investigating the perception of speed and difference. Participants sat in the passenger seat of a car, wearing a helmet fitted with a translucent visor and wearing ear shields to block out sounds. They were asked to raise the visor by the driver on four occasions during each drive, at four different speeds. The tests were also carried out under three conditions: day, night with low beam headlights; and night with high beam headlights. Participants had a one-second view of the road before writing down their estimations of the speed of the vehicle.

Triggs and Berenyl found that speed judgements made during the two night-time conditions were more accurate than those made in daytime, although people consistently underestimated speeds across all conditions. The implication is that something associated with night driving helps us to judge speed, and the researchers suggested that this might be delineation markings like cats-eyes, or the relative highlighting of road lines. More importantly, however, the study also implies that underestimation of vehicle speeds may be an important factor in road accidents.

Errors do not just happen – they can be significantly reduced, as long as we take the trouble to understand where they are coming from. Chen and Dhar (1990) observed 30 people performing subject-based searches in an online catalogue system. In particular, they noted how reference librarians helped users with subject search and what the problems were that the users encountered. The research participants were 30 business school students, who had been asked to perform a search for documents within a subject area of their interest. The students were asked to think aloud during the interaction. This was taped, and the interaction between the user and system logged. Then the subjects were interviewed briefly about the search process and problems encountered.

The results revealed between one and seven misconceptions per user, which produced errors, either by stopping them from finding the relevant material or by prolonging the search. These misconceptions fell into three categories: about the subject area itself; about the classification scheme; and about the system capabilities. The researchers developed a taxonomy of these misconceptions and suggested that if attention was paid to the taxonomy of misconceptions when people were designing library catalogue systems, the number of errors could be effectively minimized. Doing so would provide a retrieval system which could become a useful information intermediary capable of providing interactive support to a variety of users, not least because it would enable them to make effective and relevant decisions during the course of their search.

One of the main sources of errors which we encounter in everyday life is plain, simple boredom. When attention wanders, it is easy to commit quite major errors and these can sometimes have dramatic effects. As human factors specialists acknowledge, part of the design of good human–machine systems involves ensuring that the task which is required of the human being is not so mind-numbingly tedious as to encourage the person to fail to pay attention to important information.

Sustained attention

Research into both selective and sustained attention became particularly important as a result of the development and application of new technology in the Second World War. The implementation of the radar defence network, for instance, meant that people would have to scan screens for very long periods of time and detect any abnormal signal which showed up. The task was complicated by the existence of variable amounts of 'noise' – very high waves showing up on coastal radar, static interference, and so on.

Consequently, it became essential to discover how long a human being could reasonably be expected to stay alert and operating at peak performance while undertaking what was a relatively unstimulating, but very important, task. Mackworth (1950) conducted numerous studies using signal detection tasks, in which the subject

Figure 4.18 The task of spotting changes on the radar display might appear to be straightforward. However, the task requires considerable skill, judgement and vigilance.

was required to press a key when they noticed an anomalous signal: an unexpected image on a radar screen, a double-jump made by a second-hand pointer; a tone which lasted slightly longer than other tones in a series. Attention was assessed operationally: the absence of mistakes meant that the subject was attending to the task.

Mackworth identified a number of factors enhancing performance on vigilance tasks. These included characteristics of the task itself; such as the intensity and duration of the signal, and the probability of occurrence of signals; factors affecting the individual doing the task, such as feedback on their performance (whether true or false); introversion as a personality trait and the use of stimulant drugs; and factors which concerned the situation that the person was in – like whether there were others in the room and how quiet the room was. Perhaps not surprisingly, one of the most significant factors influencing how accurately the person would perform at the task was the presence of their boss, or superior officer in the case of military personnel!

Key reference: MACKWORTH, N. H. (1950) Researches on the measurement of human performance. *Medical Research Council Special Report,* **268**, HMSO, London.

There are a number of jobs where sustained attention is essential. Pilots, train drivers and air traffic controllers all need to display sustained attention because any slip or loss of concentration can result in a major disaster. Thackray, Jones and Touchstone (1973) looked at the characteristics of individuals in sustaining attention, to see whether some were unable to sustain attention under monotonous conditions. The 50 male college students in the study performed a monotonous but perceptually demanding task for approximately 30 minutes without rest. They had previously been tested to see how easily distracted they were, using a questionnaire.

Work

All the research participants showed changes in respiration, heart-rate variability and skin conductance during the task period. But, interestingly, and counter-intuitively, the researchers found that those participants who reported themselves as easily distracted did not show lapses of attention during the task, whereas those who had scored low in 'distractibility' showed a decline in attention. The researchers suggested that their data implied that certain people would find it difficult to sustain attention in low task-load conditions, and would therefore be more likely to commit errors or be able to deal with a sudden emergency. However, it seems to be more likely that studies involving self-report questionnaires – and indeed college students – are not really a good equivalent for what, say, a real air traffic controller is doing. There is, after all, a considerable difference in motivation between the two.

Davies (1970) discussed the difference between laboratory studies of monitoring and the real-life situation in the industrial setting. In such situations, it is often not feasible to provide knowledge of results, which Mackworth showed to be one of the most effective way of reducing performance decrement. But injecting artificial signals into the task, or providing frequent rest breaks, seem to be almost as effective in reducing a decline in performance. Davies argued that these, particularly the latter, were more practical for a real industrial setting.

Health

In a rather more **ecologically valid** study by Orton and Gruzelier (1989), 20 junior hospital doctors completed a battery of performance tests at the end of a normal working day or after working for up to 31 continuous hours with reduced sleep. The tests included a measure of vigilance performance in which the subjects had to detect the occurrence of the letter x, but only when it had been preceded by the letter f, in a sequence of random presentations of letters. The researchers found that after working long hours, reaction times on the vigilance task were significantly slower and more variable than after a normal day's work.

ecological validity *A way of assessing how valid a measure or test is (i.e. whether it really measures what it is supposed to measure), which is concerned with whether the measure or test is really like its counterpart in the real, everyday world. In other words, whether it is truly realistic or not.*

This study provides strong evidence that working continuously may have an adverse effect on doctors, and may be detrimental to their welfare and that of their patients. Since a modern hospital doctor is typically dealing with a considerable amount of highly technical machinery, and is also involved in making decisions which can sometimes be quite literally about life and death, the fact that junior doctors are forced to work for extremely lengthy periods at a time amounts to a very serious medical risk on the part of the general public, not to mention the detrimental effect for the doctors themselves.

Society

It is a common complaint of parents and teachers that children have a limited attention span. Popular folklore would have us believe that a combination of television and Sonic the Hedgehog is destroying the cognitive abilities of our children, although evidence on this is hard to come by. Attention has also attracted the interest of criminologists, in the form of a syndrome known as **attention deficit disorder** (ADD), which involves poor attention, impulsivity and hyperactivity. Children with this condition are said to experience 'chronic success deprivation' – in other words, not being good at anything – and a range of behavioural problems, especially in school.

attention deficit disorder *A disorder characterized by marked impulsivity, inattention and hyperactivity.*

In a longitudinal study, Farringdon (1990) found that ADD in 8–10-year-old boys was a predictor of adult criminal behaviour. It also links with a higher than average risk of unemployment, marital instability and criminal behaviour in adulthood. The question is, however, what produces the attentional deficit disorder – research shows that ADD interacts with a number of other factors including socioeconomic deprivation and the quality of the home situation, and some psychologists argue that all that is really happening with this 'syndrome' is a form of labelling, whereby the individual child (or its physiology) is blamed for what are really social problems.

Fry (1983) observed 30 fifth-and sixth-grade (age 9 to 11 years) teacher–pupil interactions in classrooms for a 4-month period, to see if there were differences in teachers' interactions with 'problem' and non-problem children. Fry found that a certain deterioration was noticeable in teachers' interactions with these children, in that problem children received more displays of negative emotion from their teachers and less encouraging feedback. Observations of these children's interactions showed that this teacher behaviour was linked with an increase in serious misdemeanours and a decline in sustained attention. Fry concluded that the critical factor in low levels of sustained attention on the part of children is the interaction between teacher and pupil, which ultimately can produce attentional 'deficits'.

Education

Olney, Holbrook and Batra (1991) looked at how people pay attention to adverts and, in particular, at whether people's attitudes had an effect on their attention. The research participants in the study were MBA business students, who were asked to watch a number of different advertisements. The researchers measured selective attention by recording the viewing time of various adverts, in terms of 'zipping' (fast-forwarding pre-recorded adverts) and 'zapping' (changing channels while an advert is on). Attitude was measured in terms of three components: hedonism; utilitarianism; and interestingness, which are considered to relate to the 'pleasure and arousal' produced by the appeal of the advertisements.

Not surprisingly, the researchers found that the uniqueness of the advert had a great effect on the attention levels. Advertisements which elicited emotions in the viewer were linked with high attention levels, but those which contained a lot of facts were avoided. In terms of attitudes, they found that hedonism and interestingness had a great effect on attention, but utilitarianism does not – in other words, people use advertisements for entertainment and interest, but not as worthy sources of information. The implication of the study, therefore, is that advertisers have to keep coming up with novel and varied ideas for advertising. The study also showed that emotion-provoking images and situations were more efficient in the capturing of consumers' attention than product information, which reflects the trend in advertising for obscure images and very little, if any, mention of the product.

Sport

Understandably, the ability to sustain attention for prolonged periods of time has been a focus of research in sports psychology. In many sporting fields, such as snooker and motor racing, the ability to concentrate without distraction is vital to success – indeed, in pretty well all competitive sports it is essential that the competitor maintains a high level of concentration – the difference between success and failure can be a single momentary lapse. Sports psychology's interest in attention has led to the development of a number of different techniques for training athletes to focus their attention on the task at hand and also to investigations of how that attentional focus can become disrupted.

Jones (1988) compared levels of anxiety in cricketers leading up to an important match. The players were asked about their level of anxiety four days, one day and one hour prior to the start of the match, and immediately before batting (one is left wondering whether this somewhat intrusive procedure influenced the outcome of the match). Those players who showed an increase in anxiety just before batting also made more errors, and Jones suggested that this was because anxiety interferes with the player's ability to sustain a focused attention on the task, by introducing distracting thoughts.

The methods used to explore attention in this study raise a number of questions about how attention can be measured in sport. Cox (1990) argued that these fall into three kinds: behavioural; physiological; and self-report, which are described in Figure 4.19. Some psychologists have tended to use the idea of personality traits when exploring success in sport, although, as with so many other examples of the trait approach, these are often of limited value in terms of their approach, since they ignore the changing motivational variables in different situations.

For example, Nideffer (1976) developed a test of attentional and interpersonal style, which aimed to assess the width of a person's attentional focus (wide or narrow) and the direction of the focus (internal or external). Bergandi and Witting (1988) administered Nideffer's test to 335 college athletes from 17 different squads. They found that those athletes

Figure 4.19 Three main ways in which attention in sport can be measured.

> **1. Behavioural methods**
> For example, the reaction time problem techniques; in this procedure, the attention demands of a primary task are estimated by measuring a person's performance on a secondary reaction time task.
>
> **2. Physiological indicators**
> For example, measures of arousal.
>
> **3. Self-report methods**
> For example, the Test of Attentional and Interpersonal Style (TAIS) developed by Nideffer (1976).

who scored high on 'attentionally affective' and low on 'overloaded' and 'performance anxiety' factors were more prone to injury than athletes with different scoring combinations.

However, it is uncertain how much value there is in assuming that attentional focus remains constant for a given individual. For example, Hemery (1988) reported how champion tennis players tended to use a wide-range attentional focus when the ball is in the other player's hand ready for serving, but to narrow it down to a tight focus the moment the ball was hit. In other words, champion players (as opposed to college athletes) were able to adopt the appropriate attentional focus for their situation, rather than just having a fixed attentional style. Of course, it is possible that this may represent a qualitative difference between first-class players and amateurs; but it is equally possible that the use of personality trait measurements leads us to think that there is a consistency in how people act which does not really exist.

Decision-making

Research into decision-making has tended to focus on how we use probabilities to make decisions – how we weigh up advantages and disadvantages or judge whether a course of action is likely to be successful. A typical example might involve something like deciding which subject to study at college. This would involve a number of factors, like the advantages or disadvantages of going away from home, the probability of getting on the desired course and some consideration of the outcomes of that choice: 'If I choose to study psychology, what are the chances of my getting a job at the end of the course?'

The logical, computational approach is to assign plus or minus values to each option, add them up, subtract one from the other and choose the option which comes out on top. But in reality, we do not operate as mechanistically as that. Instead, we use **heuristics** – strategies which will aid us in decision-making – and it is these heuristics which have formed the focus for much research into decision-making.

There are three major heuristics which human beings use in decision-making: representativeness; availability; and anchoring. Representativeness is concerned with how or whether we estimate an example of something to be typical of other similar ones. It is easy for us to think our own particular sample is typical of all the rest, when really it may not be. We use the availability heuristic when we estimate how common different situations or cases are: the more easily

Tversky and Kahneman (1974) asked people to estimate various quantities. For example, 'Estimate the number of African countries in the United Nations'.

Before asking the question the experimenter spun a 'wheel of fortune' while the subject watched. The wheel came to rest at a number (between 1 and 100) entirely at random. The subjects were asked to indicate whether the answer to the question was higher or lower than the number on the wheel and then to give their answer to the question by moving upwards or downwards from the wheel number.

The study found that subjects used the wheel number as an anchor; for example, if the wheel had stopped on 2 they might estimate 25, whereas if the wheel stopped on 65 they might estimate 45.

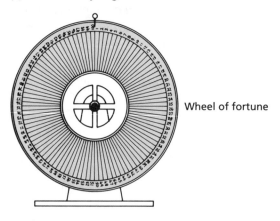

Wheel of fortune

Figure 4.20 Anchoring. Judgements can be anchored in chance events.

we can remember them, the more likely we are to see them as happening often. Anchoring is concerned with the way that our first guess tends to set a 'baseline' for later judgements and so influences whether estimates tend to be high or low.

In addition to the study of heuristics, research into decision-making has also explored the effects of situations like **entrapment** – when a person, committee or government feel unable to withdraw from a losing situation because they have invested too much in it already; and the way that over-confidence also exerts a powerful influence over the decisions which we make.

The heuristical model of decision-making is concerned with looking at the logic or otherwise of the decisions which human beings make. But human decisions are also affected by a number of other factors. For example, the decision about which subject to study at college will be influenced by choices that friends make, the self-image of the person deciding, the influence of parents and teachers, prevailing social representations of different subjects and many other factors. These influences are hard to quantify and hard to fit into a

entrapment *The way that people, committees, etc. can become unable to withdraw from unwinnable situations because they feel that they have already invested too much in them to give up.*

logical model of decision-making. They can also change from moment to moment.

In studying decision-making, then, we have to take into account social factors, past experience, emotions and, on some occasions, sheer wilfulness – it is not unknown for people to say: 'I know it's stupid, and I know it will probably end in failure, but I'm going to try anyway'. It might even be argued that the search for the underlying structure of human decision-making could be better explored by social psychologists rather than cognitive psychologists.

> **Key reference:** TVERSKY, A. and KAHNEMANN, D. (1974) Judgements under Uncertainty: heuristics and biases. *Science,* **185**, 1124–31.

In everyday life, we make decisions all the time. Sometimes, these are based on minimal thought and sometimes on careful deliberations, but making decisions is a daily imperative. Shall I get up? Shall I have Marmite on my toast? Shall I go to work? Shall I replace my old car or save up for a house? Shall I put on my new pullover? Often, we only become aware of the sheer amount of decision-making which normal life involves when it is taken away, for some reason. For many people, the worst part of being in hospital is not the medical treatment, but the total loss of control over day-to-day decision-making: having to be passive (or patient, as it were) in the institution and to accept what happens.

For long-term institutions, this can be very serious, since being without the ability to make everyday decisions or effective plans can produce the syndrome known as **institutionalization** – characterized by apathy, lack of initiative, submissiveness, a loss of individuality and a lack of interest in the future (Barton, 1976). Herbert (1986) described 19 different types of decisions which may be allowed or restricted in an institution. These are listed in Figure 4.21. Although this is not an exhaustive list, it gives some indication as to how far a given institution may restrict or encourage decision-making on the part of residents.

Society

The idea of the therapeutic community was aimed at challenging these effects of institutionalization. One model, described by Rapaport (1960), emphasized five features, which are listed in Figure 4.22. These principles were based on the idea of maximizing the amount of control which residents had over their everyday lives, in order to challenge the effects of institutionalization and help people to be able to cope with day-to-day living in the outside world.

institutionalization A *pattern of experience and behaviours associated with people in institutional settings, in particular a lessened sense of personal agency.*

Decision-making has also occupied the attention of consumer specialists, because we make so many purchasing decisions every week. One trip around the local supermarket requires us to choose which type of

What time to get up and go to bed
What to wear
What to eat for breakfast and other meals
Planning future meals
Whether to make a drink or snack
Whether to visit the local shops
Whether to go to the pictures
How to spend own money
When to have a bath
When to have a haircut
Whether to have medicine
Deciding arrangement of own room
Whether to smoke
Whether to play the radio or TV
When to invite friends in
Whether to have a sexual relationship with a friend
Planning decoration or repair of the place
Deciding how to care for or control others
Deciding policy

Figure 4.21 Decisions which may be allowed or restricted in an institution. (Herbert, 1986.)

- **active rehabilitation** as opposed to custodialism

- **democratization** shared decision-making between the unit's members

- **permissiveness** that distressing or deviant behaviour should be tolerated rather than suppressed

- **communalism** that there should be an informal climate with close but never exclusive relationships, and

- **reality confrontation** that patients should continually be given interpretations of their behaviour as other members of the community see it.

Figure 4.22 Features of the therapeutic community. (Rapaport, 1960.)

each product we are going to buy: the total sum of decisions made can be huge. But we do not always make each decision fresh each time: we often rely on habits, favourite brands, and what we have done in the past – 'Let's have a change this week...' – to reduce the cognitive load when we go shopping.

Consumer

Cultural aspects of family role and structure can influence decision-making, too. O'Guinn, Faber and Imperia (1986) asked 250 Mexican–American and 250 Anglo wives, living in a medium-sized city in the south-western United States, about the purchase of 8 different goods and services. They found that ethnicity significantly affected the women's perceptions of family decision-making roles, in ways that had nothing to do with other variables, like income, education or employment status. There were, for instance, stronger perceptions of the husband having dominance over the family's decision-making among Mexican–American families than among Anglo families. Anglo households tended to emphasize family decision-making as being a joint process.

But that does not mean that all the Mexican–American wives were living strictly stereotypical roles. The researchers found that there had been a number of changes away from husband-dominant decisions which had occurred over the years – even though most of them had lived their whole lives in the United States. These changes seemed to have produced an increase in joint decision-making in the families. The researchers took this change as evidence of the impressive power of cultural influence on decision-making. But there are a number of reasons why we might want to question this conclusion. For example, the researchers tended to assume that the differences came from the ethnic culture, but did not control for basic socioeconomic disparities. In addition, to make a full evaluation of this it would be necessary to get the husband's perceptions as well, not just one side of the partnership.

In another study of consumer choice behaviour, Hayer and Cobb-Walgren (1988) looked at the decision strategies used by shoppers. In one study they observed 542 single adult shoppers in 3 supermarkets, while a further study involved asking 175 consumers from a medium-sized south-western city (124 women, 51 men) to report their likely choices of 19 different products, and followed this up by an additional questionnaire. The results of both studies showed considerable variation in the rules which shoppers used to make their choices. The most popular principles which shoppers used were judgements of the performance of the product and their satisfaction with it. Habit was the least popular, and price was not as important as the researchers had expected, either.

The findings provide some tentative support for the idea that consumer choice tactics are influenced by a number of factors, including how the product is presented. They also showed that shoppers employ different heuristics across product purchases. The researchers also suggested that their findings implied that some people are more influenced by contingent factors, such as display or product reputation, than others.

Figure 4.23 How do you choose your washing powder? Habit? Colour? Smell? Cost? Advertiser's message? Name? Because your mum used it?

Work

The ability to make successful decisions is also the concern of organizational consultants. Driskell and Salas (1991) studied 78 male volunteers at the Navy Technical School. The aim of the study was to investigate how status and stress affect decision-making. Each volunteer was informed that his team members were of either of a higher or lower military status in comparison to his own position. They were then required to perform a decision-making task – judging which of two chequerboard patterns contained the most white – under either normal or acute stress. The researchers found that those in the low status condition were much more likely to accept their partner's choice than to stay with their own, and the introduction of the stress factor made them even more willing to acquiesce.

The conclusion, then, was that group decision-making was significantly influenced by the status of fellow group members, and particularly so in stressful situations. Although this might seem relatively unimportant, there are a number of situations in which it could be important that someone makes their own judgements heard, even if they are of lower status than someone else, such as on a flight crew.

Group decisions are almost as common as individual decisions in everyday life, and can range from decisions made by a family about where to go for their annual holiday, to a decision about the future of a company plant made by a board of directors, to the decision that someone has been guilty of a crime made by a jury. When we are making decisions as a group, a number of social mechanisms come into play, and we will be looking at these more closely in Chapters 7 and 8. But some research into group decision-making has looked explicitly at how making decisions can be influenced by the group itself.

Society

A detailed analysis of jury decision-making was carried out by Hastie *et al.* (1983). They showed 69 different simulated juries a videotape of the same case, constructed in 3 1-hour programmes. This simulated trial for murder was based on a real trial but used actors and was edited to present a summary of the most important scenes for the simulation juries to use as information. The jury was allowed to return one of five possible verdicts: first degree murder, second degree murder, manslaughter, not guilty or 'hung' (in other words, the jury were unable to agree on what the verdict should be).

In the trial that the simulation was based on, the verdict was second degree murder. However, as can be seen from Figure 4.24, a surprising 38 out of 69 of the simulation juries came to a different conclusion. The researchers compared those juries who got the answer 'right' by deciding that it was second degree murder with those who got it 'wrong', by opting for either first degree murder or manslaughter. The data suggested

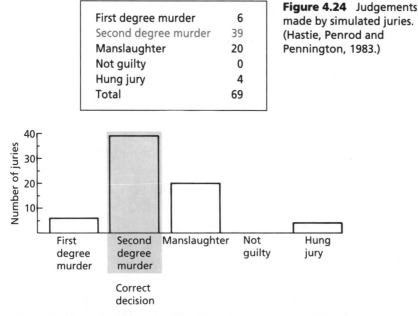

First degree murder	6
Second degree murder	39
Manslaughter	20
Not guilty	0
Hung jury	4
Total	69

Figure 4.24 Judgements made by simulated juries. (Hastie, Penrod and Pennington, 1983.)

Figure 4.25 Judgements made by simulated juries.

that the 'wrong' verdicts were associated with errors of comprehension and memory, for example in the recall of legal definitions and in details of witness testimony. In other words, those who had remembered the details correctly and understood what was going on made the 'correct' verdict.

This study tends to assume that the task of a jury is always to arrive at the right decision – the truth. However, a relatively cursory look at legal precedents shows that often, decisions made by juries have been over-turned by later evidence, which has shown that they were actually inac-curate (particularly in the West Midlands). Reskin and Visher (1986) argued that the task of arriving at the correct decision actually takes second place to the importance of obtaining agreement between the jury members. Reskin and Visher looked at the results of 38 real trials (not simulations) involving sexual assault. They evaluated the strength and type of the evidence, both during the trials and according to the press at the end of the trials.

The outcome of the study showed that where there was 'hard' evidence of assault (for example, injuries to the woman or possession of a weapon by the assailant), then a verdict of guilty was most likely. But when 'hard' evidence was not available, the outcome tended to be affected by various subjective responses to the character of the woman victim such as whether she worked or not, how attractive she was, whether she was 'careless' on the occasion of the assault, and so on.

Although these factors are irrelevant to the legal judgment of proof, the jury would use them when it lacked conclusive 'hard' evidence, because of the importance which they attached to reaching agreement between the members of the jury.

Sometimes, too, people make major life decisions which change the course of their lives. Cusson and Pinsonneault (1986) interviewed 17 Canadian ex-robbers (self-defined) to discover the reasons why they had stopped their criminal activity. They found that the decision was usually triggered off by a 'shock' – something which highlights the costs of criminal behaviour and leads the person to a reassessment or recalculation of the relative gains of crime and going straight. The shocks described by the interviewees included being wounded by the police and being assaulted by an accomplice. The researchers also found that estimates of the likelihood of punishment, dread of further time lost in prison, fear of longer sentences and fear of the uncertainty of it all increased with age and experience of the criminal justice system, until, eventually, going straight appeared to be a more attractive alternative.

A decision that has less time for consideration and less room for manoeuvre, is the decision American police officers have to make whether to pull out their guns or not. Holzworth and Pipping (1985) investigated the judgement and decision processes of 1 female and 12 male police officers facing the possible use of deadly force. The police officers were given a series of hypothetical situations, such as dealing with a disabled motorist, a suspicious person, a domestic argument etc. They were then asked to indicate the likelihood that they would draw their firearms in response to the situation.

According to the police officers, whether they would use firearms or not depended more on the nature of the offence and on the way that the person was acting, than on the characteristics of person with whom they were dealing. Whether bystanders were present or not did not matter, they said. However, the researchers also found that the police officers' judgements were somewhat inconsistent and individualistic, and it seems very clear that a self-report measure of this kind would be unlikely to represent what would really happen on the street. A finding which might perhaps have slightly greater validity was that the researchers also found a significant negative relationship between years of experience and the tendency to draw a firearm – the more experienced officers were less likely to threaten people with guns than their newer colleagues.

One type of decision which has attracted a lot of research attention is the democratic decision to vote for one political party rather than another. Felsenthal and Brichta (1985) discussed how a rational voter may sometimes decide to vote for a candidate or party that does not constitute her or his first preference – a procedure known as tactical voting (as opposed to 'sincere voting', in which people always vote for their first preference regardless of how others are likely to vote).

Felsenthal and Brichta interviewed 1024 Israeli citizens about their voting behaviour and demographic background, and categorized them as either sincere or tactical voters. They found found that tactical voters, although in the minority (only 121 of the total sample), tended to have a significantly higher educational level than the 855 sincere voters, and that they also tended to believe that polls influence voters' decisions and so delayed their own final voting decisions. They also were more likely to support small parties, but still tended to be reasonably consistent in their general party support.

Making decisions also sometimes involves a definite level of risk. In one study of medical decision-making, Elstein *et al.* (1986) gave 50 doctors 12 imaginary case descriptions of menopausal women. The case studied carried information about the likelihood of the women contracting cancer, vasomotor symptoms and osteoporosis. The doctors were then asked to estimate the probability that they would prescribe oestrogen (hormone replacement) therapy for the patient. The logical move would be to recommend treatment on the basis of applying a logical decision-making procedure, using the probabilities of various outcomes which had been given. But Elstein *et al.* found that doctors placed undue importance on the risk of patients getting cancer, which meant that they tended to be unwilling to prescribe any treatment at all. The way that we judge risks can exert a powerful influence on our decision-making and it is worth looking at this in greater detail.

Risk

Risk taking is all about making decisions which involve some possible loss, but which also offer the possibility of some obvious or hidden gain. A number of suggestions have been put forward to explain risk taking behaviour. Panagopoulos (1992) classified these into four main categories. In this categorization, *reductive explanations* look for the reasons why people take risks in biological or genetic features, like suggesting that risk taking is sensation-seeking: an attempt to maximize stimulation and therefore generate a physiological state of arousal.

A second set of theories to explain risk taking may be classified as *causal explanations,* which suggest that future rewards may be the key feature in why people take risks – or alternatively, that high risk taking behaviour can be considered as 'indirect self-destructive behaviour' that acts as a defence mechanism against depression and despair. Essentially, risk taking is seen as purposeful, or functional for the individual or group taking the risk.

Constructive explanations of risk taking look for causes within the individual's needs for **self-actualization** or self-determination. Sometimes, therefore, they are related to a conscious decision to test one's own limits, and/or to ensure that one has made the most of opportunities. This would seem to be a major motivation for risk takers such as mountain-climbers or cavers, but can also apply to those who make unusual life decisions, such as to leave their paid employment and form their own business.

A fourth group of explanations, *historical explanations,* look at the influence of social reference groups, cultural norms, and also how the development of cognitive processes might affect people's personal evaluation of risk. For example, cultural norms can exert a strong influence on the choice of sexual behaviour and can therefore be a significant influence in the reluctance of some groups of people to change from high AIDS-risk behaviour to lower risk behaviour.

The risks involved in certain behaviours can be calculated relatively accurately. For example, we know that smoking cigarettes will increase the risk of heart disease, poor circulation, limb amputation, lung cancer and a range of other health problems. But, there is a marked difference between the computation of health statistics and whether we perceive ourselves to be at risk. One of the most obvious examples of this is in responses to travel. Some people find air travel nerve-racking and fear the consequences of an accident. Yet the same people do not express the same fear of car travel, even though there is actually a much higher chance of death or injury. As a consequence, a large amount of research has focused on looking at the disparity between statistical risks, and perceived risks, and evaluating how real and perceived risks influence our behavioural choices.

> **Key reference:** YATES, F. (1992) *Risk-taking Behavior.* Wiley, Chichester.

Sport

The arousal-seeking feature of risk taking has often been seen as an important motivator in sport. Smith, Ptacek and Smoll (1992) investigated sensation seeking in a study of high school athletes. Interestingly, they found that athletes who were low in sensation seeking also showed a link between unpleasant sporting events – like losing badly – and time lost in injury afterwards. Those who scored highly on sensation seeking measures did not lose injury time after unpleasant events. The researchers suggested that sensation seeking as a trait has a potential stress-buffering effect.

It is questionable, however, how useful looking for 'risky' personality traits really is. Leon, McNally and Ben-Porath (1989) studied the personality characteristics, mood and coping patterns in a successful North Pole Expedition team. This kind of activity involves considerable personal risk, with real dangers of permanent physical damage or even death, so the researchers were interested to see whether the people who choose to take such risks have distinctive personality characteristics. The researchers administered a battery of personality tests to the members of a North Pole expedition team, which consisted of 7 men and 1 woman, aged between 26 and 41, prior to their departure, and also asked the explorers to complete a mood-scale test during the expedition.

The findings showed that the explorers scored low on measures of stress reactivity, anxiety and depression, and relatively high on measures of achievement orientation, self-control and feelings of well-being. In other words, their scores demonstrated good psychological adjustment, but showed little evidence of sensation seeking or risk-taking tendencies – suggesting that looking for 'risk-taking traits' is probably not an appropriate way to understand why people take risks. Interestingly, the study also showed that the coping strategies which the explorers used during the expedition were mainly centred on the cognitive activities of planning and reappraising which we looked at in Chapter 2. Effective social support in this highly task-oriented group did not seem to involve a great deal of sharing of personal feelings.

A number of studies have shown the clear personal benefits of encouraging risk taking. A common part of management training in many

Work

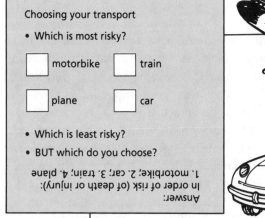

Choosing your transport

- Which is most risky?

  [ ] motorbike   [ ] train

  [ ] plane   [ ] car

- Which is least risky?
- BUT which do you choose?

Answer:
In order of risk (of death or injury):
1. motorbike; 2. car; 3. train; 4. plane

Figure 4.26 Risk taking.

large companies involve adventure-based experiential learning, much like outward-bound courses. The participants spend some time in a rural environment, and pursue challenging and sometimes risky activities such as mountain-climbing, white-water rafting or caving. The common belief among those who send their managers on such courses is that they encourage the development of initiative, team-building and decision-making skills.

There is relatively little evidence that such skills do actually transfer back to the organizational context, but it is apparent that the courses do involve considerable personal benefit, particularly in terms of personal development. Gall (1987) discussed the benefits of these courses for managers and argued that the key is getting people to risk trying something they are sure they cannot do. The heightened sense of **self-effi-cacy** which results from this achievement then contributes to confidence and a greater sense of self-worth. Gall went on to discuss how studies have shown that a by-product of these 'adventure' programmes has been the subsequent reduction of alcohol and drug abuse by participants. Those who are initially sent on such courses are often resistant at first, and Gall identified a number of sources for this resistance, including fears of physical risk and misunderstanding of the proper applications of the training

Environment

The social judgement of risk has been found to be totally unrelated to real risk in judgements of environmental dangers. Baird (1986) examined factors affecting risk estimates and tolerance among people who were directly exposed to environmental health risks. Baird distributed questionnaires at public hearings about proposed air-pollution standards for an arsenic-emitting copper smelter in Tacoma, Washington. Approximately 80% of the area residents who attended the hearings completed the questionnaires, which meant that the responses of 347 people were analysed.

Baird found that the amount of factual knowledge of formal risk estimates and proposed standards people had was irrelevant to how risky they judged the smelter to be. Similarly, how close a person lived to the smelter was not related either. What was more important in terms of whether they judged the smelter to be an actual risk for themselves was actually much more irrelevant information, including the benefits which they expected to come from the smelter (for example, increased local employment), a personal acceptance or denial of vulnerability, judgements about whether the exposure was voluntary or not and the individual's general environmental attitudes. In other words, judgements of risk had little or nothing to do with scientific evidence or factual information about the pollution, but everything to do with how the person saw the social influences on the decision which they were being asked to take.

A different kind of research into risk concerns how people deal with stressful life events. Bereavement is a universal experience, yet there can be many problems in working through it. There are four main areas that affect the pattern of recovery from bereavement: the type of death; the characteristics of the relationship between the deceased and the bereaved; the characteristics of the bereaved; and the social circumstances. Each of these factors carries its own risks, which are described in Figure 4.27.

Health

Health risks are something that we all take. 'Oh well, you've got to die some time,' you might say as you eat your third cream cake after the fish and chip supper which you picked up after five pints of lager in the Dog and Partridge. We are constantly being bombarded with information on health, and the risks to ourselves, our families and our environment. Why, then, do we respond to some risks and not others? Ferguson and Valenti (1991) explored individual differences in risk taking, to see

Type of death	Cause for blame on survivor
	Sudden/unexpected/untimely death
	Painful/horrifying/mismanaged death
Characteristics of the relationship	Symbiotic/dependent relationship
	Ambivalent relationship
	Spouse dies
	Child under 20 dies
	Parent dies (esp. mother) leaving young children
	Parent dies leaving older unmarried adult
Characteristics of the bereaved	Grief-prone personality
	Insecure, over-anxious
	Previous psychiatric illness
	Excessively angry
	Excessively self-reproachful
	Physically disabled/ill
	Previous unresolved loss
	Inability to express feelings
Social circumstances	Family absent/seen as unsupportive
	Detached from cultural/religious support system
	Unemployed
	Dependent children at home
	Low socioeconomic status
	Other losses

Figure 4.27 Risk factors in bereavement. Factors are ranked in approximate order of importance in each section. (Hodgkinson and Stewart, 1991.)

Figure 4.28 All these constitute risks to your health. How 'sensible' can you be?

whether it was linked with different ways of getting messages across to the general public.

In their study, 506 adults were asked to complete 2 surveys, which looked at a number of different message variables about risk, including the kind of targets who were at risk and how people had been informed about them. The researchers found that their sample tended to fall into three groups, which they classified as adventurous risk takers, impulsive risk takers and rebellious risk takers. They found that only those in the adventurous risk-taking group would seek out information: those in the rebellious and impulsive groups did not bother – and the impulsive group scored in ways which implied that they were not concerned about risks either.

Moreover, Ferguson and Valenti found that different groups seemed to respond more strongly to different kinds of messages. Rebellious risk takers showed higher levels of concern at a newspaper article with a state agency source, than at a newspaper article with the surgeon-general as its source. For the impulsive risk taker, however, concern was greatest when the message was from a State agency source and in a brochure. The researchers suggested that a successful media strategy for one type of risk taker might therefore have no effects or even negative effects with another type of risk taker.

Risk taking in sexual behaviour has attracted a lot of research attention, mainly because of HIV infection and the rise in incidence of acquired immune deficiency syndrome (AIDS). One of the outcomes of this research is the finding that public evaluations of risk do not always relate to medical evaluations of risk. Holly (1989) investigated the effect of public health campaigns on sixth-form girls in Milton Keynes. Holly met ten girls over a number of lunch-time meetings and addressed these two major issues: 'What do they know about HIV and other sexually transmitted diseases?' and 'What information do they need to know to make informed choices?'

Society

Although the girls showed themselves to be fairly well informed about AIDS, their knowledge did not appear to relate to their beliefs of contracting the virus. They accepted that casual heterosexual sex had become quite dangerous, but they believed that their own chances of contracting the virus were not great. They also rejected the idea of using condoms, seeing love and serious relationships as defences against AIDS and other sexually transmitted disorders.

This finding fits with the major longitudinal study of nearly 5000 16–19-year-olds, reported by Breakwell (1992). Breakwell found that one of the major factors which inhibited the adoption of safe sex practices, particularly among teenage girls, was the social representation that serial monogamy was safe – in other words, that as long as you and your partner were faithful to one another, you would not contract AIDS. The fact that these monogamous relationships tended not to last for very long, and that a single individual might experience several of them during a five-year period, was not seen as relevant to the assessment of HIV risk. In other words, both of these studies imply that judgements about AIDS risk were based on the medically worthless criteria of depth of affection rather than on scientific or factual information.

AIDS has traditionally been associated with high-risk major city populations, but the scientific evidence indicates that it is also widespread in

Some statements from the girls interviewed by Holly suggested that they felt the best defence against HIV and AIDS is through the careful choice of partners. For example, one girl said: 'If you mix with people who value themselves and value others and care, then it's avoidable.'

Another feature of these responses was the idea of trust and the integrity of the partner. For example: 'When you love someone you've got to trust them. By that time you'll know if someone's got AIDS or anything.'

Figure 4.29 Teenage girls and AIDS. (Holly, 1989.)

Glynis Marie Breakwell, born 26 July 1952, West Bromwich, England.

'Charlie Chan, that great fictional detective, said "theory, like mist on eyeglasses, obscures facts", he was right but only about weak, over-simplified theories.'

Breakwell, after gaining her PhD from Bristol University in 1976, spent some years at Nuffield College, Oxford, before moving to the University of Surrey where she became Professor of Psychology, Head of the Psychology Department, and Director of the newly founded Social Psychology European Research Institute in 1991. Breakwell has evolved Identity Process Theory, explaining the social psychological processes which operate to shape individual and group identities in the context of empirical research on such social problems as interpersonal violence, unemployment, environmental pollution, political and scientific alienation, and sexually-transmitted diseases. Her contributions to the development of social psychological theory and its application were recognized by the British Psychological Society in 1993 with the Myers Award. Breakwell developed methods to elicit data on identity and social representations and her multivariate approaches to the integrated analysis of such data are now widely used.

quieter communities. In view of its image, however, it is questionable whether people living in smaller towns and cities appreciate the level of risk. Ruefli, Yu and Barton (1992) looked at sexual risk taking in Buffalo, New York. They used a questionnaire on sexual behaviour to assess HIV risk taking by 487 gay men, aged between 17 and 73, and found that this group reported much higher levels of sexual risk taking than other homosexual populations had done.

The researchers also found that those in their sample who took more sexual risks were also more sexually opportunistic, less able to use social skills to reduce their risk of AIDS and more likely to frequent gay bars than those who also adopted safer sexual practices. They tended to be ambivalent in their feelings about condom use and inconsistent in their behaviour. The researchers suggested that sexual risk taking may be considerably higher in cities such as Buffalo which are outside the epicentres of the AIDS epidemic (San Francisco, New York, Los Angeles etc.), and that the community environment may be a critical factor affecting AIDS-related behaviours.

Holland *et al.* (1990) collected questionnaire data from 496 young women, conducted 150 in-depth interviews, and asked a small number of women to keep diaries based on their relationships and sexual practices. The interviews showed that most of the young women's sexual activity was ultimately determined by men. Many said that they had sexual intercourse when they would have enjoyed or preferred non-penetrative sex, which they were aware of as a means of avoiding HIV infection. The researchers argued that many women define sex to a large extent according to what they believe gives men pleasure and fail to assert their own preferences.

According to the researchers, male control over sexual encounters extended beyond the straightforward definitions of sex and sexual pleasure. One young woman, when describing her first experience of condom use, explained that her boyfriend had been certain that the condom should be 'blown up' first. In spite of the fact that she had strong doubts about this, she allowed her views to be overridden on the assumption that 'men knew better' (Holland *et al.*, 1990). The researchers argued that the fact that men are as socialized into their roles as women should not be forgotten by sex educators: practical information about safe sex practices was as important as general information about AIDS risks.

Risk taking and creativity sometimes seem to go hand in hand: the creative artist or entrepreneur is often the one who challenges existing boundaries, and takes risks with their material, stepping into new ventures and exploring new ideas. Many of the greatest thinkers in Western history did so at great personal risk – for example, Galileo's ordeal at the hands of the Spanish Inquisition. But, at the same time, creativity is much more than simply taking risks. It also involves the ability to synthesize – to put old materials together in a new and dynamic way, until what is produced is something entirely new.

Creative thinking

Identifying what creativity actually is is a difficult task for the research psychologist. One way of beginning to look at it is to study the biographies of eminent artists, musicians and scientists, in order to see whether there are systematic regularities which appear in accounts of how they go about their work. Wallas (1926) looked at the self-reports of eminent scientists to establish the components of creative thinking, and described four phases, which have also been found in later studies of how artists work (e.g. Ghiselin, 1952). The first was a period of preparation; formulating the problem, collecting information and making an initial attempt to solve it. The second was of incubation; setting the problem aside and not thinking about it for some time. This was followed by illumination; gaining insight into how to solve the problem. Then came verification; checking the solution to make sure it really works.

Wallas's identification of the period of preparation followed by incubation echoes some of the findings from studies of highly creative artists and musicians. Ghiselin (1952) found that creative activity requires a lengthy period of 'submersion' – years of hard work in which the artist, musician, writer or scientist familiarizes her or himself with various techniques and 'tools of the trade'. This is then followed by a period of incubation in which the idea seems to lie dormant in the unconscious mind, only to emerge later almost fully-fledged, leading into a period of intensive activity as the individual works to capture the idea in their chosen medium.

Almost by definition, however, this type of highly creative process is impossible to capture in the laboratory, since it is often unforeseen and does not just appear to order. As a result, some psychologists involved in the study of creativity have looked at it in terms of a more restricted approach, such as the ability to handle novelty. Hudson (1966) performed an extensive study of schoolchildren and found that there seemed to be two different types of cognitive style shown by different pupils. Pupils who showed a **'convergent' thinking** style tended to be extremely logical, to prefer science or mathematical subjects and to adopt a linear, focused style of reasoning if they were asked to solve a particular problem. **Divergent thinkers** were often more intuitive or impulsive in their style of thought, tended to prefer arts subjects at school and would range widely across several possible options if they were asked to solve a problem.

convergent thinking
Thinking which is directed towards getting a single 'right' answer to a problem, concentrating on strict logic and ruling out creative or intuitive thinking.

divergent thinking
Thinking which is intuitive or creative, often involving non-logical 'leaps' or sudden ideas.

Uses for a brick
One of the tests which Hudson used to distinguish between these two cognitive styles was to ask the schoolchildren to think of unusual uses for everyday objects. So, for example, he would ask them 'How many uses can you think of for a brick?' and they would have a set period of time to write down as many as they could think of. He found that divergent thinkers would tot up many more uses than convergent thinkers, often coming up with ideas which their more convergent colleagues regarded as quite bizarre.

Figure 4.30 Uses for a brick.

Hudson suggested that these divergent thinkers were actually the more creative ones and that the education system undervalued their particular cognitive style, and therefore tended to act against the development of creativity. However, there is some doubt as to how far students can really be classified this neatly: further studies suggested that the process is more complex than it appears from Hudson's study.

> **Key reference:** HUDSON, L. (1966) *Contrary Imaginations*. Penguin, Harmondsworth.

There are two puzzles for psychologists in the study of creative thinking. The first of these is how to define and measure it. We all have an implicit understanding of what we mean by creativity – or at least, we would all be likely to cite certain outstanding people as creative, such as great writers and artists. But actually defining what we mean by creativity so clearly as to be able to measure it is a much more difficult task.

Creativity in composers was investigated by Simonton (1991), who explored the life achievements of 120 classical composers of 12 nationalities. Simonton looked at their early experience, the emergence of their talent and the dates of their major achievements. The ages of their first, best and last outputs were calculated, together with the ages when they produced maximum and minimal output, and the age at which they had achieved their total lifetime output. The raters who Simonton used to undertake these calculations were not aware of what the study was about.

Society

Like other researchers who have taken a biographical approach to the study of creativity, Simonton found that the emergence of genius seemed to rest on an extensive prior period of acquiring skills, which apparently needed to be undertaken during childhood. For most of the composers, their first production was generally at about 26 years of age. Those who started formal training at younger ages often produced later compositions, higher annual productivity and a higher final list of accomplishments.

Biographical studies, of course, are concerned with identifying general trends from the data, and there are always individual exceptions, so we cannot be sure how essential childhood experience is. There have, for example, been instances of highly successful writers who did not write their first book until they were in their 40s. What does emerge, however, is the need for an intensive period of learning, as the artist, musician, or writer familiarizes themselves with the different techniques and forms of knowledge in their trade. It seems as if creativity emerges once the person has become so good at the basic techniques that they do not need even to think about them – once they can use the medium to do pretty well whatever they like, their creative talents begin to find expression. This observation has implications for art schools and other such institutions, since it implies that the teaching and practice of specific techniques in the early stages may be more important to later creativity than a curriculum which is simply based on 'self-discovery'.

This brings us to the second puzzle facing psychologists studying creativity, which is the question of how to enhance it – and how far. It is generally accepted, for instance, that creativity at work can be a good thing, but a company would not want a work force being too creative every day. On the other hand, creativity is necessary for innovation and change. Peters (1987) argued that, in a modern, competitive environment, top industrial managers need to encourage a continual process of change, adaptation, innovation and creativity, and should get away from the idea that if everything is running 'smoothly' then things are all right – since that usually means the company has become static and is not responding to changes in the external marketplace. For many managers, however, creativity is more difficult to handle: employee tasks are well established and too much creativity on the part of employees could produce unanticipated results which, unlike Peters, they tend to see as undesirable.

Work

Sometimes, managers will adopt systematic creativity-enhancing procedures. Osborn (1963) developed the technique which has become known as **brainstorming**. Brainstorming is a group-based technique in which people are deliberately encouraged to develop as many unusual and unorthodox ideas as possible. It consists of an ideas-generating period, in which people concentrate on thinking up new ideas, followed later by an evaluation period.

brainstorming   A group-based technique in which people are deliberately encouraged to develop as many unusual and unorthodox ideas as possible. It consists of an idea-generating period, in which people concentrate on thinking up new ideas, followed by an evaluation period.

There are some very important principles underlying brainstorming. The first, and probably the most important, is that any judgement about the value or sensibleness of any of the ideas mentioned is carefully withheld until the later stages. Trying to judge whether ideas are good or bad can make it difficult for people to suggest them and often an idea which sounds ridiculous at first turns out to be extremely useful. So, during the first phase of brainstorming, no judgements are made and any idea that occurs to any member of the group is recorded for scrutiny later.

Shalley (1991) found that creative performance in an organizational setting can be enhanced when the word 'creativity' is mentioned. Two hundred and seventy research participants were asked to undertake a task as if they were the personnel director of a company. They were told that their goals were to maximize either 'creativity' or 'productivity', and were given either high or low levels of personal discretion in how they went about tackling the task. Some of the research participants were told that the task was difficult, some were just told to 'Do your best', and some were not given any expectations at all. Shalley found that the people who had been assigned 'creativity' goals, whether it was a 'difficult' or 'Do your best' condition, had higher levels of creativity than those assigned performance goals. If the research participant was in the 'difficult' condition with a high level of personal discretion, their creativity level – in terms of whether the person tackled the problem in a novel and appropriate way – was highest of all.

Attempts to investigate how far creativity can be enhanced raise the contrast between the idea that there is a particular kind of personality which produces creativity – a creativity 'trait' – and the idea that creativity is something which can be demonstrated by all or most people, given the right kind of conditions. Earlier approaches in psychology and education tended to adopt the idea of the creative person, usually resting their case on the evidence from people who have made outstanding discoveries, such as the scientist Henri Poincaré, or who have produced great works of art or music.

> The following is an account given by the French mathematician Henri Poincaré about his attempts to develop a theory of Fuchsian functions:
>
> Then I wanted to represent these functions by the quotient of two series: this idea was perfectly conscious and deliberate; the analogy with elliptic function guided me. I asked myself what properties these series must have if they existed, and succeeded without difficulty in forming the series I have called theta-Fuchsian.
>
> Just at this time I left Caen, where I was living, to go on a geological excursion under the auspices of the school of mines. The change of travel made me forget my mathematical work. Having reached Coutances, we entered an omnibus to go some place or other. At the moment when I put my foot on the step the idea came to me without anything in my former thoughts seeming to have paved the way for it, that the transformations I had used to define the Fuchsian functions were identical to those of non-Euclidian geometry. I did not verify the idea: I should not have had time, as upon taking my seat in the omnibus, I went on with a conversation I had already commenced, but I felt a perfect certainty. On my return to Caen, for conscience sake, I verified the result at my leisure.

Figure 4.31 Creativity. (Poincaré, 1913.)

Education

The 'gifted person' approach tends to present creativity as something which is only achieved by a special élite, but other approaches take the view that creativity is something that most people can display given the right circumstances. For example, Isen *et al.* (1987) found that cheerful situations tend to foster creativity. Students did significantly better on creativity tests after they had watched an amusing film or been given a small present of sweets. In contrast, if they had watched a distressing film about concentration camps or a neutral film on mathematics, there was no improvement in creativity, nor was there if they had exercised for two minutes to energize themselves. The researchers suggested that, for many people, elation may be a key to creativity – an interesting idea which goes against the social stereotype of the creative artist as a tortured and less than chirpy person.

The social climate in which we are asked to work also appears to be a factor which can enhance creativity. Ziller, Behringer and Goodchilds (1960) asked 64 small groups (with between 2 and 4 members) to produce as many captions as possible for a *Saturday Evening Post* cartoon, in a given time limit. They varied the stability of the groups by removing, adding or replacing group members, and found that open groups, which had a changing membership, were more creative than closed groups whose members stayed the same. However, the open groups were also aware that there were other groups working on the same problems, whereas the closed ones were not. It is possible therefore that people in the open groups were more competitive or more highly motivated because of **social facilitation**.

social facilitation The observation that the presence of other people can influence how well they perform on a task, often improving their performance.

Another factor which seems to influence creativity is whether someone has **intrinsic** rather than **extrinsic** motivation. Extrinsic motivation is when actions are motivated by the thought of external rewards, such as wanting money, fame, attention etc. Intrinsic motivation, on the other hand, includes a sense of accomplishment, intellectual fulfilment, curiosity and the sheer love of the activity. Amabile (1985) asked 72 young poets and writers to create 2 poems. Before writing their second poem half of the writers were asked to evaluate a list of extrinsic motives for writing (e.g. 'I enjoy the public recognition of my work'). The other half were asked to evaluate a list of intrinsic motives (e.g. 'I like to play with words').

intrinsic motivation Sources of motivation inside the individual, for example, drives, rather than outside the individual, for example rewards.

extrinsic motivation Sources of motivation outside the individual, for example rewards, rather than inside the individual, for example, drives.

A panel of 12 experienced poets were then asked to judge all of the poems for originality and creativity. The results showed that the writers who had been exposed to the list of extrinsic motives showed a significant drop in creativity between the first and the second poem, whereas those writers who had been exposed to the intrinsic motives wrote two poems of equal merit.

One of the many concerns raised about film and television is that they may stunt the imagination and therefore the creativity of children. Evidence for this idea, though, is hard to come by. Some studies seem to show that creative abilities are stable and relatively impervious to short-term influences like television; others report that the media can have a considerable effect on imaginative thinking. Runco and Pezdek (1984) suggested that one problem of these studies is the way that each uses its own measures of creativity, rather than using a standardized test of some kind.

Runco and Pezdek presented 64 children (half of whom were in the third grade at their American school and half in the sixth grade) with a story on TV or radio. Then they administered the Torrance tests of creative thinking, which required the children to generate ideas in response to a hypothetical situation which followed from the story. The childrens' responses were scored in terms of ideational fluency, flexibility and originality. Their results indicated that the two media did not seem to influence the childrens' creativity. It would appear that the folk-wisdom about the dangers of television is not supported by the evidence.

Intelligence

The history of intelligence testing has been fraught with competing theories, questionable evidence and, at times, vitriolic abuse. Much of the debate focused on the rather spurious question of whether intelligence was inherited or learned and the social implications which followed from adopting one position or the other. Often, the various early theories were ideological in nature rather than resting on evidence, but some recent theories have attempted to develop a model which can integrate the whole range of research evidence, rather than just focusing on some and ignoring the rest.

The triarchic theory of intelligence put forward by Sternberg (1985) proposes that there are three distinct aspects to human intelligence, which work together to produce what we consider to be intelligent behaviour or intelligent action on the part of a given individual. The theory therefore consists of three separate sub-theories, each of which deals with one of these aspects.

The first sub-theory is that of *contextual intelligence*, which is intelligence within its sociocultural setting. This sub-theory sees intelligence as mental activity which is directed towards purposive action, helping the individual select, shape or adapt to relevant environments in the real world. This aspect of the theory, therefore, recognizes the diversity of cultures and environments in which human

Robert J. Sternberg, born 8 December 1949, Newark, NJ, USA.

Robert Sternberg first became interested in human intelligence as a child when he did poorly on intelligence tests due to test anxiety. The test anxiety eventually disappeared, but not the interest in intelligence. This interest landed him in trouble as a secondary-school student, when he was reprimanded after being caught administering intelligence tests to schoolmates, and still gets him in trouble because of his belief that conventional tests measure only a small part of human intelligence. According to his 'triarchic theory' human intelligence comprises three aspects: analytical ability; creative ability; and practical ability, only the first of which is measured by conventional tests. Sternberg has devised instruments to measure creative and practical as well as analytical abilities, and has devised training programmes to help people develop all three aspects of their intelligence. Sternberg has also proposed an 'investment theory of creativity', according to which creative people, like good investors, 'buy low and sell high' – figuratively, they come up with ideas that are unpopular and generally rejected by others, and then try to convince other people of the worth of those ideas. When they do, they move on to the next unpopular idea. Sternberg has also proposed a triangular theory of love, according to which love has three aspects: intimacy; passion; and commitment. Sternberg has been recognized in various ways for his contributions, including awards from the American Psychological Association, American Educational Research Association, National Association for Gifted Children, Society for Multivariate Experimental Psychology, and Guggenheim Foundation, among others. He is Editor of the *Psychological Bulletin* and has been a president of the Divisions of General and of Educational Psychology of the American Psychological Association. His advice to students: If you have a really creative idea, expect opposition to it, from your teachers and others. All creative people encounter obstacles, but the successfully creative ones are those who fight to overcome these obstacles.

beings live, and acknowledges cultural differences in intelligent behaviour. Indeed, Sternberg argues that it is not possible to understand intelligence outside of a sociocultural context, since although there may be some aspects of intelligence which are universal, cultural factors would influence how much importance was placed on them.

The second sub-theory of the triarchic model is that of *experiential intelligence,* which concerns how people's own past experience affects the way that they tackle a given task or situation. Sternberg considers that it involves two fundamental skills: the ability to deal with situational demands, including novel tasks, people and/or situations; and the ability to automatize information processing, so that a given task presents a smaller cognitive demand for the individual. Sternberg argues that, since individuals vary considerably in terms of how much opportunity they have had to develop these fundamental skills, any attempt to explain what intelligence is must be able to recognize and explore the nature of this variation.

The third sub-theory in the triarchic model is that of *componential intelligence*, which is concerned with the cognitive mechanisms by which intelligence behaviour is achieved. This sub-theory actually represents an older theory of intelligence (Sternberg, 1977), in which the components of intelligence were classified in terms of function and level of generality. This resulted in three categories of components: metacomponents – the higher order processes involved in, for instance, planning and decision-making; performance components – the mental processes involved in actually carrying out a task; and knowledge-acquisition components – the mental processes involved in learning new information.

Although it is the third aspect of Sternberg's theory which is most highly developed, the integration of the three different sub-theories presents a model of intelligence which draws together a range of research. It is also capable of acknowledging the diversity and multiplicity of human cultures and experience, while at the same time recognizing that human beings all over the world do have something in common.

Key reference: STERNBERG, R. J. (1985) *Beyond IQ: a triarchic theory of human intelligence.* Cambridge University Press, Cambridge.

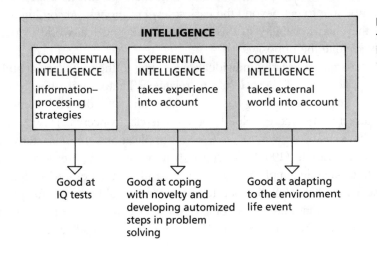

Figure 4.32 Sternberg's triarchic theory of intelligence.

The concept of intelligence has been a political battleground since the introduction of the first intelligence tests, as we saw in Chapter 1. There are a number of issues which are raised by the debates about intelligence. The first, and most obvious of these, is the question of what intelligence actually is and, more specifically, whether it is a general intellectual quality or simply a way of doing things. Rose, Kamin and Lewontin (1984) argued that the idea that there is a 'thing' called intelligence is a **reification** – that the idea has become treated as if it were a noun, whereas really it is an adverb. We can do something 'intelligently', but that means doing it appropriately in its context. It does not necessarily mean that we have an independent 'thing' called intelligence.

The idea of intelligence as a separate entity, however, became firmly fixed in early psychology and led to other questions, such as whether intelligence is a stable quality which can be measured, and what use such measurement might be. Traditionally, the idea has been that measuring intelligence may be useful because it allows individuals with high intelligence to be acknowledged and given appropriate opportunities, although Hayes (1988) argued that the history of intelligence testing showed that it served a much more negative purpose, being a justification for social stratification rather than providing opportunities for people to do well.

Education

According to Sternberg (1985) many current **IQ (intelligence quotient) tests** are of doubtful relevance to the real world. He cited an example told to him by an educational psychologist, who turned up at his first job as a school psychologist to find that the students who he was to see had just successfully escaped from the very restricted grounds of the school. When they were returned, the psychologist's first task was to give the same students an intelligence test based on tracking through mazes. The students who had been ringleaders of the real-life escape were not able to get beyond the easiest level of the test. According to the test, they had no ability in this area at all, yet the real-world evidence showed quite the opposite.

Work

IQ tests aim to classify individuals according to their intellectual ability. The applications of these tests are relatively limited and often tests of aptitude for particular jobs based on skills, and attitudes and attentional abilities etc., are more helpful for commercial concerns. However, IQ tests have been shown to have some applications. In one study, for instance, Ghiselli (1966) investigated how useful IQ tests were for selecting suitable employees for several different types of occupation. Ghiselli found that intelligence tests were reasonably successful predictors of success in training for some types of skilled work, in particular for electrical and computing staff. By contrast, non-intellectual tests of

1. Which of the five numbered figures completes the top line?

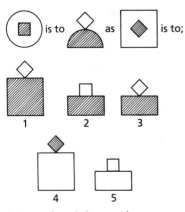

2. Insert the missing number

3. Which of the first numbered figure fits into the vacant space? (Insert the number in the square)

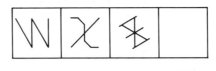

4. Underline the word that completes the sentence

Palimpsest is to palindrome as erase is to:
repeat   reverse   retire   relive   reduce   resell

5. Insert the word that completes the first word and starts the second

DE (. . .) CH

6. Underline which of these is not an island

BAUC
POWRARS
LIDNARE
PICRA

Figure 4.33 Examples of IQ test items. (Eysenck, 1962.)

dexterity were relatively useless for these occupations, although they were reasonably successful at predicting whether someone would train well for observational and manipulative occupations, like packing, assembly work or supervision. For those occupations, intelligence tests had little or no predictive validity.

The implication, then, is that intelligence tests may have some usefulness in some contexts, but not as all-encompassing predictor of performance. The fact that computing and electrical occupations often involve a high level of mental calculation may provide an indication as to why mental intelligence tests were useful – being more similar to the job itself, they may have tapped on to some of the same skills. Sternberg (1985) argued that the most critical need in ability testing is to develop a wider range of measures which can assess real-world intelligence, as opposed to just intellectual ones.

A common misconception is that intellectual abilities decline quite steadily with age and the relative forgetfulness of older people is often seen as a sign of this. Bromley (1968) pointed out that during maturity and old age, intellectual activity is mainly concerned with the application

Society

of acquired techniques and the assimilation of experience to established frames of reference. The younger person, on the other hand, has to work everything out from first principles. As a result, Bromley argued, older people can often learn applied skills more rapidly than younger ones. It is the focus of the activity that changes rather than the quality of it.

Many of the studies which suggested that performance in IQ tests declined with age were based on cross-sectional studies – in other words, the researcher performing the study had taken groups of people of different ages and compared how well they did on the same IQ tests. But this way of studying intelligence had serious problems, because it did not take account of the way that older people had experienced very different social conditions and educational practices than the younger ones.

Education

Burns (1966) reported a longitudinal study of teachers which began in the 1920s, when they first qualified and followed them up until they reached an average age of 56 years old. Unlike the findings of the cross-sectional studies, the mean IQ of this group was 7 points higher than it had been when the group had an average age of 22. When the group was separated into 'science' and 'arts' teachers, Burns found that the science teachers showed an increased score on scales which involved number and diagrammatic skills and a decrease in verbal scores, while the arts teachers showed the opposite. The implication was that it is practice which is important in whether the individual retains intelligence or not. Skills which are relatively unused may show a decrement, whereas those which are used regularly are likely to improve with age, not decline. The findings from this and other research suggests that performance on IQ tests does not show much decline until a person is very advanced in years, unless, of course, they suffer from a biological dementia.

These studies tend to assume that intelligence comprises a number of skills, working together to produce a general estimate of intelligence. But a different view of intelligence was put forward by Gardner (1985), who argued that the mind is not a holistic entity, but instead consists of distinct, independent modules. Intelligence, Gardner argues, is the composite name that we give to reflections of the activities of those modules, but intelligence is not a single thing. According to Gardner, there are seven entirely different intelligences, which are listed in Figure 4.34. Furthermore, each of these intelligences, according to Gardner, has a distinct biological source in the brain.

There is certainly some evidence that some people may have distinctive skills in some specific areas. Gladwin (1970) studied how men in the Puluwat Islands of Micronesia train to become master navigators. This

The seven intelligences outlined by Gardner are:

1. **linguistic intelligence** – that used when reading, writing or comprehending speech;

2. **musical intelligence** – used in musical appreciation, composition and
   performance;

3. **mathematical-logical intelligence** – that used in arithmetic, numerical calculation and logical reasoning;

4. **spatial intelligence** – that used in arranging objects spatially, as well
   as in visual art and finding one's way around;

5. **bodily-kinaesthetic intelligence** – that used in sport, dancing, or
   simply everyday movement and dexterity;

6. **inter-personal intelligence** – that used in relating to others and
   interpreting social signals, and predicting social outcomes;

7. **intra-personal intelligence** – that used in understanding and
   predicting one's own behaviour, and in identifying aspects of the self
   and one's own personality.

Figure 4.34 Gardner's model of intelligence. (Gardner, 1984.)

position is achieved by very few individuals – maybe only about half a dozen or so at any one time – but this is not because the necessary information is kept secret. Rather, it is because it demands an extremely high aptitude, involving a combination of different kinds of intelligence. The 'theoretical' part of the training, for example, involves memorizing vast amounts of factual information: the identities and locations of all the islands to which anyone might voyage from the Puluwat Islands; the identities and courses of all of the stars which a navigator might conceivably need to know; and the ways in which this information might conceivably be combined. Eventually, the aspiring master navigator must be able to start with any island in the known ocean and describe the stars which could be seen in any direction, both coming and going, between that island and any other reachable island.

The theoretical component demands a high level of linguistic intelligence, but the individual also needs to be adept at other kinds of skills. The most important part of the training involves the practical skills and knowledge which are involved with being at sea: knowing how to read the currents, the weather, the stars and the different waves; knowing procedures for navigation under all conditions; and being familiar with all of the practical skills required for active sea life. This involves spatial and bodily-kinaesthetic knowledge, as well as the sophisticated development and application of sensory abilities.

Lord (1960) studied how singers of oral verse in a rural Balkan community became epic singers. This involves a high degree of linguistic and musical intelligence, since the singer has to achieve a level of familiarity with the musical and linguistic formulae such that they are able to construct appropriate songs in that context. Since each song lasts throughout the evening, and a different song is sung on each of the 40 days of the holy month of Ramadan, it is a skill which takes a considerable time to acquire. Moreover, learning consists almost exclusively of observation: the would-be singer listens to the performances night after night, for many years, and only then begins to practise the formulae himself in private. This then continues for even more years, until finally the person will perform his songs in front of an audience, and will receive the critical response which informs him whether he has achieved his goal. The profession, then, involves a high level of both linguistic and musical intelligence, and is almost entirely self-taught.

There are a number of criticisms which can be made of Garder's approach. One of the most serious of these is the way that the theory treats the different intelligences as if they existed in a vacuum, independent of any social or cultural context. Language, for instance, is treated entirely as if it were an individual skill and the social functions of language are entirely ignored. In fact, social and motivational influences in general are ignored in this approach, which may be a problem in real life. Perhaps the most useful modern approach to looking at intelligence might be a synthesis of Gardner and Sternberg's model, which integrates the idea of distinctive groups of abilities with the idea of contextual, experiential and componential intelligence.

Summary

1. *A schema is a hypothetical cognitive structure which is used to represent information in the mind, and to organize planning and activity concerned with that information.*

2. *During the 1970s and 1980s many psychologists began research into artificial intelligence and computer simulation of human skills.*

3. *Research into human reasoning suggests that what appear to be mistakes in logic actually arise from applying a more sophisticated social knowledge to the problem.*

4. *Relatively minor errors can sometimes produce major disasters. In general, errors tend to be of three kinds: skill-based lapses, knowledge-based errors, and rule-based errors.*

5. *Research into sustained attention has identified a number of factors which can reduce performance decrement. Many of these involve stimuli which are likely to increase the person's arousal level, such as the presence of other people.*

6. *Human decision-making involves the use of heuristics to streamline the process of weighing up the odds. It is also influenced by social factors.*

7. *There have been a number of explanations for why people take risks, including causal explanations, needs for self-determination, and the influence of reference groups and cultural norms.*

8. *Creativity is sometimes seen as a four-stage process, involving an initial period of intensive preparation and skill acquisition, a period of incubation, an insight into the problem, and then a period of activity and verification of the solution.*

9. *The triarchic theory of intelligence sees it as deriving from three sources: the cultural and social context within which intelligent acts happen, the individual's personal experience, and the mental components of information-processing.*

PRACTICE QUESTIONS AND ACTIVITIES – 4

Creativity

Creativity is one of those qualities that we would all like to have but seems to elude most of us. Put a blank piece of paper and some paints in front of us, and we are likely to fret about what to draw before giving up and going to put the washing on. Given a problem, however, many people can be quite ingenious.

The much quoted test for creativity is to suggest a number of uses for a brick. Many psychology text books suggest this actual example for students to try out which strangely illustrates the general lack of unstructured creativity in psychologists. To demonstrate a startling originality in the authors of this text we are going to suggest some DIFFERENT objects to consider. What could you do with the following:

- An empty Marmite jar;
- An empty oil can;
- A set of Esso World Cup coins from 1972.

Award points for usefulness, humour and star quality, and deduct points for gross obscenity.

Now that you're getting the hang of it, try and suggest what each of these patterns could be.

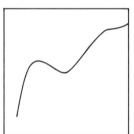

Figure 4.35
Creativity with patterns.

It is remarkable how creative you can be if you are given even a limited amount of structure for a creativity task.

PRACTICE QUESTIONS AND ACTIVITIES – 4

Ergonomics

Ergonomics is the study of the relationship between people and machines. The problem with the design of many work environments is that they are based around what a machine can do and then people are asked to do the rest. Many would suggest that this is the wrong way round.

It is worth considering the relative advantages and disadvantages of machines and people for a variety of tasks. Make a list of a number of tasks that people and machines can do, and identify the strengths and weakness of a person or a machine carrying out this task.

The 'Fitts list' is often quoted and you may like to use this as a starting point if you get stuck with this task. It is printed below.

Advantages and disadvantages of humans and machines (From Gregory and Burrows, 1989)

Function	Machine	Human
Speed	superior	
Power	consistent at any level large constant standard forces	2.0 hp for about 10 secs 0.5 hp for a few minutes 0.2 hp over a day
Consistency	ideal for routine; repetition; precision	not reliable
Complex activities	multi channel	single channel
Memory	best for literal reproduction and short term storage	large store, multiple access, better for principles and strategies
Reasoning	good deductive	good inductive
Computation	fast, accurate, poor at error correction	slow, subject to error, good at error correction
Input sensitivity	some outside human senses, e.g. radioactivity	wide energy and variety of stimuli dealt with by one unit, e.g. eye deals with relative location, movement and colour, good at pattern recognition, good at signal detection
Overload reliability	sudden breakdown	graceful degradation
Intelligence	none	can deal with unpredicted and unpredictable, can anticipate
Manipulative abilities	specific	great versatility

PRACTICE QUESTIONS AND ACTIVITIES – 4

Intelligence

Intelligence is one of those qualities that we are happy to talk about in everyday conversation, but if you were asked to identify the various skills involved in intelligent activity you might find the task quite hard. To help with this task, and to illustrate how important intelligence is in our everyday judgements of people, carry out the following task.

Make a long list of everyday terms that are used to make judgements about intelligence. Many of these are insults. Some examples are idiot, moron, imbecile, stupid, thick, brainbox etc.

You should be able to come up with 30 at least.

Now, make a list of things that you do when you might use one or more of these terms – 'Oh, that was very stupid of me'. You might have locked yourself out of your house, for example. Think of as many 'stupid' acts as you can. Now identify what psychological quality or skill you are commenting on. In the example of locking yourself out, the skills are forward planning and memory.

The list of skills that you develop gives you an insight into what you think intelligence is.

5

Learning
and
remembering

Introduction

How do we learn how we should act and how do we store information? These two questions are among the earliest studied by psychologists and still provide a focus for a substantial amount of research. The ability to learn and to reason was thought of by European scientists in the 19th century as the factor which distinguishes human beings from animals. Animals were thought to acquire their behaviour and knowledge by 'instinct', whereas people developed their own knowledge through enquiry and had the gift of reason.

Darwin's theory of evolution pointed to the biological connections between animals and people, and suggested that there were straight-line links between human beings and animals in biological terms. As interest in psychology, and particularly in human behaviour, developed, the question of behavioural connections became important. Pavlov was investigating the physiological or **reflex** actions in dogs when he noticed that these reflexes could be learned – dogs would salivate, not just in response to their food, but also when they saw the assistant approaching with it. So, challenging the idea that reflexes were simply mechanical inherited responses, Pavlov proposed that reflexes could be learned – an idea which developed into the theory of classical conditioning. The idea rapidly became adopted as an explanation for human learning, coinciding with the advent of behaviourism in America through Watson's work on stimulus-response associations.

Other work on animal learning was identifying a different form of learning: the idea that learning may take place if an action has pleasant effects. Largely based in America, this research into animals, spearheaded by Thorndike at the turn of the century, was subsequently developed into the concept of operant conditioning by the behaviourist B. F. Skinner. Operant conditioning still took the form of stimulus-response

reflex An automatic reaction to a stimulus; often inborn but can also be learned or modified by experience.

associations, but the association was considered to have been formed as a result of the consequences of performing an action, rather than simply as a result of two events occurring together.

As research into operant conditioning became more sophisticated, it generated a range of research avenues and new concepts of learning. These included the idea of learning sets: the use of operant conditioning to produce the ability to respond correctly to a type of problem rather than just to one specific problem; investigations of what kinds of events or occurrences would act to reinforce or strengthen a learned association; and the use of social approval as an intrinsic reward for human beings.

As the century progressed, this research developed into a major challenge to behaviourism, led by Albert Bandura, who maintained that

Working at the University of St Petersburg in Russia, Ivan Pavlov (1849–1936) studied the digestive system. His study of the digestive reflex led him to the discovery that an animal can learn to display the reflex in new situations. He turned his attention to the mechanisms of the learnt reflex and developed the theory of classical conditioning. By 1917, when the Russian Revolution occurred, Pavlov was an established scientific figure, and despite being valued and honoured by the new government, he opposed the new political order for many years. He was finally reconciled to it in 1933 and spent his last years in relative harmony with the Russian scientific community. One unusual local consequence of this research developed from the large production of saliva by Pavlov's dogs. These gastric juices were sold to the local population and became so popular that the proceeds from the sale doubled the laboratory's income which was already quite substantial. The picture below shows Pavlov's early work at the Soviet Military Medicine Academy.

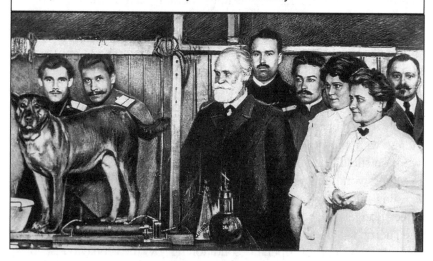

Figure 5.1 Pavlov and the conditioned reflex.

human learning did not consist entirely of stimulus-response associations, but also encompassed cognitive and social forms of learning, such as learning by imitation and through identifying with role models. Bandura's **social learning theory** presented a view of the human being as able to learn large sequences of behaviour, and to generate role-appropriate behaviour, in a way that was quite different from the mechanistic stimulus-response assumptions of the behaviourists.

Social learning theory, however, still operated within the assumption that human behaviour was essentially learned, rather than, say, inherited, and that inappropriate behaviour therefore arose because of inappropriate learning. This led naturally to the idea that people who showed behavioural disturbances could be taught new ways of acting, which would help them to lead more 'normal' lives. The process of applying operant conditioning and social learning principles to behavioural problems was known as **behaviour modification**, and became widely adopted for treating several specific behavioural problems, with a certain degree of success.

Research into animal and human learning also led to investigations of the way that information is stored. One of the major figures in this was Tolman, whose research into animal learning in the 1930s led to an increased awareness of the process which he called latent learning – the way that learned experiences could be stored by the animal and applied later, when they became useful or appropriate. Although he called himself a behaviourist, Tolman's research set the foundation for investigations of more cognitive forms of learning, such as research into **cognitive maps** and other forms of mental representations.

One of the forms of mental representation which attracted a considerable amount of research attention was how information can be stored in the form of mental images which can be adjusted, linked with other images, and used systematically to aid recall. Research into mental imagery provided the methodology for researchers to investigate a number of different facets of memory, including the organization of mental storage and how memory could be enhanced.

A different strand of research throughout the century was concerned with **skill learning** – how we go about learning to undertake certain skills, the role of practice, and the way that learning progresses. Although this began with the learning of relatively straightforward physical skills, as it developed models of skill learning began to encompass more complex skills. With increasing mechanization at work and in daily life, it became important for psychologists to have a clear understanding of how skills develop, and this influenced the design of both appropriate training programmes and appropriate machinery.

social learning The approach to understanding social behaviour which emphasizes how people imitate action and model their behaviour on that of others.

skill Welford (1958) suggested that all skills, of whatever kind, possess three main characteristics. The first of these is that skills consist of building an organized and co-ordinated activity in relation to an object or situation. This means that skills involve the whole set of sensory, central and motor nervous system processes which contribute to performance. The second characteristic is that skills are learned gradually, through repeated experience; and the third is that within each skill, many different processes or actions are ordered and co-ordinated in a temporal sequence.

memory *The capacity to retain and retrieve information.*

Research into **memory** goes back into the 19th century and was one of the first targets for experimental psychological research, when research into abstract forms of remembering used lists of nonsense syllables. Subsequent laboratory research produced considerable detail about memory processing and appeared to support the idea that there were at least two different memory stores – short term and long term. More recently, however, a number of psychologists have suggested that this distinction may be unnecessary, in that what seems to determine how long information is retained is how much the person processes it – whether they actually use the information mentally – rather than which store it enters.

An opposing tradition in memory research is often traced back to Bartlett's work in the 1930s. Bartlett showed how memory is a constructive process, in which memories are adjusted so that they can be fitted into the ideas, beliefs and assumptions of the person doing the remembering, rather than a passive recording of what happened. According to Bartlett, we imagine the past as much as we recall it. This led to research into various factors that might affect memory – important, for instance, when considering legal evidence obtained from eye-witnesses.

The study of memory does not just involve how we remember things. It is equally important to look at how, and why, we forget. Researchers have looked at a number of different ways that forgetting can take place, and have identified several different mechanisms which can be involved, ranging from physiological factors to the influence of the contexts and cues in how the information was stored in the first place. The idea is that a better understanding of memory-loss may help us to improve memory performance, to design messages in a style that will reduce the chance of forgetting or, at the very least, to develop strategies which will ameliorate the effect of loss of memory and allow the person to live a relatively normal life.

Classical conditioning

Ivan Pavlov was investigating the salivation reflex in dogs when his experiments became disrupted by the way that the animals would sometimes start to salivate as soon as the research assistant entered the room with their food. Pavlov studied this curious phenomenon and produced the first reports of the conditioned reflex. A reflex is made up of two components: a stimulus and a response. For example, a stimulus of a puff of air in the eye brings about the automatic response of a blink. Reflexes are not mediated by the brain, so they do not involve any thought. Instead, they occur through the simplest of neural connections, controlled directly by the spinal cord. So Pavlov's discovery that reflexes could be learned amounted to a revolution in neurology, as well as psychology.

Pavlov discovered that if he presented a new stimulus, such as ringing a bell, just before he triggered the salivation reflex by presenting food, then (after a few repetitions) the dog would begin to salivate as soon as it heard the bell. The dog had acquired what appeared to be an entirely new reflex. Pavlov named the original stimulus the **unconditioned stimulus** (US) and the original response the **unconditioned response** (UR). In the case of the salivation reflex, food is the unconditioned stimulus and salivation is the unconditioned response. Pavlov then introduced a neutral stimulus such as a bell, a picture or a light, referring to this as the **conditioned stimulus** (CS). After training, this would produce the **conditioned response** (CR) of salivation.

Pavlov discovered that if the conditioned stimulus was repeatedly presented without the reflex occurring, then the response of the animal would diminish, and eventually disappear. He named this

unconditioned stimulus
A stimulus which automatically, or reflexively, produces a response.

unconditioned response
A response which occurs automatically to a particular stimulus and doesn't have to be learned.

conditioned stimulus *A stimulus which only brings about a response because it has been associated with an unconditioned stimulus.*

conditioned response *A learned response which is produced to a conditioned stimulus.*

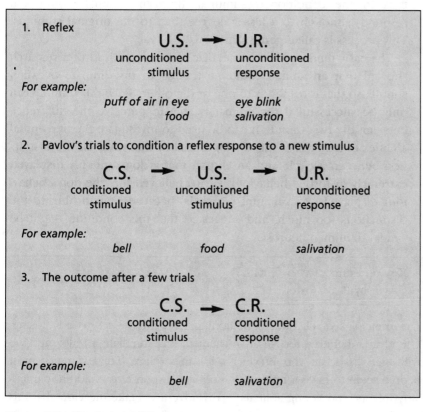

Figure 5.2 Classical conditioning.

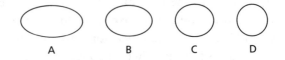

C.S. →	U.S. →	U.R.
Conditioned stimulus	Unconditioned stimulus	Unconditioned response
STIMULUS 1: CIRCLE	FOOD	SALIVATION
STIMULUS 2: ELLIPSE	NO FOOD	NO SALIVATION

If the dog is able to distinguish between a circle and an ellipse, then it will learn to salivate when shown the circle and not to salivate when shown the ellipse. It was easily able to do this.

Figure A is a clear ellipse, but as the figure changes through B and C it comes to resemble a perfect circle, D. The dog became disturbed when it could no longer tell the difference between circle and ellipse.

Figure 5.3 Discrimination trials.

---

generalization A process by which a learned response will occur in more situations than those in which it was first learned.

process extinction. He also found that if he presented a similar stimulus to the conditioned stimulus, then the animal would still respond, although to a lesser degree than to the original stimulus. This process is called **generalization**.

The basic tendency is to generalize responses, but further research showed that an animal could be trained to discriminate between stimuli, so that it responds to one or the other. Since this training can only be successful if the animal is able to perceive the difference between the two stimuli, it can be used to investigate the perceptual abilities of animals. It was during a trial of this kind, on the distinction between a circle and an ellipse, that a dog suddenly displayed extremely disturbed behaviour. Pavlov believed that the dog's behaviour displayed experimental **neurosis**, because he had blurred the distinctions too much, and suggested that this condition might be similar to human neurosis.

neuroses Mental disorders, where the patient commonly suffers from anxiety but remains in touch with reality.

Key reference: PAVLOV, I. (1927) *Conditioned Reflexes*. Oxford University Press, Oxford.

Consumer

The principles of classical conditioning lend themselves to advertising. The idea is that an effective advertisement will stimulate a reflex and we will then associate the product with this reflex. For example, most people seem to have a reflexive emotional response to children, particularly infants, and young animals. Many advertisers take the view that this emotional reaction can be transferred to products. For example, showing

John Watson (1878–1958) can reasonably be credited with being the originator of behaviourism as well as the first industrial psychologist. Although Watson based some of his theory on animal studies, he was committed to trying out his ideas in everyday human situations. He became engaged in a range of projects including studying nursery behaviour in children, studying adult sexual behaviour and devising health promotion films for the American military on venereal disease. His psychology career came to an untimely close following a relationship with his research assistant, Rosalie Raynor, whom he subsequently married. He was forced to leave his teaching post and, despite his eminence and influence in the subject, he failed to obtain another psychology post. His background and his ideas probably had more to do with this than his relationship with Rosalie Raynor.

Whatever the reason, a job became a financial necessity and he took up a position with the advertising agency J. Walter Thompson, becoming one of the first, and most successful, applied psychologists. He applied the scientific rigour he had proposed for psychology to the world of business with great success. He continued to carry out research in psychology and wrote extensively until 1932 when an article entitled 'Why I Don't Commit Suicide' was turned down for publication because it might be too depressing. The article attempted to address the issue of suicide by considering the reverse question to one on everybody's lips as soon as they hear that someone has taken their own life – Why? Watson asked 'Why not?' It was one controversy too far.

Figure 5.4 J.B. Watson and advertising.

pictures of a labrador puppy jumping about in feathers and then showing pictures of a toilet roll should, according to this model, mean that people have a warm emotional response to the puppy, which then becomes associated with the toilet roll. That is the theory, at least, but does it work?

A study by Stayman and Batra (1991) examined what effect our emotional states during an advertisement have on the subsequent memory of the product and brand choice at a later time. People were shown a 30-second TV advertisement, embedded in a programme which they were watching. The advertisement was either 'emotional' or 'informational' in its approach. The research participants were then given distracting tasks, to disguise the aim of the study. Following this, they were asked to make a brand choice between two products. Stayman and Batra found that the people who saw the emotional advertisement were more likely to choose the brand that they had seen advertised than those people who had seen the advertisement which emphasized strong argument and information.

This study is not untypical of much research in this area. There are, however, some problems which may limit how easily it can be generalized to typical consumer behaviour. One of these problems comes from the fact that the research participants used in the study were all students, who were either paid or received course credits for participating. This would have been likely to result in their paying greater attention to the information that they were presented with than someone who was just watching TV in the normal run of things. The increased attention, in turn, would tend to increase the effects.

Also, there was a relatively short space of time between the students seeing the advertisement and being asked to make the brand choice, so they would have remembered more details, possibly in a different way. As we will see later in this chapter, memory changes over time, as it adjusts to the person's own views and ideas, so it is possible that the effects of a longer time gap – as happens in real life – would have been quite different. Unfortunately, these sorts of problems seriously reduce the value of the evidence.

Other studies of consumerism, however, have operated in rather more ecologically valid contexts. Milliman (1982) investigated the effects of background music on shoppers, by arranging for several different types of music to be played in an American supermarket for a nine-week period between the New Year and Easter. The background music varied between low tempo music, fast tempo music and no music at all. Milliman found that shoppers moved at a different pace, depending on the tempo of the music. In addition, the sales volume increased dramatically when slow tempo music was playing, by 38.2%. By moving more slowly, shoppers spent more time in the store and purchased more products. The researchers explained this in terms of classical conditioning: we associate fast music with fast movement and slow music with slower movement, because of our previous experiences of that association.

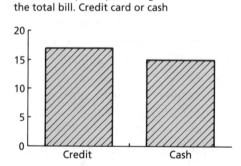

Restaurant tip as a percentage of the total bill. Credit card or cash

Figure 5.5 Credit cards and tipping. (Fernberg, 1986.)

Fernberg (1986) argued that credit cards are conditioned stimuli, which have acquired their powers to elicit spending behaviour for people, because of their prior association with the positive feelings associated with acquiring new possessions. As a result, people are more ready to part with money when they are paying by credit card than when they are paying with cash.

In an observational study of the tips left by 135 customers in a restaurant, Fernberg noted that when customers were paying by credit card, they left a tip which was significantly higher than when they were paying with cash: 16.95% of the total size of the bill, by comparison with 14.95% with a cash settlement. However, it might also be argued that the reason people are more likely to part with money on their credit cards is that they do not witness the consequences of their action for a further month when the credit statement comes. If, on the other hand, they use cash then they have immediate and direct evidence of how much they are spending, which might act as a slight deterrent.

Another study that might have some bearing on this issue was carried out by Levey and Martin (1975), and looked at the classical conditioning of human evaluative responses. Their research participants were shown 50 postcards of paintings and scenic photographs, and asked to rate them on a scale from +100 to -100. They were then asked to choose the two they liked most and the two they liked least. The research participants were then shown ten neutral cards followed immediately by their favourites, then ten more neutral cards followed by one of the two cards they most disliked. After this they were asked to rate the neutral cards again.

Levey and Martin found that in the second rating, the neutral cards which had been paired with the favourite cards had gone up by an average of 16 points, whereas the neutral cards which had been paired with the disliked cards had gone down by roughly 31 points. The researchers suggested that the research participants' emotional reactions to the pleasant or unpleasant cards had become associated with the neutral cards producing the new evaluation, purely because the stimuli had been paired together.

Avoiding food which has made us sick is a powerful survival mechanism and represents a special form of classical conditioning known as **one-trial learning**. For example, chemotherapy produces strong feelings of nausea, which patients often associate with items in their regular diet. This sometimes makes them aversive to these foods, so they refuse to eat them again. Broberg and Bernstein (1987) used classical conditioning in attempting to reduce the unpleasant effects of chemotherapy in children, by linking the nausea with one particular unimportant food

Health

one-trial learning *A rapid form of learning, usually associated with classical conditioning, which only takes one event to be learned, such as avoiding a food which has made you sick.*

which would act as a 'scapegoat', so that the child would not associate the nausea with its regular food.

Children who were about to undergo chemotherapy for cancer were given a strong-tasting sweet after eating a meal, about four and a half hours before they were given the drug treatment (four and a half hours is the period of time in which one-trial learning seems to be most effective). The researchers measured the amount of the foods which were part of the child's normal nutritious diet that the children ate at mealtimes after their treatment. Compared with the control condition in which no sweet was given, children receiving the 'scapegoat' ate more of the normal foods. The aversion resulting from the nausea seemed to have been successfully redirected towards a harmless target.

Enuresis (bedwetting) is a common childhood condition and many children find it deeply upsetting. One problem, though, is that some children sleep so soundly that they fail to wake up or dream that they are on the toilet. Mowrer (1980) described the 'bell and pad' technique for use with regularly enuretic children, where a sensitive pad underneath the sheet causes a bell to ring as soon as it detects moisture. This wakes the child, so it is able to use the toilet. The idea is that the child will come to associate waking up with the feeling of having a full bladder and so will be able to get to the toilet before urination actually begins. The technique has been used with some success in many institutions, as well as by private families – although, as with most techniques, not all children seem to benefit from it.

Environment

People who have experienced severely stressful events, such as the Lockerbie plane crash, or other disasters, frequently suffer from a syndrome known as post-traumatic stress disorder, which we looked at in Chapter 2. This involves vivid dreams and flashbacks, high levels of anxiety and hyper-vigilance, insomnia and emotional instability, and other problems, which may last for months or even years. Fairbank and Keane (1982) adopted a procedure based on classical conditioning to treat an American veteran of the Vietnam War who was experiencing severe post-traumatic stress disorder. The procedure which they used was **imaginal flooding**, in which the man was asked to imagine the combat scenes and to follow it up by imagining a positive, relaxing scene, repeatedly.

imaginal flooding *Used to conquer fear and anxiety, the patient is required to imagine the fear stimulus in a controlled setting.*

Fairbank and Keane reported that this procedure produced a decrease in the numbers of nightmares and flashbacks associated with that particular scene which the man experienced. In theoretical terms, they argued that what had happened was that the fear response to the imagined scene had become extinguished through a combination of the repeated exposure to the stimulus, resulting in a lowered emotional response

The behaviourism of Watson and Pavlov was egalitarian in that they proposed that the differences between people could be accounted for by their learning experiences and not their inheritance. This notion of equality made the movement popular in both America, where equality is written into the constitution, and the newly formed Soviet Union which was committed to notions of personal equality.

The behaviourist movement took hold of psychology for the next 30 years until it became clear that the early discoveries were not going to be built on substantially and the problems with environmental determinism became harder to ignore. So important was the early work and so little have been the subsequent discoveries, that many textbooks still use Watson's study on learnt fear in an infant (little Albert) as a behavioural explanation of phobias, despite the work being based on one case, being highly unethical and being reported differently every time Watson wrote about it.

Figure 5.6 Behaviourism.

purely through habituation, and the provision of an alternative response suggested by the relaxing scene.

Operant conditioning

At around the turn of the 20th century, the American psychologist Edward Thorndike began to investigate how animals learn. In one series of observations he would place a cat in a 'puzzle box' and measure the time it took to escape. Over a number of trials that time decreased, until eventually the cat would leave the box almost as soon as it was placed in it. From his observations, Thorndike formulated the Law of Effect, which states that behaviour which has positive or rewarding outcomes is more likely to recur in similar circumstances.

This work was amplified by the behaviourist B.F. Skinner, who argued that all behaviour in human or non-human animals is caused, shaped and maintained by its consequences. The consequences can shape behaviour in two main ways. **Positive reinforcement** occurs when a pleasant consequence follows a particular response. It strengthens that response, making it more likely to happen. In theory, for instance, giving your pet a doggo-choc when it sits on command will make it more likely to sit next time you tell it to, although the authors' experiences are that it makes the dog more likely to check whether you have a doggo-choc in your hand or not before it decides whether to sit.

Negative reinforcement occurs when an aversive stimulus is

positive reinforcement In operant conditioning, strengthening learned behaviour by direct reward when it occurs.

negative reinforcement Encouraging a certain kind of behaviour by the removal or avoidance of an unpleasant stimulus.

removed or avoided by making a particular response. Doing one's homework to avoid getting into trouble, is an example where a particular behaviour allows the avoidance of an aversive situation. Providing an elaborate excuse for not having done the homework could, if successful, be taken as an example of escaping an aversive situation, and both of these would make the behaviour more likely to happen again.

Punishment occurs when an aversive stimulus follows a behavioural response. In theory, it weakens that response and makes it less likely to recur. Skinner, however, regarded punishment as an extremely inferior form of behavioural control, on the grounds that at best it will suppress a specific form of undesirable behaviour, but it does not produce rewardable or desirable behaviour. There is nothing to stop the child, animal or adult human from doing something else equally undesirable.

Positive and negative reinforcement are used to shape entirely new behaviours, by reinforcing actions which approximate to the required response, and requiring those approximations to become successively more like the end goal. For example, if you wanted your pet to learn to jump through a hoop, you would not start by showing it a hoop and saying 'Jump!' You would begin by rewarding the animal for walking through a hoop on the ground (or swimming through if it were a goldfish), and then gradually raising the hoop and rewarding the animal for every new height achieved.

Skinner believed that the mechanisms of operant conditioning provided an adequate explanation for the whole range of learned human and animal behaviour. He saw this type of learning as the fundamental basis for the behaviour of all 'organisms' (the behaviourist's word for animal or human being). It was unnecessary, Skinner argued, to look for underlying causes of behaviour. Instead, we just need to look at the **reinforcement contingencies**, which can be used to change that behaviour.

reinforcement contingencies The conditions under which positive or negative reinforcement are given.

	Presented	Removed
Pleasant stimulus	Positive reinforcement (reward)	Omission
Unpleasant stimulus	Punishment	Negative reinforcement (escape)

Figure 5.7 Table of reinforcement.

Key reference: SKINNER, B. F. (1938) *The Behavior of Organisms.*
Appleton-Century Crofts, New York.

Positive reinforcement in the form of incentives for desired behaviour can have a considerable effect on the way that people act. Skinner (1972) argued that society should take a systematic approach to the use of positive reinforcements, encouraging people to act in a socially responsible manner by providing them with incentives. Perhaps inspired by this, Powers, Osborne and Anderson (1973) provided plastic garbage bags to people who were visiting a town park. Those who filled their bags were given a choice of incentives: either a direct reward of 25 cents; or entry in a lottery, with $20 as the first prize. The amount of littering in the park dropped dramatically while the incentive scheme was in operation. It is open to question, however, whether it produced a lasting effect on people's behaviour, since when the scheme was not in effect, a much higher level of littering was observed.

Environment

Other attempts to produce socially responsible behaviour using operant conditioning have been attempted. Foxx and Shaeffer (1981) explored ways of decreasing petrol consumption. They began by monitoring the number of miles driven each day by employees of a particular company. The company then introduced a lottery ticket system, whereby those employees who reduced their number of miles most each week were given a small cash prize. Another, larger prize was given for the greatest reduction over a four-week period. The researchers found a significant reduction in the number of miles which were driven by employees each week while the scheme was in force.

Operant conditioning has been used in a wide range of settings to deal with a wide range of problems and sometimes it has proved useful with problems which have defied other methods. **Biofeedback** is an extension of a simple operant conditioning paradigm in which people can be taught to gain control over the autonomic nervous system – normally not under conscious control – by being given sensory feedback about their bodily functioning. The awareness that they are succeeding is generally considered to be an adequate reward to reinforce this learning.

biofeedback The use of electronic signals as indicators, in order to learn voluntary control of autonomic responses.

Cerulli *et al.* (1979) used biofeedback to deal with the distressing problem of incontinence – a problem which they described as 'a stigma of great magnitude'. The condition is difficult to treat by drugs or surgery, so psychological interventions have considerable potential value. In Cerulli's study, 50 patients with poor levels of bowel control were taught to increase the contraction of the external sphincter muscle. This was achieved by getting them to respond to artificial rectal distension using the process of inflating balloons. The act of blowing up a balloon makes

Health

Figure 5.8 A person receives information about the state of their bodily functions – biofeedback.

a person contract their rectal sphincter (try it!). Cerulli *et al.* gave the patients feedback about their sphincter contraction by showing them manometric (pressure) tracings.

The results of the study showed that, as a result of this feedback, 36 out of the 50 patients managed to achieve a far better level of bowel control. In some, the problem disappeared altogether, while others showed a 90% reduction in the frequency of incontinence. By showing the patients that they were able to control this muscle, and how to go about it, the biofeedback had allowed them to learn some control over its operation. It is uncertain how long the newly acquired skill persisted outside the clinic or laboratory, but it seems likely that the patients would have been highly motivated to maintain it, and so would have made an effort to do so.

Isaacs, Thomas and Goldiamond (1960) used the technique of shaping a person's behaviour through the use of positive reinforcement in an attempt to encourage a long-stay psychiatric patient to talk. The patient, who was diagnosed as schizophrenic, had been hospitalized for 22 years and had not spoken to anyone for the last 19 of them. The first problem which Isaacs faced in dealing with this patient was to establish something which would act as a reinforcer for any learning to take place. Isaacs *et al.* noticed that the patient would look at the therapist whenever he picked up some chewing gum, so this was chosen as the reward. They reasoned that the first step towards conversation was engaging the patient's attention, so at first, whenever the patient looked at the therapist, he would hold up the gum and give it to the patient.

Over a two-week period the patient began to show this behaviour more and more often, so the therapist was then able to withhold the gum until the patient made a lip movement. Once this was established, the patient was not given the gum until he made a sound. In the final phase of the therapy the therapist would hold up the gum and say 'Say gum'. After six weeks of therapy the patient suddenly requested the gum. This proved to be the breakthrough: from then on, he would answer simple questions from the therapist. This formed a dramatic improvement in the quality of life of the patient, though whether it was directly due to operant conditioning, or whether the intensive amount of individual attention the patient received had more to do with it, is open to question.

The method of successive approximations

Summary of shaping a mute psychiatric patient to speak
End goal: speech
Reinforcement: chewing gum

Steps to the goal
1. Engaging attention
2. Making lip movement
3. Making vocal sound
4. Making words
5. Answering questions

Figure 5.9 Shaping. (Isaacs, Thomas and Goldiamond, 1960.)

In an early study, Hurlock (1925) showed how valuable positive reinforcement could be for children in school. Hurlock gave ten-year-old school children practice in performing a set of equally difficult arithmetic tests. They were divided into four groups. One group was kept separate from the other group and simply given a set of tasks to do. One group was systematically praised for their day's work, regardless of their actual level of performance. A third group was systematically reproved: told off for careless mistakes or poor work, or for any other excuse which could be found; and a fourth group was ignored, but undertook the same tests in the same classroom as the other two groups, and could hear what was said to them.

Education

On the first day, the performance of all the groups of children was much the same. From then on, however, the praised group were far more successful than the others. The reproved group improved for a couple of days, but soon showed a decline in performance. The ignored

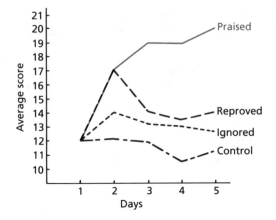

Figure 5.10 The effects of praise and reproofs on school performance. The students who received praise showed the greatest improvement in their test scores. (Hurlock, 1952.)

group performed at a consistently low level throughout – even lower than the reproved group – and the control group, who had been in a separate room, performed worst of all (see Figure 5.10).

Allen *et al.* (1964) described an instance where nursery school teachers were unconsciously reinforcing the social isolation of a particular four-year-old, named Ann. Ann typically would play by herself and not with other children, and the teachers would often try to encourage her to play with the other children. Ann found this attention from the teachers to be very rewarding and consequently continued to play by herself. In order to break the cycle, the teachers began to give Ann attention only when she played with other children or at least approached them. When she was playing by herself they left her alone and whenever Ann tried to get individual attention from a teacher this was withheld. Within ten days of beginning the new programme, Ann had changed from spending less than 20% of her time with others, to spending about 70% of it with them.

Teachers can have a considerable impact on how children get through their school days. Devlin and Williams (1992) reported a survey of over 1600 people in Britain who had achieved fame through various professions. Over 85% of the eminent scientists whom they contacted reported that they had enjoyed school and particularly singled out specific teachers who had taken an interest in their studies. The encouragement they had received from those individual teachers, they reported, had given their interest in science a boost which had lasted for the whole of their careers.

Society

A classic example of operant conditioning was developed by Skinner (1960) for the American military during the Second World War. Skinner reasoned that if, as his laboratory experiments had shown, pigeons could be taught to vary their responses depending on the visual display which was in front of them, then it would be possible to use pigeons to guide

missiles. Specifically, Skinner proposed that pigeons could be put into the nose cones of missiles to guide them in seeking out and destroying selected targets.

Skinner demonstrated the feasibility of this idea in a military project named Project ORCON (organic control). A set of pigeons were trained to peck at the centre of a target which appeared in the shape of an enemy ship on a screen. When a gold electrode on the pigeon's beak touched the screen, an electric circuit in the screen recorded the exact location of the peck. The missile could then be directed towards the target while the pigeon happily pecked away. Skinner showed that the pigeons could discriminate very effectively between different types of ship, so they could be trained to fly past friendly ships and dive to a glorious destruction on an enemy ship. However, the American military showed some concern at arming a flock of pigeons with enough explosives to wipe out the whole American fleet, so the pigeon pilots never had a chance to show their military skills.

The value of the pigeon as a navigator and spotter, though, has not been totally ignored. Stark (1981) reported that the American Coastguard had trained pigeons to spot people who are lost at sea. Carried in special observation pods beneath a helicopter, the pigeons search the seas for any sign of international orange – the colour of life-jackets. If they find any, they are immediately rewarded. Their wide range of vision and their attention allows them to spot targets that human observers miss.

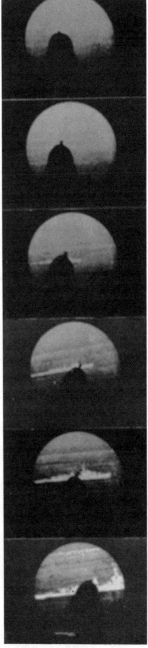

Figure 5.11 The heroic pigeons of project ORCON. (Skinner, 1960.)

Extensions of operant conditioning

Operant conditioning theory has been extended in many directions. For example, Harlow (1949) showed that it is possible to explain seemingly more complex types of learning using the concepts of conditioning. It had been believed that abstract problems required higher mental processes such as insight. Harlow, however, in an ingenious range of experiments with monkeys showed that they could be taught to solve types of problems, if they were given enough experience. The monkeys generalized from the tasks which they had originally learned and produced evidence that they had learned concepts such as 'pick the odd-one-out'. Harlow referred to these as **learning sets**.

learning sets *A preparedness to undertake certain familiar types of learning.*

Other psychologists have extended the concept of reinforcement. A reinforcer which satisfies a basic need, such as food or water, is known as a primary reinforcer. Skinner (1972) discussed the concept of secondary reinforcement, which is the way that a stimulus can acquire reinforcing properties through being associated with a primary reinforcer. For example, a rat will learn to press a lever in a box in order to hear a click if, on previous occasions, it has heard the click when food was being delivered. The sound becomes associated with the food and eventually becomes able to reinforce the rat's behaviour on its own.

Another extension of the concept of reinforcement is that of social reinforcement. There has traditionally been some debate between the strictly behaviourist view that only physical reinforcers satisfying a direct physical need are primary reinforcers (food for a hungry animal, water for a thirsty one and so on), and the broader view that social phenomena such as attention, approval or group acceptance are in themselves primary reinforcers for the human being.

This means that the distinction between a primary and secondary reinforcer can get a bit blurred at times. Is providing company a primary reinforcer for a social mammal? Is attention a primary reinforcer for a human being or is it a secondary reinforcer associated with feeding in early childhood? Some secondary reinforcers are much clearer, though. For humans, the classic secondary reinforcer is money, which does not satisfy any direct need or drive itself, but which becomes intrinsically reinforcing because it is associated with satisfying such needs.

Key reference: SKINNER, B. F. (1972) *Beyond Freedom and Dignity.* Penguin, Harmondsworth.

Thomas, Becker and Armstrong (1968) showed that teacher attention in itself could reinforce children's behaviour. They observed a class of 28 'well behaved' children. The teacher was asked to stop praising the children for a while and the amount of disruptive behaviour shown by the children increased. Then, the teacher was asked to express frequent disapproval of disruptive behaviour and the disruption increased still further. The implication was that having any kind of attention from the teacher was more reinforcing for the children than being ignored.

In another study of classroom behaviour, Barrish, Saunders and Wolf (1969) showed the effects of peer pressure, as well as teacher behaviour, in modifying how children act. They divided a class of children who normally showed a high level of disruptive behaviour in the classroom, into two teams. When any member of each team showed disruptive behaviour, a mark was made on the board. The team which had least marks by the end of the day received special privileges. Barrish, Saunders and Wolf reported that the time spent on disruptive behaviour reduced from 90% to roughly 15%.

Society

An extension of the use of reinforcement to deal with crime was described by Makin, Cooper and Cox (1989), who discussed how Merseyside Police used to concentrate their activities on trying to catch those who were stealing cars and car equipment, with relatively little success. Then, they switched their attention to the question of where the stolen stereos were going – after all thieves steal stereos because they can re-sell them and get money. The police therefore attempted to identify cars whose owners might have purchased a stolen stereo. They examined parked cars looking for incongruities, like an old car with an expensive, modern stereo, and then contacted the owners for an explanation. As soon as it became known that this was happening, the market for stolen stereos declined sharply. In operant terms, the removal of the reinforcement had reduced the frequency of the behaviour.

Work

Secondary reinforcement was also found in incentive schemes by Rank Xerox and American Airlines (Makin, Cooper and Cox, 1989). At Xerox, X certificates, which could be exchanged for $25 in cash, were introduced into the personnel department. Every member of the

secondary reinforcement
Something which reinforces learned behaviour because it has previously been associated with a primary reinforcer.

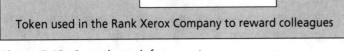

Token used in the Rank Xerox Company to reward colleagues

Figure 5.12 Secondary reinforcement.

department was able to give X certificates to other employees for work-related behaviour, like being exceptionally co-operative or having excellent attendance. At American Airlines, coupons were distributed to passengers who were encouraged to give them to staff they felt deserved some recognition. Both of these schemes produced a considerable effect on staff morale and productivity.

Makin, Cooper and Cox (1989) also reported another company, which had a fleet of tankers transporting hazardous liquids. They introduced a bonus scheme whereby drivers could phone for advice and received a pay bonus as reinforcement each time they did so. Although the scheme was, of course, open to abuse by drivers making unnecessary calls, the company reasoned that it wanted to encourage them to call whenever they were uncertain about anything. They preferred to carry the cost of a few trivial calls than to carry the cost of a dramatic accident caused by drivers not knowing how to handle the materials properly. The consequences of that for the company would have been much more expensive in the long run.

Sport

Behavioural methods in sports have been used to change behaviours that are not directly to do with sporting achievement, like encouraging people to attend training sessions or to reduce disruptive behaviour. There are, however, some studies that illustrate the power of positive reinforcement to improve actual sporting skills. Komaki and Barnett (1983) reported the use of behavioural techniques with pre-adolescent American football players. They chose three 'plays' (set-piece actions in a game). Each play was broken down into five steps, in which the correct behaviour was specified, and players were given immediate feedback and positive reinforcement for correct actions. Komaki and Barnett reported that each play showed a 30–40% improvement after the positive reinforcement was introduced.

It is worth noting, too, that the process of operant training is interactive. Although it is usually described as an operation that one person conducts on another, it is clear that it works both ways. A child is rewarded by a teacher for behaving in a required way, but at the same time the teacher is being rewarded by the child's behaviour. The behaviours are locked together. The image of two rats in a Skinner box with one saying 'I've trained that psychologist to give me food every time I press this lever' has some grain of truth, as any dog or cat owner will verify.

Social learning

Social learning theory was an attempt to integrate the rather simple models of operant and classical conditioning into a more complete description of human social behaviour, by including other forms of learning in the picture. Conditioning theories do not assume any cognitive processes in the animal or person, but suggest that we act without thought, simply learning by association or through trial and error. This type of explanation, though, does not describe our everyday experience, which involves a wide range of cognitive activities, including forward planning, evaluating the possible consequences of our actions and sometimes just daydreaming.

Social learning theorists argue that we can learn through the processes of operant and classical conditioning, but that we also use other kinds of learning, particularly observational learning. In observational learning, we can learn simply from witnessing behaviour rather than doing it ourselves.

In observational learning, the person who is observed is called the model. There are effectively two kinds of observational learning: imitation, in which specific acts, or behaviours, are copied; and identification, in which whole styles of interaction are adopted from the model. Research into social learning showed that various features of the model, as well as the relationship of the model with the observer, would affect the degree of learning. The theory has been applied to a wide range of behaviour, from the development of individual moral rules to the development of complex patterns of social organization.

Key reference: BANDURA, A. (1977) *Social Learning Theory*. Prentice-Hall, Englewood Cliffs, NJ.

Social learning theory is concerned with how people come to imitate the behaviours which they observe other people doing. It suggests, therefore, that it is important to monitor the examples of behaviour that people are exposed to, particularly through television. In a classic study by Bandura, Ross and Ross (1961) young children were individually exposed to a display of stylized adult aggression. The children saw an adult attack a large inflatable doll in a physically and verbally hostile manner. When they were given the opportunity to imitate this behaviour, many of the children showed similar patterns of hostile verbal and physical behaviour (Figure 5.13).

Society

Subsequent studies of this kind investigated the factors that would increase imitative behaviour in children. Among the most powerful of these were, first, whether the child saw the model being rewarded for the behaviour; secondly, whether the model was like the observer; and thirdly, whether the model was warm and/or powerful. The clear implication was that children who were exposed to violent but successful models would be likely to emulate them, particularly if they believed

Albert Bandura, born 4 December 1925, Mundare, Alberta, Canada.
'Human accomplishments and well-being ride on an optimistic sense of personal efficacy.'

Bandura is the leading proponent of social cognitive theory. After receiving his doctoral degree from the University of Iowa in 1953, he joined the faculty at Stanford University where he has spent his entire career. His initial research centred on the prominent role of social modelling in human thought, affect and action. The extraordinary advances in the technology of communications have made modelling a key vehicle in the social diffusion of ideas, values and styles of behaviour. Another major focus of Bandura's work concerns the human capacity for self-directedness. This research has added greatly to our understanding of how people exercise influence over their own motivation and behaviour through self-regulative mechanisms. His most recent research is adding new insights on how people's beliefs in their efficacy to exercise control over events that affect their lives contribute importantly to their attainments, resilience in the face of adversity and psychological well-being. These different lines of research address fundamental issues concerning the nature of human agency.

that those models in any way resembled themselves.

Systematic research into this kind of effect is difficult to design, however, because of the wide range of influences that we are all exposed to on a daily basis. Wharton and Mandell (1985) described two cases in which children were admitted to the emergency department of a hospital after having apparently been suffocated by a pillow placed over their face by their mother. The children had apparently been assaulted because of their incessant crying: one child was dead and the other survived. In both cases, the mothers had seen a film on television within the previous two days in which a distraught mother had been planning to suffocate her child with a pillow because the child's crying was uncontrollable. These case studies imply that the principles of social learning are not just relevant for child behaviour, but apply to adults as well.

One of the social learning mechanisms used by advertisers is often referred to as the **imitation effect**. This is concerned with how quickly a new product will be adopted by consumers. If it is successfully adopted, their rate of purchase typically shows a curve which is gentle at first, but then rises ever more steeply. This is explained in terms of the way that a relatively small number of innovators are likely to adopt a new product

imitation *Copying someone else's behaviour and specific actions.*

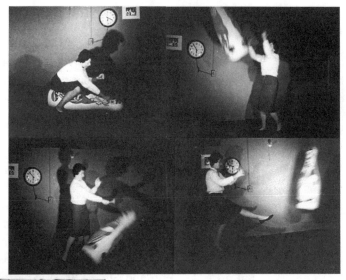

Figure 5.13 Scenes from the 'Bobo Doll' study. The pictures show various scenes from the study, including the aggression by an adult towards the Bobo doll witnessed by the child, and the subsequent aggression of the child.

in the first place, but if they do accept it, others will imitate and follow their example.

Work

In view of the imitation effect, it is pretty important that innovators should obtain the opportunity to adopt a new product easily and quickly. Thompson (1984) described how the initial marketing of Post-it notes involved conventional marketing promotions through office supply stores, but these did not have very much success. In Denver and Tulsa, however, the dealers themselves ran promotions which involved giving out free samples of the product and this was much more successful. The company therefore decided to perform a market test in a town, in which samples were mailed out to every office in the city. Since these were 'free', the employees also took them home. The result of this was that not just office workers, but also their families and friends, began to demand the product, creating a market for widespread distribution.

Health

Venn and Short (1973) explored how modelling can be an important factor in the acquisition of everyday fears. Having obtained parental permission, the researchers showed children a short film which showed a five-year-old child reacting fearfully to a plastic Mickey Mouse figure, but calming down when his mother showed him a Donald Duck one. The researchers took measures of the physiological responses of the children as they watched and found that the children showed much higher levels of arousal when watching the Mickey Mouse cartoon. When the children later participated in a task involving the two plastic figures used in the film, they tended to avoid the Mickey Mouse one and to play much more with the Donald Duck figure. However, a day or two later, this effect had almost entirely disappeared. (It is not known what the Disney Corporation thought of this study!)

Modelling can also be used to reduce fear. Melamed *et al.* (1975) showed that symbolic modelling, produced using films, was an effective way of reducing stress experienced by children recovering from surgery. The children in the study were all aged between 4 and 17 years old, and watching films of other children recovering well seemed to produce a positive effect, although the child's own previous experience was a very significant factor too. Similarly, Bandura (1969) showed how children who were afraid of dogs could have their fear significantly reduced by watching other children play with dogs and the same process has been applied to adults who were phobic about snakes.

Behaviour modification

The combination of conditioning and observational learning led to a number of applications in the area of psychotherapy. Until the 1950s, this had been dominated by the psychoanalytic theories, but in 1958, Wolpe published a paper showing how conditioning theories could be used systematically to modify disturbed behaviour. This led to a number of explorations of different techniques based on behaviourist principles, which, as Eysenck claimed in a highly controversial study in 1963, had demonstrably positive effects – a contrast with psychoanalysis, which seemed to have almost no effect at all.

Behavioural forms of therapy became loosely divided into two groups. On one side were the approaches which were explicitly based on pure stimulus-response classical conditioning, such as aversion therapy, systematic desensitization and implosion therapy, and these became collectively referred to as **behaviour therapies**. On the other side were techniques loosely based on operant conditioning and modelling, such as token economy systems, various forms of programmed learning and modelling therapies. These tended to be referred to collectively as **behaviour modification techniques**.

behaviour therapy The process of treating abnormal behaviour by looking only at the symptoms and using conditioning techniques to modify them.

There has always been a certain amount of tension between the strict stimulus-reponse behaviourists, who interpret any positive outcomes in therapy as straightforward consequences of new stimulus-reponse associations, and those therapists who utilize behavioural techniques, but also recognize the importance of cognitive factors such as understanding, expectation and planning, and of social relationships such as the rapport between therapist and patient. It was the influence of these therapists which formed the foundation for the cognitive therapy used by so many modern therapists today.

> **Key reference:** BANDURA, A. (1969) *Principles of Behavior Modification*. Rinehart & Winston, New York.

One of the most popular uses for behaviour modification techniques has been in adjusting disturbed interactions between parents and their children. Gilbert (1976) described a case in which a mother who was physically abusing her child was helped by a systematic programme of behaviour modification, aimed at teaching her how to interact with her child without feeling anxious or threatened by doing so. At the onset of the intervention, the mother, Kathleen, could not cuddle or kiss Sarah, her four-year-old girl, and had twice tried to kill her, although she was fine with her second daughter, born two years later. She was coping with the problem by keeping herself extremely busy and avoiding the child as much as possible, but still found that she was shouting at the child and that nothing the child could do was right in her eyes.

Society

The behaviour modification treatment was based on modelling, with specific targets of interaction such as talking to Sarah, praising Sarah, sitting next to her, picking her up, smiling at her, cuddling her etc. Kathleen and Sarah together attended therapy sessions, and Kathleen was encouraged to copy the therapist's interactions with Sarah. This involved games of increasing contact and intimacy. Kathleen was also encouraged to act in a warm and caring way towards the child, even though she remarked that as she did not 'feel' anything for the child she did not see how this could be helpful. The therapists were taking the view that if they changed Kathleen's behaviour, attitudes appropriate to that behaviour would follow. Kathleen was also visited at home, and they were encouraged to interact, with the father intervening if the child's behaviour became too demanding.

Gradually, Kathleen became aware that she could sometimes actually enjoy Sarah's company and this was a new experience. The treatment programme began in July and, by Christmas, Kathleen had achieved five of the eight original target behaviours. At this time, a programme of self-directed and self-maintained therapy was initiated, involving activities such as reading to Sarah, joining in indoor games, putting her arms round the child and so on. A year after commencement of treatment, both mother and child were demonstrably happier, and it was felt that the child was no longer at risk.

Herbert (1986) described how social workers could help parents to reinstate 'stimulus control' of their children – in other words, to become effective in guiding their child's behaviour through the use of appropriate reinforcements at the right times. By showing parents how they could encourage children to act appropriately, rather than simply punishing them if they did not (which did not contribute at all to the child learning appropriate behaviour), both parents and children could establish a more positive relationship. That does not mean that the intention was to turn children into good little robots. Rather, Herbert defined the task of the social worker as bringing the child's behaviour within a range which is socially acceptable, in cases where the child is acting in an anti-social or disturbed way most of the time, or in a very extreme manner.

Other therapists using behaviour modification have also found it helpful to work with parents and other members of the family when they were trying to help delinquent children. Alexander and Parsons (1973) described a behavioural programme with delinquent adolescents which used social learning principles, in particular modelling and reinforcement, to teach family members new ways of interacting with one another. They particularly emphasized the importance of communicating clearly and negotiating with one another, rather than simply issuing an ultimatum.

Alexander and Parsons compared the outcome of this programme with that of three other groups. One was a similar group of delinquent adolescents who were simply receiving the usual form of social work contact. Another group consisted of delinquent boys and their families, who met with the social worker for a similar period of time, but did not go through any structured programme of intervention, and the third group met as families and experienced a treatment programme which was based on fairly eclectic psychodynamic principles. Outcomes of the approach were assessed by measuring the recidivism rate over a period of time ('recidivism rate' refers to the rate of repeated offending). The results can be seen in Figure 5.14 and show that the behaviour modification treatment was strikingly more successful than any of the other approaches, with the psychodynamic approach appearing to be the worst of all. It is worth noting that the adolescents were not **randomly allocated** to the treatment programmes, so the different treatments could have been dealing with different problems.

Patterson *et al.* (1975) undertook a family-based behaviour modification programme with the families of 27 conduct disordered boys, who had been referred for treatment. The treatment which the families received involved several elements. One of these was about factual knowledge and, in order to obtain this, parents read a semi-programmed text followed by a multiple-choice test. Another element was concerned with learning to identify exactly what was going on, and in the programme staff taught parents directly how to pinpoint problem areas and collect appropriate data on them. The parents also joined a parent

Non-treatment control group	50%
Behaviour modification	26%
Family group, unstructured contact	47%
Eclectic psychodynamic family group programme	73%

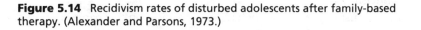

Recidivism rate

20 40 60 80 100%

No treatment

Behaviour modification

Family group

Psychodynamic

Figure 5.14 Recidivism rates of disturbed adolescents after family-based therapy. (Alexander and Parsons, 1973.)

training group to learn appropriate change techniques and to gain some social support from others in similar situations, and the social workers concerned made home visits to the families where necessary.

Once they had received a general awareness of the programme, the parents opted to work on specific behaviours which presented problems in their interactions with their children. Most of them chose the problem of their children's non-compliance to requests, but in all cases, a range of other behaviours was also covered. The families were trained for a total of 31.5 hours of professional time, with the treatment programme lasting from 3–4 months. There was a significant drop in the level of reported daily problems during follow-up observations: average of a 60% reduction in the targeted undesirable behaviours was achieved and about two-thirds of the families reported marked reductions in other problems as well.

recidivism Habitual relapse into crime.

There is a considerable amount of evidence which shows that sending young people to prison tends to increase their **recidivism** rate, rather than reduce it. The recidivism rate for young people who have been locked up tends to be over 70%, but is very much lower for those who receive non-custodial sentences. Buchler, Patterson and Furniss (1966) showed how a large part of the reason why this effect happens is because of the social reinforcement which the young people receive in the institution. Effectively, they learn to become even more anti-social.

Buchler *et al.* showed how in institutions, behaviour which is deviant or anti-social is reinforced by peers much more often than it is proscribed or punished by members of staff. Also, behaviour which is pro-social, or would be socially approved by staff, is punished by peers more often than it is rewarded by staff. In addition, the reinforcements and punishments from peers occur much more immediately and matter much more to the person concerned than staff responses do. All this boils down to the fact that, most of the time, the person is being encouraged to show deviant or anti-social behaviour and punished for being 'good'. It is not surprising, then, that locking young people up produces such high levels of recidivism.

The behaviour therapists also made a number of criticisms of psychiatry, arguing that it was inefficient, did not help people to change, neglected the social and personal context in which people lived and, above all, did not work. Interestingly, almost exactly the same criticisms were made of social work by Fischer (1978), whose criticisms are given in Figure 5.15. Herbert (1986) argued that applying behavioural techniques systematically to social work practice would address a number of these criticisms.

However, using the tool of behaviour modification to change people's

1. It is inefficient of professional time.
2. It is not oriented towards social–environmental change.
3. It does not make adequate use of people in the client's natural environment.
4. It gives disproportionate attention to diagnosis and assessment while paying insufficient attention to intervention. This is encouraged by a low correlation between the assessment and choice of treatment techniques.
5. It places an excessive reliance on talking therapies which have doubtful outcomes.
6. It focuses on client self-understanding rather than on changes in social functioning, and seldom changes the disruptive environmental patterns which instigate and maintain the problems.
7. Clients are minimally involved in any sense in the change process.
8. There are wasteful, high drop-out rates which come from mis-perceptions between client and social worker about what the process is all about.
9. Research into the effectiveness of social work reveals questionable results.

Figure 5.15 Criticisms of social work practice. (Fischer, 1978.)

behaviour raises a number of ethical issues about the conduct of social work, education or health care. One of these issues concerns who defines behaviour as 'inappropriate' or 'unacceptable', and under what circumstances we have the right to intervene and 'modify' someone. The question of human rights and freedom of choice becomes crucially important when we are talking about methods of controlling people's behaviour in this kind of way.

Behaviour modification, as we have seen, can be applied in a number of contexts. This, too, raises questions. It may be regarded as acceptable to decide that we want to change the behaviour of a dangerous criminal, but what of the child who is disruptive in class because it is bored? Such children are easily labelled as 'hyperactive', when really they are simply not receiving enough challenges, both physical and mental. But once the label has been applied, the next step is to modify the 'disturbed' behaviour, making the child dull, but satisfyingly 'normal' for the teacher.

Another, related issue concerns the power relationship between the 'modifier' and the 'modified'. By changing someone, we are taking control of them in some way: adjusting them because they cannot, or will not, adjust themselves. The language of modern social work practice, however, talks of 'empowerment', meaning that people should be encouraged to take control and responsibility for their own lives rather than be controlled by others. So there are also questions about where we draw the line: is it OK to modify the behaviour of the dangerous criminal but not the hyperactive child? Should, as Skinner (1972) proposed, society take on the right to adjust the behaviour of all of its members? Or is human autonomy and freedom of choice something we should aim to establish, and protect against all manipulation? It is not a question with any easy answers, but it is a question which must be considered, none the less.

There are, however, some contexts in which the ethics of behavioural modification become a bit less tricky. Even the most hardened civil rights activist would regard it as acceptable for a company manager to look for ways to help people to work more efficiently, and behavioural modification techniques have often produced some very useful outcomes in this respect. Taylor (1964) reviewed a number of different research programmes conducted by American companies in the late 1950s, which had compared the effectiveness of programmed learning systems and lectures, for learning factual information.

Taylor found that, taking these studies as a whole, the best results from programmed learning systems tended to be in teaching employees drills, rules and operating procedures. They were also useful for the training of specific skills such as micrometer reading, equipment maintenance, sorting and inspection. A number of other studies also showed that programmed learning was useful in teaching some industrial manual skills.

Implementing programmed learning systems in industry or commerce, however, is not simply a matter of whether the method can be effective. There are also questions of cost and development. Programmed learning systems are very expensive and demanding to set up, although once they have been established they involve relatively little maintenance. In view of this, Bass and Barrett (1972) suggested that only programmed learning systems which have been developed for tasks involving large numbers of trainees would be likely to justify their initial cost, and this seems to have been borne out by industrial practice since then.

Cognitive maps

The idea of the cognitive map was suggested by Tolman, in 1948, who showed that even rats seem to be able to develop a 'mental picture' of where they are which helped them to get to a particular goal when they needed to. In one study, rats learnt to run a maze over a number of trials. The maze was then flooded, so that the rats had to use an entirely different set of muscle actions (swimming) to get around the same maze. The rats completed the maze successfully, showing that what they had learned in the early trials was far from a simple association between the immediate stimulus and the muscular response of running.

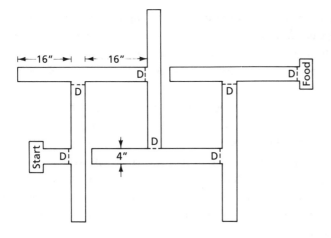

Figure 5.16   An example of a T-maze used by Tolman to investigate cognitive maps in rats. (Tolman, 1948.)

In human terms, we use cognitive maps frequently, and a number of researchers have shown how these maps reflect our personal involvement with the world. For example, Saarinen (1973) found that when college students were asked to draw maps of their campus, they tended to enlarge the areas which were most well known and important to them, and to underestimate the size of those areas which they did not go into very much.

Interestingly, though, an opposite effect seems to occur when we are judging distance. Briggs (1971) showed that people tended to underestimate the length of a well-known journey, whereas when they were asked to estimate distances between two landmarks that they did not know very well, they tended to overestimate. You may have found this yourself: the first time you visit a place it often seems very large, or the distances between two points seem very far; but, as you become more familiar with it, everything seems to become smaller and closer.

> **Key reference:** TOLMAN, E. C. (1948) Cognitive maps in rats and men. *Psychological Review,* **55**, 189–208.

When we first encounter a new institution or a new town, we tend to learn one or two routes about the place and one or two key locations, and then keep to these until we feel we have 'found our feet' a bit, and can begin to explore. As we do explore further, our mental representation of the location changes. Moar (1979) gave one group of people a

Environment

three-minute tour of an unfamiliar building and asked a second group to look at a ground plan of the building for the same amount of time. Along with a third group, who were familiar with the building, all the participants were asked to recall directions and distances between places on the ground floor.

Moar found that the 'tour group' gave answers that were fragmented and route-dependent, whereas the 'map group' gave answers that conformed to the geometric structure of the building. The 'building-familiar group' also produced answers which showed they had a cognitive map that correlated highly with this geometric structure. Moar suggested from this that the more we experience a particular place, the more our internal representations of that location tend towards its physical structure.

There are, however, some differences between cognitive maps and survey maps. People who come to know a city by using its transport systems primarily – in particular, those who know London through the London Underground – often experience some surprising reorientations if they begin to walk around central London. Places which they assumed were very distant from one another turn out to be close neighbours, while others which seemed adjacent can be quite a way apart. This is because the familiar Underground map of the central part of London bears no relationship to the survey map in direction or distance, or even in the spatial relationship of various stations. It is a network map,

Figure 5.17 The London Underground map bears little relationship to a surface street plan, but many people attempt to find their way around on the surface using a cognitive map based on this railway map.

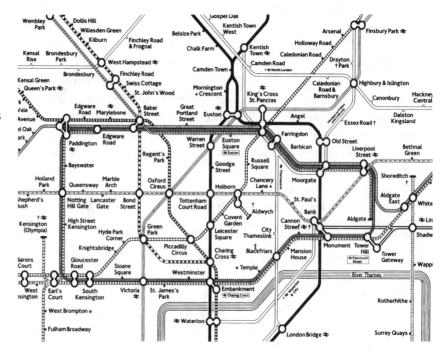

showing connections and junctions, and not a geographical representation of London.

Byrne (1979) asked long-term residents of a town to estimate the length of several routes. He found that they tended to overestimate town centre routes and routes with changes of direction, and suggested the cognitive maps tend to be based on turns and landmarks. This suggests that cognitive maps are more like a network map such as the London Underground map than a survey map which gives a geographical image of the area. Byrne also found that if people were asked to draw a particular road junction, they tended to draw right angles, even if the real junction was not anything of the sort. This, too, confirmed the impression that cognitive maps are more like network maps than survey ones.

Stanley Milgram (1977) carried out a study of the cognitive maps of Paris held by 218 Parisians. These people were given a variety of tasks including drawing the city of Paris, recognizing photographs of various key features and responding to questions such as, 'Suppose you were about to go into exile, and had a chance to take only one last walk through the city. What would be your itinerary?' Responses to these tasks showed Milgram how people's personal representations of space in cities tend to be very distorted and selective, even though they are just as useful to the person concerned as an accurate geographical representation would be (Figure 5.18).

Milgram also showed that the cognitive maps which people form of cities are multidimensional. They do not just contain cognitive representations of what is actually there, but also have strong emotional and intuitive components, associated with people's experiences of the place and with their expectations of what is likely to be the case. These impressions, Milgram emphasized, do not just come from the person's own experience. They are also shaped by social factors – people tend to hold the same expectations and beliefs about specific areas, and these are different from the beliefs which they share about other neighbourhoods. Cognitive maps, therefore, acquire some of the status and characteristics of the **social representations** which we looked at in Chapter 3.

Antes, McBride and Collins (1988) looked at how changes in travel routes through a city affected the cognitive maps of people living in the area. They asked 109 residents in a particular town to assess the distances between selected points in the city, before and after the construction of a connecting street between them. Interestingly, the researchers found that female residents showed changes in their judgements on the second occasion, becoming more accurate in their assessments. Male residents' judgements, on the other hand, remained unchanged by the opening of the connecting road.

Education

Geographical representations of an area can also be used as a teaching tool. Bruner (1961) described an experimental teaching method which was adopted with a class of American 10 to 12 year olds, who were handed charts of North America which consisted only of the major rivers, lakes and natural resources. Using these charts, the children were asked to identify where they might find the main cities, and where main roads and railways would run. The children discussed the work together and

Figure 5.18 Cognitive maps of Paris. (Milgram, 1977.)

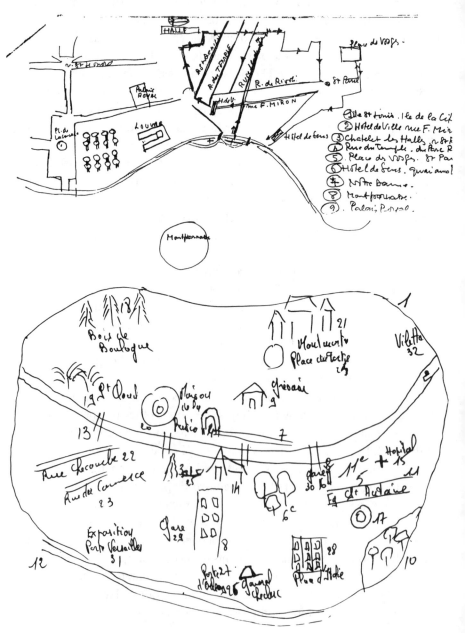

so were able to pool their existing knowledge. They were also asked to justify their choices of location, using information obtained from their previous geography classes. Then, once their choices had been made, they were able to identify which were the correct ones and what their mistakes had been. From this active learning, Bruner argued, the children obtained a much clearer understanding of geographical processes than they would have done from a more conventional, passive learning approach.

Imagery

No definition can do justice to the richness of experience that is included in the notion of imagery. Imagery is seen by psychologists as a mental activity that enables us to represent the perceptual properties of our environment. These properties can be the physical properties of objects such as shape, distance, colour and sound, and they can also be the properties of actions in the environment, for example mentally rehearsing a dance movement. Because of its close relationships with sensory experience, the rules of the imagery system are rooted in our perceptual knowledge and skills.

Interest in mental imagery goes back to the ancient Greeks and probably beyond: some of the earliest recorded mnemonics – strategies for enhancing memory – involved the use of visualization. Psychologists have investigated many different aspects of imagery, including the development of **eidetic imagery**. Eidetic imagery is a visual image of a scene that persists a long time after stimulation, that is accurate in detail and can be scanned in the same way that a picture might be scanned. About 1 in 10 Western children show remarkable abilities of eidetic imagery, yet this ability is present in less than 1 in 1000 Western adults. According to Bruner's theory of the development of representation, this occurs because, as the child matures, symbolic representation comes to supersede imagery as the major representational mode.

eidetic memory
'Photographic' memory –
visual or acoustic memory
which is so accurate as to be
almost like a factual record.

Symbolic representation has an advantage over mental imagery because it can be more readily manipulated and changed. Imagery, it seems, is for the most part tied quite closely to reality. This is supported by research into how mental images may be manipulated. In a number of studies, researchers have investigated the time which people take to match up images of rotated shapes with an original. For the most part, the time taken to complete the task tends to be proportional to the angle of rotation, suggesting that the mental world is structured using similar rules to those of the physical world.

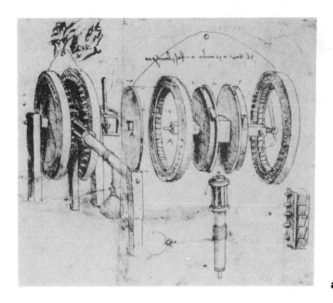

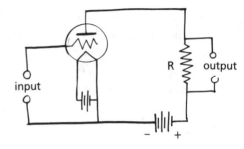

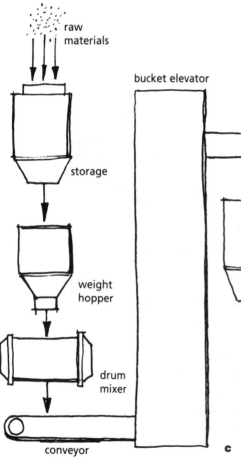

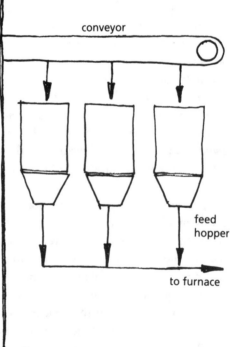

Figure 5.19   Idea sketching. (a) This sketch by Leonardo da Vinci (complete and exploded drawings of a weight-driven rachet) was an innovative form of idea sketching. (b) The approximate cross section of a vehicle and a wiring diagram are more abstract representations of objects. (c) This flowchart is more abstract still, representing relationships rather than objects.

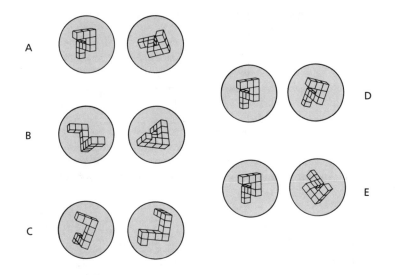

Figure 5.20 The task is to decide which of these pairs of shapes are the same. It is necessary to mentally rotate one of the shapes to see it if matches its pair. (Pair C are the only ones that do not match). (Shepard and Metzler, 1971.)

Key reference: SHEPARD, R. N. (1978) The Mental Image. *American Psychologist, 33*, 125–37.

Raugh and Atkinson (1975) developed a 'key word' system for remembering information using mental imagery. Using this technique, they showed that people who were asked to learn Spanish vocabulary using imagery were much more successful than those who tried to learn the same words using straightforward repetition. To encourage the use of memory in the study, Raugh and Atkinson gave research participants a list of Spanish words, and asked them to think of an English word which had a similar sound. The Spanish word for tent, for instance, '*carpa*', sounds like 'carp' in English. Once the participants had found a key word of this type, they were then to form an image using the key word to link the Spanish word with its English meaning. So to connect '*carpa*' and 'tent', they might envisage something like a fish in a tent.

In the test, research participants were given a list of 60 Spanish words to learn. One group was asked to use the 'key-word' method and the other group were not given any instructions about how they should go about remembering. Those using the 'key-word' method recalled an average of 88% of the words on the list, while those in the control group recalled an average of 28%. The researchers concluded that the use of

Education

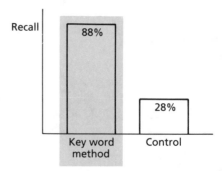

Figure 5.21 The use of imagery in vocabulary learning. (Raugh and Atkinson, 1975.)

imagery as mental representation can produce a dramatic improvement to our ability to remember information – although it must be remembered that recalling straightforward, concrete words like 'tent' and 'horse' may involve different mental processes than remembering less easily visualized words like 'justice' and 'freedom'.

Studies of mental imagery have shown that some people have quite extraordinary abilities. Stromeyer (1970) described a case study of a young teacher, Elizabeth, who worked at Harvard University and was also a painter. She appeared to be able to 'project' an image from her mind on to a blank canvas. Once on the canvas the image would remain still and she would be able to scan it. In one remarkable experiment, Elizabeth looked at one-half of a stereographic image with her right eye. This appeared as a pattern of random dots. On the next day she looked at the other half of the stereoscopic image, also a random-dot pattern, with her left eye. Because of her outstanding eidetic memory, she was able to superimpose one image on the other and recognize that the two images made up a picture of a square.

Consumer

While applications of this kind of rare ability have been elusive (or possibly top secret, if thriller writers are to be believed), we all seem to respond very much better to words which evoke concrete images than we do to words which are simply names that have no meaning. The message for marketers is that the name of any product which they are trying to sell should be easy to visualize. This was learned by the American Matex Corporation, who had developed a product for inhibiting rust and began by marketing it under the name of 'Thixo-Tex'. Sales were extremely disappointing. After some discussion, according to White (1980) the product was remarketed as 'Rusty Jones'. As a result, sales rose enormously, from $2 million worth of sales in 1976, to $100 million worth of sales in 1980.

Techniques for training people to use mental imagery have also proved helpful in the health field. Bridge *et al.* (1988) described how imagery was used to help to lessen the unpleasant emotional consequences of radiotherapy for women who had breast cancer. In the study, women who were undertaking this treatment were allocated to one of three groups. Two of the groups were relaxation training groups, one of which just emphasized physical training, particularly control of muscle tension and breathing, while the other used relaxation training along with mental imagery (asking each person to concentrate on a peaceful scene of her own choice). The control group were encouraged to meet and simply talk about themselves for an equal amount of time.

Health

Bridge *et al.* assessed the women's moods, using standard inventories, and found that women in both of the groups which had involved relaxation training were significantly less disturbed than those who were in the control groups. However, it was also clear that those women who had been encouraged to use imagery techniques as well were more relaxed than those whose intervention had focused only on physical relaxation. This appears to show the benefits of imagery, although it is less easy to pin down exactly how imagery works in this context.

In sports studies, the topic of imagery has been extensively used and is frequently associated with the idea of mental practice. Most sports psychology self-help books will give examples and exhortations to practise visualizing the successful undertaking of one's event, carrying it through from beginning to end. In a talk at the British Psychological Society's annual conference in 1988, David Hemery (Olympic 400m hurdles gold 1968, bronze 1972) described how he had used visualization in order to train himself systematically for the event. Hemery visualized running his event in every lane, under every conceivable condition of weather and competition, in his search for perfection.

Sport

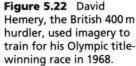
Figure 5.22 David Hemery, the British 400 m hurdler, used imagery to train for his Olympic title-winning race in 1968.

Since this experience, Hemery had interviewed many other top sporting personalities about their mental preparations for events and found that many of the most successful used visualization techniques similar to those he had adopted himself. He also emphasized the importance of positive visualization, contrasting the year when he had tried to prepare himself mentally for defeat, and lost, with the year in which he had won his gold medal, when his mental visualization included only positive images of completing the course successfully, never of failure. Hemery, then, is a convinced adherent of the method, as are many other sportspeople.

There appear to be two forms of mental imagery which sportspeople use. Internal imagery is mainly **kinaesthetic** in nature – athletes develop 'muscle images' of their performance and imagine themselves doing the action successfully. This technique, then, involves a kind of internal visualization, but not one which involves picture images: they can feel the performance but they cannot see themselves. External imagery, on the other hand, is mainly visual in nature: athletes pretend to watch themselves from the outside. There is a suggestion that internal imagery is the more effective. Mahoney and Avener (1977), for example, reported that their study of élite gymnasts indicated that they used more internal imagery than a comparison group of less successful gymnasts.

Smith (1987) identified five principles of the application of imagery to sport which are given in Figure 5.23. Fenker and Lambiotte (1987) used these principles in a performance enhancement programme based on the development of imagery skills. They reported that a major American college football team used the programme and achieved its best record in 20 years.

Internal imagery can be used by amateurs too: one of the authors found it a helpful approach when attempting to learn basic skating techniques for the first time at age 39. As with any psychological technique, however, there is a question as to whether the effects which can be observed come from the method itself or from the fact that people believe in it. There is some evidence that mental practice is better than

kinaesthetic senses *The bodily senses which inform us about the position and state of the muscles, skeletal system and internal organs.*

---

1. It is possible to develop imagery skills
2. The sportspeople must have a positive view of the effectiveness of imagery
3. Imagery has the greatest benefit for skilled athletes
4. Relaxation is a necessary part of imagery use
5. There are two kinds of imagery – internal and external

Figure 5.23 Principles of applying imagery in sport. (Smith, 1987.)

none, while not as good as actual physical practice. So, if the effects do come from the imagery itself, then how do they come about?

There are several different views on this question. Some sports psychologists argue that the benefits of mental activity mainly come from general tension or isometric muscle effects, caused by minute movements of the body which occur while the person is imagining their muscle movement. Some other psychologists argue that the effects of imagery may be psychological rather than physical – mental imagery may operate to help mental planning, helping the person to integrate correct muscular actions into their existing mental schemas. It is possible, too, that imagery serves a trace rehearsal function, revitalizing existing memories and reminding the person of the plan-to-be-executed.

A different set of explanations for the effects of mental imagery focus on the cognitive outcomes of thinking about the sporting activity rather than about anything else. One of these explanations is that, by providing a focus for the athlete's thoughts, imagery helps the person to control cognitive anxiety and make sure that worrying or irrelevant thoughts are excluded. Alternatively, it may serve as a kind of therapy for anxiety by operating in the other way: by imagining anxiety-arousing circumstances, the athlete may gradually become desensitized to the circumstances and no longer feel as anxious when they really happen. This type of desensitization is a common technique among some sports coaches. A final note is that, despite his use of imagery, David Hemery needed the shock of a false start by another competitor to focus his mind in the 1968 final.

Skill learning

A dictionary definition of skill refers to 'practised ability'. It is generally thought that skill, unlike talent, is developed from training and practice, so a skilled worker is one who has been trained over a long period of time. However, the psychological notion of skill also includes skills which are 'untrained' or, at least, which have not received formal instruction. For example, the manipulatory skill of reaching for a glass of water and drinking it without spilling any is, in psychological terms, as much a learned skill as potting a ball in pool or knitting a cardigan, although it commands somewhat less in terms of social respect.

Psychologists make an important distinction between skills and habits. The critical feature of this distinction is the idea that skills are usually adaptable and flexible, whereas habits are performed without reference to their consequences or appropriateness. In terms of the conceptual origins of the distinction, some psychologists see habits as relatively simple associations, possibly developed as a result of the forms of conditioning described earlier in this chapter, whereas skills involve more complex forms of learning.

Skills are of many kinds. Discussion of various forms of skill acquisition has encompassed physical skills, linguistic skills, social skills and intellectual ones. However, Welford (1958) suggested that all skills, of whatever kind, possess three main characteristics. The first of these is that skills consist of building an organized and co-ordinated activity in relation to an object or situation. This means that skills involve the whole set of sensory, central and motor nervous system processes which contribute to performance. The second characteristic is that skills are learned gradually, through repeated experience; and the third is that within each skill, many different processes or actions are ordered and co-ordinated in a temporal sequence.

Psychological research suggests that there are two key features of successful skill training schemes: guidance and feedback. Guidance tells us what to do and feedback tells us how successful we have been. Skill learning does not just involve developing a set of physical actions, but learning a set of rules which will lead to the development of appropriate movements. For instance, Schmidt (1975) argued that with practice at a task we learn a relationship, or rule, linking the size of muscle parameters (for example, the force used to hit an object) to the size of the outcome (for example, the distance the object moves). As we practise this, we become more sophisticated at applying the rule and guidance is an important part of the process.

It is a common notion that 'practice makes perfect'. Strictly speaking, though, psychologists would qualify this by saying it is not practice, but practice the results of which are known which makes perfect. If we do not know what the outcomes of our actions have been, we have no way of getting better at doing them. It would be impossible to learn to play darts blindfolded, unless, of course, some other system was introduced to give feedback in a different form.

Key reference: ANNETT, J. (1989) Skills. In A. M. Colman and J. G. Beaumont (eds) *Psychology Survey*, **7**, BPS /Routledge, London.

As we saw earlier in this chapter, research into association learning showed that the time taken to learn a task could be plotted as a learning curve, which had a distinctive shape. The learning of more complex skills, however, shows a correspondingly more complex pattern (Figure 5.24). Learning to type, for instance, is a highly complex skill. Its

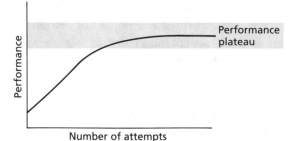

Figure 5.24 The learning curve. The diagram shows how performance improves with practice on simple tasks. Initially we show quick and substantial improvement, but the pace improvement starts to decline until we reach a limit, or plateau.

acquisition follows a pattern known as **plateau learning**, in which the person improves quite quickly for a while, showing a classic learning curve and then reaches a point where they seem to stick, not really getting much better for some time. This is known as a plateau and seems to serve some kind of function in consolidating the basics of the skill which have been acquired so far. After a while, the plateau is followed by another period of improvement, which is then followed by another plateau.

In typing, these plateaux correspond to the different stages of acquiring the skill. Initially, the person is learning the position of the keys on the keyboard and will become faster at doing so. But this improvement can only go so far. The second level of learning is as they begin to acquire muscular patterns representing whole words. Rumelhart and Norman (1982) explained this process in terms of the development of muscular schemata. In the first of these, we develop individual muscle schemata for each letter, so that our fingers 'know' where to find the letter on the keyboard, without our having to seek them out or even look at the keyboard.

Once an optimal speed for this has been obtained, the learning tends to show a plateau. But it emerges from this stable period as we begin to acquire schemata for particular words and then whole familiar phrases. As we become more proficient, we also acquire higher-order schemata about the typing itself, to do with how letters should be combined: the existence of a letter-doubling schema, for instance, can be observed from the way that people will sometimes make mistakes like typing 'bokk' instead of 'book'. At each stage, Rumelhart and Norman argued, it is the integration of the different levels of muscular schemata with continual sensory feedback that produces the smooth skill of typing.

Annett (1982) suggested that skill performance involves 'action prototypes', in which we have a mental representation of the skill in the form of a muscle image. This provides a template for learning, as we try to ensure that our physical actions match up to our impressions of how they ought to feel. Whiting *et al.* (1987) showed how this idea could be applied in ski training, by getting novices to use expert models for learning to ski. In this study, an expert model stood on a simulator platform, making leg and body movements to produce the effect of skiing. Research participants observed the model and then had practice sessions themselves, with full feedback on how accurately they were replicating what the expert had done. These learners achieved fluent movement very much more quickly than people who had experienced similar practice sessions without observing the model.

Work

Having good feedback is useful when we are acquiring skills involving fine motor control, as well as those involving movement of the whole body. Belbin, Belbin and Hill (1957) investigated ways of training employees to do a job involving invisible mending. This involved matching the repair exactly to the weave pattern of the cloth, so it is important that the person has a good understanding of the way that the weave pattern is constructed and how the repair fits with it. Since the work is so fine, however, this can be difficult to see.

Belbin *et al.* used specially made, large-weave cloth and trained employees on this while they acquired the basic understanding of what they were supposed to do. Once they were able to mend the large-weave cloth properly, the trainees transferred to working with normal cloth, but using a large magnifying glass. After relatively few training sessions, the trainees were able to dispense with the magnifying glass and work with the ordinary cloth. Belbin *et al.* found that this method of training reduced the overall training time for a skilled mender from several months to a few weeks.

During this study, Belbin *et al.* also found that, contrary to expectation, the older workers learned faster than the younger ones. Belbin (1964) went on to investigate the training needs of older workers in skill learning and found that there were a number of factors which would facilitate learning in older workers – so much so, that if these factors were built into training schemes, they would result in older people picking up new skills quicker than younger ones. One of the most important of these was timing. It was important that older trainees should be allowed to control the amount of time they had to master task objectives and the speed at which instruction was given. Possibly their previous experience and better self-knowledge made them more able to pace their learning than younger people.

Belbin also found that older workers learned best when the instruction allowed them to utilize some of their existing knowledge. It is possible that this helped them to integrate the new knowledge into their existing schemata more efficiently. Perhaps connected to this, it was also important for older workers that the instruction should be related as directly as possible to the task that was to be taught and that opportunity for practical exercising of the skill should follow instruction as quickly as possible. They were much less tolerant of abstract instruction which did not relate obviously to the job that they were being asked to do.

Education

Playing music is a skill that requires very large amounts of practice, in order to achieve a remarkably precise level of muscle control. Gruson (1988) studied rehearsal behaviour in 40 piano students taking individual lessons and 3 professional concert pianists. The experience of each pianist was assessed by noting their level of achievement on an examination board scheme of grading from one to ten. Each grade was thought to represent around one year's study on the piano, although the concert pianists were obviously well in advance of level ten. In the study, each of the pianists was given three novel pieces appropriate to their particular level and allowed half an hour for practice.

The researchers made audiotapes of the practice sessions, which were then scored using a detailed observational scale. Some of the most significant outcomes are given in Figure 5.25. As can be seen from the table, Gruson found that uninterrupted playing accounted for about a quarter of the total practice time. The next most frequent acts of practice were repeating a single note, repeating a bar, slowing down and making errors. Two of these events (repeating a single note and making errors) run counter to the advice of music tutors, who argue that the aim of rehearsal is to build up fluent performance. So, for instance, it is better for a novice to start off by playing so slowly that errors are never made. On the other hand, some features of rehearsal that were often recommended by tutors were not carried out by the students, such as playing with hands separately or repeating sections which are longer than a single bar.

Uninterrupted playing	25.0%
Repeating a single note	16.9%
Repeating a bar	16.7%
Slowing down	16.0%
Making errors	14.3%
Repeating sections longer than a bar	2.6%
Self-verbalizing (total)	1.6%
Repeating the whole piece	1.3%
Playing with hands separately	1.0%

Figure 5.25 Approximate proportions of activities during musical rehearsal by students. (Gruson, 1988.)

Positive correlations (i.e. the more expert the player, the more they performed the technique)	
	r
Repeating sections longer than a bar	.72
Playing with hands separately	.49
Time spent practising each piece	.40
Making self-guiding verbal remarks	.37
Negative correlations (i.e. the more expert the player, the less they performed the technique)	
	r
Making errors	−.31
Pausing for more than two seconds	−.31
Repeating single notes	−.31
Other person intervenes to correct	−.26

Figure 5.26 Correlations coefficients (*r*) between expertise and musical rehearsal which highlight the differences in rehearsal techniques between expert players and novices. (Gruson, 1988.)

Gruson went on to compare differences in style between pianists with different levels of expertise. An analysis of the style of rehearsal, compared with the level of skill of the pianist, showed four significant relationships, which are given in Figure 5.26. As can be seen, the higher the skill level the more the pianists played with separate hands, repeated sections larger than a bar and verbalized to themselves things like 'slow down' or 'try that one again'. When the research participants were classified into three groups, corresponding to apprentice, senior student and professional, similar results emerged, and it became apparent that those at the higher level were significantly more likely to repeat whole sections of the music when they were practising.

It would seem, then, that the practice style of pianists changes to conform to the pattern recommended by tutors as the pianist develops their skill on the instrument. However, an unfortunate feature of the study was that the high skill pianists were also the older pianists, so it is possible that the style of practice might also contain some age-related features, rather than be purely about skill acquisition.

Sport

control group *A group which is used for comparison with an experimental group.*

Athletes who need to perform to the peak of their skills have explored many different methods of enhancing skilled performance. One method that has been investigated is transcendental meditation. Reddy, Bai and Rao (1976) randomly assigned subjects to control and experimental meditation training conditions for six weeks. At the end of the training period the subjects were tested on a range of athletic tasks. The group who had learned transcendental meditation did better than the **control group** in a number of these tasks, including the short sprint, an agility test and the standing broad jump, as well as in general tests of reaction time and co-ordination. There was no difference between the groups, however, in strength tests and the shot put. The researchers concluded that transcendental meditation enhances gross motor skills, which involve large muscle movements, rather than fine motor skills, which require delicate muscle control.

Skill learning is not just about the learning of physical skills. We also acquire **metacognitive skills**, such as knowing how to memorize information effectively or learning to scan a text book for relevant information. There is an increasing emphasis on education as the teaching of skills, rather than as simply imparting knowledge: a principle which underlay the introduction of GCSE examinations in the 1980s, as well as a number of other educational changes. However, while educationalists may perceive education as skill acquisition, that does not necessarily mean that those involved in providing or acquiring education see it in the same way. A report on teaching in English polytechnics published in 1989 (DES, 1989) was critical of the overdependence of students on teachers as sources of knowledge and the effects of this lack of independence on the learning outcomes of their courses.

Saljo (1979) carried out an interview study, asking students to say what they understood by learning. Their responses were classified into five different categories, which are listed in Figure 5.27. As we can see, the first three of these ideas suggest that learning is something external to the learner – in other words, something that is done to the learner. Understandings four and five, on the other hand, emphasize the internal aspects of learning – in other words, learning is seen as something the learner does in order to make sense of the world.

Saljo found, not altogether unsurprisingly, that adult students who had experienced higher education were more likely to express understandings four and five, whereas younger students who had gone directly from school to college tended to take a more external view. Saljo also pointed out that the scheme of understanding represented by the five levels in Figure 5.27 is hierarchical: students who think of learning as understanding reality are also able to see it as increasing their knowledge. Each higher level of understanding implies all the other levels beneath it.

Education

metacognitive skills
Higher level skills, for example, memory is a skill, and learning to use and develop our memory skill is a metacognitive skill.

---

1. Learning brings about an increase in knowledge (knowing a lot)
2. Learning is memorizing (storing information for easy recall)
3. Learning is about developing skill and methods, and acquiring facts that can be used as necessary
4. Learning is about making sense of information, extracting meaning and relating information to everyday life
5. Learning is about understanding the world through reinterpreting knowledge

Figure 5.27 Students' ideas of what learning comprises. (Saljo, 1979.)

This links with a number of theoretical models of skill acquisition, notably that of Fisher (1980), who saw skill acquisition as a hierarchical process, with each higher order skill building on a complex of basic skills underpinning it.

Theories of memory

The idea that there are two types of memory store – dual memory theory – is one which has a long psychological history. In its conventional form, this model argues that we have a short-term memory (STM) with a very limited capacity, of roughly seven items, and a long-term memory (LTM) with a far greater capacity. Short-term memory is regarded as highly susceptible to interference, requiring continuous attention and rehearsal to prevent the loss of information in just a few seconds. Long-term memory, as the name implies, lasts much longer and is generally coded semantically – that is, according to the meaning of the information rather than according to its visual or auditory form.

A commonly accepted account of the relationship between long-term and short-term memory was put forward by Atkinson and Shiffrin (1977), who proposed that short-term memory was an initial entry phase for long-term memory. All incoming information, they argued, would pass automatically into short-term memory, where much of it would be lost through displacement. Information would only be transferred to long-term memory as a result of continuous rehearsal.

Dual memory theory attracted considerable criticism from other

Figure 5.28 Traditional model of short-term and long-term memory.

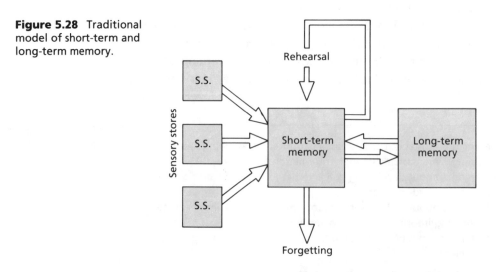

researchers, who saw the distinction as being somewhat artificial. They argued that there were differences between different forms of long-term memory as well: that it was inaccurate to classify a memory which lasted for only half an hour, which would count as long-term storage, with a memory which had lasted for many years. Craik and Lockhart (1972) proposed that it was more productive to think of memory storage in terms of a continuum, from a very fleeting short-term memory to deeply-established long-term memories, with many different grades in between.

The factor which would most influence how long an item was remembered, Craik and Lockhart argued, was how intensively the information had been processed. Information which had been coded in a superficial manner would be unlikely to be retained for very long. If it were processed by representation (e.g. by converting a visual stimulus into an auditory one), it would be retained longer; if it were processed for meaning, it would be retained for longer still and if its meaning were considered in terms of its full implications of ramifications for other information possessed by the individual, it would be retained longer still. So directly meaningful information, like speech, would be unlikely to be forgotten, whereas information which was unimportant to the individual, like the lists of meaningless digits traditionally used to measure short-term memory, would not.

> **Key reference:** CRAIK, I. F. M. and LOCKHART, R. S. (1972) Levels of Processing: a framework for memory research. *Journal of Verbal Learning and Verbal Behaviour,* **11**, 671–84.

Processing, as opposed to rehearsing, information seems to be far more effective in enhancing memory. Morris *et al.* (1981) asked research participants to learn a list of word–digit pairs, which is a task that usually produces poor performance. In this study Morris *et al.* (1981) asked research participants to memorize lists of word–digit pairs consisting of 64 of that day's football results, read out on the radio on Saturday afternoon. The control group was made up of people who were totally uninterested in football, and the experimental group was made up of football fans. Each group was asked to listen to the list of results and to recall as many as possible afterwards. The football fans recalled significantly more of the scores than the other people.

Sport

In order to control for simple familiarity, both groups were also asked to memorize a set of invented scores, knowing that they were not the real thing. There was no difference between them in their ability to recall these meaningless scores.

The researchers construed this finding in terms of levels of processing: for the football fans the material was deeply meaningful and linked with other information that they already knew. For the non-supporters, it was simply another set of word–digit pairs. The real and current nature of the results was an important factor in the mental processing of the information.

Health

There are other fields in which it is important to know how people go about remembering information. A study, which had a large impact in terms of teaching health care professionals, was described by Ley *et al.*, in 1973, who investigated how accurately people remember medical statements. Patients attending a general practice surgery were given a list of medical statements and were then asked to recall them. The same list was also given to a group of students. The statements were either given in an unstructured way or were preceded by information about how they would be organized. For example, a structured presentation might involve the researcher saying something like, 'I'm going to tell you three things: first, what is wrong with you; secondly, what tests we will be doing; and thirdly, what is likely to happen to you'.

When they were tested to see how much they remembered, Ley *et al.* found that structuring the information had made a very clear difference. The patients who had received the information in a clearly categorized form remembered about 25% more than those who had received the same information in an unstructured way. The students, who were more used to learning information, were about 50% better if they received categorized information than if it were unstructured. The clear implication of this study is that giving people a means of processing or coding information can help them to store it more effectively, which suggests that practical benefits, in terms of remembering what the doctor said, can be achieved by applying levels of processing approaches in real-life settings.

In a further study in this area Ley (1978) undertook a study of memory for medical information. After people had visited the doctor, they were asked what the doctor had instructed them to do. This would be compared with a record of what had actually been said to them and the differences were noted.

Ley found that people were quite inaccurate in remembering medical information. In general, patients remembered about 55% of what their doctor had said to them. But the inaccuracies were not random ones. In particular, Ley found a number of systematic outcomes which are listed in Figure 5.30. Each of these findings could be deduced from existing psychological knowledge about memory processes. In a follow-up to the study, Ley prepared a small booklet giving advice to doctors on how to

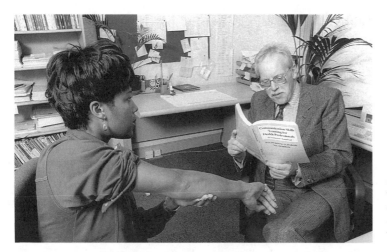

Figure 5.29 Doctors who read a booklet on communicating with people obtained better recall from their patients.

communicate more clearly with their patients. Patients whose doctors had read the booklet recalled on average 70% of what they had been told, which was a significant increase on the previous figure (see Figure 5.30).

Understandably, perhaps, the bulk of applications of memory research seems to have occurred in the field of advertising. It is, after all, essential to advertisers that people should recall the name of the product which they are advertising, preferably positively, and the whole purpose of the advertisement is to make sure that this happens.

Consumer

Dual memory theory implies that rehearsing information should encourage its transfer into long-term memory. Research evidence from advertising, however, questions whether that is really the case. Belch (1982) investigated the effects of repeating advertisements during the course of a one-hour television show. Two hundred and sixty research participants, recruited from two church groups, each watched a one-hour programme. During this time, a commercial for an imaginary toothpaste was shown once, three times or five times. Belch found that those research participants who saw the advertisement most often were less

Figure 5.30 Patients' memory for medical information. (Ley, 1978.)

General findings were that patients:
- Remember the first thing that they had been told well (the primacy effect).
- Did not improve their memorizing as a result of repetition – it did not matter how often the doctor repeated the information.
- Remembered information which had been categorized (like, say, which tablets they should be taking) better than information which was more general.
- Remembered more than other patients if they already had some medical knowledge.

likely to recall its details or to respond positively to the toothpaste being advertised.

Further evidence to suggest that repetition is not an optimal strategy for learning came with Bekerian and Baddeley's study of housewives' memory for radio frequencies, in 1980. When the BBC was changing the frequencies of its major radio stations, radio and TV announcements and wayside hoardings all informed consumers of the new wavelengths. Bekerian and Baddeley estimated that the housewives in their study had each heard the new wavelengths about a thousand times. But when they were asked to recall these frequencies, either by writing down the numbers or by marking a dial, only about a quarter of them could do so. Simple repetition without processing, apparently, is remarkably ineffective.

On the other hand, different advertisements for the same product seem to be much more effective. Unnava and Burnkrant (1991) showed research participants the same or different versions of advertisements and assessed both how much attention they paid to them, and how much they recalled of the advertisement. The researchers found that people were more likely to recall the name of the product if they had seen different versions than if they had seen the same version twice. Improved recall was found for the message as well as the brand name, even though the research participants paid just as much attention to each of the advertisements. Attention, interestingly, did not seem to have much effect on whether it was remembered or not.

Advertising jingles, perhaps regrettably, have been a feature of everyday living ever since Pepsodent toothpaste asked where the yellow went (not a reference for our younger readers). But do these jingles have any effect on our memories and purchasing choices? Yalch (1991) examined whether we remember an advertising slogan better if it is presented in the form of a jingle and also whether a jingle – or at least music – was more effective in certain circumstances than others. In this study, consumers were presented with advertising slogans in one of three forms: using a jingle; using a memory test with cues for retrieval; or showing the advertisement twice.

Music was found to enhance memory for advertising slogans when the slogans were incorporated into an advertisement in the form of a jingle or song. Slogan information that was presented with music was found to be easier to retrieve than similar information presented without music. However, due to the phonetic nature of slogans they are unlikely to be very effective in conveying complex communications about a product. Yalch found that the effectiveness of jingles was limited and almost disappeared when individuals were given sufficient cues to aid the retrieval of the brand–slogan association. So, if an advertisement, say, reflected features of someone's everyday life, a jingle would be likely to be less effective because other cues would be present to aid recall.

Yalch also found that individual differences influenced how effective jingles were. The most important of these was people's ability to process musical information and their prior knowledge of musical forms. Overall, then, it seems that the jingle has some effect on recall, but not as much as advertisers seem to believe.

Another technique that is often used to attract consumers' attention is including information in an advertisement which challenges people's expectations. There are a couple of possible explanations for this. One popular belief among advertisers is that doing so makes us pay attention, and so is thought to increase how much we will process the information. But as we saw earlier, there is no guarantee that paying attention is going to have this effect. A different explanation for why incongruent information seems to have such an effect is the argument that it disturbs our cognitive balance, producing **cognitive dissonance** (see Chapter 7). Because it does not fit with our existing schemas, we process the information until we have an adequate explanation for it.

Heckler and Childers (1992) combined visual and verbal information in print advertisements to find out how incongruencies influence how we perceive complex marketing messages. Research participants were given 30 seconds to examine the images and words in 4 advertisements. They were then asked to give their general impressions of the advertisement, and to complete a short attitude questionnaire for it. After they had seen the adverts the subjects were given a four-minute task, to make sure that they were not concentrating on trying to remember what they had seen – in dual memory terms, to clear short-term memory. They were then allowed 12 minutes to recall everything they could about each of the 4 advertisements.

Heckler and Childers found that information which was both unexpected and irrelevant to the advertisement was better remembered, and had received more processing than information which was expected but irrelevant. They suggested that providing unexpected information is one way of encouraging people to remember product information, although it is a bit unclear how the advertiser would persuade the consumer to remember the product information rather than the irrelevant information.

Mick (1992) identified four 'levels of subjective comprehension' as an attempt to use the levels of processing model of memory, to describe how we make sense of messages. The four levels are listed in Figure 5.31. Mick used this model to explore the relationship between subjective comprehension levels, and how advertisements are perceived and

cognitive dissonance
The tension produced by cognitive imbalance – holding beliefs which directly contradict one another or contradict behaviour. The reduction of cognitive dissonance has been shown to be a factor in some forms of attitude change.

Level 1:	The message-based level of meanings, including meanings related to the explicit or asserted message content.
Level 2:	The message-based level of meanings related to logical inferences derived directly from the explicit or asserted message content.
Level 3:	The receiver-based level of meaning related to non-logical, non-personalized inferences or elaborations triggered by the message content derived from general product or situational knowledge.
Level 4:	The receiver-based level of meanings related to personalized embellishments (the individual consumer) triggered by the message content, derived from self-knowledge and self-experiences.

Figure 5.31 Levels of subjective comprehension. (Mick, 1992.)

remembered. The study was carried out in two phases. First, Mick looked at people's attitudes to five national brands of compact disc players. Then, they were told that, at the end of their participation in the study, they would have to indicate from a list which brand of CD player they would choose if they won a raffle. They were then shown an advertisement for the second CD player on the list. The raffle was intended to heighten the research participants' motivation when processing the advertisement.

The research participants were divided into two groups. One group was asked to give their thoughts and feelings immediately after the target advertisement was shown: these were known as the protocol group. The second group – the non-protocol group – saw the same advertisement, but were not asked to verbalize their thoughts and feelings. After this, all of the research participants were asked to rate the advertisement in terms of how easy it was to understand, how credible it was and whether they liked it or not.

All of the protocol responses were coded into levels of subjective comprehension using the four-level comprehension framework in Figure 5.31. Mick found that more positive meanings (levels three and four) resulted in the advertisement being perceived as more credible and an increase in overall liking of the advertisement. People producing surface level comprehension judged the advertisement as less credible and liked the advertisement less. Levels three and four were also found to have a stronger relation with recall compared with levels one and two – people remembered more about the advertisement generally.

Constructive memory

As early as 1932, Sir Frederick Bartlett showed that human memory is not just a factual recording of what occurred. Instead, Bartlett argued that we make an 'effort after meaning' – we try to ensure that information is congruent with what we already know; and in the process that information often becomes changed or adapted.

Using the method of **serial reproduction** of stories, Bartlett identified seven types of changes which occurred to information as it became adjusted or adapted to fit the individual's prior knowledge: (a) changes in emphasis or the significance of details; (b) affective distortions brought about by the person's own feelings and reactions; (c) a gradual drift away from the meaning of the original information; (d) shortening; (e) changes to increase the personal coherence of the information to the subject; (f) an increase in the conventionality of the information; and (g) the omission of names and numbers.

serial reproduction A *method of examining the accuracy of memory by asking people to reproduce what they recall of a story, on several successive occasions.*

These mechanisms amount to the process of confabulation, whereby memories are adjusted to conform to a subject's prior expectations, opinions and ideas. Researchers (e.g. Loftus and Loftus, 1975) have shown that expectations, even subtle ones generated by choice of language, can be enough to distort memories such that entirely new information is included and remembered as if it were fact. Some studies, too, have shown how this is particularly likely to occur when people are asked to retrieve memories, since by

Original drawing

Reproduction 1   2

3   4   5   6

7   8   9   Reproduction 10

Figure 5.32 Bartlett's method of successive reproductions. The original figure is a stylized drawing of an owl. In successive reproductions it becomes increasingly ambiguous; by the tenth drawing it has definitely become a figure of a cat. (Zimbardo, P. and Ruch, F., 1977, *Psychology and Life*, 9th edn, p. 172. Reprinted by permission of HarperCollins College Publishers.)

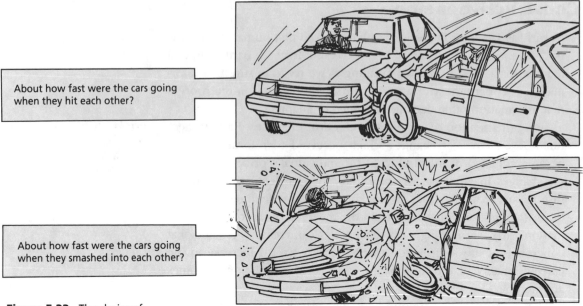

About how fast were the cars going when they hit each other?

About how fast were the cars going when they smashed into each other?

Figure 5.33 The choice of language in the questions supports a different picture to the witness. (Roediger, *et al.*, 1984,)

definition the hypnotized person is in a highly suggestible state and very ready to pick up subtle cues from the person asking the questions.

A number of studies, then, tell us that human memory works in a very different way from a factual, objective, 'tape-recording' of events, despite the fact that it feels subjectively like an accurate record. Memory is an active process, interlinked with, and directly influenced by, perceptions, expectations, emotions and cultural assumptions.

Key reference: LOFTUS, G. R. and LOFTUS, E. F. (1975) *Human Memory: the processing of information*. Halsted Press, New York.

Society

One of the difficulties with the finding that our memories are so susceptible to influence is that, subjectively, it always feels as though it is veridical – as though we are recalling exactly what happened. Neisser (1981) reported the case of John Dean, an eye-witness of the Watergate trials in America which eventually resulted in the impeachment of President Nixon. Dean was reported to have an extremely accurate memory. He recounted conversations in very precise details and testified on oath that these were exactly what he had heard. There was no doubt that he, and others who worked with him, were convinced that he had an eidetic memory for detail.

When the Watergate tapes were discovered, however, they were found to include tape-recordings of many of the conversations which Dean had

Elizabeth F. Loftus, born 16 October 1944, Los Angeles, California.

Elizabeth Loftus has made major contributions to our understanding of human memory and its foibles. Her research showing how memory can be skewed when people assimilate new data uses an elegant procedure. Participants first witness a complex event, such as a simulated violent crime or an automobile accident. Subsequently, half the participants receive new and misleading information about the event. The other half get no misinformation. Finally all participants attempt to recall the original event. From these studies she has solidly demonstrated the power of misinformation to contaminate prior memories. People have recalled non-existent broken glass and tape recorders, a clean-shaven man as having a mustache, straight hair as curly, and even something as large and conspicuous as a barn in a bucolic scene that contained no buildings at all. In later studies, Loftus showed that, with subtle suggestion, entire childhood memories could be implanted into the minds of unsuspecting subjects. She has taught us well how misinformation can alter a person's recollection in powerful, predictable ways.

In 1983, she was invited to present her early work to the Royal Society of London. She has received two honorary doctorates for her research, the first in 1982 from Miami University (Ohio) and the second in 1990 from Leiden University in the Netherlands. She served as the 1984 President of the Western Psychological Association, as the 1985 President of the American Psychology-Law Society, and as the 1988 President of Division 3 (Experimental) of the American Psychological Association.

Loftus received her PhD from Stanford University in 1970, and has spent most of her academic career in the Department of Psychology at the University of Washington in Seattle, Washington.

recalled. Interestingly, Dean's memory was found to be inaccurate in almost every detail, although his memory for the social meaning of what had occurred in the conversation – the gist of it – was completely accurate. He had remembered what had been said, not by remembering the exact words which had been used, but by remembering what they had really meant. But he had no idea that his memories were not exactly the same as a tape-recording.

Gibson (1982) discussed how the increasing use of hypnosis in police investigations of eye-witness accounts in both America and Britain is disturbing in this respect, since the effect of hypnosis is to make subjects particularly co-operative. Since they want to help the police they often unconsciously construct details of the events which they then believe are entirely true. Since there is no way of distinguishing between a 'real' memory and one which has been constructed unconsciously by a co-operative subject during hypnosis, Gibson suggested that the use of hypnosis by police should be regarded as equivalent to tampering with the evidence.

Howitt (1991) described how a variation on the classic work of Bartlett can be used in anti-racism training. The following was a story presented to people who were then asked to recall it.

> The time was 5.30 p.m. in London and the Underground train was overcrowded as usual at this time of day. In one particular crowded carriage a number of passengers were standing up very close to one another. Two men of different ethnic origins were standing up facing each other: one of them had an open double-edged knife and newspaper in his hand. When the train stopped at the next station both men stepped out on to an equally crowded platform. There were many young people at the station. In the struggle to get in and out of the train a passenger stepped on the foot of one of the men. A fight ensued involving a large number of passengers and London Transport staff. Some people were badly hurt. The police were called and they were taken to the local police station. One man rang home and informed his family that he had been remanded in custody at the police station. His wife was furious at the news; she scolded him for his irresponsibility and blamed him for what had happened to him that day. The children and some of the people involved were not charged with any offence. The following day one of the men could not go to work so his boss fired him.

Howitt reported that the recall of the story often shows distortion, in a way that reveals the effects of stereotyped sexist and racist thinking. He records the following recall from a group of people, who were overtly anti-racist.

> Five-thirty on a London Underground station and there were two black people there. One was carrying a rolled-up newspaper with a knife partly hidden in the newspaper. There was some kind of scuffle or fight on the tube train itself which involved some people and the police. One person was arrested and the other person got away. And when they got home, the other got home, he was told off by his wife.

Even though the participants believed that they were not racist, a brief look at the distortions involved in their recall shows a number of preconceived ideas and stereotypes.

Sometimes, it is possible for advertisers to use constructive memory deliberately. For example, some research has indicated that the use of open-ended messages might be persuasive in advertising, since this leads the consumer to draw a conclusion which will fit with their own ideas. To do this, they also have to think about the message and derive their conclusion by processing the information, which means that they are more likely to remember it.

To test this idea, Sawyer and Howard (1991) examined the effects of open and closed-ended advertising messages. Research participants were asked to look through a booklet of 12 advertisements and then complete a questionnaire which included recall questions, semantic differential ratings and the choice of a branded product. The researchers attempted to ensure that some of the participants would be motivated by offering them a free gift.

The results showed that open-ended advertisements worked best with motivated research participants – more of them said that they would be likely to buy the product. Less involved subjects (who did not receive a free gift for participating in the study) who viewed the open-ended advertisement and people who viewed the closed-ended advertisement, were less affected. But we do need to remember that, in real life, consumers are rarely manipulated to such a high degree, so therefore their motivation is likely to be lower and this type of effect would be much less.

Constructive memory does not just reflect our own individual beliefs and ideas. It reflects the social beliefs with which we are surrounded, as well – the social representations which we looked at in Chapter 3. Echabe and Paez-Rovira (1989) interviewed 365 people about their beliefs on the causes of acquired immune deficiency syndrome (AIDS). They asked these people who were the most likely people to be affected by AIDS and what the likely modes of transmission of AIDS are.

Health

The responses were found to reflect the two major social representations of AIDS: a conservative-blaming representation, in which the individual who contracted AIDS was seen as having deserved it because of their irresponsible lifestyle; and a more liberal representation. The interviewees were then given technical information about AIDS, followed, two weeks later, by a free recall test and a recognition test. The results of these tests confirmed the tendency which people have to remember only that information which is congruent with their pre-existing beliefs and to distort the recall of contradictory information to make it compatible with their pre-existing representations.

Theories of forgetting

There have been many psychological explanations put forward for why people forget. Here are some of the main ones.

1. Decay of a memory trace or 'engram'

This was one of the earliest ideas about how we forget things: that memories leave traces in the brain which gradually decay if they are not strengthened by being recalled. Despite its appeal to subjective experience, however, this idea has proved virtually impossible to investigate empirically and of little value in understanding the many everyday manifestations of memory.

2. Brain damage or disease

Amnesias may result from brain damage or disease. Post-traumatic amnesia can occur following a severe blow or wound to the head and may result in loss of memory for the events leading up to the accident. It is thought to interfere with a period of consolidation, needed for new information to become established in memory stores. Brain disease or injury can also produce **anterograde amnesia**, in which the individual is unable to store new memories. Anterograde amnesia has been known to result from surgical accident, but its most common source is **Korsakoff's syndrome**, brought about by long-term alcoholism accompanied by inadequate nutrition. It can also result from Alzheimer's disease and Huntingdon's chorea.

Korsakoff's syndrome A condition of severe memory loss and anterograde amnesia brought about by long-term alcohol abuse and inadequate nutrition.

3. Motivated forgetting

Freud (1901) believed that the reason why we forget things is because to do so protects the ego from threat. We repress memories which might be disturbing to the dynamic balance maintained between the ego, id and super-ego; and we therefore also repress anything which might indirectly cue us in to any disturbing memory. Another version of motivated forgetting is that such forgetting is a manifestation of some unconscious wish-fulfilment – like forgetting that you have a dental appointment.

4. Interference from other material

This theory is the idea that forgetting may occur because it is displaced or preceded by other, similar information which interferes with its recall. Proactive interference is where newly learned information is imperfectly recalled or forgotten because old information is remembered instead: someone who has previously learned French may not recall newly learned Spanish terms, because they remember the French words instead. Retroactive interference is when new information is recalled at the expense of the old: the person who has newly learned Spanish may only think of Spanish words when they try to think of something in French.

5. Lack of context

Contexts have been shown to be an effective part of recall: even mentally recreating context has been shown to aid people to retrieve information which was previously forgotten (Williams and Hollan, 1981). The implication of this is that some forgetting takes place purely because the individual is in an inappropriate context for recall. Internal context is also influential in recall: state-dependent learning is a form of learning in which information laid down during a particular internal state (e.g. while drunk) is forgotten until that state is re-entered (Goodwin *et al.*, 1969).

6. Lack of cues

Memories can be enhanced by providing appropriate cues, which lead to the relevant information. The corollary of this observation is that some forgetting occurs because of lack of cues. Many researchers (e.g. Tulving and Pearlstone, 1966) have shown how people asked to free recall without cues forgot very much more information than those asked to remember using cues. Mnemonics – aids to memory – work on the principle of helping people to remember things by providing them with additional cues to that information.

> **Key reference:** BADDELEY, A. (1983) *Your Memory: a user's guide.* Penguin, Harmondsworth.

| Decay |
| Brain damage |
| Motivation |
| Interference |
| Lack of context |
| Lack of cues |

Figure 5.34 Summary of factors responsible for forgetting.

The idea that forgetting happens because the brain trace fades with lack of use is not one which has received much experimental support. There are some cases where we can remember events very clearly that we have not thought of for years, and others where we are unable to remember things that we see every day. One of the oddest phenomena of forgetting, for example, is our inability to recall accurately objects that are very familiar to us.

Nickerson and Adams (1979) carried out a series of experiments to see how accurately Americans call recall a penny coin, without looking at one. You might like to try a personal version of this by trying to draw a £5 note or a £1 coin. The researchers found that free recall of the coin was very poor. Of the eight main features of the coin, the average number recalled and correctly located on the drawing was only three, which seems strange given how often the research participants handled these coins. Even when they asked people to recognize the coin from a series of pictures, a remarkable number of people made incorrect selections. Jones (1990) repeated Nickerson and Adams's studies by asking people to draw a British penny from memory. If anything, their drawings

Society

Figure 5.35 Recall of everyday objects is remarkably poor. The top two drawings show a coin as it actually is, and the bottom two drawings show the most common response of people attempting to draw it from memory. (Adapted from Jones, 1990.)

Health

were even more inaccurate than the original study (Figure 5.35).

In his collection of case studies, *The Man who Mistook his Wife for a Hat,* Sacks (1985) described the case of Jimmy, a man whose mind seemed to have stopped at the year 1945. He was interviewed by Sacks in 1975 and had no awareness that it was not still 1945. Jimmy was unable to hold any information in recent memory, so when Sacks went out of the room for a few minutes, he had to introduce himself again to the man on his return. Records showed that Jimmy had been in the navy until 1965 and had not developed his condition until the early 1970s, as the outcome of prolonged and heavy drinking – a classic case of Korsakoff's syndrome The amnesia produced by the brain damage from the alcohol had eaten backwards through his life, as happens in other cases of Korsakoff's, stopping at the year 1945.

Although he occasionally produced very brief flashes of memory from the 1960s, in all other respects Jimmy behaved and responded like a bright young man of 1945 – he was shocked, for example, when Sacks showed him a picture of the Earth taken from space, because someone would have had to go into space to take it, and he did not believe that had happened. Sacks described him as a 'man without a past (or future), stuck in a constantly changing, meaningless moment'.

Temporary concussion can also influence memory, particularly for the twenty minutes or so immediately after the accident. Yarnell and Lynch (1973) studied American football players who experienced concussion as a result of collisions in the field. The researchers were present at the matches, so they could ask the players questions immediately after the injury, and again 20 minutes later. They found that, immediately after the injury, the players could recall the strategy which their team had been using, but that this memory had disappeared completely 20 minutes later. The implication was that some kind of consolidation period is needed in order for material to become completely integrated with other knowledge and that this had been interrupted by the concussion.

Burke and Srull (1988) investigated interference in memory. They found that consumers' memories for magazine advertisements tended to be quite strongly influenced by competing advertisements for similar products. People remembered far less brand information about the advertisements that they had seen when these were followed by advertisements for different products in the same general category, than when the advertisement was the only one of its kind in the magazine. The researchers suggested that effect happens because of interference between the two different items of information.

Consumer

Advertisers, naturally, are concerned to make advertising effective. This means encouraging people to remember the advert when they are in a shop and in a position to buy the product. But we are bombarded by so much commercial material every day that if we did not forget most of it our minds would be completely cluttered with advertising messages.

One suggestion is that retrieval cues can be used to enhance memory for a particular product. One possible way for activating some retrieval cues is to place pictures from television advertising on the packaging of the product. Laboratory and field research has suggested that this can be very effective, particularly in helping people to recall the advertisement's claims. The Campbell Soup Company, for example, reported that sales increased by 15% when their point-of-sales materials were directly related to their television advertising (Keller, 1987).

The role of environmental context in remembering was demonstrated by Godden and Baddeley (1975) in their work with deep-sea divers. An acquaintance had previously been in charge of a team of divers attempting to watch the behaviour of fish about to enter, or escape from, trawl nets. Attempts to de-brief the divers on their return to the surface produced disappointing results because the divers appeared to have forgotten the behaviour they had observed, and it was only when they were sent to observe the fish and record their observations underwater that they produced an accurate record.

Environment

Following this up, Godden and Baddeley asked divers to listen to 40 unrelated words either on the beach or under about 10 feet of water. The divers were then tested to see how many of the words they remembered. When they were in the same environment in which they had learned the words in the first place, they remembered far more of the words than they did when they were in a different context. However, this study may not be terribly revealing, largely because of the simplicity and irrelevance of the task.

In a later study, Godden and Baddeley (1980) trained divers in a simple manual task which involved transferring nuts and bolts from one brass plate to another – very like the kinds of tasks which they might need to do when performing maintenance operations on boats or oil rigs. Typically, divers would learn to do tasks of this kind on land first and then transfer that learning to the underwater context, but the outcomes of the earlier study suggested that this might not be the best possible way for them to learn.

Accordingly, one group of divers began work learning the task immediately underwater, while the other group were given some practice trials on land before they carried out the underwater task. In both conditions the divers were required to work entirely by touch, to simulate the experience of many commercial divers who often work in very muddy water. The researchers found that the land-based training actually impeded underwater performance: the first underwater run of these divers was worse than that of divers who had no training at all.

Society

sensory deprivation *The cutting out of all incoming sensory information or at least as much of it as possible.*

Elderly people in institutions or homes often appear disorientated or confused and this is often taken as simply a sign of ageing. But Coleman (1981) suggested that we should consider the results of **sensory deprivation** experiments when looking at this problem, arguing that the living condition of elderly people might be a major contributor in their declining intellectual performance. When people are isolated, deprived of stimulation or 'brain washed', they also show signs of disorientation and confusion, and the experience of spending two days ill in bed can have a similar disorientating effect on the average adult. Herbert suggested that the restricted social contact and physical mobility of elderly people might lead to the feelings of disorientation in space and time that are so debilitating.

Summary

1. *Classical conditioning is based on the idea of learning by association: the pairing of an unconditioned stimulus with a neutral one, until eventually the neutral one produces the response*

2. *Operant conditioning is based on the idea of learning through effects. It can involve positive reinforcement, when behaviour is rewarded, or negative reinforcement, when unpleasant situations are escaped or avoided.*

3. *Variations in the application of reinforcement meant that operant conditioning could be applied to produce novel forms of behaviour in a wide range of contexts.*

4. *Social learning theory introduced an observational dimension to the process of learning social behaviour, with concepts of modelling and imitation.*

5. *Behaviour modification is a method of changing human behaviour which draws on both conditioning and social learning principles.*

6. *Cognitive maps are mental representations of our surroundings, which are instrumental in providing contexts for memories as well as learning our way around.*

7. *Mental imagery involves remembering by representing a visual or auditory impression in the mind. It can be useful in developing techniques of memorizing.*

8. *Research into skill acquisition has involved the study of many different kinds of skills. Guidance and feedback are crucial concepts in skill learning.*

9. *Some theories of memory described separate types of memory store for short-term and long-term memory. However, levels of processing theory interpreted apparent distinctions as the outcome of different degrees of processing.*

10. *Human memory is often constructive, altering details and even basic meanings to fit with existing schemas and social expectations.*

11. *There have been several different theories of forgetting, ranging from amnesia through brain damage to retrieval failure through lack of cues or inappropriate contexts.*

PRACTICE QUESTIONS AND ACTIVITIES – 5

Behaviourism and everyday life

The concepts of behavourism were thought to describe the development of all learning. Look at the list of behaviours below and consider which of these can be explained by the behaviourist approach and which can not.

(Note: **classical conditioning** is the pairing of a reflex with a neutral stimulus; **operant conditioning** is the shaping of behaviour by reinforcement (sometimes described as trial and error learning).

When you are considering these behaviours, try and explain why the behaviour occurs and also how it develops.

Take, for example, swimming. *Why does it develop?* Behaviourists may argue that it comes from a need to explore water. Monkey colonies that are exposed to water learn to swim. *How does it develop?* By the trial and error of various attempts at thrashing around in water.

Here are some examples of other behaviours:

- riding a bike;
- fighting in a pub;
- playing football;
- falling in love;
- wearing fashionable clothes;
- opera;
- painting the ceiling;

- painting the Sistine Chapel ceiling;
- dancing at a party;
- alcoholism;
- getting married;
- eating a Big Mac;
- phobias;
- going to work.

Try and think of some other everyday behaviours that cannot be explained by the behaviourist approach.

Reinforcement

Reinforcement is described as anything that will change the probability of a behaviour occurring. But why? You could explore this idea by making a list of the things that can change your behaviour, like money or a smile, or fear of humiliation. Then look for common features. What is the base of your reinforcement?

To put it another way, what is pleasure and why is it pleasurable?

Everyday memory

A simple test of the constructivist approach to memory is to attempt to draw the street where you live or even the place you live in. Put in as much detail as you can, then compare your sketch to the real thing. Some aspects will be correct, some will be missing, but, most interestingly, some will actually be wrong. If you study these errors you might be able to tease out the reasons for them and derive some insight into how you construct your personal memories.

On a similar theme, you could try drawing a map of the area you live in, or your place of work, or a nearby shopping centre. The road map is the easiest to compare because street plans are readily available. Look for the distortions in your map compared to the surveyed map.

6
Perception and motivation

Introduction

The themes of this chapter are seeing, understanding and acting in the world. Some of the earliest research and theorizing in psychology was concerned with our experiences of sensation and perception. These phenomena still interest us today and the knowledge which we have obtained about them from psychological investigations has been applied in a range of settings.

One of the first distinctions which we need to make when we are looking at this area is the difference between sensation and perception. At a basic sensory level there are a number of ways that we receive information: we can receive visual information from the eyes, auditory information through the ears, olfactory information from the nose, tactile information from the skin, gustatory information from the taste buds on the tongue, and kinaesthetic information about the movements of the body from our muscles and joints. All of these are forms of **sensation**.

Perception, however, is much more than sensation. We process and organize our sensory information so that we can make sense of the physical and social world that we live in. The early Gestalt psychologists identified a number of principles in how we organize sensory information and these have been applied in a number of contexts, including advertising and ergonomics. The Gestalt principles also seem to have an echo in the physiological organization of the visual system, suggesting that our basic tendency to organize visual information into figures against backgrounds is something which is 'hard-wired' into the nervous system, not something which we have to learn (although recognizing what those figures actually represent is another matter).

Our ability to recognize people is one of the most important features of human perception and we are remarkably skilled at it. We can distinguish between very similar faces with accuracy and also recognize the

sensation The detection or direct experience of physical energy in the external or internal environment, due to stimulation of receptors in the sense organs.

perception The process by which the brain organizes and interprets sensory information.

same familiar face in a range of contexts. But we can make mistakes too. One of the important consequences of psychological research in this area has been a growing awareness of problems of eye-witness testimony. There is a special authenticity that goes with the assertion 'I was there, I saw him, it was that man over there!', and yet sometimes, the person being recognized may actually have been someone seen in a different context. Given the importance of these judgements, understanding exactly how face recognition works is a vital area of psychological research.

All the time, we are bombarded with sensory information and, if we did not have some way of reducing our awareness of it, we would be overwhelmed. We select which information we will attend to and the way that we do this has generated a great deal of interest from psychologists. Some have argued that we have a limited capacity for processing information, others that we have to learn to structure how we select it, but in either case, flooding people with too much information means that they make mistakes. Another phenomenon in this area concerns our ability to monitor information that we are not consciously attending to. We only realize we are doing this when we suddenly catch our own name in another conversation. In Western countries, daily life is often accompanied by background media 'noise', but how much are we paying attention to it and what are the consequences of having our attention divided in this way?

Perception is a constructive process, not just a question of passively receiving information. We actively make sense of the world, and we use our knowledge, our imagination and our expectations in doing so. We

Figure 6.1 The ambiguous drawing of a woman. Some see a young woman, others see an old woman. What do you see first?

make intelligent guesses about what the world is like and what is likely to happen in it, and respond to these guesses. This means that we are ready to perceive certain things rather than others – our perception is 'set' towards particular kinds of information, and we are more ready to notice that type of information than anything else. This **perceptual set** is an integral feature of Neisser's perceptual cycle, in that the process of perception is seen as a continual process of selection and feedback in the way that we perceive the world.

perceptual set A state of readiness to perceive certain kinds of stimuli rather than others.

The study of how we make sense of the physical world leads us on to look at what motivates us to be active in the world. One well-known approach to motivation is to see it in terms of a range of drives and personal needs which energize us into action. Maslow's theory of motivation takes the view that individual needs are organized as a hierarchy, ranging from basic biological motivators like hunger to 'higher' motivators like the need for self-actualization and personal fulfilment.

Many other psychologists, however, are critical of the hierarchical approach to motivation, on the grounds that there are so many examples of people being motivated by higher goals at the expense of 'basic' ones. Other approaches to understanding human motivation have looked at social mechanisms, such as the way that people like to belong to groups or to gain respect from other people, as consistent human motives energizing a great deal of our behaviour. Each of these approaches to motivation has provided insights for work in a range of applied contexts.

Sensory modes

We are continually responding to information which we receive from the outside world and this information can come in many forms. Human beings receive information in six major sensory modes. We possess specialized sensory receptors which enable us to receive information in the 'distance' modes of visual, auditory and olfactory information (sight, hearing and smell); the 'immediate' modes of tactile and gustatory information (touch and taste); and the 'internal' kinaesthetic modes (feelings about the body).

Visual information arrives in the form of electromagnetic radiation, which is received by photo-receptors in the retina of the eye. These are of two kinds: rod cells, which are highly sensitive to minute changes in the stimulus; and cone cells, which are less sensitive but detect colour. These cells transduce (change) electromagnetic radiation into neural impulses, which pass along the optic nerve to the regions of the brain concerned with decoding visual information, in the thalamus and the cerebral cortex.

Auditory information arrives in the form of rhythmic changes in air pressure, which are detected by a taut membrane inside the ear – the ear drum. They are then amplified by special bones in the middle ear, before passing to the inner ear where they are transduced into neural impulses by specialized hair cells, which respond to vibration. The information is coded according to loudness and pitch, and passed along the auditory nerve to the specialized regions of the brain, in the thalamus and cerebral cortex, for decoding.

Olfactory information arrives in the form of chemicals carried in the air and in many animals olfaction is developed to a tremendously sensitive degree. Being the first of the 'distance' senses to evolve, olfactory information can exert a powerful influence on non-cerebral functioning like moods, emotions and motivational states like hunger or sexual attraction. Some chemicals detected by olfactory receptors act directly to stimulate hormonal responses: these are known as **pheromones**. The receptors of the olfactory system are hair cells which protrude directly into the airflow inside the nostril, to which chemical molecules adhere. This produces an electrical impulse in the cell, which is then transmitted to the olfactory cortex of the brain along the olfactory nerve.

pheromones Chemicals released into the air which, when received by another animal, exert a direct influence on its hormonal system and sometimes its behaviour.

Tactile information arrives in the form of direct contact with the skin and can take one of three forms: pressure; temperature; and pain. Specialized receptors for each of these types are located in the various layers of the skin, either as capsules, or as free nerve endings. Those for pressure and temperature transduce the information and pass it, via the thalamus, to the somatosensory area on the cerebral cortex; but those for pain transmit the information directly to the spinal cord, often in a neural **reflex** arc, which results in rapid muscle action to withdraw from the stimulus and so minimize damage.

reflex An automatic reaction to a stimulus; often inborn but can also be learned or modified by experience.

Gustatory information also involves the detection of chemical molecules, but in this case they are dissolved in saliva – a saline-like fluid produced by special glands in the mouth. Taste receptors are located on the tongue and soft palate of the mouth, forming groups known as taste buds. Hair cells come into contact with the saliva and respond to the different chemical combinations of dissolved food, producing a neural impulse which is then transmitted to the brain. Taste appears to be coded by the action of different combinations of receptors and its strength by the rapidity of neural firing.

Kinaesthetic information is a general term used to refer to information about the internal states of the body. It has a more specialist meaning too: strictly speaking, kinaesthetic information is information about body movement, transmitted to the brain by special receptors in the skeletal system and the joints. There are also proprioceptors, which transmit information to the brain from the muscles and tendons, and the semicircular canals of the inner ear contain receptors which are directly concerned with the sense of balance and the detection of body movement. Each of these sensory receptors has links with parts of the cerebellum, the part of the brain which co-ordinates voluntary movement, as well as with the cerebral cortex of the brain.

> **Key reference:** VAN TOLLER, S. and DODD, G. H. (1988) *Perfumery: the psychology and biology of fragrance.* Chapman & Hall, London.

Advertisements need to attract our attention from a background full of interest and information, and producing large advertisements with eye-catching colour is an obvious way of doing so. Gronhaug, Kvitastein and Gronmo (1991) undertook a meta-analysis of tests of 333 magazine advertisements in Norway between 1973 and 1979 (during that time in Norway there was no radio or TV advertising). The researchers found a positive correlation between the size of the advertisement, the number of colours which it had and how much readers were likely to notice it. They also found that women were more likely to read advertisements than men, although how much attention an individual advertisement received, of course, depended on the interests of the reader.

Consumer

Examining the way in which we process visual information can also be useful to advertisers. The structure of the visual system means that information from the right side of the visual field is processed by the left hemisphere, while that from the left side of the field is processed by the right hemisphere. Some physiological research suggests that the left side of the brain appears to be dominant in language functions, whereas the right hemisphere is more dominant in spatial and imagination tasks, and possibly emotions (although that is more contentious). Horowitz and Kaye (1975) proposed that this implies that the most effective advertisements will have text on the right side of the display, and emotional and spatial features on the left side of the display (see Figure 6.3).

Gregory and Wallace (1963) studied a man, S. B., who had been blind since birth, but was given sight through an operation when he was 52 years old. He had often tried to imagine what it would be like to be sighted and when he was able to see they found that he could recognize some objects. For example, he was able to recognize windows because he had touched them while he was blind, but he was unable to interpret the view from them, because he had never had tactile experience of

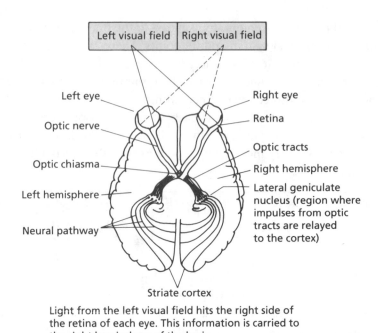

Figure 6.2 The visual system.

Light from the left visual field hits the right side of the retina of each eye. This information is carried to the right hemisphere of the brain.

Figure 6.3 The left side of the brain is dominant for language, and the right side is dominant for visual and imaginative information. Horowitz and Kaye (1975) suggested that advertisements should be like the one here, which presents visual information into the right side and text into the left side of the brain.

them. In fact he thought he would be able to touch the ground from a top-storey window if he lowered himself out by his hands although it was actually 40 feet above ground level.

Perhaps the most disturbing sensation of all is pain – something that we all experience, but which can take many different forms – and even change its character depending on whether we are thinking about it or concentrating on something else. Melzack and Wall (1982) proposed the 'gate theory' of pain which attempts to account for (a) the high degree of specialization of pain receptors and pain nerves in the nervous system; (b) the influence of psychological processes on pain perception and response; and (c) the persistence of clinical pain after healing. The theory argues that the nerve impulses which produce pain pass through a series of 'gates' on their way to the brain, and that these gates are influenced by messages descending from the brain and by other information that we are receiving. This theory can explain why, for example, someone who is engaged in a strenuous or demanding physical task may not notice an injury until they have finished it, whereupon the pain comes flooding in. Other kinds of sensory information can also close the 'gate', so concentrating very hard on a task can sometimes ease pain by 'taking your mind off it'. A summary of the conditions that can open or close the gate are shown in Figure 6.5.

Health

The central assumption of the gate theory is that a number of structures in the central nervous system are involved in the experience of pain. These mechanisms affect the 'gatelike' mechanism in the spinal column that controls the flow of pain stimulation to the brain.

Figure 6.4 The gate theory of pain. (Melzack and Wall, 1982.)

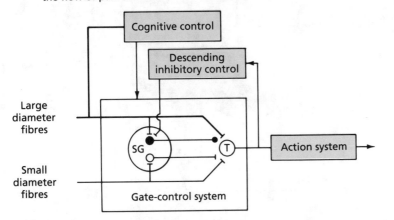

The large diameter fibres and small diameter fibres project into the substantia gelatinosa (SG) and the transmission cells (T) in the spinal column. The central control trigger is represented by a line running from the large fibre system to the central control mechanisms.

CONDITIONS THAT OPEN THE GATE	CONDITIONS THAT CLOSE THE GATE
Physical conditions	**Physical conditions**
Extent of the injury	Medication
Inappropriate activity level	Counterstimulation, e.g. massage
Emotional conditions	**Emotional conditions**
Anxiety or worry	Positive emotions
Tension	Relaxation
Depression	Rest
Mental conditions	**Mental conditions**
Focussing on the pain	Intense concentration or distraction
Boredom	Involvement and interest in life activities

Figure 6.5 Conditions that can open or close the pain gate. (Sarafino, 1991)

Youngson (1992) argued that, even though there is a great deal known about pain as a result of psychological and neurophysiological research, this knowledge is almost never put into practice in medical treatment – particularly with respect to pain after surgery. According to a 1990 survey of attitudes to pain in British hospitals, staff chose pain-relieving drugs randomly, did not take account of the nature of the pain and did not

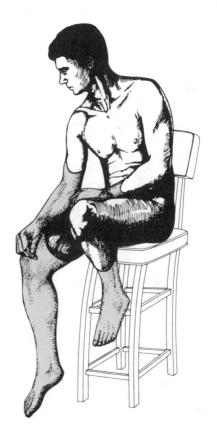

Figure 6.6 The figure shows the phantom limbs most commonly reported. (Melzack, 1992.)

even hold relieving the pain completely as a professional aim. Moreover, despite clear evidence that applying an anaesthetic block to the nerve tissues closest to the site of the operation before surgery could make a significant difference to post-surgery pain, very few medical staff actually did it.

This was also the case in the study of **phantom limb** pain. Phantom limbs are commonly experienced after someone has had to have a limb amputated – they feel, very strongly, as though the limb is still physically there. Even quite small children feel this, which Melzack (1992) used as evidence for the idea that the brain has an internal, pre-wired 'map' of the body, which it uses to structure experience. Melzack described how these phantom limbs could also hold the memory of pain experienced before the amputation, which was often quite excruciating for the patient and difficult to treat by conventional medical methods. But by applying an anaesthetic block for a period of time before the amputation, Melzack discovered that it is possible for surgeons to reduce the pain felt in phantom limbs afterwards.

phantom limbs The name given to the phenomenon experienced by amputees, of still feeling the limb as present and alive, even though it has been surgically removed.

Less traumatic disturbances to the senses are sometimes deliberately sought out by people through the use of social drugs, hypnosis and meditation. Altered states of consciousness have been sought out for as long as recorded history and form a major consumer industry today. On the other hand, deliberately distorting the senses has a disorienting effect on the individual – a phenomenon which has not been ignored by the military. Watson (1980) discussed research into sensory isolation carried out by Hebb for the Canadian Defense Research Board. The experimental techniques included fitting men with cuffs and goggles, semi-immersing them in tepid water, and playing them monotones and meaningless noise, in order to cut out normal sensory stimulation (Figure 6.7). This **sensory deprivation** appeared to produce some bizarre effects. Research participants sometimes reported hallucinations and many were unable to complete the goal of undertaking a whole day under these conditions.

Society

sensory deprivation The cutting out of all incoming sensory information or at least as much of it as possible.

Myers (cited in Watson, 1980, pp. 201–6) looked at the consequences of monotony rather than sensory deprivation, on the grounds that it would be impossible to reduce sensation to zero. In a similar set of studies, Myers produced conditions that would minimize any change in sensation, so that people's experience would be as monotonous as possible. His extensive studies showed that, although these conditions do seem bring about some psychological changes, these changes are minimal and not particularly harmful.

It is uncertain, however, just how much the effects of these sensory deprivation studies actually resulted from sensory deprivation and how

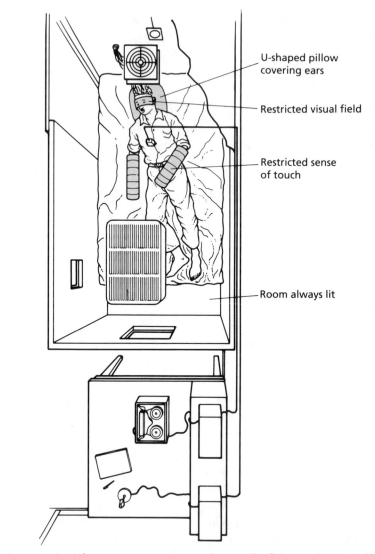

U-shaped pillow
covering ears

Restricted visual field

Restricted sense
of touch

Room always lit

Figure 6.7 Sensory
deprivation chamber.
(Adapted from Watson,
1980.)

far they resulted from expectations. In almost all of the studies conducted
in the early 1970s or before, research participants were warned that they
might experience some psychological effects and given a way of
signalling that they wanted to be released. This may have set up expectations which they then lived up to. In addition, the studies received
considerable publicity at the time. Follow-up studies conducted in a later
period failed to produce such dramatic results.

Shallice (1973) reported on the military use of sensory deprivation on
12 men who were subjected to special interrogation procedures. When
they were not being actively interrogated, the men were fitted with
hoods resembling tightly woven black bags, subjected to high decibel
noise and forced to stand with their hands above their heads for up to 16

Figure 6.8 Situations where smell is important.

hours at a time. They wore loose-fitting clothing, had a restricted diet and were deprived of sleep. The temperature was either very hot or, when the men were allowed to sleep, very cold. The interrogation lasted for 6 days and prisoners had between 9 to 43 hours under these conditions. The effects were dramatic, and included a range of psychological and physical symptoms such as hallucinations, suicidal thoughts, perceptual distortion, incontinence, severe anxiety, depression, insomnia and peptic ulcers.

The use of sensory deprivation and maltreatment in producing psychological disorientation followed a well-established tradition of military practice. Shallice was describing the treatment of Irish prisoners by the British army and the methods used were strikingly similar to the treatment of suspected Irish rebels by the English military in the 17th century. Sargant (1957) described how these techniques formed the nucleus of 'brainwashing' methods, which had been used in a number of military contexts, and discussed how prisoners of war in Korea and elsewhere had sometimes been 'converted' to the other side as a result of the disorientation produced by their systematic application.

We are often influenced by sensory stimulation, even though we are not particularly aware of it. Broadbent and Little (1960) worked on the effect of loud noise on the efficiency of operators working on film perforation. These people typically moved between different machines during the course of the day. In their study, the researchers reduced the noise levels in the work place significantly by placing absorbent material between half of the machines. By comparing the performance of the same operators, they found that work bays with lowered noise levels showed a greatly reduced rate of mistakes and also far fewer equipment shutdowns.

Work

For human beings, vision is the primary sensory mode, although the others are also important – more so than is often thought. In Western cultures, children are systematically trained in visual perception: they are encouraged to look at picture books and learn how to perceive a cartoon

Environment

representation of, say, a telephone as being the 'same' as the object in their own house (which may have a totally different shape and form). But the other senses, too, can become very highly developed with training, even though this is often neglected in the education of Western children.

For example, Dodd (1989) discussed how Native Australian children are explicitly trained in the identification of smells, from a very early age. They are taught, for instance, how to identify the smell of the same plant at different times of year or how to disentangle a combination of smells so that each component can be identified; and the training process which they receive is a very systematic one. The not surprising result is that Native Australian people are much more proficient at using smell as a major source of information than white Australians or other members of Western-style cultures.

That does not mean, however, that Westerners are not susceptible to the effects of perfumes. Smell is the only sense which has direct contact with the brain, since the neural fibres carrying information about smell pass directly to the limbic system, a part of the brain which is also strongly involved in the experience of emotion. Other sensory information passes through the thalamus, which relays it on to other parts of the brain. Hines (1977) argued that sensory information about smell is mainly processed by the right cerebral hemisphere, which is believed by many to be the part of the brain involved in artistic, religious and creative states (Ornstein, 1986). Hines suggested that this connection might explain why incense and perfumes are so important in religious and creative states.

Many people are aware that smell can sometimes have a powerful subliminal effect, operating unconsciously to influence people's behaviour. But attempts to use this to manipulate people in situations where they are suspicious of being manipulated can sometimes backfire. Baron (1983) asked students to act out the role of a personnel manager and to interview another person for an entry-level management position. They were given pre-scripted questions, and asked to rate the people whom they had interviewed afterwards. The interviewees either wore scent or did not. Male interviewees wore 'Brut' and female interviewees wore 'Jontu' perfumes.

Baron found that those who wore perfume tended to be less likely to be recommended for hire, particularly by the male interviewers. They were also rated as less intelligent and less friendly. Interestingly, too, Baron also found that these male interviewers rated themselves as less effective in the presence of those wearing perfume. It appeared that they were suspicious of being manipulated by the interviewee and their resentment at this had produced the low ratings. The female interviewers, Baron suggested, knew that they were less susceptible to these effects (as was indicated from other measures too) and so responded less negatively to an interviewee wearing perfume.

Perceptual organization

Sensation and perception are not the same thing. It is one thing receiving sensory information, but if that information is to be any use to us, we have to analyse and interpret the information which is being received through our sensory receptors. The first step in this is identifying the basic ways that information is organized: how it becomes grouped into meaningful units and what a meaningful unit actually is.

Most of the research in this area has been concerned with visual information, as it is the primary sense for human beings and the one which we seem to be able to describe most easily. The **Gestalt** psychologists were extremely interested in perceptual organization and identified four basic processes by which we combine information into meaningful units. Together, these are known as the laws of Prägnanz and are listed in Figure 6.9.

The principle of similarity
If a number of stimuli are present, then we will tend to group together those which are similar to one another

The principle of proximity
We tend to group together stimuli which are close to one another and see them as 'belonging' together

The principle of closure
The way that we tend to look for complete shapes and to 'fill in' the gaps mentally if such a shape is suggested

Figure 6.9 The Gestalt laws of Prägnanz. The tendency to organize visual information into complete rounded or satisfying shapes rather than fragmented and 'bitty' ones.

Figure 6.10 Two faces or a vase? We can see one or the other but never both at the same time. Which do you see?

These four principles are not equal in the way that we organize information: proximity will override similarity, for example, and closure will override proximity. But together, they add up to a powerful tendency to perceive visual information in terms of figures against backgrounds: we see objects and items, not random patterns of colour and brightness. Ambiguous figures, which can represent two different and opposing stimuli simultaneously, show us how powerful this tendency is (see Figure 6.10). If we choose one image to look at, the other disappears and becomes background; if we change our attentional focus to the second, the first becomes background instead. We can alternate rapidly between the two, but we do not see the two figures at the same time, because our perceptual tendency to see figures against background is so strong.

Key reference: KOFFKA, K. (1935) *Principles of Gestalt Psychology.* Harcourt Brace, New York.

Environment

Figure 6.11 The background to portraits will affect how we judge the subject.

The Gestalt principles of perception have always appealed to designers, since they appeal to their need to understand and apply visual forms at a broad and holistic level. According to Lang (1987), formal aesthetic approaches to design have been heavily dependent on Gestalt theory. The assumption, in aesthetic design terms, is that an environment which conforms to these principles will be perceived as a 'good environment' – in other words, as one which is judged to be pleasing by people who live or work in it.

Beautiful room

Average room

Ugly room

There is a considerable amount of research which suggests that the aesthetic quality of a room will affect the judgements that we make when we are looking at it. Attractive environments have been shown to affect mood, sociability, productivity and judgements about whether someone was likeable or not. For example, Maslow and Mintz (1956) asked research participants to rate pictures of people in different situations. The background to each portrait was one of three kinds: a 'beautiful' room, which was well decorated and well lit; an 'average' room, which was an office of a member of the academic staff; and an 'ugly' room, which looked a bit like a caretaker's cupboard. The ratings which the research participants made were affected by the background of the picture. The most positive ratings went to the people in the 'beautiful' room, but when the same portraits were shown in the 'ugly' room they received much more negative ratings.

Gestalt principles have also been used by advertisers. Myers and Reynolds (1967) described how the Kellogg's company used the principle of closure in a poster campaign. Kellogg's produced a series of large posters with the second 'g' cut off by the edge of the hoarding and found that people remembered this much more than a similar poster with the whole word presented to them. In a similar study, Heimbach and Jacoby (1972) showed one group of people a complete commercial and another group a commercial cut at the end. Both sets of researchers found that the incomplete advertisements led to greater recall of the product than the complete advertisements.

The explanation for these findings is that people remember the information more effectively because they are engaging in a certain amount of mental processing to complete the information into a whole and meaningful unit. In the last chapter, we saw how processing information helps us to remember things. Our perceptual tendency to complete missing parts, so as to perceive the whole unit, is one way of making sure that the information does get processed by a consumer looking at an advertisement. The recent trends towards advertisements which show only part of a well-known slogan or catch-phrase operate on much the same principle.

It is possible that the tendency to perceive complete figures is closely linked with the arrangement of nerve cells in the visual system. In 1968, Hubel and Wiesel showed that cells in the thalamus responded to different types of visual information. Since the **thalamus** is where the cells of the optic nerve synapse, before transmitting visual information on to the cerebral cortex, this implies that there is some preliminary sorting out of visual information at a very early stage – and this involves the kinds of information required for figure-ground perception.

Consumer

Figure 6.12 Kelloggs used the principle of closure to attract attention to their product.

thalamus The sub-cortical structure in the brain which receives sensory information and relays it to the cerebral cortex.

Hubel and Wiesel found a hierarchical arrangement of cells, responding to different categories of information. Simple cells responded only to the smallest bits of information: dots, or lines at a particular angle, in a particular part of the visual field. These, in turn, were connected with complex cells, which combined information from several simple cells to respond to slightly more complex stimuli, like, say, a line of a particular orientation found anywhere in the visual field. Complex cells in turn connected with hypercomplex cells, which would respond to simple figures or shapes.

Nearly 40 years earlier, the Gestalt psychologists had argued that figure-ground organization was such a strong mechanism of perception that it was likely to be innate. Hubel and Wiesel's findings supported this idea, seeming to suggest that perhaps the tendency to see figures against backgrounds really is built in to the wiring of the nervous system. This, in turn, would give us a powerful tendency to perceive complete figures rather than partial ones, which was likely to be found in all human societies.

Education

That does not mean, though, that all of our perceptual abilities are inherited. As we become more skilled at a given task, we will learn to perceive information in different ways and to group it into meaningful units. Bean (1937) used a tachistoscope (a piece of equipment that can present visual material for very short intervals of time) to flash pieces of music to musicians and non-musicians. Bean found that the musicians could play up to five notes of the music which had been presented to them, even though they had seen it for less than a second. Non-professional musicians, on the other hand, could only play one or two notes.

In a much later study, Wolf (1976) interviewed a number of professional musicians. Some of these were very good at sight-reading music, while others were poor at it. Wolf found that those who were good at sight-reading tended to be very highly organized in how they looked at music, tending to see it in terms of sets of recognizable patterns and specific pattern cues. Those who were poor at sight-reading, on the other hand, tended to use an analytic strategy, examining one note at a time, when they were looking at music and not a pattern recognition one. They were better at memorizing music than the expert sight-readers, but less good at perceiving whole patterns.

Work

Our perception of a machine and its actions will affect the way we interact with it. This makes it necessary for designers to understand aspects of human perception when they are creating visual display panels. There has been a considerable amount of research into the nature of visual displays, since they are the main way that a machine sends information to a human operator (see Figure 6.13). Human beings

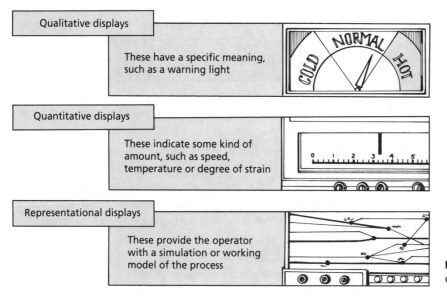

Figure 6.13 Types of displays.

generally prefer analogue-type displays (such as a clock face) to digital readouts and find that they are able to interpret them more quickly and efficiently.

When we are interpreting any display, however, there is a trade-off between accuracy and speed. Simple scales with few divisions may be fast to read, but they are also less accurate. Singleton (1969) investigated the optimal pattern for analogue scales in displays, by testing how accurately and rapidly operators could read them. Singleton concluded that the best type of display was a scale which was divided into four or five sub-divisions, with numbers to be marked only against the major scale divisions.

In reading information, too, our perceptual characteristics are important, and efficient design of machine displays needs to take that into account. Morgan *et al.* (1963) collated a vast amount of research into the effectiveness of different dimensions of letters, numbers and scale-strokes in designs. From this, they produced recommendations as to which types of designs, typefaces and so on would be most useful in different working situations.

The visual design of equipment is a common cause for error in industrial situations. HMSO (1990) described how new control panels in a British Midland aeroplane which crashed on a motorway in the mid 1980s might have contributed to the disaster. The designers of the new Boeing had recently changed their dial style from analogue to digital displays. Digital displays allow for a more accurate reading, but they do not show the rate of change as effectively and people often do not notice the information as quickly. A constantly changing number is not nearly as graphic an illustration as a needle moving on a dial and so the display is not so effective. The report suggested that, in the case of the Kegworth disaster, the difficulty in processing digital information was one factor – among several others – which inhibited the pilot's ability to respond appropriately when the plane's engine cut out.

Lee (1976) suggested that drivers use specific visual information to make judgements of relative speed between their own cars and the car in front. One of these images is the relationship between the separation of the rear lights of a car and the rate of change of this separation. Lee went on to suggest that road safety could be improved by amplifying the visual information at the back of a vehicle, to enhance this effect. For example, it would be possible to add a reflecting strip to the rear of a vehicle, so that the driver would see a progressively wider band of light when approaching a vehicle at night.

Sport

On a similar theme, but in a very different area of human behaviour, Hubbard and Seng (1954) studied the performance of baseball batters. They filmed the batters and observed that they always began to step forward when the ball was released by the pitcher (the person who throws the ball). The duration of the step and the timing of the swing were geared to the speed of the ball, even though the duration of the bat swing was relatively constant from one hit to the next. Although their filming methods were relatively insensitive, their data suggest strongly that the batters did not track the ball or fixate on it during the last part of its flight, nor when it actually made contact (or otherwise) with the bat. It appears that the most important information is picked up in the first part of the flight of the ball and that it is that initial information which determines the action of the batter.

Work

Much quality control in industry relies on the ability to spot impure or unexpected forms. Chaney and Teel (1967) developed a set of visual aids as part of a training programme for machine parts inspectors. Their job involved examining precision-machined parts to identify small defects, like wrong dimensions or misplaced holes and screw threads, and to assess the quality of the finish. Usually, this was done by practical training and telling the trainees what was needed, but in their training programme, the researchers also used simplified drawings that illustrated which features of the parts needed particular attention and what the acceptable tolerances were for minor variations. By drawing attention to the important details visually, the researchers aimed to heighten the trainees' awareness of what the finished product should actually look like.

Chaney and Teel compared four groups of trainees: one group was just given practical training in picking out the defects, without any use of

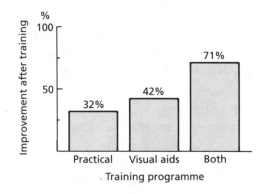

Figure 6.14 Improvement in the detection of defects after training. (Chaney and Teel, 1967.)

the special visual aids; one group was given training based only on the visual aids; a third group received a combination of the two, and a control group received neither. When they were tested, all of the groups except the control group had become better at spotting defects. The practical training group had improved by 32%, and the visual aids alone group by 42%. The group which had combined visual aids with practical training, however, had improved their effectiveness by 71%. Clearly, having a visual image of what the finished article should look like is useful in learning new tasks of this kind. This study also has some implications for the Kegworth plane disaster because the pilots had only received visual aid training on the new design plane and had not been given any simulator training.

Recognizing people

From their very earliest moments – as young as nine minutes old – infants respond to stimuli which are like human faces (Goren, Sarty and Wu, 1975) and from then on our ability to distinguish and identify faces becomes ever more sophisticated. Adult human beings can recognize very subtle differences between faces, as well as recognizing the same face on different occasions and with different expressions.

Face recognition serves many different social purposes, allowing us to identify friends, to make judgements about strangers and to understand social interaction. Some research suggests that these functions are entirely independent of one another. For example, there seems to be a difference in how we process familiar and unfamiliar faces. When we are looking at familiar faces, we concentrate more on internal features, like eyes, nose and mouth; but when we are looking at unfamiliar faces we concentrate on external details like hair and outline.

One possible explanation is that we develop cognitive

face recognition unit A *hypothetical information-processing unit in the mind which is involved in identifying known people by their faces.*

face recognition units for people that we know, so we process information about them in terms of our knowledge of their personality, interactive style and so on. This means that when we look at familiar people we gather information which will contribute to this knowledge and for this the internal features of the face are more useful. But when we look at strangers, we have no such recognition units, so we fall back on descriptive criteria, like the colour of the hair.

Putting names to faces also seems to be a different cognitive process from recognizing the face itself. It is not at all uncommon for an individual to remember a considerable amount of semantic information about someone – such as their likes, dislikes, abilities – without being able to remember their name. People who have to remember names as an important part of their job often fall back on mnemonic strategies, developing artificial memory links to 'fix' the name to the face. Names are not very useful, either, in helping us to recognize a face if we do not remember it from a picture.

Key reference: BRUCE, V. and YOUNG, A. W. (1986) Understanding face recognition. *British Journal of Psychology,* **77**, 305–27.

Vicki Bruce was born in England in 1953. She studied Natural Sciences at Cambridge, where she took experimental psychology as a second year course, and became 'hooked' on cognitive psychology, and chose to specialize in psychology in her final year (1974). She remained in Cambridge where she completed a PhD in 1977, supervised by Alan Baddeley, Director of the Medical Research Council's Applied Psychology Unit.

She then taught at the University of Newcastle for one year, before moving to the University of Nottingham where she was promoted to a Readership in 1988 and a personal Chair in 1990. She moved to an established Chair in Psychology at the University of Stirling in 1992. She has served on numerous committees of the British Psychological Society (and was Chair of the Scientific Affairs Board, 1989–1992), the Medical Research Council, and the Economic and Social Research Council (where she was Chair of the Research Programmes Board and a member of the Council, 1992–1996).

Vicki began empirical and theoretical work on face recognition during her PhD and this has been the major focus for her research throughout her career. She also helped in the design of recent UK coins through human factors research conducted for the Royal Mint. She has published several books, including advanced undergraduate textbooks on visual perception and cognition, and numerous scientific articles and chapters.

Face recognition seems to be an entirely different perceptual skill from being able to perceive objects. In the study of S. B. by Gregory and Wallace (1963), the man who became able to see for the first time at age 52, the researchers found that face recognition eluded him. Despite his ability to recognize objects and his extensive experience with people, S.B. was never able to interpret facial expressions like smiles and frowns. He was aware of moods and could read them through intonation in the voices of people who were interacting with him, but did not ever manage to interpret the facial messages which were being conveyed.

Health

The idea that a 'face recognition unit' is a cognitive structure which can operate independently of other forms of recognition, including that of recognizing or remembering names, has been supported by clinical studies of brain-damaged patients. Temple (1992) described a case study of someone who could copy drawings of faces and identify whether faces at different angles were the same person, but could not recognize familiar faces. Campbell (1992) described someone who had difficulty recognizing faces at all, whether familiar or unfamiliar, and seemed to have particular problems with the spatial proportions in faces, which give clues to expressions. In all other respects, however, both of these people lived normal, everyday lives and did not appear to suffer any intellectual or wider cognitive impairments.

Other people who have been studied by psychologists have experienced different problems with face recognition: one patient could only recognize familiar faces, but could not match up pictures of unfamiliar ones, where another could identify facial expressions with no problem, but was completely unable to recognize the faces of friends or family. The implication is that recognising people involves a number of separate cognitive abilities, which normally work together, but which can equally well operate independently of one another.

Figure 6.15 We are able to identify the face in the cartoon, even though it is very different from the photograph.

The failure to recognize a face can be socially very embarrassing. It can also be very distressing for the person who is unrecognized and therefore feels unacknowledged. It is, sadly, a feature of some forms of cognitive deficits associated with ageing that their progressive development eventually leads to the sufferer being unable to recognize their nearest friends and relatives – a situation which is distressing both for them and for their family.

Lipinska, Backman and Herlitz (1992) wondered whether the prior experience in face recognition someone had would influence their abilities to recognize faces or not, if they later acquired Alzheimer's disease. They showed normal older adults and people with a mild Alzheimer's disease, a set of pictures of famous faces, which were both dated and contemporary (for example, Greta Garbo and Stefan Edberg). The pictures were given name tags and the research participants were asked to think of unique statements about each person.

The results showed that people in both groups were able to say more about the dated figures than they could about the contemporary ones. They also found that in an episodic face recognition task, when people were unexpectedly presented with the faces, both groups performed better with the dated faces than with the contemporary ones. The researchers concluded that their results showed, first, that people know more about dated famous people than they do about contemporary famous people, and secondly, that they can use this prior knowledge to enhance their ability to remember and recognize people. In this respect, there were relatively few differences between people who were 'normally' old and those suffering from mild Alzheimer's disease, and the researchers suggested that those differences were probably only in the amount that could actually be remembered, and did not come from a different kind of remembering.

Society

Recognizing faces is a complex skill which we continuously develop and improve upon. But, in order to do this, we need to have experience of the face types we want to recognize. It is often observed that Western people sometimes experience difficulties in recognizing faces of Japanese people. Similarly, to many Asian or black people, whites all look very similar. But these effects mainly seem to come from lack of experience in meeting people from the different social group: with experience, we soon learn to be more sensitive to the differences in people's faces – if we want to, that is.

Goldstein and Chance (1985) performed a study in which Western research participants were intensively trained to learn face–digit pairs. The training sessions were explicitly designed to improve their ability to learn general rules about Japanese faces, rather than to improve their memory for individual Japanese people. There were eight people in the study, four of whom received the intensive training, while the others belonged to a control group. Each person was tested immediately after training, and on two subsequent occasions, one and five months afterwards.

When they began the study, the people in each of the groups had almost identical recognition memory handicaps. They were unable to recognize Japanese faces to any significant degree. But once they had been given the intensive training, the researchers found that people's performance was significantly enhanced, by comparison with those in the control group. Moreover, once they had learned to recognize Japanese faces, the research participants retained this ability over the whole five-month period, suggesting that once we have learned a face-recognition skill, it does not go away.

Markham, Ellis and Ellis (1991) discussed how children's cognitive abilities are often very different from those of adults. They showed how these differences also emerge in a study of the effect of context on face recognition. Three groups of 30 children (aged 6–7, 8–9, and 10–11 years), and a comparison group of 28 adults, were presented with children's faces in the same or different backgrounds from those in which they originally appeared. The faces might also have the same or different expressions. The research participants were also shown some other faces in an old or a novel background to act as distractors from the experimental task. The question was whether they would be able to recognize those faces they had seen before, even if the backgrounds were different.

Education

The researchers found that the older the child was, the better it was at recognizing the faces. Whenever they changed the background context, the success rate would drop, but it would drop less for older children and adults than for younger children. On the other hand, the adults were more affected than the children by changes in the expressions of the faces. All this suggests that children and adults are concentrating on different features when they are processing pictures of faces. For adults it is the features of the face and, possibly, its personality characteristics, whereas for children, the most salient feature seems to be the context in which the face appears.

One aspect of face recognition that can have dramatic consequences is in eye-witness testimony. Eye-witness testimony has a particular dramatic appeal to us all. Such first-hand accounts seem to have a special social authenticity – an account of what actually happened from someone who was really there. The courts, too, pay special attention to eye-witness testimony. A survey by Kassin *et al.* (1989) of 63 leading American psychologists in eye-witness testimony found that over half of them had

Society

testified on the subject in court and many had done so often – their average number of court appearances was between seven and eight.

The increasing number of court appearances by specialist psychologists in this field appears to be an outcome of the growing body of research illuminating the nature of eye-witness testimony. This research has illustrated a number of issues which might directly concern the courts. For example, in one study, O'Rourke *et al.* (1989) showed people of varying ages a film of a robbery and asked them to identify the robber. They found that correct identification decreased with age – younger people were more likely to identify the robber accurately. The researchers suggested that perhaps older people tend to rely on their stereotypes and also to transfer ideas from previous experiences instead of coming to the situation fresh (see Figure 6.16).

The identification parade is an important part of prosecution evidence and also has a particular place in the public imagination – probably as a result of endless television dramas that make use of this procedure. In 1976 the Devlin Committee analysed all the identification parades that had been held in England and Wales during the year 1973. Over 2000 parades were recorded and a suspect was identified in roughly 45% of them. In those cases, 82% of the people who were picked out were subsequently convicted. Often, the eye-witness testimony was the only evidence of guilt, and even in these cases 74% of the people were convicted. So it is important that we should be sure that eye-witness testimony is as accurate as it can be and that means researching into any of the possible factors which can influence it.

There are numerous factors that will influence the selection of a person from the identity parade by the witness. Stephenson (1992) argued that there was a serious omission in the psychological study of eye-witness testimony, in that very little research had looked at the perspective of the witnesses themselves. There are a number of issues

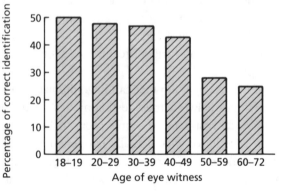

Figure 6.16 Accuracy of eye-witnesses of different ages. (O'Rourke *et al.* 1989.)

Correct identification decreases with age

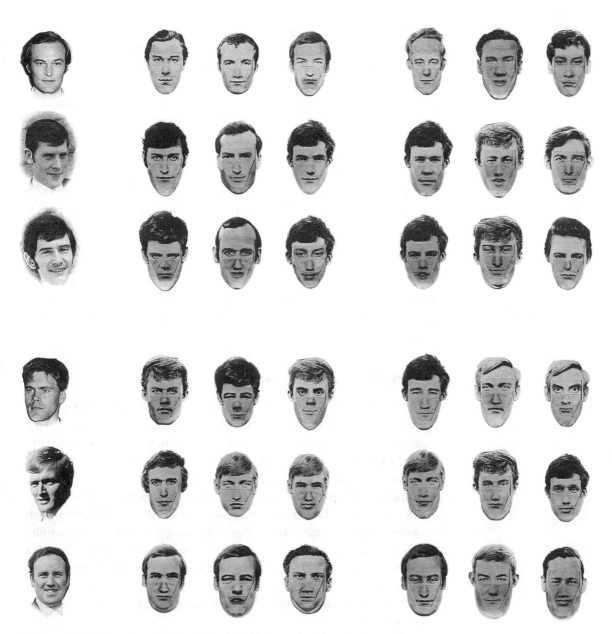

Figure 6.17 Examples of attempted photofit reconstruction. Each row shows a 'target face' (the left hand picture) that was seen by the observers, and their attempts to immediately reconstruct the face in a photofit. (Bruce, 1988.)

that might affect the quality of the witness report, such as possible coercion by relatives, pressure from lawyers, prejudice from court personnel or threats from other people involved in the court case. Memory researchers seem to assume that people in their experiments will always answer questions to the best of their ability. This may be true of laboratory studies of word list recall – although Silverman showed that, even there, research participants have their own motives for acting as they do – but it can hardly be taken for granted with witnesses in a courtroom.

Stephenson (1992) described a study which illustrates the unconscious influences on the witness. The research participants were asked to participate in a task which was similar to an identity parade. The first 41 research participants were tested by the experimenter when he knew what the correct answers to the task were. Then, the researchers decided to improve the design of the study and, when the remaining 30 research participants were tested, the experimenter was unaware of the correct answer. To the surprise of the researchers, the second set of tests produced a substantially different result to the first set. The experimenter had unconsciously communicated his knowledge to the witnesses. Since the police officers who conduct witnesses to identity parades are usually aware of the suspect, this study implies that they may, unconsciously, bias the outcome of the parade in the direction of their own expectations.

Selective attention

How is it that you can be in a crowded room, listening only to your immediate conversation, yet instantly become aware that someone nearby has mentioned your name? Known as the 'cocktail party problem' (a name which in itself dates the research), this problem engaged research psychologists for several years.

Early explorations of selective attention suggested that we adopt relatively basic filtering strategies, attending only to information with certain physical characteristics and ignoring the rest – for example, ignoring sounds which are coming from a different location. But that did not answer the cocktail party problem. Clearly, highly meaningful information can catch our attention even if has different physical characteristics, so this type of filter is not an adequate explanation for our experience.

Later models suggested that the information which reaches our awareness has got through some kind of semantic filter, which allows information in on the basis of its meaning. Various filter models were proposed, of which perhaps the most elegant is that suggested by Triesman. Triesman suggested that initial filters did not actually cut out information with the wrong physical characteristics: instead, they attenuated the signal, so that it still passed through the filter, but in a much weaker form. So, if the information had a particularly powerful

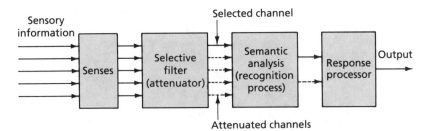

Figure 6.18 Treisman's attentuation model of attention.

content – like one's own name – then it would become strengthened again and would pass through a second-stage filter to reach awareness. Other information would be filtered out at the second stage (see Figure 6.18).

> **Key reference:** TRIESMAN, A. (1964) Verbal cues, language and meaning in attention. *American Journal of Psychology, 77*, 206–14.

Cooper and Fairburn (1992) carried out a study of women with the eating disorders anorexia or **bulimia nervosa**, to see whether their problem influenced the way that they paid attention to different types of stimuli. They used a Stroop colour-naming task, in which people were asked to look at words and state what colour ink the words were printed in, as quickly as possible. They were compared with a control group of 'normal' dieters, and another of women who were not dieters and did not show any symptoms of an eating disorder. The words with which they were presented in the Stroop task were either neutral ones, or words which related to eating, weight or shape (e.g. 'fat', 'diet', 'thighs', 'cakes').

The groups with eating disorders took significantly longer to name the colour of the target words than to name the neutral words. The control groups, however, showed no difference between the two conditions. The fact that the women with eating disorders took longer to name the colour of the target words implies that they were less able to ignore the meaning of the word presented to them – in other words, that they would particularly attend to words which had salience for them. The authors suggested that this kind of selective attention may be one way in which eating disorders are maintained: people with eating disorders simply notice food-related stimuli a great deal more than other people do.

As the **cocktail party phenomenon** shows, we can be listening to one conversation and suddenly become aware that we are being talked about in another part of the room. Another example of this kind of selective attention comes in the way that some people are able to tune in, and

Health

bulimia A disorder characterized by alternate gorging on food, followed by purging of that food by vomiting, or using laxatives or diuretics.

cocktail party phenomenon The phenomenon in selective attention in which someone may be attending only to an immediate conversation, yet may none the less catch their own name if it is mentioned elsewhere.

Figure 6.19 Subliminal advertising. Can advertising messages be sent to us without our awareness of them? It is not clear whether subliminal perception has any effect on us, but it still generates controversy; some people look for hidden messages and images in advertisements.

PEOPLE HAVE BEEN TRYING TO FIND THE BREASTS IN THESE ICE CUBES SINCE 1957.

The advertising industry is sometimes charged with sneaking seductive little pictures into ads.

Supposedly, these pictures can get you to buy a product without your even seeing them.

Consider the photograph above. According to some people, there's a pair of female breasts hidden in the patterns of light refracted by the ice cubes.

Well, if you really searched you probably *could* see the breasts. For that matter, you could also see Millard Fillmore, a stuffed pork chop and a 1946 Dodge.

The point is that so-called "subliminal advertising" simply doesn't exist. Overactive imaginations, however, most certainly do.

So if anyone claims to see breasts in that drink up there, they aren't in the ice cubes.

They're in the eye of the beholder.

ADVERTISING
ANOTHER WORD FOR FREEDOM OF CHOICE.
American Association of Advertising Agencies

subliminal perception
The ability to perceive and respond to stimuli which are presented below the level of conscious awareness.

Consumer

tune out, of watching television and listening to the radio, only noticing it if something that they are interested in comes on. These observations imply that incoming information is being processed at some level without our being aware of it. In turn, this leads to the idea of subliminal perception – that we will perceive and process information unconsciously.

In the world of advertising, the discovery of **subliminal perception** led to the question of whether advertising messages could be conveyed subliminally. Subliminal messages are messages that are too weak to reach conscious awareness, perhaps because they occur too rapidly or are too faint. Brean (1958) described a market researcher who arranged with a cinema owner for the use of a second special projector to deliver subliminal messages. This projector flashed the words 'EAT POPCORN' and 'DRINK COCA-COLA' on to the screen every five seconds, during the

One of the phenomena of selective attention is that we are able to tune in to background information if it appears to have some importance. This tuning in might mean that we have missed some early important information. This might well have contributed to the famous mass panic in America that accompanied Orson Welles and the 'Mercury Theatre of the Air' radio production of the H. G. Wells' classic War of the Worlds. Breaking the conventions of radio drama, Welles presented the play to America in 1938 as an outside broadcast with 'news bulletins' interrupting 'regular' programmes. These bulletins described an invasion by Martians and because people had only tuned in their attention to the emergency messages many people believed the descriptions to be true. Many people took action to deal with this emergency by leaving home and heading for safety in the remote parts of America.

Figure 6.20 *War of the Worlds.*

showing of a regular film. The exposure was extremely brief – only 1/3000th of a second, which is well below the ordinary human perceptual threshold for visual information so the cinema-goers were unaware that the information had been transmitted.

More than 45 000 people were exposed to the subliminal message during the six weeks that this trial lasted. According to the report, the sales of Coca-Cola at the cinema rose by 18% and popcorn sales rose by nearly 60%. However, the details of the study are not well reported and the film itself (*Picnic*) contained several scenes of eating and drinking, so it is uncertain how far the effect really came from the subliminal message. A second trial, in which the words 'ICE-CREAM' were presented subliminally shortly before the cinema interval, was reported to have produced a rise in sales of ice-cream, but also a number of complaints to the management that the cinema was too cold!

Whether these trials really demonstrated the effectiveness of subliminal perception or not, they were sufficiently powerful to ensure that subliminal advertising of this type was banned in both the US and the UK. That does not mean, however, that advertisers cannot use other ways of getting messages across, and sometimes these, too, can be so subtle as to operate unconsciously on the consumer. The use of colour and visual images in advertisements are very carefully selected so as to evoke moods, associations and impressions unconsciously, as is the use of background music in supermarkets.

Calvert *et al.* (1982) performed a study of children's TV watching, looking particularly at what children pay attention to when they are watching TV and whether their attention is necessary for comprehension of the programme's content. They showed 128 children, aged between 5 and 8, a pro-social cartoon. Each child watched the cartoon in the

Society

company of another child, of the same gender. The researchers recorded each child's visual attention continuously and then later related the tape of the child watching TV with each of ten formal features of the cartoon which they had watched. The children were also asked to complete a lengthy multiple-choice test, designed to see how much they recalled and how much they had understood of what they had seen.

Perhaps not surprisingly, Calvert *et al.* found that the more the child had attended to the TV, the more it understood what was going on. But there were also differences between older and younger children in what they understood, which linked with what they had paid attention to. Both age groups comprehended the central story content, which had been presented with rapid and moderate action levels. But the younger children's comprehension was associated with attending to during notice-able auditory parts of the action, like sound effects, but not with periods in which an adult narrated the story. Older children, on the other hand, tended to pay attention to dialogue between the child characters in the cartoon, and to moderate character action, and these were the parts which they comprehended most clearly.

Anderson *et al.* (1979) studied how children watch television. Their observations revealed that most children look at the screen for only a short time before looking away. In fact, over half of the looks lasted for only three seconds or even less. But once a child looks at the screen for 15 seconds or more, then it is likely that it will continue viewing for a longer period of time. Anderson *et al.* also observed that when a child looked at the TV for ten seconds or more, the body would relax, the head would slouch forward and the mouth would drop open. Anderson *et al.* suggested that TV watching involves a trance-like state, which includes a form of **attentional inertia**, in which it is easier to keep one's attention on the screen than to look away.

attentional inertia *State of fixed attention, for example, watching the television.*

Consumer

A study that looked at how advertisements influence our attention was described by Janiszewski (1990), who asked research participants to read an article in a mock newspaper. An advertisement was placed directly next to the article, and this consisted either of a picture or of a verbal message, in the form of a slogan. When they had read the article, the research participants were asked to complete a series of questions designed to establish how much they remembered of what they had seen in the newspaper.

Janiszewski found that those people who had been presented with the verbal advertisement had a lower recall of the complexity of the passage and also recalled fewer quotations than those research participants whose article was accompanied by a pictorial advertisement. But the people who had seen a pictorial advertisement showed lower overall recall of the passage and were less able to distinguish between the different implications of the text. In other words, they remembered more of the detail, but less of the meaning in the passage that they had read.

The study has a number of implications, not only in terms of unconscious information processing, but also in terms of competition from other information. For example, it would seem to imply that visual advertisements form a distraction from the content of the article, and possibly that whole-page advertisements might have less competition in terms of the reader's attention, and so might be more effective.

Another feature of selective attention relates to the importance we attach to incoming information. The more important we judge something to be, the more we are likely to attend to it and the converse seems to be equally true. Mackenzie (1986) asked research participants to study an advertisement for a set time period and then fill in a questionnaire about the product which was being advertised – a watch. The only attribute mentioned about the watch was that it was water-resistant, but although they all mentioned this point, some advertisements emphasized it far more than others.

Mackenzie found that the amount of attention which the advertisement directed to the watch's water-resistance directly influenced people's perceptions of the importance of this attribute – an effect which was equally strong whether the advert was shown singly or in among others.

Mackenzie also found that those advertisements with highly concrete messages tended to attract more attention than advertisements with abstract messages. On the other hand, whether the picture in the advertisement was relevant to what the advertisement was promoting made no difference at all to people's attention. Nor did the number of times the person was exposed to the advertisement or the amount of prior knowledge they possessed about the product.

The study of selective attention also highlights some of the limitations on our ability to process information. An example of this problem was reported by Barber (1988), in a description of an aircraft accident in the area of Zagreb which was then part of Yugoslavia. A British Airways Trident collided with a DC-9 of Inex Adria Airways, resulting in the loss of 176 lives. One of the factors identified as leading to the collision was the cognitive overload of the air traffic controller responsible for the sector the planes were flying in.

Work

At the time of the accident the controller's assistant was missing, there were 11 aircraft in his sector, he was in simultaneous radio communication with 4 other aircraft and he was taking part in a telephone conversation with Belgrade concerning two further aircraft. The controller had received very short notice of the arrival of the DC-9 into his sector, and it appears that the short notice and the overload of information contributed to the final error. Nevertheless, he was prosecuted and jailed. This is a graphic illustration of the limitations of our information processing capacities, as well as of the way that public responses to disasters are often to blame individuals, when it is the systems within which the individuals are working which are actually at fault.

People differ in how much information they can process at any given time. It has often been assumed that this is an 'ability', which is unlikely to change much over time. Working on this principle, Gopher (1982) argued that it would be advantageous to consider these differences when selecting people for jobs that require attentional skills. Gopher investigated the introduction of a **dichotic listening task** of selective attention, as part of the pilot selection test battery of the Israeli air force. In this study, 2000 flight cadets were presented with 4 auditory messages, each of which was composed of strings of words and digits. Different information was simultaneously presented to each ear. The cadets were asked to identify whenever a digit name appeared in the relevant channel – in other words, to indicate if they heard the name of a number in, say, the right ear – and to swap over channels (from right to left ear or vice versa) when they received a particular signal.

Gopher found that these measures of selective attention did not correlate with any of the other tests which were being used as part of the pilot selection procedure. Moreover, cadets who had completed a two-year training programme had significantly lower error scores on all attention measures – implying that they had actually improved their abilities to attend selectively to some stimuli rather than others. Gopher concluded that attention capabilities are an independent dimension and that introducing tests for them could enhance the predictive validity of the overall test battery. However, it could equally well be concluded that there was little point in introducing such a test at the beginning of training, since all they measured was the person's existing skill and not how good at it they might become after a couple of years' training.

We need to pay attention to little things in everyday life, too, such as the way that we speak. Baars (1980) designed a series of laboratory studies to investigate how we produce spoonerisms – the speech errors in which the initial letters of words become changed over. Baars observed that people will easily produce examples of spoonerisms which create new words, such as 'barn door', for 'darn bore', but they find it much harder to produce examples that create non-words, such as 'bart-doard' for 'dart-board'. Baars also noted that it was difficult to get people to produce rude spoonerisms, which suggests that we are 'editing' our spoken output at a number of different levels. Baars proposed that

dichotic listening task
A way of studying selective attention by presenting different messages simultaneously to each ear and asking people to report what they hear.

speech errors which conform to our personal dictionary are likely to escape the attention of the 'editor' – unless, of course, the output is going to be socially unacceptable. However, the repeated personal experience of one of the authors suggests that these errors can still emerge, now and again, despite the presence of the 'editor'.

Perceptual set

Psychologists use the word 'set' in very much the same way as the starter of a race, who says 'Get ready, get set, go!' In other words, 'set' is used to describe a state of readiness – of being prepared. But unlike the race starter, whose 'set' means get physically ready to take action, the psychological version of 'set' refers to mental preparedness: readiness to think, perceive or learn in certain kinds of ways.

Perceptual set, then, is a state of readiness to perceive certain kinds of things in preference to others. Sets can be generated in several ways, the most usual being through expectation: people who have just been looking at sets of numbers will be more ready to perceive an ambiguous figure as a number, than those who have been looking at sets of letters (Bruner and Minturn, 1955). Perceptual sets can also be generated through motivational states: hungry people are more likely to identify pictures of food or to interpret ambiguous stimuli as food related. Primacy effects, personality traits, personal values and social prejudices have all been shown to generate perceptual sets of one sort or another. So, while it would not be entirely true to say that we only see what we expect to see, it is certainly true to say that we are often much more prepared to see some things and not others.

Neisser (1976) drew together research into perceptual set with research on visual search and on selective attention to challenge the idea that we filter out unwanted material. Instead, Neisser argued, we actively choose what we will attend to. Our perceptual processes form a continuous, cyclic process of anticipating what is likely to happen in the perceptual world, scanning that world to see if these expectations are supported and then modifying our expectations in the light of the perceptual information we receive.

Our expectations about what we are likely to perceive take the form of **anticipatory schemata**, which direct or channel our perceptual exploration of the external world. As a result of that perceptual exploration, we take samples from the available information – we do not take in everything around us, but only the information to which our attention is directed. But, although we have selected what we

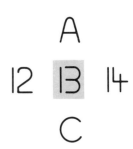

Figure 6.21 Perceptual set. The central figure can either be perceived as a B or a 13, depending on the context in which it is viewed.

anticipatory schemata
Sets of ideas about what is likely to happen, which in turn directs how we respond to things that do happen.

will pay attention to on the basis of our expectations, we will still sometimes receive information that is not exactly what we expected. So this incoming information, in turn, modifies the anticipatory schema.

Neisser's theory, then, shows how perception is not just a matter of receiving factual information; but at the same time it is not just a matter of expectation either. We do both: as a general rule, our anticipatory schemata mean that we tend to notice what we expect, but because it is the external world that we are scanning, we still remain open to the unexpected. Neisser saw this perceptual cycle as forming the basis for all cognition: seeing cognition as an active, selective process, and not simply the passive receipt and processing of information.

> **Key reference:** NEISSER, U. (1976) *Cognition and Reality.* W. H. Freeman & Co., San Francisco.

Consumer

'Readiness' or 'set' is an important condition for receiving advertising messages, and advertisers take this into account when placing their advertisements. Mathur and Chattopadhyay (1991) selected two advertisements and sections from two TV programmes, and showed them to research participants. One advertisement and one TV programme were designed to induce a happy mood in the viewer, while the others were designed to induce a sombre mood. The selected viewers saw one of the four possible advertisement/programme combinations (happy advertisement, sombre programme etc.) and then answered a questionnaire designed to measure their mood, and the amount they recalled of what they had seen.

Mathur and Chattopadhyay found that the mood which was induced by the TV programme segment had a significant effect on how people looked at the advertisement and what they remembered of it. Those viewing the 'happy' programme had greater recall of the advertisement and more happy responses to it than those viewing the 'sombre' programme. The effectiveness of an advertisement, then, depends on a great deal more than viewing figures and time slots, and the recent increase in TV advertisements which are clearly 'targeted' to the audience of a specific programme shows that this is something which is taken into account.

Another implication of this study is that advertisements can be affected by the mood which has been created by other advertisements. This influences the placing of public service advertisements, for example, such as those against drinking and driving or for crime prevention. These advertisements deliberately aim to create a sombre mood in their viewers, so it is no surprise that they usually appear at the end of a television advertising break, rather than immediately before advertisements for unrelated commercial products.

Perceptual judgements form an important part of successful driving. When driving, people need to be able to judge speed, acceleration and distance, and estimate the time it will take for a moving car to arrive in a new position. Tricky stuff, but most of us are able to take this in our stride most of the time. But when our perceptions have become distorted by travelling at high speeds, it is a different matter: when we are coming off a motorway, we often feel as if we are going very slowly when actually we are still travelling very fast.

Environment

Bruce and Green (1985) pointed out that the major North–South trunk road in England (the A1) is particularly dangerous in this context, because it is almost a motorway – many parts of it have motorway regulations – and this encourages fast driving. However, it also contains numerous roundabouts which require the driver to stop. The combination of high and low speeds means that accidents are frequent, as people fail to adjust perceptually and continue to apply perceptual expectations based on the motorway experience as they approach the roundabout.

Although perceptual set is usually thought of as a visual experience, it can also affect the other senses. A study by Beal (1985), for example, explored the effect of musical expectation on the recognition of musical forms. In the study, 68 undergraduates were compared in their ability to discriminate musical chords. They were played pairs of chords on different instruments, and asked to identify when the same chord was being played. Thirty-four of these students were music students, while the other 34 studied other subjects and were not musicians even in their spare time.

Education

Beal found that the musicians were better than the non-musicians at recognizing the same chord played on two different instruments – as long as the chord took the usual Western forms. But if the chords which were being played were unusual – if the chord structures did not conform to the rules of Western music for tonal harmony – then both musicians and non-musicians were equally poor at recognizing similar chords. The implication, then, is that the different abilities of musicians and non-musicians in distinguishing chords comes from practice and familiarity rather than from intrinsic ability, since if it were intrinsic it would be reasonable to expect that musicians would also be better at unfamiliar chords. Beal suggested that musicians develop perceptual and cognitive skills specific to their culture's music. In other words, they have expectations about how the sound ought to be structured and use these expectations in processing musical information.

Neisser's model of the perceptual cycle reminds us that perception is not only about expectation – it is also influenced by the real information we receive from the outside world. Gibbons and Kassin (1987) reported a study of 176 undergraduates, who were asked to evaluate some artwork supposedly painted by either mentally retarded or non-retarded children. Judgements about artistic merit tend to be affected by our expectations of the people producing the work, so the students were expected to produce more favourable judgements when they perceived the work as coming from ordinary children, than they would if they believed that the work came from mentally retarded children.

However, Gibbons and Kassin found that it was not quite as simple as that. The judgement also depended on the quality of the work itself. When the quality of the work was good the students did not value the work any more when they were informed it was produced by ordinary children than when they thought it had been produced by mentally retarded ones. But a negative evaluation was very evident when the work was of a poor quality. If the students were told this work came from non-retarded children they gave it a reasonable evaluation, but if they were told it was from retarded children the evaluation was very negative. (The evaluation was meant to be strictly based on artistic merit, not on the artists' efforts.) So this study suggests that the nature of the material itself influenced how it was perceived. Expectations about people's capacities to produce good work only came into play if the work itself was poor and not if it was good. Real-world information influences our perceptual judgements too.

Figure 6.22 Expectations and judgement. How would you judge this picture if you were told it was either a) a great work of art worth millions or b) an example of a child's painting?

The process of reading is an interesting combination of gleaning information from the external world – the printed page – and applying our own expectations. Pichert and Anderson (1977) asked research participants to read a passage about a boy bringing a friend home from school, while his parents were out. The research participants were asked to read the passage first and then imagine that they were particular people when they were asked questions about how much they recalled of what they had read. People who were asked to imagine that they were a prospective house-buyer remembered entirely different items of information from the passage than those who were asked to imagine that they were a prospective burglar. Although much of the early research into reading saw it as largely a process of word recognition, the work of Pichert and Anderson, and others, shows that expectations and context are just as important in reading for meaning as any ability to recognize the patterns of words or letters.

With some material, though, the objective information that we have available is less clear. When we are looking at other people, for instance, we are bombarded with information, because people act in many different ways in different situations. That means that we select which particular bits of information we will take notice of, and so our expectations and anticipatory schemata become much more important than in situations where more objective information is available. As we saw in Chapter 2, this can make a big difference to how we interpret personality. When Newcomb (1961) recorded the behaviour of boys at a summer camp, the records showed that each boy had acted in both introverted and extroverted ways during the course of the camp. But the staff had only noticed those acts which conformed to their expectations about each boy: if a boy had been deemed to be 'extrovert', then the staff only observed his sociable acts and did not notice it when he was quiet or solitary.

Lawler (1967) studied the beliefs which managers hold about the pay of others in the organization. Organizations vary in how secretive they are about other people's levels of pay and Lawler found that, in organizations where levels of pay were kept secret, people consistently overestimated the amount that their subordinates were paid and consistently underestimated the levels of pay of those above them in the hierarchy. As a consequence, there was a general tendency for people to underestimate differential rates of pay in the organization as a whole. This, Lawler found, tended to lead to dissatisfaction on the part of senior managers.

Work

This finding also has implications for the question of motivation. Typically, money has been used in industry as the main incentive for promotion and as a way of providing knowledge of the results of successful performances. But Lawler suggested that the fact that junior staff underestimate senior salaries might reduce their incentives to seek promotion – they would not think it worth while for the rewards that were offered. Remaining secretive about salary levels for managers, Lawler argued, also lowers the effectiveness of money as a method of providing knowledge-of-results for the individual, because the benefits of attempting to do well were not immediately apparent. In the next section, we will look at the question of money as a motivator in a little more detail and at some other aspects of human motivation.

Motivation

drive theories *Theories of human motivation which explain why we do things, using the idea that our behaviour is directed towards reducing some inner need. The need then sets up an internal tension and the desire to reduce this tension forms a pressure to act (the drive) which is only reduced when the need becomes satisfied.*

homoeostasis *A state of physiological balance or equilibrium in the body.*

Early approaches to understanding motivation, both in human beings and in animals, tended to use the idea of **drives**. Drive theories of motivation consisted of inferences about the underlying state of the organism (animal or human being), made on the basis of the behaviour which the animal was showing. So, for example, observation of an animal seeking out and eating food produced the inference that the absence of food had created an internal motive – a drive – which energized the behaviour of food seeking.

Drive theories are based on the concept of **homoeostasis**. Homoeostasis is about maintaining a steady state within the body to keep it functioning in an optimal manner. The concept implies that once homoeostasis has been restored, there is no further need for goal-directed behaviour and so it is unlikely to happen. In other words, motivation only happens while there was some kind of internal need: if every need were satisfied, there would be nothing to energize action.

The humanistic psychologist Maslow argued that, in the case of human beings at least, motivation was a complex process involving much more than physiological homoeostasis. Although still working within the drive concept, Maslow proposed that human needs encompass both basic biological and survival needs, and highly complex and cognitive ones, ranging from the need for adequate food, drink and shelter to a need for personal fulfilment and self-actualization. According to Maslow's formulation, once more basic needs were satisfied, then needs higher up in the hierarchy would become important and demand to be satisfied.

The implication of Maslow's work, then, was that human motivation is a dynamic and ever-changing process, which builds on what has gone before. Although there are a number of criticisms of Maslow's ideas, particularly in his assumption that people would not

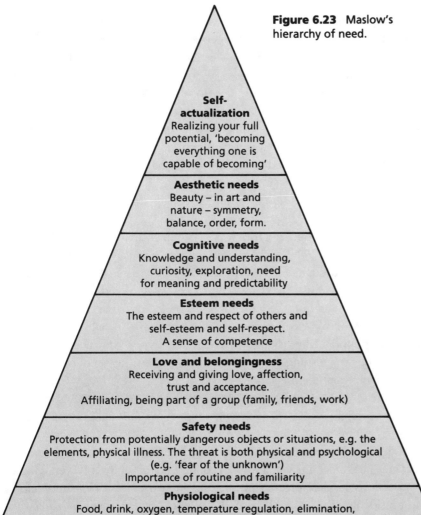

Figure 6.23 Maslow's hierarchy of need.

Self-actualization
Realizing your full potential, 'becoming everything one is capable of becoming'

Aesthetic needs
Beauty – in art and nature – symmetry, balance, order, form.

Cognitive needs
Knowledge and understanding, curiosity, exploration, need for meaning and predictability

Esteem needs
The esteem and respect of others and self-esteem and self-respect. A sense of competence

Love and belongingness
Receiving and giving love, affection, trust and acceptance. Affiliating, being part of a group (family, friends, work)

Safety needs
Protection from potentially dangerous objects or situations, e.g. the elements, physical illness. The threat is both physical and psychological (e.g. 'fear of the unknown') Importance of routine and familiarity

Physiological needs
Food, drink, oxygen, temperature regulation, elimination, rest, activity, sex

work to satisfy 'higher' needs unless lower ones were already satisfied, his model proved useful in many contexts and widened out the study of motivation to include many more of those motives which we consider to be important for human beings.

Key reference: MASLOW, A. H. (1954) *Motivation and Personality.* Harper & Row, New York.

In human beings, even apparently basic drives like hunger are affected by a host of social variables, such as mood, body stereotypes and social representations about what is or is not appropriate food. As we saw in Chapter 3, Fischler (1930) showed how cultural beliefs about food form

Society

social representations which reflect changes in society: for example, the acceptance of the pizza and burger as appropriate meals in Britain reflects the increased acceptance of eating as something which is slotted in between work and leisure time, in contrast to the idea of the family meal as the major event of the day. In Maslow's model, this would be taken as reflecting the idea that society in general had moved higher up the motivational hierarchy. In the post-war years, food had been rationed and satisfying basic hunger was a very important task. In modern society, for most people basic food needs are more than satisfied, so social and other needs become more important.

As society became more affluent, social trends shifted towards increasing slimness, despite increasing medical evidence that being slightly plump (though not obese) is healthier than being skinny. As Jodelet showed in 1984, social representations about what constitutes an ideal body have changed dramatically over the years. Wade and Tavris (1990) report that Miss Sweden of 1951, who was judged to be the 'most glamorous' woman in the competition, was 5 ft 7 in tall and weighed 151 pounds. However, Miss Sweden of 1983 was 5 ft 9 in tall and weighed only 109 pounds. This change in ideal stereotypes has meant that the basic act of replenishing energy through eating has become loaded with social meanings and expectation.

It is little surprise, then, that so many people define themselves as having a weight problem and seek help either through purchasing a range of 'slimming' products or through therapy. Some work places, too, have developed programmes to encourage employees to lose weight and become healthier. Brownell (1984) described a study of weight-loss competitions in different businesses and industries. In one competition the presidents of three banks issued challenges to each other's banks for a weight loss contest over a three-month period. Each bank put up a team and each member of the team put money into the pool, which would go to the winners at the end of three months. Each team member was given a goal, although a maximum weight loss of 20 pounds was set, in order to avoid crash dieting.

Two similar competitions were set up in manufacturing companies, so that in the end the 3 competitions had included 277 participants. Brownell studied the 213 people who had been overweight by 10% or more of their calculated healthy weight at the beginning of the competition. Of these, only one person dropped out of the competition and after 3 months the average weight loss was 12 pounds. In a follow-up study six months later, the researchers found that the overweight people had kept off over 80% of the weight they had shed during the competition. This is an interesting effect, since it suggests that social variables presented by the competition can override the seemingly basic drive of eating and represents another challenge to Maslow's idea that basic drives must be satisfied before higher needs become important.

For all the concern about excessive weight, it must be said that the consequence of eating too little can be very serious. In an intriguing series of experiments which became known as the Minnesota Starvation Studies, Keys (1952) put 26 normal men on a 6-month semi-starvation diet. In all other respects, such as in terms of living quarters, social life and exercise, they were given entirely normal facilities, but their food was restricted. Within a relatively short time, all of the men became obsessively preoccupied with food, to the point where some of the men displayed serious mental disorders.

Health

Some modern psychologists see the Minnesota Starvation Studies as providing a clue as to why Freud regarded sex as the main significant motivator for human beings. His theory was developed in the context of a very strait-laced Victorian culture, in which sexual exploration or even curiosity were tightly suppressed. It is not surprising, therefore, that it came to become a dominant concern in his patients' unconscious minds. A more open society, in which sexual knowledge is widespread, would be more likely to produce individuals who were accepting of sexual motivation and less obsessed with it.

What studies about food, eating and dieting, then, seem to add up to, is the idea that a physiological drive which is unsatisfied becomes psychologically absorbing, whereas if it has some degree of satisfaction, it becomes far less important. But if there is enough social motivation – such as gaining respect from other people or avoiding failure in a competition, these factors can be overridden. In the next section, we will be looking more closely at social factors in motivation, but for now we will look at some other different types of motivational needs.

In another seeming disconfirmation of the Maslow hierarchy, Hankins and Clarke (1989) investigated the motivation behind career choices for teaching. They thought that students who had chosen to be teachers would tend to be more self-actualized than other students, since teaching was a vocational choice, which people certainly did not make for the money. However, when they actually explored the degree to which trainee teachers **self-actualized**, by comparison with students who intended to go into other professions, they found that trainee teachers were less self-actualized, according to a questionnaire analysis, than the others. They were less inner-directed, showed less capacity for intimate contact and were lower in self-esteem.

Education

self-actualization *The making real of one's abilities and talents: using them to the full.*

It is possible, though, that this outcome results more from the researchers' assumptions about the nature of motivation for teaching than

Figure 6.24 The 'I want to be a slug' effect. The pictures show some motivational statements used in the advertisements by the Prudential Assurance Company.

from weaknesses in Maslow's theory. Teaching is essential as a social profession and a social activity, and it might just as well be hypothesized that people would enter teaching because, say, esteem needs were more important to them than they were to other people. The finding that would-be teachers were lower in self-esteem and less inner-directed than others would be perfectly congruent with this.

Market research has also concerned itself with identifying the motives behind consumption of various products. Much of this has resulted in the development of various typologies, designed to indicate a 'kind' of person towards whom advertisements can be targeted. For example, Ackoff and Emshoff (1975) identified four general 'types' of drinkers, with different motivations for drinking. The four types are listed in Figure 6.25.

Consumer

Figure 6.25 Motivational 'types' of drinkers. (Ackoff and Emshoff, 1975.)

1. **The ocean drinker**: tends to drink so as to become more gregarious and extroverted
2. **The indulgent drinker**: tends to drink in order to become withdrawn and introverted
3. **The reparative drinker**: tends to drink in order to wind down from work and ease into leisure, and also as a reward for all their efforts
4. **The social drinker**: tends to use alcohol as a social lubricant

Ackoff and Emshoff then recruited a number of beer drinkers to take part in a study based on this approach. Each drinker took a test that categorized them as one of the four types. They were then shown four commercials for four different brands of beer. Each commercial followed a similar pattern, but had been made with one of the personality types in mind. The first segment of each commercial identified the main character as one of the motivational types. This was followed by a second segment that showed the actor drinking and finally a third segment that showed a change in behaviour in line with the motivation for drinking. So, for example, the commercial featuring the 'Oceanic Drinker' showed the actor becoming more extroverted.

After seeing the commercials the drinkers were asked to sample the four beers shown – although the only difference between them was name and packaging – and asked to choose a case of one of the 'brands' to take home as a reward for participating in the study. Ackoff and Emshoff reported that the drinkers consistently expressed a preference for the beer that was associated with their motivational type. Most of the drinkers were sure they could tell the brands apart and most described at least one of the brands as not fit for human consumption, despite the fact that they were drinking exactly the same beer!

One unexpected motivational effect was discovered by market researchers investigating the introduction and uptake of cake mixes in the 1960s. Myers and Reynolds (1967) described how instant cake mixes were not particularly popular when they first appeared on supermarket shelves. These cake mixes were intended to simplify the home baking of cakes and only required the cook to add water, but housewives did not like that. When the company changed its recipe, so that the cook had to add an egg to the mixture, however, sales increased dramatically.

The explanation for this was to do with cultural expectations. In the 1950s and early 1960s it was taken for granted that regular cake-making was a routine part of housewifely tasks and many women saw the ability to produce a good cake as an important visible sign that they were good at their job of housekeeping. A mixture which reduced the activity to simply adding water did not allow any sense of involvement, but beating and adding an egg was much more like 'real' cooking, and so allowed people to feel that they had actively taken part in the baking process, and deserved some of the credit for the outcome. Although it may seem trivial to a modern and more affluent society in which bought cakes have become the norm, the ability to make good cakes was at that time important not only in providing cheap wholesome food, but also in satisfying self-esteem needs, and this was reflected in the purchasing behaviour of women.

Work

A considerable amount of research into human motivation has been concerned with motivating people at work. One of the very first investigations of the individual at work, and arguably the most influential, was reported by Taylor (1911), of a labourer asked to load pig-iron into railway trucks. By putting the man on a piece-work rate, directing all of his movements explicitly, Taylor showed that the amount of pig-iron which could be loaded daily by one man could be dramatically raised. Taylor's labourer loaded 47 tons on that day, as opposed to the normal average of 12 ½ tons.

scientific management
Begun by Taylor, a method of applying scientific principles to improve job productivity and efficiency through procedures such as time-and-motion analyses.

From this, and other studies, Taylor went on to develop what he described as '**scientific management**', which was basically about using people as components in an industrial process, with their actions and movements tightly scripted. Taylor, naïvely and somewhat patronizingly, assumed that levels of pay were the only important motivator for working people. Because the new 'time and motion' approach allowed people to be more productive and so earn more pay, he expected that it would therefore be welcomed.

However, it rapidly became apparent that people at work object to being treated like robots rather than human beings and that simply assuming pay to be the only requisite motivator was completely inadequate. The Hawthorne studies conducted by Elton Mayo and his colleagues in the 1930s became legendary, not so much because of their scientific rigour, but because they encapsulated the idea that there is more to working life than just pay. Mayo, Roethlisberger and Dickson showed how the social and personal dimensions of working life are not simply diversions, they are active factors in encouraging motivation to work, and they did so in a way which was overtly 'scientific', and so seemed incontrovertible.

Although the Hawthorne studies and the vast quantity of subsequent research which they generated showed that pay was not in itself an adequate intrinsic motivator for human beings at work, it is none the less the case that pay levels can become important. Lawler (1971) summarized five conditions which have to be met if pay levels are to be motivating for the work force, which are given in Figure 6.26. As can be seen from the table, pay on its own does not motivate people. But, as Lawler pointed out, pay as a sign that people are appreciated, valued and that their efforts are worthwhile, does.

Motivation, then, is highly influenced by social influences and social factors, and these can sometimes influence even events which are apparently out of human control. For example, Phillips (1970) investigated rates of death in Jewish communities and found that far fewer people died immediately before the holy day Yom Kippur (the day of atone-

1. Employees must attach importance to higher pay.
2. Employees must believe that good performance at work does, in fact, lead to high pay.
3. Employees must believe that good performance at work reflects the efforts which they are putting into it.
4. Employees must see the benefits of good performance as outweighing negative effects.
5. Employees must see good job performance as the most attractive option out of all the possible behaviours available.

Figure 6.26 Conditions which need to be met if pay is to be an important motivator. (Lawler, 1971.)

ment) than at other times during the course of the year. The implication is that even the timing .of dying can be influenced by psychological and social factors, if they are important enough. In recent years, investigations of human motivation have focused much more closely on the nature and influences of social needs.

Social motivation

Social motives for human beings seem to be very fundamental, rather than just an afterthought tacked on to the psyche once physiological needs have been satisfied. There are a number of social needs which seem to recur time and time again as motivators of human behaviour, in one form or another.

One group concerns affiliative needs – the needs that we all have for relationships, positive regard from others and to mix with other people. These needs can form a major source of human motivation and take several different forms. In this context, Rogers (1961) argued that one of our most basic psychological needs is to have positive regard – love, friendship or affection – from other people. Lack of this positive regard, or life experiences in which such regard was always made conditional upon appropriate behaviour, would produce neurosis and impede psychological health.

Tajfel and Turner (1979) showed how membership of social groups, and the **social identifications** which result, form an important part of social life and social motivation. Seeing social life in terms of in-groups and out-groups, or 'us' and 'them', seems to be a basic trait in social experience and the membership of different groups reflects on the individual's own sense of self-esteem, as well as on their views of reality. But internal cohesion in these groups is also important. De Waal (1989) argued that reconciliation is an important feature in the life of all social animals, including apes and

social identity theory A theory which emphasizes how membership of social groups forms a significant part of the self-concept, and can determine reactions to other people and events, such that people respond primarily as group members and not as individuals.

human beings. He identified a number of different reconciliation strategies which are shared by both ape and human social groups, ranging from the use of touching and gestures as signals of 'forgiveness' to the 'collaborative lie', in which tension between two individuals is reduced by both feigning interest in some relatively trivial situation or event and so gradually re-establishing communication. Mechanisms of reconciliation allow a group to continue to function socially after tense or aggressive encounters and, de Waal argued, are important for restoring a kind of 'social homoeostasis' to the group.

Harré (1979) argued that social respect is a fundamental motive in human behaviour – people will go to great lengths to avoid looking ridiculous or stupid in front of others, or even to themselves. This tendency, Harré argued, is manifest even from childhood: the child wishes to be noticed and for its achievements to be recognized. It continues throughout adult social life and forms an important constituent of the social glue which co-ordinates social activity. The implication here is that gaining respect and avoiding ridicule – 'saving face ' – are major motivators for human beings.

> **Key reference:** HARRÉ, R. (1979) *Social Being*. Basil Blackwell, Oxford.

Sport

Competitive gymnasts
competence
fitness
challenge

Recreational gymnasts
competence
fitness
fun
situation

Former gymnasts
competence
fun
challenge
action

Figure 6.27 Reasons for beginning competitive sport. (Klint and Weiss, 1986.)

One important aspect of human motivation is the ability to engage in sustained effort over a long period of time. Some people appear to find this a relatively straightforward thing to do, while others find it difficult to sustain effort if they do not experience an immediate result. In some areas of human activity, such as sport, sustained motivation is essential for success, so the question of why people persist in their efforts is very important.

Klint and Weiss (1986) interviewed 106 competitive, recreational and former youth gymnasts about their motivations for beginning, and for dropping out of, the sport. The gymnasts gave a number of reasons for their initial attraction to the sport, and these differed slightly between competitive gymnasts, recreational gymnasts and those who had previously been successful but had now dropped out of gymnastics (see Figure 6.27). Understandably, challenge was an important motive for those who had engaged in competitive gymnastics, either now or in the past, but not for those who simply undertook gymnastics for recreational purposes.

However, when they looked at the reasons which the gymnasts gave for quitting the sport, they did not find any connection between these and the motives for starting. The most important reasons which people gave for leaving gymnastics were having other things to do, injuries, not liking the pressure, not having enough fun and the sport being too time-consuming. It is apparent, then, that the reasons why people take up a sport cannot be used to predict whether they will sustain it or not.

Other studies have investigated different types of achievement motivation. In an early study, Sears (1940) sorted children aged 10–12 years into three groups. One group consisted of children who were successful at both arithmetic and reading. A second group consisted of children who tended to be unsuccessful at both subjects. The third group consisted of children who were successful at reading but unsuccessful at arithmetic. The children were given several arithmetic and reading tests, under normal classroom conditions. After each task, the child was asked to give an estimate of how long it would take to carry out the next one. The estimates were taken as indicators of the child's expectations.

Sears found that experiencing success was necessary in order for the children to develop realistic expectations about their abilities. Those in the first group made realistic estimates of how long it would take them to do the tasks. Those in the second made unrealistic estimates and those in the third made realistic estimates for reading, but unrealistic ones for arithmetic. In other words, practical experience of success made the children's expectations much more realistic.

This finding fitted with research by McClelland (1953), who found that levels of achievement motivation were highest in those who had experienced success followed by failure. McClelland manipulated the experiences of different people under research conditions and compared the nAch scores which they gave (nAch is the abbreviation used to refer to need for achievement). The outcome is given in Figure 6.28 and shows that people who had only ever experienced success tended to try far less hard than those who had experienced some degree of failure after a period of success. One possible explanation for this is that it would tie in with the idea of social respect as a major motivator of human behaviour: if we have once experienced respect for achievement, and then fail, it may be much more important for us to regain that respect, than it is for someone who has never had it or for someone who has always had it.

Hertzberg (1966) explored the question of motivation at work. As we saw in the last section, the straightforward assumption that people work to earn money does not really explain a lot of observations about why people do go to work and why being unemployed is so very harmful psychologically. At the same time, though, money does count for something: as we shall see, paying people too little produces very different effects from paying them more than they feel they are worth. In what became a classic series of studies, Hertzberg interviewed 200 engineers and accountants, who were asked to recall critical incidents that had led

Education

Situation	Mean nAch score
Relaxed	1.95
Neutral	7.33
Success	7.92
Achievement-oriented	8.77
Failure	10.10
Success then failure	10.36

Figure 6.28 Achievement motivation scores under different conditions. (McClelland, 1953.)

Work

them to feel either good or bad about work, which were used as an indication of the sources of job dissatisfaction and the sources of job satisfaction. The outcome of the interviews indicates that the sources of each were entirely different.

Job dissatisfaction, Hertzberg argued, came from factors which he referred to as hygiene factors. These concerned issues like physical working conditions, pay levels and the quality of supervision. If you do not get a fair rate of pay, if your working conditions are bad, or if your supervisor is stupid or sarcastic, you are likely to feel dissatisfied with your job. But that does not mean that if these things are OK, you will feel positively satisfied. Job satisfaction, Hertzberg found, came from factors which were concerned with responsibility, achievement, recognition and appreciation from management, and the characteristics of the job itself. In other words, we experience job satisfaction when we feel appreciated and valued, or when we are doing work which we find intrinsically interesting and satisfying.

A management strategy in which attention is only paid to hygiene factors, Hertzberg showed, might remove sources of dissatisfaction but would not necessarily produce a highly motivated and hard-working work force. For that, more appreciation of the personal and social aspects of working life was necessary, as was a management style which shows respect for the individual. This finding resulted ultimately in the development of a number of attempts to improve the quality of working life, ranging from 'job enlargement' schemes in manufacturing industries, designed to give workers more opportunity to participate in the manufacture of whole units, rather than just single components, and therefore more sense of achievement, to 'total quality management' (TQM) schemes, designed to train managers into running their departments in such a way as to demonstrate respect for the contributions of all the members in their team.

Although it might be expected that work satisfaction would arise automatically from working competently, investigations between job satisfaction and work performance have found only a relatively limited correlation between the two. Carlson (1969) studied job satisfaction and performance in 500 workers, and found that what was most important was the fit between the individual's own personal qualities and the work that they were expected to do. Those who showed a large mismatch between their own abilities and skills, and the requirements of the job that they were doing, were likely to show little relationship between satisfaction and performance. But, among those who showed a good match between their abilities and their job requirements, there was a high correlation between job satisfaction and performance. It is difficult to get satisfaction out of doing a job which is well below what you are capable of doing!

Despite the findings of Hertzberg and others, however, pay is by far the most common method of attempting to motivate good performance at work than other strategies. In part, this may be because the other strategies tend to produce long-term, implicit outcomes rather than short-term, visible ones. Paul, Robertson and Hertzberg (1969) studied laboratory technicians who were suffering from low morale. They divided them into two groups, without the individuals concerned being aware that they were the subjects of a study. One group then experienced a 'job enrichment' programme, in which a number of 'motivators' were varied, although 'hygiene factors' such as pay and working conditions remained constant.

The technicians in the experimental group were encouraged to become more involved with their work, writing final reports on research projects, having increased responsibility and authority with respect to being able to order supplies, and being given opportunities for self-initiated work. Members of both the experimental and control groups were asked to write monthly reports, and these were used as a measure of work performance.

By comparison with the control group, which did not experience these changes but which was in all other respects similar, the quality of the monthly reports of the experimental group became far superior, being eventually judged to be almost as good as those of the research scientists. Morale as a whole seemed to be much higher in the group. Explicit measures of job satisfaction, however, did not change during the experimental period, although the researchers believed that this could be explained by reasons which were not to do with the actual intervention. So anyone looking for instant, visible effects would have found little evidence that the situation had been improved, but a longer term investigation of motivation and the quality of reports – or possibly also of staff turnover rates – might tell a different story.

Social exchange theory is all about how people perceive the balance of obligations, duties and rewards that they experience in society. Adams and Jacobsen (1964) applied a version of social exchange theory to looking at how people respond to feeling overpaid or underpaid at work. They asked research participants to perform a variety of experimental tasks resembling production work and paid them at different rates. What they found was that people, understandably, would tend to decrease their output when they felt underpaid. But they would also increase their output if they felt overpaid – they would not just accept the extra money. This, the researchers argued, showed how people seek to establish a 'fair' exchange between their own efforts and the rewards that they receive for them, rather than an unbalanced one.

Adams and Jacobsen also found that the way in which they were paid directly affected how people responded to the tasks which they were set. If they were overpaid on an hourly basis, they tended to increase the quantity of their work. But if they were overpaid on a piece-work basis, they tended to decrease the overall amount, but increase the quality of their work. For example, when the research participants were asked to undertake a proofreading task, those who were overpaid on a piece-work basis read fewer pages in an hour, but detected more errors than other groups, including those who felt that their pay levels were fair.

It seems apparent, then, that motivation for working involves more than just earning enough money to live on. In a study by Harpaz (1989), workers in seven different countries were asked the 'lottery question' – whether they would give up work if they won, or inherited, a large sum of money. The question was intended to be an evaluation of people's non-financial commitment to working. In the study nearly 9000 people were interviewed and workers from different countries were compared. The results are given in Figure 6.29.

Percentage of respondents who would continue working		
	Men	Women
Belgium	84	79
Britain	69	71
Germany	70	62
Israel	87	86
Japan	93	91
Netherlands	86	86
USA	88	86

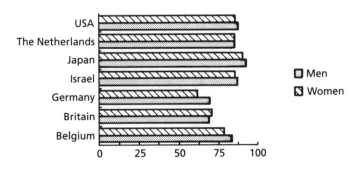

Figure 6.29 Response to the lottery question in seven countries. (Harpaz, 1989.)

Among the seven national groups included in the study, British men emerged as the most keen to give up work and Britain was the only national group where the women were keener to continue working than the men. It is also worth noting the striking disparity between the expressed commitment of British workers and Japanese workers. The overall conclusion we would draw from this study, though, is that given the choice, most workers would continue working rather than enter a life of continual leisure. The increasing number of people who take up alternative careers after retirement also supports this idea. It is so much more of a tragedy, then, that so many people should have no opportunity to work.

Summary

1. *Information is received by the brain through six major sensory modes: visual, auditory, olfactory, tactile, gustatory, and kinaesthetic.*
2. *Perceptual organization is the process by which we group together and structure the sensory information that we are receiving in order to interpret it.*
3. *The study of face recognition shows that recognizing people we know, putting names to faces and making judgements of strangers' faces each involve different cognitive mechanisms.*
4. *Selective attention is the way that we pick out relevant information from among a mass of other stimuli. It has often been explained using filter models.*
5. *Perceptual set is a state of readiness to perceive certain types of things rather than others. It can be induced by expectation, motivation, or experience.*
6. *Early theories of motivation saw behaviour as energized by drives and needs. This model was extended by Maslow to include 'higher' human needs as well as basic physiological ones.*
7. *Human social motivation has been shown to involve needs for affiliation with others, for social identification, and for social respect.*

PRACTICE QUESTIONS AND ACTIVITIES – 6

Recognizing faces

It is remarkable how quickly we are able to recognize a face. It is also remarkable how often we make mistakes. A study by Young, Hay and Ellis (1985) looked at the mistakes we make in facial recognition and asked their 22 researchers to keep a diary of their errors of recognition. Some of the major incidents that were recorded in this study were (a) person unrecognized – for example being told after you watched a film that Arnold Schwarzenegger was in it, but you had not noticed; (b) person misidentified – mistaking a person for someone else; (c) difficulty in recalling full details – so you might remember some features about the person but you cannot remember their name.

You could carry out a similar diary method of your own. For a day, note down every time you have a problem recognizing a face, either in your everyday life or when you are watching television. Watching television programmes can often provoke that infuriating discussion on where you have seen one of the actors before. Try to identify what was the problem in recognizing the face and how you resolved that problem.

Sensory modes

A much quoted, though still excellent exercise, is to explore the limits on your directional hearing. The basic idea is that you will have trouble identifying what direction sound is coming from without some other cues.

The best way to check this out is to get someone to sit blindfolded in the middle of a large room. Then you move about the room, very quietly and occasionally bang two spoons together. The blindfolded person has to point to where he or she thinks the noise is coming from. Make some mark on the floor of the direction which was pointed out and also the actual location of the sound.

Repeat this process several times and you will build up a chart of the errors that are made by your blindfolded colleague. It is worth looking for the directions of sound that are most accurately identified and the directions that are least accurately identified.

Motivation at work

Imagine the following situation. A local lace factory has found that productivity has dropped over the last few months. In discussions with the staff of the factory it is discovered that the production workers feel the drop in performance is due to poor management. They feel that they are not given clear instructions and they experience management 'getting at them'. On the other hand, the management believe that the fault lies with the production workers not working to instruction.

You have been asked to advise the company on how to improve performance at work.

1. What psychological concepts and theories might be relevant to this situation?
2. Suggest how the company might improve the motivation of the production staff and the management, and therefore improve productivity.

7

Attitudes and groups

Introduction

Attitudes are cognitive frameworks we use to make sense of the social world. They structure our world and how we act in it. Some people have attitudes and opinions on most issues and events, and are happy to express them and argue them regardless of their level of knowledge. Other people prefer to refrain from expressing their attitudes in public, while maintaining private beliefs or opinions about what is important. Attitudes provide us with a framework for evaluating our experience – they permit us to decide, relatively quickly, where we stand with respect to new events or ideas and to assess whether or not we should take some type of action.

In terms of psychological research into attitudes, one of the more difficult problems has always been finding out exactly what people's attitudes are. There are a range of attitude measurements used by psychologists, in a variety of different contexts. However, many of these measures have flaws when they are used as ways of predicting how people will act: partly because people do not always tell the truth when responding to an attitude measure, but partly also because there is often a difference between the overall attitude that we hold towards a general issue and the specific way that we think about a particular example of that issue when it actually happens.

Sometimes, it is important that we should change our attitudes, in the face of new social situations, new health risks or new constraints on action. Over the past 20 years, there have been many examples of attitude change, such as the acceptance of seat-belt wearing in cars, changes in awareness of ecological issues and changes in assumptions about the nature of sexual relationships arising from growing public awareness of HIV and AIDS. There are a number of different models of attitude change, some of which have been more effective than others in initiating

attitude *A relatively stable opinion towards a person, object or activity, containing a cognitive element (perceptions and beliefs) and an emotional element (positive or negative feelings).*

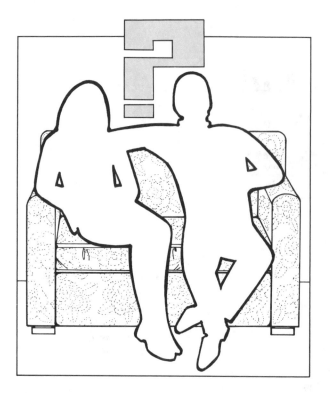

Figure 7.1 Sexual behaviour and HIV and AIDS.

Figure 7.2 Examples of political propaganda in the Second World War.

cognitive dissonance
The tension produced by cognitive imbalance – holding beliefs which directly contradict one another or contradict behaviour. The reduction of cognitive dissonance has been shown to be a factor in some forms of attitude change.

and maintaining attitude change. Some of these apply only in a particular area, such as the health belief model; others, such as the Yale model of communication, are intended to apply more widely.

One of the classic theories of attitude change was developed in the 1950s by Leon Festinger. Festinger was interested in the way that we like to appear rational, or balanced, at least to ourselves. As a result of this, when we notice that there are apparent contradictions between our beliefs or actions, it acts as a powerful stimulus for attitude change. The theory of **cognitive dissonance** stimulated a range of psychological research into the nature of explanations as well as attitude change and still has many uses today.

As political events throughout the 20th century demonstrated, social prejudice can be a major social problem, sometimes with tragic outcomes. After the Second World War, a considerable amount of psychological research was devoted to understanding prejudice, with a view to reducing or changing prejudiced attitudes in society. This research, for the most part, adopted one of two approaches to the issue of prejudice. It has either seen it as a pathological response in the individual, usually brought about by unresolved conflicts in childhood, or as a function of social categorization and social identification. The first model, by and large, focuses on the individual rather than on social and cultural factors; the second emphasizes the importance of political and historical factors very much more strongly. Both approaches have helped us to understand some of the factors in prejudice and suggested some ways that it may be reduced.

Membership of social groups influences our lives in many other ways, too; not least in the way that groups develop norms about what type of behaviour is acceptable and what is not. Social norms affect our daily life continually, from the clothes we put on in the morning, to the way we behave at work, to the way we act at the bus stop. We know there are certain things we can do and certain things we can say, and we are aware when we are stepping near to the line of social unacceptability. This is intimately linked with the concept of social role: we play a variety of parts in our daily lives and the way that we act out these parts is scripted, much as if they were parts in a play. The way that we interpret our parts, however, is up to us, and the interaction between role demands and individual choice has been an interesting area of study.

Social identity theory looks at how the social groups we belong to affect the way we see ourselves and, therefore, the way we interact with other people. We often act as representatives of one group or another, and with that membership comes a range of attitudes and responsibilities. Moreover, social groups differ from one another in terms of real power and status, and this too affects the way that people belonging to those groups interact. Rather than simply being abstract categorizations, the social groupings that we identify with exist in the real world, with all its political, historical and social ramifications.

In our modern society, most decisions are made by groups of one form or another, such as committees, working parties or working teams. So one important area of investigation has been the way that groups make decisions. Two issues in particular have been explored by psychologists working in this area. One of these concerns the tendency which groups have to polarize decisions, making judgements which are either more risky or more conservative than the same people would make if they were acting as individuals. Another problem of group decision-making, closely linked with the question of social identity, is the phenomenon of **groupthink**, in which the group develops a consensus about the problem or what they should do which is nothing like the real world, and can have disastrous consequences.

One of the key influences in groups is the effect of the leader. Sometimes leaders are placed in position by others, such as managers at work; at other times, more rarely, people become leaders through force of their personality or vision. Leaders occur in a variety of contexts, such as in business, sport, politics and military; and can adopt a range of

groupthink The way that a committee, members of a club or other group of people may become divorced from reality as a result of their own special consensus. Groupthink means that they may make decisions which are dangerous or stupid because the group fails to question their own assumptions or to take into account unwelcome aspects of reality which may have a bearing on the situation.

different styles. Some of these styles are clearly more effective than others in certain situations and a considerable amount of psychological research has been devoted to exploring this question.

Leaders can exert a powerful influence on their subordinates. All of us respond to the ideas which other people have about us and it is hard not to try to do well when others are clearly expecting you to be successful. Leadership expectations are a vital source of influence, not only in organizational life, but also in teamwork of other kinds.

The quality of the interactions between leaders and subordinates is another facet of leadership which has attracted the attention of psychologists. Transactional theories of leadership emphasize the way that leaders communicate with their subordinates and how they are perceived by them. Transformational leadership is concerned with how leaders can produce change through their vision and charisma, to an organization or even, at times, a society.

Attitudes

The problem of defining exactly what an attitude is has engaged the attention of many psychologists. One of the more useful definitions was produced by Allport (1935), who defined an attitude as 'a mental state of readiness, organised through experience, exerting a directive or dynamic influence upon the individual's response to all objects and situations with which it is related'.

The definition highlights four features of attitudes. First, it implies that attitudes are related to objects or some aspect of the individual's world. Secondly, it makes the point that attitudes are relatively enduring, not just instantaneous switches of opinion or mood. A third feature contained in this definition concerns the way that attitudes contain implicit evaluations and feelings; and the fourth is the way that attitudes are seen as forming a framework for experiencing and acting in the world.

Smith, Bruner and White (1956) suggest that attitudes have three major functions for the individual. One of these is object appraisal – attitudes provide us with a ready aid for 'sizing up' events and objects we encounter. This saves us having to work out which side we stand on all the time. Some people, for example, will hear of a dispute between a trade union and management, and instantly form an opinion, without knowing any of the specific details of the issue. In this way, attitudes may save a great deal of cognitive 'work'.

Another function which attitudes have is in social adjustment: attitudes structure our social encounters, allowing us to 'fit in' with particular social groups. For example, our attitudes will influence which charitable concerns we support, and this in turn may define our social reference group. Supporting Cancer Research suggests a different social grouping to supporting Greenpeace, or Friends of the Earth. The third function of attitudes is known as externalization. Attitudes offer an outlet for our inner needs and feelings, and provide us with a sense of consistency for the self-concept. Through our attitudes, we gain a picture of what we ourselves are like.

Key reference: SMITH, M. B., BRUNER, J. S. and WHITE, R. W. (1956) *Opinions and Personality.* Wiley, New York.

Society

It is hard to define what the key factors are which shape, and sometimes distort, our attitudes. Television is an obvious source of social information, and is likely to have some shaping effect on our attitudes towards a range of events and interactions. Gerbner, Gross, Morgan and Signorielli (1980) looked at the difference in attitudes to crime between people who are heavy watchers of television and people who are light watchers. The proportion of people who said that 'fear of crime is a very serious personal problem' was consistently greater for the heavy watchers in all categories.

The reasons for this are, of course, debatable, but a plausible hypothesis is that, by watching television, people build up a picture of there being more violence in the outside world than there really is, due to the regular use of violence as a central part of action shows and the relatively limited portrayal of ordinary, non-violent living. In addition, modern suburban lifestyles tend to limit the amount of contact which most people have with strangers, so there is little interaction with 'real' life to keep the television images in perspective. The researchers

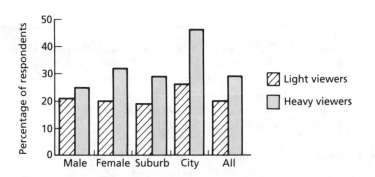

Figure 7.3 The bar chart shows that people who watched more television express a greater fear of crime. (Gerbner, *et al.,* 1980.)

particularly found that women who were heavy watchers of television tended to hold fearful attitudes of this type, which may be because women are more consistently victimized in the television world, so they receive a double dose of the fear message.

One of the biggest problems in studying attitudes is how to measure them. This information is essential for a number of social purposes, such as the development of health programmes, political campaigning and consumer actions. Attitudes are complex cognitive structures and assessing them requires the analysis of a number of different dimensions. Some of these are listed in Figure 7.4.

One of the basic problems with most methods of measuring attitudes, though, is that they often rely on a high level of both self-awareness and personal honesty in the people who are being tested. Various attempts have been made to overcome this, including some which are distinctly questionable, in ethical terms. Alternatively, some researchers have used indirect measures of attitude, like choice of magazines or the selection of subject matter for personal photographs, and inferred attitudes from these. It is open to question, however, how accurate these inferences actually are.

Health

Attitude measurements are carried out every day by market analysts. But one of the major problems of attitude measurement is the fact that simple measures of how someone feels about a particular product, person or idea are not actually very good predictors about how that person will act – partly because we often hold a number of different attitudes, which become tangled together. For example, Marteau (1990) carried out a study to try to disentangle people's attitudes towards medicine from people's attitudes towards doctors. The outcome of a test of a set of questions compiled for this purpose showed that some groups distinguished between doctors and medicine more clearly than others. Women attending an ante-natal clinic tended to hold similar, positive

• **Valence**	The degree of positive or negative feelings expressed
• **Breadth**	Some attitudes are very specific, for example towards people who sneeze on buses, whereas some are very broad, for example towards war
• **Stability**	How resistant the attitude is to change
• **Centrality**	How important the attitude is to our perception of self-identity
• **Salience**	How much awareness it occupies from total pre-occupation to virtual absence

Figure 7.4 Dimensions of attitudes.

Figure 7.5 Your choice of reading material says something about your attitudes.

attitudes towards both medicine and doctors. Nurses regarded the two rather differently, being more negative towards doctors than they were towards medicine, while behavioural scientists tended to regard both doctors and medicine in a negative light.

What all this implies is that developing a simple attitude questionnaire about, say, attitudes towards general medical practice might actually tap into a number of conceptual confusions and disagreements, which would confuse the outcome of the questionnaire and limit its usefulness.

Attitudes structure how we see our world and how we act in it; so as the world changes, so do attitudes. Bell *et al.* (1990) described the changing attitudes of white Americans to wilderness landscapes. The early settlers to the continent had found themselves in a threatening environment of harsh winters and poor soil. This, combined with their conservative religious beliefs, meant that they saw the wilderness around them as a hostile threatening landscape, inhabited by servants of the devil (Native Americans). These attitudes led to the notion that they should tame and conquer the environment, and make it as much like the familiar European one as possible.

Environment

However, as people started moving west across the American continent, and also as the Eastern seaboard became more urbanized, the prevailing attitude changed and people started to look more favourably on the wilderness. President Thomas Jefferson, for example, believed that it was better to try to understand nature rather than conquer it, and encouraged an expedition in 1803 to provide detailed reports of natural phenomena. Nowadays, the American wilderness ·holds a powerful symbolic role for many people, while some hold ambivalent attitudes, viewing it with both fear and awe.

What we can see here is a **dialectical** relationship between attitudes and society. As society changed, so did attitudes; those attitudes in turn shaped the actions of people towards the physical world; and the

dialectical An interrelationship in which two apparently opposite or opposing entities or ideas combine to form an entirely new synthesis. Each influences the other and is influenced by it, such that together the relationship produces something new.

Figure 7.6 The wilderness is a powerful symbol for many.

Health

changes in the physical world changed the nature of society. When we are dealing with the type of group-held attitudes which are closely associated with social structure, like this, then the study of attitudes begins to connect closely with the research into social representations which we looked at in Chapter 3.

Other attitudes, however, operate on a much more individual level. Owens and Naylor (1989) discussed how the attitudes of friends and relatives to death frequently made it very difficult for a dying person to conduct their everyday lives in a normal fashion, even when they wished to do so, and when the general prognosis for their illness was such that death was many months away. In their description and discussion of Naylor's lengthy and terminal illness, Owens and Naylor showed how the relatively unfamiliar experience of death in modern Western society had produced many highly negative attitudes. For the dying person, these attitudes make things worse, as they tend to produce avoidance or to mean that people act as if the dying person has somehow become somebody else entirely.

People's attitudes towards particular types of illness can influence how they act towards the people who have those illnesses quite considerably. During the late 1980s, a random sample of licensed psychologists in the United States were asked to read a passage about a male college student who was diagnosed as having a terminal illness. The passages were identical, except that the student was described as either heterosexual or homosexual, and as having contracted either AIDS or leukaemia. When they had read the passage, the psychologists were asked to complete a number of attitude scales.

When they analysed the results, St Lawrence *et al.* (1990) found extremely negative attitudes towards the AIDS patient, which were not applied to the leukaemia one. The AIDS patient was considered to be more responsible for his illness, more dangerous to other people, to deserve quarantine and sometimes even to be a person for whom suicide is the best solution. By comparison with the leukaemia patient, they also expressed less willingness to see the AIDS patient professionally, to work in the same office, to continue a past friendship or to allow children to visit him.

However, there were a great many problems with this study, so there are limits to the conclusions we can draw from it. One of these problems was that the object of the study was not very well disguised. Another, more serious problem is that the survey was conducted by mail and, as with many mailshot surveys, the response rate was poor – only 185 of the 500 psychologists responded, which was only 37% of the sample. In mail surveys of this kind, those who respond tend to be those who are highly motivated to do so – and that often means that it is because they already have strong opinions. As market researchers have found, people who have more moderate, or tolerant, opinions frequently do not bother to respond to postal surveys.

Surveys can have their uses, though. One of the very first major attitude surveys in industry was conducted in 1930 at a Kimberley-Clarke Corporation mill in Wisconsin. The outcome of the survey was news at the time, but as more and more attitude surveys were completed, eventually it became a commonplace view and illustrated the usefulness of the approach. Essentially, what the survey showed, and what has been shown by many industrial surveys since, is that many industrial disputes or sources of industrial discontent are entirely unnecessary and come about because the management has not bothered to find out what the employees are really thinking. As Hollway (1990) remarked, 'Too often, the workers' attitudes are guessed at, ignored, or damned' (p. 90).

Work

Hayes and Lemon (1990) described a consultancy model for training managers in small-but-growing businesses to become more aware of how their employees were seeing the company, in order to help them to deal with increasing staff management issues as the company grew in size. Essentially, this consisted of a single report for the company directors, based on interviews with the company staff. Showing directors how very different employee attitudes were from those that they had expected, or guessed at, and highlighting areas about which the staff were concerned, Hayes and Lemon argued, could provide a catalytic effect, helping directors of new companies to develop employee

Figure 7.7 Measuring attitudes.

THE LIKERT SCALE

One of the most popular methods developed has been the Likert Scale (Likert, 1932). Using this method, people are asked to respond to a series of statements using a five-point scale which ranges from 'strongly agree' through a 'don't know' middle point, to 'strongly disagree' at the other end. The trick is to produce an appropriate list of statements for people to respond to. One of the strengths of this approach is that it gives a measure of the strength of an attitude as well as its content.

THE SEMANTIC DIFFERENTIAL

This technique was developed by Osgood, Suci and Tannenbaum (1957) and can be used to build up a more sophisticated picture of a particular attitude than the Likert Scale can achieve. The semantic differential uses a number of different dimensions and people are required to use them to respond to a single target word. The responses are on a seven-point scale and differences between individual responses can be observed visually.

SOCIOMETRY

This technique, which was developed by Moreno (1934) is most commonly used with groups to find out how members of the group see each other. The individual group members are asked to name another member of the group who would be their preferred partner for some activity, or their friend, or the group leader. From this information a sociogram can be drawn up that illustrates the social network of the group. The individual group members are represented as circles and each arrow represents their choice of group members.

SOCIAL DISTANCE SCALE

The Social Distance Scale was developed by Bogardus (1925) and is made up of a series of statements concerned with the amount of 'social distance' which people perceive between themselves and others. People are provided with a list of groups, for example ethnic and national groups, and asked to tick or cross a number of statements. The outcome of the scale is used to identify prejudiced attitudes of one form or another, although it may be that responses bias and an increasing social awareness of the outcomes of bigotry have meant that it is less useful in modern times.

INTERVIEW ANALYSIS

Many forms of interview or account analysis are concerned with identifying the underlying attitudes. For example, Eiser (1983) proposed that a careful examination of the emotive words people use in interviews can provide a valuable indication of what their underlying attitudes are. And many researchers will analyse interviews by going through transcripts and recordings, and isolating key quotes or statements which summarize the underlying attitude that has been revealed through the interview (see discourse analysis in Chapter 3).

Read the following statements and rate your agreement using the scale below.

'Hanging should be brought back'

Strongly Agree	Agree	Dunno	Disagree	Strongly Disagree
—	—	—	—	—

'The song *"Chirpy Chirpy Cheep Cheep"* was the peak of British popular music'

Strongly Agree	Agree	Dunno	Disagree	Strongly Disagree
—	—	—	—	—

How would you rate the phrase CUP CAKES on the following scales?

	+3	+2	+1	0	−1	−2	−3	
Good	—	—	—	—	—	—	—	Bad
Beautiful	—	—	—	—	—	—	—	Ugly
Strong	—	—	—	—	—	—	—	Weak
Active	—	—	—	—	—	—	—	Passive
Skilful	—	—	—	—	—	—	—	Lucky

Responses to the question, 'Who are your friends?' Each line represents a friendship link.

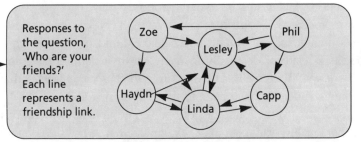

Examples of 'social distance' statements

Which of the following would you agree with for, say, a member of the Conservative Party?

- would admit to close kinship by marriage
- would admit to my club as personal chums
- would admit to citizenship in my country
- would exclude from my country
- would admit to my street as neighbours

Howitt (1991) points out the underlying culturally biased assumptions that are evident in the introductory text by Atkinson *et al.* (1990) The emphasis is added

'Behaviour that is considered normal by one **society** may be considered abnormal by another. For example, members of some african **tribes** do not consider it unusual to hear voices when no one is actually talking or to see visions when nothing is actually there, but such behaviours are considered abnormal in most **societies**'. (Atkinson, *et al.* 1990, p. 592)

So, according to Atkinson, Africans live in tribes, whereas other people live in societies. Who else lives in tribes?

'In another chimpanzee border war observed during the 1970s, a **tribe** of about 15 chimpanzees destroyed a smaller neighbouring group by killing the members off one male at a time'. (Atkinson, *et al.* 1990, p. 427)

management systems which were based on listening to employees, and taking their attitudes and ideas into account.

A considerable amount of research has looked at the way that organizations can develop general climates, which influence the attitudes and behaviour of the people who work in them. Miller and Gwynne (1972) examined a number of homes catering for people with irreversible and severe physical handicap. They identified two types of institutional climate in these institutions. One was a 'warehousing' philosophy, in which the prime emphasis was that the residents were dependent on the provision of good physical care, so that was what the institution should be providing. The other was a 'horticultural' approach, which emphasized that the residents' psychological well-being was in the institution's hands, as it were, so the staff of the institution should be working to cultivate the residents' interests and abilities.

These two organizational climates produced very different behaviour on the part of the care staff; and individual staff attitudes too (or at least the ones which they expressed openly) were consistent with the climate in the institution. Miller and Gwynne proposed that each of these approaches represented a **coping** response to the very serious nature of the residents' handicaps, in which the most likely end of the residence came about as a result of death. By focusing on their defined task, and ensuring that it was done well, staff were able to satisfy themselves that they had done as much as they could, to the best of their ability.

coping The process of managing external or internal demands that are perceived as taxing or exceeding a person's resource.

Different staff vary in their attitudes of course and, to some extent, this links with personality variables. For example, staff who have more authoritarian personalities (see later in this chapter) tend to express more custodial attitudes. But there are systematic differences between institutions which relate far more to institutional climate than to individual differences. Although people will vary in how they act, if the general institutional policy is custodial and authoritarian, its staff will tend to show custodial and authoritarian attitudes. So how this comes about is an interesting question.

Society

Herbert (1986) suggested that three main processes are at work in establishing consistency between staff and **organizational climates**. The first of these is selection in. Some people will be more attracted to work in a particular institution than others, and interview panels will look for those likely to 'fit in', so by and large the institution will tend to recruit people who conform to its ideas. In a similar way, there will be selection out: people whose attitudes are in line with the prevailing institutional climate will be likely to remain with the institution, but those who find that they do not agree with its approach will tend to look for jobs elsewhere.

organizational climate The psychological or social atmosphere of an organization.

The third factor which establishes consistency between institutions and staff attitudes is that, over time, a certain amount of attitude change will take place. Employees will be subtly pressured to conform to the prevailing institutional climate and not to be socially deviant by going against the conventional approach. In addition, other employees in the institution will have explanatory **social representations**, which 'show' that the policy is the 'right' one for this particular situation. These pressures combine to produce attitude change in individual members of staff over a period of time. In this context, it is striking how much attitude change can take place when someone leaves one job and begins another. Being away from those subtle pressures can often feel like a real release for people who have been unconsciously conforming to them.

Moos (1974) developed a measure of institutional attitudes for use when comparing the different climates found in different hospitals. The Ward atmosphere scale evaluates the perceptions of members of institutions and organizations according to ten dimensions. The ten dimensions are organized into three groups. The first group deals with the interpersonal relationships which exist between people in the institution. The

---

RELATIONSHIP DIMENSIONS

Involvement   How active patients are in the everyday social functioning of the ward

Support   How helpful and supporting patients are, towards other patients, and staff are towards patients

Spontaneity   How well the environment encourages patients to act openly and express feelings freely

PERSONAL DEVELOPMENT DIMENSIONS

Autonomy   How self-sufficient and independent patients are and are encouraged to be

Practical orientation   How far the patient's environment allows preparation for the future

Personal problem orientation   How far patients are encouraged to be concerned with their feelings and problems, and seek to understand them

Anger and aggression   How far patients are allowed and encouraged to argue or become openly angry

SYSTEM DIMENSIONS

Order and organization   The importance of order and planning of the ward

Programme clarity   How far patients know what to expect in day-to-day routine, and in ward rules and procedures

Staff control   How strict rules, schedules, regulations and other measures are

Figure 7.8 Dimensions of the Ward atmosphere scale. (Moos, 1974.)

second is concerned with the personal development of individuals within the institution and the third is concerned with the nature of the system itself. A summary of these relationships is shown in Figure 7.8.

Herbert (1986) described a study which compared the failure rates of 16 hostels for boys on probation. Failure was judged in terms of the percentage of residents leaving the hostel as a result of absconding or being reconvicted. The attitudes of the wardens were assessed and what emerged was that there were two components which correlated positively with success in dealing with these boys. The first of these was strictness as opposed to permissiveness – wardens who were strict tended to be more successful than those who were lenient. The second was 'warmth' – a willingness to discuss the resident's problems. Wardens who displayed more warmth and willingness to discuss problems were more successful than those who did not.

The ideal combination, then, for the warden of a probation hostel appears to be that they should be simultaneously warm and strict. Unfortunately, however, these two characteristics tend to be uncommon in the same individuals: warmth is more often found to be associated with permissiveness, while strictness is often associated with emotional distance. There were some individuals, however, who showed that the two could be combined and these people tended to be particularly successful.

Persuasion and attitude change

Much attitude research has centred around the question of how people's attitudes can be changed – not surprising, when you consider the tremendous payoffs, in both commercial and political fields, for achieving this successfully, particularly if that attitude change is then translated into action.

There have been a number of attempts to model the process of attitude and behavioural change. The information-processing approach proposed by Hovland and Janis (1959) stated that what was important in attitude change was the way that the information was processed. This could be broken down into five features which are listed in Figure 7.9. However, although this was a very popular model for some time, it does not really address the question of how attitudes can actually be changed, and it fails to address any of the social, motivational and personal aspects of attitude change. Human beings do not really process information like computers.

One of the more recent alternatives to information-processing models is the *theory of reasoned action*, proposed by Ajzen and

1. The source of the message, e.g. whether it comes from a recognized 'authority' in the field or a popular TV personality.

2. The message itself, e.g. whether it is high in information content or focuses on creating an emotional impact.

3. The target of the message, e.g. whether it is aimed at young people, house-wives or professionals.

4. The medium that is used to carry the message, e.g. whether it uses visual, verbal and/or auditory stimuli, and if so what types of stimuli it adopts.

5. The context that the message is received in, e.g. whether a business computer advert appears immediately after a business oriented TV programme.

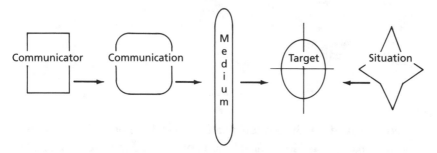

The Yale model of communication

Figure 7.9 Factors identified in information-processing models of attitude change. (Hovland and Janis, 1959.)

Fishbein (1980). This was particularly developed to address the problematic relationship between attitudes and behaviour – specifically, the way that people often act in ways that are quite different from the attitudes which they hold. So, for example, someone might have an attitude concerning the positive value of looking after one's health, yet continue to smoke or lead an unhealthy lifestyle in other ways.

There are good reasons for this apparent contradiction, according to Ajzen (1988). One of them is the way that researchers tended to gather information about attitudes in general, but then to expect them to be manifest in very specific contexts, where additional factors also came into play. A restaurateur in the 1930s might express segregationist attitudes when asked in a survey, but actually turning away an ethnic minority couple from the doorstep involves interpersonal dimensions which run contrary to the professional practice of being a restaurant owner – being openly rude to potential customers is not good practice and would be difficult, particularly if those people were accompanied by a white friend.

Ajzen and Fishbein pointed out that what is important in determining what people will do is not the attitudes which they express, but their intentions. The theory of reasoned action is all about how intentions interact with attitudes and form the best predictor of what

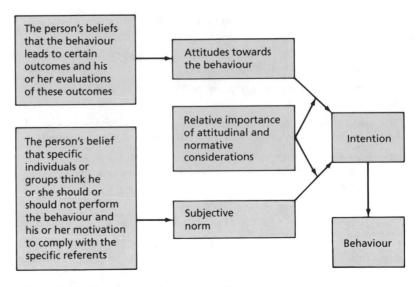

Figure 7.10 The theory of reasoned action.

people will do. Other, often related, models of attitude and behavioural change have been developed and applied in specific areas. For example, the *health belief model* is used to explore the relationship between people's personal health behaviour and attitudes.

Key reference: AJZEN, I. and FISHBEIN, M. (1980) *Understanding Attitudes and Predicting Social Behavior*. Prentice-Hall, Englewood Cliffs, NJ.

Society

Advertisers, understandably, have been directly concerned with attitude changes as manifest by purchasing behaviour or lowered accident rates, as the intention underlying a new advertising campaign is usually to change behaviour directly. Often, however, people's reported attitudes are not particularly helpful. For example, Cowpe (1989) reported how, when asked about chip pan fires, people claimed that they always adopted safe practices, although fire brigade statistics, and the ideas which the survey uncovered, showed that this was not always the case. Consequently, the television advertising campaign which was developed took a different tack, showing a dramatic sequence of pictures which showed exactly how these fires develop and how people should deal with them. The adverts ended with a simple statement, such as, 'Of course, if you don't overfill your chip pan in the first place, you won't have to do any of this.'

By comparing fire brigade statistics for the areas which had received the advertisements and those for the areas which had not, the advertisers

INATTENDANCE

Figure 7.11a
The television campaign on chip-pan fire protection.

If you go out of
the kitchen

and leave your
pan of cooking
fat or oil with
the heat on

it's going to
get very hot.

When it gets
hot enough

it'll catch fire.

When you notice it

the first thing

you'll have
to do

is turn off the
heat. The second
thing you'll

have to do is get a
tea towel, run it under
the tap and wring it out
until it's just damp.

The third thing you'll
have to do is place it
over the area of the fire.
And the fourth thing is
to leave it alone until
it is completely cooled
down.

Of course, if you don't
leave your pan unattended
in the first place you
won't have to do any of this.

Figure 7.11a *contd*

OVERFILLING

If you fill your
chip pan more than
half full of cooking
fat or oil

it will bubble over
when you add the chips.

When it touches the
heat it will naturally
catch light.

Having started a fire
you should set about
putting it out.

The first thing you
should do if you can
reach the knob safely
is turn off the heat.

The second thing you'll
have to do

is get a towel, run it
under the tap,

and wring it out
until it's just damp.

The third thing you'll
have to do is place it
over the area of the
fire

and if you haven't already
done it, turn off the heat.
The fourth thing is

leave the pan alone for half
an hour or so . . . until it's
completely cooled down.

Of course, if you don't
overfill your chip pan in
the first place, you won't
have to do any of this.

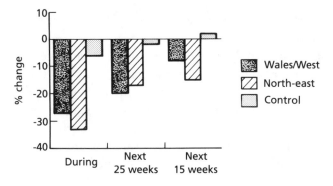

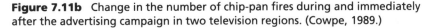

Figure 7.11b Change in the number of chip-pan fires during and immediately after the advertising campaign in two television regions. (Cowpe, 1989.)

found that the advertisements had produced a 25% reduction in the number of chip pan fires in some areas, with a 12% reduction overall. Surveys taken after the series of advertisements showed that people had more accurate knowledge about what they should do in the event of a chip pan fire than before.

The use of fear in attempts to change peoples' attitudes has attracted a considerable amount of attention. Some early research was carried out by Janis and Feshbach (1953). In their study they divided college students into three groups and gave them messages designed to produce low, medium or high fear about the relationship between teeth brushing and gum decay. The most effective message was moderate fear appeal when accompanied by instructions on effective tooth brushing. High fear, it would appear, tends to have a negative effect on behavioural change.

Health

Less extreme emotions, too, can influence our responses to advertisements. People who are in a positive mood tend to perceive and evaluate advertisements more favourably than those in a negative mood. Positive moods are also known to influence how well the message is accepted – they tend to shape how people respond partly by producing more varied responses, such as support arguments and counterarguments. People in negative moods seem to develop just one line of argument and stick to it, for the most part.

Batra and Stayman (1990) investigated how the strength of an advertising message would interact with the mood of the reader to produce a change in attitude. Their experiment contained two phases, which were presented to the research participants as two different studies. In the first phase the mood of the research participants was manipulated into either a positive or a neutral state. Then, they were asked to examine a printed advertisement, and to use this to weigh up an organization and how effective its marketing efforts were. The advertisement which they looked

Consumer

at contained either three strong arguments for the organization, or three weak arguments.

The results of the study showed that when people were in a neutral mood, the strong argument had a significantly greater effect on their attitudes. But, if they were in a positive mood, then either type of argument was likely to have an effect – the strong arguments remained just as effective while the weaker arguments gained in strength. It seemed that people who were in a good mood were simply more prepared to pay attention to information – it did not have to be presented in a very strong form.

What this study shows is that whether we are receptive to information or not is not simply to do with the form of the information or any of the other factors identified by the information-processing model. Instead, how we feel is equally important, if not more so. Advertisements which are designed to entertain people, or to make them laugh, may therefore be just as effective as ones which deliver a powerful informative message, because the uplifting of mood may make the consumer more receptive to the information.

Environment

Who we consider responsible for things will also influence how prepared we are to change our behaviour. Belk, Painter and Semenik (1981) developed a system for categorizing consumers in terms of their beliefs about energy conservation. Their categorization focused on the attributions which people made about the source of the energy crisis: whether they thought it was attributable to excessive personal energy use or to impersonal sources such as the international oil companies. Belk, Painter and Semenik found that people who attributed the energy problem to personal causes were likely to favour personal solutions (brick in the cistern, lagging the loft etc.), whereas those who blamed the oil companies favoured political solutions and did not tend to take personal action.

This study has a number of implications for the attempt to raise environmental awareness on the part of the population. It showed that the same environmental message can be received in different ways by different people, which is not particularly surprising. But it also shows how important it is for ecological pressure groups to show people that personal action can be effective: those who spend their time blaming multinationals, the capitalist system, consumerism etc. may be doing more harm to their cause, by indicating to people that personal action is not worth while, than those who attempt to work with existing practices and emphasize that everyone can make a contribution.

Health

There have been numerous attempts to encourage health behaviour through mass media appeals, though their effectiveness has been hard to

	Town 1	Town 2	Town 3
CONDITION	Control; no campaign	Massive media campaign concerning smoking, diet and exercise over two-year period via TV, radio, newspapers, posters and mailshots	Massive media campaign concerning smoking, diet and exercise over two-year period via TV, radio, newspapers, posters and mailshots; PLUS, face-to-face instruction directed at high-risk people on how to modify risk behaviours
EFFECT	No change	Increased awareness but relatively little behavioural change	Greater change where people had received behavioural instruction

judge – it is not like product advertising, where the effect can be measured in sales. There are, however, some indications that simply presenting people with mass media information-based campaigns is not enough. Taylor (1986) described the Stanford heart disease prevention programme, which involved three towns, of similar size and socioeconomic status, and differing amounts of health information (see Figure 7.12). The results suggested that mass media campaigns alone produce only marginal changes in behaviour – they need to be accompanied by personal intervention of some kind before people will change their behaviour.

Figure 7.12 The Stanford heart disease prevention programme.

Mass media campaigns have also been used for political **propaganda**, though again it is difficult to tell whether they had any success or not. Shils and Janowitz (1948) reviewed the wartime propaganda of the Second World War, in which the Allies made extensive use of propaganda leaflets, which they air-dropped over German lines. '*Nachrichten fur die Truppe*', a daily newsheet published by the Allied Psychological Warfare Division, showed that each copy which was picked up had an average readership of between four and five soldiers, according to German prisoners of war. Studies such as this suggested that as many as 80% of the German soldiers had seen Allied propaganda.

Society

propaganda *Traditionally defined as an attempt to influence public opinion and public behaviour through specialized persuasion techniques: can supposedly be contrasted with education.*

Although it is difficult to assess the effectiveness of these campaigns, some clues might be seen in the responses of captured German soldiers to various measures of opinion. The evidence suggested that there was no decline in their attachment to the Nazi ideology until the spring of 1945, when the war was all but lost for the Germans and their army was in disarray. In other words, despite a high level of penetration of the propaganda, it no had appreciable effect on the German soldiers until

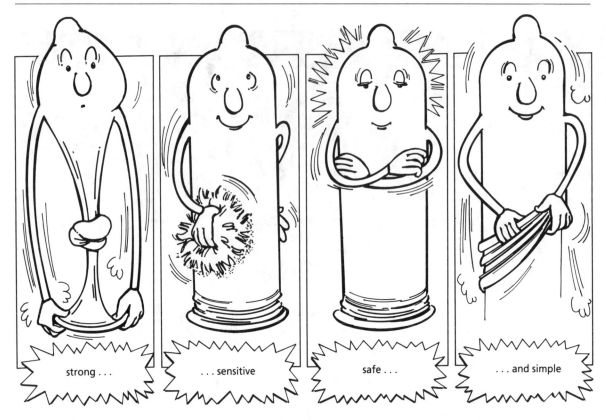

strong . . .   . . . sensitive   safe . . .   . . . and simple

Figure 7.13
The illustrations above, redrawn from a Local Authority Health leaflet, were part of a campaign to change attitudes and behaviour towards safer sex practices.

Consumer

their own leadership was cast into doubt. At that time, however, it appeared to become more effective.

All of this evidence combines to suggest that people's own personal involvement is important if attitude change is to take place. As the theory of reasoned action states, it is intentions which are important in attitude change, not whether we are the passive recipients of convincing information. Understandably, the theory of reasoned action has generated a lot of interest in the world of marketing. Mullen and Johnson (1990) showed how the theory has been successfully applied to such diverse phenomena as the purchase of clothing items, dating behaviour and the use of coupons.

Mullen and Johnson suggested that the intention to use a product generally comes from a positive overall evaluation of the product, along with norms supporting the use of the product. Actual use of the product can generally be predicted from a stated intention to use the product. However, there are alternative ways of looking at this question, which link much more closely with the attributions which we make and the underlying values that they reveal.

Many studies have revealed a discrepancy between attitudes and behaviour. For example, there is a growing awareness in the Western consumer that behaviour can have an effect on the environment and an attitude is developing that we should make positive choices to protect the environment. But when Heslop, Moran and Cousineau (1981) looked at the environmental attitudes of family homes and also their energy consumption, they found that attitudes towards energy consumption or conservation seemed to have no effect on the actual use of energy in the home. In fact, the only factors that seemed to influence the amount of energy used were the number of people living in the home and the cost-consciousness of the family members.

The reason for this apparent contradiction may lie in the distinction between approving of a product and actually choosing to buy it. Drawing from data gained from market research interviews over a three-year period, Stratton and Siviter (1993) showed that consumers make a clear distinction between approval and choice, and that this distinction emerged in every area that they looked at, whether it was between GPs talking about therapies for ulcers, TV viewers talking about soap operas or mothers talking about convenience foods; and it also emerged in cross-cultural data.

Essentially, the analysis undertaken by Stratton and Siviter showed that there were two underlying questions which consumers were asking when they evaluated products. The first was whether that brand was intrinsically worth while, and a positive answer to that question signified that the consumer approved of it. But the second question was whether that brand allowed the person to achieve something which was important to them, and that was the question which would result in the consumer actually choosing to purchase the product.

For the most part, the values and attitudes which consumers expressed when they were talking about approval and choice were different. However, there were some core values which were used as criteria for both approval of a product and choosing it. Stratton and Siviter argued that these core values provided the clue to understanding brand positioning. Brands which were seen as tapping into core values for both approval and choice would achieve a reputation as an important example of that type of product; brands which did not would tend to be regarded as less significant.

A different model of attitude change is known as the health belief model. This model argues that the likelihood that individuals will take preventive action depends directly on two assessments that they make. The first of these concerns their evaluations of the perceived threat, and the second a cost–benefit analysis of what taking action will involve and whether it will feel personally worth while. Figure 7.14 identifies some of the components involved in these two assessments.

Health

Evaluating the threat

Several factors influence a person's perceived threat of illness, including:
- perceived seriousness in terms of both organic and social consequences;
- perceived susceptibility – how vulnerable you feel to the dangers;
- Cues to action – the reminders and models for action.

Cost–benefits analysis

The cost–benefit assessment looks at whether the perceived benefits exceed the perceived barriers. The barriers might be financial, situational (difficult to get to a health clinic), social (don't want to acknowledge getting old). The benefits might be improved health, relief from anxiety and reducing health risks.

Figure 7.14 Components of health belief assessments.

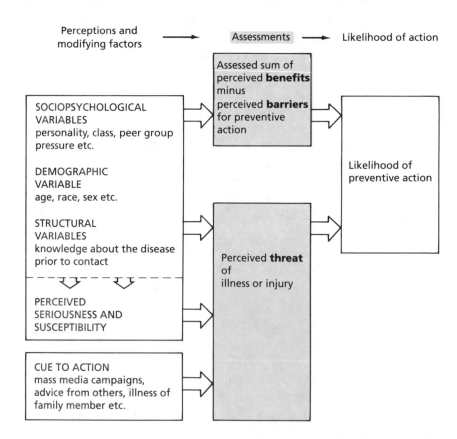

Figure 7.15 The health belief model.

The health belief model has been used to help researchers to predict who will make use of free health examinations, yearly medical check-ups and screening programmes. For example Kasl (1975) found that participants in disease prevention programmes were more likely to value their health highly, to feel susceptible to the disorder in question and to believe in the power of modern medicine to cure disease if detected early. Results from this and similar studies suggest that health beliefs are an important factor in the decision to adopt health behaviours or not.

Although the health belief model appears to be useful in some respects – and certainly seems to be more useful than a straightforward 'attitude' measure – it does have its limitations. Hunt and Martin (1988) looked at the development of 'healthy eating' in the context of the health belief model. They had two groups of volunteers, who were recruited by means of an advertisement. One group was asked to keep a health diary for a period of a month. The other group acted as interviewers in a survey of people buying fibre-rich foods. The researchers found that those people who were in the interviewing group showed an increase in some aspects of healthy eating, by comparison with the others. They concluded that bringing habitual eating behaviour into consciousness, in this case by asking others about their dietary habits, had generated self-initiated behaviour change from the research participants. This showed how important it is to take account of habits as well as beliefs when looking at attitude change.

Cognitive dissonance

A different, motivational approach to the way that attitudes may sometimes change is suggested in the theory of **cognitive dissonance**, proposed by Leon Festinger, in 1957. Festinger based his work on Heider's idea of cognitive balance (Heider, 1958), which asserted that people generally try to maintain cognitive balance between the different beliefs which they hold, so that each is reasonably congruent with the others. Festinger argued that consistency between attitudes, behaviour and values was also important, and that if an incongruence developed, then the person would be motivated to change their beliefs accordingly.

Essentially, the processes of attitude change through cognitive dissonance are as follows: inconsistencies between cognitions in an individual generate a feeling of dissonance, because they produce a state of cognitive imbalance. The dissonance is unpleasant, so the individual is motivated to remove it. Moreover, the individual will actively avoid situations and information that may increase it. The motivation to avoid or remove dissonance increases with the amount of dissonance, and the amount of dissonance depends, in turn, on the amount of difference between the cognitions.

An experimental demonstration of dissonance was provided by the forced compliance studies of Festinger and Carlsmith, in 1959.

Figure 7.16 Cognitive dissonance: balancing a lie with a bribe.

1. BALANCE

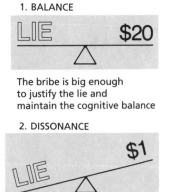

The bribe is big enough to justify the lie and maintain the cognitive balance

2. DISSONANCE

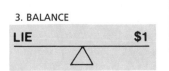

The bribe is not big enough to justify the lie, so the only way to restore cognitive balance is for the lie not to be so big after all.

3. BALANCE

LIE $1

College students were brought one at a time into a room to work for 30 minutes on 2 repetitive and dull tasks. On completion of the task they were offered either $1 or $20 to try to persuade a potential subject for the study that it was interesting and enjoyable. Common sense would suggest that the greater bribe would produce greater attitude change in the subjects. The theory, however, predicts the opposite and the outcome of the study supported the theory.

According to the theory, telling a lie will create cognitive dissonance in most people, as there is a discrepancy between what they experienced and what they say they experienced. Consequently, they will need to see themselves as having had a reason for lying. This dissonance can be reduced by a large reward, because the person can convince themselves that they did it for the money, but a small reward is not enough. The only way for the small reward people to reduce the dissonance was, therefore, to reduce the size of the lie. By rationalizing that the task was not that dull or repetitive after all, people could minimize the amount of dissonance which they experienced.

> **Key reference:** FESTINGER, L. (1957) *A Theory of Cognitive Dissonance.* Row, Peterson, Evanston, Ill.

Health

The effects of cognitive dissonance are very marked in studies of personal risk evaluation. For example, McMasters and Lee (1991) investigated the knowledge and beliefs of smokers. When they compared smokers, non-smokers and ex-smokers, they found that all of the groups had a similar amount of factual knowledge about the effects of smoking. Moreover, the smokers estimated their general risk of contracting lung cancer as being greater than the people in the other two groups. But when they were asked to estimate their personal risk, they rated it as lower than it would be for the 'average smoker', and they were much more likely to support rationalizations and distortions of logic regarding smoking than the non-smokers or ex-smokers. McMasters and Lee suggested that it was the dissonance produced by knowing that they were engaged in risky behaviour which produced these different beliefs.

Environment

Burger and Gochfeld (1991) looked at the response of Puerto Rican fishermen to mercury contamination of their fishing grounds. When they surveyed crabbers and fishermen in the polluted estuary, they found that nearly everyone interviewed at the polluted site was aware of the mercury threat, but either denied its importance, believed the contamination was restricted to a distant part of the estuary, or assumed that the estuary would be closed if the threat was real. The fishermen were all still consuming the fish and crabs they caught. A control group of fishermen and crabbers from ecologically similar control sites argued that they would not eat fish or crabs from that location.

The researchers suggested that the fishermen were experiencing cognitive dissonance between their own experience and the technical assertions of risk, media reports of pollution and lack of a governmental prohibition of fishing. The way that they were resolving this cognitive dissonance was to devalue the threat and continue with their fishing which, for some, was an essential part of their livelihoods.

A remarkable study by Festinger, Riecken and Schachter (1956) described the process of cognitive dissonance in a religious cult based in a large American city. The cult was led by a medium, Mrs Keech, who prophesied that the northern hemisphere would be destroyed by flood on a certain day, when everyone would be killed. The cult members sold all of their possessions and spent the night on top of a hill outside the city, praying to be spared. They were joined by Festinger and his colleagues, who were interested to know how the cult members would cope when their beliefs were disconfirmed. When the next day failed to bring the promised flood the cult members asserted that their actions had averted the flood and that they had saved the world – a belief which saved them from having to face the cognitive dissonance implied by the idea that their actions might have been entirely futile.

Society

According to cognitive dissonance theory, once we have made the decision to buy, say, a particular type of washing machine, we will then justify that decision by enhancing our opinion of the product choice and devaluing our opinion of the alternatives. For example, Ehrlich *et al.* (1957) interviewed 125 men in an advertising survey to find out information on the car advertisements which they read. Sixty-five of the men had recently bought new cars. They found that new car owners tended to read advertisements about the make of car which they had bought much

Consumer

The theory of cognitive dissonance has been used in wide contexts. For example, it offers an explanation for the enhancement of group cohesion through harsh initiation rites. The dissonance is created by the submission to the humiliation/hardship of initiation and reduced by the increased value put on to the group the individual has been initiated into. So, for example, having to work 120 hours a week for a couple of years or more used to act as a mechanism which cemented doctors' identification with the medical profession and convinced them that those who hadn't been through it were 'outsiders', and not worthy of communicating with. Fortunately, this seems to be an attitude which is dying away, although not very quickly.

Figure 7.17 Group cohesion and cognitive dissonance.

more often than adverts for other types of car. It was also apparent that new car owners generally tended to read car advertisements less than other people. Ehrlich *et al.* concluded that they were seeking information which was consonant with their decision and avoiding potential sources of cognitive dissonance.

Later studies, however, showed a rather more complex picture. Bell (1967) interviewed 234 car buyers after purchase, asking questions designed to reveal any cognitive dissonance which they might feel. Measures of persuasibility and their perception of quality of service were obtained from these interviews, and from additional information supplied by the car salesman. Bell did not find any relationship between persuasibility and dissonance, but did find that the self-confidence of the customer, and their perception of quality of service, influenced their feelings about the car. So cognitive dissonance was interacting with other social variables, rather than acting as a single factor in attitude change.

Hunt (1970) investigated the effects of post-transaction communications on 152 purchasers of refrigerators at a department store. The store sold several varieties of refrigerators, with a large variety of special features, so there was considerable potential for cognitive dissonance. Customers who had purchased refrigerators the day before were chosen from a list supplied by the department store and randomly assigned to one of the three groups. The first group was the control and did not receive any post-transaction messages. Those in the second group were sent a letter about the refrigerators available in the store and people in the third group received a telephone version of the letter.

The researchers found that the second group had a lower dissonance score (implying greater satisfaction) and more intention to purchase from the store again, than either of the other groups. Contrary to expectation, though, the third group had the highest dissonance score of all – they felt anxious about their purchase and did not intend to go to that store again. In other words, where the written presentation had been effective, the oral strategy had been counterproductive. Perhaps people had felt hassled, or harassed, by the personal contact or maybe it had led them to feel that there might be reason to doubt the integrity of the store.

Environment

Cognitive dissonance theory has been employed in the search for ways to encourage more 'environmentally friendly' behaviour by consumers. Kantola, Syme and Campbell (1983) conducted an experiment on electricity conservation and cognitive dissonance among householders in Perth, Western Australia, who owned properties with ducted air conditioning. This type of air conditioning involves a high level of energy consumption. The 203 householders in the study were given an attitude measure beforehand, and all of them indicated that they were

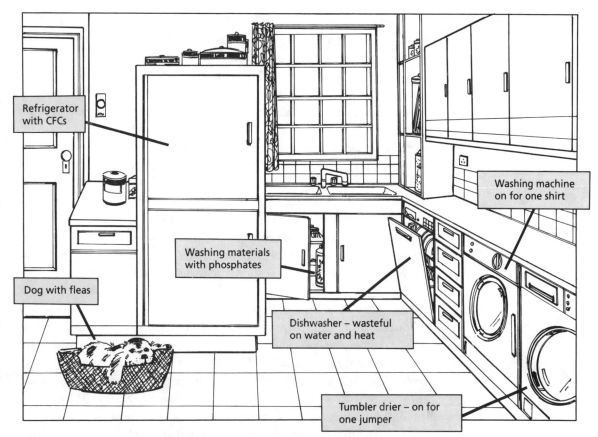

Refrigerator with CFCs

Washing machine on for one shirt

Washing materials with phosphates

Dog with fleas

Dishwasher – wasteful on water and heat

Tumbler drier – on for one jumper

Figure 7.18 Energy conservation and cognitive dissonance. Many people have pro-environmental attitudes and anti-environmental life styles. Pointing out the inconsistency might provoke dissonance and bring about changes in behaviour.

concerned about energy conservation and felt it was their duty as responsible citizens to conserve energy.

The householders were then divided into four experimental groups. Group 1 (the 'dissonance group') was informed of an inconsistency between their expressed attitude and their actual practice, in terms of their high consumption of electricity. Group 2 were notified of their high electricity consumption and also given tips on how to conserve energy. Group 3 were only given the tips, but their own domestic activity was not discussed, while Group 4 were the control group, who were simply sent a letter thanking them for participating in the study.

In the first two weeks of the study, Group 1 conserved more electricity than all other groups. In the third and fourth week after the intervention, though, Groups 2 and 3 equalled them in electricity consumption. The results of the researchers' measures indicated that there was an effect of dissonance in consumption of electricity, but that it did not seem to affect people's expressed attitudes. They also found that self-reported behaviour change and requests for additional conservation materials were not reliable indicators of actual conservation behaviour.

A study by Dickerson, Thibodeau, Aronson and Miller (1992) had a similar pro-social aim, applying cognitive dissonance theory to encourage water conservation, although their methods were somewhat ethically questionable. Dickerson *et al.* asked swimmers to make a public commitment to water conservation, by urging other people to take shorter showers. They aroused dissonance by making them feel hypocritical about their showering habits, suggesting that they wasted water when they showered. Some of the swimmers made the public commitment after being reminded of their past behaviour – designed to arouse a feeling of dissonance; others were not made to feel guilty or were not asked to make a public statement at all. The researchers found that those in the 'hypocrisy' group took shorter showers than the others.

The process of adjusting attitudes and beliefs as a response to social realities may also have something to do with the cognitive dissonance produced by having to accept that an unpleasant reality has come to pass. Granberg and Nanneman (1986) looked at attitudes towards the two American presidential candidates, Jimmy Carter and Ronald Reagan, before and after the 1980 election, which Reagan won. They interviewed 1614 voters 8 weeks before the election and reinterviewed 1408 of the same people afterwards. What they found was that those voters who had not received the outcome that they expected showed the greatest change in attitude. After the election, Granberg and Nanneman found that the voters who had expected Carter to win now held much more favourable attitudes to Reagan and had become less positive towards Carter.

Theories of prejudice

A prejudice is, literally, a pre-judgement: a mental state in which the way that someone will evaluate information is already established, long before the information actually arrives. It is possible to be prejudiced in favour of something, as well as against things, but for the most part psychological research into prejudice has tended to focus on hostile social prejudice rather than any other kind. For example, prejudice was defined by Allport (1954) as '… an antipathy based on a faulty and inflexible generalisation. It may be felt or expressed. It may be directed toward a group as a whole, or toward an individual because he is a member of that group'.

Understandably, the aftermath of the Second World War saw a dramatic increase in research into prejudice, as psychologists struggled to explain what had happened in Nazi Germany and else-where in Europe. The psychological theories of prejudice which emerged were of two kinds: those which saw the source of prejudice as being in the individual and those which looked for it in social influences.

Of the individual approaches, the most prominent theory was the psychoanalytic model of the authoritarian personality, proposed by Adorno *et al.* in 1950. This characterized prejudice as being a conse-quence of excessively rigid childhood discipline, producing unre-solved childhood hostility. Although it provides a possible explanation for why some people are more rigid in their attitudes than others within the same social context, this approach does not serve to explain prejudice shared by whole communities, cultures or institutions.

The alternative is to see prejudice developing from interactions between social groups. Sherif (1956) demonstrated that competing groups will develop ethnocentric behaviours and attitudes, which lead to intergroup rivalry. Tajfel (1969) suggested that the mere existence of categorization into groups is enough for intergroup hostility to emerge. Such categorization produces a tendency to undervalue the out-group and overvalue the in-group, and a pressure for conformity and group cohesion. Social categorization was also seen as resulting in increased hostility and rejection to out group members, although more recent research challenges the inevitability of intergroup rivalry, which does not appear to occur in conditions of equal status.

These mechanisms of social identification operate along with the fact that in the real world, social groups differ in power and status, and that real economic and political conflicts exist. The result, according to Tajfel and his colleagues, is social prejudice – sometimes of the most extreme kind.

Figure 7.19 The fictional character of Alf Garnett, created by Johnny Speight, is a classic example of the authoritarian personality. He projected hostility on to minority groups, he was narrow-minded, he was rigid about rules and values, unquestioningly submissive to authority, sexually inhibited, intolerant of ambiguity and politically conservative.

> **Key reference:** TAJFEL, H. (1969) Cognitive aspects of prejudice. *Journal of Social Issues*, **25**(4), 79–97.

Earlier research into prejudice and stereotyping showed that highly preju-diced individuals tend to make sharper distinctions between racial cate-gories than those who are less prejudiced. Secord, Bevan and Katz (1956) showed research participants pictures of different people and asked them to classify the pictures into 'black' or 'white' groups. Those who scored highly on measures of prejudice were much more rigid in their choices and also perceived the photographs as being more different than those who were more relaxed in their attitudes.

Society

This type of approach to prejudice, which was typical of much early psychological research, may help us to understand individuals. But it is of limited value when we are trying to understand racism, sexism or ageism in society, because it tends to treat prejudice as if it is a personal, not a social problem, and ignores the economic and political factors which underlie it. None the less, within a given society some individuals are more inclined to show prejudiced, bigoted or rigid behaviour than others, and the individual approach can be useful in understanding how these particular people have come to be as they are.

For example, the British psychiatrist Dicks (1972) carried out an analysis of eight Nazi mass killers from the Second World War. They were compared with other Nazis and other captured German servicemen. He found that the most 'fanatical' of the people he interviewed tended to have had difficult relationships with their fathers, expressed no feelings towards their mothers, were intolerant of tenderness, showed tendencies to anti-social sadism and to project hostile intent outside themselves. They also displayed extreme neurotic anxiety. Taken together, these findings amount to a fair summary of the authoritarian personality, as described by Adorno.

Dicks found that these men had a number of other characteristics in common. They tended to be volunteers rather than conscripts and were more likely to come from rural rather than urban backgrounds. In terms of their personal inclinations they tended to be unreflective people, who preferred action to thinking or discussion. They also, Dicks found, tended to remain single longer than most other people in their position, had entered the service younger and quite a number of them had a brother killed in action. Although they are interesting, we could not conclude that these characteristics were important factors in creating their high levels of racism without knowing how many other people shared the same kinds of backgrounds, and yet did not become mass killers.

It is important to remember, too, that the general ideology of a society creates a context for the development of prejudice. An authoritarian personality may be inclined to become prejudiced, but the targets of that prejudice will depend on the particular economic, political and ideological circumstances of the society in which that person lives. Tajfel (1969) proposed that people engage in a 'search for coherence' to justify their group behaviour and social identification. They develop group beliefs, which serve to bind the group more closely together and also, importantly, to justify its practices towards 'outsiders'.

In this context, Gould (1981) showed how an important dimension to Nazi practices was their belief in genetic inferiority, supported by the bigoted and even fraudulent research of certain psychologists and biologists. By linking a belief in an 'evolution' of races and of the desirability of aggression, based on an extremely spurious biology, with a belief in genetic inferiority, based on an equally spurious psychology, the Nazis produced a set of cultural beliefs which allowed them to convince themselves that their murderous actions would benefit humanity. As Arendt (1963) showed, many of them confidently expected that the rest of Europe and America would share their views, and were surprised to find that they did not

Before the Second World War, Dollard *et al.* (1939) had developed a model of prejudice which saw it as the displacement of social frustration. Groups which were economically frustrated – perhaps by unemployment, impoverished housing conditions or other forms of social inequality, would use another group as the scapegoat for their frustrations. In support of this, Hovland and Sears (1940) analysed the incidence of lynchings of Black Americans in the rural areas of the southern United States. They found that the number of lynchings correlated with the price of cotton – the lower the price of cotton, the more lynchings had taken place. What was happening, they argued, was that the economic frustration being experienced by the white farmers was being vented on the black population.

We can see, then, that both individual and social factors are important in the expression of prejudice. Clearly, social phenomena like racism cannot be understood purely as the outcome of individual personalities, since social and cultural factors are so powerful. On the other hand, it is individuals who carry out these practices. Tajfel (1969) proposed a model of prejudice which took the categorization underlying social identity as its starting point. Social identity theory is based on the idea that there are very real social differences between groups, and that some groups are much more limited in their access to power and to the resources of society. Because of this, social comparison and social beliefs reflect social and political factors.

A considerable amount of research has taken place which uses social identity theory as a useful framework for exploring the psychological dimensions of political conflict. For example, studies have investigated the perceived importance of religious, ethnic and political social categories among young people living in Northern Ireland (Cairns and Mercer, 1984); the different situations in which ethnopolitical identity in Northern Ireland is important and when it is not (Waddell and Cairns, 1986); and how living in a society in conflict leads to the ability to classify people as belonging to one 'side' or the other of the conflict (Stringer and Lavery, 1987).

Hunter (1991) investigated intergroup **attributions** in the context of

attribution theory *The explanation of social perception by examining how people allocate intention or meaning of the behaviour of others.*

1. There must be equal status for participants
2. There must be the potential for members of the two groups to make personal acquaintance
3. There must be contact with non-stereotypical individuals
4. There must be social support for contact between the groups
5. There should be some occasion for co-operative effort

Figure 7.20 Criteria for reducing prejudice. (Cook, 1978.)

the conflict between Catholics and Protestants in Northern Ireland. TV scenes showing Protestants and Catholics committing intergroup-oriented violence were shown to two groups of research participants, one Catholic, one Protestant. They were then asked to explain why the violence was taking place. In general, the two groups attributed their own sect's violence to external factors – i.e. it was provoked by circumstances – whereas they attributed the opposite sect's violence to internal factors – i.e. they are 'bad' or 'unfair'. This principle seems to be helpful in explaining why intergroup violence can escalate so much: a situation of intergroup hatred evolves, not simply from opposing points of view, but from a long history of differently perceived retaliatory acts.

Describing how intergroup prejudice occurs is one thing: working out how it can be changed is quite another. Cook (1978) described five main criteria which need to be met if social prejudice is to be seriously challenged and these are listed in Figure 7.20. Looking at them, we can see that one of the prerequisites for eradicating social prejudice would be a society in which one group is not seriously disadvantaged by comparison with another: the idea that the participants would need to have equal status, for example, may well be accurate, but is difficult to achieve easily in societies which have systematically disadvantaged one group economically and socially.

Environment

A much-quoted study of equal status contact was performed by Deutsch and Collins (1951), who compared two kinds of housing projects. One project was thoroughly integrated, with black and white residents being assigned to houses regardless of their race. The other housing estate was segregated. The researchers interviewed residents in both projects and found, not surprisingly, that casual and neighbourly contact between the racial groups was higher in the integrated estate. They concluded also that this contact was accompanied by a decrease in racial prejudice on the part of the white residents, thus supporting the equal status **contact hypothesis**.

contact hypothesis *The idea that prejudice can be effectively reduced simply as a result of two groups having frequent contact with one another. In practice, however, there are other conditions which also need to be met, such as that the two groups would have equal status.*

However, there is some evidence which challenges this approach, though not with that particular housing estate. For example, Stephan (1978) evaluated the short-term consequences of school desegregation policies in the United States and claimed that the evidence did not

The pursuit of common goals has stimulated the development of the **jigsaw classroom technique** by Aronson *et al.*, 1978. In this technique, children are assigned to small inter-racial learning groups in which each member is given material that forms one piece of the lesson to be learned. Each child has to learn their particular information AND communicate it to the other members of the group. The child is eventually tested on all the available information so it becomes essential to communicate effectively with group members to find out their piece of the jigsaw. Aronson claims that the method has a number of positive consequences including enhanced self-esteem, improved academic performance, increased liking for classmates and the reduction of negative inter-racial perceptions. He goes on to note, however, that the improved perceptions of particular members of different ethnic groups were not generalized to the group as a whole.

Figure 7.21 The jigsaw technique.

support the idea that contact reduces prejudice. He noted that the prejudice towards black pupils showed very little reduction, while black prejudice towards white pupils had actually increased. The only positive consequence of the desegregation, Stephan argued, was the improved academic performance of the black pupils – although if one takes the long-term view into account, this is quite an important consequence!

There are other kinds of prejudice in society, too. For example, Sigelman *et al.* (1986) performed an investigation of attitudes towards women in Britain. In their study, people were given fictitious profiles of election candidates and asked which candidates they would vote for. The researchers found that male voters discriminated against female candidates, describing them as less qualified, giving them ratings and voting for them less. Female voters, on the other hand, chose evenly between male and female candidates.

Social identity

Social identity theory was developed by Henri Tajfel and forms one of the main theories in 'European' social psychology. Essentially, social identity theory states that the social groups and categories to which we belong constitute an important part of our self-concept, and that therefore a given individual will at times interact with other people, not as a single individual, but as a representative of a whole group or category of people. This means that someone may shift from interacting with another on a personal level to interacting in terms of a social identification even during the course of a single conversation, if circumstances warrant it. In business meetings people sometimes suggest that they are wearing 'a different hat' to convey the idea that they are adopting a different social identity.

categorization *The first stage in the process of social identification, which involves grouping other people into social categories or sets. Research shows that such categorization in itself, even if based on minimal criteria, can lead to a strong bias in favour of the in-group.*

social comparison *The process of comparing one's own social group with others, in terms of their relative social status and prestige. Social comparison is important, in that people will tend to distance themselves from membership of a group which does not reflect positively on the self-esteem by comparing favourably with other groups.*

self-esteem *The evaluative dimensions of the self-concept, which is to do with how worth while and/or confident the person feels about themselves.*

There are three fundamental psychological processes underlying social identification. The first of these is **categorization** – a basic tendency to classify things into groups. Categorization of both animate and inanimate stimuli has been shown to result in an exaggeration of the similarities of those in the same group and an exaggeration of the differences between those in different groups. This means that when we categorize people, we accentuate the similarities to ourselves of people in the same group and exaggerate the differences from ourselves of people in other groups.

The second psychological process is that of **social comparison**. Social groups do not exist in isolation, but in a social context in which some groups have more prestige, power or status than others. Once a social categorization has been made, the process of social comparison means that the group is compared with other social groups and its relative status is determined. Social comparison also results in a tendency for members of a given group to take more account of the beliefs and ideas expressed by members of their own group, and to disregard the beliefs and ideas of people from different groups. This is partly because we have more social contact with members of our own group and so have a better understanding of them, and partly because the group is, by definition, composed of people who are regarded as being 'like' the self.

The third psychological mechanism underlying social identity concerns the way that membership of social groups affects the self-concept. Through social comparison, people weigh up how their social group compares with others. According to Tajfel and Turner (1979), people seek to belong to groups which will reflect positively on their **self-esteem**, since maintaining positive levels of self-esteem is a basic motivation for human beings. If the group does not compare favourably with others, so membership of it results in a lowered self-esteem, then people will seek to leave the group or to distance themselves from it. If leaving the group is impossible, then they may look for ways that group membership can provide a positive source of self-esteem, either by attempting to change the group's status or by adopting some other strategy, like emphasizing comparison with another group of lower status rather than with higher, unreachable groups.

Key reference: TAJFEL, H. and TURNER, J. C. (1979) An integrative theory of intergroup conflict. In W. G. Austin and S. Worchel (eds) *The Social Psychology of Intergroup Relations*. Brooks/Cole, Monterey, Cal.

Figure 7.22 Using social identity to sell wine.

Butterfield (1989) described a British advertising campaign for Californian wine carafes, which had drawn on social identity to establish shared meanings between the consumers and the advertising figure. The advertisements drew on a well-known and very 'English' figure to present the wine, contrasting American slang phrases ('A red that knows where it's coming from') with British understatement ('It's really jolly good'). The advertising campaign consisted of two such television advertisements, and resulted in a hugely increased market share for the wine in those parts of the country which had experienced the advertising campaign.

Consumer

Qualls and Moore (1990) asked 103 black research participants and 107 white ones to watch an advertisement for a new beer, to rate the advertisement, the actor and the beer, and then to taste the beer and evaluate it. The advertisements were varied in terms of the race and social class of the people portrayed, and the research participants also varied along the same dimensions. Qualls and Moore found that, with regard to race, people tended to prefer those advertisements portraying the same social group: white research participants viewed white actors more positively than black actors, and black research participants viewed black actors more positively than white ones. This was consistent over social class and also influenced how the product was rated. The researchers saw this as an example of in group bias resulting from social identification, although it is important to remember that these were extreme examples – the experimenters did not investigate the effects of mixed groups portrayed in advertisements, for instance.

Social identifications occur in working life, too. Hayes and Stratton (1992) suggested that human resource management could be usefully understood in terms of social identity theory. Many of the existing practices recommended as 'good' management practice could be seen as being ways of encouraging members of a working group or team to form

Work

positive social identification with the organization. Hayes and Stratton presented a model of consultancy in which three aspects of social identity theory were operationalized in terms of managerial tasks. One of these was the setting of clear 'in group/out group' boundaries, so that people could all feel that they were working as a team against their external competitors. Another was to firm up intragroup cohesion, through effective formal and informal communication. The third was to provide people with opportunities for enhanced self-esteem by encouraging people to feel proud of belonging to their working team or to the organization.

Health

Social identification forms an important contribution to the self-esteem. Zani (1987) showed that social identification played a crucial part in understanding psychiatric nurses' responses to changes in the psychiatric services. In a study of 331 nurses involved to different extents in the process of decentralization of psychiatric services, Zani found that the nurses adopted a number of distinctive strategies to maintain a sense of group distinctiveness in the face of these changes. By insisting that they were a special, distinct group, they were able to make sure that they could retain their own sources of self-esteem and their professional values.

Society

Deyhle (1986) performed a three-year study of social identifications among members of three different ethnic communities: Ute; Navajo; and Anglos. Part of the study focused on the popularity of break dancing among Ute and Navajo teenagers. Deyhle proposed that the Native American students turned to breakdancing to emphasize their social identification. By having a distinctive form of dance at which they could excel, they were able to express their own uniqueness while at the same time developing a feeling of belonging to a distinctive group and a shared communication with others in that group. In part, Deyhle argued, their emphasis on breakdancing was a response to the continual academic failure and social isolation which they experienced as members of an ethnic minority. The breakdancing provided them with a way of achieving success in a community environment which was otherwise indifferent to them.

The fact that people belong to more than one social group in society also means that they can categorize themselves in more than one way. Sometimes, this can give people the opportunity to emphasize their membership of a positive group, rather than one with a more negative social status. In a study of women living in senior citizen homes, for instance, it was found that those who participated regularly in a course of gymnastics were less likely to see rigid distinctions between stereotypes of 'the old woman' and 'the young woman', than elderly people who did not engage in gymnastics. The idea was that belonging to the gymnastic group, which had a positive social status, compensated for personal effects of belonging to a low-status group (Rehm, Lilli and Van Eimeren, 1988).

One of the predictions of social identity theory is that those who are unable to derive positive self-esteem from membership of their social group will seek to leave that group or to distance themselves from it. In this context, it is interesting to note that as early as 1957, Hertzberg *et al.* described a continuum of withdrawal behaviour in the working context, which ranged from absenteeism to the decision to leave the job altogether and included membership of countercultural groups. Lyons (1972) reviewed studies of absenteeism and staff turnover, and came to the conclusion that the available evidence supported the idea that these behaviours were linked in a kind of continuum of withdrawal.

Work

However, Porter and Speers (1973) suggested that there might be a case for regarding absenteeism and staff turnover as different, alternative behaviours, rather than being two ends of a continuum. For many employees, leaving would not be an option owing to the economic consequences. Such people would therefore fall back on absenteeism as an alternative withdrawal strategy. If, as Hayes and Stratton (1992) suggested, good management behaviour can be construed as maintaining positive social identification within the working group, it follows that failing to maintain positive social identification would result in withdrawal: the implication being that a high rate of turnover and absenteeism is a pretty reliable indicator that something is seriously wrong with the approach to management in that group or company.

Hayes (1991) argued that the degree to which an organizational culture would be adopted by members of that organization is intimately linked with the social identifications made by its members. Following the model suggested by Van Maanen and Barley (1985) of organizational cultures as collections of smaller working groups, which share the general assumptions and beliefs of the culture to a greater or lesser degree, Hayes showed how social identification involves adopting the beliefs and ideas of the in-group. In a 'strong' organizational culture, in which smaller working groups share many if not all of the beliefs of the organization as a whole, this leads to people identifying with the general organizational culture itself and so perpetuating the culture in their everyday working practices. In a weaker, more fragmented culture, social identification with the working group can lead to the emergence of 'canteen cultures', with practices and goals which are very different from the expressed goals of the leadership of the organization.

Education

Social identification does not just involve favouring the in-group: it also often results in people seeing the members of their own group as very different, whereas members of other groups are seen as being pretty much the same. Lorant and Deconchy (1986) studied the 'in-group/out-group' effects produced by different types of sports training. One group of French school-age children was given a rigorous, 'hard' physical training regime, designed to foster a very strong sense of identification and teamwork. A similar group was given a 'soft' physical training system. The researchers found that the children who had experienced the hard training system tended to over-evaluate their own performance and under-evaluate the performance of members of the other group. They also discriminated much less between the performances of the people in the other group.

It is a feature of social identification that differences between groups become exaggerated, particularly if the grouping is seen as relevant or significant to that particular context. McGarty and Penny (1988) asked research participants to listen to and evaluate a number of political statements. The statements were said to come from a number of different authors. McGarty and Penny found that people who had strong political views tended to judge the political statements in a more extreme way than people who were not interested in politics. Their judgements were even more extreme if the author of the statement seemed to be connected with, or representative of, the message itself.

Doise, Deschamps and Meyer (1978) asked research participants to rate people who were apparently being interviewed for a job. The people were of either white Canadian or Native American origin. The researchers found that when the research participants were asked to evaluate the people who were supposedly being interviewed, they tended to exaggerate those aspects of behaviour which fitted with their stereotypes of the social categories, but not the non-stereotypical behaviours. By doing this, they made the members of the two groups seem more similar to one another and so accentuated the differences between the two groups.

Hewstone, Jaspars and Lalljee (1982) looked at the intergroup images of public and comprehensive schoolboys, and proposed that group identifications had also influenced the attributions which the boys made for success or failure. In the first part of the study, all the schoolboys were asked to write essays about how they and the boys from the other type of school were similar or different. The two groups identified the same sorts of differences, particularly in relation to things like future prospects, social background and intellectual ability (Figure 7.23). In the second part of the study, the boys were asked to give reasons for why these differences happened. They gave very different types of explanations:

Public schools childrens' attributions of themselves and others

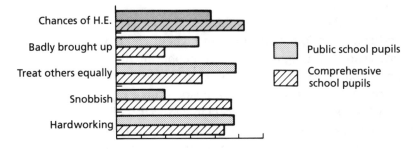

Comprehensive schools childrens' attributions of themselves and others

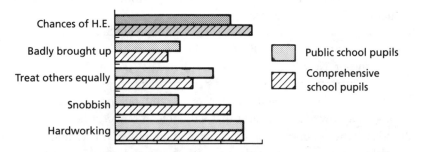

Figure 7.23 Attributions of school children. (Hewstone, Jaspus and Lalljee, 1982.)

public schoolboys were more likely to give attributions which explained the differences in terms of ability or skill, whereas comprehensive schoolboys tended to attribute them to luck.

Social and group norms

Belonging to social groups also means conforming to group norms. We learn how to behave, socially, from the other people around us, and that social behaviour is regulated by unconscious expectations about what counts as 'normal' or acceptable behaviour. These expectations are known as social norms. Conforming to social norms involves acting in ways which are predictable and appropriate to the social role which the individual is playing at the time. Goffman (1959) argued that when an individual is first learning a social role, they act out the part as if they were participating in a play; but that later it becomes internalized and part of their personal repertoire of social action. Garfinkel (1967), in a series of studies, showed that when people are faced with someone acting in a manner which is inappropriate to their role, they become agitated and sometimes even distressed.

The implicit but highly sophisticated understanding of social roles and role behaviour is learned throughout childhood, as a result of interaction with significant other people in the person's life. The peer group is the group of similar others with whom the individual is in contact, and this provides a major source of information about social expectations and acceptable social behaviour. Reference groups, also, provide social role models, particularly for those who have aspirations or ambitions in a given respect: a girl who is fond of music, for example, may take other musicians as her reference group when learning social behaviours pertinent to that interest; someone who is interested in sports may choose to model their behaviour on that of other sportspeople.

> **Key reference:** GOFFMAN, E. (1959) *The Presentation of Self in Everyday Life.* Anchor, New York.

The desire to be accepted by our peers and belong, rather than not belong, is a powerful motivator that will affect a range of behaviours and attitudes. One example comes from Witt (1969), who identified close friendship groups among male students at Pennsylvania State University

The gap of annoyance

Figure 7.24 Group norms. Somehow or other, we learn the norms of social behaviour. For example, how should we behave in a bus queue? If we stand too close to, or too far away from, the next person in the queue it creates annoyance in the other members of the queue.

and found that group cohesiveness significantly influenced the students' consumer decisions when it came to choices of beer and after-shave lotion, though not their purchasing decisions for deodorant and cigarettes.

Similarly, Witt and Bruce (1972) investigated 25 groups, each containing 3 or 4 women from Austin, Texas, who were already shopping companions or friends – participants had been asked to recruit 2 or 4 friends to participate in the study as well. The researchers investigated their brand choices for seven different types of product: cook-in-bag frozen vegetables; instant coffee; ground coffee; rug cleaner; laundry detergent and presoaker; and furniture cleaning spray. They found a **correlation** between what the women had decided to purchase in some of these categories and measures of group cohesiveness. The highest was frozen vegetables, with a correlation coefficient of 0.72 between the two variables, and the lowest was furniture spray, with a correlation coefficient of 0.45.

The researchers concluded that there were two important factors in the relationship between group cohesiveness and purchasing decisions. One was how conspicuous the product was – in other words, whether other people would see or know that the women were using it. Another was the nature and extent of the product's symbolic involvement with the purchaser's social interaction framework – cook-in-bag frozen vegetables say something about a certain kind of lifestyle (as compared with, say, earthy vegetables from a market which have to be cleaned and trimmed). The researchers concluded that some products are used to show social belonging, and the reference group is important in these, whereas others are used to define individuality.

correlation *A measure of how strongly two, or more, variables are related to each other.*

Figure 7.25 The type of food you decide to put in your shopping basket says something about how you see yourself and how you want to be seen.

It is a noticeable finding that younger people tend to be more readily influenced by reference groups than older people and this was illustrated in a study by What Park and Parker Lessig (1977). The researchers compared 100 Kansas women and 88 unmarried marketing students with respect to the way that different reference groups were likely to influence their brand choices. The students were consistently more susceptible to reference group influence on brand selection, and for a greater number of products, than the women.

Education

Cocanougher and Bruce (1971) investigated the attitudes of 114 male undergraduates towards a business career. Each participant was given two identical decks of cards, with the name of a product printed on each card. They were asked to sort each deck, from most to least descriptive of what the person intended to own five years after graduation. Then they were asked to sort them again, for what was owned by a typical business executive. The researchers found a high correlation between identification with the reference group, as measured by the matching of the two decks, and the undergraduates' attitudes towards having a business career.

Work

Roethlisberger and Dickson (1939) performed a number of observations of working groups at the Hawthorne works of the Western Electric Company in Chicago in the early part of the 20th century. One of these observations – the 'Bank Wiring Observation Room' study – provided a detailed account of the way that group norms could influence how people behave at work. (See 'Motivation' in Chapter 6 for a further discussion of the Hawthorne studies.)

The Hawthorne studies had been concerned with exploring ways to increase output at work. In other parts of the factory, various strategies had been shown to improve work output. But in the bank wiring room, the existence of a long-standing group with particularly strong group norms meant that the group kept up a steady output, regardless of the manipulations of the researchers. The group's norms could be summarized in three main points, which are listed in Figure 7.26. Since the

Figure 7.26 Group norms. (Roethlisberger and Dickson, 1939.)

1. A member of the group should work at the same rate as other members of the group. Working too hard or too little would put pressure on other members of the group, either to keep up or to make up the slack, and so this was unacceptable.
2. A member of the group should never say anything to a superior in the work hierarchy which might have the result of getting a colleague into trouble.
3. People in positions of authority, such as the group foreman or others, should not act officiously.

members of the group were spending almost all of their working time together, these norms operated powerfully to ensure that a steady output was maintained throughout the period of investigation.

Hill and Trist (1962) investigated 'accident repeaters'. While accidents at work may happen to anyone, it is demonstrable that they occur far more frequently with some people than with others. Hill and Trist suggested that this might be construed in terms of group norms and compliance – or, rather, refusal to do so. On investigating absenteeism and accident rates in a steel works in the early 1950s, they found that strong social norms operated as to which types of absenteeism were acceptable and which were not. Absences which had been certified (for example, by a sick note) were regarded as acceptable; unexpected ones and those due to accidents were not. Consequently, the researchers argued, the 'accident repeaters' were actually showing a form of withdrawal from work and a refusal to comply with group norms. It should be noted, though, that an attempted replication of these findings with workers in a photographic process plant failed to produce the same observations (Castle, 1956).

From the outside a group appears to be made up of a number of similar people doing similar things. But in the 1950s, a number of researchers adopted models of groups as having a social structure with a number of distinct roles for people to take on.

According to Watson (1980), the Israeli psychologist Teichman was part of a small unit near the Sinai front during the Yom Kippur War of 1973, and spent much of his time observing the leadership and group processes which were going on. At first, the formal leader was very much in command, mainly because what the group most needed was information and he was in charge of communications. Later on, however, other informal leaders gained prominence and provided better emotional support for the men. The topics of conversation changed, too: at the start of the week, information about such things as money, food and equipment made up 70% of all conversation, but this had dropped to 30% by

Society

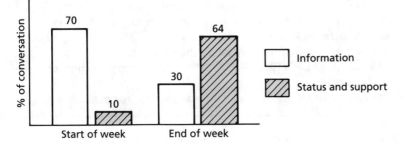

Figure 7.27 Changing pattern of conversation among Israeli troops during the Yom Kippur War of 1973.

Group task roles

Initiator-contributor   Recommends new ideas about, or novel solutions to, a problem

Information seeker   Emphasizes facts and other information from others

Opinion seeker   Solicits input concerning the attitudes and feelings about ideas under consideration

Information giver   Contributes relevant information to help in decision making

Opinion giver   Provides own opinions and feelings

Elaborator   Clarifies and expands on the points made by others

Co-ordinator   Integrates information from the group

Orientor   Guides the discussion and keeps it on topic when the group digresses

Evaluator-critic   Uses some set of standards to evaluate the group's accomplishments

Energizer   Stimulates the group to take action

Procedural technician   Handles routine tasks such as providing materials or supplies

Recorder   Keeps track of the group's activities and takes minutes

Group building and maintenance roles

Encourager   Encourages others' contributions

Harmonizer   Tries to resolve conflicts between group members

Compromiser   Tries to provide conflicting members with a mutually agreeable solution

Gatekeeper   Regulates the flow of communication so that all members can have a say

Standard setter   Sets standards and deadlines for group actions

Group observer   Makes objective observations about the tone of the group interaction

Follower   Accepts the ideas of others and goes along with the group majority

Self-centred roles

Aggressor   Tries to promote own status within group by attacking others

Blocker   Tries to block all group actions and refuses to go along with group

Recognition seeker   Tries to play up their own achievements to get group's attention

Self-confessor   Uses group discussion to deal with personal issues

Playboy   Engages in humour and irrelevant acts to draw attention away from the task

Dominator   Attempts to monopolize the group

Help-seeker   Attempts to gain sympathy by expressing insecurity or inadequacy

Special interest pleader: Argues incessantly to further own desires

Figure 7.28 Roles in working groups. (Benne and Sheats, 1948.)

the end of the week. By contrast, talk about status, feelings and giving support had risen from 10% at the start of the week to 64% at the end.

A fairly typical set of group roles was developed by Beene and Sheats (1948) and is listed in Figure 7.28. Although these models of group behaviour became very popular, particularly as the basis for group exercises on management selection courses, many people found them unnecessarily restricting, in that they failed to take account of the dynamic nature of social groups, and the way that the roles in a group may shift about from minute to minute, depending on what is going on at the time. Instead, more recent research into groups has tended to look at group processes, rather than group norms.

One of these group processes is the phenomenon of **group polarization**. In 1961, a graduate student, James Stoner, showed that when people were acting as members of a group, they would often make far riskier decisions than they would when they were simply acting as individuals. The 'risky-shift' phenomenon, as it became known, attracted a considerable amount of research. One explanation which received some support was the diffusion of responsibility hypothesis put forward by Wallach, Kogan and Bem (1962) – the idea was that the group members felt less individually responsible for the end result and so were more daring than they might have been.

One of the reasons for the interest in risky-shift was because it contravened the idea that groups would always tend to act conservatively and seemed to suggest that the opposite was true. In 1969, however, Moscovici and Zavalloni showed that sometimes groups would make more conservative decisions. What actually happened was that groups would polarize decision-making, either towards safety or towards risk. Which it was would depend on the initial stance of the group: groups which were in favour of approaching the problem cautiously at the beginning would tend to become more conservative, while those in favour of taking a chance would show the risky-shift.

Moscovici and Zavalloni suggested that one reason for group polarization is that the group discussion provides people with additional information, so that they can clarify their ideas and become more aware of why they are either in favour of a cautious approach or of a risky one. It also – perhaps more importantly – allows people to become aware of whether risk or safety are more likely to gain social approval from the group members.

In a different context, it has been found that anonymity may sometimes produce polarization of attitudes. Lea and Spears (1991) reported that groups of research participants who were asked to communicate with one another using computers tended to produce more polarized

group polarization The observation that people will often make more extreme decisions when they are working in a group than the members of such a group would make as individuals. Such decisions may be more extreme in either direction: they may be more risky or more conservative.

decisions than groups who interacted with one another in a face-to-face setting.

We are all affected by social norms to some extent – even those who engage in anti-social behaviour. There are many public perceptions about criminal activity but relatively few studies – hardly surprising, since a request for 'people engaged in crime' is not likely to get many volunteers coming along to a psychology department. In one study, however, Cromwell *et al.* (1991) were able to look at group effects on the decision-making of burglars. They interviewed 30 self-confessed active burglars, between 16 and 43 years old, over a period of 16 months. The burglars were asked to evaluate a number of sites which had been burgled, either by the respondent or by someone else.

The researchers found that when the burglars evaluated the sites by themselves they tended to see them as more vulnerable to burglary than if they evaluated them in a group – in other words, the group made the burglars more cautious in their judgements. On the other hand, the interviews with the burglars revealed that they committed more crimes when working as part of a group than when working alone. The other finding from the interviews was the report that the burglars concerned felt greater apprehension and anxiety when they were working in groups than they did when they were working alone.

groupthink *The way that a committee, members of a club or other group of people may become divorced from reality as a result of their own special consensus. Groupthink means that they may make decisions which are dangerous or stupid because the group fails to question their own assumptions or to take into account unwelcome aspects of reality which may have a bearing on the situation.*

One of the most disturbing features about how people operate in group concerns the phenomenon of **groupthink**, identified by Janis in 1972. Janis studied a number of poor decisions made by high-level decision-making groups where the consequences had been disastrous. He looked at a number of decisions by American presidents that history has shown to be blunders, such as President Kennedy's decision to back a group of exiles in their attempt to invade Cuba which was then under the new administration of Fidel Castro. They landed at the Bay of Pigs, and the exercise was a total disaster both militarily and diplomatically. Another 'blunder' was President Johnson's decision to escalate the Vietnam War in the middle of the 1960s. Janis also investigated some disastrous business decisions, for example, the decision to market the drug Thalidomide which led to thousands of birth deformities, and the decision of the Ford Motor Company to market the Edsel, which was one of the greatest failures in the history of mass produced car manufacture.

Janis noticed that there were a number of similarities in the decision-making processes which had produced these incidents and identified eight symptoms of groupthink, which are listed in Figure 7.30. In particular, the group had defined itself in such as way as to make sure that it was not open to external, realistic information, and was making its decisions on the basis of a highly consensual and unrealistic view of what

One feature to note here is the description of a decision as 'risky' or 'bad', or a result of 'groupthink'. All of these descriptions are applied after the event and the judgement is affected by the consequences of the decision. If, for example, the dramatic military escalation of the Vietnam War ordered by American President Johnson had resulted in a speedy resolution of the conflict and increased stability in the area, then it would not be judged as a bad decision. It has to be noted that the consequences of a decision do not always match the quality of the decision making. Sometimes you get lucky and sometimes you get very unlucky. This problem is perhaps best described by considering accidents. When we are driving a car, we often make minor errors of judgement, but only sometimes do they result in an 'accident'. The accident only follows the error if there are a number of other factors in the environment that happen at the same time; in other words, you are unlucky. So, to study errors by looking at accidents misses the vast majority of cognitive slips that could result in accidents. Likewise, to look at group decision making from examples of where it went wrong ignores the many errors or deficient discussions that precede decisions.

Figure 7.29 The judgement of history.

1. **Illusion of invulnerability**   The highly cohesive decision-making group members see themselves as powerful and invincible. Their attraction to and faith in the group leads them to ignore the potential disastrous outcomes of their decision.

2. **Illusion of morality**   Members believe in the moral correctness of the group and its decision. Members view themselves as the 'good guys' and the opposition as bad or even evil.

3. **Shared negative stereotypes**   Members have common beliefs that minimize the risks involved in a decision or belittle any opposing views.

4. **Collective rationalizations**   Members explain away any negative information that goes against the decision of the group.

5. **Self-censorship**   Members suppress their own doubts or criticisms about the decision.

6. **Illusion of unanimity**   Members believe, mistakenly, that there is a general consensus for the decision because there are no alternative views being expressed.

7. **Direct conformity pressure**   When an opposing view is expressed, pressure is exerted to get the dissenter to agree to the decision.

8. **Mindguards**   Some members protect or insulate the group from any opposing views or negative information.

Figure 7.30 The eight symptoms of groupthink. (Janis, 1972.)

was really going on in the world. Because the groups were so cohesive – usually because of their desire to placate or keep in with an exceptionally strong leader – the members' desire to maintain cohesiveness had overridden the uncomfortable and disruptive process of criticism.

That does not mean that groupthink is inevitable in social groups, although it does seem to happen quite often. But a number of studies have shown that dissenting minorities can be valuable to a group's decision-making. It has been found, for example, that when a minority persists in its judgement, and argues its case, the group as a whole tends to make more thoughtful and creative decisions compared with when there is no minority influence – in other words, minority influence encourages a more active consideration of the problem and leads to a better quality decision. Also, some studies have shown that when people are exposed to a consistent minority view, they remember the information better than if they are only exposed to a majority view or to a set of changing viewpoints. Zimbardo and Leippe (1991) suggested that there are three qualities necessary for effective minority influence: the minority must appear confident; it must avoid appearing rigid and dogmatic; and it must be skilled at social influence.

Leadership style

An early theory of leadership is that leaders fall naturally into two types: one concerned with the task demands of the group; and the other concerned with the interpersonal and social dynamics of the group's functioning, and with maintaining high levels of motivation among group members. As early as 1939, Roethlisberger and Dickson showed that supervisors who concentrated most strongly on production had departments which were less productive than those with supervisors who were concerned with maintaining positive social relationships in the work force. Some saw this as a fundamental distinction between different types of managers: that most managers were either interpersonally considerate towards their staff or highly task-oriented, but rarely both. Bales and Slater (1955) argued that a typical functional group would generally have two leaders, each of which fulfilled one of these functions but not the other.

This idea was challenged by a number of researchers. Blake and Moulton (1982) disputed the idea that the two qualities were mutually exclusive, arguing that effective leadership actually required both qualities and could readily be combined in the same individual. Studies of the most effective leaders, they argued, showed that these were people who scored highly on both dimensions of leadership. The idea of the single consistent leader was also challenged. Other researchers suggested that, rather than just having a single leader (or even two), groups will choose whichever of their members has the qualities required for dealing with the current situation. So a group may have several different leaders, depending on how the situation varies. Moreover, the research suggested that the different approaches might be more to do with leadership style, than fixed and invariant traits.

Key reference: BLAKE, R. R. and MOULTON, J. S. (1982) Theory and research for developing a science of leadership. *Journal of Applied Behavioural Science,* **18**, 275–92.

The relative effectiveness of leadership styles was illustrated in what became a classic study of a boys' after-school hobbies club, in which leadership styles were systematically varied and produced differing outcomes. Lewin, Lippitt and White (1939) divided those attending the club into three groups. One group was given an **authoritarian leader**, very task-oriented and strict, who supervised the boys closely. The second group had a 'democratic' leader, who operated by means of discussion and consultation, showing a personal interest in what the boys were doing, and listening to their ideas and opinions. The third group had a *laissez-faire* leader, who left the boys very much alone, working without guidance.

Education

authoritarian leaders
Leaders who act in an autocratic fashion, giving commands and directing action without showing interest in the views of their subordinates, unlike 'democratic' leaders.

Under the autocratic leader, the boys worked hard while supervised, but stopped work when they were not being watched. They operated individualistically and in competition with one another. Under the democratic leader, co-operation was more the norm, and the boys would help one another out and offer ideas. They also worked steadily, regardless of whether the leader was present or not. Unlike the other two groups, this group also showed a high level of morale: the boys were cheerful and friendly, and stated that they enjoyed what they were doing. The boys with the *laissez-faire* leader did very little work at all. Rotation of the leaders around the groups showed that these outcomes did seem to relate to the style itself, rather than simply resulting from the personalities of the people concerned. The choice of the term 'democratic' by Lewin *et al.* to describe the successful leader can be interpreted as an attempt to endorse the political system of the United States. The activities of this leader could just as easily have been called 'socialist' – encouraging debate and co-operation – and the results of the study would have been seen very differently.

Certainly, there seems to be a great deal of evidence that purely autocratic leaders do not tend to be very successful. During the Vietnam War there were some incidents of 'fragging', in which officers were assaulted or sometimes killed by the soldiers in their command. It was noted that this usually occurred to officers who had considerably less combat

Society

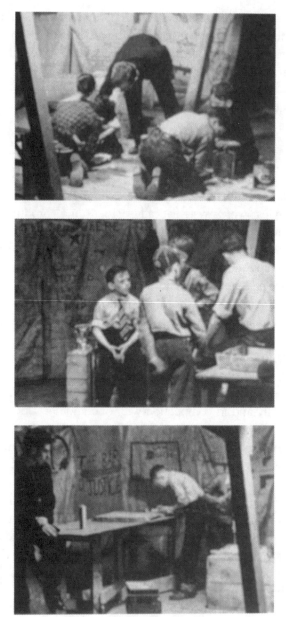

Figure 7.31 The three leadership styles used in the Lewin, Lippett and White study, 1939. They are autocratic (top), democratic (middle) and laissez-faire (bottom).

experience than their NCOs and who had demanded that their troops carry out a manoeuvre the troops believed to be impossible.

Clarke (1953) found that effective military squads shared a better 'emotional climate' than ineffective ones. This was not, however, a simple matter of friendship patterns. Clarke found that a soldier in the effective squads might choose one colleague to spend the night in a bunker with, but then chose entirely different squad members as people they would want to go on leave with. Clarke suggested that this confirms the idea that there are several human relations functions which have to be successfully carried out if the squad is going to be effective.

Some studies of leadership style are difficult to interpret because of the way that the same form of language can set up different expectations. For example, Sadler (1968) showed that, although most employees in an interview study said that they preferred a participative leadership style, a significant number said that they preferred an authoritarian style. In fact, the blue collar workers were much more likely to say they preferred authoritarian styles of leadership than were the white collar workers. But the research did not go on to investigate exactly what the employees meant by 'authoritarian' – whether they were saying that they wanted a leadership style in which they were never consulted or whether they were saying that they wanted clear decision-making from their leaders. Without identifying more precisely the meaning underlying the choice of language, it is impossible to know how findings of this kind should be interpreted.

Work

Field experiments tend to show that supervisors with a more participative style are more effective, and more likely to promote satisfaction among their employees, than those with an authoritarian style. For example, Vroom (1962) studied delivery men at 27 different stations and showed that those who had participative supervisors were far more likely to meet delivery quotas than those who had authoritarian or more distant ones. However, laboratory studies of leadership style have consistently failed to find differences between the two. Although some theorists have taken this as implying that the finding is somehow not valid, it is possibly more useful to argue that this tells us something about the lack of validity of laboratory studies.

Leadership behaviour in sport is often seen in terms of the behaviour of the coach, and the relationship between the coach and the team members. Danielson, Zelhart and Drake (1975) gave an extensive coaching behaviour questionnaire to American school ice hockey players in an attempt to discover the dimensions of leadership behaviour in ice hockey coaches. The responses of the players were analysed to reveal eight general dimensions of coaching behaviour, which are listed in Figure 7.32. The most striking finding of the research, and one that contradicts some of the more lurid popular perceptions of coaching behaviour, was that the behaviour of the coaches was largely communicative in nature, rather than domineering or aggressive.

Sport

The leader of a team is often thought to be responsible for the climate of the group and in sports this climate might give a team the edge to win matches. Fisher, Mancini, Hirsch, Proulx and Staurowsky (1982) designed

Dimension	Description
Competitive training	Behaviours associated with training, performance and motivation
Initiation	Behaviours associated with an open approach to solving problems using new methods
Interpersonal team operation	Behaviours associated with getting members to work together for efficiency
Social	Behaviours associated with social interaction outside athletics
Representation	Behaviours concerned with representing the team favourably in contacts with outsiders
Organized communication	Behaviours associated with a concern for organization or communication with little concern for interpersonal support
Recognition	Behaviours concerned with feedback and reinforcement as rewards for performance and participation
General excitement	Behaviours associated with arousal and activation: involves a disorganized approach to team operation

Figure 7.32 Dimensions of coaching behaviour.

a study to look at the link between the interactions of coaches and athletes, and the feelings of satisfaction. American school basketball players were videotaped at practice and also asked to complete a social climate scale. The videos were coded into a number of verbal and non-verbal behaviour categories. The results showed that athletes who were members of teams with a high satisfaction rating received more praise and were more likely to initiate communication with the coach. Coaches of these high satisfaction teams often designed creative and imaginative practices, and spent very little time just getting information across.

Smith, Smoll and Curtis (1979) attempted to improve the performance of baseball coaches through a training programme. They developed a list of coaching behavioural guidelines (do's and don'ts) and gave them to an experimental group of coaches. Throughout the season the coaches were given feedback on their behaviour and encouraged to use this feedback to help them implement the do's and don'ts list. The research looked at the results of the teams, the players' perceptions of the coaches, and the players' self-esteem levels; these were recorded and compared with another set of teams who were not using the training programme.

The researchers found that the coaches' behaviour improved, along the lines of the advice that they had been given. They also recorded that the players had more positive perceptions of the coaches and themselves than did the players in the control teams. On the other hand – and perhaps most importantly – the results obtained by the teams were no different from those with 'untrained' coaches – as one sports fan put it, the players lost just as often but felt better about it.

Leadership and expectation

A different view of leadership is the idea that the quality of leadership is all to do with the expectations which the leader has about the work force. McGregor, in 1960, proposed that managers tended to hold either Theory X or Theory Y about their workers. Theory X was that workers were effectively lazy and would only work if they were made to; Theory Y was that workers liked to work, and would work hard and readily if they were placed in a situation where that was expected and appreciated. (See the section on Rogers' theory of personality in Chapter 2.)

Following on from this, House (1971) argued that people tend to live up to the expectations that the leader has of them: if they are trusted and treated as responsible adults, they act in trustworthy and responsible ways, but if they are treated as lazy and untrustworthy, they will tend to live up to these expectations. Moreover, House argued, the most effective leaders are those who make sure that those in their group can fulfil their own personal goals at the same time as those of the group – an idea congruent with treating group members of employees as responsible adults rather than simply followers of leaders.

Other theories of leadership see the leader as the manager of the group's values. Krech, Crutchfield and Ballachey (1962) described five characteristics of effective group leaders. These were: first, that they should be seen as belonging to the group; secondly, that they should maintain the qualities and beliefs of the group; thirdly, that they should provide role models for members of the group; fourthly, that they should be visibly helping the group to achieve its goals; and fifthly, that they should represent the group positively to outsiders.

Smith and Peterson (1988) argued that the leader's ability to articulate or exemplify the goals and the values of the group or organization is important in providing common goals with which all of the team members can identify. In other words, it is how the leader 'stands for' the goals of the group which is seen as the most essential feature of effective leadership in this model.

Key reference: SMITH, P. B. and PETERSON, M. F. (1988) *Leadership, Organisations and Culture*. Sage, London.

Work

Likert (1961) conducted a series of studies of departments within many different types of organization. The departments were assessed as 'good' or 'bad' using criteria such as productivity, the rate of absenteeism, staff turnover and employees' motivation. Likert found that 'good' departments tended to have supervisors who were 'employee centred', focusing on the interpersonal dynamics within the department, while the departments which were rated as 'bad' tended to have supervisors who concentrated solely on rates of production. Ironically, these departments scored less well on the production criteria, as well as on the other measures.

Stodgill and Coons (1957) performed a large-scale research project into supervisory behaviour, by collecting a total of 1800 statements about supervisory behaviour from a range of employees in different organizations. They combined these with the results of employee surveys to develop the leader behaviour description questionnaire. This showed that supervisory behaviours could be clustered into two major categories: 'consideration' and 'initiating structure'. The consideration dimension linked closely with the person-centred approach described by Likert, in that this dimension was concerned with the way that the supervisor related with the work force, such as whether ideas and opinions were sought on important matters, whether they were informed about changes or consulted about possible new developments. The initiating dimension, however, was to do with task centredness, and included behaviours such as a rigid approach to deadlines, authoritarian decision-making and a rigorous maintenance of standards.

Unlike Likert's findings, however, Stodgill and Coons found that the two dimensions of consideration and initiating structure were independent of one another. Where Likert had described employee-centredness and job-centredness in supervisors as opposites, in the sense that people would conform to one or the other style, Stodgill and Coons found that it was perfectly possible for the same individual to score highly on both dimensions – and, in fact, that the most effective supervisors were those who scored most highly on both dimensions. Those scoring low on both tended to be the most ineffective.

Society

It is not just in the organizational context that expectations can be so important. Lerner and Fiske (1973) showed how the expectations of therapists were crucially important when they were conducting therapy with people with severely disturbed backgrounds or from lower socio-economic groups. When therapists had accepted the idea that work with these clients was more difficult and had a poor prognosis, therapy tended to produce relatively poor outcomes. But when the therapists were unimpressed by this view and had sustained their beliefs that they could help whatever the circumstances, they had actually been very

effective, producing highly successful outcomes. These 'committed' therapists managed to convey optimism to their clients through their own attitudes and their non-verbal communication, and this was very different
from the unconscious messages transmitted by the others. They also
demonstrably invested more effort with these cases than did those who
perceived such work as difficult and unpromising.

Barbara Tizard, born 26 April 1926, London, England.

Barbara Tizard's first social science research project, at the age of
41, was a study of the interrelationships between the social structure
of residential nurseries, the quality of staff–child interactions, and the
language development of the child inmates. This involved weeks of
rewarding observation, from waking till bedtime. Her own experience of child rearing helped her to recognize the stranger aspects of
institutional environments, and led her to go on to contrast the rich
learning potential of the home with the supposedly more educational formal adult-child interactions at nursery school. It also led
her to a longitudinal study of the residential nursery children, who
are being followed into adult life. Because of her own experience of
adopting, she went on to studies of the diverse social identities of adolescents. She thinks that
students should not be afraid to draw on their own experiences in studying psychology.

An important aspect of expectation in leadership is the principle that
staff are able to act as responsible, autonomous individuals, making their
own decisions. Tizard *et al.* (1975) observed 13 residential nurseries, all
of which had been modernized to provide 'family group' care, in which
mixed-age groups of 6 children each had their own suite of rooms, and
their own nurse and assistant nurse. The nurseries varied considerably in
the amount of autonomy which they granted to the nurses running the
units. The researchers identified three main groups. The first group
consisted of small units which were effectively run centrally, by a
matron. Only routine decisions were made by the staff – all else was
referred. The days were strictly timetabled and the nurse would have
little autonomy, having, for instance, to ask permission to take the
children for a walk or turn on the TV set.

The second group comprised small units over which the staff had
considerable autonomy: shopping, cooking, making their own plans for
the day. This also spread to the children, who could move freely around

the house and garden. Although there was an overall matron in charge, the staff rarely referred decisions to her, unless it was something which they really did not feel able to handle. The third group of nurseries involved something in between these two extremes. The researchers found that the more autonomous staff spent much more time talking to children, playing with them, reading with them and giving information to them. Children in these units also scored higher on a test of verbal comprehension.

Staff autonomy does not just affect the staff themselves. It can also be an important feature in how far inmates of residential institutions are permitted the freedom to make their own decisions. Canter and Canter (1979) found a difference in how staff responded to disabled children in their care, depending on whether they were working in a small independent unit or in a small unit which was part of a larger institution. In the latter example, staff adopted more institution-oriented as opposed to child-oriented practices. The size of the unit itself was irrelevant: the degree of autonomy was what really counted.

Transactional and transformational leadership

More recent theories of leadership see leadership as being much more of a two-way process, involving interactions between the leader and those in subordinate positions. These fall broadly into two groups: transactional leadership, which is to do with how leaders and subordinates interact; and transformational leadership, which is to do with the role of the leader in providing a clear vision of the organization's direction and goals.

The concept of *transactional leadership* is based on the idea that leadership can be seen as a series of transactions between the leader and the team members. This focuses attention on the exchanges which take place between individual members and the leader, and suggests that it is the quality of the relationships between the leader and each individual team member which produces effective leadership. Issues like responsibility, fairness and the honouring of agreements are therefore extremely important in positive leadership, since they will determine the nature of the leader–member exchange.

Another, related concept of leadership emerged with the interest in organizational culture which dominated organizational research in the 1980s. *Transformational leadership* concerns the type of leadership needed in order to produce organizational change. Although it often draws on the idea of charismatic leaders – people with the personal qualities which inspire confidence and co-operation on the part of their subordinates – much of the work on transformational leadership has been concerned with the idea of the leader as the person who manages accepted meanings and assumptions within the organization. Since organizational culture is predominately viewed as shared assumptions about how the world works and why it is like it is (Schein, 1990), the role of the transformational leader is to manage the symbolic and practical life of the organization in such a way as to induce the acceptance of a different set of assumptions, so that organizational change can take place.

Key reference: BURNS, J. M. (1978) *Leadership*. Harper & Row, New York.

Williams, Podsakoff and Huber (1992) collected information from 369 people who worked in nursing homes, about the styles of leadership which they experienced and about the quality of the interactions which they had with their managers. By comparing various measures of both group and individual leader behaviour, they found that the transactional approach was far more useful in explaining people's attitudes towards their managers than the idea of leadership styles. People responded most strongly to the specific exchanges and interactions which they had with their manager, and took relatively little notice of the overall management style which the manager used towards the group.

Work

Deluga and Perry (1991) looked at the perceived quality of exchanges between managers and subordinates among a mixed group of 166 men and 202 women, who were mainly employed as managers or professionals. They found that managers who maintained a high quality of exchanges with their subordinates were also seen as being likely to take into account their views and ideas. They were also seen as being less likely to adopt authoritarian or extremely assertive strategies in managing their teams.

Interestingly, though, there is often quite a discrepancy between how leaders believe that they interact with their subordinates and how their subordinates actually perceive that interaction. Callan (1993) investigated 273 manager–subordinate pairs, drawn from middle management. Callan found that the managers in general believed that they communicated more often with their subordinates than their subordinates thought they did. This was particularly true of very task-oriented female managers and it was also the case that female subordinates reported a far lower degree of interaction from their managers than male subordinates did.

Society

Ragins and Sundstrom (1990) looked at gender differences in how people perceived the type of power which their managers had. Contrary to what they had expected, they found that people rated female managers as having higher levels of expertise than male managers did and also that male managers with female subordinates were rated as having the least impressive amounts of expertise.

Burns (1978) performed a study of major political leaders, looking at historical data as well as contemporary evidence. Burns concluded that these leaders, too, could be seen as either transforming or transactional in their approaches, with the transformational leaders sometimes presiding over periods of massive social change, during which time the basic assumptions about political and social reality across the country were altered. Burns' analysis took place before the Thatcher years in Great Britain, but it is easy to see how the model can be seen as an example of transformational leadership.

A possibly less confrontational example of transformational leadership was displayed by Bob Geldof, during the Live Aid campaign for emergency relief to starving people in Africa. Westley and Mintzber (1988) identified four dimensions which are useful in examining visionary leadership. The first of these is the aptitudes and acquired skills of the leader; the second is their background experiences; the third is the context of the organizations and institutions that they are working in and with; and the fourth is the larger social, historical and political context in which they are operating.

Westley (1991) discussed how Geldof's work provided a clear example of how visionary leadership could produce global change. Visionary leaders, according to Westley, are people who can perceive and manipulate structures, as well as interacting with the individual people and groups who make up the human context in which they are active. Westley discussed how Geldof's own personal background and experiences provided him with the skills which he used in the Live Aid work, and how his awareness of political and social structures enabled him to put in motion massive projects which were both dynamic and effective.

Westley does not refer to it in the article, but one very good example of how Geldof's past experiences facilitated his work with Live Aid was in his mastery of crowd control. One of the authors recalls seeing his band, the Boomtown Rats, perform on stage during the punk rock era, in the late 1970s. Unlike other punk rock bands of the time, the Boomtown Rats showed a striking awareness of crowds, and an outstanding ability to generate and control crowd excitement. These skills were to stand Geldof in good stead during the organization and performance of the Live Aid events, as did his clear and outspoken, but never self-interested, views.

Transformational leadership can be catching, it appears. Bass *et al.* (1987) studied New Zealand managers and showed how, where a manager was seen as transformational, their subordinates, too, were perceived as transformational by other members of the organization. And Waldman, Bass and Einstein (1987), also in New Zealand, showed that people who work for transformational leaders are particularly likely to receive positive performance appraisals when their turn comes round. These findings suggest that an approach to leadership which sees the work in terms of positive change and forward vision is one to which people will respond, and which they will often adopt as their own.

Summary

1. *Attitudes are consistent ways of looking at the world, which serve the functions of object appraisal, social adjustment, and externalization.*
2. *Theories of attitude change and persuasion were initially based on information-processing models, and more recently came to address the question of intentions as well.*
3. *Cognitive dissonance is a mechanism which often produces attitude change, as a result of an inescapable discrepancy between experience and attitude.*
4. *Theories of prejudice have ranged from individual, trait-based explanations to explanations based on power and inequality and society, reflected through social identity processes.*
5. *Social identification involves three fundamental processes: categorization, social comparison, and the need for group membership to be a source of positive self-esteem.*
6. *Social roles and group norms play an important part in social life, and often determine the type of interaction in which we engage with other people.*
7. *Early investigations of leadership distinguished between those who concentrated on social issues, and those who focused only on task demands, although later approaches suggested that good leaders combined the two.*
8. *Recent approaches to leadership focused on the importance of positive expectations in getting the best out of the work force, and on the idea of the leader as encapsulating the group's values.*

PRACTICE QUESTIONS AND ACTIVITIES – 7

Violating norms

You can learn a lot about social norms by deliberately breaking them. Mind you, it is important to choose very carefully which norms to break and where to break them. Here are some relatively safe suggestions.

1. When someone asks you how you are, give them a brief review of your general state of mind, health and bowel movements for the day so far.
2. Dress unusually for work or college. This does not mean hiring a zebra outfit, but just wear some clothes that would be unusual for you.
3. When you are visiting a friend, ask if you can make a telephone call. Then pretend to call your aunt in Australia and stay on the phone as long as you can. You can test your powers of ingenuity by carrying on a one-sided conversation with the dialling tone.

You might find it impossible to carry out any of these exercises because the power of social norms is so strong that you do not feel able to break them, even for a short while. If you do manage to try one of these exercises, observe how people react, and marvel.

Knowing your lemon

Go to the local greengrocers and buy ten lemons. No really, this will be OK. Then with a group of work colleagues/fellow students/friends carry out the following exercise. Everyone has to pick one of the lemons for themselves. Take your lemon, look at it, get to know it, look for any blemishes or quirks and basically get to know it as an individual. After five or ten minutes, when everyone has got to know their own lemon, put them all together in a bowl and mix them up. The task is to be able to find your lemon again. This might sound incredibly difficult (to say nothing of pointless!), but it will be easier than it looks. Only to the unknowing and unobservant do all lemons look the same.

Try and figure out how you knew it was your lemon, and try and list the distinguishing features. Then, if you still do not see any value in this exercise, take your lemon, get a bottle of tonic and go home!

PRACTICE QUESTIONS AND ACTIVITIES – 7

Informational appeals to change health behaviour

Research has suggested the following principles:

1. communication should be colourful and vivid rather than steeped in jargon and statistics;
2. communication sources should be prestigious and trustworthy;
3. discuss both sides if audience is not inclined to accept message and one side if audience is inclined to accept message;
4. strong arguments should be presented at the beginning and end of the message;
5. the message should be short, clear and direct;
6. state conclusions explicitly – do not leave them implicit;
7. extreme messages produce more attitude change, but only up to a point;
8. creating fear is only likely to produce short-term benefits at best and is likely to have a number of negative effects.

Your task is to use the criteria above to assess a piece of health promotion literature. How many of the research findings are adhered to? What explanation can you offer for not adhering to all of them?

The Yale model of communication

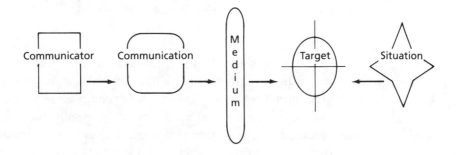

Use the Yale model to examine some popular advertisements and look for differences between the advertisements. In particular look for the following.

- Who is the communicator?
- What is the message?
- Who is the target audience?
- Look at a range of commercials, maybe one for a shampoo, one for a car, one for a beer and one for a food product.

8

Interacting
with
others

Introduction

We interact with other people almost all of the time, directly or indirectly. Even the presence of other people can influence our behaviour and a great deal of our everyday behaviour is carried in front of people without involving them in what we are actually doing. So, one of the first areas of psychological research which we will be exploring in this chapter is the way that the presence of other people can influence human behaviour.

The agenda of psychology is often set by social concerns and social problems. A pivotal event of the twentieth century for Western society was the Second World War (1939–1945) when an initial European conflict managed to involve a large proportion of the world population in warfare. During this conflict the combatants brought terror and destruction to civilian populations, and unthinkable acts of brutality and genocide were carried out. It was a direct challenge to Western society's belief that it was a civilized and advanced society. The subsequent attempts to make sense of this, and other similar events, have had a powerful influence on the focus of social psychology.

One of the social psychology studies that has caught the imagination is the demonstration of obedience to authority by Stanley Milgram. The key question is how far will we go when following orders from someone in a supervisory position over us. Milgram's frightening conclusion was that we will inflict pain and death on innocent people under no more justification than that a scientist told us to do it. The continuing history of barbarous acts against humanity alerts us to this possibility, but the startling feature of the Milgram study was that the perpetrators of these acts were ordinary citizens and not the deranged serial killers of popular fiction. Not surprisingly, it is difficult to design real life studies that do not contravene almost every ethical principle you can think of, but the implications are clear for organizations – if you put barriers in the way of dissent then people will be led to obey even ridiculous or damaging orders from their supervisors.

When social demands are not followed, the conflict which follows can sometimes be expressed as **aggression**. There have been several different psychological theories of aggression, ranging from the idea that aggression is an innate, instinctive characteristic of people to the idea that it arises from frustration and difficult situations. Most psychological research has focused on identifying those factors, like television, which can accentuate or exaggerate the aggressive behaviours which people sometimes show.

A certain amount of psychological research has been concerned with the way that aggression can sometimes be manifested by crowds – the old idea of 'mob psychology'. Crowds are usually perceived in a negative way by researchers, following a tradition which derives from political issues of social control and workers' demonstrations. More recent approaches in psychology, such as **deindividuation**, follow the old tradition of 'mob psychology' and aim to explain how the individual can behave quite differently in a crowd. Alternative models, however, have looked at collective behaviour in less emotive contexts, and at how situational factors and differing expectations influence crowd behaviour.

Another aspect of human behaviour, which was once thought to be intimately concerned with aggression, is the idea of **territoriality**. This concept has changed its meaning considerably since it was first developed from animal studies and now tends to focus on two aspects of human behaviour. One of these is the idea of 'ownership' of physical areas, while the other is to do with how close or distant we are from the person that we are interacting with. Breaking the unwritten rules of territorial behaviour can lead to social tension and possibly even conflict.

Although the agenda of psychology has been influenced by the definition of social problems, it has not been completely taken over by it. Not all social action is centred around conflict and aggression, and psychology has studied some of the more positive aspects of our behaviour and experience. Many people choose to take action that has no obvious benefit for themselves and which could sometimes result in personal loss or injury. This type of action is known as **altruistic behaviour** and psychologists have investigated several facets of altruism, such as the circumstances under which we are likely to help others and the factors which inhibit such action. In many aspects of our daily lives we co-operate with other people, and the chapter goes on to look at examples of co-operation. Strangely, a lot of research has been laboratory based, but there are a number of applications of co-operation research particularly in the fields of organization, therapy and sports.

aggression *A term used in several ways, but generally to describe negative or hostile behaviour or feelings towards others.*

deindividuation *A state of awareness where a person develops a changed sense of personal identity which, in particular, leads to a feeling of reduced personal agency (feeling that you are in control of your behaviour). The development of this state is often a response to conditions in the social environment.*

territoriality *The name given to a set of behaviours which involve establishing and maintaining access to a particular area, while refusing the same to potential competitors of one's own species.*

altruism *Acting in the interests of other people and not of oneself.*

In recent years, too, psychology has become increasingly concerned with the way that social living takes place within the human context of relationships. The quality of interpersonal relationships has a considerable effect on the way that we conduct our social lives and there are a number of factors that will seriously affect these relationships. Although this is one of psychology's 'newer' areas, it is one which is growing rapidly, as psychology recognizes the importance of relationships in almost every area of life.

The last section in this book looks at how a merger of cross-cultural psychology and anthropology is helping to explore how the wider social dimensions of living can influence social and personal life. Although much traditional psychology adopted a rather narrow 'Western' perspective, psychology is changing fast and there is an increased awareness of the importance of a pluralistic view of culture in social psychological research. This broadening of outlook has been reflected in many different aspects of psychology, and is enriching our understanding of human beings and their interactions considerably.

Audiences

One of the earliest experiments in social psychology was performed by Triplett in 1898, who asked children to turn a fishing reel as fast as they could. Triplett compared how fast children turned the reel when they were alone with how fast they would do it if there were other children doing the task as well and showed that this made a significant difference – they would turn the reel faster when others were present than they would when alone. Triplett referred to this phenomenon as 'social facilitation' and argued that the competitive element had meant that the children worked harder.

Further studies showed that competition was not necessarily as important as all that. In fact, the key feature in social facilitation seemed to be the presence of an audience, which appeared to be able to improve performance regardless of whether the task was competitive or not. Subsequent research showed that there was an interaction between the nature of the task and **audience effects**, finding that while a passive audience enhances performance on a simple motor task, it tends to inhibit performance on new and complex conceptual tasks. One interesting finding emerging from audience effect research was that the audience does not actually have to be present – simply telling people that others are present, or performing the same task, can lead to improved performance.

Zajonc suggested that audience effects occur because having an

audience effects *The way that people will often act differently when there are others present or observing than they would if they were alone and unobserved.*

Figure 8.1 Audiences encourage better performance.

audience increases the person's **arousal**. As we saw in Chapter 2, a familiar or easy task tends to be facilitated by increased arousal. But a complex, poorly learned or new task will tend to be inhibited by a high arousal levels. A complementary effect is found in the phenomenon of **coaction** – when people work side by side on similar or identical tasks and their level of performance improves. Research on coaction shows that it produces an improvement in the quantity of work, because people work harder, but that the quality of the work deteriorates. Zajonc suggested that coaction increases a person's arousal level, resulting in a competitive urgency to complete the task.

coaction *Describes the phenomenon where people work side by side on similar or identical tasks and their level of performance improves.*

Key reference: ZAJONC, R. B. (1965) Social facilitation. *Science,* **149,** 269–74.

Research into audience effects has a number of implications for those who are engaging in skilled activities which are observed by other people, such as sport or musical performance. One of these implications is the finding that tasks which are well learned seem to be less subject to performance impairment when there is an audience present, than tasks which are new or poorly learned. It seems likely, from this, that an audience will increase the performance of people who are confident of their skill, and impair the performance of those who are less skilled and less confident.

Sport

Bell and Yee (1989) investigated whether this effect was valid in a study of karate skills. A group of 16 skilled and 17 unskilled American karate students kicked a target as many times as possible, during 4 trials which each lasted for 15 seconds. They carried out this routine drill in the presence of an audience of karate experts and also without any audience being present. The results showed that the skilled karate students performed equally well whether they were alone or in front of an audience. But the unskilled students performed fewer kicks when they were performing in front of an audience. It seems that the unskilled students sacrificed performance to avoid an increase in errors.

It would be interesting, too, to note whether the fact that the audience was composed of karate experts made a difference – perhaps the novices were concentrating particularly on their technique because of the expertise of the audience and might have acted differently had the audience consisted of people whom the novices believed did not know anything about karate. Research into the different types of audiences, and their effects on sportspeople, shows that there are several different classes which will have different effects on performance. The five classes described by Streng (1980) are listed in Figure 8.2.

Education

The other issue which becomes relevant here is performance anxiety. Performing a task in front of an audience has a quality all of its own and we sometimes become unable to do what in any other situation would be easy. Steptoe and Fidler (1987) investigated stage fright in orchestral musicians. They asked 65 experienced professional orchestra musicians, 41 undergraduate music students and 40 amateur musicians to complete a number of questionnaires, which looked at different aspects of performance anxiety, such as musical performance anxiety, the person's own level of neuroticism and the number of everyday fears which they tended to experience. In addition, the researchers asked the research participants to describe their own feelings about performing in front of audiences

Figure 8.2 Types of audience. (Streng, 1980.)

1. **Passive spectators**	People who show no evidence of approval or disapproval
2. **Active positive spectators**	People who take a positive stance with respect to the performances of the player or team
3. **Active negative spectators**	People who take a critical or negative stance towards the performances of the player or team
4. **Imaginary spectators**	Audiences who are not really present, but are 'imagined' by the athlete or performer
5. **Co-actors**	Team-mates or other people working with or alongside the person concerned

and any behavioural coping strategies which they tended to adopt to help them to deal with the situation.

Steptoe and Fidler found that in all of the musicians, performance anxiety was related to neuroticism and everyday fears. The research participants particularly expressed fear of crowds and social situations, although, given the context of the study, that may not be too surprising. Essentially, then, what they found was that those people who tended to experience performance anxiety most keenly were people who tended to be anxious about other things as well: people who were phlegmatic by nature tended not to experience performance anxiety as badly.

Another interesting finding from this study was the way that performance anxiety also seems to be linked to aspects of cognitive style and attribution. As we saw in Chapter 2, the way that we think about events can have a serious impact on the amount of stress and anxiety that we feel, and Steptoe and Fidler found that performance anxiety was particularly linked to what the researchers called 'catastrophizing'. By this, they meant that the person tended to be inclined to imagine that something really awful and socially humiliating would happen if they failed to perform perfectly. Those who experienced less performance anxiety, on the other hand, tended to view the consequences of failure rather more realistically.

Society

The presence of other people has been shown to have an apparent effect on all manner of activities. For example, de Castro (1991) looked at how much people eat, to see whether the presence of other people influenced it. In this study, 315 people were asked to keep detailed diaries of their eating over a 1-week period. These research participants recorded everything they ate and drank, where they consumed it and with whom they consumed it. De Castro found that people were more likely to eat in the presence of others at weekends than during the week and that they also ate more food on those occasions. De Castro concluded from this that eating is affected by social facilitation.

However, it is not at all certain that this is an adequate conclusion to draw from the data, since there are a number of other variables involved when we compare social and individual meal-taking. For example, by definition people are more likely to engage in conversation during social meals, and this can easily result in their taking longer over the meal and eating more for that reason. Another factor is that social meals are more of an 'occasion' and so often involve far more food than would be necessary for eating to stay alive: the preparation and presentation of food has enormous cultural significance, and people will go to some trouble to present others with food which is attractive to eat. Moreover, at weekends there is often more time to prepare food than there is during the

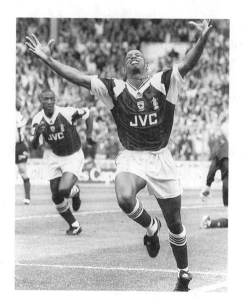

Figure 8.3 Black foot-ballers experience more hostility from crowds than their white team-mates and are more likely to have disciplinary problems on grounds away from home.

social facilitation *The observation that the presence of other people can influence how well they perform on a task, often improving their performance.*

Sport

week. So, to conclude that the reason why people eat more when in company is simply a function of **social facilitation** is rather simplistic, to say the least.

Audiences can have a dramatic effect on the performance of team sports players. Glamser (1990) investigated the number of disciplinary cautions received by football players during a single season. Looking at one London club it was found that the further the match was played away from London, the greater the likelihood that players would receive a caution during the game. The importance of venue for the game was particularly great for black players, who tend to experience the greatest level of hostility from the crowds. Glamser found that many black players, whose home disciplinary record was similar to that of white players, were almost seven times as likely be cautioned in out-of-London games. Glamser concluded that the behaviour of the audience was an important factor in this, although potential racism on the part of referees cannot be discounted as a possibility.

Conformity and compliance

Social conformity is the crucial ingredient of social living. It allows us to develop expectations of the behaviour of others and simplify the daily range of interactions that we encounter. Traditionally, confor-mity has been viewed by social psychology as a relatively negative quality, mainly due to the social context of the research, which was concerned with trying to explain the atrocities of the Second World War and the Vietnam War. For the most part, social conformity is often an acceptance of social responsibility rather than a character weakness, but there is also a point, as was shown at the Nuremberg trials, where blind conformity in the face of human cruelty becomes morally unacceptable.

In the classic experiments of Solomon Asch, a group of people were asked to make simple perceptual judgments in turn about comparative line lengths. Unknown to one person, the rest of the group were confederates of the experimenter and primed to give incorrect answers. Asch wanted to know how often the other person would deny the evidence of their own eyes. Asch found that the isolated person would conform in about one-third of the trials.

Inspired by the work of Asch, Stanley Milgram investigated the response of people to requests from an authority figure. In his classic demonstration of obedience he asked for volunteers to come to his laboratory at Harvard University to take part in a study into the effects of punishment on learning. The participants were unaware that the real purpose of the investigation was to measure the extent of their obedience in administering a series of electric shocks of increasing intensity to another person.

The results confounded the expectations of experts and ordinary people, because a majority of participants continued with the shocks, despite the screams of the person, to the end of the scale and only stopped when requested to by the authority figure. Although the other person was a confederate of the experimenter and the screams of pain that followed the shocks were pre-recorded, as far as the research participants were concerned, the effect was real.

The study generated considerable debate at the time of its publication and continues to provoke strong reactions today. It illustrates, as did the experiences in Nazi Germany, Vietnam and Cambodia, that destructive and life-threatening behaviour can be performed by ordinary people, not just by psychopaths. Milgram suggested that we respond to people in authority by suppressing our personal autonomy and denying responsibility for our own actions.

Key reference: MILGRAM, S. (1963) Behavioral study of obedience. *Journal of Abnormal Psychology,* **67**, 371–8.

In the Asch studies, the research participant had been in a room with several other people who all, very positively, gave the same wrong answer to a very easy problem. But that leaves us with the question of whether the conformity occurred as a result of the majority opinion or as a result of the physical presence of other people. Consequently

Obedience

In Milgram's study, the subject was required to give an electric shock of increasing intensity to a 'learner' every time the 'learner' made a mistake in a memory test. The learner, who was really a confederate of Milgram, was seated in another room, and made a number of complaints and screams as the intensity of the shocks increased. The diagram below shows a record of complaints made by the learner and the level of obedience shown by the subjects.

The cries of the 'learner'

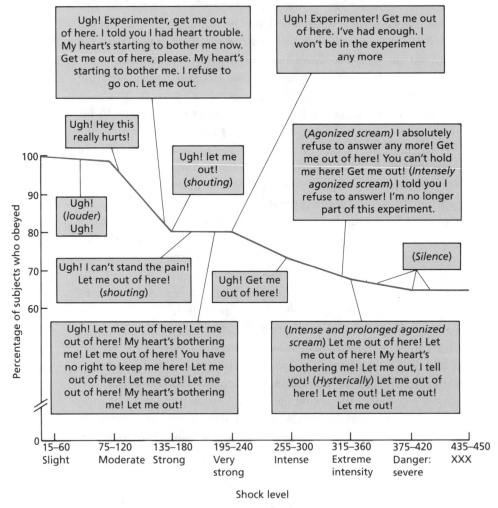

Crutchfield (1955) investigated whether the presence of other people was actually necessary to induce conformity.

Society

The research participants in this study were military personnel undergoing a management training course. They were made aware of the responses of 'other people' by a display of lights – each research participant was seated, alone, in a special booth. By manipulating these lights,

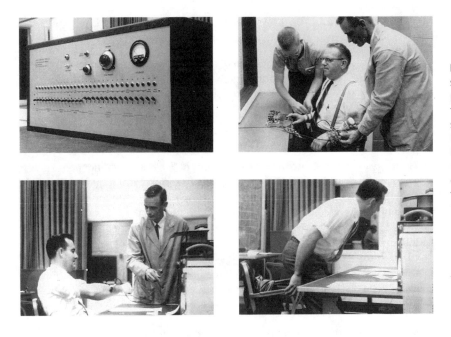

Figure 8.4 Milgram's study of obedience. The pictures show (clockwise from top left) the bogus shock generator used by Milgram, the 'learner' being strapped in ready to receive the shocks, a concerned 'teacher' leaving the study and an obedient 'teacher' following the instruction of the 'experimenter'. (© 1965 by Stanley Milgram. From the film OBEDIENCE, distributed by the Pennsylvania State University Audio Visual Services.)

Crutchfield was able to create a 'bogus majority' in the minds of the people under study, and again this majority would, unanimously, give the same wrong answer to an easy problem. Crutchfield found similar levels of conformity to those of Asch: under this sort of pressure, the research participants agreed with statements such as '60 to 70% of Americans are over 65 years old', 'The average American sleeps 4 to 5 hours a night', and 'The average American male has a life expectancy of 25 years'.

Crutchfield asked 'expert psychologists' to rate the various participants in the study on a range of personality scales, without having witnessed their performance in the test. When these ratings were correlated with the conformity trials, Crutchfield reported that they indicated two different personality profiles: 'independents' and 'yielders'. The differences between the two are listed in Figure 8.5. There are problems, though, with trying to classify people by type in this way, since people tend to respond differently in different situations. Our behaviour is affected by its context, as well as by the perceived consequences of certain behavioural choices. This was illustrated by the issues raised in studies by Perrin and Spencer.

Perrin and Spencer carried out three sets of replications of the Asch study. In the first replication (Perrin and Spencer, 1980) they used engineering undergraduates as the experimental stooges who had been instructed to give incorrect answers. The experimental participants were also engineering undergraduates. This replication produced no

According to Crutchfield, it is possible to identify 'yielders' and 'independents' who can be described as follows.

Yielders   Submissive, inhibited, indecisive, lacking insight into their own motivation and behaviour, confused, unadaptive under stress and exploitable.

Independents   More efficient, ascendant, resourceful, active, outgoing, unaffected, self-reliant, imaginative, masculine and sensuous.

A cursory glance at Crutchfield's descriptions of 'yielders' and 'independents' gives an insight into the value system of social psychology at the time. It clearly values independence over co-operation (or, in their words, yielding) and masculine over feminine. It is no surprise then that women were found to appear more often in the yielders category, along with members of ethnic minority groups. A particular quirk of the study is that the post-experimental interviews suggested that as many as 17 per cent of the people taking part had realized that a deception was taking place. Crutchfield does not indicate how this affected the experimental outcome.

Figure 8.5 Compliance in context.

conformity and the researchers initially concluded that it was 'a child of its time' – a product of the pressures towards social conformity in the 1950s.

This finding, however, was challenged by Doms and Avermaet (1981), who pointed out that engineering students were particularly inclined to value accurate measurement, so to use them as the participants in a study of conformity based on line judgements was to introduce a bias against conformity which did not show in replications performed with other students.

Following this, Perrin and Spencer (1981) performed two further replications, which did not involve students. In one, the experimental 'stooges' were probation officers and the experimental research participants were young men on probation. They had an average age of 19 and so were very different from the majority group on the basis of three factors: age; professional status; and power. In this case, Perrin and Spencer achieved conformity levels which were similar to those achieved by Asch. In the third replication, the experimental stooges were unemployed young men from inner London of Afro-Caribbean backgrounds, again with an average age of 19. The experimental participants were also Afro-Caribbean youths and the experimenter was white. In this case, too, the researchers obtained a similar conformity level to those obtained by Asch.

In each of these cases, the level of conformity which was being displayed by the research participants made extremely good social sense, given the situation and context. Perrin and Spencer argued that

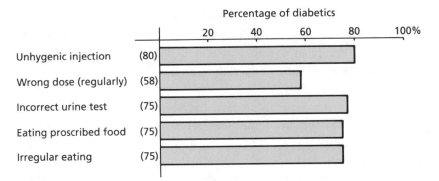

Percentage of diabetics

Figure 8.6 The self-reports of insulin administration and diet by diabetics. Wing *et al.,* 1986)

conformity is actually a socially adaptive strategy, rather than a social problem. They concluded that those social problems which are associated with conformity arise from people exploiting the social responsibility of their fellow citizens, not from a personal weakness in the general population.

In the area of health treatment, too, conformity is usually a manifestation of socially responsible behaviour. **Compliance** to treatment regimes is more important for some disorders than others. Some kinds of kidney failure (especially those requiring dialysis) and some kinds of **diabetes** need people to keep very carefully to special diets. In both cases noncompliance is a major problem. For example a survey of diabetics by Wing *et al.* (1986) reported that 80% of patients administered insulin in an unhygienic manner; 58% of them regularly administered the wrong dose of insulin; 77% tested their urine incorrectly or made incorrect interpretations of the result; 75% did not eat the prescribed foods; and 75% did not eat with sufficient regularity. Clearly, compliance is not as easy to induce as Asch suggested (Figure 8.6).

Developing an accurate picture of treatment compliance can be tricky, because the estimates which have been made about whether people conform to their treatment instructions vary widely. This is partly a matter of definition. Taylor (1990), for example, suggested that 93% of patients fail to adhere to some aspect of their treatment regimes, whereas Sarafino (1990) argued that people adhere 'reasonably closely' to their treatment regimes about 78% of the time for short-term treatments and about 54% of the time for chronic conditions. In other words, the two researchers were using different definitions: Taylor was talking about precise conformity to every detail of the recommended treatment; but Sarafino was allowing for the way that most people 'customize' their treatments to fit in with their own lifestyles, but recognize that they may still be complying with the general features of the treatment.

Health

compliance *The process of going along with other people – i.e. conforming – but without accepting the views on a personal level.*

diabetes *Type I diabetes involves a complete failure of the pancreas and requires insulin replacement by injection. Type II diabetes is far more common. In this condition individuals retain some endogenous insulin and are able to maintain homeostatic glycemic control through diet, weight management and oral medication.*

Sarafino also found that the average adherence rates for taking medicine to prevent illness is roughly 60% for both long-term and short-term regimes, but compliance with a requirement to change one's lifestyle, such as stopping smoking or altering one's diet, was generally quite variable and often very low. There are limits, it seems, to how far people will conform to medical demands if they seem to involve too great a change. Similarly, Sarafino found that people were much more likely to keep to scheduled appointments for medical treatment if they had made the appointment, than if it had been made by the medical practitioner. All this can be seen as linking very closely with the need for people to control their own lives, as we saw in Chapter 2.

Non-compliance to health requests is not just a Western phenomenon. For example, Barnhoorn and Adriaanse (1992) found a similar problem in India. They interviewed two groups of patients who had completed or not completed a tuberculosis control programme. The researchers found that the two groups were different in a number of ways. One of the most important was social support – people who had completed the tuberculosis control programme were more likely to report that at least one family member helped them in taking anti-tubercular medication. This is just one indication of the way that, in order to be effective, health professionals have to take into account a whole range of personal, relationship and social variables.

Consumer

In a different area of applied research, Venkatesan (1966) asked 144 male students to choose the 'best' suit from a selection of three identical suits. In the control condition, the research participants evaluated the suits individually, but in the experimental condition they were grouped with three confederates who had each been instructed to choose suit B. After examining the suits, each research participant had to state his choice, with the confederates giving their answers first, in the same way as they had in the Asch studies. The research participants were then interviewed. Venkatesan found that those people who were exposed to the group norm tended to conform by choosing the suit chosen by all of the others, whereas those who had not been exposed to the majority view were equally likely to choose any of the suits.

Weber and Hansen (1972) interviewed 232 white Florida women shoppers and asked them to describe their purchasing behaviour for five products: ground coffee; instant coffee; gelatin dessert; frozen orange juice; and toothpaste. The women were then categorized into groups on the basis of the preferences which they had expressed. Each research participant was sent a letter expressing appreciation for her co-operation and naming the most popular brand which had supposedly been selected from the three most frequently bought products – as 'feedback'

A particular example of non-compliance that has concerned health workers has been the reluctance of people to carry out simple screening exercises. For example, breast self examination (BSE) by women has been found to be useful in the early detection of breast cancer. Pitts and Phillips (1991) suggest that less than 30 % of British women carry out BSE despite the health advantages (see *Practice questions and activities* at the end of this chapter). There are many reasons for this 'non-compliance', and while some are to do with the cognitions and feelings of women, some are also to do with the way women are thought of and dealt with by the medical profession.

One attempt to increase BSE has been to increase the impact of health education messages by emphasizing the gains of BSE rather than emphasizing the losses of not carrying out BSE. Meyerowitz and Chaiken (1987) gave women students health education pamphlets that either emphasized gain or loss.

GAIN	LOSS
By doing breast self-examinations now, you can learn what your normal healthy breasts feel like so that you will be better prepared to notice any small, abnormal changes that might occur as you get older	*By not doing breast self-examinations, you will not learn what your normal, healthy breasts feel like so you will be ill-prepared to notice any small, abnormal changes that might occur as you get older*
Research shows that women who do breast self-examination have an increased chance of finding a tumour in the early, more treatable stages of the disease	*Research shows that women who do not do breast self-examinations have a decreased chance of finding a tumour in the early, more treatable stages of the disease*

This simple manipulation in the message had an effect on attitudes to BSE and intentions to carry out BSE by the women, both at the time of the message and also four months later. The results are shown in the diagrams below.

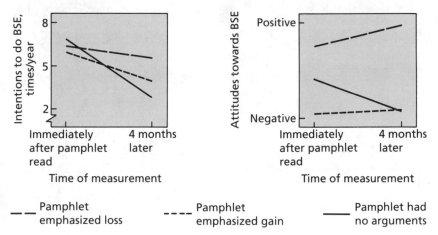

Figure 8.7 Compliance and health.

One feature of Western social behaviour that salespeople make use of is the tendency of people to stand by a commitment. Zimbardo and Lieppe (1991) describe how car salespeople attempt to gain an agreement to buy before finally agreeing a price. A very attractive price is offered and the customer agrees to buy. The salesperson then says she must check with the boss. The salesperson departs (most likely for a cup of tea) and returns to inform the customer that the boss or the computer will not agree to the deal. How about ...? The new price is a little higher, still decent, but not attractive. To decline to purchase now requires a more active decision on the part of the purchaser than the decision to buy did in the first place. One of the authors confirms this technique from his recent experience of buying a car, and found his knowledge of the technique was absolutely no help whatsoever, and so he paid up. The principle of this technique is that the customer should freely enter into an agreement before the rules are changed slightly. Compliance is then likely to follow.

from the study, although it was manipulated by the researchers – and then asked to give their brand preferences again.

Weber and Hansen found that people were more likely to change their preferences under three conditions: first, if they did not already have a particular favourite brand preference; secondly, if the non-favoured brand was high in the preference hierarchy that they had identified earlier; and thirdly, if it was favoured by the majority. The implication is that if consumers who aren't really interested in which brand they buy obtain information suggesting that a large number of group members use a certain brand, they will probably be induced the change to that brand – especially if they see the brand as being OK. So if you believe that nine out of ten cat owners all go for the same cat food, you are more likely to buy it yourself, unless there is some good reason not to.

Friedman and Fireworker (1977) asked 240 persons at several shopping centres to taste and evaluate a new wine. Before tasting the wine, each group of tasters was given one of five statements, e.g. 'Some people say this wine is awful'. Other groups were told that the wine was 'unsatisfactory', 'average', 'satisfactory', or 'fantastic'. The results showed that informing the tasters that an unseen and unknown group considered the product 'fantastic' had a definite influence on their evaluations of the product. Telling them about any of the other opinions, though, made little difference.

Figure 8.8 Selling: gaining compliance by creating a commitment.

These consumer studies seem to contradict the health studies in the ease with which it is possible to induce conforming behaviour. However, a closer look at the Asch studies might suggest an answer. It has been suggested that one of the reasons Asch was able to induce conformity was that the task he presented was relatively meaningless and that the people taking part had no investment in the outcome. In this case they did not really care what the answer was and so conformed because there was no good reason not to conform. The same applies to some of these studies of purchase choices, particularly when the products to choose between are similar in quality and price. Conformity seems to occur most when the product is similar or when it is considered to be a reasonably acceptable option anyway: nobody will switch to a brand which is right at the bottom of their preference hierarchy purely because other people buy it.

This is clearly an important finding for those who are competing by producing several virtually identical products. However, when an issue or choice is important to us, we are less likely to conform to other people. This means that changes in health behaviour which involve considerable thought and behavioural restraint are less likely to be complied with. For example, the current message about condom use during penetrative sex is widely known and understood, yet all of the evidence suggests that condoms are not used as widely as they ought to be.

Children, of course, are obliged to comply with the authority of the school – indeed, Jackson (1968) argued that the **hidden curriculum** of schooling was all about teaching children compliance, obedience and coping with delay, and that education came second to that. Perhaps as a result, non-conformity in school has traditionally been perceived as a problem and there have been many studies which have tried to examine the factors that either enhance or diminish the risk of 'delinquency' within a school. Hargreaves (1980) summarized six organizational options facing school authorities and linked these with the type of delinquency which could result from them. These are listed in Figure 8.9. This work suggests that research into conformity needs to take account of the world in which the behaviour is occurring, as well as the individual who is conforming or being 'independent'.

Organizations can generate a context in which compliance becomes virtually inescapable on the part of employees. A worrying study in this context was conducted in a working hospital by Hofling *et al.* (1966). In this study, a nurse in charge of a ward was telephoned by a doctor, whom they had not met before, and asked to administer some medication to a patient. The request broke a number of hospital rules. First, medication could not be given on telephone request, but must be written

Education

hidden curriculum *What is really being taught rather than what is purported to be taught.*

Health

Problem area/ Organizational options	Delinquency-prone	Non-delinquent
Streaming	Flexible: pupil demotion and promotion	Rigid and stable: setting and streaming
Teacher assignment	Discriminatory	Non-discriminatory
Discipline and curricula	High teacher autonomy	Strong control and supervision by head of department
Rule enforcement	Rigorous enforcement of minor rules	Creation of 'truce'
Attitude to pupils who are difficult to teach	Leaves to own devices provided not disruptive	Expect them to behave like all other pupils
Attitude to deviant pupils	Distrusted and categorized as irresponsible	Optimistically given trust and responsibility

Figure 8.9 School management and delinquency-prone schools.

in the notes by the prescribing doctor before administration. Secondly, this doctor was unknown to the nurse in charge. Thirdly, the drug prescribed by the doctor was not on the list of prescribed drugs for that ward and was, in fact, a fictitious medication. Fourthly, the label on the bottle stated that the maximum daily dose was 10 mg but the request from the doctor was to give 20 mg. In other words, the nurse was asked to give an unknown drug, at double the recommended dose, to a patient at the request of an unknown doctor as a result of a telephone instruction.

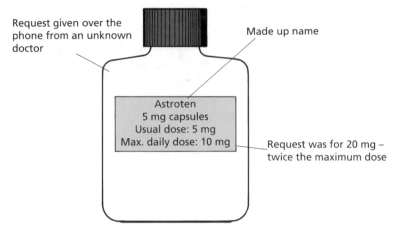

Request given over the phone from an unknown doctor

Made up name

Astroten
5 mg capsules
Usual dose: 5 mg
Max. daily dose: 10 mg

Request was for 20 mg – twice the maximum dose

Figure 8.10 Hofling *et al.*'s study of nursing obedience.

Hofling *et al.* found that 21 out of the 22 nurses studied prepared the medication to comply with this request and were stopped shortly before they administered it to the patient. Again, this study shows the importance of context in such decisions – particularly the social contexts of power and status. Although, on paper, it is obvious that the nurses should have refused to comply with the request, the reality is that in a hospital setting, nurses are expected to obey doctors and not to challenge what they ask. These nurses were simply conforming to standard hospital practice – which was not at all the same as complying with hospital rules.

Encouraging compliance to simple requests is an important component of selling techniques. One of the strategies that has been explored is known as the door-in-the-face technique. This is the strategy of first making a large request which will almost certainly be refused – the 'door slammed in the face'. Then a smaller request is made, which people find much harder to refuse. Mowen and Cialdini (1980) carried out a study on pedestrians in a large university campus. The pedestrians were approached and asked to fill out what seemed to be an insurance survey

Society

Figure 8.11 Obedience in war. (Zimbardo and Ruch, 1977.)

Real-life accounts of obedience under pressure have been gathered in various studies. Zimbardo records the following exchange with an American veteran of the Vietnam War.

Veteran: The most particular experience I had was one time in the DMZ (de-militarized zone). We were in a small village and there was a machine gunner in the schoolhouse firing at us. We all spread out and hit the ground. I said I was a medical corpsman (no weapons) but I was the only one in position. So they handed me a grenade and said to throw it in a window and wipe it out. So when I got close enough to see inside to drop it in, I noticed there was about 20 to 30 children sitting in the back of the room in the corner with about two or three ladies. I threw in a grenade and ... blew them all to hell.

Zimbardo: Was there any way you could knock out the machine gun without...

Veteran: No. There was no way at all, 'cause like you were about three feet away from them. And this grenade is set to explode around a diameter of about 40 or 50 feet at least, killing power. You don't have time to think 'cause either you get shot or you kill them. It's them or you. So it's survival is all it is. Save your ass.

Zimbardo: What about afterwards? I mean after you threw it, everybody get killed, or...

Veteran: Right. All the children were killed, the building destroyed, that was that.

on safety in the home. One group were told that it would take 15 minutes to complete and only 29% of these people agreed to answer the questions. A second group were first asked to complete a survey that would take two hours. Not surprisingly, all of this group refused, but when they were then asked to take part in the 15 minute survey 53% of the sample agreed.

Environment

Another example of how commitment might affect compliance was described by Moriarty (1975). New Yorkers who were sunning themselves on a sandy beach were asked to keep an eye on a nearby radio, left on a blanket, while its owner was briefly away. In a control group, the nearby person was not asked to look after the radio, but contact was made through a request for a time check. Soon after the radio was abandoned an experimental confederate attempted to walk off with it in full view of the neighbouring sunbather. Only 20% of the people who had been asked the time attempted to intervene in the theft, whereas 95% of the people who had been asked to mind it attempted to prevent the theft.

Theories of aggression

aggression A term used in several ways, but generally to describe negative or hostile behaviour or feelings towards others.

The many different theories which have been put forward to explain **aggression** can be classified into four groups: those which see aggression as an innate trait in human beings; those which see aggression as a learned behaviour; those which see aggression as a response to frustration; and those which see aggression as a response to environmental stimuli.

The idea of aggression as an innate trait was very popular up until the 1960s. Lorenz (1966) drew on some highly-selected animal studies to propose that all animals, including human beings, had an innate 'reservoir' of aggressive energies, which needed to be drained periodically or it would overflow. Freud, in the later part of his life, attempted to explain the carnage of the First World War in terms of a negative aggressive energy, known as 'thanatos', which accounted for the darker side of human nature. And Jacobs, Brunton and Melville (1965) argued that the slightly higher percentage of people with XYY chromosomes to be found in prison rather than in the general population (1.5% as opposed to about 0.01%), suggested that this argued a genetic basis for aggression (although this observation was not supported by later evidence).

A contrasting argument was to see aggression as a learned behaviour. Bandura (1977) suggested that people behave aggressively as a result of **social learning**. Seeing people engage in aggressive behaviour, whether in real life or through television, provides models for social learning through imitation. Seeing such behaviour pay off encourages vicarious learning – people identify such actions as having instrumental value and store this learning for future occasions. In a series of demonstrations, Bandura and others showed that children were quick to pick up aggressive behaviour from watching a film, although they did not necessarily show it immediately. In a situation where these behaviours could give an advantage, however, they would use the aggressive behaviours they had learned.

Dollard *et al.* (1939) proposed that aggressive behaviour results from frustration in attempts to achieve personal goals. Personal goals may be as implicit as just wishing to get on quietly with one's own life, but interruption of them produces tension and aggression. Dollard *et al.* believed that this occurs because motivational energies become displaced and spill over into aggression. Although there has been some criticism of the extreme version of this theory, which was the proposition that all frustration will inevitably lead to aggression, many psychologists believe that there is some value in the basic concept.

Another set of explanations explained aggression in terms of environmental factors, such as noise, crowding or heat. One idea is that such factors serve to heighten physiological arousal, which then

Figure 8.12 Some psychological explanations of aggressive behaviour and feelings.

Frustration (Dollard)

Role Models (Bandura)

Genetic predisposition (Jacobs, Brunton and Melville)

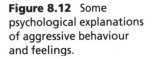

This person feels aggressive because of . . .

Environmental features such as noise or temperature

Deep motivation of Thanatos (Freud)

makes the individual more sensitive to stimuli that are potentially irritating. The baseline level of general irritation is then readily displaced on to more specific targets.

As with most other human characteristics, it seems likely that each of these types of factor – disposition, social learning, frustration and environment – may contribute to a specific instance of human aggression. Single factor explanations, however, seem to be far less likely, despite their popularity in the media. Moreover, studies of aggression are very susceptible to **reification**, with widely differing behaviours, ranging from simple competition to outright murder, being classified as manifestations of 'aggression'.

Key reference: BANDURA, A. (1979) Psychological mechanisms of aggression. In M. von Cranach *et al.* (eds) *Human Ethology: claims and limits of a new discipline.* Cambridge University Press, Cambridge.

Education

The Bandura studies of aggression stimulated a range of replications and modifications. Wood, Wong and Chachere (1991) performed a meta-analysis of 28 experiments, taken from 23 published studies of children or adolescents being exposed to either aggressive or non-aggressive films in school and then asked to play with others while being observed unobtrusively. The mean effect of the studies as a whole revealed a significant increase in aggression after exposure to violent media, implying that exposure to media violence does increase the viewer's aggression.

Of course, that does not show an inevitable connection: there is always the argument that aggressive children might simply prefer to watch violent programmes – in other words, that the aggression comes first, while the TV watching follows. Investigating this idea, Singer and Singer (1981) asked parents to record detailed observations of their child's viewing during four separate weeks of the year. They recorded each programme the children watched, the length of time they watched it, whom they watched it with and the amount of attention they gave the programme. At the same time, each child was observed at nursery school by independent observers, who were unaware of the TV watching records.

Singer and Singer found that children who watched aggressive television one day were much more likely to be aggressive in nursery school the next. On the other hand, on the days when the children were aggressive at nursery school, they were no more likely to watch aggressive television later that day or the following day. So these results suggest a clear direction of effect from television to action and not the other way round.

One of the other problems in trying to analyse the connection between violent TV and aggressive behaviour is that, often, the connection is very far removed in time. As we saw in Chapter 3, social life is also lived in accordance with social scripts: we gain an understanding of what is expected of us and what episodes in living are like, from observing other people. By bringing fictional situations to life on the TV screen, the scriptwriters introduce different definitions of what living is all about and these become incorporated into the social scripts which we use for guiding our actions. So, even though people may not copy the violence directly, the possibility that they will revert to violent action when a situation reminds them of one portrayed that way in the media is much stronger than if the TV violence had not been so graphically portrayed in the first place.

O'Moore and Hillery (1989) performed a study of bullying in schools. They interviewed 285 boys and 498 girls from 4 state schools, about being bullied and bullying others, and found that bullying was extremely common. Most of the children in their study reported some experience of at least the common types of bullying, such as teasing, rejection, being hit and kicked, and being picked on. The researchers also found that 10.5% of the children whom they interviewed said that they were often involved in bullying other children – implying that bullying is not only widespread, but so accepted by the children themselves that they saw no need to conceal it from the interviewers.

The researchers also found that children who were in remedial or special needs classes were more likely to be bullied than those in regular classes. Overall, 17.5% of children in remedial classes and 14.3% of children in special needs classes were bullied. The researchers took this as implying that acceptability by schoolchildren of this age is in part dependent on a child's being 'normal' within a group of schoolchildren, and not being different in any way.

To see bullying as simply a matter of 'bullies' and 'victims', however, is to oversimplify the problem. Lane (1988) pointed out that there are broader organizational implications in school bullying as well. In an interview study with children, Lane found that they also described about 10% of their teachers as bullies. Reviewing research into bullying, Lane (1989) showed how in many schools teachers accepted bullying on the part of children and considered it helpful to do nothing about it. But in schools where bullying was taken seriously as a problem, it could be considerably reduced, if not eradicated altogether.

Lane (1988) argued that school bullying involves a combination of three factors. The first is to do with the individual's own preferred action style – personality differences which mean that some children are more likely to engage in violent behaviour than others. The second factor is multiple stress: those involved in bullying – from either side – are more likely to suffer from multiple sources of social and physical stress, having more health problems, poor peer relationships, higher levels of social disadvantage and fewer compensating positive features in their lives. And the third factor was the action taken by schools: there are large differences between schools in terms of the amount of bullying which goes on and those schools which ignored it as a problem were those which had the highest levels.

Both Lorenz and Freud argued that watching violent sports has a **cathartic** effect on the spectators. Aggressive feelings, they believed, would be discharged by observing an aggressive contest. However, the empirical research evidence challenges this idea. In one study, for example, Arms *et al.* (1980) asked 127 women and 87 men to watch an ice hockey game, professional wrestling and a swimming contest. They measured levels of aggressiveness, using paper and pencil tests, before and after their research participants watched the sport. From these, Arms *et al.* found that those watching the contact sports (ice hockey and wrestling) showed higher aggressive scores than the swimming viewers – not less, as would have been predicted by the catharsis idea.

Measured aggression is one of the few psychological qualities that consistently shows a gender difference. Pollack and Gilligan (1982) asked 88 men and 50 women to write stories in response to six **thematic apperception** test pictures. (These are ambiguous pictures, so to describe them the person has to 'read in' a meaning. It is thought that the meaning which they infer will indicate their unconscious motivation.)

Sport

catharsis *The idea that aggressive or other energies can be safely discharged through harmless channels (e.g. highly competitive spectator sports).*

Society

Figure 8.13 Thematic apperception test. The ambiguous picture allows the viewer to impose his or her own meaning on to it.

The pictures used in this study showed either a man and woman in close affiliation or people at work in impersonal achievement situations.

When the pictures were analysed, Pollack and Gilligan found that the men projected more violence into situations of personal affiliation than impersonal situations of achievement. The women, on the other hand, saw more violence in impersonal situations. They suggested that men and women perceive danger in different social situations – that women perceive aggression as being tied to disturbances in human relations, whereas violence in male fantasy arises from a problem in communication and lack of knowledge about human relationships. The problem, of course, is that both men and women differ widely within their own groups, so it is clearly unrealistic to make sweeping generalizations about how half the human race sees aggression from a study of this type.

There is a considerable amount of evidence to show that people learn how to handle aggression. Drinkwater and Feldman (1982) showed that experienced nurses in psychiatric hospitals are less likely to be assaulted than inexperienced ones. Davies (1989) observed that the same applies to prison officers and concluded that this has little to do with age. Instead, it is because the person develops a larger repertoire of potential behaviours which they can use in dealing with potentially explosive situations. This included the practical skill of taking precautions to minimize the likelihood of attack, as well as second-order skills, such as the ability to spot that there is more than one possible course of action. Experienced people, Davies argued, are more likely to analyse aggressive incidents which do occur, in order to learn from them.

McGurk *et al.* (1981) showed that habitually violent people have a wider 'body-buffer zone' than most other people. This meant that they were likely to become aroused, feeling that their personal space was invaded, when conversations were conducted at what most people would consider to be 'normal' speaking distances. In a potentially violent situation, such as in an interview between such a person and a social worker or other representative of authority, this could easily provide the trigger which initiated a violent outbreak. Accordingly, McGurk *et al.* suggested that it would be sensible for professionals to maintain a slightly wider distance than normal when dealing with such people.

Davies (1988), in a paper entitled 'How not to get hit', discussed the problem of violence in the helping professions, and showed how very often aspects of non-verbal communication could exacerbate the situation and actually make violence more likely. One of the main examples of this was the idea that it was always appropriate to present a cool, calm, professional demeanour. As Davies pointed out, in many domestic situations, remaining calm can be one of the most irritating tactics possible and the same can be the case when a social worker is trying to deal with an exasperated client. At such times, revealing some of the social worker's own personal feelings should not be regarded as 'unprofessional', but as a realistic way to deal with a potentially explosive situation.

This last study highlights one issue that is often ignored when studying aggression. Aggression is often seen as an action that is carried out by one person on another (or on an object); so the complaint 'She hit me!' is an account of an aggressive act. However, by looking at how not to get hit we are acknowledging that some aggressive acts, at least, are an inter-action between people. So the response to the above complaint might be 'Well he deserved it!'. The aggressor understands the experience in a different way to the victim, and that understanding means we have to look at the relationship between the people and the incidents leading up to the aggressive act, not just at the action in isolation.

Crowds and deindividuation

Psychological research into crowds began at the end of the 19th century, with the work of Le Bon (1895). As with much psychological research, this work was stimulated by social conditions of the time, which included increasing unrest on the part of working people against repressive social conditions and the emergence of strategies of collective political action, such as mass strikes and demonstrations. These demonstrations frequently led to violence as police and army forces attempted to suppress them.

Le Bon proposed that the source of this violence lay in a kind of 'mob psychology' – when people were in a crowd, their individual conscience and autonomy was suppressed, and they reverted to what Le Bon described as a primeval, animalistic state in which they would commit acts of aggression which were unthinkable to the same people when acting as individuals.

A more recent formulation of the same idea was contained in Zimrardo's theory of deindividuation. Zimbardo (1970) described this as a state of awareness where an anonymous individual develops a reduced sense of personal agency. This produces weakened restraints against impulsive behaviour; increased sensitivity to immediate cues of current emotional states; a lowered ability to engage in rational planning; less concern about what other people will think; and an inability to monitor or regulate personal behaviour.

These approaches to understanding human behaviour in crowds, however, fail to take account of both situational and perceptual factors in the crowd 's experience. While it has always been politically expedient to deny that a demonstrating crowd may have an internal logic and justification for its actions, studies of political crowds show that crowd actions are very rarely purely impulsive or random. This is not to deny the existence of a collective consciousness, since studies of peaceful crowds as well as aggressive ones show this can be a very meaningful part of human experience. But it does challenge the idea that collective consciousness is necessarily accompanied by irrational and potentially violent behaviour.

> **Key reference:** ZIMBARDO, P. G. (1970) The human choice: individuation, reason and order versus deindividuation, impulse and chaos. In W. J. Arnold and D. Levine (eds), *Nebraska Symposium on Motivation.* University of Nebraska Press, Lincoln.

Society

In an early study on this topic, Zimbardo (1970) attempted to create a sense of deindividuation in female students. He asked the students to wear identical white coats and hoods so that their faces could not be seen, and the loose clothing disguised any distinguishing features. The students were seated in darkened rooms and never referred to by name, further increasing the anonymity. When given the opportunity to deliver electric shocks to other female volunteers, as a test of their empathy and the volunteers' ability to perform under stress, the women in costume gave twice the level of shock as did women who were not in costume and who wore large name tags. Zimbardo concluded that the creation of a deindividuated state leads to increased levels of anti-social behaviour and identified four conditions of deindividuation, which are listed in Figure 8.14.

This conclusion was challenged, however, by Johnson and Downing (1979), who argued that the hoods and coats worn by Zimbardo's research participants were highly suggestive of violence, since they resembled Ku Klux Klan costumes, so that therefore the research

---

- A sense of personal anonymity (for example, when a person is in a part of town where they are not known).
- A high level of arousal, possibly induced by being in a crowd.
- An increased focus on external events rather than personal feelings or interpersonal events.
- Close group unity.

According to Zimbardo, this array of conditions can lead to reduced self-awareness and shifts in perception causing a deindividuated state.

Figure 8.14 Environment conditions that can induce deindividuation. (Zimbardo, 1970.)

participants had gained expectations as to how they ought to behave in the study and acted accordingly. They replicated the study, comparing a group dressed in the same way as those in Zimbardo's study with a group dressed in nurse uniforms. Johnson and Downing found that those wearing nurse uniforms, while just as anonymous, gave fewer shocks than the others.

In a simulation of the prison experience conducted by Haney, Banks and Zimbardo (1970), research participants were asked to act out the roles of 'prisoner' or 'guard' in a situation which was as realistic as possible. The experiment had to be stopped after five days, because of the cruelty of the guards as they acted out their roles. In this study, one of the key elements that was manipulated was the appearance of both prisoners and guards. Both groups were given uniforms that would reduce their sense of self-involvement in the project and deindividuate them – in particular, the guards wore mirrored sunglasses, so that they did not make personal eye contact with the 'prisoners'. The implication was that giving people a uniform and removing their personal identifiers would make them more inclined to act out the social role and less inclined to act as conscientious individuals.

Education

Rehm, Steinleitner and Lilli (1987) tested this idea using games of field-

Figure 8.15 The theory of deindividuation suggests that giving a person a uniform removes their personal identifiers and makes them more inclined to act out a social role.

ball with schoolchildren in Germany. Observers watched the games and noted down the number of aggressive acts which the children made. For some games, the children were asked to wear uniforms as they played and the experimenters found that this increased the number of aggressive acts which they made. However, it is possible that, again, the children took the uniform as a cue to how they should act and so acted more aggressively. Also, of course, 'dressing up' in childhood is almost always associate with some form of play-acting in accordance with the costume which has been adopted, so it would probably be more surprising if the children had not acted in accordance with the uniform.

The concept of deindividuation has also been used to explain some health phenomena, notably in the controversial idea of **mass sociogenic illness**. Moss and McEvedy (1966) studied the timing of episodes of dizziness and fainting among schoolgirls. The study was based on the notion that these effects were a function of being part of a crowd or large group, which was why they tended to occur together. The researchers found that repeated outbreaks tended to affect the same people and spread more rapidly when the group was together than when they were alone. They also found that those affected scored higher on extroversion and neuroticism. One conclusion from this is that what was happening was part of a process of **deindividuation** and that therefore effective action would be to separate the people concerned.

Interestingly, the concept of deindividuation has also been used as a mitigating defence plea in a court of law. Colman (1991) described how expert psychological testimony given in two murder trials in South Africa had influenced the legal judgments. In 1989, in the extenuation trial of eight workers found guilty of murdering non-strikers, Colman and another social psychologist (called as expert witnesses) invoked deindividuation, extreme frustration, relative deprivation, group polarization, bystander apathy and learned helplessness to explain why some of the defendants had watched passively while others committed the murders. The Court of Appeal withdrew the death penalty.

In another retrial (of six men found guilty of murdering a police informant), Colman invoked relative deprivation, obedience to authority, conformity, group polarization, frustration-aggression and deindividuation. The death penalty was commuted and the 6 men sentenced to 60 months' imprisonment. This was the first time that psychological evidence had been taken into account as extenuating evidence in South Africa and there is currently no record of the British court accepting such evidence as a defence of murder. It might be, however, that the very special political circumstances of South Africa in the late 1980s contributed to the the acceptance of this evidence.

mass sociogenic illness
Colloquially 'mass hysteria': a social situation where a number of people report similar symptoms, often fainting or dizziness, where no organic cause is found.

deindividuation *A state of awareness where a person develops a changed sense of personal identity which, in particular, leads to a feeling of reduced personal agency (feeling that you are in control of your behaviour). The development of this state is often a response to conditions in the social environment.*

Society

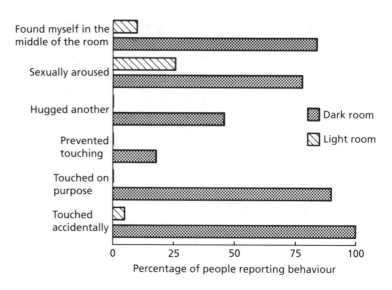

Figure 8.16 Frequency of assorted behaviours under light and dark conditions. (Gergen and Gergen, 1973.)

Environment

Other studies have shown that anonymity need not lead to the anti-social deindividuation that was described by Zimbardo. In a study by Gergen and Gergen (1973), for example, people were monitored as to how they would act with strangers. In one condition, the research participants were asked to spend one hour of their time in a closed room with people they had never seen before and were not likely to see again. Once in the room, the research participants tended to spread themselves out fairly evenly in the space available and carried out friendly conversations with the other person, from the same position. Most people described the experience as friendly, but not intimate (Figure 8.16).

In the experimental condition, the research participants were given the same instructions, but this time they were asked to stay in a room that was completely dark. In this condition, people moved about much more, and the conversation was patchy and usually stopped after a short while. Several people reported developing intimate and deep emotional contact with other people in the room. The researchers suggested that anonymity may reduce some social inhibitions, allowing the person to experience intense positive emotion more readily – much like the intimacy that some people can develop with a stranger, such as in conversation on a train. They concluded that this was evidence of deindividuation, although the observations are very different from the anti-social deindividuation described by Zimbardo.

Moreover, there are some significant other factors involved in this study. There are extensive cultural beliefs concerned with darkness which would have affected this situation. For example, darkness is portrayed in the mass media as a situation in which people are vulnerable – a recurrent theme which occurs in a range of settings, from horror movies to the recurrent but unsubstantiated social belief that better street lighting will reduce crime (the introduction of street lighting in London in the 19th century was celebrated in the newspapers as the end of street crime). It could well be that feelings of vulnerability led the research participants to form closer friendships in order to establish better defences against a nebulous threat, rather than resulting from a reduction in personal inhibitions.

One difficulty which is involved in discussion of deindividuation is that, all too often, psychologists have used the term deindividuation as if it were synonymous with anonymity. But it is possible to be anonymous without becoming deindividuated: Zimbardo's model of deindividuation contains many other elements, most notably the disinhibition of aggression. Other forms of collective experience do not involve collective aggression, even though they might involve a shared awareness and collective consciousness. There are several studies of peaceful crowds which show that being anonymous within a large group can also be accompanied by positive forms of collective consciousness, such as are experienced by members of sporting crowds at times of excitement or in other types of large gatherings such as rock festivals. It does not necessarily result in deindividuation, as described by Zimbardo.

Benewick and Holton (1987) conducted a series of interviews with members of the crowd during the Pope's visit to Britain in 1982. Eighty-two thousand people had celebrated an open-air Mass together and their descriptions of the event showed that it had been an almost overwhelming experience for many of them. One of the central themes in the interviews was the experience of unity with other people which they had experienced, but this was not accompanied by any sense that they had abandoned their own personal identity. On the contrary, they saw it as an intensely personal experience – and a very joyful one. The collective experience was of positive affirmation and belonging, and of sharing with complete strangers.

Society

Even apparently violent and deindividuated mobs are rarely as irrational as the traditional psychological models would suggest. In the 1981 riots in Liverpool, for instance, it was notable that the community centre and other buildings perceived as making a positive contribution to the community were not damaged, despite widespread damage to buildings all around them. Parry, Moyser and Wagstaffe (1987) reported a study of a similar riot which had occurred in Moss Side, Manchester and had lasted for a couple of days. Their investigations showed that the people

Crowd disturbances at sporting events are often incorrectly described as being modern phenomena. However the Byzantine empire of the 5th and 6th centuries also had problems, and the wooden stadium at Constantinople was burned by crowds in AD491, 507 and 532, at which point the emperor decided to build a marble stadium. The rival supporters would dress in outlandish clothes and roamed the streets attacking anyone who was there. All of this makes Millwall Football Club (We are Millwall, Nobody likes us, we don't care) look soft.

Figure 8.17 Sports crowds.

in the crowd perceived, very clearly, a link between their social deprivation and the behaviour and attitudes of the authorities, and that the crowd's perceptions of its actions against the police needed to be seen in that context, not as a spontaneous explosion of deindividuated aggression. Similar findings emerged from a study of the St Paul's riot in Bristol conducted by Potter and Reicher (1987).

One of the several social factors which has often been identified as liable to provoke aggressive behaviour concerns the question of overcrowding. This brings us to the whole question of territoriality and the way that people interact in defined areas.

Territorial behaviour and personal space

The concept of territoriality originally developed from animal studies, from which it was falsely concluded that a basic 'instinct' to defend a territory was inherited by human beings from their animal forebears, and that this accounted for forms of aggression such as wars, as well as the human activity of, say, putting fences around gardens. The fact that possessive territoriality only occurs in most species of animal during a very specific time of year was overlooked, as were other, more social, explanations for human wars and garden fencing.

Since that time, research into human territoriality has extended into a range of descriptive accounts. Altman (1975) suggested that human beings have three types of territory, which differ in their importance to the individual or the group. Primary territories are the most important, followed by secondary territories and public territories. A summary of the three types is given in Figure 8.18. As can be seen, Altman's concept refers to almost any place or spatial zone which might be occupied by a human being and bears little connection to territoriality as described by Lorenz or the early comparative psychologists.

A different, but related, concept is concerned with the question of *proxemics* or personal space. This is all to do with how closely we interact with other people, in physical terms. It is sometimes conceptualized as a bubble around the individual, which is of varied size depending on the relationship which the person has with those 'outside'. This personal space is seen as a mechanism for regulating social interaction, although there is considerable potential for social misunderstandings, since both cultural and individual differences influence what are considered to be socially desirable distances. The anthropologist Hall (1963) suggested that there are four major zones of proximity, which are listed in Figure 8.19. Hall emphasized that the actual distances considered socially acceptable would vary between people, and between cultures, but that the types of space would be likely to be consistent between cultures.

	Sense of ownership	*Personalization defence*
Primary territory (for example, home or office)	HIGH: perceived to be owned in a relatively permanent manner by the occupants and by other people	Extensively personalized/unwelcome entry to the space is a serious issue
Secondary territory (for example, classroom)	MODERATE: the occupant is perceived as one of a number of qualified users of the space	Could be personalized during occupancy/ some chance of defence when the person has the right to be there
Public territory (for example, part of the beach)	LOW; control is difficult to assert and the occupant is perceived as just one of many possible users	May be personalized in a temporary way/very little likelihood of defending the space

Figure 8.18 Forms of territory and territorial behaviours. (Altman, 1975.)

	Relationships and activities	Sensory qualities
Intimate distance	Intimacy, for example, snogging, or comforting: also some sports	Intense awareness of a range of senses, for example smell, body heat; touch is an important communicator
Personal distance	Social contacts with friends and acquaintances	Less awareness of the others' sense; vision is the major information source; words and sounds are the major form of communication
Social distance	Impersonal, maybe business contacts	Touch not possible, words for communication
Public distance	Formal contact between a person and the public, for example at a press conference	Exaggerated non-verbal behaviour to give emphasis to the verbal communication since the distance has removed some of the subtle inflections of intonation

Figure 8.19 Zones of proximity. (Hall, 1963.)

Key reference: HALL, E. T. (1963) A system for the notation of proxemic behavior. *American Anthropologist,* **65**, 1003–26.

Environment

defensible space *Clearly bounded or semi-private areas that appear to belong to someone.*

Newman (1972) applied the concept of territoriality to the design of housing estates in cities, introducing the idea of 'defensible space'. Newman had noted that many acts of vandalism were carried out in housing estates and that these estates often had wide areas of public space, which did not belong to anyone in particular and which were also difficult to monitor. This, Newman believed, invited vandalism, partly by making it easy for people to damage the property anonymously and partly by depersonalizing the property itself so that it did not seem to matter. Newman believed that if **defensible space** – areas which were clearly defined and seemed to belong to the residents of the area – was created in housing estates, then vandalism would be less likely, and residents would feel more responsible for the area and more inclined to take care of it. It would also be likely to create greater social cohesion between neighbours.

A demonstration of the defensible space concept was reported by Fowler, McCall and Mangione (1979), who described a housing project in a small town in Connecticut, USA where these design features were introduced. By comparison with people living in comparable areas,

Defensible space

Support for the ideas of Newman comes from a study by Wilson (1978) on vandalism on London housing estates. The study collected data from council repair records on a range of different buildings and estate designs. Some of these are shown below. Wilson found that the majority of damage was to public facilities rather than private and the damage that did occur to private dwellings was mainly the breakage of windows on ground floor properties. She also found that the higher the block, then the greater the level of vandalism in the communal entrance areas. She suggested that this was due to the extensive semi-public space that could not be looked after by the tenants.

Some examples of semi-public space that received a lot of vandalism and semi-private space that receive little vandalism.

(a)

An entranceway which acts as a through-route to other locations (vandalism prone)

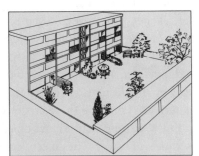

Semi-private open space (low vandalism)

An entranceway which implies residents' access only (low vandalism)

Semi-public open space (vandalism prone)

Figure 8.20
(a) Defensible space;
(b) Location of damage of 6200 reports of vandalism on London housing estates;
(c) Storey height and damage in communal areas. (Wilson, 1978.)

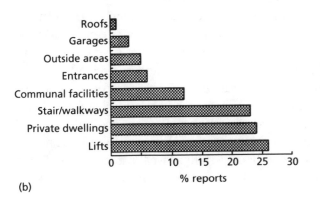

(b)

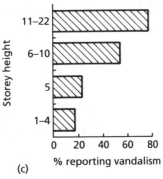

(c)

which had not been designed in this way, residents described themselves as having a reduced risk of crime. They also reported walking more often in the neighbourhood, because it felt safer and believed that it was easier to recognize if someone was a stranger. That this was not all their imagination was indicated by the fact that there were also fewer burglaries reported in the area.

Education

The concepts of personal space and territoriality have also been applied to the learning environments. In a study by Miller (1978) students received instruction from their teacher at one of the four personal space zones defined by Hall. Miller found that when the instruction occurred at the intimate distance, it produced the greatest learning. In other words, if the teacher is in a one-to-one session with a student, then the effectiveness of the interactions is dependent on the space between them. However, since close personal space is traditionally an expression of trust and personal intimacy, it would seem necessary that the student and teacher should already have a good relationship, since otherwise such an experience could be quite anxiety-producing for the student.

In the current educational climate, a one-to-one session with a student is quite unusual. The more common experience is for a teacher to address large classes or seminar groups. In those situations, it seems that the seating position chosen by the student can influence the interaction which the student experiences with the teacher. Kinarthy (1975) observed the amount of communication between students and teachers in large classrooms, and found that the students sitting in the middle or front sections of the class received more attention and more verbal interaction. These people also got the best grades in the class.

The problem with all of these studies, however, is that they rely on observing a correlation between two variables, but that does not mean that it is possible to assume causality. It is very possible – in fact, quite likely – that the students who were most educationally competent opted to sit closer to the teacher, while those who did not feel as confident in an educational setting did not like to be as close.

Health

The personal space adopted by medical personnel also seems to correlate with subsequent behaviour. In a study by Greene (1977) the patient was more likely to follow a diet if the doctor gave them positive feedback and was in close physical proximity, but less likely if they were not close and neutral feedback was given. Since positive interpersonal feedback and close proximity are powerful signals of liking, it is likely that this stimulated a feeling of well-being and being liked on the part of the patient, and therefore made them more co-operative. But being too close to somebody can be a threat gesture as well, particularly when the person who is standing too close is in a position of authority. So the patient may have construed that interpersonal style as indicating dislike or as an aggressive demonstration of power and become less co-operative as a consequence.

Power also seems to be a factor when people are deciding whether to use space which has been 'marked' as belonging to someone else – like a chair having a set of files or a jacket on it. Haber (1980) studied how these markers operate in a working context and found that markers which obviously belonged to a man were a much more effective form of territorial 'defence' than markers which obviously belonged to a woman. Haber also found that men's desks are less likely to be invaded than women's desks. This finding was related to the way that, for the most part, women tend to be perceived as being less powerful than men.

As any sports fan knows, the performance of a team is often different, in all manner of ways, when they are on their own territory than when they are 'away'. This is particularly true of sporting contests. Varca (1980) looked at the game statistics for an American college basketball league over a whole season. Several different kinds of data were available, including the number of successful scoring attempts, the number of turnovers (when the team lost possession of the ball), and the number of blocked shots, fouls and rebounds. Varca noticed that when teams were playing away, their statistics showed a different pattern of play to when they were playing at home. Although there were no differences in the rate of successful scoring attempts or turnovers, there were marked differences in the 'aggressive skills' of blocking shots and rebounding. The home team was better at these and was also deemed to have made fewer fouls by the referee. The implication may be that teams are, metaphorically, more in control when playing on familiar ground and so they tend to reflect this in their styles of play.

Sport

Urban environments bring a galaxy of pressures, among which one of the most important is population density. Ruback and Pandey (1992) looked at the very hot and really crowded urban environment of an Indian city. They interviewed 250 passengers of 3-wheeled motorized rickshaws – a popular mode of transport throughout India and South-east Asia. Ruback and Pandey found that the attitudes expressed by the passengers reflected the level of crowding and also the temperature. High levels of crowding and high temperatures had a negative effect on both behaviour and attitudes. However, the researchers also found that informing passengers about the negative psychological effects of this environmental feature helped them to deal with it. They speculated that this was because the information gave the passengers a greater feeling of control over their environment, which, as we saw in Chapter 2, meant that the stress which they experienced was lower.

Environment

Figure 8.21 Looking at a picture of a crowded shopping centre can create a sense of dread or excitement: the same crowd, a different experience. Mental preparation can help reduce the negative aspects of shopping in crowds.

A similar effect occurred in a study of crowds and shopping conducted by Langer and Saegart, in 1977. They gave information about crowding and what it would feel like to a set of shoppers in their study, while a control group was not given any such information. All of the shoppers were asked to buy a number of items, which would take some time and these shopping expeditions occurred in shops with varying degrees of crowding. Perhaps not surprisingly, the performance of the shopping task was worse when the density was highest. However, Langer and Saegart found that having information about crowding helped the people to cope with the task better. They reported a more positive emotional experience in the shop than the non-informed shoppers. Again, as we have found repeatedly throughout this book, our responses to situations do not simply depend on the physical situation – they also depend on how we look at the situation and how we understand what is going on.

Sommer and Dewar (1963) argued that one of the most difficult problems for a hospital patient is the fact that there is no way for them to retain their own personal space. Whereas most people have a small zone of personal privacy around themselves, patients in a hospital have to put up with nurses and doctors, and sometimes even ward assistants, approaching them at extremely close distances and even making body contact, with no acknowledgement of the idea that this might be stressful or difficult for the person to handle. Since personal distance is one important strategy that we use for retaining personal identity, Sommer and Dewar argued, the taken-for-granted nature of the invasion of personal space by medical staff is another factor in depersonalizing people in the hospital environment.

In institutional life, any indicators of personal identity become doubly important, since so many of the everyday personal things which most people take for granted are missing. Lipman (1968) observed where old people commonly sat in the sitting rooms of their residential homes and found that there was a very strong principle of **territoriality** in operation. Although staff commonly saw it as unfair or undesirable if residents had their 'own' chairs, the residents themselves took very stringent views about whose chair was whose and were quick to inform newcomers about it. Essert *et al.* (1965) argued that this type of territoriality in institutions should be seen as a sign of positive mental health rather than a nuisance, since it was a way for the residents to maintain and assert their personal identity. Someone who had given up caring about their identity so much that they could not even assert their right to a familiar chair is in a very bad way indeed.

There has been considerable public debate in Britain about the question of overcrowding in prisons. One of the reasons for this is that the prison population in Britain has steadily increased without a commensurate increase in the prison space, so prisons now contain many more prisoners than they were designed to hold. Wener and Keys (1988) looked at the effects of changes in jail population densities on crowding, the amount of sickness and spatial behaviour. The researchers collected data before and after a court order that caused population levels to be decreased in one unit, which was already overcrowded, and increased in another prison unit, until the final population density in both units was the same.

Wener and Keys studied 75 adult jail inmates assigned to one of these prison units. They found that when population levels were equal, the perceived crowding and sickness rate was higher in the unit which had become more full, than in the unit which had had its population reduced. Also, as the population levels increased, the inmates showed more isolated passive behaviour and less isolated active behaviour in public areas, suggesting that withdrawal and isolation were coping responses for the increased level of stress.

Society

territoriality *The name given to a set of behaviours which involve establishing and maintaining access to a particular area, while refusing the same to potential competitors of one's own species.*

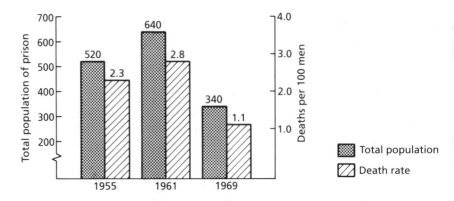

Figure 8.22 Death rate and population size in a prison. (Paulus, McCain and Cox, 1978.)

More dramatically, a study by Paulus, McCain and Cox (1978) showed that prisoners living in settings with greater space and less social density had less sickness than prisoners in high density settings. In fact, as we can see from Figure 8.22, population density has been found to be closely related to the death rate in prison, even when the incidence of violent death is controlled for.

Although it is aggression, crowding and territoriality which seem to hit the headlines more often, people also engage in altruistic and pro-social ways, helping one another out and co-operating with one another in many different ways. Everyday life is full of examples of co-operation and helping. We may not hear about these as much, or even notice them, but this is partly because they are so familiar that we barely think of them as happening. In the same way, they have been less of a focus for research, although there has none the less been some psychological investigation of this area.

Altruism

An altruistic act is one which benefits others, but not the person who performs it. Laboratory studies of helping behaviour identified several factors which seem to be involved in determining whether or not a given individual would be likely to help someone who needed it. These resulted in a theoretical formulation in social impact theory, which proposed that the social impact of a source decreases as the number, immediacy and importance of targets increase. So, if several potential helpers are present, the immediate pressure on a single individual to help is less than if there are only a few.

Piliavin *et al.* (1981) proposed the arousal:cost–reward model of helping. In this, helping is seen as determined by (a) the person's level of **arousal**, such as distress caused at the sight of the victim, and (b) the cost–reward equation – a cognitive evaluation of the likely consequences of helping or not helping. High costs for helping might be, say, fear of the sight of blood or the chance of personal injury; a cost of not helping might be social disapproval from friends or family. Some studies have attempted to operationalize these costs and benefits, and have offered support for the model, but its relevance may be limited as, like social impact theory, it largely ignores the social context in which people live and the sense of community which they share, or do not share, with the victim.

A third theoretical orientation is offered by the version of evolutionary theory known as sociobiology. This theory suggests that the basic drive of all living creatures, including human beings, is simply to perpetuate their genes – to ensure gene survival through reproduction. Altruism is explained in terms of kin selection: an individual may lay down its life to save a close relative, because that enables the shared genes to survive. The problem, of course, is that this argument is unable to explain the numerous examples of animal species in which non-related individuals protect the young in a colony; and even less able to explain many of the altruistic behaviours which occur in human societies.

Other researchers have suggested that altruism forms a kind of social glue in society: people help one another voluntarily, because in the long term such behaviour is liable to be repaid by similarly helpful behaviour from others. There is a growing body of evidence which suggests that, like reconciliation, altruism may be an important and frequent form of social behaviour which serves to ensure social cohesion.

> **Key reference:** LERNER, M. J. and LICHTMAN, R. R. (1968) Effects of perceived norms on attitudes and altruistic behavior towards a dependent other. *Journal of Personality and Social Psychology,* **9**, 226–32.

arousal *A general physiological state in which the sympathetic division of the autonomic nervous system is activated.*

Research interest into bystanders and helping began during the 1960s, particularly following a case in which a young woman was murdered in full view of the residents of a block of flats, but nobody attempted to intervene or even telephone the police. A number of laboratory studies were conducted by psychologists, which generally involved research participants in a waiting room while some kind of 'emergency' was simulated, such as cries for help coming from the next room (Latané and Rodin, 1969), smoke pouring from a ventilator shaft (Latané and Darley, 1968) and the like.

Society

These studies showed that the way people defined the situation was crucial in determining whether they responded or not. In this, clues were also obtained from other people present, so that if others appeared unperturbed, a state of what the researchers referred to as **pluralistic ignorance** was generated, in which the situation was deemed to be non-urgent. A third factor which emerged was diffusion of responsibility: the presence of others witnessing the same situation meant that the single individual felt less personally responsible for taking action.

These studies, however, were all conducted in laboratories and mostly involved students as research participants. Studies conducted in more natural environments produced much higher rates of helping. For example, Piliavin, Rodin and Piliavin (1969) set up a situation in which someone would 'collapse' while travelling on the New York subway. In some conditions, the 'victim' seemed weak and ill, while in others he smelled of drink. But even in the latter case, help was offered on 50% of the occasions and, when the person appeared to be ill, he was helped on 95% of occasions.

Although Piliavin *et al.* saw altruism as being based on an evaluation of costs and benefits, there is very little evidence to support that idea. In one study, for example, Lerner and Lichtman (1968) showed that over 70% of people would voluntarily choose to endure pain in an experiment rather than select another person to do so, simply because they were told that the other person was 'really scared'. But in a situation where they had no personal information about the other – in which the other person was not made 'real' – fewer than 10% would do so. The implication is that the tendency to act altruistically towards other people is a far stronger mechanism in human social behaviour than has previously been acknowledged and does not just depend on our being able to do so at no cost to ourselves.

Although neither social impact nor arousal:cost–reward models of helping seem to be adequate, there is some evidence that the way that

pluralistic ignorance The tendency for people in a group to mislead each other about a situation; for example, an individual might define an emergency as a non-emergency because others are remaining calm and not taking action.

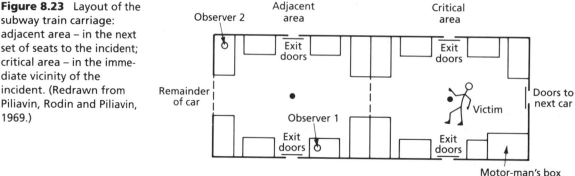

Figure 8.23 Layout of the subway train carriage: adjacent area – in the next set of seats to the incident; critical area – in the immediate vicinity of the incident. (Redrawn from Piliavin, Rodin and Piliavin, 1969.)

we define the situation matters. Darley and Latané (1970) set up a study in which passers-by were approached by an actor in the street and asked for a small coin (10 cents). Sometimes, the actor gave no reason for the request and, in this situation, would receive the money about a third of the time. Sometimes, he said that he needed the money to make a phone call and then received the money about two-thirds of the time. When he said that he needed the money because his wallet had been stolen, he would be given the money over 70% of the time.

In another study, a student took a set of coins to a number of dealers and said that he had inherited them, and wanted to sell them. The coins were valued at $12, but the amount which the dealers offered depended on why they believed the student wanted the money. When the student said he needed the money to buy text books for his course, they offered more money than when no reason was given – offers in the former condition averaged over $13, while those when no reason was given averaged under $9. So we do seem to be more ready to give help for what we see as a worthy cause.

Voluntary work and donations to charity form a massive (though often ignored) part of the infrastructure of modern industrial societies, and depend entirely on altruistic behaviour on the part of ordinary people. People are faced with charitable appeals all the time and will generally give to some but ignore others. Warren and Walker (1991) identified two constructs which seem to be helpful when organizations are soliciting money from the general public. The first of these was empathy – a self-conscious awareness of the consciousness of others – and the second, how effective the helping behaviour is perceived as being.

Warren and Walker carried out a study in conjunction with the International Red Cross sending a mailing to 2648 randomly selected residents of Perth, Western Australia. The people were asked to respond either with a support form, which did not ask for money, or a donation, or both. As part of the study, levels of empathy were manipulated by asking the reader to 'picture a person' or 'imagine yourself' and also varied in how persistent they represented the need as being.

The researchers achieved astoundingly low response rates to these requests, which may perhaps reflect the saturation mailing of requests for money sent to those on charity lists. Only 37 people in total replied, which was a response rate of 1.5%, and they only donated A$390 in total, which did not even cover the postage. Despite this very low response the researchers were able to perform some analyses of the data. For example, they found that the response rate was higher when the information focused on an isolated case rather than the whole situation and when it presented the need as short term rather than long term. The

Figure 8.24 Types of helping strategy. (Hopson, 1986.)

1. **Giving advice**   Offering someone your opinion of what would be the best course of action based on your view of their situation.

2. **Giving information**   Giving a person the information they need in a particular situation, e.g. about legal rights, the whereabouts of particular agencies etc. Lacking information can make one powerless; providing it can be enormously helpful.

3. **Direct action**   Doing something on behalf of somebody else or acting to produce for another's needs, e.g. providing a meal, lending money, stopping a fight, intervening in a crisis.

4. **Teaching**   Helping someone to acquire knowledge and skills; passing on facts and skills which improve somebody's situation.

5. **Systems change**   Working to influence and improve systems which are causing difficulty for people – that is, working on organizational development rather than with individuals.

6. **Counselling**   Helping someone to explore a problem, clarify conflicting issues and discover alternative ways of dealing with it, so that they can decide what to do about it, i.e. helping people to help themselves.

These are not ranked in any particular order.

counselling *The key features of counselling are as follows. (a) At least two people are required. One must identify themselves as in need of help (the client) and one must identify themselves as the person providing help (the counsellor). (b) The participants must be in psychological contact, though not necessarily face-to-face. (c) Both the counsellor and the client must identify the process as counselling rather than some other kind of helping relationship. (d) Counselling is freely entered into by the person seeking help. (e) The counsellor acknowledges the central role of, and actively uses relationship variables in, the counselling process. (f) The counsellor will share with the client the common key purpose of the activity.*

manipulation of empathy failed to produce any effect on the number of returns or the amount of money donated.

A number of people, of course, are involved in helping others as part of their day-to-day work. Hopson (1986), in a discussion of interventions appropriate for the caring professions, identified six different types of helping strategies, which are listed in Figure 8.24. One of the main professions which is all about helping others is counselling, and this has become a growth industry in modern society.

Hopson and Scally (1979) described the kind of helping involved in counselling as having five characteristics: self-empowerment; goals; values; skills; and information. Carkhuff (1974) identified three stages in the helping process: (a) exploration, (b) understanding, and (c) action – a model which was later extended by Brammer (1973), as given in Figure 8.25. Carkhuff went on to define the skills needed by the helper at each stage in the process, and developed a system for selecting and training people to do this. These skills, Carkhuff argued, are basically life skills – they are needed in life, work, learning and relationship building. Carkhuff saw the process of helping as being to do with bridging the gap between the helper's skills and the client's skill level.

Hopson and Scally argued that **counselling** has as its ultimate goal the eventual redundancy of the helper, and the activity should discourage dependency and subjection. It should promote situations in which the person's views and feelings are heard, respected and not judged, building personal strength, confidence and inviting initiative and growth. This idea is similar to that of the 'father' of counselling, Carl Rogers (see Chapter 2), who, in reviewing his life's work in 1978, had realized that the process of enabling people is in itself a highly political action – that the process of empowerment can, ultimately, change society.

Not everyone, however, would agree that these idealistic goals are actually reflected in the counselling process. Carkhuff and Berenson (1976) argued that no matter how benevolent the counsellor is, the relationship and existence of the counsellor is effectively disabling rather than enabling, because it encourages dependency and consciously or unconsciously promotes inadequacy in clients. People are ultimately being encouraged to turn to 'professionals' for help and this weakens them, whereas they would gain strength from dealing with their own problems themselves.

Scally and Hopson (1979) emphasized that counselling is merely the expression of a set of beliefs, values and behaviours to be found in the community at large. They argued that a licence for counselling becomes a danger if (a) those who have it see themselves as qualitatively different from the rest of the population and (b) it symbolizes to the non-licensed that they are incapable, or inferior, or calls into question valuable work they may be doing but are 'unqualified' to do.

Altruism is often seen as a solitary act made by an individual, manifested in a decision to help by action or by making a financial donation. It may, as we have seen, involve putting yourself at some disadvantage for the sake of a cause or friendship. However, there are other ways that people show their commitment to other people and ideas, and perhaps the most important of these is the process of social co-operation.

| 1. Entry |
| 2. Classification |
| 3. Structure |
| 4. Relationship |
| 5. Exploration |
| 6. Consolidation |
| 7. Planning |
| 8. Termination |

Figure 8.25 Stages of helping behaviour. (Brammer, 1973.)

Co-operation

Traditionally, psychology has tended to look at people as individuals, separated from other people, with personal rather than collective motives and individual rather than collective identities. This approach has tended to ignore, or minimize, the social co-operation that is a central feature of everyday life. However, in recent years the concept of co-operation has generated increasing amounts of research and applications.

Argyle (1991) defined co-operation as 'acting together in a co-ordinated way at work, leisure, or in social relationships, in the pursuit of shared goals, the enjoyment of the joint activity or simply furthering the relationship.' This all-purpose definition specifies a joint activity

Co-operation towards material rewards
People could work together for mutual self-interest, for example building houses, providing food, dealing with hostile situations etc.

Communal relationships
People develop a range of social links during their lives based on family, friendship, political affiliation, religion etc.

Co-ordination Most social interaction requires some level of social co-ordination and even in competition it is necessary to co-operate by keeping to the rules.

Figure 8.26
Forms of co-operation.

and also a common sense of purpose, which distinguishes co-operation from competition. Argyle identified three main forms of co-operation, which are listed in Figure 8.26.

Co-operation can lead to a number of emotional rewards. For example, co-operative relationships can be powerful sources of joy, satisfaction, fulfilment, positive mental adjustment and physical health. Co-operation can also lead to the development of affiliative bonds between the people involved. Working with people, experiencing some hardship together, often seems to lead people to feel positively about the people they co-operated with.

> **Key reference:** ARGYLE, M. (1991) *Co-operation*. Routledge, London.

Work

quality circle *Small groups of employees from the same work areas who meet regularly to solve quality-related work problems.*

The benefits of a working environment which emphasizes co-operative values, as opposed to competitive ones, have been shown in developments such as **quality circles**. Traditionally, the Western approach to industrial relations has been largely adversarial, structured, at least in part, by class distinctions and industrial conflict. The Japanese, however, credit much of their industrial success to the way that all members of the organization see their interest as lying in the success of the organization itself and so aim to work co-operatively. This has led to the development of quality circles, which are semi-autonomous work groups that meet voluntarily to identify, discuss and recommend solutions to production and quality problems.

Quality circles are actively encouraged by Japanese management practices. Members are trained in problem-solving techniques, industrial engineering processes and quality control procedures. The technique is one which has been successfully exported to a number of international companies, including General Motors and Ford. In a review of the practice, Barrick and Alexander (1987) found that properly implemented quality circles resulted in increased productivity, better attendance and higher self-esteem of the workers.

In a further study of the impact of quality circles, Elizur (1990) examined the impact of quality circle participation on job satisfaction and on the quality of working life for those employees who participated in them. The study was conducted in one of the manufacturing divisions of a large industrial corporation in Israel. A total of 143 employees, half of them participating in quality circles and half not doing so, were surveyed. Elizur found a positive relationship between participation in quality circles and many different measures of the quality of life – for example, employees saw their work as rewarding, challenging and giving personal satisfaction. Elizur concluded that quality circle activities act as an extension and enrichment of working life, as well as benefiting the company concerned.

Co-operation is an obvious advantage in team sports. If footballers do not co-operate then they will never score a goal. In the area of sports psychology, researchers have generally looked at co-operative behaviour in terms of group cohesion: how far a team actually acts as a cohesive group. Co-operation is essential in teamwork, and studies of team sports that require a high level of interaction like football and basketball have, not surprisingly, found a strong connection between group cohesion and success.

Sport

More surprisingly, co-operation has also been found to have positive effects on non-interactive sports like golf. Johnson, Bjorkland and Krotee (1984) reported a study in which male and female college students were randomly divided into co-operative, competitive and individualistic groups. The three groups were matched for skill levels and research participants were given the same golf coaching, while also being encouraged to practise co-operative, competitive or individualistic behaviours. Johnson, Bjorkland and Krotee found that the co-operative group developed better putting skills and more positive attitudes towards the coach. It is possible that the increased level of co-operation meant that the players were able to concentrate more whole-mindedly on their game, since they were less likely to be concerned with how others were competing with them.

Society

Another area in which the benefits of co-operation are very apparent

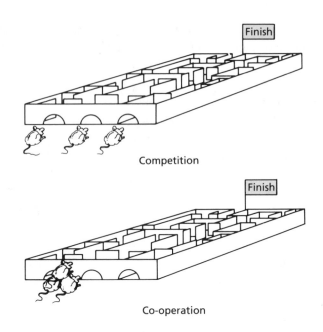

Figure 8.27 Competition and co-operation. (Redrawn from Cox, 1990.)

is in group therapy and other types of support group for people having to deal with problems of one kind or another. The basic principle of these groups is to provide a vehicle in which people can share relevant experiences and support the personal development or re-adjustment of the group members. Cancer patients have to deal with a number of psychological changes alongside the physical discomfort, such as withdrawal from family members or friends and avoidance of social contact in the face of embarrassment (Owens and Naylor, 1989). Because of these, and other problems, cancer patients often benefit greatly from support groups.

In one study by Cain *et al.* (1986) cancer patients in a support group received social and professional support on issues of diet, exercise and their illness. When the progress of these patients was compared with another group of patients who had similar levels of illness, but who did not participate in the support group, Cain *et al.* found that the support group patients were less depressed, had fewer sexual problems and took part in more leisure activities.

Work

Many different facets of living involve some degree of negotiation with other people and this, by definition, requires co-operation. Stephenson (1981) discussed how negotiation in industrial relations situations involves a complex interplay between people interacting as individuals and as representatives of their groups. Interestingly, Stephenson found that interacting as representatives is often a hindrance to successful

---

1. Announce the intention of reducing tension by making a number of concessions.
2. Announce each move in advance.
3. Invite the other side to reciprocate.
4. The concessions continue for some time regardless of reciprocation.
5. Initiatives are risky but do not reduce the capacity to retaliate if necessary.
6. If there is no co-operation, the level of concessions is increased.

Figure 8.28 The six stages of the graduated and reciprocal initiative in tension reduction. (Osgood, 1962.)

industrial bargaining: outcomes which are more acceptable to all concerned – including those who are being represented – are much more likely to occur when those doing the negotiating are free to interact as individuals.

Osgood (1962) proposed a strategy to resolve international hostilities, called GRIT (graduated and reciprocal initiative in tension reduction). This involved six stages, which are listed in Figure 8.28. The model was tested using laboratory simulations of co-operative situations, such as the 'prisoner's dilemma' problem, and was found to be fairly successful in encouraging co-operative behaviour. However, attempts to try the approach experimentally in the international arena might be a little tricky, although one suspects that any systematic approach might be better than the seemingly random policies which seem to be popular with many governments.

There is some question, though, as to how useful laboratory simulations, such as the prisoner's dilemma game, are for letting us know how people will really act. Some laboratory studies have used more realistic simulations, such as a simulation of escape from a crashed aircraft used by Muir and Marrison (1989). However, they also tend to be limited in that they tend to give strong hints to the research participants as to how they should behave. For example, in one condition of the Muir and Marrison study, research participants were paid £5 if they were among the first 50% of passengers to get out. This, not surprisingly, led to violent competition to get out and people frequently got jammed in the some of the exits. But it is hard to know exactly what this study showed, except that research participants try to co-operate by providing the behaviour which they believe the experimenters are expecting.

It has often been thought that co-operation at work means giving up some degree of individualism, although that is a fairly questionable assumption. Hofstede (1984) carried out a study on individualism at work. Using a questionnaire method, Hofstede collected data from

Environment

The Prisoner's Dilemma

This is a game where two people each have to make a choice of pleading guilty or not guilty – if they both plead not guilty, they receive a medium sentence, if they both plead guilty they both receive a light sentence, but if one pleads guilty and the other pleads not guilty then the person who pleads guilty receives the longest sentence possible and the not guilty plea receives the shortest sentence possible. The co-operative strategy is to plead not guilty, hope your partner pleads the same and obtain the medium punishment. The individualistic strategy is to plead not guilty and hope your partner pleads guilty so that you can obtain the minimum punishment.

Sentences and pleas:

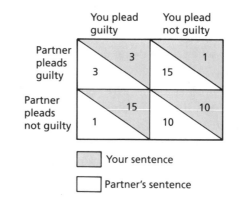

Figure 8.29 The prisoner's dilemma.

Figure 8.30 Co-operation in exceptional circumstances.

Some evidence from various natural disasters tends to support the idea that social co-operation can collapse under extreme risk conditions. For example Hodgkinson and Stewart (1991) record that a survivor of the Bradford football stand fire fled the stand at Valley Parade forgetting that her son had gone to the game with her. Also, the members of one family of four on the 'Herald of Free Enterprise' which capsized in Zeebrugge harbour, forgot that they had children, parents, and brothers and sisters, and only remembered each other when they were reunited in the tug boats. However, these have to be offset against the numerous accounts of people acting to help others in similar situations: people differ in their reactions and there isn't just one single response to this type of situation.

Figure 8.31 Factors which correlated with collectivism at work. (Hofstede, 1984.)

- Less economic development
- Less social mobility, less development of middle class.
- Nearer the equator
- Traditional agriculture, less industry and urbanization
- Extended families, more children per family
- Traditional educational system for a minority of population
- Better health

116000 people in 40 countries, and found a high correlation (r = 0.82) between a national individualism score and the gross national product. Hofstede also found that more collective approaches to working also seemed to correlate with a number of other social criteria, which are listed in Figure 8.31. However, there were some exceptions to this, of which the most striking was Japan, in which a high level of industrialization was achieved, while retaining traditional social structures of hierarchical leadership, close-knit groups and a high level of co-operation.

Relationships

There have been two major approaches to the study of relationships: those which have adopted an 'economic' approach, seeing relationships in terms of costs, benefits and 'profit', and those which have seen relationships in terms of cognitive similarity on the part of the people concerned. Economic theories of relationships have been based around social exchange theory: a model of social behaviour which sees social behaviour in terms of implicit social contracts, in which one party makes a deal with the other (or with society) involving mutual exchange and a certain amount of bargaining for the best deal.

Following the social exchange model, Thibaut and Kelley (1959) proposed a four-stage model of relationships, based on economic principles. Stage 1 was sampling, in which the potential costs and rewards of various associations are explored. Stage 2 involves bargaining: giving and receiving various types of reward to see whether this potential relationship could be seen as profitable. Stage 3 is commitment, in which the partners contract (implicitly) to devote their attention to the relationship itself rather than to other people, and Stage 4 is institutionalization, in which the couple 'settle down', and establish mutual norms and expectations.

Equity theory is an extension of social exchange theory which emphasizes a long-term balance in the distribution of rewards and incentives, rather than a short-term, immediately 'fair' exchange. Applying this approach to relationships, Walster, Walster and Berscheid (1978) identified four basic principles, which are listed in Figure 8.32. It is unclear, however, how far this approach to understanding relationships is really helpful: equity and social exchange theory can explain anything after the event, but they have very limited predictive value when it comes to judging what is likely to develop in the future.

Duck (1973) argued that the crucial variable in long-term relation-

Steve Duck, born 4 January 1946, Keynsham, England.

'How can you NOT be interested in understanding relationships?'

Steve Duck did his undergraduate work in Psychology and Philosophy at Oxford University and gained his PhD in Personality and Social Psychology from Sheffield University. After lecturing at Glasgow University and the University of Lancaster, he was invited to become the first Daniel & Amy Starch Distinguished Research Professor at the Communication Studies Department, University of Iowa, USA in 1986.

Steve Duck has conducted research on relationship processes, particularly the development of friendship and the breakdown of relationships, and is particularly well known for his theoretical work on the nature of relationships. He also has investigated relationship maintenance and definition through everyday talk, using the Iowa Communication Record, a procedure for recording impressions of conversations.

Steve Duck has been the prime mover in the formation and organization of the field of personal relationship research, having founded the *Journal of Social and Personal Relationships*, the International Network on Personal Relationships, and international series of conferences. He has published 30 books and some 150 articles on relationships and is the Editor of the *Handbook of Personal Relationships*.

Figure 8.32 Principles of equitable relationships. (Walster, Walster and Berscheid, 1978.)

1. People try to maximize reward and minimize unpleasant experiences in a relationship.
2. Rewards may be shared out in different ways: a group or couple may develop their own 'fair' system.
3. An inequitable ('unfair') relationship produces personal distress. The more inequitable it is, the more distressing it is to the person on the losing side.
4. Someone in an inequitable relationship will try to restore equity to the relationship. The more the inequity, the more effort they make to do so.

ships is not social exchange, but cognitive similarity. Duck proposed that we are attracted to those who share our ideas, because that implies that they have similar personal construct systems and see the world in the same way. Since we find it easier to interact with those who see the world in the same way that we do, a similar construct system implies that the initial attraction to them will be able to deepen into a longer term relationship.

In addition to stressing the importance of cognitive similarity,

Duck also emphasized that relationships are based on the interaction between two individuals and that they are ongoing social processes which change over time. Social exchange and equity models, on the other hand, tend to present a static rather than a dynamic view of relationships and this, too, limits their long-term usefulness.

Key reference: DUCK, S. (1988) *Relating to Others*. Open University Press, Milton Keynes.

Society

When the term 'relationship' is used, the attention seems to turn towards family relationships, using a model of the nuclear family of mother, father and two or three children. The assumption is that domestic arrangements largely consist of a single heterosexual couple and their children. However, the *General Household Survey* produced by HMSO for the UK reveals a very different story. A glance at the figures in Figure 8.33 shows that in 1990 over half of all households in Britain contained just one or two people. This is very different from the conventional assumption and shows that we have a long way to go in understanding the broad range of relationships.

Number of people in household	% of households 1971	% of households 1990
6 or more	6	2
5	8	5
4	18	15
2	31	35
1	17	26

Chart showing the proportion of different household sizes in Britain in 1971 and 1990.

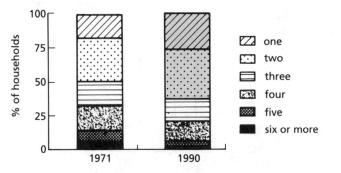

Figure 8.33 Household information for Britain in 1971 and 1990. (HMSO, 1992, *General Household Survey* 1990.)

Family life is an issue that everyone seems to have an opinion about. Politicians blame a break-down in family values for the social ills of society, and various newspaper columnists and tap room philosophers will chip in with their version of how family relationships are not what they used to be. However, for every account that purports to show the disastrous consequences of family break-up, there are others which support alternative views. For example, Power, Asch, Schoenberg and Sorey (1974) looked at delinquency in boys, defined by a court appearance and their family circumstances. They found that boys from 'broken homes' were less likely to reoffend than boys who were in a family with ongoing stress.

The issue of 'working mothers' is one that is recycled on a regular basis. This can be traced to a set of post-war studies, conducted at a time when the then government was aiming to close down the day-care facilities that had been needed during the war, which seemed to show that children who were deprived of the full-time care of their mothers in the first five years of life would suffer emotionally and might become juvenile delinquents. Although massive amounts of subsequent research showed that whether the mother worked or not was totally irrelevant to the quality of the care the infant received, the myth was too politically attractive to be laid to rest and so it continues, even to this day.

Rutter (1982), in reviewing psychological research in this area, showed that what is important for healthy emotional development is that parents should be able to be relaxed and happy in interacting with their infant. The amount of time is not as significant as the quality of the interaction, so a child can obtain all the emotional support which it needs for healthy development just as well if the interaction takes place for a relatively short period of time in the evening, as if the parent is with the infant all the time.

Despite assumptions that 'latch-key kids' will inevitably turn to

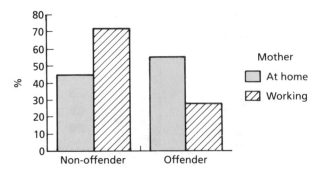

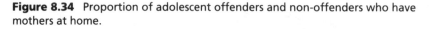

Figure 8.34 Proportion of adolescent offenders and non-offenders who have mothers at home.

juvenile delinquency, there is little evidence that this is really the case. A study of delinquency in a north Nottinghamshire town by Banyard, Fletcher and Stratford (1980) involved over 100 interviews with teenagers, of whom half had at least one recordable offence. The interview schedule was designed to see if there were any differences between the offenders and a similar group of non-offending teenagers in a number of variables, including family size, the jobs of the parents, where they lived, their attitudes to the area and to school, their available money and their friendships.

The most striking outcome of the research was that the teenagers who were known offenders were more likely to have a non-working mother than those who had stayed out of trouble. The researchers reasoned that, far from being a negative influence, having a working mother brought a lot of positive benefits to the family. They identified three major factors in this; the first one of which was that she brought in more money and therefore the standard of life for the family was improved. The second factor was that the home was less likely to be dominated by traditional gender roles, so that domestic chores were shared by other family members, and stereotyped assumptions about gender and domestic work were less likely to be maintained. The third factor was that the teenager was usually required to be more independent and responsible. Other studies of delinquency have found similar results for the effects of working mothers, although these have often been rather underplayed and certainly have received very little publicity.

The question of how far imitation can influence relationships is a tricky one. It has often been claimed, for instance, that parents acting out conventional gender roles in the home are essential if a child is to develop appropriate gender identity and form heterosexual relationships with others when they are older. However, Golombok, Spencer and Rutter (1983) compared 37 children aged between 5 and 17 who had been raised in households with lesbian couples, with 38 children, of the same ages, who had been raised in heterosexual, single-parent households.

The researchers measured as many different aspects of gender role as they could, including gender identity, gender role behaviour and sexual orientation. However, they found no differences between the two groups of children on any of the measures which they used. These research findings support the observations which are often made in less formal settings, that children brought up with homosexual parents are in no danger of gender role confusion.

Gender roles between husband and wife pairs seem to be becoming increasingly flexible. However, to some extent, this seems to depend on the type of occupations of the people concerned. In one study, for instance, Biernat and Wortman (1990) took a sample of married couples with young children who had roughly equal professional status, and interviewed them about their home and work life, to determine the distribution of childcare and who generally took responsibility for household chores.

Biernat and Wortman found that if the couples were academics, then it depended on the hours which each person worked: the person who was able to be at home at any given time took responsibility for childcare. But with couples in a 'business' line of work, childcare was determined by the husband's work hours, income and education. For the most part, it was seen as being the wife's responsibility, with the husband 'helping out'. In both types of marriage, though, the researchers found that the wives were more self-critical than husbands about their performance in home roles and were more highly rated by their husbands than by themselves.

What is also important to those trying to bring up a family is some degree of social support. The long-term study of depression in London women, conducted by Brown and Harris (1978), showed that the presence of a friend or a close relationship with their husbands made a great deal of difference: those without a source of social support were very much more vulnerable to depression. Having a close friend or a member of the family that one can confide in makes a great difference to everyone, and being without that kind of support can have dramatic psychological, and even physical, effects.

For example, Achterberg and Lawlis (1977) showed that psychological factors such as having a history of poor social relationships or the absence of supportive social relationships could also be crucial factors in terminal illness. Although the disease itself which the person had might originate from physiological causes, patients who had no or little social support showed poorer prognoses – in other words, the prospects for their future were less good – and they tended to die sooner than people who had a good network of supportive relationships. Those with good personal and social relationships did not just live longer – they also seemed to be experiencing less apparent pain than the others.

Health

It works the other way too, in that a number of health problems have often unforeseen psychological consequences, particularly for the relationships of the patient. For example, people who suffer kidney failure tend to experience major life changes which require considerable changes of lifestyle. In many cases, people need haemodialysis, which involves two or three sessions of several hours per week attached to a dialysis machine. This can produce a number of social problems, such as

1. **Family problems**: the patient is unable to continue with the lifestyle they had before the kidney failure.
2. **Marital problems**: there is an inevitable strain on close personal relationships.
3. **Financial burdens**: the problems of dealing with increased burdens with, most likely, less income.
4. **Severe role disruption in work and social spheres**: unemployment is a likely outcome because of the time taken on dialysis and the general weakened state of the individual, and within the family, holidays will be difficult because the patient cannot be away from the dialysis for very long.
5. **Patients exercise excessive control over family**: every one has to look out for the sick member of the family.
6. **Children of patients**: 30% show high levels of anxiety, depression or psychosomatic problems.
7. Studies show that **partner stress** increases with time on dialysis – 61% felt depressed at how their partner had changed during first year of dialysis and 54% were exhausted with effort of coping.

Figure 8.35 Social consequences of haemodialysis. (Long, 1989.)

those listed in Figure 8.35, and both the patient and their family and friends need to adjust their lives to deal with this. Long (1989) found that almost half of the renal patients examined during a survey of lifestyle adaptation suffered some form of emotional maladjustment in coming to terms with this.

Long emphasized that psychological care was needed to help people to deal with both the social and the physical changes. There is a range of psychological interventions which can help people to learn to deal with some of the problems, such as the use of operant methods to control gagging and vomiting or the use of hypnotherapy to deal with excessive thirst. It is also possible for psychologists to give useful guidance as to how people can go about making the necessary adjustments in their social relationships. Too often, however, people are simply left trying to cope with the changes, with the only assistance that is offered being physical care.

Masters and Johnson (1970) discovered that problems of sexual dysfunction affect a great many people at some stage during their marriages and that this can produce considerable strain on the couple. They developed a range of sex therapies, which emphasized the couple rather than the individual as the most appropriate treatment unit. Part of their therapy involved discussion and advice from a counsellor, coupled with 'homework assignments' which the partners were expected to carry out at home in between therapy sessions. They found that these techniques were highly effective in resolving many forms of marital disturbance – perhaps because, by focusing on shared sexual experience, they showed the partners how to become more relaxed with one another and this helped them to resolve other sources of tension too.

There has been a growing interest in the changes associated with mid-life and, in particular, how parents adjust to their children leaving home. One of the prime functions of parenting is to prepare children to become adults and to 'launch' them into their independent adult lives. But once the children have left, the couple are then left together, in what is known as the 'empty nest'. White and Edwards (1990) interviewed over 400 parents, and found that the 'empty nest' was associated with significant improvements in marital happiness for all parents.

Society

This increase in marital happiness was particularly strong in the period just after the last of the children had left. For many parents, though, there was a gradual diminishing of that feeling of well-being unless they remained in close contact with their children. While parents do seem to experience a modest 'honeymoon' as they reaffirm their relationship with one another and enjoy having their own lives again, some aspect of the parental role, not surprisingly, remains important to their psychological well-being. Very few people could, or would want to, simply abandon their children entirely once they have left home.

Some children do not leave home at all, but remain with their parents even as adults. In a survey of such families, Aquilino (1991) found that children were more likely to remain at home if the parents had not remarried at some point and they were still with their original partners. This was particularly likely if the family had close relationships and if the parents accepted the idea of the child continuing to be supported by them. But, in fact, Aquilino found, continued financial dependency of the child formed a negative pressure for the parents, who often found it to be a strain. This was particularly so for middle-class parents, who generally seemed to find the dependence of a resident child stressful. Working-class parents tended to accept it more and to find it less stressful.

Some parents, of course, have children who are unlikely ever to be able to leave the 'nest'. Children with severe learning difficulties, for example, are unlikely to be able to lead independent lives and the general lack of sheltered environments means that they will usually stay at home. Quine and Pahl (1992) looked at the parents of children with learning difficulties to find out what the major concerns were. They found that when the children reached their late teenage years they still required a lot of supervision and attention – and this meant that only 29% of the mothers were in employment compared with 69% of mothers of comparable age in the general population. Inevitably, this puts such a household at a financial disadvantage, which increases their general levels of stress. Such parents also tended to be very worried about the

The writings of Kübler-Ross (1969) suggested that there were five stages of psychological adjustment to death:

1. **denial** (it's a mistaken diagnosis);
2. **anger** (why me?);
3. **bargaining** (dealing with fate for more time);
4. **depression** (sadness and crying);
5. **acceptance.**

This work has been heavily quoted with the unfortunate consequence that it has been seen as the 'natural' way to approach death. Although these stages are widely believed, there is little empirical evidence to support their existence (Wortman and Silver, 1987).

There are also a number of assumptions about the responses of people to loss that have been found to be incorrect. For example, it is commonly believed that a response to loss is the absence or drastic reduction of the experience of positive emotions. Wortman and Silver (1987) investigated the emotional response of parents following the sudden death of an infant (SIDS). They discovered that the parents, on average, still experienced a considerable amount of positive effect (see Figure 8.36b).

Another commonly held belief about bereavement is that it is important to 'work through' grief to an emotional and cognitive resolution. Wortman and Silver (1987) point out that there is also very little evidence to support this idea and in their study they found evidence for the reverse effect. They found that the parents who had done the most 'working through' of their grief showed the greatest distress at the time and also 18 months after the loss (see Figure 8.36c)

(a)

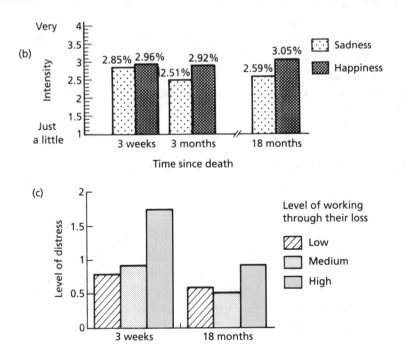

Figure 8.36 (a) The five stages of psychological adjustment to bereavement. (b) Intensity of positive and negative effect of SIDS parents. (c) The relationship between 'working through loss' and distress for SIDS parents. (Wortman and Silver, 1987.)

Health

schizophrenogenic families *Families which appear to encourage the development of schizophrenia in certain members through disturbed interactions.*

double bind *A disturbed pattern of social interaction in which a person becomes trapped by two conflicting and equally unpleasant injunctions, with a third implicit injunction preventing them from escaping from the situation altogether.*

family therapy *An approach to psychotherapy in which individual dysfunction is seen as a family problem, rather than a personal one, and in which communication patterns and alliances within the family are explored, and sometimes challenged.*

future and anxious about their child's communication skills – essential for any degree of independence.

Not every family is a relaxed and supportive one, and some families can be seriously disturbed. Bowen, in 1960, observed how many schizophrenic patients seemed to improve while they were in hospital, but then relapsed again when they got back to their families. Bowen suggested that it was possible that some families directly contributed to mental disturbance on the part of their family members and suggested that some families might be **schizophrenogenic** – liable to induce schizophrenia in people who were susceptible to it.

This idea was taken up by Bateson *et al.* (1956), who showed how the families of schizophrenics often indeed had very disturbed forms of interaction, often revolving around a communication pattern known as a **double bind**. The five ingredients of a double bind are listed in Figure 8.37, but essentially what it means is that the person becomes repeatedly trapped in interpersonal situations in which whatever they do is wrong and subtly punished by family members.

The radical psychiatrist R. D. Laing also investigated disturbed interactions in the families of schizophrenics and showed how such families often engage in a process of mystification, which involves insisting that everything is fine, when really there are powerful undercurrents of hostility and tension. In such families, an emotionally vulnerable person is often labelled as 'sick' and used as a scapegoat for any unpleasant realities which the family does not want to face up to (Laing, 1961).

As a result of all this, many therapists began to feel that it was more appropriate, in some situations, to deal with clinical problems by interacting with the whole family rather than just the individual. **Family therapy** as a method of clinical psychology began in the early 1960s and has been used in many clinical contexts ever since, with some degree of success. Most current family therapists operate within a systems approach, seeing the family as a working system, which needs to gain a balance in satisfying the needs of the different people within the system. An important part of achieving that balance is the provision of feedback: by letting family members recognize what is going on between them, the belief is that the family can adjust itself to a more psychologically healthy mode of interaction.

Families, of course, do not exist independently of their cultural mileu. What counts as important in a family, the way that the family interacts, and the assumptions about individuality and relationships, are strongly dependent on the culture within which the family is located. Psychology is just beginning to come to terms with how these cultural differences shape human experience and the way that we interact with one another.

1. **Two or more persons**
   The 'victim' and other family members.

2. **Repeated experience**
   The double-bind is not a single event, but a recurrent experience.

3. **A primary negative injunction**
   e.g. 'Do not do this or I will punish you' or 'if you don't do this, I will punish you'.

4. **A secondary injunction**
   This is often non-verbal and conflicts with the first one at a more abstract level (e.g. 'If you don't do this, I will be offended' or 'If you do this, I will despise you'). Because this one isn't stated directly, it can be difficult to pin down, but the 'victim' is well aware that it exists, as are other family members.

5. **An injunction preventing escape**
   So that the person can't sidestep the whole question by withdrawing from it.

Figure 8.37 The necessary ingredients for a double bind. (Bateson *et al.*, 1956.)

Cultural psychology

Cultural psychology came about as a kind of merger between two different areas of study: psychological anthropology and cross-cultural psychology. It is concerned with exploring the different ways that culture can influence social and personal life in human beings across the world. Unlike cross-cultural psychology, which is specifically concerned with comparing two or more different cultures, cultural psychology also includes the study of how the characteristics of a single culture may influence the beliefs, social practices and interactions within it.

In this sense, of course, it might be possible to argue that all psychology is cultural psychology, since culture is one of the levels of explanation which are influential in almost every aspect of human practice. Cultural psychology, like physiological psychology, focuses attention on this specific level of explanation and explores how cultural explanations may be integrated with other levels to gain a more complete awareness of the human being.

One major area of study within cultural psychology centres around the question of universality versus cultural relativity. Some aspects of human behaviour are clearly culturally relative, in that they only appear in some cultures and not in others. The dating behaviour of the North American undergraduate might be taken as a case in point. Other aspects of human behaviour, however, may be universal: it is possible, for example, that all human beings make use of social representations, schemata and personal constructs to make sense out of their personal and social experience. In many cases, an underlying phenomenon may be universal, while its behavioural manifestation may be specific to the culture: all known human societies, for instance, involve some form of socially sanctioned, long-term hetero-sexual attachment; but the ways in which these are manifest vary greatly from one culture to another.

Another important aspect of cultural psychology focuses on the question of personal identity, and the location of the individual within an immediate and wider social context. It is a moot point whether the American ideal of the free and independent individual is actually a human possibility: the increase in cult membership and leisure group networks in the United States has been taken as indication of a fundamental human need to be rooted in a social network. Certainly, many other societies perceive individual identity in very different terms, and the concept of the individual as an independent, separate entity from the family and social group appears to be relatively rare in cultural terms.

> **Key reference:** PRICE-WILLIAMS, D. R. (1985) Cultural psychology. In G. Lindzey and A. Aronson (eds). *The Handbook of Social Psychology Vol. II,* 3rd edn. Random House, New York.

Environment

Yang (1988) conducted a study that was cross-cultural both in the style of the landscape it looked at and the samples of people chosen for the study. The chosen landscapes were Korean, Japanese and Western. The ..lso looked at three landscape elements (water, vegetation and as well as the layout of the environment. Yang presented Korean and American subjects with 40 photographs of scenes representing typical examples of the different types of landscape. Both the Western and Korean research participants gave the highest ratings to the Japanese landscapes, and rated their own landscapes second. Both groups rated the water scenes as most attractive and the rock scenes as least attractive.

In a study on visual preferences for outdoor space in Egypt, Stino (1983) carried out over 100 interviews with people living in a community near Cairo. They were asked to look at a series of 42 photographs and state how much they liked them by using a 10-point scale, as well as answering a series of questions about the neighbourhood in the pictures, including issues such as sense of safety and sense of privacy. The photographs represented several local environments which were defined by their function: active streets, squares, avenues and so on. Stino found that people tended to prefer environments which showed signs of vegetation, as long as this was not excessive. They did not, though, like vegetation which interfered with the function of the location, for example where trees obscured the view of the street or blocked out the sunlight.

Music and musical form vary greatly from one culture to the next, but can also indicate how different cultures might be related to one another. Nettl (1964) discussed how different forms of music might be organized into a kind of 'world map' by grouping together those cultures whose forms of music seem to be the most similar. Following this method, for example, a division between North and Southern Africa can be identified, with music from the North African cultures following what seems to be a Pan-Islamic tradition in which the voice is paramount, with relatively little instrumental music and a distinctive type of voice production. Southern African cultures, by contrast, tend to have traditional musical styles which involve groups of people, often with a soloist singing a short phrase followed by a group response. The music has a heavy emphasis on instrumentation, particularly with respect to drums, and is polyphonic – that is, there are often several independent but co-ordinated things going on at the same time.

In a multicultural society, very small differences can sometimes become major factors in social interaction. Gumperz (1982) described how the sounds of language, as well as its meanings, can affect relationships between people of different cultures, because of the differing uses of intonation and inflections. For example, Gumperz observed Indian and Pakistani women working in a staff cafeteria in Britain, who were often perceived as being surly and unco-operative. Gumperz noticed that there were differences in the intonation which they used, which seemed to be producing these perceptions. When serving food, for instance, a white cafeteria assistant would say 'Gravy?' with a rising intonation that implied a question. The Indian women, on the other hand would use the same word, but pronounce it with a falling intonation, like a statement of fact. To the people being served, this apparent statement of fact seemed to be pointless or rude.

Work

Gumperz played the women tape-recordings of these exchanges, contrasting the two forms of intonation. At first, they found it difficult to hear any differences between what they were saying and what the white assistant was saying, but with experience, they became more able to tell the difference and also more fluent in using this form of intonation themselves. This language training also had a number of positive spin-offs, not least of which was the fact that the women came to understand why their fellow workers had shown negative attitudes. This helped them to regain their confidence to learn, and eventually resulted in more positive interactions between them and the other people that they interacted with.

The question of differences between cultures becomes even more important in a multicultural society when those in positions of power are making decisions about what are 'appropriate' forms of behaviour. This becomes particularly apparent in the case of psychiatric diagnosis. Admission rates to psychiatric hospitals show an uneven distribution of different ethnic groups and there is some evidence that the reason for this has more to do with a lack of awareness of sub-cultural norms on the part of the psychiatrists making the diagnosis, than it has to do with a real difference in susceptibility to **schizophrenia**. Horsford (1990) discussed how a white, middle-class psychiatrist can often misinterpret behaviour which is perfectly ordinary within an Afro-Caribbean culture, as being abnormal, simply because it is not the sort of behaviour shown by white, middle-class people.

There is also a need to be sensitive to the very real differences in social stressors experienced by members of different groups. Tewfik and Okasha (1965) studied patients from Caribbean backgrounds, who had been admitted to British hospitals diagnosed as schizophrenic. The study found that only 15% of the patients conformed to the classical description of either schizophrenic or manic depressive psychosis. The remaining 85% had a distinctive pattern of symptoms, which some psychiatrists referred to as 'West Indian psychosis'. Littlewood and Lipsedge (1989) suggested that this so-called 'West Indian psychosis' is actually an acute psychotic stress reaction, which ought not to be confused with schizophrenia and which does not require the same treatment. They pointed out that mental illnesses of people in minority groups often involve feelings of being persecuted, which reflect the disadvantaged social conditions of many of these people.

Littlewood and Lipsedge showed that paranoid reactions of this type have been noted in many minority groups, including West Indians in Britain and the United States, German-speaking servants in England in the 1920s, Arab immigrants in France, Turkish migrant workers in Germany, Eastern European immigrants in Australia and so on. In short, these reactions can be found in any disadvantaged minority group in society. In the Caribbean, delusions of persecution are not common in most of the community, the exception being among the white minority. Littlewood and Lipsedge argued that these delusions of persecution are a response to the experience of discrimination, not a characteristic of the cultural group itself.

The cultural history of a given society extends its influence to the institutions which develop in that society. For example, Misumi (1990)

Health

schizophrenia *A mental disorder marked by some, or all, of the following symptoms: delusions, hallucinations, incoherent word associations, inappropriate emotions or lack of emotions.*

Work

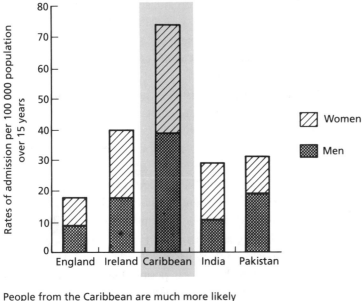

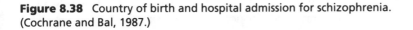

People from the Caribbean are much more likely
to be diagnosed as schizophrenic in British
hospitals than those from other national groups

Figure 8.38 Country of birth and hospital admission for schizophrenia.
(Cochrane and Bal, 1987.)

pointed out that one of the distinctive qualities in the Japanese approach
to work is that hard work was much more of a universal fact of life in
Japan. In the West, hard physical labour was traditionally done by serfs
and slaves, whereas in Japan it was a cultural norm for almost everyone
in the society. So, for that reason, it has never been disparaged in the
same way as it has in the West. This means that everyone, bosses as well
as workers, is perceived as working hard for the success of the company,
and there is less of a gulf between management and work force. It also
means that management is more ready to listen to the work force, and
take into account what people working on the factory floor have to say.

Azuma, Hess and Kashiwagi (1981) described how Japanese children
are disciplined from a very early age into an awareness of how their
actions affect other people. Because of this, Japanese people are often
very sensitive to feelings of guilt and social shame. De Vos (1985)
discussed how this results in a search for a secure 'belonging' in a
network or social group, which is reflected in working practices, as well
as in family life. Even large manufacturing organizations in Japan are
organized into autonomous small groups, in such a way as to ensure that
the potential egalitarianism of Japanese culture and the desire to belong
to a group has some expression within the company.

A number of researchers into organizations have looked at cultural differences, both in management practices and in assumptions about employees. Hofstede (1980) reported on a large-scale study of cultural differences, which surveyed over 116 000 employees of the multinational company IBM, in over 70 countries.

As a result of this research, Hofstede identified four basic dimensions which could be used to compare national cultures. The first of these dimensions was power–distance which is all about how far those in authority are expected to exercise their power. Some cultures, such as France and India, were seen by Hofstede as being high power–distance cultures in which subordinates did not feel that they had the right to disagree with their managers, whereas others, such as Austria and Israel, were low power–distance cultures in which leaders and subordinates considered one another to be colleagues in similar tasks.

The second dimension which Hofstede identified was uncertainty-avoidance. This is to do with how far people like things to be clear and orderly, with roles being rigidly defined and everyone having a strict position in the hierarchy. Some cultures, such as Denmark and Hong Kong, score as weak on the uncertainty-avoidance dimension. Both people and organizations from these cultures can tolerate a high level of change and uncertainty, and do not experience anxiety and stress as a result.

A third dimension in Hofstede's model was individualism, which is to do with how far the culture encourages individualistic ambitions and concerns on the part of its people, and how far people are seen as members of a collective group. Figure 8.31 illustrates some of the characteristics of collectivism at work, as drawn from Hofstede's research.

The fourth dimension in Hofstede's model was named masculinity–femininity. Highly 'masculine cultures' were ones which emphasized performance and money above all else. Hofstede identified Australia and Italy as examples of these cultures. By contrast, 'feminine cultures' such as The Netherlands or Sweden were those which valued the quality of life, and considered environmental and other issues to be important.

Shackleton and Ali (1990) used Hofstede's dimensions to compare manager's attitudes in seven different organizations. Four of these were in the Sudan and three in Britain, with one of the latter consisting of an organization which only employed staff from families of Pakistani origin. They looked particularly at the power–distance and uncertainty-avoidance dimensions, and found that the Sudanese companies showed marked similarity to other African and Arab companies, and were different from the British ones, with respect to power–distance, although both showed weak uncertainty-avoidance. The managers of the Pakistani–British company showed values which were much more similar to those of managers in Pakistan than to those of managers in Britain, even though they had all been born in the UK.

The general beliefs as to how progress should be made are also different from those in the West. Imai (1986) discussed how Japanese industry adopts the idea of '*kaizen*', or continuous change towards improvement, as a working principle in industry. This meant that where Western industries would remain the same for some time and then suddenly introduce 'innovations' which changed everything they had previously been doing, Japanese industries would make continuous minor adjustments, all the time, and so would always be improving their manufacturing practice.

It is not just Japan which emphasizes the social context for the individual. Many other cultures, too, perceive the relationship between the individual and their culture as being much closer than is perceived in the West. Mbiti (1970) described how the African philosophical tradition sees the individual self as firmly located within the collective self of the tribe or the people. This provides the context for being oneself and it is regarded as inconceivable that the self could exist independently. A similar awareness is apparent in the traditional beliefs of the Native Australian cultures, who have a deep mistrust for the sort of alienated individualism shown by white Australian culture. In both traditional African and Native Australian cultures, placing the individual self before the good of all is seen as being irresponsible and uncivilized.

Summary

1. People perform tasks differently when they have an audience, or when other people are present. It is possible that this is because it produces a heightened level of arousal.

2. Research into conformity shows that people tend to comply with a majority rather than confront and oppose it. They are also prepared to obey authority, for the most part, to quite extreme degrees.

3. Theories of aggression can be classified into four types: biological, learning theories, frustration–aggression theories, and environmental stimulus theories.

4. Theories of crowd psychology began with the idea of the crowd as a primeval mob. The concept of deindividuation takes a similar view, although other studies of crowds suggest that they may often be more rational than this.

5. There are different types of territory: primary, secondary and public. The study of territoriality also includes the concept of proxemics, or personal space.

6. There have been a number of explanations for altruism, including the arousal:cost–reward model and the idea that altruism forms the social glue which holds society together.

7. Studies of co-operation have shown that it can lead to a number of emotional rewards for people, including enhanced affiliation, positive mental adjustment, and mental health.

8. Psychological theories of relationships have shifted from economic theories such as social exchange and equity models, to process and cognitive similarity theories.

9. Cultural psychology involves questions about how far aspects of human behaviour or experience are universal, and how far they are culturally-specific. One of its main concerns has been the question of personal identity.

PRACTICE QUESTIONS AND ACTIVITIES – 8

Aggression
Look at the following statements and consider whether you think they represent aggressive acts. When you have noted your response to each statement go back over the list and try to analyse how you made the distinction between aggression and non-aggression.

- A cat kills a bird then drags it into your kitchen.
- A farmer wrings a chicken's neck to get it ready for supper.
- A soldier shoots an enemy soldier.
- A notorious gossip speaks badly of someone they know.
- A man kicks a cat viciously.
- An angry son does not write home to his mother even though he knows she is expecting a letter and will be hurt when she does not receive one.
- A politician votes to send troops to a foreign war.
- A tennis player smashes her racket after missing a shot.
- A prisoner warden administers capital punishment to a convicted murderer.
- A dog barks at the postman but does not bite.
- A person commits suicide.
- A girl kicks a waste basket.
- Two men fight in a public house in a dispute over a game of pool.
- An ice hockey player is charged into the side of the rink by an opponent.
- Someone dreams of killing their boss ... slowly.
- A nurse restrains a psychiatric patient who is trying to leave the hospital against the wishes of the doctor.

Encouraging breast and testicular self-examinations
Look at the following pieces of information (from Pitts and Phillips, 1991):

- 1 in 14 British women will develop breast cancer during their lifetimes;
- each year 13 000 women die of breast cancer in the UK;
- breast cancer accounts for 20% of all female deaths;
- if it is detected and treated when it is localized, then the five-year survival rate is 85%;
- however, if the cancer has spread to the ancillary nodes the five-year survival rate drops to 53%;
- breast self-examination (BSE) is a relatively brief and simple way of checking for lumps in the breast;
- less than 30% of women practise BSE monthly.

1. Suggest as many reasons as you can why women do not practise BSE.
2. Although the danger of testicular cancer is not as great as breast cancer, it still affects a significant proportion of men. Testicular self-examination is also a simple and brief method of

PRACTICE QUESTIONS AND ACTIVITIES – 8

checking for growths in the testes. Suggest as many further reasons as you can why men are even more reluctant than women to carry out a simple procedure to enhance health.

'Sudso', the wonder washing powder from the shores of sunny Cathay

A detergent company wants to introduce a new washing powder on to the market. It is not sure how to present it to the consumers. Your task is to prepare a report for the company on the psychological aspects of consumer behaviour. In your report you should:

1. Identify some psychological ideas that help explain the behaviour of consumers;
2. Suggest how the company might encourage people to buy its new product.

Afterword

In this book, we have tried to show you how broad the span of applied psychology can be. As you have read through it, you will have encountered psychological theories applied to many different aspects of everyday life and in a wide range of contexts. Obviously, it has not been possible for us to do a comprehensive review of all of the potentially relevant studies, but we hope that what we have covered has managed to give a taste of the diversity which is applied psychology. Whatever your own area of work, or whatever area of work you intend to enter, we hope that you will have found something to interest you in this book, and that you will carry away with you a keen awareness of the value of psychological theories and research.

Glossary

ability tests *Psychometric tests which are designed to measure what someone is already able to do, as opposed to what they might be able to learn in the future.*

accent *A distinctive pattern of pronunciation in a given language, shared by a regional or socioeconomic group.*

accounts *People's own descriptions or explanations of events or phenomena, usually given in interviews or conversation.*

achievement motivation *See need for achievement.*

Acquired immune deficiency syndrome (AIDS) *AIDS is a contagious disease, most likely caused by a virus, that attacks the immune system making the host vulnerable to a variety of diseases that would be readily controlled by a healthy immune system.*

action research *A method of undertaking social research which acknowledges that the researcher's presence is likely to influence people's behaviour, and so incorporates the researcher's involvement as a direct and deliberate part of the research, with the researcher consciously acting as change agent.*

adrenalin *A hormone secreted by the adrenal glands, which causes increase in blood pressure, release of sugar by the liver and a number of other physiological responses to threat.*

affective *To do with feelings or emotions, such as the component of an attitude concerned with feelings.*

aggression *A term used in several ways, but generally to describe negative or hostile behaviour or feelings towards others.*

AI *See artificial intelligence.*

alarm reaction *A term used to describe the series of physiological responses brought about by the activation of the sympathetic division of the autonomic nervous system.*

algorithm *A problem-solving operation which, if repeated often enough, will eventually lead to a solution.*

alternate forms method *A system for judging how reliable a psychometric test is, which involves comparing the results produced by two different versions of the same test, if they are given to the same subjects.*

altruism *Acting in the interests of other people and not of oneself.*

amnesia *The loss of memory, usually through physical causes.*

anchoring *A feature of human problem-solving in which people use one item of information as a comparison for further judgements.*

ANS *See autonomic nervous system.*

anterograde amnesia *The loss of memory for events taking place after the damage which produced the amnesia.*

anthropologist *A person who studies human cultures.*

anthropometric *Concerned with measuring the human being ('metric' = measurement; 'anthropo' = to do with human beings).*

anticipatory schemata *Sets of ideas about what is likely to happen, which in turn directs how we respond to things that do happen.*

arousal *A general physiological state in which the sympathetic division of the autonomic nervous system is activated.*

artificial intelligence *Computer systems which are able to 'learn' and to produce the same kinds of outcomes as are produced by human thinking.*

assertiveness training *Group therapies with a behavioural focus designed to model and role-play appropriate ways to stand up for your rights.*

attention *A state of specific alertness or readiness to react to particular sensory input.*

attention deficit disorder *A disorder characterized by marked impulsivity, inattention and hyperactivity.*

attentional inertia *State of fixed attention, for example, watching the television.*

attenuation *The weakening of a signal, usually one which is being processed in terms of selective attention.*

attitude *A relatively stable opinion towards a person, object or activity, containing a cognitive element (perceptions and beliefs) and an emotional element (positive or negative feelings).*

attribution *The process of giving reasons for why things happen.*

attribution theory *The explanation of social perception by examining how people allocate intention or meaning of the behaviour of others.*

attributional style *The distinctive pattern of attributions which an individual makes, in terms of whether events are usually perceived as external, stable, controllable, etc.*

audience effects *The way that people will often act differently when there are others present or observing than they would if they were alone and unobserved.*

authoritarian leaders *Leaders who act in an autocratic fashion, giving commands and directing action without showing interest in the views of their subordinates, unlike 'democratic' leaders.*

authoritarian personality *A collection of characteristics found by Adorno to occur together, implying a rigid approach to moral and social issues.*

autism *A condition of social withdrawal characterized by (a)*

impairment in reciprocal interaction, (b) impairment in verbal and non-verbal communication, and in imaginative activity, (c) restricted repertoire of activities and interests.

autonomic *To do with the actions of the autonomic nervous system; sometimes used vaguely as a general term for unconscious, automatic neural functioning.*

autonomic nervous system *A network of nerve fibres running from the brain stem and spinal cord to the internal organs, which can activate the body for action or set it into a quiescent state.*

availability heuristic *A problem-solving strategy in which judgements are based on the most current or immediate information.*

aversion therapy *A technique of behaviour therapy which involves associating unpleasant stimuli with things that are to be avoided.*

behaviour shaping *A process whereby novel behaviour can be produced through operant conditioning, by selectively reinforcing naturally-occurring variations of learned responses.*

behaviour therapy *The process of treating abnormal behaviour by looking only at the symptoms and using conditioning techniques to modify them.*

behavioural psychotherapy *Psychotherapy which aims to teach people new ways of coping with problems by learning new ways of acting, e.g. through imitation and modelling.*

behaviourism *A reductionist school of thought which holds that the observation and description of overt behaviour is all that is needed to comprehend the human being, and that manipulation of stimulus-response contingencies is*

all that is needed to change human behaviour.

biofeedback *The use of electronic signals as indicators, in order to learn voluntary control of autonomic responses.*

bodily-kinaesthetic intelligence *One of Gardner's seven independent types of intelligence.*

brainstorming *A group-based technique in which people are deliberately encouraged to develop as many unusual and unorthodox ideas as possible. It consists of an idea-generating period, in which people concentrate on thinking up new ideas, followed by an evaluation period.*

bulimia *A disorder characterized by alternate gorging on food, followed by purging of that food by vomiting, or using laxatives or diuretics.*

burnout *A problem incurred by workers in which consistent and frustrating hard work over years produces a sense of numbness, lethargy and a lack of motivation.*

bystander intervention *The issue of when and under what circumstances passers-by or other uninvolved persons are likely to offer help to those who look as though they need it.*

case study *A detailed description of a particular individual or group under study or treatment.*

catastrophe theory *A mathematical model used to illustrate how gradual increases in the intensity of a stimulus can produce sudden and dramatic discontinuities.*

categorization *The first stage in the process of social identification, which involves grouping other people into social categories or sets. Research shows that such categorization in itself, even if based on minimal criteria, can lead to a strong bias in favour of the in-group.*

catharsis The idea that aggressive or other energies can be safely discharged through harmless channels (e.g. highly competitive spectator sports).

causal attributions The reasons which people give for why things happen.

cerebral cortex The outer covering of the cerebral hemispheres in the brain.

charismatic authority Authority which someone has acquired because of their distinctive personality or abilities.

chemotherapy Treatment for physical or psychiatric disorders which involves the use of drugs.

circadian rhythms Biological rhythms based on a 24-hour cycle or near equivalent.

classical conditioning A form of learning which involves the pairing of a neutral stimulus with a reflex.

client-centred therapy An approach to psychotherapy developed by Carl Rogers, in which the client is regarded as the best person to understand and resolve their own psychological problems, and the therapist's role is to provide a supportive environment to enable that to happen (more recently referred to as person-centred therapy).

closure The Gestalt principle of perceptual organization, which describes how, perceptually, we tend to complete fragmented images, so that they form whole shapes.

co-operation Acting together, in a co-ordinated way, at work, leisure or in social relationships, in the pursuit of shared goals, the enjoyment of the joint activity or simply furthering a relationship.

coaction Describes the phenomenon where people work side by side on similar or identical tasks and their level of performance improves.

cocktail party phenomenon The phenomenon in selective attention in which someone may be attending only to an immediate conversation, yet may none the less catch their own name if it is mentioned elsewhere.

coercive power Power which is based on the fact that the person is in a position to force others to obey them, through threat of punishment of some kind.

cognition Mental processes. Cognition includes the processes of perception, memory, thinking, reasoning, language and some types of learning.

cognitive dissonance The tension produced by cognitive imbalance – holding beliefs which directly contradict one another or contradict behaviour. The reduction of cognitive dissonance has been shown to be a factor in some forms of attitude change.

cognitive maps Mental images about where things are. People develop cognitive maps as they get to know a town or an institution; rats develop one as they explore mazes.

cognitive science A multidisciplinary approach to studying artificial intelligence and similar phenomena, bringing together psychologists, linguists, information scientists and others.

cognitive style A distinctive pattern of thinking or problem-solving.

cognitive therapy A form of psychotherapy which is based on changing people's beliefs, attitudes and attributions about their worlds, and so helping them to act more positively and to change things for the better.

compliance The process of going along with other people – i.e. conforming – but without accepting the views on a personal level.

componential intelligence The part of Sternberg's triarchic model of intelligence which is concerned with, and consists of, mental process and skills.

computer simulation The attempt to develop computer programmes which will replicate human processes such as skill learning or problem-solving.

concurrent validity A method for assessing whether a psychometric test is valid (i.e. really measures what it is supposed to), by comparing it with another measure which has been taken at the same time, i.e. which is occurring concurrently.

conditioned response A learned response which is produced to a conditioned stimulus.

conditioned stimulus A stimulus which only brings about a response because it has been associated with an unconditioned stimulus.

conditions of worth The internalized ideas about what personal qualities or achievements will make someone a valuable or worthwhile person, which are developed as a result of experiences with other people. According to Carl Rogers, the realism of the individual's conditions of worth is the main factor in the maintenance of self-esteem, or lack of it.

conformity The process of going along with other people, i.e. acting in the same way that they do.

confounding variable A variable which changes along with the independent variable, and so makes it impossible to infer a cause in the experiment.

construct validity A method for assessing whether a psychometric test is valid (i.e. really measures what it is supposed to) by seeing how it matches up with theoretical ideas about what it is supposed to be measuring.

constructive memory The idea that in recalling an event we mentally reconstruct it from a series of cues.

contact hypothesis The idea that prejudice can be effectively reduced simply as a result of two groups having frequent contact with one another. In practice, however, there are other conditions which also need to be met, such as that the two groups would have equal status.

contextual intelligence The part of Sternberg's triarchic model of intelligence which emphasizes that intelligent acts always take place in a context – something which is an intelligent thing to do in one context may be stupid in another. Contexts range from being very specific, like an immediate circumstance or situation, to very broad, like an entire culture or society.

control group A group which is used for comparison with an experimental group.

controllable attributions Judgements about why things happened which contain the idea that they could potentially be directed or controlled – generally by the the person who is making the attribution.

convergent thinking Thinking which is directed towards getting a single 'right' answer to a problem, concentrating on strict logic and ruling out creative or intuitive thinking.

coping The process of managing external or internal demands that are perceived as taxing or exceeding a person's resource.

correlation A measure of how strongly two, or more, variables are related to each other.

correlation coefficient A number between -1 and +1 which expresses how strong a correlation is. If this number is close to 0, there is no real connection between the two; if it is close to +1 there is a positive correlation – in other words, if one variable is large the other will also tend to be large; and if it is close to -1, there is a negative correlation – in other words, if one variable is large, the other will tend to be small.

counselling The key features of counselling are as follows. (a) At least two people are required. One must identify themselves as in need of help (the client) and one must identify themselves as the person providing help (the counsellor). (b) The participants must be in psychological contact, though not necessarily face-to-face. (c) Both the counsellor and the client must identify the process as counselling rather than some other kind of helping relationship. (d) Counselling is freely entered into by the person seeking help. (e) The counsellor acknowledges the central role of, and actively uses relationship variables in, the counselling process. (f) The counsellor will share with the client the common key purpose of the activity.

creativity The uninhibited imaginative thought processes involved in the act of creating; the occurrence of uncommon or unusual, but appropriate, responses to situations.

criterion validity A method for assessing whether a psychometric test is valid (i.e. really measures what it is supposed to) by comparing it with some other measure. If the other measure is

assessed at roughly the same time as the original one, then the type of criterion validity being applied is concurrent validity; if it is taken later, it is predictive validity.

deconstructionism Originally a form of literary criticism, but more recently recognized for its value in philosophy. Developed by the French philosopher Jacques Derrida, it is a theory of meaning in which the assumptions behind language are exposed.

defence mechanisms Protective strategies that the mind uses to defend itself against unwelcome or disturbing information.

defensible space Clearly bounded or semi-private areas that appear to belong to someone.

deindividuation A state of awareness where a person develops a changed sense of personal identity which, in particular, leads to a feeling of reduced personal agency (feeling that you are in control of your behaviour). The development of this state is often a response to conditions in the social environment.

demand characteristics Those aspects of a psychological study (or other artificial situation) which exert an implicit pressure on people to act in ways that are expected of them.

democratic leaders Leaders who make decisions only after consulting with subordinates and discussing issues with them (hypothetical construct).

dependent variable The thing which is measured in an experiment and which changes, depending on the independent variable.

depressive attributional style A distinctive pattern of making attributions which is often shown by those who are chronically *depressed and which helps to perpetuate the depression.*

diabetes *Type I diabetes involves a complete failure of the pancreas and requires insulin replacement by injection. Type II diabetes is far more common. In this condition individuals retain some endogenous insulin and are able to maintain homeostatic glycemic control through diet, weight management and oral medication.*

dialect *A distinctive pattern of language use shared by a regional or socioeconomic group, which has its own vocabulary and grammatical forms.*

dialectical *An interrelationship in which two apparently opposite or opposing entities or ideas combine to form an entirely new synthesis. Each influences the other and is influenced by it, such that together the relationship produces something new.*

diary method *A way of studying what human beings do in everyday life by asking them to note down specific items of information at regular intervals or on appropriate occasions.*

dichotic listening task *A way of studying selective attention by presenting different messages simultaneously to each ear and asking people to report what they hear.*

diffusion of responsibility *The idea that people are less likely to intervene to help someone who seems to need it if there are others present because they perceive responsibility as being shared between all present and therefore see themselves as being less responsible personally.*

diglossia *The ability to speak in more than one form of language, e.g. 'posh' English and colloquial English, as the situation demands.*

discourse analysis *A method of studying human experience by analysing the things people say to one another and how they express them, both symbolically and behaviourally.*

dispositional attribution *When the cause of a particular behaviour is thought to have resulted from the person's own personality or characteristics, rather than from the demands of circumstances.*

dissonance *See cognitive dissonance.*

diurnal rhythms *Biological rhythms shown by animals based on the day/night cycle.*

divergent thinking *Thinking which is intuitive or creative, often involving non-logical 'leaps' or sudden ideas.*

double bind *A disturbed pattern of social interaction in which a person becomes trapped by two conflicting and equally unpleasant injunctions, with a third implicit injunction preventing them from escaping from the situation altogether.*

double blind control *A form of experimental control which aims to avoid self-fulfilling prophecies by ensuring that neither the subjects nor the experimenter who carries out the study are aware of the experimental hypothesis.*

drive theories *Theories of human motivation which explain why we do things, using the idea that our behaviour is directed towards reducing some inner need. The need then sets up an internal tension and the desire to reduce this tension forms a pressure to act (the drive) which is only reduced when the need becomes satisfied.*

DSM-IIIR *Published in 1987, it is the revised third edition of the* Diagnostics and Statistical Manual of Mental Disorders, *developed by the American Psychiatric Association.*

dyad *Two people interacting.*

ecological validity *A way of assessing how valid a measure or test is (i.e. whether it really measures what it is supposed to measure), which is concerned with whether the measure or test is really like its counterpart in the real, everyday world. In other words, whether it is truly realistic or not.*

eidetic memory *'Photographic' memory – visual or acoustic memory which is so accurate as to be almost like a factual record.*

Einstellung *A form of mental set in which the person becomes unable to solve problems because they are trying to do so within self-imposed constraints.*

elaborated language codes *Ways of using language characterized by extensive vocabulary, complex grammatical structure and an attempt to make meaning verbally explicit.*

empathy *In client-centred therapy, the accepting and sharing of the client's expressed emotions.*

enactive representation *Representing information in the mind by means of impressions of actions – 'muscle memories'.*

encounter groups *Self-help groups originated by Carl Rogers, designed to generate unconditional positive regard between their members in order to facilitate personal growth.*

engram *The name given to a theoretical 'memory trace' in the brain.*

entrapment *The way that people, committees, etc. can become unable to withdraw from unwinnable situations because they feel that they have already* invested too much in them to give up.

episodic memory *A store of personal experiences and events, tied to specific contexts – memory for things which have happened.*

ergonomics *The area of work psychology concerned with designing tools, machines, work systems and work places to fit the skills and abilities of workers.*

ethics *A set of rules designed to distinguish between right and wrong.*

ethnocentricity *Being unable to conceptualize or imagine ideas, social beliefs or the world, from any viewpoint other than that of one's own particular culture or social group. The belief that one's own ethnic group, nation, religion, scout troop or football team is superior to all others.*

ethogenics *An approach to studying social experience developed by Harré, which emphasizes the importance of complete episodes and verbal accounts.*

ethology *The study of behaviour in the natural environment.*

eugenics *The political idea that the human race could be improved by eliminating 'undesirables' from the breeding stock, so that they cannot pass on their supposedly inferior genes. Some eugenicists advocate compulsory sterilization, while others seem to prefer mass murder or genocide.*

experiental intelligence *The part of Sternberg's triarchic theory of intelligence which is concerned with what the individual has learned from their own personal experience.*

experiment *A form of research in which variables are manipulated in order to discover cause and effect.*

experimenter effects *Unwanted influences in a psychological study which are produced, consciously or unconsciously, by the person carrying out the study.*

expert systems *AI systems designed to provide human experts with an extended information source, to aid them in making decisions.*

external locus of control *The feeling or belief that events are caused by situations or by others and cannot be influenced by oneself.*

extroversion *A general tendency towards outgoing, social behaviour.*

extrinsic motivation *Sources of motivation outside the individual, for example rewards, rather than inside the individual, for example, drives.*

eye contact *Mutual gaze or when two people are each looking at the other's eyes at the same time.*

face recognition unit *A hypothetical information-processing unit in the mind which is involved in identifying known people by their faces.*

face validity *Whether a test or measure looks on the surface as though it probably measures what it is supposed to.*

facilitator *One who aims to encourage interpersonal processes to take place, e.g. in an encounter group.*

factor analysis *A method of statistical analysis which examines intercorrelations between data in order to identify major clusters of groupings, which might be related to a single common factor.*

family therapy *An approach to psychotherapy in which individual dysfunction is seen as a family problem, rather than a personal one, and in which communication patterns and alliances within the family are explored, and sometimes challenged.*

feedback *Knowledge about the effectiveness of one's performance on a task or set of tasks. Feedback appears to be essential in most forms of learning and is more effective if it is immediate.*

feminist research *Mary Gergen (1988) suggested the following as the main themes of feminist research: 1. recognizing the interdependence of experimenter and subject; 2. avoiding the decontextualization of the subject or experimenter from their social or historical surroundings; 3. recognizing and revealing the nature of one's values within the research context; 4. accepting that facts do not exist independently of their producer's linguistic codes; 5. demystifying the role of the scientist and establishing an egalitarian relationship between science makers and science consumers.*

fight or flight response *A physiological reaction produced by the sympathetic division of the ANS in response to threat or anger, which results in the body being activated for energy.*

figure-ground organization *The structuring of visual experience into shapes (figures) against backgrounds.*

filter theory *Theories of selective attention which see unwanted information as being excluded, as opposed to wanted information being actively sought.*

five robust factors *The recurrent finding that personality questionnaires produce results which, when factor analysed, fall into five groups, thought to represent basic personality traits.*

flashbulb memories *Fully complete contextual memories associated with dramatic happenings or events.*

frustration–aggression hypothesis *The idea that frustrating circumstances or events, in which someone is prevented from reaching or achieving a desired goal, can produce aggression. Goals in this context do not need to be specific: for example, oppressive or impoverished social circumstances may frustrate a goal of leading a secure and comfortable life.*

g *The abbreviation for 'general intelligence': a kind of intelligence which is supposed to underpin all different types of mental operations, as opposed to more specific types of talents or aptitudes.*

GAS *See general adaptation syndrome.*

general adaptation syndrome *The process of physiological adaptation to long-term stress, resulting in lowered resistance to illness and other negative outcomes.*

general mental ability tests *Another term for intelligence tests, which is preferred in occupational testing circles.*

General Problem Solver (GPS) *An early computer simulation programme which used means-end analysis to solve simple problems.*

generalization *A process by which a learned response will occur in more situations than those in which it was first learned.*

Gestalt psychology *A school of psychology which opposed the S-R reductionism of the behaviourists and instead emphasized a human tendency towards wholeness of experience and cognition.*

GPS *See General Problem Solver.*

group polarization *The observation that people will often make more extreme decisions when they are working in a group than the members of such a group would make as individuals. Such decisions may be more extreme in either direction: they may be more risky or more conservative.*

group therapy *A form of psychotherapy in which several patients interact with one another and the therapist, as opposed to the one-to-one situation of individual therapy.*

groupthink *The way that a committee, members of a club or other group of people may become divorced from reality as a result of their own special consensus. Groupthink means that they may make decisions which are dangerous or stupid because the group fails to question their own assumptions or to take into account unwelcome aspects of reality which may have a bearing on the situation.*

hermeneutic *Concerned with the nature of social meaning and interpretation.*

heuristics *Strategies for solving problems which involve taking the step which looks most likely to lead towards a solution, even if this is uncertain.*

hidden curriculum *What is really being taught rather than what is purported to be taught.*

homoeostasis *A state of physiological balance or equilibrium in the body.*

human immunodeficiency virus (HIV) *HIV is the virus that is believed to cause AIDS by attacking the immune system.*

hypertension *Pathological elevation of blood pressure in the arteries.*

iconic representation *Coding information in the mind by means of sensory image, usually, though not always, visual ones.*

ideology *A set of overriding political or philosophical beliefs which govern the assumptions of a particular culture or society.*

idiolect *The personal or idiosyncratic form of language used by a single individual.*

idiots-savants *People who appear mentally disabled with respect to general intellectual abilities, yet show outstanding mental ability in one narrow area – like being able to add up extremely rapidly and accurately, or calculate the day of the week of any specific date in the past few thousand years.*

imagery *Forms of mental representation which are based on, and seem to take the form of, physical sensations (e.g. mental pictures).*

imaginal flooding *Used to conquer fear and anxiety, the patient is required to imagine the fear stimulus in a controlled setting.*

imitation *Copying someone else's behaviour and specific actions.*

implosion therapy *A form of behaviour therapy based on 'overkill' in which the person is continually faced with the feared stimulus until their fear dies down.*

independent variable *The conditions which an experimenter sets up to cause an effect in an experiment. These vary systematically, so that the experimenter can draw conclusions about changes.*

independent-measures design *When a study involves comparing the scores from two or more separate groups of people.*

infant schema *Mental expectations of the features of young organisms.*

insight learning *Learning which takes place as a result of making a sudden mental connection and seeing the solution all at once; as opposed to more gradual forms of learning in which the solution is arrived at a little bit at a time, like trial and error learning.*

instinct theories *The name given to the suggestion that the reasons why people do things or act in certain ways is because they are driven by some kind of inborn pressure or 'instinct'.*

institutionalization *A pattern of experience and behaviours associated with people in institutional settings, in particular a lessened sense of personal agency.*

intelligence quotient *A numerical figure, believed by some to indicate the level of a person's intelligence and by others to indicate how well that person performs on intelligence tests.*

intelligence *An inferred characteristic of an individual, usually defined as the ability to profit from experience, acquire knowledge, think abstractly or adapt to changes in the environment.*

interference *The distortion or disruption of memory which happens as a result of other information being learned or already stored in memory.*

intergroup rivalry *Competition between different social groups, which can often lead to powerful hostility.*

internal attribution *The judgement that a behaviour or act is caused by sources within the person, i.e. their character, personality or intentions. This is also known as dispositional attribution.*

internal locus of control *The belief that important life events are largely caused by one's own efforts, abilities, etc. as opposed to being caused by external circumstances.*

interpersonal *Literally 'between persons', this term is used to describe actions or occurrences which involve at least two people affecting one another in some way.*

intrinsic motivation *Sources of motivation inside the individual, for example, drives, rather than outside the individual, for example rewards.*

introversion *A general tendency towards solitary, withdrawn behaviour.*

ipsative tests *Tests which are used to show the balance of different characteristics within one individual, but not to compare people with one another.*

IQ *See intelligence quotients.*

jet lag *Disruption of the circadian rhythms of the body caused by the need to adjust rapidly to different time zones.*

job aptitude tests *Psychometric tests which assess whether someone is likely to be good at a particular job – in other words, whether they have the right type of mental skills or talents, so that they should be able to learn the job quickly and easily.*

kinaesthetic senses *The bodily senses which inform us about the position and state of the muscles, skeletal system and internal organs.*

Korsakoff's syndrome *A condition of severe memory loss and anterograde amnesia brought about by long-term alcohol abuse and inadequate nutrition.*

labelling theory *The approach to understanding social behaviour which is based on the idea of the self-fulfilling prophecy – that expectations can become self-confirming, because the people concerned act as if they were already true.*

latent learning *Learning which takes place without producing an immediate change in behaviour.*

lateral thinking *An approach to problem-solving which deliberately steps outside conventional assumptions and frameworks in seeking solutions.*

law of effect *The learning principle that actions which have a pleasant effect on the organism are likely to be repeated.*

laws of Prägnanz *A set of perceptual principles identified by the Gestalt psychologists through which visual information is given shape and form.*

lay epistemology *The study of how everyday beliefs and social representations are adopted, transmitted and changed, and of what counts as valid knowledge in socially accepted belief systems.*

learned helplessness *The way that the experience of being forced into the role of passive victim in one situation can generalize to other situations, such that the person or animal makes no effort to help themselves in unpleasant situations, even if such effort would be effective.*

learning *A change in behaviour, or the potential for behaviour, that occurs as a result of environmental experience, but is not the result of such factors as fatigue, drugs or injury.*

learning curve *A distinctive graph pattern produced when mapping the time taken to learn a new behaviour.*

learning sets *A preparedness to undertake certain familiar types of learning.*

levels of processing theory *The idea that what determines whether information is remembered, and* for how long, is how deeply it is processed, i.e. thought about and linked with other information.

linguistic relativity hypothesis The idea that thinking depends on language and so people who speak a different language also inhabit different conceptual worlds.

locus of control Where control of what happens is perceived to come from. An internal locus of control means that the person sees it as coming from within themselves – so they are largely in control of what happens to them or at least in a position to influence it. An external locus of control means that it is perceived as coming from sources outside of the person and so is not something which the individual can influence.

longitudinal study A study which monitors changes occurring over a period of time.

LTM The common abbreviation for long-term memory.

mass sociogenic illness Colloquially 'mass hysteria': a social situation where a number of people report similar symptoms, often fainting or dizziness, where no organic cause is found.

medical model The approach to understanding abnormal behaviour adopted by members of the medical professions, e.g. psychiatrists.

memory The capacity to retain and retrieve information.

menarche The onset of menstruation.

mental imagery See imagery.

mental representation A theoretical model of how we hold information in the brain.

mental set A state of readiness to learn, think or perceive in certain ways.

meta-analysis A research method which analyses the outcomes of several studies investigating the same issues.

metacognitive skills Higher level skills, for example, memory is a skill, and learning to use and develop our memory skill is a metacognitive skill.

metaphorical frame The set of ideas invoked by the use of a particular metaphor, which then sets the context for further discussion.

minimal group paradigm An approach to the study of social identification which involves creating artificial groups in the social psychology laboratory on the basis of spurious or minimal characteristics (e.g. tossing a coin) and then studying the in-group/out-group effects which result.

mnemonics Strategies for helping people to remember information, usually involving cues such as rhyme or imagery.

modelling Providing an example which a child can imitate in order to learn styles of behaviour.

moral reasoning Using cognitive processes to make judgements about right and wrong.

motivated forgetting Forgetting which indicates an unconscious desire to forget, e.g. forgetting an unpleasant event, or an unwelcome appointment.

motivation That which drives, or energizes, a human being or animal's actions – that which makes it active rather than quiescent.

nAch See need for achievement.

natural experiments Events in which variables change as a result of natural, political, social or economic circumstance, such that the outcome of these changes can then be studied.

natural killer cells Natural killer cells are part of the immune system and play an important role in killing some types of tumour cells and also can kill cells infected with viruses or bacteria.

nature–nurture debates Fairly pointless theoretical debates, popular in the 1950s, concerning whether a given psychological ability was inherited or whether it was learned through experience.

need for achievement An internal motivation to succeed in life or in attaining particular goals.

need for affiliation An internal motivation to belong to a group or family, or at least to be accepted by others.

need for positive regard An internal motivation to be loved, approved of or respected by other people.

need for self-actualization An internal motivation to develop one's own talents and abilities to the full.

negative reinforcement Encouraging a certain kind of behaviour by the removal or avoidance of an unpleasant stimulus.

neuroses Mental disorders, where the patient commonly suffers from anxiety but remains in touch with reality.

non-directive Acting in such a way as to allow interaction with another person to continue without actually indicating how the other person should act, or hinting, implicitly or explicitly, at what they ought to be saying.

non-reactive measures Research measures that are designed to produce the minimum influence on the behaviour of the research participants.

non-verbal communication Communication which does not involve language or words of any form.

non-verbal cues *Acts or signs which communicate information to other people, deliberately or unconsciously, but which do not involve the use of words.*

normative *Representing the norm; typical.*

observational study *A study which involves watching and recording what happens, rather than intervening and causing changes.*

occupational psychologists *Psychologists who deal with people at work. Some occupational psychologists are concerned with recruitment or selection: fitting people to jobs. Others are concerned with human interactions at work: how organizations and departments are managed.*

one-trial learning *A rapid form of learning, usually associated with classical conditioning, which only takes one event to be learned, such as avoiding a food which has made you sick.*

operant conditioning *The process of learning identified by B. F. Skinner, in which learning occurs as a result of positive or negative reinforcement of an animal or human being's action.*

organizational climate *The psychological or social atmosphere of an organization.*

paradigm *The framework of ideas, theories and assumptions which is implicitly adopted by an academic community or group of people.*

paralanguage *Non-verbal cues contained in how people say things, such as in tones of voice, pauses, or 'um' and 'er' noises.*

parallel distributed processing *A form of computer simulation in which several different logic pathways are at work simultaneously, with interconnections between them.*

paramnesia *A clinical condition in which memories become distorted rather than lost altogether.*

paranoia *Unreasonable and excessive suspiciousness, jealousy or mistrust.*

participant observation *A method of study in which the investigator joins in the social process being observed.*

PDP *See parallel distributed processing.*

peer group *A group of people who are considered to be the equals of, or like, the person concerned.*

perception *The process by which the brain organizes and interprets sensory information.*

perceptual defence *A process whereby objects or events which are threatening or unconsciously unwelcome are less easily perceived than more innocuous stimuli.*

perceptual set *A state of readiness to perceive certain kinds of stimuli rather than others.*

performance decrement *The decline in accuracy which occurs over time as an individual performs a task requiring sustained attention.*

personal constructs *Individual ways of making sense of the world, which have been developed on the basis of experience. Personal construct theorists argue that getting to understand the personal constructs which someone applies to make sense of their experience is essential for effective psychotherapy, as well as for effective interaction in day-to-day living.*

personal space *The physical distance which people like to maintain between themselves and others. This varies according to their relationship with and*

attitude to other people, and according to norms and contexts.

personality *A distinctive and relatively stable pattern of behaviours, thought, motives and emotions that characterize an individual.*

phantom limbs *The name given to the phenomenon experienced by amputees, of still feeling the limb as present and alive, even though it has been surgically removed.*

phenomenological *Concerned with the person's own perceived world and the phenomena which they experience, rather than with objective reality.*

pheromones *Chemicals released into the air which, when received by another animal, exert a direct influence on its hormonal system and sometimes its behaviour.*

phi phenomenon *The perceptual phenomenon in which discrete stimuli presented in rapid sequence are perceived as linked together.*

physiological arousal *See arousal.*

physiological drives *Motives which are concerned with satisfying physiological needs such as hunger, etc.*

placebo effect *An inactive substance or fake treatment that produces a response in patients.*

pluralistic ignorance *The tendency for people in a group to mislead each other about a situation; for example, an individual might define an emergency as a non-emergency because others are remaining calm and not taking action.*

polygraph *A machine often used to measure stress or anxiety – and therefore sometimes as a 'lie-detector' – which works by measuring many ('poly') different physical indicators that the person is under stress, such as blood* *pressure, pulse rate, heart rate and galvanic skin response.*

population norms *A set of scores for a particular population (e.g. females aged 18–24) which establishes the normal range of scores for that population, on a particular psychometric test or measure. Tables of population norms are used to judge whether an individual's test result is typical for their population group or not.*

positive regard *Liking, affection, love or respect for someone else.*

positive reinforcement *In operant conditioning, strengthening learned behaviour by direct reward when it occurs.*

post-traumatic stress disorder *An anxiety resulting from experience with a catastrophic event beyond the normal range of human suffering, and characterized by (a) numbness to the world, (b) reliving the trauma in dreams and memories and (c) symptoms of anxiety.*

postural echo *The way that people who are in intense conversation or rapport will often unconsciously mimic one another's stance or posture.*

predictive validity *A method of assessing whether a psychometric test is valid (i.e. really measures what it is supposed to) by seeing how well it correlates with some other measure, which is assessed later, after the test has been taken.*

prejudice *A fixed, pre-set attitude, usually negative and hostile, and usually applied to members of a particular social category.*

proactive amnesia *A memory disorder in which the person becomes unable to store new information.*

programmed learning *A technique for applying operant conditioning to the schooling process.*

projective tests *Psychometric tests which involve providing the person with ambiguous stimuli and seeing what meanings they read into them. The idea is that this will illustrate the concerns of the unconscious mind.*

propaganda *Traditionally defined as an attempt to influence public opinion and public behaviour through specialized persuasion techniques: can supposedly be contrasted with education.*

proprioceptors *Nerve cells which receive information from the muscles and skeleton.*

pro-social *Altruistic, helpful, friendly or otherwise acting in ways that are beneficial to others.*

Protestant work ethic *The idea that being productive and working hard is a good thing, and is an attitude that will bring the person closer to God: divinity through industry.*

psychiatrist *A person who trains as a doctor and then specializes in mental disorders.*

psychoanalysis *Freud's theory of personality which describes how human behaviour is affected by unconscious thoughts and feelings.*

psycholinguistics *The study of language and language structure, particularly in terms of its interaction with thinking.*

psychology *The scientific study of experience and behaviour.*

psychometric tests *Instruments which have been developed for measuring mental characteristics. Psychological tests have been developed to measure a wide range of things, including creativity, job attitudes and skills, brain damage and, of course, 'intelligence'.*

psychosomatic disorders *A group of disorders in which actual physical illness is caused or influenced by psychological factors.*

psychotic *A mental state characterized by profound disturbances in reality testing, thought and emotion.*

qualitative methods *Ways of collecting data which are concerned with describing meaning, rather than with drawing statistical inferences from frequency counts.*

quality circle *Small groups of employees from the same work areas who meet regularly to solve quality-related work problems.*

quantitative methods *Ways of collecting data which focus on numbers and frequencies rather than on meaning or experience.*

random assignment *Allocating research participants to experimental conditions by using chance, such as a toss of a coin.*

random sample *A way of selecting a sample where every person from the defined population has an equal chance of being chosen.*

rational–emotive therapy *A form of psychotherapy which mixes rational argument with positive reward systems.*

recidivism *Habitual relapse into crime.*

reductionism *An approach to understanding behaviour which attempts to explain complex actions in terms of simple causes.*

reflex *An automatic reaction to a stimulus; often inborn but can also be learned or modified by experience.*

rehearsal *Practice, e.g. the continuous repeating of information to be memorized.*

reification *The process of treating an adverb as if it were a* noun – e.g. seeing 'acting intelligently' as if it were a manifestation of some kind of entity called 'intelligence'.

reinforcement The strengthening of learning in some way. The term is usually applied to learned associations, acquired through operant or classical conditioning, but it may also be applied to other forms of learning.

reinforcement contingencies The conditions under which positive or negative reinforcement are given.

relationship-oriented leaders Leaders who make it their prime responsibility to ensure that all the team get on well together and communicate effectively, in the belief that if this is running right, then the necessary tasks will be done. This contrasts with task-oriented leaders.

repertory grid technique A system for eliciting personal constructs and showing how individuals use them to interpret their experience.

restricted language codes Ways of using language characterized by limited vocabulary, simple grammatical structures, and a heavy reliance on shared implicit meaning and paralinguistic cues.

retrograde amnesia A form of memory disorder in which the person becomes unable to recall events or information stored before the disorder occurred.

retrospective study A study which involves collecting data about events which happened in the past.

risky-shift phenomenon A form of group polarization which involves the observation that some people will tend to make riskier decisions when acting as members of a group or committee than they

would when they are acting as individuals.

role A social part that one plays in society.

role-schema The total set of memories, actions and intentions associated with a particular social role: the understanding of that role.

S–R learning See stimulus–response learning.

sample The group of subjects used in a study: the selection of people, animals, plants or objects drawn from a population for the purposes of studying that population.

Sapir-Whorf hypothesis See linguistic relativity hypothesis.

scapegoating The process of putting the blame for difficult economic circumstances or other sources of frustration on to some disliked but 'inferior' social group, so increasing prejudice and intergroup hostility.

scattergram A diagram used to illustrate correlations.

schema A mental framework or structure which encompasses memories, ideas, concepts and programmes for action which are pertinent to a particular topic.

schizophrenia A mental disorder marked by some, or all, of the following symptoms: delusions, hallucinations, incoherent word associations, inappropriate emotions or lack of emotions.

schizophrenogenic families Families which appear to encourage the development of schizophrenia in certain members through disturbed interactions.

scientific management Begun by Taylor, a method of applying scientific principles to improve job productivity and efficiency through procedures such as time-and-motion analyses.

script A well-known pattern of

social action and interaction which has been socially established and accepted, and is implicitly and automatically followed by people in the relevant situation.

secondary reinforcement Something which reinforces learned behaviour because it has previously been associated with a primary reinforcer.

selective attention The phenomenon by which people select what information they will pay attention to and what they will ignore.

self-actualization The making real of one's abilities and talents: using them to the full.

self-concept The idea or internal image that people have of what they themselves are like, including both evaluative and descriptive dimensions.

self-efficacy beliefs The belief that one is capable of doing something effectively. Self-efficacy beliefs are closely connected with self-esteem, in that having a sense of being capable and potentially in control tends to increase confidence. But the concept is often thought to be more useful than the generalized concept of self-esteem, since people may often be confident about some abilities, or in some areas of their lives, but not in others.

self-esteem The evaluative dimensions of the self-concept, which is to do with how worth while and/or confident the person feels about themselves.

self-fulfilling prophecy The idea that expectations about a person or group can become true simply because they have been stated.

self-image The factual or descriptive picture which a person holds of themselves, without the *evaluative component implicit in the concept of self-esteem.*

self-schema *The total set of memories, representations, ideas and intentions which one holds about oneself.*

semantic differential *A form of attitude measurement which involves asking people to evaluate a concept by weighing it up according to several different verbal dimensions.*

semantic *To do with meaning.*

sensation *The detection or direct experience of physical energy in the external or internal environment, due to stimulation of receptors in the sense organs.*

sensitivity training *A technique of experience-based training in which individuals learn interpersonal skills.*

sensory deprivation *The cutting out of all incoming sensory information or at least as much of it as possible.*

sensory mode *The route by which information comes to the brain, e.g. through vision, hearing, smell, etc.*

serial reproduction *A method of examining the accuracy of memory by asking people to reproduce what they recall of a story, on several successive occasions.*

set weight *The phenomenon detected by physiological studies of obesity, that the body appears to have an internal established ideal weight and that eating or fasting behaviour will tend to maintain that weight.*

sexism *Using the pervasive power imbalance between men and women to oppress women by devaluing their experience, behaviour and aspirations.*

signal detection tasks *Procedures used in studies of sustained attention in which the*

person is required to notice, or detect, a small signal whenever it occurs.

situational attribution *A reason for an act or behaviour which implies that it occurs as a result of the situation or circumstances that the person is in at the time.*

skill *Welford (1958) suggested that all skills, of whatever kind, possess three main characteristics. The first of these is that skills consist of building an organized and co-ordinated activity in relation to an object or situation. This means that skills involve the whole set of sensory, central and motor nervous system processes which contribute to performance. The second characteristic is that skills are learned gradually, through repeated experience; and the third is that within each skill, many different processes or actions are ordered and co-ordinated in a temporal sequence.*

social cognition *The way that we think about and interpret social information and social experience. In developmental psychology, the term refers to a theory of cognitive development which states that social interaction is the most important factor in a young child's cognitive development.*

social comparison *The process of comparing one's own social group with others, in terms of their relative social status and prestige. Social comparison is important, in that people will tend to distance themselves from membership of a group which does not reflect positively on the self-esteem by comparing favourably with other groups.*

social facilitation *The observation that the presence of other people can influence how*

well they perform on a task, often improving their performance.

social identity theory *A theory which emphasizes how membership of social groups forms a significant part of the self-concept, and can determine reactions to other people and events, such that people respond primarily as group members and not as individuals.*

social learning *The approach to understanding social behaviour which emphasizes how people imitate action and model their behaviour on that of others.*

social norms *Socially or culturally accepted standards of behaviour, which have become accepted as representing how people 'ought' to act and what is 'normal' (i.e. appropriate) for a given situation.*

social representation theory *A theory which looks at how shared beliefs develop and are transmitted in social groups and in society as a whole. Such shared beliefs serve an important function in explaining reality and in justifying social action.*

sociometry *An approach to examining attitudes and social groupings by charting relationships within a group, and who refers to whom in terms of influence.*

somatic therapies *Forms of treatment which are based entirely on the body, e.g. using drugs to suppress disturbed behaviour rather than attempting to deal with the disturbance using psychotherapy.*

speech register *The form of language deemed appropriate for a particular social occasion. There are different speech registers to suit different types of occasions, and also to suit different relationships between people – for example,* friends would use an intimate speech register, while a patient consulting a doctor would use a formal one.

split-half method *A system for judging how reliable a psychometric test is which involves splitting the test into two, and administering each half of the test to the same people, then comparing the results.*

standardization *(a) The process of making sure that the conditions of a psychological study or psychometric test are always identical. (b) The process of establishing how the results of a psychometric test will usually come out in a given population, by drawing up sets of population norms.*

state-dependent memory *A form of remembering which is dependent on its physiological context, e.g. the influence of drugs or emotion.*

stimulus *An external environmental event to which an organism responds.*

stimulus–response learning *The name given to the behaviourist approach to learning, which viewed it as a simple association between an external stimulus and the behavioural response, denying any cognitive or mental processing.*

STM *The abbreviation used for short-term memory or memory which lasts for only a few seconds.*

stress experience *How we perceive the situation and the experiences we are having. The experience of stress is affected by our cognitive appraisal of the situation that we are in, so stress is not inevitable. We might easily see an event as exciting rather than stressful.*

stress response *Physiological changes, such as autonomic*

arousal, which occur as a result of stress.

stressors *Environmental changes that can induce a stress response.*

Stroop effect *A phenomenon demonstrating automaticity of information-processing, in which the identification of colour is interfered with by the name of a colour given in the stimulus material.*

subliminal perception *The ability to perceive and respond to stimuli which are presented below the level of conscious awareness.*

survey *A technique of collecting opinions from large numbers of people, generally involving the use of questionnaires.*

sustained attention *The process of concentrating consistently on one set of stimuli for a prolonged period of time.*

symbolic representation *The coding of information in the brain by means of symbols as opposed to sensory images.*

synaesthesia *A condition in which sensory input becomes distorted and confused, such that sounds may be experienced as touch etc.*

systematic desensitization *A classical conditioning technique for reducing fear and anxiety by replacing it with a calm response.*

task-oriented leaders *Leaders who focus explicitly on the tasks which have to be done by the team, and who show little or no interest in interpersonal concerns within it, unlike relationship-oriented leaders.*

temperament *The stable aspects of the character of an individual, which are often regarded as biologically based, and as providing the basic dispositions which interact with the environment to develop personality.*

territoriality *The name given to a set of behaviours which involve establishing and maintaining access to a particular area, while refusing the same to potential competitors of one's own species.*

test–retest method *A system for judging how reliable a psychometric test or measure is which involves administering the same test to the same people on two different occasions and comparing the results.*

thalamus *The sub-cortical structure in the brain which receives sensory information and relays it to the cerebral cortex.*

token economy *A system involving the use of tokens as secondary reinforcers used, for example, in the rehabilitation of long-term psychiatric patients.*

trait *A specific facet of personality.*

triangulation *Using several different methods of study to investigate a phenomenon is known as triangulation. If several different methods of study all come up with similar implications, we may conclude that the phenomenon we are investigating is a real one even if it is not possible to perform a single absolutely definitive study which proves it once and for all.*

triarchic theory of intelligence *A theory of intelligence developed by Sternberg (1958) which argues that intelligence needs to be understood from three distinct viewpoints: (a) the cultural and social context in which an intelligent act occurs; (b) how the person's own previous experience has shaped their responses; and (c) the mental skills and abilities involved in solving problems.*

two-process theory of memory *The idea that short-term and long-term memory are actually two entirely different systems, as* opposed to different levels of processing.

type A and B personalities Personality syndromes in which A is characterized by impatience, intolerance and a high level of stress, while B involves a relaxed, tolerant approach and noticeably lower personal stress.

unconditional positive regard Love, affection or respect which does not depend on the person's having to act in particular ways.

unconditioned response A response which occurs automatically to a particular stimulus and doesn't have to be learned.

unconditioned stimulus A stimulus which automatically, or reflexively, produces a response.

unconscious messages Information which we receive and are able to respond to without being aware of it.

validity The question of whether a psychometric test or psychological measure is really measuring what it is supposed to.

vasoconstriction The constriction of blood vessels which occurs as a response to cold.

verbal deprivation hypothesis The idea that children who do not experience extended forms of language may suffer cognitive

deficits as a consequence.

vigilance More commonly referred to as sustained attention: relates to the ability of an individual to maintain concentration on a task.

vocational guidance tests Psychometric tests which are designed to help people to find out what kind of jobs they are suited for.

Yerkes-Dodson law of arousal The principle that performance of any given task can be improved if the person is aroused; but that if the arousal increases beyond an optimal point, performance then declines.

References

ABELSON, R.P. and CARROLL, J. (1965) Computer simulation of individual belief systems. *American Behavioural Science,* **8**, 24–30.

ABRAMSON, L.Y., SELIGMAN, M.E.P. and TEASDALE, J.D. (1978) Learned helplessness in humans: critique and reformulation. *Journal of Abnormal Psychology,* **87**, 49–74.

ACHAMAMBA, B. and KUMAR, K.G. (1989) I-E locus of control and job satisfaction among the workers of public and private sector undertakings. *Journal of the Indian Academy of Applied Psychology,* **15**, 83–6.

ACHTERBERG, J. and LAWLIS, G.F. (1977) Psychology factors and blood chemistries as disease outcome predictors for cancer patients. *Multivariate Experimental Clinical Research,* **3**, 107–22.

ACKOFF, R.L. and EMSHOFF, J.R. (1975) Advertising research

ADELSTEIN, A.M. (1952) Accident proneness: a criticism of the concept based on an analysis of shunters' accidents. *Journal of the Royal Statistical Society,* **115**, 111–18.

ADAMS, J.S. and JACOBSEN, P.R. (1964) Effects of wage inequities on working quality. *Journal of Abnormal and Social Psychology,* **69**, 19–25.

ADORNO, T.W., FRENKEL-BRUNSWICK, G., LEVINSON, D.J. and SANFORD, R.N. (1950) *The Authoritarian Personality.* Harper, New York.

AIELLO J. and AIELLO, T. (1974) The development of personal space: proxemics behaviour of children 6 through 16. *Human Ecology,* **2**, 177–89.

AJZEN, I. and FISHBEIN, M. (1980) *Understanding Attitudes and Predicting Social Behaviour.* Prentice-Hall, Englewood Cliffs, New Jersey.

AJZEN, I. (1988) *Attitudes, Personality and Behaviour.* Open University Press, Milton Keynes.

ALEXANDER, J.F. and PARSONS, B.V. (1973) Short-term behavioural intervention with delinquent families. *Journal of Abnormal Psychology,* **81**, 219–25.

ALLEN, H. (1987) *Justice Unbalanced: gender, psychiatry and judicial decisions.* University Press, Milton Keynes.

ALLEN, K.E., HART, B.M., BUELL, J., HARRIS, F.R. and WOLF, M.M. (1964) Effects of social reinforcement on isolate behaviour of a nursery school child. *Child Development,* **35**, 511–18.

ALLPORT, G.W. (1935) Attitudes, in C.M. Murchison (ed.) *Handbook of Social Psychology.* Clark University Press, Worcester, Massachusetts.

ALLPORT, G.W. (1954) *The Nature of Prejudice.* Addison-Wesley, Cambridge, Massachusetts.

ALTMAN, I. (1975) *The Environment and Social Behaviour.* Brooks/Cole, Monterey, California.

AMABILE, T.M. (1985) Motivation and creativity: effects of motivational orientation on creative writers. *Journal of Personality and Social Psychology,* **48**, 393–9.

AMERIO, P. and GHIGLIONE, R. (1986) Cambiamento sociale, sistemi di rappresentazione e d'identita di attori vs. agenti sociali (Social change, systems of representation and identity of social actors vs agents). *Giornale Italiano di Psicologia,* **13**, 615–36.

AMMANN, R. (1987) Attributionsprozesse und soziales Wissen (Attribution processes and social knowledge). *Zeitschrift für Sozialpsychologie,* **18(2)**, 106–17.

ANDERSON, D.R., ALWITT, L.F., LORSCH, E.P. and LEVIN, S.R. (1979) Watching children watch television, in G. Hale and M. Lewis (eds) *Attention and the Development of Cognitive Skills.* Plenum, New York.

ANDERSON-KULMAN, R.E. and PALUDI, M.A. (1986) Working mothers and the family context: predicting positive coping. *Journal of Vocational Behaviour,* **28**, 241–53.

ANHEUSER-BUSCH INC. *Sloan Management Review,* **16**, 1–15.

ANNETT, J. (1989) Skills, in A.M. Colman and J.G. Beaumont (eds) *Psychology Survey 7.* BPS/Routledge, London.

ANTES, J.R., McBRIDGE, R.B. and COLLINS, J.D. (1988) The effect of a new city traffic route on the cognitive maps of its residents. *Environment and Behaviour,* **20**, 75–91.

AQUILINO, W.S. (1991) Predicting parents' experiences with coresident adult children. *Journal of Family Issues,* **12**, 323–42.

ARBOUS, A.G. and KERRICH, J.E. (1951) Accident statistics and the concept of accident proneness. *Biometrics,* **7**, 340–429.

ARCHIBALD, H.C.D., LONG, D.M., MILLER, C. and TUDDENHAM, R.D. (1963) Gross stress reactions in combat. *American Journal of Psychiatry,* **119**, 317.

ARENDT, H. (1963) *Eichmann in Jerusalem: a report on banality of evil.* Viking Press, New York.

ARGYLE, M. (1975) *Bodily Communication.* Methuen, London.

ARGYLE, M. (1991) *Co-operation.* Routledge, London.

ARGYLE, M., TRIMBOLI, L. and FORGAS, J. (1988) The bank manager/doctor effect: disclosure profiles in different relationships. *Journal of Social Psychology,* **128**, 117–24.

ARMS, R.L., RUSSELL, G.W. and SANDILANDS, M.L. (1980) Effects of viewing aggressive sports on the hostility of spectators, in R.M. Suinn (ed.) *Psychology in Sports: methods and applications.* Burgess Publishing Company, Minneapolis.

ARONSON, E. *et al.* (1978) The effects of a co-operative classroom structure on student behaviour and attitudes, in D. Bar-Tal and L. Saxe (eds) *Social Psychology of Education.* Wiley, New York.

ASCH, S.E. (1956) Studies of independence and conformity: a minority of one against a unanimous majority. *Psychological Monographs,* **70**, 9.

ATKINSON, R.C. and SHIFFRIN, R.M. (1977) Human Memory: a proposed system and its control processes, in G.H. Bower (ed.) *Human Memory: basic processes.* Academic Press, New York.

AZUMA, H., HESS, R.D. and KASHIWAGI, K. (1981) *Mother's Attitudes and Actions and the Intellectual (Mental) Development of Children.* Tokyo University Press, Tokyo.

BAARS, B.J. (1980) Eliciting predictable speech errors in the laboratory, in V. Fromkin (ed.) *Errors in Linguistic Performance: slips of the tongue, ear, pen, and hand.* Academic Press, New York.

BADDELEY, A. (1983) *Your Memory: a users's guide.* Penguin, Harmondsworth.

BADDELEY, A.D. and HITCH, G. (1974) Working memory, in G.H. Bower (ed.) *The Pyschology of Learning and Motivation* (Vol. 8), pp. 47–90.

BAINBRIDGE, L. (1987) The ironies of automation, in J. Rasmussen, K. Duncan and J. Leplat (eds) *New Technology and Human Error.* Wiley, London.

BAIRD, B.N. (1986) Tolerance for environmental health risks: the influence of knowledge, benefits, voluntariness, and environmental attitudes. *Risk Analysis,* **6**, 425–35.

BAKER, L.J., DEARBORN, M., HASTINGS, J.E. and HAMBERGER, K. (1984) Type A behaviour in women: a review. *Health Psychology,* **3**, 477–97.

BALES, R.F. and SLATER, P.E. (1955) Role differentiation in small decision-making groups, in T. Parsons *et al.* (eds) *Family Socialisation and Interaction Process.* The Free Press, New York.

BALTAXE, C.A. and SIMMONS, J.Q. (1977) Bedtime soliloquies and linguistic competence in autism. *Journal of Speech and Hearing Disorders,* **42**, 376–93.

BANDURA, A., CIOFFI, D., BARR TAYLOR, C. and BROUILLARD, M.E. (1988) Perceived self-efficacy in coping with cognitive stressors and opioid activation. *Journal of Personality and Social Psychology,* **55**, 479–88.

BANDURA, A., ROSS, D. and ROSS, S. (1963) Imitation of film mediated aggressive models. *Journal of Abnormal and Social Psychology,* **66**, 3–11.

BANDURA, A. (1969) *Principles of Behavior Modification.* Rinehart & Winston, New York.

BANDURA, A. (1973) *Aggression: a social learning analysis.* Prentice-Hall, Englewood Cliffs, New Jersey.

BANDURA, A. (1977) Self-efficacy. *Psychological Review,* **84**, 191–215.

BANDURA, A. (1977) *Social Learning Theory.* Prentice-Hall, Englewood Cliffs, New Jersey.

BANDURA, A. (1979) Psychological mechanisms of aggression, in M. von Cranach *et al.* (eds) *Human Ethology: Claims and limits of a new discipline.* Cambridge University Press, Cambridge.

BANDURA, A. (1989) Perceived self-efficacy in the exercise of personal agency. *The Psychologist,* **2**, 411–24.

BANYARD, P., FLETCHER, C. and STRATFORD, E. (1980) *Delinquency and Working Mothers.* Trent Papers in Education 80/2.

BARBER, P. (1988) *Applied Cognitive Psychology.* Routledge, New York.

BARGER, J. (1991) Coping behaviours of US Army flight nurses in World War II: an oral history. *Aviation, Space, and Environmental Medicine,* **62**, 153–7.

BARNHOORN, F. and ADRIAANSE, H. (1992) In search of factors responsible for noncompliance among tuberculosis patients in Wardha district, India. *Social Science and Medicine,* **34**, 291–306.

BARON, R.A. (1983) Self-presentation in job interviews: when there can't be too much of a good thing. *Journal of Applied Social Psychology,* **68**, 709–13.

BARRICK, M.R. and ALEXANDER, R.A. (1987) A review of quality circle efficiency and the existence of positive-findings bias. *Personnel Psychology,* **40**, 579–92.

BARTLETT, F.C. (1932) *Remembering.* Cambridge University Press, Cambridge.

BARTON, R. (1976) *Institutional Neurosis,* 3rd edn. Wright, Bristol.

BARRISH, H.H., SAUNDERS, M. and WOLF, M.M. (1969) Good behaviour game: effects of individual contigencies for group consequences on disruptive behaviour in a classroom. *Journal of Applied Behaviour Analysis,* **2**, 119–24.

BASLER, H.D. and REHFISCH, H.P. (1990) Follow-up results of a cognitive-behavioural treatment for chronic pain in a primary care setting. *Psychology and Health,* **4**, 293–304.

BASS, B.M. and BARRETT, G.V. (1972) *Man, Work and Organisations.* Allyn and Bacon, Boston.

BASS, B.M., WALDMAN, D.A., AVOLIO, B.J. and BEBB, M. (1987) Transformational leadership and the falling dominoes effect. *Group and Organisation Studies,* **12**, 73–87.

BASSOFF, E. (1985) Neglecting the negative: shortcomings in reasoning. *Journal of Counselling and Development,* **63**, 368–71.

BATESON, G., JACKSON, D., HALEY, J. and WEAKLAND, J. (1956) Towards a theory of schizophrenia. *Behavioural Science,* **1(4)**, 251–64.

BATRA, R. and STAYMAN, D.M. (1990) The role of mood in advertising effectiveness. *Journal of Consumer Research,* **17**, 203–14.

BAUM, A., FLEMING, R. and REDDY, D.M. (1986) Unemployment stress: loss of control, reactance and learned helplessness. *Social Science and Medicine,* **22**, 509–16.

BEAL, A.L. (1985) The skill of recognizing musical structures. *Memory and Cognition,* **13**, 405–12.

BEAN, K.L. (1937) An approach to the reading of music. *Psychological Monographs,* **226**, 1–80.

BEATTIE, G. (1988) *All Talk: why it's important to watch your words and everything else you say.* Weidenfeld, London.

BEAUTRAIS A.L., FERGUSSON, D.M. and SHANNON, F.T. (1982) Life events and childhood morbidity: a prospective study. *Pediatrics,* **70**, 933–40.

BECK, A.T., RUSH, A.J., SHAW, B.F. and EMERY, G. (1980) *Cognitive Therapy of Depression.* Wiley, Chichester.

BEKERIAN, D.A. and BADDELEY, A.D. (1980) Saturation advertising and the repetition effect. *Journal of Verbal Learning and Verbal Behaviour,* **19**, 17–25.

BELBIN, E. (1964) Training the adult worker. *Problems of Progress in Industry,* No. 15. D.S.I.R., London.

BELBIN, E., BELBIN, R.M. and HILL, F. (1957) A comparison between the results of three methods of operator training. *Ergonomics,* **1**, 39–50.

BELCH, G.E. (1982) The effects of television commercial repetition on cognitive response and message acceptance. *Journal of Consumer Research,* **9**, 56–65.

BELK, R., PAINTER, J. and SEMENIK, R. (1981) Preferred solutions to the energy crisis as a function of causal attributions. *Journal of Consumer Research,* **8**, 306–12.

BELL, G.D. (1967) The automobile buyer after purchase. *Journal of Marketing,* **31**, 12–16.

BELL, P.A. and YEE, L.A. (1989) Skill level and audience effects on performance of a karate drill. *Journal of Social Psychology,* **129**, 191–200.

BELOFF, H. (1988) The eye and the me: self-portraits of eminent photographers. *Philosophical Psychology,* **1**, 295–311.

BENEWICK, R. and HOLTON, R. (1987) The peaceful crowd: crowd solidarity and the Pope's visit to Britain, in G. Gaskell and R. Benewick (eds) *The Crowd in Contemporary Britain.* Sage, London.

BENNE, K.D. and SHEATS, P. (1948) Functional group members. *Journal of Social Issues,* **4**, 41–9.

BENNETT, W.L. and FELDMAN, M.S. (1981) *Reconstructing Reality in the Courtroom.* Tavistock, London.

BERGANDI, T.A. and WITTING, A.F. (1988) Attention style as a predictor of athletic injury. *International Journal of Sport Psychology,* **19**, 226–35.

BERNSTEIN, B. (1973) Social class, language and socialisation, in V. Lee (ed.) (1979) *Language Development.* Croom Helm/Open University, London.

BIERNAT, M. and WORTMAN, C.B. (1990) Sharing of home responsibilities between professionally employed women and their husbands. *Journal of Personality and Social Psychology,* **60**, 844–60.

BILLIG, M. (1990) Collective memory, ideology and the British Royal Family, in D. Middleton and D. Edwards (eds) *Collective Remembering.* Sage, London.

BILLIG, M., CONDOR, S., EDWARDS, D., GANE, M., MIDDLETON, D. and RADLEY, A. (1988) *Ideological Dilemmas. A Social Psychology of Everyday Thinking.* Sage, London.

BLAKE, R.R. and MOULTON, J.S. (1982) Theory and research for developing a science of leadership. *Journal of Applied Behavioural Science,* **18**, 275–92.

BLAU, G. (1987) Locus of control as potential moderator of the turnover process. *Journal of Occupational Psychology,* **60**, 21–9.

BOAS, F. (1911) *Handbook of American Indian Languages.* Smithsonian Institute, Washington, D.C.

BOLZMAN, C., MUGNY, G. and ROUX, P. (1987) Comparaisons entre groupes de statut social different: attributions sociocentriques ou logique d'une representation sociale? *Social Science Information,* **26**, 129–54.

BOSKIND-WHITE, M. and WHITE, W.C. (1983) *Bulimarexia: the binge/purge cycle.* Norton, New York.

BOWEN, M. (1960) A family concept of schizophrenia, in D.D. Jackson (ed.) *The Etiology of Schizophrenia.* Basic Books, New York.

BOWMAN, K. (1951) The problem of the sex offender. *American Journal of Psychiatry,* **108**, pp. 250–7.

BRADLEY, C., GAMSU, D.S., MOSES, J.L., KNIGHT, G., BOULTON, A.J.M., DRURY, J. and WARD, J.D. (1987) The use of a diabetes-specific perceived control and health belief measure to predict treatment choice and efficacy in a feasibility study of continuous subcutaneous insulin infusion pumps. *Psychology and Health,* **1**, 133–46.

BRAMMER, L.M. (1973) *The Helping Relationship.* Prentice-Hall, Englewood Cliffs, New Jersey.

BREAKWELL, G.M. (1992) *The AIDS Generation, Thatcher's children ... identity, social representations and action.* Inaugural lecture, University of Surrey.

BREAKWELL, G.M. (1994) The Echo of Power: a framework for social psychological research. C.S. Myers Commemorative Lecture. *The Psychologist,* **7**(2), 65–72.

BREAN, H. (1958, 31 March) What hidden sell is all about. *Life,* 104–14.

BREWIN, C.R. (1984) Attributions for industrial accidents: their relationship to rehabilitation outcome. *Journal of Social and Clinical Psychology,* **2**, 156–64.

BRIDGE, I.R., BENSON, P., PIETRONI, P.C. and PRIEST, R.G. (1988) Relaxation and imagery in the treatment of breast cancer. *British Medical Journal,* **297**, 1169–72.

BRIGGS, R. (1971) Urban cognitive distances. Unpublished doctoral dissertation, Ohio State University, cited in Matlin, M. (1983) *Cognition.* Holt, Rinehart & Winston, New York.

BROADBENT, D.E. and LITTLE, E.A.J. (1960) Effects of noise reduction in a work situation. *Occupational Psychology,* **34**, 133–40.

BROBERG, D.G. and BERNSTEIN, I.L. (1987) Candy as a scapegoat in the prevention of food aversions in children receiving chemotherapy. *Cancer,* **60**, 2344–7

BROMLEY, D.B. (1968) *The Psychology of Human Ageing.* Penguin, Harmondsworth.

BROPHY, J. and GOOD, T. (1970) Teachers' communication of differential expectations for children's performances: some behavioural data. *Journal of Educational Psychology,* **61**, 365–74.

BROWN, G.A. (1975) *Micro-teaching.* Methuen, London.

BROWN, G. and HARRIS, T. (1978) *The Social Origins of Depression. A Study of Psychiatric Disorder in Women.* Tavistock, London.

BROWNELL, K.D., COHEN, R.Y., STUNKARD, A.J., FELIX, M.R. and COOLEY, N.B. (1984) Weight loss competitions at the work site: impact on weight morale and cost-effectiveness. *American Journal of Public Health,* **74**, 1283–5.

BRUCE, V. and GREEN, P. (1985) *Visual Perception: physiology, psychology and ecology.* Lawrence Erlbaum Associates, London.

BRUCE, V. and YOUNG A.W. (1986) Understanding face recognition. *British Journal of Psychology,* **77**, 305–27.

BRUNER, J.S. and KENNEY, H. (1966) The development of the concepts of order and proportion in children, in J.S. Bruner *et al.* (eds) *Studies in Cognitive Growth.* Wiley, New York.

BRUNER, J.S. (1964) The course of cognitive growth. *American Psychologist,* **19**, 1–15.

BRUNER, J.S. and MINTURN, A.L. (1955) Perceptual identification and perceptual organisation. *Journal of General Psychology,* **53**, 21–8.

BRUNER, J.S. (1961) The act of discovery. *Harvard Educational Review,* **31**, 21–32.

BRUNER, J.S. (1973) *Beyond the Information Given: studies in the psychology of knowing.* W.W. Norton, New York.

BUCHLER, R.E., PATTERSON, G.R. and FURNISS, J.M. (1966) The reinforcement of behaviour in institutional settings. *Behaviour Research and Therapy,* **4**, 461–76.

BUGARD, P., CHEYNE, W.M. and JAHODA, G. (1989) Children's representations of economic inequality: a replication. *British Journal of Developmental Psychology,* **7**, 275–87.

BURGER, J. and GOCHFELD, M. (1991) Fishing a superfund site: dissonance and risk perception of environmental hazards by fishermen in Puerto Rico. *Risk Analysis,* **11**, 269–77.

BURKE, R.R. and SRULL, T.K. (1988) Competitive interference and consumer memory for advertising. *Journal of Consumer Research,* **15** (June), 55–68.

BURN, S.M. and KONRAD, A.M. (1987) Political participation: a matter of community, stress, job autonomy, and contact by political organizations. *Political Psychology,* **8**, 125–38.

BURNS, J.M. (1978) *Leadership.* Harper & Row, New York.

BURNS, R.B. (1966) Age and mental ability. *British Journal of Educational Psychology,* **36**, 116.

BUTLER, J.M. and HAIGH, G.V. (1954) Changes in the relation between self-concept and ideal concepts consequent on client centred counselling, in C.R. Rogers and R.F. Dymond (eds) *Psychotherapy and Personality Change.* University of Chicago Press, Chicago.

BUTTERFIELD, L. (1989) Paul Masson California Carafes: 'They're really jolly good!', in C. Channon (ed.) *Twenty Advertising Case Histories* (2nd series). Cassell, London.

BYRNE, R.W. (1979) Memory for urban geography. *Quarterly Journal of Experimental Psychology,* **31**(1), 147–54.

CAIN, E.N., KOHORN, E.I., QUINLAN, D.M., LATIMER, K. and SCHWARTZ, P.E. (1986) Psychosocial benefits of a cancer support group. *Cancer,* **57**, 183–9.

CAIRNS, E. and MERCER, G.W. (1984) Social identity in Northern Ireland. *Human Relations,* **37**, 1095–102.

CAIRNS, E. and WILSON, R. (1984) The impact of political violence on mild psychiatric morbidity in Northern Ireland. *British Journal of Psychiatry,* **145**, 631.

CALLAN, V.J. (1993) Subordinate-manager communication in different sex dyads: consequences for job satisfaction. *Journal of Occupational and Organisational Psychology,* **66**, 13–27.

CALVERT, S.L., HUSTON, A.C., WATKINS, B.A. and WRIGHT, J.C. (1982) The relation between selective attention to television forms and children's comprehension of content. *Child Development,* **53**, 601–10.

CAMARGO, C.A., VRANISAN, K.M., THORESEN, C.E. and WOOD, P.D. (1986) Type A behaviour pattern and alcohol intake in middle-aged men. *Psychosomatic Medicine,* **48**(8), 575–81.

CAMPBELL, A. (1984) Girls' talk: the social representation of aggression by female gang members. *Criminal Justice and Behavior,* **11**(2), 139–56.

CAMPBELL, R. (1992) Face to face: interpreting a case of developmental prosopagnosia, in R. Campbell (ed.) *Mental Lives: case studies in cognition.* Blackwell, Oxford.

CANTER, D. and CANTER, S. (1979) *Designing for Therapeutic Environments: a review of research.* Wiley, Chichester.

CANTER, D. (1980) *Fires and Human Behaviour,* Wiley, Chichester.

CARKHUFF, R.R. and BERENSON, B.G. (1976) *Teaching as Treatment.* Human Resource Development Press, Amherst, Massachusetts.

CARKHUFF, R.R. (1974) *The Art of Helping.* Human Resource Development Press, Amherst, Massachusetts.

CARLSON, R.E. (1969) Degree of job fit as a moderator of the relationship between job performance and job satisfaction. *Personnel Psychology, 22*, 159–70.

CARMICHAEL, L., HOGAN, H.P. and WALTER, A.A. (1932) An experimental study of the effect of language on visually perceived forms. *Journal of Experimental Psychology,* **15**, 73–86.

CARROLL, J.S., GALEGHER, J. and WIENER, R. (1982) Dimensional and categorical attributions in expert parole decisions. *Basic and Applied Social Psychology, 3*(3), 187–201.

CARUGATI, F.F. (1990) Everyday ideas, theoretical models and social representations: the case of intelligence and its development, in G.R. Semin and K.J. Gergen (eds) *Everyday Understanding: Social and scientific implications.* Sage, London.

CASTLE, P.F.C. (1956) Accidents, absence and withdrawal from the work situation. *Human Relations,* **9**, 223–33.

CERULLI, M.A. NIKOOMANESH, P. and SCHUSTER, M.M. (1979) Progress in biofeedback for fecal incontinence. *Gastroenterology,* **76**, 742–6.

CHANEY, F.B. and TEEL, K.S. (1967) Improving inspector performance through training and visual aids. *Journal of Applied Psychology,* **51**, 311–15.

CHEN, H. and DHAR, V. (1990) User misconceptions of information retrieval systems. *International Journal of Man-Machine Studies,* **32**, 673–92.

CHEYNE, W. (1970) Sterotyped reactions to speakers with Scottish and English regional accents. *British Journal of Social and Clinical Psychology,* **9**, 77–9.

CHODOROW, N. (1974) Family structure and feminine personality, in M.Z. Rosaldo and L. Lamphere (eds) *Woman, Culture and Society.* Stanford University Press, Stanford.

CHOY, S.J. and DODD, D.H. (1976) Standard-English-Speaking and Nonstandard Hawaiian-English-Speaking children: comprehension of both dialects and teacher's evaluations. *Journal of Educational Psychology,* **68**, 184–93.

CHRISTANSEN-SZALANSKI, J.J. and BEACH, L.R. (1984) The citation bias: fad and fashion in the judgement and decision literature. *American Psychologist,* **39**, 75–8.

CLARIDGE, G. (1988) *Temperament, personality and individual differences.* Lecture given at Psychology Teachers Workshop, Oxford University, March 1988.

CLARKE, R. (1953) *Analysing the group structure of rifle squads in combat.* Paper presented to the APA Convention, Cleveland, Ohio.

COCANOUGHER, A.B. and BRUCE, G.D. (1971) Socially distant reference groups and consumer aspirations. *Journal of Marketing Research,* **8**, 379–81.

COCHRANE and BAL (1987) in R.Littlewood and M. Lidsedge, M. (eds) (1989) *Aliens and Alienists,* 2nd edn, Unwin Hyman.

COHEN, D. (1979) *J.B. Watson: The Founder of Behaviourism.* Routledge and Kegan Paul, London.

COHEN, S., EVANS, G.W., KRANTZ, D.S. and STOKOLS, D. (1980) Physiological, motivational and cognitive effects of aircraft noise on children. *American Psychologist,* **35**, 231–43.

COHEN, S., GLASS, D.C. and SINGER, J.E. (1973) Apartment noise, auditory discrimination and reading ability in children. *Journal of Experimental Social Psychology,* **9**, 407–22.

COLBY, K.M. (1981) Modelling a paranoid mind. *Behavioral and Brain Sciences,* **4**, 515–60.

COLBY, K.M., WEBER, S. and HILF, F.D. (1972) Artificial paranoia. *Artificial Intelligence,* **2**, 1–25.

COLEMAN, P. (1981) Ageing and Social Problems, in M. Herbert (ed.) *Psychology for Social Workers,* pp. 279–94. British Psychological Society/MacMillan, London.

COLMAN, A.M. (1991) Expert psychological testimony in two murder trials in South Africa. *Issues in Criminological and Legal Psychology, 1*(17), 43–9.

CONDRY, J. (1989) *The Psychology of Television*. Lawrence Erlbaum Associates, Hillsdale, New Jersey.

COOK, M. (1978) *Perceiving Others*. Routledge, London.

COOPER, M.J. and FAIRBURN, C.G. (1992) Selective processing of eating, weight and shape related words in patients with eating disorders and dieters. *British Journal of Clinical Psychology*, **31**, 363–5.

COOPER, D.E. (1984) Labov, Larry and Charles, *Oxford Review of Education*, **18**, 177–92.

COTTERILL, P. (1992) Interviewing women – issues of friendship, vulnerability and power. *Women's Studies International Forum*, Vol. **15**, 615–17.

COWPE, C. (1989) Chip pan fire prevention 1976–1984, in C. Channon (ed.) *Twenty Advertising Case Histories* (2nd series). Cassell, London.

COX, R.H. (1990) *Sport Psychology: Concepts and Applications*. Wm C. Brown, London.

CRAIK, I.F.M. and LOCKHART, R.S. (1972) Levels of processing: a framework for memory research. *Journal of Verbal Learning and Verbal Behaviour*, **11**, 671–84.

CROMWELL, P.F., MARKS, A., OLSON, J.N. and AVARY, D.W. (1991) Group effects on decision-making by burglars. *Psychological Reports*, **69**, 579–88.

CRUTCHFIELD, R.S. (1955) Conformity and character. *American Psychologist*, **10**, 191–8.

CUMMINS, R. (1989) Locus of control and social support: clarifiers of the relationship between job stress and job satisfaction. *Journal of Applied Social Psychology*, **19**, 772–88.

CURTISS, S. (1977) *Genie: A Psycholinguistic Study of a Modern-Day 'Wild Child'*. Academic Press, New York.

CUSSON, M. and PINONNEAULT, P. (1986) The decision to give up crime, in D.B. Cornish and R.V. Clarke (eds) *The Reasoning Criminal*, pp. 72–82. Springer-Verlag, New York.

DAINO, A. (1985) Personality traits of adolescent tennis players. *International Journal of Sport Psychology*, **16**, 120–5.

DANE, F.C. and WRIGHTMAN, L.S. (1982) Effects of defendants' and victims' characteristics of jurors' verdicts, in N.L. Kerr and R.M. Bray (eds) *The Psychology of the Courtroom*. Academic Press, London.

DANIELS, G.S. (1952) *The 'average man'?* Technical note WCRD 53–7 Wright-Patterson Air Force Base, OH: Wright Air Development Centre, USAF 9AD-10203.

DANIELSON, R.R., ZELHART, P.F. and DRAKE, C.J. (1975) Multidimensional scaling and factor analysis of coaching behaviour as perceived by high school hockey players. *Research Quarterly*, **46**, 323–34.

DARLEY, J.M. and LATANÉ, B. (1970) Norms and normative behaviour: field studies of social interdependence, in J. Macauley and L. Berkowitz (eds) *Altruism and Helping Behaviour*. Academic Press, New York.

DAVIES, D.R. and SHACKLETON, V.J. (1975) *Psychology and Work*. Methuen, London.

DAVIES, D.R. (1970) Monotony and work. *Science Journal*, **6**(8), 26–31.

DAVIES, W. (1988) How not to get hit: violence and the helping professions, in N.J. Hayes (ed.) Teaching psychology to social workers. *Group of Teachers of Psychology Occasional Papers No. 7*. British Psychological Society, Leicester.

DAY, D.V. and BEDEIAN, A.G. (1991) Work climate and Type A status as predictors of job satisfaction: a test of the interactional perspective. *Journal of Vocational Behavior*, **38**, 39–52.

DE BENEDITTIS, G., LORENZETTI, A. and PIERI, A. (1990) The role of stressful life events in the onset of chronic primary headache. *Pain*, **40**, 65–75.

DE CASTRO, J.M. (1991) Social facilitation of the spontaneous meal size of humans occurs on both weekdays and weekends. *Physiology and Behavior*, **49**, 1289–91.

DE VOS, G. (1985) Dimensions of the self in Japanese culture, in A.J. Marsell *et al.* *Culture and Self: Asian and western perspectives.* Tavistock Publications, London.

DE WAAL, F.B.M. (1989) *Peacemaking Among Primates.* Harvard University Press, Cambridge, Massachusetts.

DELUGA, R.J. and PERRY, J.T. (1991) The relationship of subordinate upward influencing behaviour, satisfaction and perceived superior effectiveness with leader-member exchanges. *Journal of Occupational Psychology,* **64**, 239–52.

DEPOLO, M. and SARCHIELLI, G. (1983) Le rappresentazioni sociali del lavoro (The social representations of work). *Giornale Italiano di Psicologia,* **10**(3), 501–19.

DEUTSCH, M. and COLLINS, M. (1951) *Interracial Housing: A psychological evaluation of a social experiment.* University of Minnesota Press, Minneapolis, Minnesota.

DEVELLIS, D.L., DEVELLIS, B.M. and MCCAULEY, C. (1978) Vicarious acquisition of learned helplessness. *Journal of Personality and Social Psychology,* **36**, 894–9.

DEVLIN, LORD PATRICK (1976) Report to the Secretary of State for the Home Department of the Departmental Committee on Evidence of Identification in Criminal Cases, HMSO, London.

DEVLIN, T and WILLIAMS, H. (1992, 26 September) Hands up those who were happy at school. *New Scientist.*

DEYHLE, D. (1986) Break dancing and breaking out: Anglos, Utes, Navajos in a border reservation high school. *Anthropology and Education Quarterly,* **17**, 111–27.

DI GIACOMO, J.P. (1980) Intergroup alliances and rejections within a protest movement (analysis of the social representations). *European Journal of Social Psychology,* **10**, 329–44.

DICKERSON, C.A., THIBODEAU, R., ARONSON, E. and MILLER, D. (1992) Using cognitive dissonance to encourage water conservation. *Journal of Applied Social Psychology,* **22**, 841–54.

DICKS, H. (1972) *Licensed Mass Murder: a socio-psychological study of some SS killers.* Tavistock, London.

DODD, G.H. (1989) *Aromacology.* Paper delivered at the British Psychological Society London Conference, December.

DOHERTY, W.J. (1983) Impact of divorce on locus of control orientation in adult women: A longitudinal study. *Journal of Personality and Social Psychology,* **44**(4), 834–40.

DOISE, W., DESCHAMPS, J.C. and MYER, G. (1978) The accentuation of intra-category similarities, in H. Tajfel (ed.) *Differentiation Between Social Groups.* Academic Press, London.

DOLLARD, J., DOOB, L.W., MILLER, N.E., MOWRER, O.H. and SEARS, R.R. (1939) *Frustration and Aggression.* Yale University Press, New Haven.

DOMS, M. and AVERMAET, E. VAN (1981) The conformity effect: a timeless phenomenon? *Bulletin of the British Psychological Society,* **34**, 383–5.

DRINKWATER, J.M. and FELDMAN, M.P. (1982) *Violent incidents in a British Psychiatric Hospital: a preliminary study.* Unpublished manuscript, University of Birmingham Library.

DRISKELL, J.E. and SALAS, E. (1991) Group decision making under stress. *Journal of Applied Psychology,* **76**, 473–8.

DRIVER, R. (1983) *The Pupil as Scientist?* Open University Press, Milton Keynes.

DUCK, S.W. (1973) *Personal Relationships and Personal Constructs: A study of friendship formation.* Wiley, London.

DUCK, S.W. (1988) *Relating to Others.* Open University Press, Milton Keynes.

DUNKEL-SCHETTER, C., FOLKMAN, S. and LAZARUS, R.S. (1987) Correlates of social support receipt. *Journal of Personality and Social Psychology,* **53**, 71–80.

DWECK, C. (1975) The role of expectations and attributions in the alleviation of learned helplessness. *Journal of Personality and Social Psychology,* **31**, 674–85.

DWECK C. *et al.* (1987) Sex differences in learned helplessness II: the contingencies of evaluative feedback in the classroom and III: an experimental analysis. *Developmental Psychology,* **14**, 267–76.

EARN, B.M. and SOBOL, M.P. (1990) A categorical analysis of children's attributions for social success and failure. *Psychological Record,* **40**(2), 173–85.

ECHABE, A.E. and PAEZ-ROVIRA, D. (1989) Social representations and memory: the case of AIDS. *European Journal of Social Psychology,* **19**, 543–51.

EDWARDS, A.D. (1987) Language codes and classroom practice. *Oxford Review of Education,* 13, 237–47.

EDWARDS, D. and MERCER, N. (1987) *Common Knowledge: the development of understanding in the classroom.* Methuen, London.

EDWARDS, J.R. (1979) *Language and Disadvantage.* Edward Arnold, London.

EDWARDS, R. (1990) Connecting method and epistemology: a white woman interviewing a black woman. *Women's Studies International Forum,* **13**, 477–90.

EHRLICH, D., GUTTMAN, I., SCHONBACK, P. and MILLS, J. (1957) Postdecision exposure to relevant information. *Journal of Abnormal and Social Psychology,* **54**, 98–102.

EIBL-EIBLESFELDT, I. (1975) The ethology of man, in H. Brown and R. Stevens (eds) *Social Behaviour and Experience.* Open University Press, Milton Keynes.

EKMAN, P. and FRIESEN, W.V. (1969) The repertoire of non-verbal behaviour: categories, origins, usage and coding. *Semiotica,* **1**, 49–98.

ELIZUR, D. (1990) Quality circles and quality of work life. *International Journal of Manpower (UK),* **11**(6), 3–7.

ELSTEIN, A.S., HOLZMAN, G.B., RAVITCH, M.M., HOLMES, M.H., HOPPE, R.B., ROTHERT, M.L. and ROVNER, D.R. (1986) Comparison of physicians' decisions regarding replacement therapy for menopausal women and decisions derived from a decision analytic model. *American Journal of Medicine,* **80**, 246–58.

ERLENMEYER-KIMLING, L. and JARVIK, L.F. (1963) Genetics and intelligence: a review. *Science,* **142**, 1477–9.

ESSER, A. *et al.*(1965) Territoriality in institutions, in J. Wortis (ed.) *Recent advances in Biological Psychiatry.* Plenum, New York.

EYSENCK, H.J. (1947) *Dimensions of Personality.* Routledge, London.

EYSENCK, H.J. (1962) *Know Your Own IQ.* Penguin, Harmondsworth.

EYSENCK, H.J. (1965) The effects of psychotherapy. *International Journal of Psychiatry,* **1**, 99–142.

EYSENCK, H.J. (1971) *Race, Intelligence and Education.* Temple Smith, London.

EYSENCK, H.J. (ed.) (1981) *A Model for Personality.* Springer-Verlag, New York.

FAIRBANK, J.A. and KEANE, T.M. (1982) Flooding for combat-related stress disorders: assessment of anxiety reduction across traumatic memories. *Behavior Therapy,* **13**(4), 499–510.

FAIRFIELD-SONN, J.W. (1987) Using cognitive maps to learn how organisations function. Cited in Nossiter, V and Biberman, G. (1990) Projective drawings and metaphor: analysis of organisational culture. *Journal of Managerial Psychology,* **5**(3), 13–16.

FARN, C.K. and JIANG, R.K. (1990) Organisational issues in small businesses computerisation in the Republic of China. *International Journal of Psychology,* **25**, 901–15.

FARRINGDON, D.P. (1990) Implications of criminal career research for the prevention of offending. *Journal of Adolescence,* **13**, 93–113.

FELSENTHAL, D.S. and BRICHTA, A. (1985) Sincere and strategic voters: an Israeli study. *Political Behavior,* **7**, 311–24.

FENKER, R.M. and LAMBIOTTE, J.G. (1987) A performance enhancement programme for a college football team: one incredible season. *The Sport Psychologist,* **1**, 224–36.

FERGUSON, M.A. and VALENTI, J.M. (1991) Communicating with environmental and health risk takers: an individual differences perspective. *Health Education Quarterly,* **18**, 303–18.

FERNBERG, R. (1986) Credit cards as spending facilitating stimuli: a conditioning explanation. *Journal of Consumer Research,* **13**, 348–56.

FESTINGER, L. and CARLSMITH, J.M. (1959) Cognitive consequences of forced compliance. *Journal of Abnormal and Social Psychology,* **58**, 203–10.

FESTINGER, L. (1957) *A Theory of Cognitive Dissonance.* Row, Peterson, Evanston, Illinois.

FESTINGER, L., RIECKEN, H.W. and SCHACHTER, S. (1956) *When Prophecy Fails.* University of Minneapolis Press, Minneapolis.

FEUERSTEIN, M., LABBÉ, E. and KUCZMEIRCZYK, A. (1986) *Health Psychology: A psychobiological perspective.* Plenum, New York.

FINCHAM, F. and O'LEARY, K.D. (1983) Causal inferences for spouse behavior in maritally distressed and nondistressed couples. *Journal of Social and Clinical Psychology,* **1**, 42–57.

FINN, G.P.T. (1990) In the grip? A psychological and historical exploration of the social significance of freemasonry in Scotland, in T. Gallagher and G. Walker (eds) *Sermons and Battle Hymns: Protestant popular culture in modern Scotland.* University Press, Edinburgh.

FISCHER, J. (1978) *Effective Casework Practice: an electric approach.* McGraw-Hill, New York.

FISCHER, K.W. (1980) A theory of cognitive development: the control and construction of hierarchies of skills. *Psychological Review,* **87**, 477–531.

FISCHLER, C. (1980) Food habits, social change and the nature/culture dilemma. *Social Science Information,* **19**(6), 937–53.

FISHER, A.C., MANCINI, V.H., HIRSCH, R.L., PROULX, T.J. and STAUROWSKY, E.J. (1982) Coach–athlete interactions and team climate. *Journal of Sport Psychology,* **4**, 388–404.

FISKE, S.T. and LINVILLE, P.W. (1980) What does the schema concept buy us? *Personality and Social Psychology Bulletin,* **6**, 543–57.

FIVUSH, R. (1984) Learning about school: the development of kindergartens' school scripts. *Child Development,* **55**, 1697–709.

FLETCHER, S. and WOOD, R. (1993) *The efficacy of coaching in test-taking behaviour: a preliminary investigation.* Paper presented at the British Psychological Society Annual Conference.

FOLKMAN, S. and LAZARUS, R. (1988) *Manual for the Ways of Coping Questionnaire.* Consulting Psychologists Press, Palo Alto, California.

FORDEN, C. (1981) The influence of sex-role expectations on the perception of touch. *Sex Roles,* **7**, pp. 889–94.

FORER, B.R. (1949) The fallacy of personal validation: a classroom demonstration of gullibility. *Journal of Abnormal and Social Psychology,* **44**.

FOWLER, F.J., McCALL, M.E. and MANGIONE, T.W. (1979) *Reducing Residential Crime and Fear: The Hartford neighbourhood crime prevention program.* Government Printing Office, Washington, D.C.

FRANCIS, T. (1989) *Clough: A biography.* Stanley Paul, London.

FRANSELLA, F. (1972) *Personal Change and Reconstruction.* Academic Press, London.

FRASER, A. (1983) *Cromwell: A chief of men.* Weidenfeld & Nicholson, London.

FRAZIER, P.A. (1990) Victim attributions and post-rape trauma. *Journal of Personality and Social Psychology,* **59**, 298–304.

FREUD, S. (1901) The psychopathology of everyday life. Republished 1953. In J. Strachey (ed.) *The Standard Edition of the Complete Psychological Works of Sigmund Freud Vol. 6.* Hogarth, London.

FREUD, S. (1920) *Beyond the Pleasure Principle* (1975 edn.) Norton, New York.

FRIEDMAN, H.H. and FIREWORKER, R.B. (1977) The susceptibility of consumers to unseen group influence. *Journal of Social Psychology,* **102**, 155–6.

FRIEDMAN, M. and ROSENMAN, R.H. (1974) *Type A Behaviour and your Heart*. Knopf, New York.

FRY, P.S. (1983) Process measures of problem and non-problem children's classroom behaviour: the influence of teacher behaviour variables. *British Journal of Educational Psychology*, **53**, 79–88.

FULLERTON, J. and WEST, M. (1991) *Dimensions of Client-consultant Relationships in Management Consultancy*. Paper delivered at the British Psychological Society Occupational Psychology Conference, January.

FURNHAM, A. and VARIAN, C. (1988) Predicting and accepting personality test scores. *Personality and Individual Differences*, **9**, 735–48.

FURNHAM, A. (1989) Personality and the acceptance of diagnostic feedback. *Personality and Individual Differences*, **10**, 1121–33.

GALL, A.L. (1987) You can take the manager out of the woods, but .... *Training and Development Journal*, **41**, 54–8.

GALLI, I. and NIGRO, G. (1987) The social representation of radioactivity among Italian children. *Social Science Information*, **26**, 535–49.

GALTON, F. (1888) Co-relations and their measurement, chiefly from anthropometric data, in J.J. Jenkins and D.G. Paterson (eds) *Studies in Individual Differences*, 1961. Appleton Century Crofts, New York.

GAMMON, C. (1985, 10 June) A day of horror and shame. *Sports Illustrated*, **62**, 20–35.

GARDNER, H. (1985) *Frames of Mind: The theory of multiple intelligences*. Paladin, London.

GARDNER, R.C. and TAYLOR, D.M. (1968) Ethnic Stereotypes: Their effects on person perception. *Canadian Journal of Psychology*, **22**, 267–76.

GARFINKEL, H. (1967) *Studies in Ethnomethodology*. Prentice-Hall, Englewood Cliffs, New Jersey.

GASKELL, G. and SMITH, P (1985) An investigation of youth's attributions for unemployment and their political attitudes. *Journal of Economic Psychology*, **6**(1), 65–80.

GERBNER, G., GROSS, L., MORGAN, M. and SIGNORIELLI, N. (1980) The 'mainstreaming' of America: violence profile No. 11. *Journal of Communication*, **30**, 10–29.

GERGEN, K. and GERGEN, M. (1973) Deviance in the dark. *Psychology Today*, October.

GERGEN, M.M. (1988) Building a feminist methodology. *Contemporary Social Psychology*, **13**, 47–53.

GHISELIN, B. (1952) *The Creative Process*. University of California Press, Berkeley, California.

GHISELLI, E.E. (1966) *The Validity of Occupational Aptitude Tests*. Wiley, New York.

GIBBONS, F.X. and KASSIN, S.M. (1987) Information consistency and perceptual set: overcoming the mental retardation 'schema'. *Journal of Applied Social Psychology*, **17**, 810–27.

GIBSON, H.B. (1982) The use of hypnosis in police investigations. *Bulletin of the British Psychological Society*, **35**, 138–42.

GIBSON, J.J. (1979) *The Ecological Approach to Visual Perception*. Houghton Mifflin, Boston.

GIELEN, U. (1979) Naturalistic observation of sex and race differences in visual interactions. *International Journal of Group Tensions*, **9**, 211–27.

GILBERT, M. (1976, 29 January) Behavioural approach to the treatment of child abuse. *Nursing Times*.

GILES, H. (1973) Accent mobility: a model and some data. *Anthropological Linguistics*, **15**, 87–105.

GILLIGAN, C. and ATTANUCCI, J. (1988) Two moral orientations: gender differences and similarities. *Merrill Palmer Quarterly*, **34**, 223–37.

GIORGI, L. and MARSH, C. (1990) The Protestant work ethic as a cultural phenomenon. *European Journal of Social Psychology*, **20**, 499–517.

GIST, M.E., SCHWOERER, C. and ROSEN, B. (1989) Effects of alternative training methods on self-efficacy and performance in computer software training. *Journal of Applied Psychology,* **74**, 884–91.

GLADWIN, T. (1970) *East is a Big Bird: navigation and logic on Puluwat atoll.* Harvard University Press, Cambridge, Massachusetts.

GLAMSER, F.D. (1990) Contest location, player misconduct, and race: a case from English soccer. *Journal of Sport Behavior,* **13**, 41–9.

GLASS, D.C., SINGER, J.E. and FRIEDMAN, L.W. (1969) Psychic cost of adaptation to an environmental stressor. *Journal of Personality and Social Psychology,* **12**, 200–10.

GLEASON, H.A. (1961) *An Introduction to Descriptive Linguistics,* Holt Rinehart Winston, New York.

GODDEN, D.R. and BADDELEY, A.D. (1975) Context-dependent memory in two natural environments: on land and underwater. *British Journal of Psychology,* **66**, 325–31.

GODDEN, D.R. and BADDELEY, A.D. (1980) When does context influence recognition memory? *British Journal of Psychology,* **71**, 99–104.

GOFFMAN, E. (1959) *The Presentation of Self in Everyday Life.* Anchor, New York.

GOLDSTEIN, A.G. and CHANCE, J.E. (1985) Effects of training on Japanese face recognition: reduction of the other-race effect. *Bulletin of the Psychonomic Society,* **23**, 211–14.

GOLOMBOK, S., SPENCER, A. and RUTTER, M. (1983) Children in lesbian and single-parent households: psychosexual and psychiatric appraisal. *Journal of Child Psychology and Psychiatry,* **24**, 511–72.

GOLUB, S. (ed.) (1983) *Menarche,* Lexington Books, Lexington, Mass.

GOODMAN, L., SAXE, L. and HARVEY, M. (1991) Homelessness as psychological trauma: broadening perspectives. *American Psychologist,* **46**, 1219–25.

GOODWIN, D.W., POWELL, B., BREMER, B., HOINE, H. and STERN, J. (1969) Alcohol and recall: state dependent effects in man. *Science,* **163**, 1358–60.

GOPHER, D. (1982) A selective attention test as a predictor of success in flight training. *Human Factors,* **24**(2), 173–83.

GOREN, C.C., SARTY, M. and WU, R.W.K. (1975) Visual following and pattern discrimination of face-like stimuli by new-born infants. *Paediatrics,* **56**, 544–9.

GOULD, D., PETLICHKOFF, L., SIMONS, J. and VEVERA, M. (1987) Relationship between competitive state anxiety inventory – subscales scores and pistol shooting performance. *Journal of Sport Psychology,* **9**, 33–42.

GOULD, S.J. (1981) *The Mismeasure of Man.* Norton, New York.

GOULD, S.J. (1982, 6 May) A nation of morons. *New Scientist,* 349–52.

GRADBERG, D. and NANNEMAN, T. (1986) Attitude change in an electoral context as a function of expectations not being fulfilled. *Political Psychology,* **7**, 753–65.

GREENE, L.R. (1977) The effects of verbal evaluation feedback and interpersonal distance on behavioural compliance. *Journal of Consulting Psychology,* **24**, 10–14.

GREENWOOD, M. and WOODS, H.M. (1919) The incident of industrial accidents upon individuals with special reference to multiple accidents. *Industrial Health Research Board Report No. 4.* HMSO, London.

GREGORY, R.L. (1973) The confounded eye, in R.L. Gregory and E.H. Gombrich (eds) *Illusion in Nature and Art.* Duckworth, London.

GREGORY, W.L. AND BURROUGH, W.J. (1989) *Introduction to Applied Psychology,* Scott Foresmann, London.

GREGORY, R.L. and WALLACE, J.G. (1963) Recovery from early blindness. *Experimental Psychology Society Monographs No. 2.*

GRIFFIN, C. (1992) *Feminism, Social Psychology and Qualitative Research.* Paper delivered at the British Psychological Society London Conference, December.

GRONHAUG, K., KVITASTEIN O. and GRONMO, S. (1991) Actors moderating advertising effectiveness as reflected in 333 tested advertisements. *Journal of Advertising Research,* **31**, 42–50.

GROVE, J.R., HANRAHAN, S.J. and STEWART, R.M. (1990) Attributions for rapid or slow recovery from sports injuries. *Canadian Journal of Sport Sciences,* **15**(2), 107–14.

GRUSON, L.M. (1988) Rehearsal skills and musical competence: does practice make perfect? in J.A. Sloboda (ed.) *Generative Processes in Music: The psychology of performance, improvisation and composition.* Oxford University Press, Oxford.

GUERRA, N.G., HUESMAN, L.R. and ZELLI, A. (1990) Attributions for social failure and aggression in incarcerated deliquent youth. *Journal of Abnormal Child Psychology,* **18**, 347–55.

GULIAN, E. (1974) Noise as a stressing agent. *Studia Psychologica,* **16**, 160–8.

GUMPERZ, J.J. (1982) *Discourse Strategies.* Cambridge University Press, Cambridge.

HMSO (1992) *General Household Survey, 1990.* HMSO, London.

HABER, G.M. (1980) Territorial invasion in the classroom: invadee response. *Environment and Behaviour,* **12**, 17–31.

HACKER, K.L., COSTE, T.G., KAMM, D.F. and BYBEE, K. (1991) Deconstruction of TV news. *Discourse and Society,* **2**(2), 183–202.

HALL, E.T. (1963) A system for the notation of proxemic behaviour. *American Anthropologist,* **65**, 1003–26.

HANDELSMAN, M.M. and McLAIN, J. (1988) The Barnum effect in couples: effects of intimacy, involvement, and sex on acceptance of generalized personality feedback. *Journal of Clinical Psychology,* **44**, 430–4.

HANEY, C., BANKS, W.C. and ZIMBARDO, P.G. Interpersonal dynamics in a simulated prison. *International Journal of Criminology and Penology,* **1**, 69–79.

HANKINS, N.E. and CLARK, H. (1989) Self-actualization: do teachers need it? *Journal of Human Behavior and Learning,* **6**(2), 7–13.

HARDY, L. (1988) *The Inverted-U Hypothesis: a Catastrophe for Sport Psychology.* Paper delivered at the British Psychological Society Annual Conference, Leeds, April.

HARGREAVES, D.H. (1980) Classrooms, schools and juvenile delinquency. *Educational Analysis,* **2**, 75–87.

HARLOW, H.F. (1949) The formation of learning sets. *Psychological Review,* **56**, 51–65.

HARPAZ, I. (1989) Non-financial employment commitment: a cross-national comparison. *Journal of Occupational Psychology,* **62**, 147–50.

HARRÉ, R. (1979) *Social Being.* Basil Blackwell, Oxford.

HASTIE, R., PENROD, S.D. and PENNINGTON, N. (1983) *Inside the Jury.* Harvard University Press, Cambridge, Massachusetts.

HAU, K.T. and SALILI, F. (1989) Attribution of examination results: Chinese primary school students in Hong Kong. *Psychologia: An International Journal of Psychology in the Orient,* **32**(3), 163–71.

HAU, K.T. and SALILI, F. (1991) Structure and semantic differential placement of specific causes: academic causal attributions by Chinese students in Hong Kong. *International Journal of Psychology,* **26**(2), 175–93.

HAYER, W.D. and COBB-WALGREN, C.J. (1988) Consumer decision-making across product categories: the influence of the task environment. *Psychology and Marketing,* **5**, 45–69.

HAYES, N.J. and LEMON, N. (1990) Stimulating positive cultures in growing companies. *Leadership and Organisational Change Management,* **11**(7), 17–21.

HAYES, N.J. and STRATTON, P.M. (1992) Social identity and organisational consultancy. *International Journal of Psychology,* **27**, 486 (abstract).

HAYES, N.J. (1988) *The Politics of Nature and Nurture.* Lecture delivered to Association for the Teaching of Psychology student workshops, Spring.

HAYES, N.J. (1991a) *Social Identity, Social Representations and Organisational Culture.* Doctoral thesis, CNAA/University of Huddersfield.

HAYES, N.J. (1991b) Psychology teaching and children's literature. *British Psychological Society Group of Teachers of Psychology Occasional Papers,* **11**, 33–6.

HAYNES, E.G. and FEINLEIB, M. (1980) Women, work and coronary heart disease: prospective findings from the Framingham Heart Study. *American Journal of Public Health*, **70**, pp. 133–41.

HECKLER, S.E. and CHILDERS, T.L. (1992) The role of expectancy and relevancy in memory for verbal and visual information: what is incongruency? *Journal of Consumer Research*, **18**, 475–92.

HEIDER, F. (1958) *The Psychology of Interpersonal Relations*. Wiley, New York.

HEIMBACH, J.T. and JACOBY, J. (1972) The Zaigarnik Effect in Advertising. Proceedings of the annual conference of the Association for Consumer Research, 746–58.

HEMERY, D. (1988) *Sport Psychology and the Athlete*. Paper delivered at the British Psychological Society Annual Conference, Leeds, April.

HENLEY, N. (1977) *Body Politics: power, sex and nonverbal communication*. Prentice Hall, Englewood Cliffs, New Jersey.

HERBERT, M. (1986) *Psychology for Social Workers*. BPS/Macmillan, London.

HERBERT, M., HEALY, T.E.J., FLETCHER, I.R. and ROSE, J.M. (1983) The profile of recovery after general anaesthesia. *British Medical Journal*, **286**, 1539–42.

HERSEN, M. and BELLACK, A.S. (1976) Social skills training for chronic psychiatric patients: rationale, research findings and future directions. *Comprehensive Psychiatry*, **17**, 559–80.

HERTZBERG, F. (1966) *Work and the Nature of Man*. Staples, London.

HERZLICH, C. (1973) *Health and Illness: A social psychological analysis*. Academic Press, London.

HESLOP, L.A., MORAN, L. and COUSINEAU, A. (1981) 'Consciousness' in energy conservation behaviour: an exploratory study. *Journal of Consumer Research*, **8**, 299–305.

HEWSTONE, M. (1989) *Causal Attributions: from cognitive processes to collective beliefs*. Blackwell, Oxford.

HEWSTONE, M., JASPERS, J. and LALLJEE, M. (1982) Social representations, social attribution and social identity: the intergroup images of 'public' and 'comprehensive' schoolboys. *European Journal of Social Psychology*, **12**(3), 241–69.

HILL, J.M.M. and TRIST, E.L. (1972) Industrial accidents, sickness and other absences. *Tavistock Pamphlet No. 4*. Tavistock, London.

HILLOCKS, G. (1984) What works in teaching composition: a meta-analysis of experimental treatment studies. *American Journal of Education*, **93**, 133–70.

HINES, D.E. (1977) Olfaction and the right cerebral hemisphere. *Journal of Altered States of Consciousness*, **3**(1), 47–59.

HINKLE, J.S., LYONS, B. and BURKE, K.L. (1989) Manifestation of Type A behavior pattern among aerobic runners. *Journal of Sport Behavior*, **12**(3), 131–8.

HIRSCH, P.M. and ANDREWS, J.A.Y. (1983) Ambushes, Shootouts and Knights of the Round Table: the language of corporate takeovers, in L.R. Pondy *et al.* (eds) *Organisational Symbolism*. JAI Press, Greenwich, Connecticut.

HMSO (1990) Aircraft Accident Report 4/90. HMSO, London.

HODGKINSON, P.E. and STEWART, M. (1991) *Coping with Catastrophe: a handbook of disaster management*. Routledge, London.

HOFFMAN, R.E., KIRSTEIN, L., STOPEK, S. and CICCHETTI, D.V. (1982) Apprehending schizophrenic discourse: a structural analysis of the listener's task. *Brain and Language*, **15**, 207–33.

HOFLING, K.C., BROTZMAN, E., DALRYMPLE, S., GRAVES, N. and PIERCE, C.M. (1966) An experimental study in the nurse–physician relationship. *Journal of Nervous and Mental Disorders*, **143**, 171–80.

HOFSTEDE, G. (1980) *Culture's Consequences*. Sage, London.

HOLLAND, J., RAMAZANOGLU, C., SCOTT, S., SHARPE, S. and THOMSON, R. (1990) Sex, gender and power: young women's sexuality in the shadow of AIDS. *Sociology of Health and Illness*, **12**, 336–50.

HOLLWAY, W. (1990) *Work Psychology and Organisational Behaviour*. Sage, London.

HOLLY, L. (ed.) (1989) *Girls and Sexuality, Teaching and Learning*. Open University Press, Milton Keynes.

HOLMES, T.H. and RAHE, R.H. (1967) The social readjustment rating scale. *Journal of Psychosomatic Research*, **11**, 213–18.

HOLZWORTH, J.R. and PIPPING, C.B. (1985) Drawing a weapon: an analysis of police judgments. *Journal of Police Science and Administration*, **13**, 185–94.

HOPSON, B. (1986) Counselling and helping, in M. Herbert (ed.) *Psychology for Social Workers*. Macmillan/BPS, London.

HOPSON, B. and SCALLY, M. (1980) *Lifeskills Teaching: education for self-empowerment*. McGraw-Hill, Maidenhead.

HORNER, M.S. (1968) *Sex Differences in Achievement Motivation and Performance in Competitive and Non-competitive Situations*. PhD Dissertation, University of Michigan.

HOROWITZ, I.A. and KAYE, R.S. (1975) Perception and advertising. *Journal of Advertising Research*, **15**, 15–21.

HORSFORD, B. (1990, 18 December) *Cultural issues and psychiatric diagnosis*. Paper delivered at Abnormal Psychology Study Day, Nottingham University.

HORTON, R. (1967) African traditional thought and Western science, in M.F.D. Young (ed.) (1971) *Knowledge and Control*. Addison-Wesley, Cambridge, Massachusetts.

HOUSE, R.J. (1971) A path-goal theory of leadership effectiveness. *Administrative Science Quarterly*, **16**, 321–38.

HOVLAND, C.I. and JANIS, I.L. (1959) *Personality and Persuasibility*. Yale University Press, New Haven.

HOVLAND, C.I. and SEARS, R. (1940) Minor studies in aggression VI: correlation of lynchings with economic indices. *Journal of Psychology*, **9**, 301–10.

HOWITT, D. (1991) *Concerning Psychology: psychology applied to social issues*. Open University Press, Milton Keynes.

HUBBARD, A.W. and SENG, C.N. (1954) Visual movements of batters. *Research Quarterly*, **25**, 42–57.

HUBEL, D.H. and WIESEL, T.N. (1968) Receptive fields and functional architecture of monkey striate cortex. *Journal of Physiology*, **195**, 215–43.

HUDSON, L. (1966) *Contrary Imaginations*. Penguin, Harmondsworth.

HUESMANN, L.R. and ERON, L.D. (1984) Cognitive processes and the persistence of aggressive behaviour. *Aggressive Behavior*, **10**, 243–51.

HUGHES, M. (1989) The child as learner: the contrasting views of developmental psychology and early education, in C. Desforges (ed.) *Early Childhood Education: British Journal of Educational Psychology Monograph Series No. 4*. Scottish Academic Press, Edinburgh.

HULL, C.L. (1952) *A Behaviour System*. Yale University Press, New Haven.

HUNT, S.D. (1970) Post transaction communications and dissonance reduction. *Journal of Marketing Research*, **34**, 16–51.

HUNT, S.M. and MARTIN, C.J. (1988) Health-related behavioural change: A test of a new model. *Psychology and Health*, **2**(3), 209–30.

HUNTER, J.A., STRINGER, M. and WATSON, R.P. (1991) Intergroup violence and intergroup attributions. *British Journal of Social Psychology*, **30**, 261–6.

HURLOCK, E.B. (1925) An evaluation of certain incentives used in school work. *Journal of Educational Psychology*, **16**, 145–59.

HUXLEY, A. (1965) *Brief Candles*. Penguin, Harmondsworth.

HYDE, J. (1981) How large are cognitive differences? *American Psychologist*, **36**, 892–901.

IMAI, M. (1986) *Kaizen the Key to Japan's Competitive Success*. Random House, New York.

INGHAM, R., WOODCOCK, A. and STENNER, K. (1991) Getting to know you ... young people's knowledge of their partners at first intercourse. *Journal of Community and Applied Social Psychology,* **1**, 117–32.

ISAACS, W., THOMAS, J. and GOLDIAMOND, I. (1960) Application of operant conditioning to reinstate verbal behaviour in psychotics. *Journal of Speech and Hearing Disorders,* **25**, 8–12.

ISEN, A.M., DAUBMAN, K.A. and NOWICKI, G.P. (1987) Positive affect facilitates creative problem solving. *Journal of Personality and Social Psychology,* **52**, 1122–31.

ITARD, J. (1972) *The Wild Boy of Aveyron.* New Left Books, London.

ITTELSON, W.H. (1978) Environmental perception and urban experience. *Environment and Behaviour,* **10**, 193–213.

JACKSON, P.W. (1968) *Life in Schools.* Holt, Rinehart & Winston, New York.

JACOBS, P.A., BRUNTON, M. and MELVILLE, M.M. (1965) Aggressive behaviour, mental abnormality and the XXY male. *Nature,* **208**, 1351–2.

JAIN, U.C. and MEHTANI, P. (1986) Perceived causes of job-satisfaction and dissatisfaction: testing of attribution model. *Indian Journal of Applied Psychology,* **23**(2), 65–76.

JAMAL, M. and BABA, V.V. (1991) Type A behavior, its prevalence and consequences among women nurses: an empirical examination. *Human Relations,* **44**, 1213–28.

JANIS, I.I. (1972) *Victims of Groupthink.* Houghton Mifflin, Boston.

JANIS, I.I. and FESHBACH, S. (1953) Effects of fear-arousing communications. *Journal of Abnormal and Social Psychology,* **48**, 78–92.

JANISZEWSKI, C. (1990) The influence of nonattended material on the processing of advertising claims. *Journal of Marketing Research,* **27**, 263–78.

JANOFF-BULMAN, R. (1989) Assumptive worlds and the stress of traumatic events: applications of the schema construct. *Social Cognition,* **7**, 113–36.

JEFFERY, R.W., FRENCH, S.A. and SCHMID, T.L. (1990) Attributions for dietary failures: problems reported by participants in the Hypertension Prevention Trial. *Health Psychology,* **9**(3), 315–29.

JENNINGS, H.H. (1950) *Leadership and Isolation.* Longmans Green, New York.

JENSEN, A.R. (1969) How much can we boost IQ and scholastic achievement? *Harvard Educational Review,* **39**, 1–123.

JODELET, D. (1984) The representation of the body and its transformations, in R.M. Farr and S. Moscovici (eds) *Social Representations.* Cambridge University Press, Cambridge.

JOHNSON, R.D. and DOWNING, L.L. (1979) Deindividuation and valence of cues: effects on prosocial and antisocial behaviour. *Journal of Personality and Social Psychology,* **39**, 1532–8.

JOHNSON, R.T., BJORKLAND, R. and KROTEE, M.L. (1984) The effects of cooperation, competitive and individualistic student interaction patterns on the achievement and attitudes of students learning the golf skill of putting. *Research Quarterly for Exercise and Sport,* **55**, 129–34.

JOHNSON-LAIRD, P.N. (1988) *The Computer and the Mind.* Fontana, London.

JONES, G.V. (1990) Misremembering a common object: When left is not right. *Memory and Cognition,* **18**(2), 174–82.

JONES, J. GRAHAM (1988) *Pre-competition multidimensional anxiety, self-confidence and performance.* Paper delivered at the British Psychological Society Annual Conference, Leeds, April.

JUEL, C., GRIFFITH, P.L. and GOUGH, P.B. (1986) Acquisition of literacy: a longitudinal study of children in first and second grade. *Journal of Educational Psychology,* **78**, 243–55.

KAMIN, L. (1974) *The Science and Politics of IQ.* Penguin, Harmondsworth.

KANNER, A.D., COYNES, J.C., SCHAEFER, C. and LAZARUS, R.S. (1981) Comparison of two modes of stress measurement: daily hassles and uplifts versus major life events. *Journal of Behavioural Medicine,* **4**, 1–39.

KANTOLA, S.J., SYME, G.J. and CAMPBELL, N.A. (1983) Cognitive dissonance and energy conservation. *Journal of Applied Psychology,* **69**, 416–21.

KASL, S.V. (1975) Issues in patient adherence to health care regimes. *Journal of Human Stress,* **1**, 5–17.

KASSIN, S.M., ELLSWORTH, P.C. and SMITH, V.L. (1989) The general acceptance of psychological research on eyewitness testimony. *American Psychologist,* **44**, 1089–98.

KELLER, K.L. (1987) Memory factors in advertising: the effect of advertising retrieval cues on brand evaluations. *Journal of Consumer Research,* **14**, 316–33.

KELLY, G. (1955) *The Theory of Personal Constructs.* Norton, New York.

KEYS, A. (1952) Experimental introduction of psychoneuroses by starvation. *The Biology of Mental Health and Disease.* Millbank Memorial Fund 27th Annual Conference. Harper & Row, New York.

KIECOLT-GLASER, J., GARNER, W., SPEICHER, C. *et al.* (1984) Psychosocial modifiers of immunocompetence in medical students. *Psychosomatic Medicine,* **46**, 7–14.

KINARTHY, E.L. (1975) *The Effects of Seating Position on Performance and Personality in a College Classroom.* Doctoral Dissertation, University of Southern California.

KING, N. and WEST, M.A. (1987) Experiences of innovation at work. *Journal of Managerial Psychology,* **2**, 6–10.

KINSEY, A.C. *et al.* (1948) *Sexual Behaviour in the Human Male.* Saunders, Philadelphia.

KINSEY, A.C. *et al.* (1953) *Sexual Behaviour in the Human Female.* Saunders, Philadelphia.

KIRKCALDY, B.D. (1982) Personality and sex differences related to positions in team sports. *International Journal of Sport Psychology,* **13**, 141–53.

KIRMEYER, S.L. (1988, November) Coping with competing demands: interruption and the Type A pattern. *Journal of Applied Psychology,* **73**(4), 621–9.

KITZINGER, C. (1987) Introducing and developing Q as a feminist methodology: a study of accounts of lesbianism, in C. Kitzinger (ed.) *The Social Construction of Lesbianism.* Sage, London.

KLEE, H. (1991) Homelessness among injecting drug users: implications for the spread of Aids. *Journal of Community and Applied Social Psychology,* **1**, 143–54.

KLINT, K.A. (1986) Dropping in and dropping out: participation motives of current and former youth gymnasts. *Canadian Journal of Applied Sport Sciences,* **11**(2), 106–14.

KNAPP, M.L. (1978) *Nonverbal Communication in Human Interaction,* 2nd edn, Holt, Eastbourne.

KOFF, E. (1983) Through the looking glass of menarche: what the adolescent girl sees, in S. Golub (ed.) *Menarche.* D. C. Heath, Lexington, Massachusetts.

KOFFKA, K. (1935) *Principles of Gestalt Psychology.* New York: Harcourt Brace.

KOMAKI, J. and BARNETT, F.T. (1983) A behavioural approach to coaching football, in C.L. Martin and D. Hrycaiko (eds) *Behavioural Modification and Coaching.* Charles C. Thomas, Springfields.

KRAHÉ, B. (1988) Attribution to victims of rape. *Journal of Applied Social Psychology,* **18**, 50–8.

KRECH, D., CRUTCHFIELD, R.S. and BALLACHEY, E.L. (1962) *Individual in Society.* McGraw-Hill, New York.

KREMER, D. and CRAWFORD, W. (eds) (1989) *The Psychology of Sport,* BPS Occasional Paper, 41–2.

KRIKORIAN, R., WROBEL, A.J., MEINECKE, C. *et al.* (1990) Cognitive deficits associated with human immunodeficiency virus encephalopathy. *Journal of Neuropsychiatry and Clinical Neurosciences,* **2**, 256–60.

KUBLER-ROSS, E. (1969) *On Death and Dying.* Macmillan, New York.

LABOV, W. (1972) The logic of nonstandard English. In V. Lee (ed.) (1979) *Language Development.* Croom Helm/Open University, London.

LADNER, J.A. (1971) *Tomorrow's Tomorrow, The Black Woman.* Doubleday & Co., London.

LANE, D.A. (1987) Personality and antisocial behaviour: a long-term study. *Personality and Individual Differences,* **8**, 799–806.

LANE, D.A. (1988) Violent histories: bullying and criminality, in D.P. Tattum and D.A. Lane (eds) *Bullying in Schools.* Trentham Books, Stoke-on-Trent.

LANE, D.A. (1989) Bullying in schools: the need for an integrated approach. *School Psychology International,* **10**, 211–15.

Lang, J. (1987) *Creating Architectural Theory: The role of the behavioural sciences in environmental design.* Van Nostrand Reinhold, New York.

LANGER, E.J. and RODIN, J. (1976) The effects of choice and enhanced personal responsibility for the aged: a field experiment in an institutional setting. *Journal of Personality and Social Psychology,* **34**, 191–8.

LANGER, E. and SAEGART, S. (1977) Crowding and cognitive control. *Journal of Personality and Social Psychology,* **34**, 191–8.

LARSEN, S.F. and LAZLO, J. (1990) Cultural-historical knowledge and personal experience in appreciation of literature. *European Journal of Social Psychology,* **20**, 425–40.

LARSEN, S.E. (1984) En skrift der skriver sig selv–informationsteknologien set som et nyt kapitel i skriftens historie (A script that writes itself: the new information technology seen as a further chapter in the history of script). *Psyke and Logos,* **5**, 346–59.

LATANÉ, B. and DARLEY, J.M. (1968) Group inhibition of bystander intervention in emergencies. *Journal of Personality and Social Psychology,* **10**, 215–21.

LATANÉ, B. and RODIN, J. (1969) A lady in distress: inhibiting effects of friends and strangers on bystander intervention. *Journal of Experimental Social Psychology,* **5**, 189–202.

LATHAM, G.P. and SAARI, L.M. (1984) Do people do what they say? Further studies on the situational interview. *Journal of Applied Psychology,* **69**, 569–73.

LAWLER, E.E. (1971) *Pay and Organisational Effectiveness: a psychological view.* McGraw-Hill, New York.

LAWLER, E.E. (1967) Secrecy about management compensation: are there hidden costs? *Organizational Behaviour and Human Performance,* **2**, 182–8.

LAZARUS, R. and FOLKMAN, S. (1984) The concept of coping, in A. Monat and R. Lazarus (1991) *Stress and Coping,* 3rd edn. Columbia University Press, Oxford.

LE BON, G. (1920) *The Crowd: A Study of the Popular Mind.* Viking Press, New York. Reprinted 1985.

LEA, M. and SPEARS, R. (1991) Computer-mediated communication, de-individuation and group decision-making. *International Journal of Man–Machine Studies,* **34**, 283–301.

LEE, C. and GILLEN, D.J. (1989) Relationship of Type A behavior pattern, self-efficacy perceptions on sales performance. *Journal of Organizational Behavior,* **10**, 75–81.

LEE, C. (1989) The relationship between goal setting, self-efficacy, and female field hockey team performance. *International Journal of Sport Psychology,* **20**, 147–61.

LEE, D.N. (1976) A theory of visual control of braking based on information about time-to-collision. *Perception,* **5**, 437–59.

LEON, G.R., MCNALLY, C. and BEN-PORATH, Y.S. (1989) Personality characteristics, mood, and coping patterns in a successful North Pole Expedition team. *Journal of Research in Personality,* **23**, 162–79.

LERNER, B. and FISKE, D. (1973) Client attributes and the eye of the beholder. *Journal of Consulting and Clinical Psychology,* **40**, 272–7.

LERNER, M.J. and LICHTMAN, R.R. (1968) Effects of perceived norms on attitudes and altruistic behavior towards a dependent other. *Journal of Personality and Social Psychology,* **9**, 226–32.

LEVEY, A.B. and MARTIN, I. (1975) Classical conditioning of human evaluative response. *Behavioural Research and Therapy,* **13**, 221–6.

LEVINE, S. (1960) Stimulation in infancy. *Scientific American,* **202**, 81–6.

LEVINSON, R.A. (1986) Contraceptive self-efficacy: a perspective on teenage girls' contraceptive behavior. *Journal of Sex Research,* **22**, 347–69.

LEWIN, K., LIPPITT, R. and WHITE, R.K. (1939) Patterns of aggressive behaviour in experimentally created social climates. *Journal of Social Psychology,* **10**, 271–9.

LEY, P. (1979) Memory for medical information. *British Journal of Social and Clinical Psychology,* **18**(2), 245–55.

LEY, P., BRADSHAW, P.W., EAVES, D. and WALKER, C.M. (1973) A method for increasing patients' recall of information presented by doctors. Psychological Medicine, **3**, 217–20.

LIKERT, R. (1932) A technique for the measurement of attitudes. *Archives of Psychology,* **140**.

LIKERT, R. (1961) *New Patterns of Management.* McGraw-Hill, New York.

LIPINSKA, B., BACKMAN, L. and HERLITZ, A. (1992) When Greta Garbo is easier to remember than Stefan Edberg: influences of prior knowledge on recognition memory in Alzheimer's disease. *Psychology and Ageing,* **7**, 214–20.

LIPMAN, A. (1968) Territorial behaviour in the sitting-rooms of four residential homes for old people. *British Journal of Geriatric Practice,* **2**, 265–78.

LITTLEWOOD, R. and LIPSEDGE, M. (1989) *Aliens and Alienists,* 2nd edn. Unwin Hyman, London.

LITTON, I. and POTTER, J. (1985) Social representations in the ordinary explanation of a 'riot'. *European Journal of Social Psychology,* **15**, 371–88.

LOFTUS, G.R. and LOFTUS, E.F. (1975) *Human Memory: The Processing of Information.* Halsted Press, New York.

LONG, C. (1989) Renal care, in A. Broome (ed) *Health Psychology.* Chapman & Hall, London.

LORANT, J. and DECONCHY, J.P. (1986) Entrainement physique, categorisation intergroupe et representations sociales (Sports training, inter-group categorization and social representations). *Cahiers de Psychologie Cognitive,* **6**(4), 419–44.

LORD, A.B. (1960) *The Singer of Tales.* Harvard University Press, Cambridge, Massachusetts.

LORENZ, K. (1966) *On Aggression.* Harcourt, Brace & World, New York.

LOVELESS, N.E. (1962) Direction of motion stereotypes: a review. *Ergonomics,* **5**, 357–83.

LUNDBERG, U. (1976) Urban commuting: crowdedness and catacholamine excretion. *Journal of Human Stress,* **2**, 26–32.

LUTZ, C.A. (1990) Morality, domination and understandings of 'justifiable anger' among the Ifaluk, in G. R. Semin and K. J. Gergen, *Everyday Understanding: Social and Scientific Implications.* Sage, London.

LYONS, J. (1981) *Language and Linguistics: an introduction.* Cambridge University Press, Cambridge.

LYONS, T.E. (1972) Turnover and absenteeism: a review of relationships and shared correlates. *Personnel Psychology,* **25**, 271–81.

MACCOBY, E. and JACKLIN, C.N. (1980) Psychological sex differences, in M. Rutter (ed.) *Developmental Psychiatry*. Heinemann, London.

MacEVEDY, C.P. and BEARD, A.W. (1970) Royal Free Epidemic of 1955: a reconsideration. *British Medical Journal*, **1**, 7–11.

MACKENZIE, S. (1986) The role of attention in mediating the effect of advertising on attribute importance. *Journal of Consumer Research*, **13**, 174–93.

MACKWORTH, N.H. (1950) Researches on the measurement of human performance. *Medical Research Council Special Report*, **268**, HMSO, London.

MADDEN, C.C., KIRKBY, R.J. and McDONALD, D. (1989) Coping styles of competitive middle distance runners. *International Journal of Sport Psychology*, **20**, 287–96.

MAHJOUB, A., LEYENS, J.P., YZERBYT, V. and DI GIACOMO, J.P. (1989) War stress and coping modes: representations of self-identity and time perspective among Palestinian children. *International Journal of Mental Health*, **18**(2), 44–62.

MAHONEY, M.J. and AVENER, M. (1977) Psychology of the elite athlete: an exploratory study. *Cognitive Therapy and Research*, **1**, 135–41.

MAIN, C.J. and WADDELL, G. (1987) Psychometric construction and validity of the Pilowsky Illness Behaviour Questionnaire in British patients with chronic low back pain. *Pain*, **28**, 13–25.

MAJOR, B., COZZARELLI, C., SCIACCHITANO, A.M. *et al.* (1990) Perceived social support, self-efficacy, and adjustment to abortion. *Journal of Personality and Social Psychology*, **59**, 452–63.

MAKIN, P.J., COOPER, C.L. and COX, C.J. (1989) *Managing People at Work*. British Psychological Society, Leicester.

MALAMUTH, N.M. and BILLINGS, V. (1984) Why pornography? Models of functions and effects. *Journal of Communication*, **34**, 117–29.

MANDELBAUM, D.B. (1958) *Selected Writings of Edward Sapir in Language, Culture and Personality*. University of California Press, California.

MARKHAM, R., ELLIS, D. and ELLIS, H. (1991) The effect of context change on children's recognition of unfamiliar faces. *British Journal of Developmental Psychology*, **9**, 513–20.

MARKOVA, I. and WILKIE, P. (1987) Representations, concepts and social change: the phenomenon of AIDS. *Journal for the Theory of Social Behaviour*, **17**, 389–409.

MARKUS, H. (1977) Self-schemas and processing information about the self. *Journal of Personality and Social Psychology*, **35**, 63–78.

MARR, D. (1982) *Vision: a computational investigation into the human representation and processing of visual information*. W.H. Freeman & Co., San Francisco.

MARSELLA, A.J., DEVOS, G. and HSU, F.L.K. (1985) *Culture and Self: Asian and Western perspectives*. Tavistock, London.

MARSH, H.W. (1992) Content specificity of relationships between academic achievement and academic self-concept. *Journal of Educational Psychology*, **84**, 35–42.

MARSH, P., ROSSER, E. AND HARRÉ, R. (1978) *The Rules of Disorder*. Routledge, London.

MARTEAU, T.M. (1990) Attitudes to doctors and medicine: the preliminary development of a new scale. *Psychology and Health*, **4**, 351–6.

MARTEAU, T.M. (1990) *Framing of information: its influence upon decisions of doctors and patients*. Proceedings of the second conference of the Health Psychology Section, BPS Occasional Papers No. 2. British Psychological Society, Leicester.

MASLOW, A.H. and MINTZ, N.C. (1956) Effects of esthetic surrounding: I. Initial effects of three esthetic conditions on perceiving 'energy' and 'well-being' in faces. *Journal of Psychology*, **41**, 247–54.

MASLOW, A.H. (1954) *Motivation and Personality*. Harper & Row, New York.

MASSARIK, F. (1981) The interviewing process re-examined, in P. Reason and J. Rowan (eds) *Human Inquiry: a sourcebook of new paradigm research*. Wiley, Chichester.

MASTERS, W. and JOHNSON, V. (1970) *Human Sexual Inadequacy*. Churchill, London.

MATHIESON, C.M., STAM, H.J. and SCOTT, J.P. (1991) The impact of a laryngectomy on the spouse: who is better off? *Psychology and Health*, **5**, 153–63.

MATTHUR, M. and CHATTOPADHYAY, A. (1991) The impact of moods generated by television programs on responses to advertising. *Psychology and Marketing*, **8**, 59–77.

MAXWELL, G.M. (1976) An evolution of social skills training. Unpublished University of Otago, NZ, described in M. Argyle (1986) Social Behaviour, in M. Herbert (ed.) *Psychology for Social Workers*. Methuen/BPS, London.

MAYS, C.M. and POUMADERE, M. (1989) Decentralizing risk analysis in large engineered systems: an approach to articulating technical and socio-organizational dimensions of system performance. *Risk Analysis*, **9**(4), 453–61.

McAULEY, E., DUNCAN, T.E. and McELROY, M. (1989) Self-efficacy cognitions and causal attributions for children's motor performance: an exploratory investigation. *Journal of Genetic Psychology*, **150**, 65–73.

McCABE, V. (1984) Abstract perceptual information for age level: a risk factor for maltreatment? *Child-Development*, **55**(1), 267–76.

McCLELLAND, D.C. *et al.* (1953) *The Achievement Motive*. Appleton-Century-Croft, New York.

McCOWN, W. (1991) Contributions of the EPN paradigm to HIV prevention: a preliminary study. *Personality and Individual Differences*, **12**, 1301–3.

McCRAE, R.R. and COSTA, P.T. JUN. (1985) Updating Norman's 'adequate taxonomy': intelligence and personality dimensions in natural language and in questionnaires. *Journal of Personality and Social Psychology*, **49**, 710–21.

McDONALD, L.M. and KORABIK, K. (1991) Sources of stress and ways of coping among male and female managers. Special issue: handbook on job stress. *Journal of Social Behavior and Personality*, **6**(7), 185–98.

McEVOY, G.M. and CASCIO, W.F. (1989) Cumulative evidence of the relationship between employee age and job performance. *Journal of Applied Psychology*, **74**, 11–17.

McFARLANE, A.C. (1989) The aetiology of post-traumatic morbidity: predisposing, precipitating and perpetuating factors. *British Journal of Psychiatry*, **154**, 221–8.

McGARTY, C. and PENNY, R.E. (1988) Categorization, accentuation and social judgement. *British Journal of Social Psychology*, **27**, 147–57.

McGREGOR, D.M. (1960) *The Human Side of Enterprise*. McGraw-Hill, New York.

McGURK, B.J., DAVIES, J.D. and GRAHAM, J. (1981) Assaultive behaviour, personality and personal space. *Aggressive Behaviour*, **7**, 317–24.

McKINSTRY, B. and WANG, J. (1991) Putting on the style: what patients think of the way their doctor dresses. *British Journal of General Practice*, **41**, 275–8.

McMASTERS, C. and LEE, C. (1991) Cognitive dissonance in tobacco smokers. *Addictive Behaviors*, **16**, 349–53.

MEICHENBAUM, D. (1977) *Cognitive-Behaviour Modification: an integrative approach*. Plenum Press, New York.

MELAMED, B.G. and SIEGEL, L.J. (1975) Reduction of anxiety in children facing hospitalization and surgery by use of filmed modelling. *Journal of Consulting and Clinical Psychology*, **43**(4), 511–21.

MELZACK, R and WALL, P. (1982) *The Challenge of Pain.* Penguin, Harmondsworth.

MELZACK, R. (1992) Phantom limbs. *Scientific American,* April.

MEYEROWITZ, B.E. and CHAIKEN, S. (1978) The effect of message framing on breast self-examination attitudes, intentions and behaviour. *Journal of Personality and Social Psychology,* **52**, 500–10.

MICK, D.G. (1992) Levels of subjective comprehension in advertising processing and their relations to ad perceptions, attitudes, and memory. *Journal of Consumer Research,* **18**, 411–23.

MILGRAM, S. (1963) Behavioural study of obedience. *Journal of Abnormal Psychology,* **67**, 371–8.

MILGRAM, S. (1977) *The Individual in a Social World.* Addison Wesley, New York.

MILLER, A. (1986) Performance impairment after failure: mechanism and sex differences. *Journal of Educational Psychology,* **78**, 486–91.

MILLER, E.J. and GWYNNE, G.V. (1972) *In Life Apart: A pilot study of residential institutions for the physically handicapped and the young chronic sick.* Tavistock, London.

MILLER, G. (1969) Psychology as a means of promoting human welfare. *American Psychologist,* **24**, 1063–75.

MILLER, J.F. (1978) *The Effects of Four Proxemic Zones on the Performance of Selected 6th, 7th and 8th Grade Students.* Doctoral dissertation, East Tennessee State University.

MILLIMAN, R. (1982) Using background music to affect the behaviour of supermarket shoppers. *Journal of Marketing,* **46**, 86–91.

MISUMI, J. (1990) The Japanese meaning of work and small group activities in Japanese industrial organisations. *International Journal of Psychology,* **25**, 819–32.

MITCHELL, M. (1992) *GPs explanatory models of post traumatic stress disorder in Lockerbie residents.* Paper delivered at the British Psychological Society Annual Conference, Scarborough.

MITROFF, I.I. (1983) Archetypal social systems analysis: on the deeper structure of human systems. *Academy of Management Review,* **8**, 387–97.

MOAR, I. (1983) Inconsistency in spatial knowledge. *Memory and Cognition,* **11**, 107–13.

MOOS, R.H. (1974) *Evaluating Treatment Environments: a social ecological approach.* Wiley, New York.

MORGAN, C.T., COOK, J.S., CHAPANIS, A. and Lund, M.W. (eds) (1963) *Human Engineering Guide to Equipment Design.* McGraw-Hill, New York.

MORGAN, E. (1972) *The Descent of Woman.* Open Books, London.

MORIARTY, T. (1975) Crime, commitment and the responsive bystander: two field experiments. *Journal of Personality and Social Psychology,* **31**, 370–6.

MORRIS, P.E., GRUNEBERG, M.M., SYKES, R.N. and MERRICK, A. (1981) Football knowledge and the acquisition of new results. *British Journal of Psychology,* **72**, 479–83.

MOSCOVICI, S. and HEWSTONE, M. (1983) Social representations and social explanations: from the 'naive' to the 'amateur' scientist, in M. Hewstone (ed.) *Attribution Theory: social and functional extensions.* Blackwell, Oxford.

MOSCOVICI, S. (1961) La Psychoanalyse: son image et son public. Presses Universitaires de France, Paris.

MOSCOVICI, S. and ZAVALLONI, M. (1969) The group as a polariser of attitude. *Journal of Personality and Social Psychology,* **12**, 125–35.

MOSCOVICI, S. (1984) The phenomenon of social representations, in R.M. Farr and S. Moscovici (eds) *Social Representations.* Cambridge University Press, Cambridge.

Moss, P.D. and McEvedy, C.P. (1966) An epidemic of overbreathing among schoolgirls. *British Medical Journal*, **2**, 1295–300.

Mowen, J.C. and Cialdini, R.B. (1980) On implementing the door-in-the-face compliance technique in a business context. *Journal of Market Research*, **17**, 253–8.

Mowrer, O.H. (1980) Enuresis – the beginning of the work: what really happened. *Journal of the History of Behavioural Sciences*, **16**, 25–30.

Muir, H.C. and Marrison, C. (1989) Human factors in cabin safety. *Aerospace*, April, 18–21.

Mullen, B. and Johnson, C. (1990) *The Psychology of Consumer Behaviour*. Lawrence Erlbaum Associates, Hove.

Myers, D.H., Leahy, A., Shoeb, H. and Ryder, J. (1990) The patient's view of life in a psychiatric hospital: a questionnaire study and associated methodological considerations. *British Journal of Psychiatry*, **156**, 853–60.

Myers, J.H. and Reynolds, W.H. (1967) *Consumer Behaviour and Marketing Management*. Houghton-Mifflin, Boston.

National Economic Development Office (1978) Case study E. *Case Studies in Company Manpower Planning*, 41–7.

Nauta, R. (1988) Task performance and attributional biases in the ministry. *Journal for the Scientific Study of Religion*, **27**, 609–20.

Neisser, U. (1976) *Cognition and Reality*. W.H. Freeman & Co., San Francisco.

Neisser, U. (1981) John Dean's memory: a case study. *Cognition*, **9**, 1–22.

Nettl, B. (1964) *Theory and Practice of Ethnomusicology*. Free Press of Glencoe, New York.

Newcomb, T.M. (1961) *The Acquaintance Process*. Holt, Rinehart & Winston, New York.

Newell, A. and Simon, A.H. (1972) *Human Problem Solving*. Prentice-Hall, Englewood Cliffs, New Jersey.

Newman, O. (1972) *Defensible Space*. Macmillan, New York.

Newmeyer, F.J. (1973) Linguistic theory, language teaching, sociolinguistics: can they be interrelated? *Modern Language Journal*, **57**, 405–10.

Nickerson, R.S. and Adams, M.J. (1979) Long-term memory for a common object. *Cognitive Psychology*, **11**, 287–307.

Nideffer, R.M. (1976) Test of attentional and interpersonal style. *Journal of Personality and Social Psychology*, **34**, 394–404.

Noel, J.G., Forsyth, D.R. and Kelley, K.N. (1987) Improving the performance of failing students by overcoming their self-serving attributional biases. *Basic and Applied Social Psychology*, **8**, 151–62.

Nossiter, V. and Biberman, G. (1990) Projective drawings and metaphor: analysis of organisational culture. *Journal of Managerial Psychology*, **5**(3), 13–16.

O'Guinn, T.C., Faber, R.J. and Imperia, G. (1986) Subcultural influence on family decision-making. *Psychology and Marketing*, **3**, 305–17.

O'Moore, A.M. and Hillery, B. (1989) Bullying in Dublin schools. *Journal of Psychology*, **10**, 426–41.

O'Rourke, T.E., Penrod, S.D., Cutler, B.L. and Stuve, T.E. (1989) The external validity of eyewitness identification research: generalising across subject populations. *Law and Human Behaviour*, **13**, 385–95.

Ollendick, T.H., Elliott, W. and Matson, J.L. (1980) Locus of control as related to effectiveness in a behaviour modification programme for juvenile delinquents. *Journal of Behaviour Therapy and Experimental Psychiatry*, **11**, 259–62.

Olney, T.J., Holbrook, M.B. and Batra, R. (1991) Consumer responses to advertising: the effects of ad content, emotions and attitude towards the ad on viewing time. *Journal of Consumer Research*, **17**, 440–51.

ORBACH, S. (1978) *Fat is a Feminist Issue*. Paddington Press, London.

ORNE, M.T. (1962) On the social psychology of the psychological experiment: with particular reference to demand characteristics and their implications. *American Psychologist,* **17**, 276–83.

ORNSTEIN, R.E. (1986) *The Psychology of Consciousness,* 2nd edn. Freeman & Co., New York.

ORTON, D.L. and GRUZELIER, J.H. (1989) Adverse changes in mood and cognitive performance of house officers after night duty. *British Medical Journal,* **298**, 21–3.

OSBORN, A.F. (1963) *Applied Imagination.* Scribner's, New York.

OSGOOD, C.E. (1962) *An Alternative to War or Surrender.* University of Illinois Press, Urbana.

OWENS, G. and NAYLOR, F. (1989) *Living While Dying: What to do and what to say when you are, or someone close to you is dying.* Thorsens, Wellingborough.

PAAP, K.R. (1989) Applied cognitive psychology, in W. L. Gregory and W. J. Burroughs (eds) *Introduction to Applied Psychology.* Scott, Foresman & Co., London.

PALOMBO, S.R. (1985) Can a computer dream? 28th Annual Meeting of the American Academy of Psychoanalysis (1984, Los Angeles, California). *Journal of the American Academy of Psychoanalysis,* **13**, 453–66.

PANAGOPOULOS, I.S. (1992) *Why do people take risks? Explanations of individual risk-taking.* Paper presented at BPS London Conference.

PARKIN, A.J. and HUNKIN, N.M. (1991) Memory loss following radiotherapy for nasal pharyngeal carcinoma – an unusual presentation of amnesia. *British Journal of Clinical Psychology,* **30**, 349–57.

PARRY, G., MOYSER, G. and WAGSTAFF, M. (1987) The Crowd and Community. Context, content and aftermath, in *The Crowd in Contemporary Britain* (eds G. Gaskell and R. Benewick). Sage Publications, London, pp 212–54.

PATTERSON, G.R., REID, J.B., JONES, J.J. and CONGER, R.E. (1975) *A Social Learning Approach to Family Intervention.* Castalia, Oregon.

PAUL, W.J., ROBERTSON, K.B. and HERTZBERG, F. (1969) Job enrichment pays off. *Harvard Business Review,* **47**, 61–78.

PAULUS, P., McCAIN, G. and COX, V. (1978) Death rates, psychiatric commitments, blood pressure and perceived crowding as a function of institutional crowding. *Environmental Psychology and Nonverbal Behaviour,* **3**, 107–16.

PAVLOV, P. (1927) *Conditioned Reflexes.* Oxford University Press, Oxford.

PERRIN, S. and SPENCER, C. (1981) Independence or conformity in the Asch experiment as a reflection of cultural and situational factors. *British Journal of Social Psychology,* **20**, 205–9.

PERRIN, S. and SPENCER, C. (1980) The Asch effect: a child of its time? *Bulletin of the British Psychological Society,* **32**, 405–6.

PETERS, T. (1988) *Thriving on Chaos: a handbook for a management revolution.* MacMillan, London.

PETERS, T.J. and WATERMAN, R.H., JN. (1982) *In Search of Excellence: Lessons from America's best-run companies.* Harper & Row, New York.

PETERSON, K.C. (1986) Evasion and invisibility in Ninjtsu. *Combat,* **12**(6), 28–31.

PHILLIPS, D.P. (1970) *Dying as a Form of Social Behaviour.* Doctoral dissertation, Ann Arbour, Michegan.

PICHERT, J.W. and ANDERSON, R.C. (1977) Taking different perspectives on a story. *Journal of Educational Psychology,* **69**, 309–15.

PILGER, J. (1975) *The Last Day.* Mirror Group Books, London.

PILIAVIN, I.M., RODIN, J. and PILIAVIN, J.A. (1969) Good Samaritanism: an underground phenomenon? *Journal of Personality and Social Psychology,* **13**, 289–99.

PILIAVIN, J.A., DOVIDIO, J.F., GAERTNER, S.L. and CLARK, R.D. (1981) *Emergency Intervention*. Academic Press, New York.

PITTS, M. and PHILLIPS, K. (eds) (1991) *The Psychology of Health,* Routledge, London.

POINCARE, H. (1913) *The Foundations of Science* (trans., G. B. Halstead) Science Press, New York.

POLLACK, S. and GILLIGAN, C. (1982) Images of violence in thematic apperception test stories. *Journal of Personality and Social Psychology,* **42**, 159–67.

PONDY, L.R. (1983) The role of metaphors and myths in organisation and in the facilitation of change, in L. R. Pondy *et al.* (eds) *Organisational Symbolism.* JAI Press, New York.

PORTER, L.W. and SPEERS, R.M. (1973) Organisational work and personal factors in employee turnover and absenteeism. *Psychological Bulletin,* **80**, 151–76.

POTTER, J. and EDWARDS, D. (1990) Nigel Lawson's tent: discourse analysis, attribution theory and the social psychology of fact. *European Journal of Social Psychology,* **20**, 405–24.

POTTER, J. and REICHER, S. (1987) Discourses of community and conflict: the organisation of social categories in accounts of a 'riot'. *British Journal of Social Psychology,* **26**.

POTTER, J. and WETHERALL, M. (1987) *Discourse and Social Psychology: beyond attitudes and behaviour.* Sage, London.

POWER, M.J., ASCH, P.M., SCHOENBERG, E. and SOREY, E. (1974) Deliquency and the family. *British Journal of Social Work,* **4**, 13–38.

PRAPAVESSIS, H. and CARRON, A.V. (1988) Learned helplessness in sport. *Sport Psychologist,* **2**, 189–201.

PRICE-WILLIAMS, D.R. (1985) Cultural Psychology, in G. Lindzey and A. Aronson (eds) *A Handbook of Social Psychology* Vol. II, 3rd edn. Random House, New York.

QUADRIO, A., CATELLANI, P. and SALA, V. (1988) La rappresentazione sociale della politica (The social representation of politics) *Archivio di Psicologia: Neurologia e Psichiatria,* **49**(1), 5–27.

QUALLS, W.J. and MOORE, D.J. (1990) 'Sterotyping' effects on consumers' evaluation of advertising: effects of racial differences between actors and viewed. *Psychology and Marketing,* **7**(2), 135–51.

QUINE, L. and PAHL, J. (1991) Stress and coping in mothers caring for a child with severe learning difficulties: a test of Lazarus' transactional model of coping. *Journal of Community and Applied Social Psychology,* **1**, 57–70.

QUINE, L. and PAHL, J. (1992) A longitudinal study of young people and their families. *Journal of Community and Applied Social Psychology,* **2**, 1–76.

RACK, P. (1982) Migration and mental illness: a review of recent research in Britain. *Transcultural Psychiatric Research Review,* **19**, 151–69.

RAE, J.P. (1989) *Explanations and Communicative Constraints in Naturally Occuring Discourse*. PhD Thesis, University of Leeds.

RAELIN, J.A. (1985) Work patterns in the professional life-cycle. *Journal of Occupational Psychology,* **3**, 177–87.

RAGINS, B.R. and SUNDSTROM, E. (1990) Gender and perceived power in manager–subordinate relations. *Journal of Occupational Psychology,* **63**, 273–87.

RAGLAND, D.R. and BRAND, R.J. (1988) Type A behavior and mortality from coronary heart disease. *New England Journal of Medicine,* **318**, 65–70.

RAPAPORT, R.M. (1960) *Community as Doctor: New perspectives on a therapeutic community.* Tavistock, London.

RAUGH, M.R. and ATKINSON, R.C. (1975) A mnemonic method for learning a second language vocabulary. *Journal of Educational Psychology,* **67**, 1–16.

RAY, C. and FITZGIBBON, G. (1981) Stress arousal and coping with surgery. *Psychological Medicine,* **11**, 741–6.

REASON, J. (1990) *Human Error.* Cambridge University Press, Cambridge.

REDDY, J.K., BAI, A.J.L. and RAO, V.R. (1976) The effects of the transcendental meditation programme on athletic performance, in D. J. Orme-Johnson and I. Farrow (eds) *Scientific Research on the Transcendental Meditation Program* (Collected papers, Vol. 1). MERU Press, Weggis, Switzerland.

REHM, J., STEINLEITNER, M. and LILLI, W. (1987) Wearing uniforms and agression: a field experiment. *European Journal of Social Psychology,* **17**, 357–60.

RESKIN, B.F. and VISHER, C.A. (1986) The impacts of evidence and extra legal factors in jurors' decision. *Law and Society Review,* **20**, 423–38.

RIST, R.G. (1970) Student social class and teacher expectations: the self-fulfilling prophecy. *Harvard Educational Review,* **40**, 411–51.

ROBERTSON, I.T. and KANDOLA, R.S. (1982) Work sample tests: validity, adverse impact and applicant reaction. *Journal of Occupational Psychology,* **55**, 171–83.

ROBINSON, D.W. and HOWE, B.L. (1987) Causal attribution and mood state relationships of soccer players in a sport achievement setting. *Journal of Sport Behavior,* **10**, 137–46.

ROBINSON, E.J. and WHITFIELD, M.J. (1987) Participation of patients during general practice consultations. *Psychology and Health,* **1**, 123–32.

ROBINSON, P. (1991) *People and barbarians in the state of Europe.* Paper delivered at the British Psychological Society, Social Psychology Section Annual Conference, Surrey, September.

ROBINSON, R. and WEST, R. (1992) A comparison of computer and questionnaire methods of history-taking in a genito-urinary clinic. *Psychology and Health,* **6**, 77–84.

RODIN, J. (1976) Crowding, perceived choice and response to controllable and uncontrollable outcomes. *Journal of Experimental Social Psychology,* **12**, 465–78.

RODIN, J. (1983) Behavioural medicine: beneficial effects of self-control training in ageing. *International Review of Applied Psychology,* **32**, 153–81.

RODIN, J. and LANGER, E.J. (1977) Long term effects of a control-relevant intervention and the institutionalised aged. *Journal of Personality and Social Psychology,* **35**, 897–902.

ROEBUCK, J.A, JN, KROEMER, H.E. and THOMSON, W.G. (1975) *Engineering Anthropometry Methods.* Wiley & Sons, New York.

ROETHLISBERGER, J.W. and DICKSON, W.J. (1939) *Management and the Worker.* Harvard University Press, Cambridge, Massachusetts.

ROGERS, C.R. (1961) *On Becoming a Person: A therapist's view of psychotherapy.* Constable, London.

ROGERS, C.R. (1970) *Carl Rogers on Encounter Groups.* Harper & Row, New York.

ROGERS, C.R. (1978) *Carl Rogers on Personal Power.* Constable, London.

ROHLEN, T.P. (1970) Sponsorship of cultural continuity in Japan: a company training programme. *Journal of Asian and African Studies,* **5**, 184–92.

ROOK, D.W. (1985) The ritual dimension of consumer behaviour. *Journal of Consumer Research,* **12**, 251–64.

ROSE, S. (1985) Is romance dysfunctional? *International Journal of Women's Studies,* **8**, 250–65.

ROSE, S., KAMIN, L.J. and LEWONTIN, R.C. (1984) *Not in our Genes: biology, ideology and human nature.* Penguin, Harmondsworth.

ROSENTHAL, R. (1979) The 'file drawer problem' and tolerance for null results. *Psychological Bulletin,* **86**, 638–41.

ROSENTHAL, R. and FODE, K.L. (1963) The effect of experimenter bias on the performance of the albino rat. *Behavioural Science,* **8**, 183–9.

ROSENTHAL, R. and JACOBSON, L. (1968) *Pygmalion in the Classroom: teachers' expectations and pupils' intellectual development.* Holt, Rinehart & Winston, New York.

ROTTER, J.B. (1966) Generalised expectancies for internal vs external control of reinforcement. *Psychological Monographs,* **80**(1).

RUBACK, R.B. and PANDEY, J. (1992) Very hot and really crowded: quasi-experimental investigations of Indian 'tempos'. *Environment and Behavior,* **24**, 527–54.

RUEFLI, T., YU, O. and BARTON, J. (1992) Sexual risk taking in smaller cities: the case of Buffalo, New York. *Journal of Sex Research,* **29**, 95–108.

RUMELHART, D.E. and NORMAN, D.A. (1982) Simulating a skilled typist: a study of skilled cognitive-motor performance. *Cognitive Science,* **6**, 1–36.

RUMELHART, D.E. (1980) Schemata: the building blocks of cognition, in R. J. Spiro *et al.* (eds) *Theoretical Issues in Reading Comprehension.* Erlbaum, Hillsdale, New Jersey.

RUNCO, M.A. AND PEZDEK, K. (1984) The effect of television and radio on children's creativity. *Human Communication Research,* **11**(1), 109–20.

RUSSELL, R.J. and WELLS, P.A. (1991) Personality similarity and quality of marriage. *Personality and Individual Differences,* **12**, 407–12.

RUTTER, M. (1982) *Maternal Deprivation Reassessed,* 2nd edn. Penguin, Harmondsworth.

SACKS, O. (1985) *The Man who Mistook his Wife for a Hat.* Picador, London.

SADLER, P.J. (1968) Executive leadership, in D. Pym (ed.) *Industrial Society.* Penguin, Harmondsworth.

SAHOO, F.M. and NANDA, U. (1990) Socialization parameters of learned helplessness. *Psychological Studies,* **35**, 52–61.

SAHOO, F.M. and TRIPATHY, S. (1990) Learned helplessness in industrial employees: a study of non-contingency, satisfaction and motivational deficits. *Psychological Studies,* **35**, 79–87.

SALANCIK, G.R. and MEINDL, J.R. (1984) Corporate attributions as strategic illusions of management control. *Administrative Science Quarterly,* **29**, 238–54.

SALJO, R. (1979) Learning in the learner's perspective: I. Some common-sense conceptions. *Reports from the Institute of Education.* University of Gothenberg, 76.

SANDERS, P. (1993) *An Incomplete Guide to Using Counselling Skills on the Telephone.* PCCS Books, Manchester.

SAPIR, E. (1947) *Selected Writings in Language, Culture and Personality.* University of California Press, Los Angeles.

SARAFINO, E. (1990) *Health Psychology: Biopsychosocial interactions.* Wiley, New York.

SARGENT, W. (1957) *Battle for the Mind: A physiology of conversion and brainwashing.* Doubleday, New York.

SASSAN, G. (1980) Success anxiety in women: a constructivist interpretation of its sources and its significance. *Harvard Educational Review,* **50**, 13–25.

SAWYER, A.G. and HOWARD, D.J. (1991) Effects of omitting conclusions in advertisements to involved and uninvolved audiences. *Journal of Marketing Research,* **28**, 467–74.

SCALLY, M. and HOPSON, B. (1979) *A Model of Helping and Counselling: indications for training.* Counselling and Career Development Unit, University Leeds, Leeds.

SCHACHTER, S. and SINGER, J.E. (1962) Cognitive social and physiological determinants of emotional states. *Psychological Review,* **69**, 379–99.

SCHANK, R. and ABELSON, R. (1977) *Scripts, Plans, Goals and Understanding: An enquiry into human knowledge.* Erlbaum, Hillsdale, New Jersey.

SCHMIDT, R.A. (1988) *Motor control and learning.* Human Kinetics, 417–22.

SCHOEMAN, T.J., STEVENS, V.J., HOLLIS, J.F. and CHEEK, P. (1988) Attribution, affect, and expectancy following smoking cessation treatment. *Basic and Applied Social Psychology,* **9**(3), 173–84.

SCHRANK, J. (1977) *Snap, Crackle and Popular Taste.* Dell, New York.

SCHUBAUER-LEONI, M.L. and BELL, N. (1989) Rappresentazioni degli studenti nelle interazioni didattiche (Students' representations in didactic interactions). *Studi di Psicologia dell' Educazione,* **8**(2), 81–9.

SCHWABACHER, S. (1972) Male vs female representation in psychological research: an examination of the *Journal of Personality and Social Psychology,* 1970, 1971. *JSAS Catalog of Selected Documents in Psychology,* **2**, 20–1.

SCHWARZER, R. and LEPPIN, A. (1989) Social support and health: a meta-analysis. *Psychology and Health,* **3**, 1–15.

SCULLY, D. and MAROLLA, J. (1984) Convicted rapists' vocabulary of motive: excuses and justifications. *Social Problems,* **31**, 530–44.

SEARS, D. (1986) College sophomores in the laboratory: influences of a narrow data base on psychology's view of human nature. *Journal of Personality and Social Psychology,* **51**, 515–30.

SEARS, P.S. (1940) Levels of aspiration in academically successful and unsuccessful children. *Journal of Abnormal and Social Psychology,* **35**, 498–536.

SEAVER, W.B. (1973) The effects of naturally induced teacher expectancies. *Journal of Personality and Social Psychology,* **28**, 333–42.

SECORD, P.F., BEVAN, W. and KATZ, B. (1956) The Negro stereotype and perceptual accentuation. *Journal of Abnormal and Social Psychology,* **53**, 78–83.

SELFRIDGE, O.G. (1959) Pandemonium: a paradigm for learning, in *The Mechanisation of Thought Processes,* Vol. 1. HMSO, London.

SELIGMAN, M.E.P. (1975) *Helplessness: on depression, development and death.* Freeman, San Francisco.

SELIGMAN, M.E.P. and MAIER, S.F. (1967) Failure to escape traumatic shock. *Journal of Experimental Psychology,* **74**, 1–9.

SELYE, H. (1982) History and the present status of the stress concept, in L. Goldberger and S. Breznitz (eds) *Handbook of Stress: Theoretical and clinical aspects.* The Free Press, New York.

SERVAN-SCHREIBER, D. (1986) Artificial intelligence and psychiatry. *Journal of Nervous and Mental Disease,* **174**, 191–202.

SHACKLETON, V.J. and ALI, A. (1990) Work-related values for managers: a test of the Hofstede model. *Journal of Cross-Cultural Psychology,* **21**, 109–18.

SHACKLETON, V.J., WILD, J.M. and WOLFFE, M. (1980) Screening optometric patients by questionnaire: methods of improving response. *American Journal of Optometry and Physiological Optics,* **57**, 404–6.

SHALLEY, C.E. (1991) Effects of productivity goals, creativity goals and personal discretion on individual creativity. *Journal of Applied Psychology,* **76**, 179–85.

SHALLICE, T. (1973) The Ulster depth interrogation techniques and their relation to sensory deprivation research. *Cognitive Psychology,* **1**.

SHEPARD, R.N. (1978) The mental image. *American Psychologist,* **33**, 125–37.

SHERIDAN, C. and KING, R. (1972) *Obedience to authority with an authentic victim.* Proceedings of the 80th Annual Convention, APA, Part 1, 7, 165–6.

SHERIF, M. (1956) Experiments in Group Conflict. *Scientific American,* **195**.

SHILS, E. and JANOWITZ, M. (1948) The impact of allied propaganda on Wehrmacht solidarity, from cohesion and disintegration in the Wehrmacht in World War II. *Public Opinion Quarterly,* **12**, 280–315.

SIGELMAN, C.K., THOMAS, D.B., SIGELMAN, L. and RIBICH, F.D. (1986) Gender, physical attractiveness and electability: an experimental investigation of vote biases. *Journal of Applied Social Psychology,* **16**, 229–48.

SILVERMAN, I. (1977) *The Human Subject in the Psychological Laboratory.* Pergamon, New York.

SIMONTON, D.K. (1991) Emergence and realisation of genius: the lives and works of 120 classical composers. *Journal of Personality and Social Psychology,* **61**, 829–84.

SINGER, J.L. and SINGER, D.G. (1981) *Television, Imagination and Aggression: a study of pre-schoolers.* Lawrence Earlbaum Associates, Hillsdale, New Jersey.

SINGLETON, W.T. (1969) Display design: principles and procedure. *Ergonomics,* **12**, 519–31.

SKINNER, B.F. (1972) *Beyond Freedom and Dignity.* Penguin, Harmondsworth.

SKINNER, B.F. (1960) Pigeons in a pelican. *American Psychologist,* **15**, 28–37.

SLOBIN, D.L. (1971) *Psycholinguistics.* Scott Foresman, Illinois.

SLOBODA, J. (1985) *The Musical Mind: the cognitive psychology of music.* Clarendon Press, Oxford.

SMITH, A. (1983) Nonverbal communication among black female dyads: an assessment of intimacy, gender and race. *Journal of Social Issues,* **39**, 55–67.

SMITH, P.B. and PETERSON, M.F. (1988) *Leadership, Organisations and Culture.* Sage, London.

SMITH, D. (1987) Conditions that facilitate the development of sport imagery training. *The Sport Psychologist,* **1**, 237–47.

SMITH, J. (1992) Pregnancy and the transition to motherhood, in P. Nicolson and J. Ussher (eds) *The Psychology of Women's Health and Health Care.* MacMillan, London.

SMITH, M.B., BRUNER, J.S. and WHITE, R.W. (1956) *Opinions and Personality.* Wiley, New York.

SMITH, R.E., PTACEK, J.T. and SMOLL, F.L. (1992) Sensation seeking, stress, and adolescent injuries: a test of stress-buffering, risk-taking, and coping skills hypotheses. *Journal of Personality and Social Psychology,* **62**, 1016–24.

SMITH, R.E., SMOLL, F.J. and PTACEK, J.T. (1990) Conjunctive moderator variables in vulnerability and resiliency research: life stress, social support and coping skills, and adolescent sport injuries. *Journal of Personality and Social Psychology,* **58**, 360–70.

SMITH, R.E., SMOLL, F.L. and CURTIS, B. (1979) Coach effectiveness training: a cognitive-behavioural approach to enhancing relationships skills in youth sport coaches. *Journal of Sports Psychology,* **1**, 59–75.

SMITH, R.R. and LEWIS, R. (1985) Race as a self-schema affecting recall in black children. *Journal of Black Psychology,* **12**, 15–29.

SMITH, S.H. and WHITEHEAD, G.I. (1984) Attributions for promotion and demotion in the United States and India. *Journal of Social Psychology,* **124**, 27–34.

SOMMER, R. and DEWAR, R. (1963) The physical environment of the ward, in E. Friedson (ed.) *The Hospital in Modern Society.* Free Press, New York.

SONSTROEM, R.J. and BERNADO, P. (1982) Intraindividual pregame anxiety and basketball performance: a re-examination of the inverted-U curve. *Journal of Sport Psychology,* **4**, 235–45.

ST LAWRENCE, J.S., KELLY, J.A., OWEN, A.D., HOGAN, I.G. and WILSON, R.A. (1990) Psychologists' attitudes towards AIDS. *Psychology and Health,* **4**, 357–63.

STAINTON ROGERS, W. (1991) *Explaining Health and Illness*. Harvester Wheatsheaf, London.

STARK, E. (1981) Pigeon patrol. *Science*, **81**, 85–6.

STAYMAN, D.M. and BATRA, R. (1991) Encoding and retrieval of ad affect in memory. *Journal of Marketing Research*, **28**, 232–9.

STEINER, I.D. and JOHNSON, H.H. (1963) Authoritarianism and 'tolerance of trait inconsistency'. *Journal of Abnormal and Social Psychology*, **67**, 388–91.

STEPHAN, W.G. (1978) School desegregation: an evaluation of predictions made in Brown vs Board of Education. *Psychological Bulletin*, **85**, 217–38.

STEPHENSON, G. (1992) *The Psychology of Criminal Justice*. Blackwell, Oxford.

STEPHENSON, G.M. (1981) Intergroup bargaining and negotiation, in J. C. Turner and H. Giles (eds) *Intergroup behaviour*. Blackwell, Oxford.

STEPTOE, A. and FIDLER, H. (1987) Stage fright in orchestral musicians: a study of cognitive and behavioural strategies in performance anxiety. *British Journal of Psychology*, **78**, 241–9.

STERNBERG, R.J. (1977) *Intelligence, Information Processing and Analogical Reasoning: the componential analysis of human abilities*. Erlbaum, Hillsdale, New Jersey.

STERNBERG, R.J. (1985) *Beyond IQ: a triarchic theory of human intelligence*. Cambridge University Press, Cambridge.

STINO, L. (1983) A visual preference study of urban outdoor spaces in Egypt. Doctoral Dissertation, University of Michigan, summarised in R. Kaplan and S. Kaplan (1989) *The Experience of Nature: a psychological perspective*. Cambridge University Press, Cambridge.

STIPEK, D., WEINER, B. and LI, K. (1989) Testing some attribution-emotion relations in the People's Republic of China. *Journal of Personality and Social Psychology*, **56**, 109–16.

STODGILL, R.M. and COONS, A.E. (eds) *Leader Behaviour: its descriptions and measurement*. Ohio State University, Columbus, Ohio.

STONER, J.A.F. (1961) *A comparison of individual and group decisons involving risk*. Masters thesis, MIT School of Industrial Management.

STORER, B.R. (1949) The fallacy of personal validation: a classroom demonstration of gullibility. *Journal of Abnormal and Social Psychology*, **44**.

STORMS, M.D. and NISBETT, R.E. (1970) Insomnia and the attribution process. *Journal of Personality and Social Psychology*, **16**, 319–28.

STRATTON, P.M. and SWAFFER, R. (1988) Maternal causal beliefs for abused and handicapped children. *Journal of Reproductive and Infant Psychology*, **6**, 201–16.

STRATTON, P.M. and SIVITER, R. (1993) *New technology, new paradigms and the attributional cloak: qualitative research shall go to the (scientific) ball*. Paper delivered at the European Society for Opinion and Marketing Research, Rome.

STRATTON, P.M. (1991) Attributions, baseball and consumer behaviour. *Journal of the Market Research Society*, **33**(3), 163–78.

STRENG, J. (1980) *Sportpsychologie*, internal publication, Faculty of Human Movement Sciences. Free University, Amsterdam.

STRINGER, M. and LAVERY, C. (1987) The acquisition of ethnic categorization ability by British university students in Northern Ireland. *Social Behaviour*, **2**(3), 157–64.

STROMEYER, C.F. (1970) Eidetikers. *Psychology Today*, November, 76–80.

SUTTON, C. (1979) *Psychology for Social Workers and Counsellors: An introduction*. Routledge & Kegan Paul, London.

SWANK, R. (1949) Combat exhaustion. *Journal of Nervous and Mental Disorders*, **9**, 369–76.

TAFARI, S., ABOUD, F.E. and LARSON, C.P. (1991) Determinants of mental illness in a rural Ethiopian adult population. *Social Science and Medicine,* **32**(2), 197–201.

TAJFEL, H. and TURNER, J.C. (1979) An integrative theory of intergroup conflict, in W. G. Austin and S. Worchel (eds) *The Social Psychology of Intergroup Relations.* Brooks/Cole, Monterey, California.

TAJFEL, H. (1969) Cognitive aspects of prejudice. *Journal of Social Issues,* **25**(4), 79–97.

TASHAKKORI, A., BAREFOOT, J. and MEHRYAR, A.H. (1989) What does the Beck Depression Inventory measure in college students? Evidence from a non-western culture. *Journal of Clinical Psychology,* **45**, 595–602.

TAYLOR, F.W. (1911) *The Principles of Scientific Management.* Harper & Row, New York.

TAYLOR, A. and FRAZER, A. (1982) The stress of post-disaster body handling and victim identification work. *Journal of Human Stress,* **8**, 4–12.

TAYLOR, H. (1964) Programmed instruction in industry – a review of the literature. *Personnel Practice Bulletin,* **20**, 14–27.

TAYLOR, S. (1986) *Health Psychology.* Random House, New York.

TAYLOR, S. (1990) Health Psychology: the science and the field. *American Psychologist,* **45**, 40–50.

TAYLOR, S.E., LICHTMAN, R.R. and WOOD, J.V. (1984) Attributions, beliefs about control and adjustment to breast cancer. *Journal of Personality and Social Psychology,* **46**, 489–502.

TEMPLE, C.M. (1992) Developmental memory impairment: faces and patterns, in R. Campbell (ed.) *Mental Lives: Case studies in cognition.* Blackwell, Oxford.

TERRY, D.J. (1991) Predictors of subjective stress in a sample of new parents. *Australian Journal of Psychology,* **43**, 29–36.

THACKRAY, R.I., JONES, K.N. and TOUCHSTONE, R.M. (1973) Self-estimates of distractibility as related to performance decrement on a task requiring sustained attention. *Ergonomics,* **16**, 141–52.

THIBAUT, J.W. and KELLEY, H.H. (1959) *The Social Psychology of Groups.* Wiley, New York.

THOMAS, D.R., BECKER, W.C. and ARMSTRONG, M. (1968) Production and elimination of disruptive classroom behaviour by systematically varying teacher's behaviour. *Journal of Applied Behaviour Analysis,* **1**, 35–45.

THOULESS, R.H. (1974) *Straight and Crooked Thinking,* 3rd edn. Pan, London.

TIZARD, B., HUGHES, M., CARMICHAEL, H. and PINKERTON, G. (1983) Language and social class: is verbal deprivation a myth? *Journal of Child Psychology and Psychiatry and Allied Disciplines,* **24**, 533–42.

TIZARD, J., SINCLAIR, I. and CLARKE, R.V.G. (1975) *Varieties of Residential Experience.* Routledge & Kegan Paul, London.

TOLMAN, E.C. (1948) Cognitive maps in rats and men. *Psychological Review,* **55**, 189–208.

TRIESMAN, A. (1964) Verbal cues, language and meaning in attention. *American Journal of Psychology,* **77**, 206–14.

TRIGGS, T.J. and BERENYL, J.S. (1982) Estimation of automobile speed under day and night conditions. *Human Factors,* **24**, 111–14.

TRIPLETT, N. (1989) Dynamogenic factors in pacemaking and competition. *American Journal of Psychology,* **9**, 507–33.

TROWER, P., BRYANT, B. and ARGYLE, M. (1978) *Social Skills and Mental Health.* Methuen, London.

TRUAX, C.B. and CARKHUFF, R.R. (1967) *Toward Effective Counselling and Psychotherapy: Training and practice.* Aldine, Chicago.

TULVING, E. and PEARLSTONE, Z. (1966) Availability versus accessibility of information in memory for words. *Journal of Verbal Learning and Verbal Behaviour,* **5**, 381–91.

TVERSKY, A. and KAHNEMANN, D. (1974) Judgements under uncertainty: heuristics and biases. *Science,* **185**, 1124–31.

TVERSKY, A. and KAHNEMANN, D. (1983) Extensional vs intuitive reasoning: the conjunction fallacy in probability judgement. *Psychological Review,* **90**, 293–315.

UNNAVA, H.R. and BURNKRANT, R.E. (1991) Effects of repeating varied ad executions on brand name memory. *Journal of Marketing Research,* **28**, 401–16.

UOMOTO, J.M. (1986) Examination of psychological distress in ethnic minorities from a learned helplessness framework. *Professional Psychology Research and Practice,* **17**, 448–53.

VAN MAANEN, J. and BARLEY, S.R. (1985) Cultural organisation: fragments of a theory, in P. J. Frost *et al.* (eds) *Organisational Culture.* Sage, London.

VAN TOLLER, S. and DODD, G.H. (1988) *Perfumery: The psychology and biology of fragrance.* Chapman & Hall, London.

VARCA, P.E. (1980) An analysis of home and away game performance of male college basketball teams. *Journal of Sport Psychology,* **2**, 245–57.

VENKATESAN, M. (1966) Experimental study of consumer behaviour conformity and independence. *Journal of Marketing Research,* **3**, 384–7.

VERNOR, M.W. and TOMERLIN, J. (1989) Pedal error and misperceived centreline in eight different automobiles. *Human Factors,* **31**, 368–71.

VROOM, V.H. (1962) Ego involvement, job satisfaction and job performance. *Personnel Psychology,* **15**, 159–77.

WADDELL, N. and CAIRNS, E. (1986) Situational perspectives on social identity in Northern Ireland. *British Journal of Social Psychology,* **25**, 25–31.

WADE, C. and TAVRIS, C. (1990) *Psychology,* 2nd edn. Harper & Row, London.

WALDMAN, D.A., BASS, B.M. and EINSTEIN, W.O. (1987) Leadership and outcomes of performance appraisal processes. *Journal of Occupational Psychology,* **60**, 177–86.

WALLACH, M.A., KOGAN, N. and BEM, D.J. (1962) Group influence on individual risk-taking. *Journal of Abnormal and Social Psychology,* **65**, 75–86.

WALLAS, G. (1926) *The Art of Thought.* Harcourt, New York.

WALSTER, E., WALSTER, G.W. and BERCHEID, E. (1978) *Equity: Theory and research.* Allyn & Bacon, Boston.

WALUS-WIGLE, J. and MELOY, J.R. (1988) Battered woman syndrome as a criminal defense. *Journal of Psychiatry and Law,* **16**, 389–404.

WARNER, R. (1976) The relationship between language and disease concepts. *International Journal of Psychiatry in Medicine,* **7**, 57–68.

WARREN P. and WALKER, I. (1991) Empathy, effectiveness and donations to charity: social psychology's contribution. *British Journal of Social Psychology,* **30**, 325–37.

WASON, P.C. (1968) Reasoning about a rule. *The Quarterly Journal of Experimental Psychology,* **20**, 273–81.

WASON, P.C. and JOHNSON-LAIRD, P.N. (1970) A conflict between selecting and evaluating information in an inferential task. *British Journal of Psychology,* **61**, 509–15.

WATSON, P. (1980) *War on the Mind.* Pelican, Harmondsworth.

WEBER, E.J. and HANSEN, R.W. (1972) The majority effect and brand choice. *Journal of Marketing Research,* **9**, 320–3.

WEINER, B. (1985) An attributional theory of achievement motivation and emotion. *Psychological Review,* **92**, 548–73.

WEISNER, W.M. and CRONSHAW, S.F. (1988) a meta-analytic investigation of the impact of interview format and degree of structure and the validity of the employment interview. *Journal of Occupational Psychology, 61*, 275–90.

WELFORD, A.T. (1958) *Ageing and Human Skill*. Oxford University Press, Oxford.

WENER, R.E. and KEYS, C. (1988) The effects of changes in jail population densities on crowding, sick call, and spatial behaviour. *Journal of Applied Social Psychology, 18*, 852–66.

WESTLEY, F. and MINTZBERG, H. (1988) Profiles of strategic vision, in Conger, L. and Kanungo, J. (eds) *Charismatic Leadership: the elusive factor in organisational effectiveness*. Jossey-Bass, San Francisco.

WESTLEY, F. (1991) Bob Geldof and Live Aid: the effective side of global social innovation. *Human Relations, 44*, 1011–36.

WHARTON, R. and MANDELL, F. (1985) Violence on television and imitative behavior: impact on parenting practices. *Pediatrics, 75*, 1120–3.

WHAT PARK, C. and PARKER LESSIG, V. (1977) Students and housewives: differences in susceptibility to reference group influence. *Journal of Consumer Research, 4*, 102–10.

WHITE, H. (1980, 18 February) Name change to Rusty Jones helps polish product's identity. *Advertising Age*, 47–8.

WHITE, L. and EDWARDS, J.N. (1990) Emptying the nest and parental well-being: an analysis of national panel data. *American Sociological Review, 55*, 235–42.

WHITING, H.T.A., BIJLARD, M.J. and DEN BRINKER, B.P.L.M. (1987) The influence of the dynamic model on the acquisition of a complex cyclical action. *Quarterly Journal of Experimental Psychology, 39A*, 43–59.

WHITLEY, B.E. (1990) The relationship of heterosexuals' attributions for the causes of homosexuality to attitudes toward lesbians and gay men. *Personality and Social Psychology Bulletin, 16*, 369–77.

WIDIGER, T.A. and TRULL, T.J. (1992) Personality and psychopathology: an application of the five-factor model. *Journal of Personality, 60*, 363–93.

WIESENFELD, E. (1987) Residential density, locus of control, and crowding perception in popular housing projects. *Journal of Environmental Psychology, 7*, 143–58.

WILEY, M.G. and ESKILSON, A. (1988) Gender and family/career conflict: reactions of bosses. *Sex Roles, 19*, 445–66.

WILLEMSEN, T.M. and VAN SCHIE, E.C.M. (1989) Sex stereotypes and responses to juvenile deliquency. *Sex Roles, 20*, 623–38.

WILLIAMS, M.D. and HOLLAN, J.D. (1981) The process of retrieval from very long-term memory. *Cognitive Science, 5*, 87–119.

WILLIAMS, M.L., PODSAKOFF, P.M. and HUBER, V. (1992) Effects of group-level and individual-level variation in leader behaviours on subordinate attitudes and performance. *Journal of Occupational and Organisational Psychology, 65*, 115–29.

WILLIAMS, R.L., EYRING, M., GAYNOR, P. and LONG, J.D. (1991) Development of a view of life scale. *Psychology and Health, 5*, 165–81.

WILLIAMS, R.B., BAREFOOT, J.C. and SHEKELLE, R.B. (1985) The health consequences of hostility, in M.A. Chesney and R.H. Rosenman (eds) *Anger and Hostility in Cardiovascular and Behavioural Disorders*. Hemisphere, New York.

WILSON, R. and CAIRNS, E. (1992) Trouble, stress and psychological disorder in Northern Ireland. *The Psychologist, 5*, 347–50.

WILSON, S. (1978) Vandalism and 'defensible space' on London housing estates, in R. Clarke, *Tackling Vandalism*. Home Office Research Study No. 47. HMSO, London.

WINCH, C. (1985) Cooper, Labov, Larry and Charles. *Oxford Review of Education,* **11**, 193–200.

WING, R.R., EPSTEIN, L.H., NOWALK, M.P. and LAMPARSKI, D.M. (1986) Behavioural self-regulation in the treatment of patients with *diabetes mellitus. Psychological Bulletin,* **99**, 78–89.

WINTER, D.A. (1967) Construct relationships, psychological disorder and therapeutic change. *British Journal of Medical Psychology,* **55**, 257–69.

WITT, R.E. and BRUCE, G.D. (1972) Group influence and brand choice congruence. *Journal of Marketing Research,* **9**, 440–3.

WITT, R.E. (1969) Informal social group influence on consumer brand choice. *Journal of Marketing Research,* **6**, 473–6.

WOLF, T. (1976) A cognitive model of musical sight-reading. *Journal of Psycholinguistic Research,* **5**, 143–72.

WOLLMAN, N. and STOUDER, R. (1991) Believed efficacy and political activity: a test of the specificity hypothesis. *Journal of Social Psychology,* **131**, 557–66.

WOLPE, J. (1958) *Psychotherapy by Reciprocal Inhibition.* Stanford University Press, Stanford.

WOOD, W., WONG, F. and CHACHERE, J.G. (1991) Effects of media violence on viewers' aggression in unconstrained social interaction. *Psychological Bulletin,* **109**, 371–83.

WOODALL, K.L. and MATTHEWS, K.A. (1989) Familial environment associated with Type A behaviors and psychophysiological responses to stress in children. *Health Psychology,* **8**(4), 403–26.

WOODSIDE, A.G. (1972) Informal group influence on risk taking. *Journal of Marketing Research,* **9**, 223–5.

WORTMAN, C.B. and BREHM, J.W. (1975) Responses to uncontrollable outcomes: An integration of reactance theory and the learned helplessness model. In *Advances in Experimental Social Psychology,* Vol. 8 (ed. L. Berkowitz). Academic Press, New York.

WORTMAN, C.B. and SILVER, R.L. (1987) Coping with irrevocable loss, in G. VandenBos and B. Bryant *Cataclysms, Crises and Catastrophes: Psychology in action.* American Psychological Association, Washington, D.C.

WRIGHT, T. (1987) Self-ratings of health: the influence of age and smoking status and the role of different explanatory models. *Psychology and Health,* **1**(4), 379–97.

YALCH, R.F. (1991) Memory in a jingle jungle: music as a mnemonic device in communicating advertising slogans. *Journal of Applied Psychology,* **76**, 268–75.

YANG, B.E. (1988) A cross cultural comparison of preference for Korean, Japanese and Western landscape styles. Doctoral dissertation, University of Michigan, summarised in R. Kaplan and S. Kaplan (1989) *The Experience of Nature: A psychology perspective.* Cambridge University Press, Cambridge.

YANPING, Z. and DERSON, Y. (1986) The relationship of life events and stress to neurosis in China: Comparison of 105 neurotic patients to 103 normal controls. *Culture, Medicine and Psychiatry,* **10**(3), 245–58.

YARNELL, P.R. and LYNCH, S. (1973) The ding: amnesic states in football trauma. *Neurology,* **23**, 196–7.

YOUNG, A., HAY, D. and ELLIS, A. (1985). The faces that launched a thousand ships: everyday difficulties and errors in recognizing people. *British Journal of Psychology,* **76**, 495–523.

YOUNGSON, R. (1992, 21 March) Pathways to pain control. *New Scientist.*

ZAJONC, R.B. (1965) Social facilitation. *Science,* **149**, 269–74.

ZAJONC, R.B. (1968) Attitudinal effects of mere exposure. *Journal of Personality and Social Psychology,* **9**, 1–27.

ZANI, B. (1987) The psychiatric nurse: a social psychological study of a profession facing institutional changes. *Social Behaviour,* **2**, 87–98.

ZEIGLER, S.G., KLINZING, J. and WILLIAMSON, K. (1982) The effects of two stress management programs on cardiorespiratory efficiency. *Journal of Sport Psychology,* **4**, 280–9.

ZILLER, R.C., BEHRINGER, R.D. and GOODCHILDS, J.D. (1960) Group creativity under conditions of success or failure and variations in group stability. *Journal of Applied Psychology,* **45**, 43–9.

ZIMBARDO P. and LIEPPE, M.R. (1991) *The Psychology of Attitude Change and Social Influence.* McGraw-Hill, New York.

ZIMBARDO, P. and RUCH, F. (1977) *Psychology and Life,* 9th edn. pp. 643. Scott Foresman and Company, Glenview, Illinois.

ZIMBARDO, P.G. (1970) The human choice: individuation, reason and order versus deindividuation, impulse and chaos, in W. J. Arnold and D. Levine (eds) *Nebraska Symposium on Motivation 17.* University of Nebraska Press, Lincoln.

Index